+ Barry Montreal

June 7. 07

# The Measure of Faith

*The Right Reverend Andrew Hutchison,*
*10th Lord Bishop of Montreal*

# The Measure of Faith

## Annals of the
## Diocese of Montreal
## 1760-2000

M.E. Reisner

ABC Publishing
ANGLICAN BOOK CENTRE
TORONTO ■ CANADA

2002
Anglican Book Centre
600 Jarvis Street
Toronto, Ontario
Canada M4Y 2J6

Cover photo: Paul Litherland
Book and cover design: Jane Thornton
Printed in Canada

**Canadian Cataloguing in Publication Data**

Reisner, M.E.
  The measure of faith: annals of the Diocese of Montreal / M.E. Reisner

Includes bibliographical references and index.

ISBN 1-55126-384-X

1. Anglican Church of Canada. Diocese of Montreal — History.
I. Title.

BX5612.M58R43  2002     283'.71428'09     C2002-903852-9

*For I say, through the grace given unto me, to every man that is among you, not to think of himself more highly than he ought to think; but to think soberly, according as God hath dealt to every man the measure of faith.*

**Romans 12: 3**
part of the 2nd Lesson appointed for Evening Prayer, according to the Book of Common Prayer, for the day on which Francis Fulford first entered his Diocese

*This was my first progress through any portion of my diocese — with the beauties of Nature I was charmed beyond measure … I was also very much pleased with the clergy — those I met in this little tour were all of them earnest simple-minded men, devoting themselves to their work in faith & patience under many & great discouragements —*

**Bishop Fulford's Private Journal**
September 1850

# CONTENTS

# LIST OF ILLUSTRATIONS
# AND MAPS

# LIST OF
# ABBREVIATIONS

| | |
|---|---|
| ACC | Anglican Church of Canada |
| ACNAC | Anglican Council of North America and the Caribbean |
| ACW | Anglican Church Women |
| AFSA | Anglican Fellowship for Social Action |
| ANQM | Archives nationales du Québec à Montréal |
| ARM | Anglican Renewal Movement |
| AYPA | Anglican Young People's Association |
| BAM | Barnabas Anglican Ministries |
| BAS | Book of Alternative Services |
| BCP | Book of Common Prayer |
| CCCA | Christ Church Cathedral Archives |
| CCHS | Canadian Church Historical Society |
| CCSS | Colonial Church & School Society |
| *DCB* | *Dictionary of Canadian Biography* |
| *DNB* | *Dictionary of National Biography* |
| GA | Girls' Auxiliary |
| GFS | Girls' Friendly Society |
| GORA | Granby, Otterburn, Rougemont & Abbotsford (regional ministry) |
| GSA | General Synod Archives, Toronto |
| LPA | Lambeth Palace Archives |
| MDA | Montreal Diocesan Archives, Montreal |
| MDTC | Montreal Diocesan Theological College |
| MHSA | Missisquoi Historical Society Archives |
| MSCC | Missionary Society of the Canadian Church |
| NDG | Notre-Dame-de-Grâce |
| PBSC | Prayer Book Society of Canada |
| PWRDF | Primate's World Relief and Development Fund |
| QDA | Quebec Diocesan Archives, Lennoxville |
| TCPR | Trinity Church (Frelighsburg) Parish Records |
| TMR | Town of Mount Royal |
| SPCK | Society for Promoting Christian Knowledge |
| SPG | Society for the Propagation of the Gospel in Foreign Parts |
| UCC | United Church of Canada |
| USPGA | Archives of the United Society of the Propagation of the Gospel |
| WA | Woman's Auxiliary |

# THE ARMS OF THE DIOCESE OF MONTREAL

(supplied by the Venerable Peter Hannen)

PLATE 1 *Diocesan Coat of Arms*

There is a natural affinity between heraldry and faith in that both make extensive use of symbolism to refer to deeper truths. The following is a technical description, in heraldic terms, of the arms of the Diocese of Montreal:

> *Azure a pastoral staff and a key upwards and outwards in saltire Or, surmounted by an open book Proper bound Gules edged of the second between in chief a mullet of six points Argent, and in base an anchor cabled also of the second.*

In contemporary English this blazon describes a blue shield bearing an open book (white, with red bindings), over crossed crozier and key (gold), between a white six-pointed star and a white anchor and cable.

Although the formal grant of these arms was made on 5 January 1950 by the College of Arms in London, England, the design itself is much older. The Rev. Dr Robert M. Black (once a priest of this diocese) writes that these arms were "created by the first bishop, Francis Fulford, in 1850, very possibly with the assistance of his Devonshire neighbour, James Pulman, then Clarenceux King of Arms." The keys and pastoral staff stand for apostolic order, and the open book, representing the Bible, for evangelical truth. The star, Dr Black suggests, "is an heraldic symbol for the Virgin Mary (Montreal started as Ville Marie), and the anchor both stands for faith and commemorates the fact that the See city is a great port."

# FOREWORD

The year 2000 marked the 150th Anniversary of the Diocese of Montreal and the arrival of its first Bishop, Francis Fulford. He had been consecrated in Westminster Abbey, and was the last Bishop in Canada to be appointed to his See by the monarch.

The Anglican presence in Montreal in fact dates from 1759 when British troops began to worship with their chaplain in a borrowed Roman Catholic chapel. Episcopal supervision was first provided by the Bishop of Nova Scotia, and later by the Bishop of Quebec, until the Diocese of Montreal came into being in 1850.

The anniversary year sparked a new interest in the history of the Diocese. An historical exhibition was presented at the Marc-Aurèle Fortin museum in Montreal, an hour-long video was produced celebrating not only our history and present ministry, but also the rich architectural and artistic variety represented in the 124 churches remaining in the Diocese. Important historic moments were celebrated in a procession of special events and liturgies. Connecting with the Jubilee year, a diocesan debt relief programme eliminated the debts of many parishes, and reduced others to manageable size.

Amongst our most ambitious projects was the commissionning of this present work — a new history of the Diocese. This monumental task was undertaken by Dr. Mary Ellen Reisner who had recently done a similar work for the Diocese of Quebec's bicentenary in 1993.

Those who look for a chronology of events in the life of the Diocese will not find it here. Rather, Dr. Reisner's anecdotal approach gives us vignettes of the life and times of Anglicans over the almost-250 years of our presence in Quebec and Montreal. Obviously, all history is about people, but Dr. Reisner's approach is particularly people-centered, and all the more readable for that reason.

I commend the book as a welcome addition to the colourful story of an Anglican community in pilgrimage. To the author, *mille remerciements*; to the reader, *bonne lecture*!

† *Imprimatur*
**Andrew S. Hutchison**, *Tenth Bishop of Montreal*

# PREFACE

The Diocese of Montreal has already been the subject of several full-length histories devoted to its life and work. What then is the use of yet another, beyond filling in the intervening years between this and the last one?

The present volume, although it includes much of the interval already covered by previous writers, is a different kind of history. The earliest, the *History of the Diocese of Montreal*, published in 1910 to commemorate the Diocesan Synod's Jubilee in 1909, was an expanded version of a historical sketch written by one of the older Diocesan clergy to celebrate the Jubilee Year of the Diocese in 1900. Although largely a celebration of clerics, especially bishops, and more a labour of love than the fruit of orderly research, it contains much interesting material and is well worth reading. *The Blessed Communion*, published in 1960, marked "the first century of synodical administration in the Diocese of Montreal," but covered the entire period of Anglican presence in this part of Canada East from 1760 to 1960. Authored by respected Canadian historian John Irwin Cooper and published by the Archives Committee, this study not only traced the development of the Diocese under seven episcopates; it also examined such themes as "Works of Mercy," "Montreal Anglicanism in Peace and War," and "The Religious Orders," concluding with a chapter on the "State of the Diocese, 1950-1960." Except for its lack of references and bibliographical information (presumably a deliberate omission by the Committee to make the book seem more appealing to a popular rather than a scholarly readership) it continues to be a valuable study, the lack of an index being its most serious flaw. The present volume is not intended to supersede *The Blessed Communion*, but rather to look at the Diocese in another way.

Most parishes, too, have printed histories — St John the Evangelist, Montreal, among others, has several — and some, such as Thomas R. Millman's on Dunham, or Cecil Royle's on Vaudreuil, are true works of scholarship. A diocesan history, however, cannot merely conflate such histories into a single narrative or trace their corporate development in any meaningful manner.

Other specialized studies, such as John Wilfred Netten's *The Anglican Church: Its Influence on the Development of Education in the Province of Quebec from 1760-1900*, presented as a Master's thesis in 1965, Robert Merrill Black's doctoral thesis, *A Crippled Crusade: Anglican Missions to French-Canadian Roman Catholics in Lower Canada, 1835 to 1868*, presented in 1989, and Joan Marshall's *A Solitary Pillar: Montreal's Anglican Church and the Quiet Revolution*, published in 1995, all furnish useful, if specialized, insights into the history of the Diocese, but they, too, seek to analyze and formulate. *The Measure of Faith*, by contrast, presents annals of the Diocese — an almost-annual sequence of Diocesan happenings and personalities, leaving it to the reader to see contrasts, find parallels, trace issues, and draw conclusions rather than merely to receive them ready made.

By the end of the twentieth century, attitudes towards collective experience had changed radically from those in the 1950s and 1960s. Not only among academics but among people in all walks of life there was less credit given to the possibility of objective historic truth and a greater sense of the relativity of experience. In 1961, British historian E.H. Carr had maintained that "the belief in a hard core of historical facts existing objectively and independently of the interpretation of the historian is a preposterous fallacy, but one which it is very hard to eradicate." By 2001 the eradication was all but complete. The pronouncements of past critics (including historians) were seen increasingly as constructions rooted in the prejudices and preoccupations of their authors' own times, no matter what the period under discussion might be. Individual "stories" and personal judgments from the period itself came to seem more "relevant," and more "true," whether they concerned the so-called "big events" or not.

*The Measure of Faith* makes little pretense at a critical analysis of the institutions and activities of the Diocese over the last one hundred and fifty years. It does seek, however, to provide brief, detailed glimpses into Diocesan life at various periods along the way, using texts that come from those times and retain their flavour — from letters, newspaper articles, synod journals, sermons, vestry minutes, advertisements, contemporary descriptions, diaries and personal jottings, to name a few of the sources. These brief vignettes, arranged chronologically and grouped under loose historical headings, will provide, it is hoped, a series of 'freeze-frames,' often of lay people and ordinary parish clergy, but not neglecting influential citizenry, both clerical and lay, or the tasks and challenges of bishops.

Among these annals, the reader will glimpse a rural clergyman in the Richelieu district, stung to the quick by an episcopal reprimand in 1820 which he feels to be altogether undeserved, and hear about the efforts of a twenty-one-year-old young woman and her friends in the Eastern Townships to organize and staff a Sunday School in 1850. In 1889 a gruff, laconic bishop urges a hard-working missionary in the Ottawa Valley to conserve his energies and not move prematurely into an unfinished parsonage. In 1923 the reader overhears the rejection experienced by a young Black woman, newly arrived in Canada, when the rector of a Montreal church tries to send her "to the coloured Union Church." Here, too, in 1985, a choir-boy's father, anxious about his young son's travel on the Metro at night, appeals to the choirmaster to reschedule his practice for the sake of the boys' safety. There are the efforts of a group of Montreal young people to establish a drop-in centre in the downtown area in 1986. The list goes on. All are part of the story of the Diocese of Montreal. Each brings with it a wealth of implications which analysis and argument would reduce or remove.

In his preface, Cooper described *The Blessed Communion* as "a survey of the achievements" of the Anglican people of the Diocese of Montreal, "and," he added, "inevitably, detail is sacrificed." *The Measure of Faith*, by contrast, has sacrificed survey and celebrates detail.

In such a study, the selection of items could become somewhat arbitrary. Some things to be included seem obvious: the first service, the first resident clergyman, the first visitation, early settlements, the erection of the Diocese, the first Synod, and so forth. Certain kinds of things, too, such as church politics, power struggles, churchmanship, liturgy, finding clergy, planting parishes, missionary outreach, communications, episcopal supervision and lay involvement (especially by women's groups) cry out to be dealt with. Particular concerns, such as relationships with other denominations, ecumenism, French ministry, multiculturalism, human sexuality, social justice and the ordination of women to the priesthood must all find a place. The heroic efforts of missionaries to reach scatterings of rural homesteaders, or of lay people struggling to persuade Diocesan authorities to recognize them as a congregation, should not be neglected, nor the local calamities of churches burning down or being sold and deconsecrated. Some of the many public crises that have affected the Diocese seemed important to include: the ice storm of 1998, the epidemics of the past — typhus, smallpox, influenza — as well as the impact of local rebellion, distant war and widespread depression. Montreal's effort to reach out and minister to the newly-settled Canadian West could not be left out. Conditions peculiar to the Church in Quebec must find a place, too: the changing relationship between Church and State as the Colonial period drew to its close, the growing influence of the Roman Catholic Church on Government policy, the impact of the Quiet Revolution in the 1960s, the population shifts resulting from political instability, the effects of Government legislation centred on language, education and health care, and the destabilizing influence of repeated referenda. All these must be acknowledged. In the wider context of the Anglican Church of Canada, the Diocese has had its role to play in hosting General Synod, in working on the various Service Books commissioned by it, in responding, willingly or unwillingly, to its decisions. Nor should the long-term implications of such national Church involvements, as the Residential Schools issue, be neglected.

Besides settling on these givens for a start, a thoroughgoing effort was made to determine what the members of the Diocese themselves would hope to find in a new history, or, more significantly, what they would be disappointed to see left out. In response to 125 letters of enquiry sent out to the clergy and through contact with many others in person, by e-mail and by telephone, more than eighty-five people — men and women, clergy and laity — provided a cross section of priorities and concerns to be considered. Some are well worth mentioning as they have given shape to the final product.

Although 75% of Quebecers were living in cities by 2000, many people wanted to read about "smaller country parishes," and "the growth and spread of the church in the rural areas of the Diocese." The early history, when Montreal was part of the Diocese of Quebec was called for several times, not infrequently accompanied by the warning that "it should not be a glorification of our colonial past." Many wanted "a personal face to the history," with "biographical components which give 'flesh and blood' to the story." Others asked for "some personal anecdotes revealing the faith and character of leading personalities in the diocese." Most wanted a variety of things:

> So many histories only mention bishops & a few priests [wrote one correspondent]. I would like to read about people who founded parishes & worked in them — lay & clergy — and the struggle women had to have any voice despite their enormous contribution. Pictures.

Many stressed the importance of discussing changes in attitudes towards church-going, the reduced numbers on parish rolls, financial difficulties and the increasingly minority position of English-speaking Anglicans in Quebec society. Others called for "the on-again, off-again story of rela-

tions with and ministry to the French-speaking majority in the Diocese."
A very significant number stressed the importance of discussing the "transition from a totally anglophone ministry to a multi-language & multi-culture ministry," and, more particularly, "the significant contribution of the non-white to the life of the church, especially in the urban core." Acknowledging the issues of racism and race relations was mentioned, as was an awareness (or the lack of it) in the churches of "the surrounding community."

Interest was expressed in an account of church music in the Diocese and "recognition of the work of our church musicians" over the years. Calls for a discussion of the contribution of "Evangelicals and other mission-oriented groups" appeared on a number of responses, as did those for an examination of the liturgical changes instituted over the years. One correspondent hoped to find some account of "innovative Diocesan programs (e.g. Prayer & Praise Festivals, Cathedral property & Diocesan property development)."

The increasing importance of lay ministry, and the "steady faithfulness of the laity over the years as priests come and go" was mentioned frequently. The growing number of clergy in the Diocese who had entered the ministry as a second career was singled out for attention more than once, as was the importance of discussing non-parochial ministries. "I feel it would be unfortunate not to include issues arising from the death of Warren Eling and the gay issues that are with us," wrote one correspondent. A discussion of what was termed "the sexuality issue" was called for in replies to many questionnaires.

Above all, however, those who responded, whatever their particular areas of concern, did not want an empty celebration of the past:

> I would be disappointed to see where we failed left out [wrote one young priest]. Also the true history of blacks and other minorities should not be left out — I would like to see authenticity and truth, not a glorious history or a triumphant one. I would like to see a well balanced history that can make us all proud.

Others hoped for "signposts to the future," or at least "to be able to see the changes through which we have gone to bring us to where we are now."

> It would be wonderful if the history would show how the Christian faith of the people continued despite all the changes and setbacks [wrote another]. It's not simply a question of numbers or statistics but the lives and faith of the people.

It will be up to each reader to judge the extent to which these hopes have been fulfilled, always keeping in mind that there are many more stories to be found and told.

# ACKNOWLEDGEMENTS

I wish to express my gratitude to the Rt Rev. Andrew Hutchison for his confidence in giving me a free hand in researching, structuring and writing the sesquicentennial history of the Diocese, and for contributing to its completion in a variety of ways. His kindly advice, patience, and unfailing good humour have been of inestimable value throughout the project.

For giving me access to, and permission to quote from, archival material, I would like to thank the Rt Rev. Bruce Stavert, Bishop of Quebec; Dr Richard Palmer, Librarian and Archivist, Lambeth Palace; the Rev. Ian Pearson, formerly Archivist, Society for the Propagation of the Gospel, and Ms Teresa Thompson, Director, General Synod Archives, Toronto. Dr Richard Virr, archivist of the Montreal Diocesan Archives, Assistant Archivists Sophie Lemercier and Luc Lepage, and tireless and knowledgeable Archives volunteer Mary Mizuhara gave every assistance. I am grateful to James Sweeny, Quebec Diocesan Archivist, for supplying materials and information on countless occasions. I owe a special debt of gratitude to the Ven. Peter Hannen, Archdeacon of Montreal and Vicar General, who has provided a description of the Arms of the Diocese, and responded to a variety of thorny questions on the administration of the Diocese at the present time. The late Marilyn McGregor Wiseman, too, was most kind throughout the period of my research in furnishing both information and supplies. She cheerfully set up appointments, forwarded enquiries, and dealt with a multitude of details on my behalf.

In 1999, soon after taking on this project, I wrote to every priest on the active clergy list in the Diocese, as well to as those listed as retired and on leave, asking five basic questions about their thoughts on a project of this kind. There was also a second questionnaire to be passed on to a knowledgeable layperson by those clergy involved in parish ministry. Some clergy who did not respond initially I was able to track down by telephone, e-mail, or in person. Much useful material was gleaned from these enquiries. For their generosity of response I would particularly like to thank the Ven. Maurice W. Bate, Rev. Canon Horace G. Baugh, the Rev. Peter R. Blunt, the late Rev. Canon John Bonathan, the Rev. Nick Brotherwood, Karen J. Buzzell, George L. Campbell, Jr, Rev. Canon Brett Cane, the Rev. Anthony Capon, Rev. Canon Kenneth Cleator, the Ven. David Conliffe, Rev. Canon Dr Jan H.L. Dijkman, the Ven. Jack Doidge, the Rev. Frederick Dykes, Mary Irwin Gibson, Paul Gibson, Anthony D. Grainger, Mark Gudwin, Rev. Canon Robin Guinness, the Rt Rev. Russell Hatton, the Rev. Howard J. Hawes, the Most Rev. Reginald Hollis, the Rev. Gordon E. Ingram, J. Paul James, Rev. Canon Anthony G.E. Jemmott, the Rev. Raymond Jensen, the Rev. Yves-Eugène Joseph, Rev. Canon Jenö G. Kohner, Cyrus R. Lang, the Rev. Gérard Lavallée, Ralph T.R. Leavitt, the Ven. John R. Lee, the Rev. Roslyn Macgregor, Gordon McKibbin, Murray C. Magor, J. Edwin Majka, Rev. Canon Dr John I. McNab, the Rev. John Morrell, Garth R. Morrill, Charles F. Morris, Douglas A. Parrett, Rev. Canon Bryan W. Pearce, Rev. Canon Dr Monroe Peaston, Rev. Canon Norman Pilcher, the Very Rev. Walter Raymond, the Rev. Dr Elizabeth Rowlinson, Rev. Keith A. Schmidt, E. Joan Shanks, Joyce M. Sanchez, Rev. Canon Dr John Simons, Rev. Linda Borden Taylor, Rev. Canon Dr Reginald Turpin, Rev. Canon Heather Thomson, and the Rev. Marc-Philippe Vincent. Special thanks are due to the Rev. Canon Dr Lettie James and Lay Canon Quentin Robinson for making available to me their personal papers and for permission to quote from them.

Twenty parishes sent responses to the separate question-sheet included with the clergy questionnaire. Although clearly filled out by other hands, the lay people who often took such care in completing and returning these forms, seldom included their names. I can therefore only offer my thanks to the parishes themselves: St Joseph of Nazareth (Brossard), St George's (Chateauguay), St Paul's (Greenfield Park), St George's (Granby), St Paul's (Knowlton), Grace Church (Montreal), Le Rédempteur (Montreal), St Cuthbert, St Hilda and St Luke (Montreal), St George's (Montreal), St Ignatius (Montreal), St James the Apostle (Montreal), Trinity Church (Morin Heights), Trinity Memorial (Notre-Dame-de-Grâce), St Martin's (Otterburn Park), St Thomas's (Rougemont), St Mark's (St-Laurent), St Francis of the Birds (St-Sauveur), Grace Church (Sutton), St Peter's (Town of Mount Royal), and St Stephen's (Westmount). I was grateful to receive two further replies from non-parochial ministries: the Mile-End Mission and the Montreal Pastoral Counselling Centre. All contained helpful information.

Besides directing letters to Diocesan clergy, I asked for further input through the *Montreal Anglican* on a number of topics of particular concern to the laity. This, too, brought fruitful response. The people I met through this avenue of enquiry, some in person, others over the telephone, have made this project particularly rewarding on a personal level. Again and again I was struck by the faithfulness and concern for their church of the people of this Diocese.

Among lay people I received generous support which often involved their sharing with me personal recollections, specialized information, printed material, photographs and other memorabilia. Telephone conversations, e-mails and hand-written correspondence brought a dimension to the substance of this book that I would have been loath to do without. I would like to acknowledge especially the help I received from Alexander D. Addie, Chris Ambidge, Gloria Augustus, Margot A. Blackman, Connie Bridgeman, Katharine Childs, Mercia Church, Phyllis Gauthier, John Gomes, Peter Harper, Sarah Hoblyn, Marcia C. Hollis, Catherine Hughes, Elizabeth Hutchinson, Laurie Kirkpatrick, Marjorie Lee, Jean McCaw, Jean MacLean, Marjorie C. Monk, Ardyth Robinson, Bruce Russell, W.T. Duncan Shaddick, Robert L. Smith, Marion Standish, H. Nigel Thomas, Charlotte W. Turner, Patrick Wedd, and Dorothy Wilson. I am grateful to Richard D. Moysey who gave me generous access to and permission to quote from the papers of the Rev. George Slack and other documents in his possession. To those whose personal stories they have permitted me to include in these pages — Marita Archer, Elizabeth Howes and Richard L.M. Lord — I offer particular thanks.

I would like to express my sincere appreciation to Jane Thornton of the Anglican Book Centre who prepared the manuscript for publication, designed the layout and created the book's attractive cover. Her care and patience have been extraordinary.

Finally, I owe a special debt of gratitude to my husband, Dr Thomas A. Reisner on whose fine critical sense, sharp eye, and great patience I have relied throughout this project.

# INTRODUCTION

The Diocese of Montreal was erected by Letters Patent in 1850. Prior to this, Anglicans within its territory fell successively under the jurisdiction of the Bishop of London (1760-87), the Bishop of Nova Scotia (1787-93), and, finally, the Bishop of Quebec (1793-1850). This amounted to one bishop of Nova Scotia (Charles Inglis), who made a single Visitation to Montreal in 1789, and three bishops of Quebec (Jacob Mountain, the Hon. Charles James Stewart, and George Jehoshaphat Mountain, Jacob's son), who all made regular confirmation tours, consecrated churches and burial grounds, and kept close oversight of their clergy.

Jacob Mountain's episcopate lasted for thirty-two years, until his death in 1825. Stewart, who had served the Diocese as a missionary since 1807, died a short ten years after his consecration, having made provision for his successor in the person of G.J. Mountain, who was appointed by Letters Patent in 1836 to assist him under the name, style and title of Bishop of Montreal. When Stewart died in 1837, Mountain chose to retain this title — to keep before the authorities' eyes, it was said, the need for a separate diocese for Montreal. The appointment of Bishop Francis Fulford to the newly-erected See of Montreal made it necessary for Mountain to vacate the title in 1850 and assume that of Bishop of Quebec.

Since its erection, the Diocese of Montreal has undergone three divisions of its territory, ceding the area of Rouyn-Noranda to the Diocese of Moosonee in 1946, and the region of Temiscaming to the Diocese of Algoma in 1965. Also in that latter year, the Deanery of Clarendon, comprising the Quebec counties of Pontiac, Gatineau, Hull and part of Papineau, was transferred to the Diocese of Ottawa, leaving the Diocese of Montreal with an area of approximately 21,400 square kms.

In the early days, as has been the case throughout the history of the Diocese, the city of Montreal and its environs were the dynamic centre of the region, and the Montreal clergy often raised the hackles of their Eastern Townships and Richelieu brethren by presuming to speak for them as well as themselves when addressing the bishop, for example.

These rural areas together with the Ottawa region formed two distinct wings of Montreal missionary activity. To treat only the areas that form the Diocese today (and omitting the Deanery of Clarendon) would falsify the early and firmly-established relationship between the two regions and the developing congregations on and around the island of Montreal.

The earliest missionaries to serve in Diocesan territory were appointed and funded directly by the British Government, and no thought was given at first to seeking financial support from among the local people. From 1832, when the State began to withdraw the annual grant in support of the Church, the Society for the Propagation of the Gospel in Foreign Parts (SPG) shouldered much of the cost of ministry in the colony, but it was clear that some effort at local self-support had to begin. In 1836 the Diocese of Nova Scotia founded a Church Society to include lay members and encourage lay participation in the form of set subscriptions to the Society. New Brunswick followed suit the next year, as did the Dioceses of Quebec and Toronto in 1842. Until the incorporation of its own Church Society in 1850, Montreal formed part of the Church Society of the Diocese of Quebec which maintained a network of widespread parochial branches.

Montreal's first bishop, Francis Fulford, was appointed by the Crown and consecrated at Westminster Abbey by the Archbishop of Canterbury and five assisting bishops — including John Strachan of Toronto. By the time of Fulford's death in 1868, Canada's first episcopal election had taken place in the Diocese of Huron. All subsequent bishops in the Diocese of Montreal have been synodically elected, although not all its episcopal elections have ended in an appointment.

The Montreal Diocesan Synod met for the first time in 1859 and with its incorporation in 1868 the Diocesan Church Society was merged with it and ceased to exist.

In 1855, after a long and acrimonious struggle, particularly bitter in Canada West, the Canadian Legislature alienated the Clergy Reserves which had been set aside by statute to provide revenue to support "a Protestant clergy" throughout the newly-acquired colony. Although the stipends of clergy whose appointments predated the withdrawal of grants were secure until they retired or died, no funds to replace them were to be forthcoming. To establish a fund from which the ministry could find support, the clergy with such life interests were persuaded to commute them, on the understanding that the responsibility of providing for them would be assumed by the Diocese. The SPG reduced its grants and cut off subsidies for building in 1858, and then halved what remained in

1888. Fortunately, the Diocese was able to draw on the benefactions of its considerable membership among Montreal's prosperous business, financial and industrial leaders.

Prior to the Synod Act of 1856–7, diocesan bishops were virtually authorities unto themselves in all church matters. With the formation, successively, of the Ecclesiastical Province of Canada in 1860 and of General Synod thirty-three years later, these powers were significantly curtailed.

The Ecclesiastical Province of Canada — formed as the result of local representations begun as early as 1851 — consisted originally of the Dioceses of Quebec, Montreal, Toronto and Huron, with the newly-erected Diocese of Ontario added in 1861. It was the intention of the Provincial Synod to confine itself to temporalities, discipline and administration.

Although Letters Patent originally fixed the Metropolitan See at Montreal with Francis Fulford as its first Metropolitan, their validity was later challenged and they were annulled. The position of Metropolitan became elective after Montreal's second bishop, Ashton Oxenden's retirement in 1878, and John Medley, Bishop of Fredericton became the third to hold the office. The composition of the Provincial Synod of Canada was broadened to include Nova Scotia and Fredericton in 1871, only to be diminished by the withdrawal of the Ontario-based dioceses which formed their own Provincial Synod in 1912. Its jurisdiction increased again in 1949 with the addition of Newfoundland and Labrador which, as of 1976, comprised three dioceses.

Since the formation of General Synod in 1893 — the Diocese of Montreal being one of those objecting to the form it took — the setting of policy and strategic decision-making have increasingly passed to that body. The forum for such issues as remarriage after divorce, church union, the ordination of women to the priesthood, liturgical reform, and the blessing of same-sex unions has been the floor of General Synod. Thinly-populated dioceses, or those with particular regional concerns, have frequently been sidelined to the priorities of the more populous dioceses, centred west of the Quebec border, in Ontario.

In 2001, with the continued existence of General Synod in jeopardy, the increased stature of Provincial and Diocesan Synods will no doubt be felt throughout the Canadian Church. Fortunately for Montreal, none of the twenty-seven Residential Schools divided among thirteen Canadian dioceses was built or operated within its borders, but the implications for the whole Church of the abuse suffered by First Nations children in these church-operated schools can hardly fail to have an impact here.

Diocesan bishops, especially those with long episcopates, have played a decisive role in setting the tone and influencing churchmanship in their episcopates. Bishops have the power to licence, to discipline and effectively to dismiss clergy under their jurisdiction. They ordain or may choose not to ordain the candidates presented to them. They instruct and chair Synod, are ex officio members on all diocesan committees, and hold an episcopal veto. Considering the context of the society within which they function, their sway is enormous.

Of the nine completed episcopates in the Diocese of Montreal, the longest (John Cragg Farthing's) lasted for thirty years and the shortest (James Carmichael's) only two, but the majority extended for fifteen years or more. Francis Fulford, William Bennett Bond, James Carmichael and Arthur Carlisle died in office. Ashton Oxenden, Farthing, John Dixon, Kenneth Maguire and Reginald Hollis resigned. Five Montreal bishops have served as Metropolitans of the Ecclesiastical Province of Canada — Fulford, Oxenden, Bond, Dixon and Hollis — and one, Archbishop Bond, was elected Primate of All Canada.

Long before the erection of the Diocese, Montreal had a decidedly Evangelical slant. This was somewhat moderated by Bishop Fulford (1850-68), who, like his contemporary G.J. Mountain, valued the inclusivity of the Anglican tradition and sought to avoid the preponderance of any one party in the Church. Once the episcopate became elective, however, and the predominantly Evangelical clergy and laity had a voice in the choice of their diocesan, an Evangelical tone was dominant. Under Bishops Oxenden (1869-78), Bond (1879-1906) and Carmichael (1906-8), a significant period in the development of the Diocese lasting for thirty-eight years, this was certainly the case.

During this interval, in 1873, the Montreal Diocesan Theological College was founded — "the Church's right arm," as Bishop Bond called it. Bishop's College, Lennoxville, had opened in 1845, but this favourite project of G.J. Mountain's was regarded by Evangelicals as rather too High Church. The benefactions to the Montreal college by Andrew Frederick Gault, a generous layman of Irish origin, served to confirm its vocation as an initially Evangelical institution. The College, which later became affiliated with McGill University, has played an important role in shaping generations of Diocesan clergy. Funded largely by private donors, alumni and a few supporting parishes, it has remained financially independent of the Diocese. When General Synod called for a streamlining of theological training throughout Canada, the continuing seminaries to be strategically located in Toronto, Halifax and Vancouver, the MDTC felt free to ignore this directive, and as of 1970 was the only Anglican seminary in the province of Quebec.

In this sea of largely Evangelically-minded laity and clergy, there was, however, a small Anglo-Catholic undercurrent, exemplified originally by Father Edmund Wood, founder of St John the Evangelist, Montreal. This tradition, though never predominant, has strengthened over the years, largely through the force of character of individual devoted priests, and has found outlets periodically in other city churches.

Liberal, Broad Church views have been present in various forms since the mid-nineteenth century at least, and have occasionally tipped the scales in their favour in setting Diocesan priorities. This was particularly true in the mid-1960s and early 1970s, no doubt partly influenced by the liberalization of Quebec society after Premier Duplessis's death and the initial period of ecumenical and liturgical euphoria following Vatican II.

The increasing polarization of theological stance characteristic of the whole Church seems particularly marked in this Diocese. Montreal has perhaps grasped the ambiguity of modern church life in a more fully-realized form than have other parts of the Canadian Church. From the 1940s onward, it has provided a forum where some very liberal positions were discussed quite openly, such as those relating to social responsibility, and, more recently, radical theology, contemporary liturgy and other areas of theological concern. At the same time, a long-established conservatism that seems capable of endeavouring to 'wait-out' novelties seems firmly in place. The presence of active proponents of these three parties, leavening a present-day majority of moderate churchpeople, has now and then given rise to bitter antagonisms, and set at variance the liberal and conservative elements — a fact that has done nothing to diminish the dynamic, creative potential of such a mix.

Bishop Farthing, who saw the Diocese through the First World War, and led it up to the threshold of the next, favoured a more elaborate and ritualized form of service than had until then been seen in the majority of parishes or the Cathedral. Yet his energy, forthright manner and missionary zeal won the approval of High and Low Churchmen alike. His expansionism and parish-planting, using such innovative equipment as "portable churches" that could be moved in until a proper chuch was constructed and then be carried off to another site, saw church work expand at a remarkable rate, even in the hard times that marked the final years of his episcopate.

The two World Wars were devastating for Anglicans, both in the Diocese and throughout Canada, for a very high percentage of volunteers — and consequently of casualties and deaths — came from among their ranks. In 1918, for example, forty-five percent of the Canadian troops on active service were Anglicans. There was hardly a family that did not have a son, father, brother, daughter, uncle or cousin actively engaged in the Armed Forces or serving overseas. The numbers of names on honour rolls in churches throughout the Diocese stand as mute reminders of the heavy losses sustained by those communities in two World Wars. Bishop Carlisle, a former military chaplain, saw the Diocese into World War II, but did not live to see it out. He spent much of his brief episcopate struggling with Diocesan finances so that Montreal could honour its commitment to fund missionary labours in the Canadian West.

Bishop John Dixon, a no-frills, quiet family man, reconfirmed the Diocese in its Protestant heritage. His indifference to the renewed and widespread interest in vestments and ceremony that was gradually taking hold in other parts of the Church was evidenced on occasion by his donning his mitre with the tabs in front. Bishop Dixon's nineteen-year episcopate, which began during the Duplessis years and ended after the Quiet Revolution had begun, coincided with the period of greatest social change and cultural ferment that had hitherto been experienced by Quebec Anglicans.

Bishops Maguire and Hollis, in their different styles, embraced the challenge of francization which became more and more pressing during their episcopates, and endeavoured actively to set about preparing their clergy for ministry in a predominantly French-speaking society. During this period of liturgical experimentation and change, Bishop Maguire was theologically more liberal, Bishop Hollis more conservative. Unlike bishops in other episcopal jurisdictions, however, neither compelled his clergy to use either the Book of Alternative Services or the Prayer Book to the exclusion of the other. On the subject of the ordination of women to the priesthood, Bishop Maguire favoured full discussion in the parishes and at Diocesan Synod; Bishop Hollis preferred to curtail debate at Synod, to leave General Synod delegates free to vote according to their consciences, and to await the outcome of the debate at Lambeth. When that watershed was past, however, he proceeded to ordain a waiting candidate without delay. Bishop Hollis heartened and strengthened the Evangelical tradition of the Diocese after a predominantly Liberal, Broad Church interval.

As the Church moved into the twenty-first century, the Diocese of Montreal found itself ten years into a second liberal-minded episcopate, where liturgical traditionalists were treated with tolerance and the Evangelical tradition, though somewhat on the sidelines, was far from dormant. The bold transformation of Cathedral and Diocesan property into La Maison des Coopérants and Les Promenades de la Cathédrale in the mid-1980s, orchestrated largely by the present Bishop, had left the Diocese in a strong financial position with funds for a variety of special projects. Its already endowed episcopal chair, together with provision for considerable administrative support, contrasted sharply with the as-yet-unendowed and increasingly straitened sister-episcopate of Quebec.

During the last twenty years of the nineteenth century, unfamiliar faces began to appear on the streets of Montreal and other Canadian cities. With increasing numbers of immigrants entering the country, Montrealers were no longer simply French or English; they were Russian, Syrian or Italian as well. At first this had little impact on Anglican membership as the Russians were predominantly Jewish and the Italians and Syrians were Roman Catholic. Somewhat later came waves of Ukrainians, Hungarians, Greeks, Portuguese and others. Montreal was rapidly becoming a multicultural society. In the 1950s, numbers of Caribbean immigrants began to swell the small but significant Black community that had been in existence since pioneer days. Upheavals in South-East Asia, Africa, South America, and the Balkan states have more recently brought floods of refugees fleeing from wars and ethnic cleansing.

Although Anglicans have had a good record in helping refugees, they were slow initially to welcome new arrivals to their churches. In spite of the fact that a significant number of those who came from the Caribbean were Anglicans, many had difficulty in finding a congregation where they were made to feel wanted. Confirmation classes were organized specifically for immigrants in the 1950s but these were largely attended by European newcomers. For many years, Montreal's parishes showed little evidence of the increasing racial and cultural mix of the city they were part of.

Not until the late 1970s were efforts made to attract Black clergy to the Diocese, but since that time the number of predominantly Black congregations, both English and French-speaking, has increased dramatically. A Diocesan Race Relations Committee was established in 1991 (born in the wake of the Oka crisis which involved the Native Community). Among other activities, it conducted a survey of all the parishes to compile statistics on the number of members of visible minorities on the rolls and the positions that they held.

In a 1997–98 report, published by the national Church of its country-wide diocesan consultation, the Diocese of Montreal described itself as having "an abundance of gifts (people, finances, material) available locally" and as needing "to search them out and use them in creative and visionary ways." In this conjunction, its representatives who attended the consultation wanted "to empower the people in their parishes" and "invite them to serve and take risks"; they wanted to provide "specialized training for clergy," to "promote inter-cultural, inter-faith activities and understanding," to find "alternative forms of ministry: teams, [or] clusters," and to engage in "more strategic thinking around ministries to follow Alpha." They wanted "more strategic thinking regarding filling the gaps left by the national Church restructuring," "resources to help attract 35-55 year olds," and perhaps most significantly, "resources to help us find the courage to close church buildings and combine parishes."

Under the heading of Strengths (which for some dioceses numbered up to fifteen) they listed four: "youth ministry," "growth of lay ministry (tied with) alternative forms of ministry," "restructuring / reorganizing of diocesan committees," and "social service ministries."

As their weaknesses, described in the report as "Burdens," they listed four (the average number was 7.3). These were "priests [who] have not been trained to be good motivators / facilitators / managers," a church that "is not growing, not reaching the unchurched," a superfluity of buildings, and "not enough Synod staff (tied with) [a] lack of openness between clergy."

In 1960, the national Church's Anglican Directory listed church membership in the Diocese of Montreal at 93,073 souls, with 103 clergy active in parochial ministry serving 188 congregations in 108 self-sustaining parishes and 50 aided parishes and missions. Twenty-five years later the same source showed a membership of 37,095, with 77 clergy in parochial work, serving 114 congregations in 81 parishes (no longer broken down into self-supporting and aided). In 2000, there were 19,956 souls, 59 clergy in active parish work serving 117 congregations in 72 parishes. The Diocese, having passed from a pioneering situation to a settled one, has now, with changed circumstances, come full circle. This time around, at least, its people know how such challenges have been faced in the past and may be faced again.

Numbers tell only a small part of the forces that have made this Diocese what it is, and statistics reflect little of its quality of life or of its spiritual identity. It is the stories of its people, its parishes and its institutions — the struggles, failures, triumphs and transformations of its multifarious experience — that reveal the rich fabric of its centuries-old tradition or offer some hint of where its future may lie.

# BEGINNINGS
## 1760-1792

## Chaplain to the Forces (1760)

The first Anglican clergyman to serve the citizenry of Montreal was the Rev. John Ogilvie, chaplain to the forces under General Amherst. Born in New York City of a military family, Ogilvie was educated at Yale University and, as was necessary at this period, had travelled to England for ordination. Before his appointment in 1756 to the Royal American Regiment of Foot, he had been licenced to officiate as a missionary of the Society for the Propagation of the Gospel, ministering in English and Dutch "to a motley frontier flock," in Albany, New York, and in the Mohawk language at neighbouring Fort Hunter, some forty miles to the west. By the time he arrived in Montreal under orders from General Amherst, he had been a member of the clergy for eleven years.

A brief account of Ogilvie's four-year ministry in Montreal — liberally peppered with quotations from the chaplain's own reports — appears in C.F. Pascoe's history of the Society for the Propagation of the Gospel in Foreign Parts (SPG), compiled in 1893 from the Society's papers:

Another Missionary of the Society, the Rev. John Ogilvie, attended the British troops to Canada in 1759 in the capacity of chaplain to the British soldiers and their Mohawk allies, who formed part of his charge in the neighbourhood of Albany, New York.

In 1760 he was "obliged to return to Montreal for the winter season by express orders from General Amherst, who seem'd extremely sensible of removing him from his Mission [in Albany] for so long a time but said it must be so, to keep up the honour of the Protestant religion in a town where all the old inhabitants [that is, the local population] are of a contrary persuasion, by the regular and decent performance of the public offices of our Church."

On the capitulation of Montreal, as Ogilvie informed the Society, the

Roman Catholic inhabitants were granted the free exercise of their religion; their priests were permitted to remain in their respective parishes, and to continue to minister to the Native People already in their care. Ogilvie promised to do all in his power to recommend the Church of England to the established population "by the public and constant performance of its Divine Worship, and by keeping up a friendly correspondence both with Clergy and Laity."

To assist him in his work [Pascoe continues] the Society sent him a supply of French Bibles and Prayer Books and of "tracts in French on the chief points in dispute between the Protestants and Papists, wrote with the most Christian temper.

"The British merchants with the British garrison," in Montreal made 'a considerable congregation', who assembled "regularly for Divine Worship on Sundays and other Festivals."

According to a list of "Protestant House-Keepers" in the district of Montreal, drawn up by General Murray on 26 October 1764, there were forty-eight names with an additional nine names (none duplicating the householders) of Justices of the Peace. An Ordinance issued by Murray and printed in the *Quebec Gazette* of 20 December 1764, required that "All keepers of public houses at Quebec, Montreal, and Three Rivers, shall keep their doors shut during the time of Divine Service," and that anyone over twelve years of age who neglected to attend public worship at the church designated — this would presumably apply only to Protestants — "shall be fined five shillings." This goes some way toward explaining the large and regular congregations among so few inhabitants.

"As by the Capitulation [Pascoe continues]," no provision was made [by the military government] "for a place of worship for the Established Church," Mr. Ogilvie's congregation[s] were "under necessity of making use of one of the chapels [that of the Hôtel-Dieu]," which was "the cause of much discontent."

The Indians in the neighbourhood for some 40 miles distance were "extremely attached to the Ceremonials of the [Roman Catholic] Church," and had been "taught to believe the English have no knowledge of the Mystery of Man's redemption by Jesus Christ." As these Indians spoke the Mohawk language, Mr. Ogilvie "endeavoured to remove their prejudices, and by showing them the Liturgy of our Church in their Mother Tongue [which he would have used in his mission at Fort Hunter, New York]," he "convinced many of them that we were their fellow Christians."

Ogilvie urged Montreal's need for a regularly-appointed clergyman and for a school, but his own unsettled position in the city, and the need to serve the civilian population "voluntarily" and "without Fee," no doubt led to his seizing the opportunity of an appointment as Assistant Rector of Trinity Church, New York.

During his residence in Montreal [Pascoe affirms], Mr. Ogilvie succeeded in gathering congregations which became "numerous and flourishing" under his care; but after his departure, for want of shepherding, they dwindled away, and "many converts who under him had renounced the errors of Popery" returned again "to the bosom of their former Church," and carried with them "some members of ours."

Ogilvie was popular with the military and civil population in Montreal and, according to his biographer, "got along well with the Roman Catholic clergy and members of the religious orders." In ministering to the civilian population of the city, he was also mindful of the outlying areas, performing baptisms in Sorel, Chambly and Boucherville. His manner was described by a contemporary as "prepossessing," and his address and manners, "those of a gentleman." The parish of Montreal may be justly proud of such a founding father.

## "What Footing Religion Is to Be Upon" (1765)

When New France passed to the British Crown in 1763 there was a flurry of interest among churchmen over how the Church of England would fare in a hitherto exclusively Roman Catholic colony. Introducing an episcopal system with no resident bishop was an obvious problem; inducing a useful and qualified body of clergy to go to such a mission field would be another. The following letter, dated 6 April 1765, from the Rev. Mr Des Vœux, an English clergyman, examines the question in the abstract:

To a clergyman who will transplant himself & family into Canada, it is a point of no small concern to know what footing Religion is to be upon in that New world. … It is presumed, from the King's piety, & it might be expected, from even sound policy, that his Majesty's design is, by fair means of persuasion, to bring over as many of his new subjects to the Reformation as possible — To this effect, the Protestant Clergy must gain respect, & some authority in the country; which they can scarcely do, in any degree of proportion to what the Popish clergy already enjoy, if they are not countenanced by [a] Person of an equal rank with that of the head of the Papists.

At this period, it was unthinkable that a bishop could be consecrated to serve outside the British Isles. Samuel Seabury, the first American bishop, would not receive consecration until 1784, and even then Lambeth stood aloof while the Scottish nonjuror bishops performed the rite at Aberdeen.

In the supposed case [Des Vœux continued], the Presbyterian model would be preferable for the Protestant cause in general, as it carries every where with itself the whole power, authority and Hierarchy which it acknowledges. That model would have another advantage, namely of providing a sufficient exertion of a proper Ecclesiastical Discipline, which is a point of no small consideration; whereas an Episcopal clergy, without any Episcopal Authority, but what must be called for from beyond Sea, may be apt to run into courses which will not promote the Reformation —

It was precisely this argument that prompted the Bishop of Llandaff's influential sermon to the SPG on 20 February 1767 in which he pointed out the plight of the Anglican Church in the colonies:

The want of Bishops [in America] hath been all along the more heavily lamented because it is a case so singular, that it cannot be paralleled in the Christian world. ... All sects of Protestant Christians at home [in Britain] ... have the full enjoyment of their religion. Even the Romish Superstition, within a province lately added to the British dominions [Canada], is completely allowed in all points; ... only the church here by law established ... exists only in part, in a maimed state, lopt of Episcopacy, an essential part of its Constitution.

Within the territory of present-day Canada, this situation was to continue for more than twenty years, until the consecration of Charles Inglis as Bishop of Nova Scotia, in 1787.

To return to Des Vœux's letter, he was obviously pessimistic about the source and quality of clergy who would present themselves to go abroad to so new a field of labour. He continues:

It is well known how recommendations, especially to go to foreign Parts, are obtained; and there are but too many among the clergy who would be a discredit to their own order, if not restrained by the respect they owe to ... their Ecclesiastical superior ...

No doubt, an Ecclesiastical adventurer, & good recommendations, too, may be procured, either from Holland, or, above all, from Switzerland, upon much cheaper terms than a clergyman already known in England: but a saving-scheme is often the ruin of the best designs — It must be considered, whether a man who will know nothing of the Church of England but by having received Orders at one of his stages, riding Post from one Continent to another, is well qualified to recommend to his Majesty's new Subjects that mode of Protestantism which is peculiar to these Islands?

Although the first clergy appointed by the Crown (to serve the Protestant civilians at Quebec, Three Rivers and Montreal) were hardly 'ecclesiastical adventurers' — nor did their stipends suggest a 'saving-scheme' — they were indeed foreign-trained, and not particularly well versed in the doctrines of the Church of England. The desire to win the local population 'to the Reformation' had motivated the sending of French-speaking clergy. The policy was to be a total failure.

On 14 April 1766, the Rev. David Chabrand Delisle, who had left the French Protestant seminary at Lausanne with his studies in divinity unfinished, but had received ordination in England and the brief care of a French-speaking London congregation, was appointed garrison chaplain at Montreal. Two years later he was put in charge of the Protestant civilian population there.

In many aspects of his assessment Des Vœux was far from wrong.

## "Peculiar Situations and Circumstances" (1768)

On 13 August, Sir Guy Carleton, then Lieutenant-Governor of Canada, wrote to Richard Terrick, Bishop of London to outline to him the priorities and true state of affairs, as he saw them, in the newly-won colony. In touching on religious matters he addressed Terrick because London and not Canterbury at this period had jurisdiction over all Anglican clergy outside the British Isles, with the exception of military chaplains:

Your Lordship will give me leave to observe [Carleton wrote], that the peculiar Situations and Circumstances of this late Acquisition to the Crown, may not be so universally understood at Home, as were to be wished for the King's Interest therein; that at the Conquest, this Province contained about ninety or one hundred thousand souls, all Roman Catholicks, and no more than three or four Protestants among the whole; ... a very small Proportion of British Protestants have settled in the Country, and these, from various causes, too tedious to trouble your Lordship with, are daily diminishing —

In 1764, General Murray had sent home to the Government a list of 56 Protestant householders ("housekeepers") in Montreal, and of 144 in Quebec. His successor Carleton was more interested in winning the loyalty of the local French population than providing religious privileges for the small number of British civilians — the troops had their own chaplains. He did not want the Government to engage in the potentially divisive act of sending Protestant clergy into the colony. Carleton's reference to diminishing numbers in the above passage probably refers the high frequency of conversion to Roman Catholicism necessary among British subjects who wished to be married to Canadian wives by local Canadian priests. He continues, giving reasons why he has 'supplemented' the instructions of the recently arrived French-speaking Protestant clergy appointed by the Crown to serve in Montreal, Three Rivers and Quebec:

Well convinced myself [that] the only prudent Measures, at present to be pursued by Government in regard to the Canadians, are to quiet their minds, to win them by Degrees from their old attachments, to conciliate their Affections by a strict, steady, and impartial Administration of Justice; and that by good Example, far more than Precept, with infinite Tenderness for the Prejudices in which they have been trained and educated from their earliest Infancy, we shall obtain the fairest and indeed only Chance of ever gaining them over to the King's Interests, I have, for these Reasons, recommended to these Gentlemen, newly come over [David Chabrand Delisle, Legere-Jean-Baptiste-Noël Veyssière and David-François De Montmollin], to avoid religious Disputes, which can never bring about a Reformation, and may tend to Create ill Blood, and to breed a Discontent, not easily to be got the better of.

## The First Appointment by the Crown (1771)

On 14 July, the Rev. David Chabrand Delisle wrote to the SPG to request that he be adopted as one of its missionaries. He argued that he needed the salary attached to this position to enable him to serve those Protestants dispersed in the countryside in the vicinity of Montreal. He was, at this date, already receiving £115 as chaplain to the garrison, to which had been added £200 as minister to the Protestant population of Montreal, but was dissatisfied because a church for the exclusive use of his congregation had not as yet been provided. He probably hoped that the patronage of the Society would hasten his procuring one, and sought a further avenue for placing pressure on the government.

Of greater interest in this begging letter, however, is Delisle's brief reference to the habit of some Montreal Protestants "to take young Indians, whom they call 'Panis' [obviously slaves] to the services of their church." Delisle was obviously upset by this and stated that, although some of these 'Panis' were baptized, "the instruction of many others is attended with difficulty."

Delisle was in fact one of a significant number of Montreal slave owners. In 1766, the year of his appointment as chaplain to the garrison, he had purchased a slave named 'Charles,' but whether Charles was Black or Native Canadian is not recorded.

Delisle may have been uncomfortable ministering to those Native People and Blacks whose continued status as slaves had been stipulated by the French in the Articles of Capitulation signed in Montreal on 8 September 1760 by Pierre François Rigaud, Marquis de Vaudreuil. The anti-slavery movement in Britain had hardly begun; Lord Mansfield's ringing pronouncement about slavery in Britain was a year away. Among Christian denominations, the Quakers alone consistently opposed slavery as an institution. Eighteenth-century North American attitudes condoned it oftener than not. In the mid 1860s, in colonial Delaware (and apparently in Pennsylvania as well), the Rev. Charles Inglis, future bishop of Nova Scotia "was the only missionary to admit blacks to the communion table," although there were other missionaries who were willing to baptize and catechize them.

Many members of the gentry, as well as notaries, doctors, clergy, merchants and officers in the military, owned slaves. James McGill, a wealthy North West Company merchant bought "a Negro woman named Sarah, about the age of 25 years for the sum of fifty-six pounds lawful money of the Province," in 1768. With the influx of United Empire Loyalists to Canada following the War of Independence, more slaves would be brought into Canada forming part of the body of pioneers who cleared and settled the country. The Rev. John Stuart, 'Father of the Church in Upper Canada,' and for some time missionary to the Mohawks at Lachine, recorded in his diary 'that he had brought his slaves with him from Mohawk Valley where he had been a missionary to the Indians.' The Rev. John Doty wrote to Sir Frederick Haldimand asking for an allowance of provisions for a negro boy whom he had "purchased ... from Lieut Clench of the Indian Department, which boy has been allowed his provisions (drawn at Cataraquay) from the time of his coming into this province, which was with other Loyalists from New York last year."

Gradually the institution of slavery would wither away in Canada —

largely through decisions in the courts, both in Lower and in Upper Canada. In 1798 the Chief Justice, James Monk, released a runaway slave stating that he did so since in his opinion slavery "had no longer an existence in Lower Canada." The record would later be improved by the refuge provided to freedom-seeking slaves by way of the underground railway.

Yet British North America, and her churches, too, have much to answer for in their attitudes, actions — and inaction — toward the slaves.

## Fruits of Patronage and Power (1788)

Although a bishop for the Canadas would not be appointed until 1793 — in the person of Jacob Mountain, first Lord Bishop of Quebec — representations were made shortly after the erection of the Diocese of Nova Scotia, to have at least a bishop's agent or commissary in the more westerly regions of this vast new See. A member of one of Montreal's powerful merchant families — the fur-trading Frobishers who were prominent in "the Protestant Congregation of Montreal"— took it upon himself to approach the civil authorities to secure such an appointment for the city of Montreal.

Joseph Frobisher was a member of the firm of McTavish, Frobisher & Co., one of those companies that, in 1783, had united to form the North West Company with headquarters in Montreal. On 10 April 1788 he wrote the following letter to the Hon. Thomas Dunn, a puisne judge of the court of King's Bench, who would shortly become a member of both the Executive and Legislative Councils of the Province, hoping to secure Dunn's influence on behalf of his candidate:

Dear Sir: —
Being informed that a Bishop has been appointed for, and arrived in the Province of Nova Scotia, with power to appoint Commissaries, to exercise Jurisdiction spiritual and ecclesiastical in the Province of Quebec, New Brunswick, and the Island of Newfoundland, and having so often experienced your readiness to oblige, I take the liberty of troubling you on behalf of my Friend the Revd Mr Cha[brand] Delisle, whose long residence in this Country, and general Character and large Family induce me to wish to interest you so far in his favour as to recommend him to Lord Dorchester and Governor Carleton as a proper person for that appointment in this District. Should it not be a pecuniary one it will at least be a Distinction that seems due to the person who is the first Protestant Clergyman settled in this District, and who without doubt would be sensibly hurt to see a younger man placed over his head.

*Charles Inglis 1787–1793*

*Jacob Mountain 1793–1825*

*Charles James Stewart 1826–1837*

*G.J. Mountain 1837–1850*

PLATE 2　*North American Bishops who oversaw the Diocesan area before 1850*
*(Photo Credit: QDA)*

As T.R. Millman has pointed out, there seems to have been a close relationship between Frobisher and Delisle. Frobisher was godfather to one of Delisle's children, and would act as sub-guardian to those still under-age when both parents died in 1794. A year before the above letter was written, Delisle's only published sermon was preached at the funeral of Benjamin Frobisher, also godfather to one of the rector's children.

Despite Frobisher's representations to government through Thomas Dunn, it was Bishop Inglis and not the Governor or the Executive Council who named the bishop's commissaries, however. In the course of his Visitation Inglis chose not to appoint a Montrealer as his representative in Lower Canada, but the Rev. Philip Toosey, residing in the district of Quebec, and — far from tempering his decision with considerations for Delisle's feelings or long service — further named the Rev. James Marmaduke Tunstall (thirty years Delisle's junior) to act as assistant and "regular preacher" in English to his Montreal congregation.

Of the three government-appointed French-speaking clergy Inglis regarded Delisle as the most acceptable, but found his English incomprehensible. In a letter to the SPG, he went so far as to describe it as "disgusting and injurious." With the coming of the Loyalists there was increased pressure for services in the English language. Otherwise Inglis found Delisle "a sensible, well-bred man." He was to remain in his post with his duties curtailed; Tunstall was granted the right of succession in the parish on Delisle's decease or retirement.

Unfortunately, Tunstall, who had been approved by the SPG, and had appeared to Inglis as "a modest, sensible, young man, of good learning and unblemished moral character," fell victim to intemperance and, six years after Delisle's death became so "irregular in his attendance on his duties" that the wardens of the Christ Church "had been directed to write to His Lordship the Bishop of Quebec," now resident in Quebec, asking him to remove Tunstall and appoint someone else. The records show that in 1800 many of the marriages, baptisms and burials were actually performed by the Rev. Joseph Young, Presbyterian minister connected with the St Gabriel Street Church. It is worth noting here that Joseph Frobisher and James McGill, who were both vestrymen of Christ Church were also subscribers to the St Gabriel Street Church and, in one way or another, held pews there as well.

After his dismissal, Tunstall was sent to St Armand where he remained for two years, but returned to Montreal as garrison chaplain. Subsequently, as Bishop Mountain lamented to the Archbishop of Canterbury, he was publicly charged with "such gross misconduct as loudly called for the animadversion of the Bishop," which included "cruelty in the treatment of his Wife."

Tunstall had married after his arrival in the colony, and his wife's social prominence probably told against him. She was Sarah Christie, second daughter of General Gabriel Christie, Commander of the Forces in Lower Canada. Tunstall was found guilty by the Court of King's Bench in Montreal. Although he never seems to have held a position in the church from that time, and was struck from the list of SPG missionaries, Tunstall remained in Montreal until his death in 1840 and was buried in the Mount Royal cemetery.

As for Delisle, although he seems to have fared better than the other two French-speaking Protestant government apointees, his position was an anomalous one. He became a man of property, but, according to one biographer, he "found the fruits of his appointment bitter, since he tasted the aversion for him of the [French] Canadians, the insulting indifference towards him of most of his congregation, and, finally, near abandonment by the Church of England."

## The First Visitation (1789)

Until 1787 the church in Canada was under the jurisdiction of the Bishop of London. With the appointment of Charles Inglis as Bishop of Nova Scotia (the first diocese to be erected by Parliament outside the British Isles) some degree of local supervision had at last become possible. Ordinations and confirmations could take place on this side of the Atlantic. The clergy could be convoked for guidance and direction; churches and burial grounds could be consecrated.

Although British-born (Inglis was Irish), the new Bishop was no stranger to the conditions of colonial life, for his entire ministry had been spent in Delaware and New York. He was well aware of the difficulties of travel, communication and the exigencies of a frontier society.

Immediately after his arrival in Halifax, Inglis set about planning visitations of his clergy: first in Nova Scotia, then in New Brunswick. By 1788 he had completed both these undertakings and determined to push onward into Canada. On 13 May 1789 he set sail for Quebec and Montreal.

The telegraphic journal that Inglis kept on this journey makes interesting reading:

On July 2nd, a Thursday, the Bishop rose early and at 1 o'clock crossed the river to the Island of Montreal where he dined at Mr Burns.' After dinner, Mr Delisle, and eight or nine of the principal gentlemen of Montreal met him at his lodgings which were nine miles from the town, and rode into Montreal with Mr Frobisher, who assigned the house of his partner Mr McTavish for his lodgings. The Bishop noted that the house was large and elegantly furnished, that Mr McTavish had "gone to the westward," and that the inhabitants of the city were exceedingly civil and polite.

On the following day, many of the principal inhabitants called on him. He dined with Delisle and a large company, after which he was conducted to the Jesuits' Church "which Ld Dorchester proposes to give us — it is about 70 feet long, exclusive of the Chancel, by 36 wide — besides an ai[s]le at each side 9 feet wide — which give it the form of a Cross — the Turret was damaged by Lightning — it requires a new covering — the ceiling is unfinished — no floor, or Glass in the Windows — & much of the wall wants plaster, without & within —" This building would become the first Christ Church, ancestor of Christ Church Cathedral.

On July 4, Saturday, Inglis rode out in the morning with Major Hughes and Mr Frobisher "& went round the Hill above Montreal." Later in the day he received a number of callers including "several of the Romish Clergy."

It was on Sunday the 5th that the truth about Delisle's capabilities in English was made manifest. Inglis read prayers in the morning, in the afternoon Delisle preached. "I could scarcely understand him," Inglis observed.

The Bishop was impressed by the setting of Montreal and admired the "extensive & pleasing prospect" which could be seen from Mount Royal on a clear day. "The eye takes in a circle," he noted, "the diameter of which, in many places, is from 150 to 200 miles — this immense tract is quite level, & intersected by the St Lawrence, Ottawa & other smaller rivers — in some places, the horizon is bounded by distant hills — but in most places, the view is closed by a level country, as by the ocean, when we are at Sea." Delisle was once again his host for dinner on the 6th.

The following day, Inglis visited the Hotel Dieu in a party of five, and thought that the Mother Superior and the nuns behaved very politely. He was impressed with the hospital with its 46 patients, and the cleanliness and order everywhere present. He noted that Protestants were also admitted there and that the means of the sisters seemed very limited. He took an interest in the other nunneries as well: the Grey Sisters, who took care of orphans, and the Sisters of the Congregation, who had a school for girls.

On the same day he also visited the Seminary, and "saw all the

Ecclesiastics of that place," among them, Mr Montgolfier, a venerable old Gentleman, upwards of 80 years old, and very infirm. Inglis regaled his Journal with a number of details of the old man's history: that he was formerly a Captain of Horse in the French Service, and that a disappointment in love was said to have driven him into a convent. He noted also that Montgolfier was "much esteemed by Protestants as a man of probity & good sense, & knowledge of the world."

It seems hard to believe that Inglis would refer in these terms to Étienne Montgolfier, formerly Superior of the Sulpicians in Montreal, and Vicar General, but, by 1789, the latter's faculties were failing and he was no longer able to read or write. According to one of his biographers, Montgolfier "preserved a European turn of mind in the Sulpicians which made them feel closer to the new British masters than to the Canadian people." This may, in part, explain his being "esteemed by [British] Protestants."

On Wednesday, July 8, the Protestant inhabitants of the city presented an Address to Inglis requesting that an English-speaking assistant be appointed for Delisle. The Bishop returned an answer, proposing that the sum of £100 a year from the inhabitants should be secured for that purpose since there was no question of removing Delisle whose appointment (and salary) was for life.

On Sunday the 13th, Inglis preached "to a very crouded audience in the forenoon" and confirmed some 170 people, many of whom he described as "educated Dissenters." There were many more who presented themselves, but he refused to confirm anyone under fourteen years of age.

In the afternoon the Bishop preached again after which he gave 100 loaves of bread to be distributed among the poor "by Mr DeLisle, the Popish Curate, & some Magistrates." Finally, on the same day, ten gentlemen "engaged [themselves]" for the payment of £100 a year "to an English Assistant for Mr De Lisle."

The next day Inglis left for points west, continuing his journey as far as Coteau du Lac. On his return journey, he was entertained by the Lotbinières with whom he was particularly impressed — "the genteelest Canadian family I have yet seen." On Thursday the 16th he embarked "at half past 10 o'clock in an open boat, with 4 hands which I hired, to return to Quebec." As he had done on the journey up-river, he spent the night at Sorel with the Rev. John Doty.

On this brief visit to Montreal, Inglis had settled the question of a church for the Protestant inhabitants, arranged for ministry in the English language, and secured the funds to support it without disrupting the provisions of Government, conducted a sizeable confirmation, and exchanged courtesies with representatives of the Roman Catholic community.

Until the arrival of Jacob Mountain on his first visitation in 1794, this was the only appearance made by a Protestant bishop in the city of Montreal.

## Petitioners to Government (1792)

For twenty-four years Montreal Anglicans had theoretically enjoyed, free of charge, the services of their own minister, but thought themselves otherwise not very well provided for. It seemed natural to them to turn to government to meet their needs. The following petition, addressed to His Majesty's local representative, set out their situation and outlined their wants:

> To His Excellency Alured Clarke Esquire, Lieutenant Governor and Commander in Chief of the Province of Lower Canada and Major General Commanding His Majesty's Forces in America &c, &c, &c.

> The Petition of the Ministers, Church Wardens, Vestry and Congregation of Christ Church, Montreal.

> *May it please Your Excellency,*
> We His Majesty's loyal Subjects, the Ministers, Church Wardens, Vestry and Congregation of Christ Church Montreal, deeply impressed with sentiments of gratitude for the many and great benefits which we enjoy under His majesty's benign Government and your Excellency's Administration, beg leave to represent to your Excellency that your Petitioners have since the year 1789 been, and continue to be in possession of Christ Church, Montreal, repaired and fitted up by the favour and with the bountiful assistance of Government for Divine worship. — but the same (contrary seemingly to the intention of Government) being without any permanent establishment, your Petitioners apprehend that very great inconveniences, amongst others, may arise from the said Church's not being established as a Parsonage or Rectory according to the establishment of the Church of England, without which the Church Wardens have no legal Corporate capacity to sue or be sued, or to purchase or acquire property for the use of said Church — and of the Protestant Inhabitants residing within the Parish and particularly a spacious Burying ground (now very much wanted) at a proper distance from the town.

The language of the petition, both abject and grandiose to the modern ear, disguises the petitioners' determination that their wants be supplied at government cost. It was a notion typical of eighteenth-century Anglicans that endowments for ministry (here referred to as "Parsonages" or "Rectories") should be theirs by right. The persistence of this attitude well into the nineteenth century would be detrimental to the early growth and progress of Anglican ministry throughout the Canadas.

Your Petitioners therefore humbly pray that your Excellency ... establish the said Church as a Parsonage or Rectory, according to the establishment of the Church of England, for the Protestant Inhabitants who now do or may hereafter reside within the Parish until from the increase of their number further and other provisions may be made in this behalf, but without subjecting them ... to the payment either of Tithes or Parish rates, they being too few in number to be able to support these charges, even if other circumstances rendered the collection thereof practicable and legal, which is not the case; And therefore your Petitioners further pray that the present allowance for the maintenance of the Parson or Rector may be continued until Government can make some other suitable provision for that purpose; And in order to remove every doubt touching the Church Wardens' right to purchase or acquire the said Burying Ground now so much wanted, that they may be expressly authorised so to do by the Letters Patent to be granted by your Excellency.

   [dated at] Montreal, 29 October 1792

Letters Patent erecting Christ Church (then described as "the Protestant Episcopal Church of Montreal on Notre Dame Street") into a "Parish Rectory" were finally granted on 12 August 1818.

The Montreal Jewish community, which expected and received nothing which their own efforts did not provide, had founded the Shearith Israel Congregation in 1768, and by 1777 had built a synagogue, the first in Canada. Four years earlier, one of their members had purchased a piece of land "to serve in perpetuity as a cemetery for individuals of the Jewish faith who may die in the Montreal district." This proved ineffectual, unfortunately, as the land reverted to the heirs on the purchaser's death, but the will to provide for the community is quite clear. In 1828 the Jewish residents of Montreal successfully petitioned the Legislature of Lower Canada for the incorporation of a Jewish religious corporation with power for its minister to celebrate marriages and keep registers (a right which Anglicans had enjoyed since the Conquest) and to acquire property for a house of worship, cemetery and residence for its minister (all of which members of the community had already done). These achievements, in the same city by a religious group that sought no favours, form a sobering contrast to the expectations of Montreal's Anglican community.

# AN EPISCOPATE
# FOR THE CANADAS
# 1793–1835

## Bishop Mountain on the Road to Montreal (1794)

On 1 November 1793, Jacob Mountain arrived in Canada and took possession of his newly erected Diocese of Quebec. The following summer he set out on his first Visitation, accompanied by his brother Jehoshaphat and his nephew Salter, both in holy orders. As they planned to pass through settlements widely differing in accommodations for travellers, and to journey by land and by water, careful provision had to be made for themselves and the servants who accompanied them. The Bishop's habit of sharing his experiences through intimate diary-letters, written to family members left behind in England, has preserved many of the details of this formidable first venture into the hinterland of his vast diocese. On 15 July, at Maskinongé, he described the arrangements he had made prior to setting out:

I had sent off a bateau (a flat bottomed boat), with five bateaux-men, and another of my servants, two days before, with all our travelling apparatus, to meet us at Three Rivers, and again at Montreal, etc., etc. The travelling apparatus consists of a mattress, etc., and little bedstead for each, with gauze curtains to keep off mosquitoes. Trunks of robes and clothes; hampers of Wine and porter, hams and tongue; a coop with four dozen chickens; a box fitted to hold, without breaking, tea equipage, glasses, plates, dishes, spoons, knives and forks; a travelling basket for cold meat, and other dressed meat, and other dressed provisions, etc., etc., etc.; all of which will be necessary after we leave Montreal, and more especially when we enter upon Upper Canada. In our Calèches we had some cold meat and tongue, and a few bottles of wine and Porter, but unluckily these all broke in the first few miles.

As is evident from his descriptions, Mountain took a lively interest in the folkways of his *habitant* hosts and drivers, and had an eye for fine scenery, as well as an appreciation for the sublime in the forces of nature. It is also clear that the journey was filled as much with real danger as with minor inconvenience, both of which were taken more or less in stride. The party's first stop within the bounds of the present-day diocese of Montreal was at Maskinongé.

[Tuesday, July 15] We left Three Rivers ... and travelled that day as far as Masquinongé. I found the drivers on the road almost all in their holiday clothes in honour of Monseigneur l'Evêque — the time of my coming being known, by the post-master-general at Quebec having given orders for relays of horses to be ready for me all the way up to this place. Some of these gentlemen had very smart hats and jackets, and very gay moccasins, but the prevailing dress was nothing more than a clean, coarse shirt, and clean white trousers, naked feet and a black hat with black feathers, and gold and silver twists around the crown, with half a dozen tassels hanging down the middle of the back, ... Two things in these gay drivers would interest you in their favour — their humanity to their horses, which they scarcely upon any occasion touch with their whips, but drive and manage them by talking to them incessantly; and by their universal civility. I never saw an instance of their omitting to take off their hats to the poorest persons that they meet, though it were the poorest peasant, or the youngest child that can be supposed to walk along the road. ...

We got to Masquinongé pretty early in the evening, and found plenty of room in the house where we proposed to sleep, and very good beds (for the Canadians have their beds of the largest size that you see in England, very lofty, and made up with peculiar neatness), and everything clean but the floor, about which they are very little solicitous. We seemed, however, likely to fare but ill in the article of supper. Eggs and milk formed no very good treat for hungry travellers who had but a very light repast by way of dinner. We ordered our eggs to be boiled, and in tbe meantime there came about the door not less than a dozen children with little bark baskets full of ripe raspberries, fresh gathered from the woods and fields. With our eggs, therefore, by way of first course, and our raspberries, with plenty of new milk and maple sugar, we made a very refreshing supper, and such as you, take it for all in all, would have preferred to any much more various and splendid. ...

We were this night much less molested by the flies, having learned to exclude them by darkening the bed-rooms, and leaving a door a little open into a lighted room. And hitherto we have been the least troubled with mosquitoes.

[Wednesday, July 16] Early next morning we proceeded on our journey, and found much amusement in observing the birds which are entirely different from those in England, and very beautiful in their plumage, and the great variety of flowers and flowering shrubs that grow by the wayside. …

We left our carriages at a beautiful village called Berthier, and crossed the river to William Henry [Sorel] in a bateau. The passage is the finest thing that can be conceived. It is just at the upper end of Lac St. Pierre, and the number and variety of the islands there form a thousand interesting and delightful views. … William Henry is a pretty town standing upon the bank of the river Sorel, where it runs into the St. Lawrence. We were received on our landing by the officers of the garrison, and conducted by them to the Government-House, about a mile out of the town, which Lord Dorchester had ordered to be prepared for our reception …

[Thursday, July 17] Next morning all the gentlemen of the town waited upon us, and I had also a visit from all the Roman Catholic Clergy in the neighbourhood, in a body. I held a Confirmation in the town which was very fully attended. During my stay, I received every possible mark of attention and respect, not only from the two officers who had it in charge to attend upon us, but from all the people of the place. …

[Friday, July 18] On the 18th, we left William Henry, and Captain Ingram having manned a bateau with eight soldiers, and going with us himself, we recrossed the St. Lawrence to Berthier, where we found our calèches waiting for us upon the bank, and we immediately proceeded upon our journey. For the former part of the day we had most beautiful weather, but the sky gradually clouded, and a violent storm of thunder, lightning and rain, obliged us to stop for shelter. It is impossible to give you an adequate idea of a storm in this country. The immense volumes of dark clouds exceed anything that you can conceive. The flashes of lightning frequently cover the whole sky with a bright purple … The forked lightning breaks from a great many places, and three or four of the zig-zag lines unite in one point, and seem to dart into the ground.

As I was sitting in a window remarking the progress of the storm, I saw one of these unisons, so dreadfully, beautifully grand that I called out eagerly to my brother and Salter to turn their eyes in that direction. But my brother who had been long watching the storm, was just dropped asleep, and Salter was too far from the window to be in time. …

As we proceeded, we saw a barn, by the roadside, entirely burnt by the lightning, and we found that the Church of St. Sulpice, the next Parish, had also suffered in its roof. …

We had been so long detained by the storm that it was nearly dark when we came to the part of the river which we were to cross to go to the island of Montreal. ... By the time we landed on the island it was perfectly dark. We went one stage without seeing anything, and then coming at 11 o'clock to an English hotel where we were likely to be well accommodated, we stopped for the night.

We were now only three leagues from Montreal, and had the mortification to learn that fourteen gentlemen from thence had come out in the morning to meet us, in order to conduct us to the city, that they had dined there, and staid till late in the evening, and finally gone away disappointed.

On the following day, Montrealers would welcome their first bishop to reside in the Canadas, a relationship with Mountain that continued for thirty-one years.

## Murder Will Out? (1796)

Now and then an incident has occurred suggesting that the Enlightenment (associated with the eighteenth century) experienced some delay in parts of the Diocese. One of the most unusual took place during the last decade of the 1700s with the public application of the more-than-medieval practice of the "ordeal of touch" — a process whereby a corpse is used to accuse its murderer. Such an ordeal took place in the garrison town of Sorel, known at that time as William Henry. It seems to have involved the entire population, French and English, as well as the detachment of Royal Artillery stationed there.

On July 4th 1884, the centenary of the founding of the parish of Sorel, Rev. Canon William Anderson preached a sermon which called to mind the history of the parish from 1784, the beginning of Anglican work there. Anderson had served Sorel for more than half a century and had apparently immersed himself in the story of its varying fortunes over the years. His sermon, which was later printed, contained an account of the incident in question.

Another circumstance, which occurred in Sorel, in 1796, during the period of Mr Doty's incumbency a most singular case of mediæval superstition, perhaps the only instance of its kind in Canada [Anderson remarked], is deserving of passing notice.

A man named Jean Pailly [Paillé] was found murdered in his dwelling. The deed of blood, naturally created intense excitement throughout the little community. Searching enquiry was instituted, but no clue was obtained to the guilty party. Resort was then had to the *ordeal of touch*, the theory being that if the guilty party *touched* the corpse, *blood* would flow from it. The body of the murdered man, with head and breast uncovered, was publicly exposed in the market-place, and proclamation made, that under penalty of imprisonment, all the males of the town above a certain age should then and there be present. At the same time the whole of the military in garrison, by order of Captain Dickinson, R.A., the Commandant, were similarly mustered, and then marched around the body, each man in passing being made to *touch* the murdered man, "but," records an eye-witness, whose manuscript, kindly loaned to me by one of the old families of Sorel, I have seen, "but, there was no sign given by blood." "This, however," he adds, "clears the town of the innocent blood shed in it!"

Although this event took place years before Anderson arrived in Sorel as a young man of twenty-five, he obviously was fully convinced of the authenticity of the manuscript that recounted it — and which he himself had borrowed and studied. In 1887, *The Canadian Church Magazine and Mission News* regarded the incident as sufficiently interesting to reprint it in its profile of Christ Church, Sorel.

Anderson's centennial sermon must have been a fairly long one, for Charles Abrahall, a later amateur historian, devoted more than thirty-two hand-written pages of his unpublished history of the Diocese of Montreal to transcribing a large part of it:

This sermon is now out of print [Abrahall remarked], and the writer, understanding that few copies are in existence, felt that it would materially add to the interest of Church people if he included the greater part of it. —

Abrahall's extract and the article in the *Mission News* are obviously drawn from the same source.

It is worth noting that it never seems to have occurred to anyone that someone other than a soldier, or a townsman "above a certain age" was capable of the murder, but further details suggest that he (or she) must have been someone of presence and strength.

More information appears in an exchange of letters between Moses Holt, a magistrate at William Henry, and Jonathan Sewell, Attorney General at Quebec. Paillé's, it seems, was not the only murder on this occasion. His little servant girl, probably not more than a child, was also killed, both by savage blows to the head.

Paillé, who was a merchant, lived behind his shop in the Market Place. From the dispositions of the bodies and the condition of the premises, it appeared that the murderer had called Paillé into the shop after he had retired for the night, on the pretext of buying a pound of candles. The bodies were found together behind the counter "their heads exceedingly fractured with the strokes they had received."

About £100 in cash was stolen, but objects of value (a watch, shoe-buckles and a silver snuff box) which "lay in the way" were untouched. Neither the investigation, the reward of £50 offered in the *Quebec Gazette*, nor the ordeal itself — horrible as it must have been, given the cause of death — proved effective in identifying the murderer.

Presumably the Rev. Mr Doty and all the male members of his congregation submitted to a search, and took part in the ordeal as Anderson has recounted it.

# Rural Psalmody (1809)

This letter of Jacob Mountain's, written to his youthful relative Susanna Brooke (in Bath, England) was penned on 22 August at Missiskoui Bay, in the course of a confirmation tour, and on the occasion of his first visit there.

The resident clergyman, the Hon. and Rev. Charles James Stewart (he was a younger son of the Earl of Galloway) had come to Canada in 1807 and, shortly after his appointment as missionary at St Armand, had set about building churches to serve his mission: one at Frelighsburg (the first church built in the Eastern Townships) and another planned for Philipsburg (also known as Missiskoui Bay). A man of simple tastes and great sincerity, Stewart soon won the affection and respect of the surrounding settlers, and gathered a large and apparently still-increasing congregation. At the time of Mountain's first visit, Trinity Church, Frelighsburg, had been completed and open for worship for about seven months.

As is usual in Mountain's intimate correspondence, his responsiveness to the beauties of the natural scene, as well as to neatness and order in human encroachment upon it, shows him as a true eighteenth-century aesthete. His comments on psalmody show how early the tradition of excellence in church music had taken root in the present-day Diocese of Montreal:

In this remote corner of the world, I think of you, my Susanna [wrote the Bishop], &, in the leisure that is afforded me, in the preparation for my return [to Quebec], I take up my pen to tell you that I do so.—

This is the first time that I have visited this place; & of all the parts of the world that I have seen, it appears to me the most beautiful & romantic. In riding from this Bay, about twelve miles into the Country, to the Village in which the Hon[oura]ble Mr Stewart is placed, we passed thro' the most lovely series of hills & dales (with the addition of a near & lofty mountain) that it is possible to conceive; the settlements, all along, are just enough to humanize & diversify the scene; & the woods are more rich, & from their sloping & hanging positions, more picturesque than any that, even in this picturesque country, I have had an opportunity of remarking.

But a greater pleasure awaited us at the conclusion of this ride, where the Village, situated on each side of a winding rivulet, is adorned, & as it were consecrated by a very neat new Church, most happily placed on an eminence on one side, & by the snug elegance of Mr Stewart's Cottage, peeping from beneath a sweeping wood on the other.

The change in the character & the manners of the people, since this Gentleman settled here, is as wonderful as it is pleasing: & in no part of the world, perhaps, has the power of Religion more decidedly & more rapidly manifested itself than here. — Mr S. without any sort of cant, & without the least appearance of enthusiasm, has more zeal, & more persevering activity, than it has ever before been my good fortune to witness: & it has pleased God to prosper his endeavours, in an extraordinary manner. —

Great numbers of the more respectable people were introduced to me; & the whole of my time, not occupied in the business of my visitation, was occupied in conversing with them (three or four or five at a time) at Mr S's. —

On Sunday, I confirmed about 60 — & preached to a Congregation of about 600.

The Psalmody, in this part of the world, is generally very superior to what it is in England; but here, it was better than I ever heard. — The Singers, without any distinction of rank (tho' the greater part of them were of the better class) assemble in the middle aisle, men & women; many of them, especially the latter, young; but no children; they sing, in three parts, not with that vulgar twang, & discordant bawling which are too common at home, but with a softened & a chasten'd tone & manner; & with a perfectness of tune & a sweetness of voice that were really surprising. — They were between 50 & 60 in number; their instructor & leader standing among them, a little raised above the rest, & marking the time by a gentle motion of his hand. — I cannot express to you the effect that this truly devotional music had upon my mind any otherwise than by saying that if you had been with me I am sure you would have wept outright. —

I left this place with regret. — Mr S came with us hither, & means to go back with me in my Boat, to St John's, which is a distance of sixty miles. — If you look at any map that contains Lake Champlain, you may perhaps find the two places — St John's & Missiskoui Bay. ...

And now for my eight-oared Boat — Adieu, my own Susanna! Give my best love to my best friend, & to my sweet Bess, & to my dear Fanny. I return hence to Montreal, then to Sorel, & Three Rivers, & so home [to Quebec], — which I hope to reach by the end of the month; I left it on the 12th of the last.

# The Plight of a Bachelor Clergyman (1811)

Missionaries who brought their wives and families to Canada from England often had great difficulties in adjusting to primitive conditions, isolation and the lack of suitable servants. For bachelor clergy, however, the situation called for singular adjustments — particularly for men sent into the outlying areas.

Charles Caleb Cotton, who had presented himself to Jacob Mountain for ordination in 1804, was an Englishman and an Oxford graduate, recently come to Canada by way of the United States. During a stay of twenty-five days at Quebec, he was received by the Bishop and the Governor, and attended the consecration of the cathedral. He was then sent off to the distant mission of Missisquoi Bay, where there was as yet neither church nor parsonage nor conventional accommodations for a single clergyman of twenty-nine.

At first he boarded with a Dutch-American family named Strite, and then, after a move to Dunham to make way for the newly-arrived Charles James Stewart as missionary to St Armand, Cotton boarded for two years with the Ten Eyck family. It was a two-room house, and there were eight Ten Eycks. As this arrangement proved unsatisfactory, by 1808 he had bought 100 acres of 'wild land' and built a log house on it. It was still necessary, however, to bring in someone to look after his needs. He therefore employed a married couple with six children to live with him, but this was not a happy solution either, and he determined to make other arrangements.

On 24 September 1811, Cotton wrote to his sister Fanny in England to break to her the only decision he thought practicable to him under the circumstances:

Since I have commenced housekeeping for myself [he began], I have experienced a great deal of unavoidable discomfort, & a great additional expence in a variety of ways, having, as I have before mentioned a large family living with me [the Thomas Shepherd family], who are considerably indebted to me, and at present quite unable to discharge it. —

In this country the difficulty of being boarded with any tolerable comfort, is exceedingly great, so much so that I long ago made preparation for keeping my own house, but it is next to impossible for a *single man* to be suited with proper persons to live with him ... & on this account, as well as from my present time of life, I think it the most eligible step for me to endeavour to provide an agreeable Companion, by which means I should be in hopes to keep house with much greater ease & satisfaction to myself, —

I have no one, my dearest Fanny, to unbosom my thoughts to, since I am separated from our dear family, & what an irksome state this is to remain in so long, one can hardly conceive without the experience of it. — Friendship, true friendship is certainly the greatest solace in all our troubles that we can have, and marriage is, at least ought to be, a state of the most inviolable and purest friendship during life.

As to any idea of fortune (further than personal merits) in this country, it is out of the question. Neither is that finished education among your sex, which is so general in England, to be expected here. But yet, some education, and a pleasing behaviour, and the useful qualifications of good house-wifery are to be found among us. —

Being under so many disadvantages in my present way of living, I should be very willing if a favourable opportunity should be within my reach, of having a partner who might share with me my joys & sorrows, and if such a change should hereafter take place in my relative situation, I shall hasten to give intelligence of it to our family, without any delay.

Some light is cast on Cotton's hesitancy by Bishop Mountain's comments on him to the SPG at the time of his appointment to Missisquoi Bay: "He appears to be peculiarly suited to the situation, having great simplicity, becoming gravity of manners, good ability, and much facility in communicating his thoughts," wrote the Bishop. His chief qualification, however, seems to have been that, "from his residence in America [he has gained] sufficient familiarity with the manners prevalent among their new settlers, which are so apt to give an Englishman disgust."

On 20 July 1814 Cotton wrote to Anna, another sister — he was one of thirteen brothers and sisters — with the news that he had at last married:

In my last letter to my dear Fanny, I mentioned the great difficulties which I have experienced since commencing as a housekeeper, & that no other way of removing many of these obstacles presented itself but by a change in my condition of life from the single to the married state. I also mentioned this circumstance, tho' not very certain, yet as a very probable event, & have now to inform you that this alteration in my circumstances has recently taken place, by a union in marriage with a young woman of the neighbouring Township of Brome, by name Drusilla Pettis. —

I hope in the kind Providence of God that I may be blessed in this important undertaking, & that it may be the means of enabling me to lead a more comfortable life in this distant part of the world.

I hope, dearest Anna, that my conduct in taking this step (an affair long ago intended) will not be viewed in an unfavourable light by yourself & the rest of the family, for if you as well knew as I do, what frequent difficulties I have had to endure for these five or six years past, for want of having a Housekeeper of my own, you would rather wonder that I should have continued so long in a single state of life. ...

Drusilla Pettis was the daughter of a well-to-do farmer and more than twenty years Cotton's junior. The Rev. C. J. Stewart (himself a lifelong bachelor) married the couple by licence on 22 June 1814 in Trinity Church, Frelighsburg. The Register notes, quite properly, the presence of Drusilla's father, for she was a minor. The couple had a family of seven children of whom three survived the parents. Drusilla predeceased her husband by two years.

Cotton ministered to the people of Dunham for forty years, during which, according to his biographer, he celebrated 617 baptisms, 656 marriages and 187 burials, and prepared 226 candidates for confirmation.

Cotton died on 8 October 1848; he never returned to England.

# Family Prayers (1814)

The earliest collection of prayers printed in the Canadas especially for Anglican use was compiled and issued by the missionary at St Armand, Charles James Stewart.

From his first days in his mission, Stewart visited widely among the scattered settlers. Although church-building, and providing regular services were always priorities, he also believed strongly in the importance of daily devotions and family prayer. He took pains to distribute Prayer Books among the people, but nothing of the wider scope of prayers for all occasions seemed to be available. With characteristic energy he began to compile a collection himself.

The resulting book, titled *Two Sermons on Family Prayer, With Extracts From Various Authors; [a]nd a Collection of Prayers, Selected and Compiled by the Hon. and Rev. Charles Stewart* was prefaced by "An Address to the Episcopal Congregation of St. Paul's Church and Trinity

Church in St. Armand, Lower Canada." The preface captures something of Stewart's character as a missionary priest. As Thomas R. Millman, Stewart's successor in due course as incumbent at Trinity Church has remarked, "it reflects those qualities which the writer exemplified throughout his years in Canada as Missionary and Bishop. — his zeal as a pastor, his love for the Church, his simple evangelical fervour."

Stewart's Preface, dated at Frelighsburg, 1813, concludes with the words

I commit the book to the Press in humble reliance on the grace of God, that it will be profitable to the good of your souls, through His mercy and your diligent use of it. You must work together with me in the care of your souls, and in the service of the Lord; and you must pray for God's blessing on this little work, and on all your and my labours in the Lord, that God may give the increase, and that we may be a blessing and blest by and with one another. Pray for us, as we pray for you: …

Believe me in the bands of the Gospel of peace and love and union in Jesus Christ,

Dear Brethren, Your faithful Minister, And affectionate Brother …

Stewart seems to have completed the 392-page volume by 1813, but on 1 November of that year he mentioned in a letter to the SPG, that although he could not get it printed "before January or February next."

Publication was by no means straightforward in spite of the fact that Stewart paid for it himself. He placed the work in the hands of a Montreal publisher Nahum Mower, but suffered further delays because Mower "[could] not get Journeymen" to set the type. When the book finally appeared — some time after 2 May — Stewart discovered to his dismay that not only had many typographical errors slipped into the text, but also fifteen consecutive pages (22 to 36) had been entirely left out! All the copies had to be returned, reassembled, supplied with a full-page errata slip, and rebound.

Millman theorized that "the issue was undoubtedly small, and that it is improbable that the book was ever put on sale." Stewart's correspondence confirms that he published the book at his own cost and that he gave copies away to parishioners and friends. A letter written to his curate on 29 July 1815 mentions the names of twenty-seven people who were to receive copies, often listing the places where they lived to facilitate identifying them (for example, "Dr Weston [of] Hatley," "Revd Taylor [of] Eaton," "Mrs Marvin [of] St Albans" and "Powers — near Toof's"). Small x's beside some names suggest that the letter served as a checklist to distribute these gifts.

The two sermons were Stewart's own, delivered in the churches of his mission. The prayers that follow were suitable for a great variety of occasions. Their authors and sources are identified. Stewart drew on Robert Nelson's *Practice of True Devotion*, and Sir James Stonhouse's *Spiritual Directions for the Uninstructed*, for example — on Lancelot Andrewes, Jeremy Taylor, Isaac Watts and publications of the SPCK — but he also used material from little manuals of devotion published in Vermont and New Hampshire and the Prayer Book of the American Protestant Episcopal Church.

There were many prayers for the sick, such as the following "from Bishop Taylor":

Give thy servant, O Lord, patience in his sorrows, comfort in his sickness, and restore him to health if it seem good to thee. And, however thou shalt determine concerning him, yet make his repentance perfect, and his faith strong, and his hope steadfast, and his passage safe; that when thou shalt call his soul from the body, it may enter into the rest of the sons of God, and the bosom of blessedness, and be with the Holy Jesus. *Amen*

Some are highly specialized in nature, such as the "Prayer for a Sick Woman that is with Child," "for Grace and Assistance for a Woman, after Delivery, but still in Danger," "for a Person that is afflicted with Grievous Pains of his Body," or "for a Person in a Consumption, or any lingering Disease."

There are prayers specifically for young people, several for servants, and a prayer to be said for "Natural Fools or Madmen." There is a prayer "that may be used with condemned Prisoners by those who visit them." At least three prayers are for "a Prisoner for Debt." Others concern a person "under Doubts of the Lawfulness of any Action," or "engaged (or likely to be engaged) in a Lawsuit." There is a two-and-a-half-page prayer for "a Person in a state of Poverty";

More appropriate to the ordinary round of daily life are short prayers of a few lines to be said "Before you read the Bible, or other good book," "When you walk out of your house," "Before you begin your work or study," "As you are walking or riding in the fields," and "At your return home."

Stewart was a man who travelled a good deal in the course of his duties. It is therefore not surprising that there are several prayers "before a Journey," and thanksgivings after a safe return. It is tempting to regard some choices as particularly reflective of the man who selected them. The following prayer ("from Mr. Nelson"), for example, not only underscores the dangers of travel at this period, but is also particularly appropriate to the simplicity and frugality of the style in which Stewart chose to live:

Almighty God, in whom all things live, move, and have their being; who dost govern all things by thy wise providence, and whose protection is my only defence and security; I humbly beseech thy divine Majesty, to give thy holy angels charge over me in the journey I am now about to undertake. Let no temptation that may offer itself, prevail upon me to transgress any of thy holy laws; but let the power of thy grace secure me in all those places and companies where my occasions shall lead me. Let not the freedom of conversation at such times, make me forget those rules which my Christian profession obliges me to; neither let the kindness and hospitality of others betray me to the least excess, either in eating or drinking. Defend me from thieves and robbers that lie in wait to exercise acts of violence; and protect me from all dangers and evil accidents which may disturb or annoy me. Preserve my going out, and my coming in; let thy providence be my guard, thy grace my defence, and thy blessed self my portion, both now and for evermore, through Jesus Christ our Lord. *Amen.*

It is important to remember, too, the immediacy of the included "Prayer in Time of War," for during the period Stewart was compiling his book, the border region of his mission was on alert with the threat of invasion. As Stewart reported to the SPG, in November 1812 "the Enemy did come on in considerable force to the Province line on the west side of Lake Champlain … In consequence of the War many families have gone out of the part of the Province from the Townships in the neighbourhood of this Seigniory." A year later, Stewart described a more serious incursion:

about 150 men under the command of Colonel Clark attacked our Militia at Philipsburg, Missisquoi Bay … one of our men was killed & 8 were wounded … & about 90 were made Prisoners … The Prisoners were marched off immediately into the States. … In the meantime many of the families are suffering materially in consequence of their absence. … A few hours after Colonel Clark and his men arrived at Philipsburg, another party of near 300 men with two Field Pieces, came in batteaux & landed there. They plundered two stores [Shops or Warehouses] of considerable property, & a few houses of some articles. … The Lord Bishop was on the point of coming here from Montreal at the very time this disaster took place. It obliged his Lordship to give up visiting here this season, which was an additional matter of regret to me & many others. On the 27th of last month Colonel Clark came at the head of 50 Cavalry to Frelighsburg (where Trinity Church is) & collected in the neighbourhood between 70 and 80 head of cattle and drove them off. … The country has been considerably agitated & distressed of late. I have endeavoured to make improvement of it in my congregations & I hope the visitations of the Lord will not be unprofitable to us.

His book's "Prayer in Time of War" concludes:

Doubtless, O Lord, we deserve thine anger, and our sins do cry aloud in thine ear for vengeance; and it were but just with thee, if thou shouldst make us a prey and spoil unto our enemies; but, O gracious God, let us now fall into thy hands, for thy mercies are great, and let us not fall into the hands of men; let it appear that thou art in the midst of us, … And in thy due time set thou peace in our borders, and make strong the bars of our gates; especially let the gospel of thy Son sound yet louder among us, … so we thy people, and the sheep of thy pasture, shall praise thee for ever, and from generation to generation we will set forth thy glory, through Jesus Christ our Lord and only Saviour. *Amen.*

When Millman paid tribute to Stewart's collection of family prayers in an article in the *Montreal Churchman*, the "Prayer in Time of War" was the only one quoted. He noted that while it was "longer than those which are now in use, [it] might possibly be adapted to present-day need." Stewart compiled his collection during the war of 1812-14; Millman reviewed it in 1943.


# Montreal Through American Eyes (1817)

Three years after the conclusion of the War of 1812, Joseph Sansom, an American from Philadelphia, set out to visit Canada to find out the disposition of this neighbour under British rule, and wrote an account of his travels.

As his 'Preliminary Observations' state: "we [Americans] have … no information, upon which we can rely, of the sentiments of the people [of Canada], or the comparative situation and future prospects of that country. We know not whether the French, in Canada, are to be dreaded as enemies, or to be conciliated as friends."

Deeply anti-British, and uncomfortable in the garrisoned towns he visited, Sansom nevertheless tried to convey a fairminded notion of what he saw. A Protestant — although apparently not an Episcopalian — he nevertheless took particular interest in Roman Catholic institutions.

His description of Montreal provides an interesting picture of the city's expanding economy. Having just come from Quebec City, where he visited the scene of General Montgomery's defeat, comparisons with that city are never far from his mind:

The city of Montreal has thriven surprisingly within a few years [Sansom observed], and now contains as many inhabitants as Quebec, say twelve or fifteen thousand.

There has been, and in time of peace will continue to be, a great influx of Americans, chiefly from the New England States, who are winding themselves into all the most active and ingenious employments. Episcopal and Presbyterian chapels, or meeting-houses, have long been established here; and of late the Methodists, those pioneers of reformation, have broke ground within the precincts of the Catholic church ...

The relations of trade increase daily between this place and the United States; and such is the course of exchange, that the notes of our principal banks circulate freely in all the towns of Canada. The merchants of Montreal are now, however, [setting] about establishing a bank of their own with a capital of £250,000 sterling, something more than a million of dollars. This will have a tendency to limit the circulation of foreign paper [money], and promote domestic improvement, as well as facilitate the operations of trade ...

On 1 October 1817 the Bank of Montreal issued the first Canadian banknote.

Sansom next turned his attention to agriculture:

If the vicinity of Montreal is less wildly magnificent than that of Quebec, it is far more luxuriant and smiling. Here wheat and rye seldom fail to reward the labours of the husbandman (however ill-directed they may be) ... Plums, apples, pears, are likewise much better here than at Quebec; and the berry fruits, particularly currants, raspberries, and strawberries, from foreign stocks, are produced as large, and some of them as fine, as they are with us.

On his travels, Sansom sought out French-speaking contacts and found French Canadians more congenial than the "cold, calculating temperament" of the Englishmen he met with at table in hotels. He acknowledged, nevertheless, the apparent "Englishness" of Montreal, and predicted that this characteristic of the city was then on the ascendant:

As many weekly papers are already published, both in Montreal and also at Quebec, in the English language as in the French; it is evident that the former will gain the ascendency here — perhaps at no distant day.

The streets of business, and especially the shops, have the snug look of an English town; and it was amusing to see how exactly the young men of any figure were in the London cut.

The British Officers, I am told, do not mix much in society with the natives of Canada; yet military manners prevail here, as well as at Quebec. The rabble flock in crowds to regimental parades; and even women, of any appearance, make a point of stepping to a march.

Before I quit Montreal I shall not do justice to its public edifices without mentioning, as a handsome structure, the government-house, for the administration of justice, &c. with the king's arms in the pediment, elaborately executed in Coade's artificial stone; a new jail, of appropriate construction, accompanied by that eye-sore to American feelings — the Whipping Post; and a naval pillar (which has been unfavourably placed in front of the latter) intended in honour of Lord Nelson.

Although Sansom's reflections bear less on the Anglican experience in 1817 than they do on life in Montreal generally, Montreal Anglicans would have been influenced profoundly by the social, economic and judicial factors so shrewdly observed on his visit.

# Dreams of Establishment (1819)

During these early years the state regarded religious observance among the people as a stabilizing, unifying influence in its new-found colonies, and, consequently, took care to provide for the support of "a Protestant clergy," under the Constitutional Act of 1791. Although the Anglicans thought that "Protestant" was a term applying exclusively to themselves (at least as far as the Act was concerned) a good deal of bitterness was generated among those who thought they deserved a share (such as the Presbyterians) and those who resented the exclusion of others (such as the Methodists and Congregationalists). State provision, and the Clergy Reserves — the form it was take — consumed much valuable energy among the denominational leaders in both Upper and Lower Canada and in the end brought comparatively little benefit to the intended recipients.

Represented among the early Protestant settlers were many denominations, but few ministers of any kind to go around. Some communities built "Union Churches" which were used by several denominations, and particularly by any itinerant preachers passing through the countryside. Others might manage to unite their differences under one particular missionary whose own denominational affiliation would determine that of the church to be built.

Well into the nineteenth-century, many colonial Anglican clergy still dreamed of the notion of an Established Church, such as that in Britain, and longed for one overarching, state-funded church as the solution to internal strife and religious rivalry. In his annual report to the Society for the Propagation of the Gospel in Foreign Parts for 1820, Lower Canada's 'Travelling Missionary,' appointed to serve "those places which were not altogether prepared for the reception and maintenance of a resident Minister," expressed the following opinion:

It is to be regretted that the influence of the Gospel in Canada has by many obstacles been hitherto impeded; the prospect of success, however, is becoming brighter, and affords ample encouragement to the Society to continue their exertions. These obstacles arise principally from the want of unity among the people, and the variety of sects into which they are divided; each sect being desirous of a minister, and form of service, agreeable to their own religious persuasion, and consequently, indisposed to unite in erecting a house of prayer. Such being the effect of division, it is of primary importance to induce the people to unite in one communion, by contributing to the support of an ecclesiastical establishment, which affords certain provision for the regular performance of public worship, and the best security for peace and prosperity in every community.

Bishop Francis Fulford, in his Charge to the clergy at his primary Visitation in January 1852, shows how much the attitude of the Anglican clergy, even those newly arrived from England, had changed in their attitude toward Establishment:

It is my wish, in the first place [Fulford stated], to direct your attention to the real position, which, as members of the United Church of England and Ireland, we occupy in this Diocese. While spiritually we are identified with the Church in the mother-country, — emanating from her, using the same liturgy, subscribing to the same articles, blessed with the same apostolic ministry, visibly forming part of the same ecclesiastical body, and claiming as our own all her mighty champions, confessors and martyrs — yet in a political sense, and as regards temporalities, and everything that is understood by a legal establishment, or as conferring special privileges above other religious communities, we are in a totally dissimilar situation. Whether it ever was contemplated in these respects to carry out the theory of the Church of England in Canada, certainly it never has been practically effected; politically considered, we exist but as one of many religious bodies, consisting of such persons as may voluntarily declare themselves to be members of our Church; and who thus associate together because they are agreed upon certain principles and doctrines, according to which they believe it to have been from the beginning the rule of the Church to serve and worship God.

Thus the Anglican Church in the Diocese of Montreal, expressing itself through its first bishop, had come to recognize itself as one of many, and not the dominant religious voice even among non-Roman Catholics. It would be a hundred years before a similar notion took root in Anglican minds in Upper Canada.

## Disciplinary Measures (1820)

Episcopal supervision of so large a diocese was no easy task, but Bishop Jacob Mountain did his best to supervise his clergy, when not in person, at least by letter, demanding accountability for any irregularity brought to his notice. The following letter, dated, 22 September 1820 at Christie Manor, is a response to what appears to have been a stiff note from the Bishop. The recipient, the Rev. Micajah Townsend — an American by birth and a former Methodist — was obviously stung by what he regarded as unjust treatment. Townsend did his best to explain the context of his actions:

My Lord,
   Your Lordship's Letter of the 13th inst has just reached me, conveying to me your disapprobation of the arrangement for performing Divine Service with the Troops at Isle aux Noix, and your expectation that Duty will be performed at both my Churches every Sunday. — In reply to which, I beg leave to assure your Lordship, that every wish and expectation contained in your Lordship's Letter shall be forthwith complied with. —
   After this assurance, my duty to myself requires that I should respectfully state, for the information of your Lordship, the circumstances which induced me to consent to that arrangement when it was proposed to me; circumstances with which I did not think it necessary to trouble your Lordship, but which, had they been fully known, might have spared, at best, some *unnecessary*, and I think, *unmerited* severity in the manner of your Lordship's communication. —
   I beg leave to state, that by this arrangement, I "relinquished" no part of "the duties of my Mission" which ever have been performed. — As your Lordship has never before given me any instructions on this subject, I have implicitly followed the directions and arrangements made for me by the Revd Dr Stewart at the time of my appointment to this place, which were,

*to perform Service and preach a Sermon, once, on alternate Sundays, at Caldwell and Christie Manors.*

The frequent dashes and underlinings (indicated in italics) betray the writer's barely suppressed indignation. Stewart, in St Armand, had been his mentor, had brought him to seek Holy Orders and shown by his example what a missionary should be.

This has been for many years the practice both at St Armand and Dunham, (and still is unless some recent change has taken place) experience having proved that a second Service is never attended in the Country [Townsend continued]. — In addition to this, however, I have usually, at the desire of the people, performed an *extra Service* in some remote settlements in the Parish, where distance and other causes prevented the people from attending at the *two stated places* of worship. — I have also to inform your Lordship, that Isle aux Noix is within the nominal limits of my Parish, as it forms part of Noyan & Christie Manor; so that this arrangement only shifted the place of the *extra service*, without affecting the places for *stated worship*. — There are also many civilians who attend service at Isle aux Noix, who have not the means of going elsewhere. —

I have also to assure your Lordship, that as I was requested by his Excellency through the Chaplains at Quebec and Montreal, to undertake this service my impression was, that your Lordship had been consulted, and had sanctioned the arrangement, and that as one half of our Salary is paid by the Government, its wishes, especially when expressed from so high a source, are certainly entitled to some deference. —

The real issue here was probably money, for, as the Bishop well knew, such chaplaincy services were paid for. It would seem that a clergyman with a Government Salary, and further provision from the SPG, living in a parsonage, and with a stipulated contribution from the people, had no business seeking further income. Townsend proceeds to deal with this question as well:

I regret the necessity of acquainting your Lordship that the stipulations entered into by the inhabitants of this place, *to build a parsonage* for the Minister, and to pay £30 annually towards his support, have been neglected by them; that after a residence here of more than five years, nothing is done, or thought of being done respecting a *Parsonage*; and from the £30, not five has, or can be realized without a recourse to the Law. — This has driven me to the necessity of purchasing ground and building a house to shelter me, which has involved additional and unexpected expenses, to meet which, it became necessary (as the people did nothing to assist me) to accept the avails of the *extra Service* offered to me, of which your Lordship has now been pleased to deprive me. —

On 7 November 1815, Townsend had forwarded to Mountain an undertaking from the people "expressing our ready and grateful compliance with the conditions of the Government and the Society." It is worth noting, too, that this was Townsend's first parish, and that Mountain had himself ordained him prior to his taking charge at age 26.

I have long since intended, whenever our Church on Christie Manor should be fitted for use, to perform divine Service in both Churches every Sunday.

It has now been used but two Sundays, and a few weeks more would have closed my attendance at Isle aux Noix for the Season, when it was my intention to have commenced the new arrangement. —

These, my Lord, are the considerations which induced me to comply with the wishes of His Excellency; and as the Duty did not interfere with the usual parochial Services, I did not deem it necessary to trouble your Lordship with the subject. —

I can only add, I regret that the measure has incurred your Lordship's disapprobation, and conclude by repeating the assurance, that your Lordship's wishes shall be *immediately* complied with. —

I have the honour to be, My Lord, Your Lordship's Obedt Servant,

Micajah Townsend

The Bishop appears to have been unmoved by Townsend's letter. He not only insisted on the two services each Sunday, but also stipulated the times at which such services were to be held.

On 29 December of that year Townsend wrote to G.J. Mountain, the Bishop's acting secretary, "with sincere regret" that his "Wardens and principal Members of both [his] Churches" had urged him to inform the Bishop that the 10 a.m. service in one church and the 2 p.m. service in the other, instituted on his lordship's express instructions, were causing great inconvenience to both congregations:

The consequence of which change [Townsend explained] has been so general a dissatisfaction that the greater part of my people remain at home, and a sufficient number to begin Morning Service can seldom be collected before 11 O'clock. The span of time between the two services is barely sufficient to enable me to reach the other Church in season, even when not delayed by Baptisms &c, but when they occur, the second Congregation is kept waiting beyond the appointed hour. — During the short days and cold weather, 10 is so early, and 2 so late an hour, that those who have several Miles to come *can* not, or what is the same, *will* not attend at those hours.

They desire me respectfully to represent to His Lordship the serious inconvenience which the present arrangement subjects them to, and request His Lordship to give directions that, from the First day of May to the First day of November inclusive, Divine Service may be performed in both Churches each Sunday; and from the First of November to the First of May inclusive, Divine Service may be performed in the Churches on alternate Sundays. —

I forbear expressing my own opinion on the subject of this arrangement, wishing only to follow His Lordship's directions; and I should not now have troubled you, but from the serious apprehension of alienating from the Church many of its best supporters, by an arrangement which does not comport with the convenience of the inhabitants. —

Coordinating service times for multipoint parishes has more recently emerged as a continuing problem when dwindling congregations are amalgamated under the care of a single priest. At hindsight, it is obvious that greater autonomy in establishing local timetables would have benefited country churches in their early years — but such initiatives would have been (and were) unthinkable to Jacob Mountain.

## The Archdeacon Reports (1829)

Charles James Stewart had succeeded Jacob Mountain as Bishop of Quebec in 1826.

From his days as Travelling Missionary, Stewart knew the vital importance of visiting unfrequented settlements and becoming acquainted with the condition of the people. After he became bishop his efforts continued undiminished, and when it was not possible to cover a particular portion of the Diocese himself, he relied on his Archdeacon, G.J. Mountain, to visit established stations and comment on the prospect of planting new ones. Mountain had served his father in this capacity and knew the Diocese well.

In the winter and spring of 1828-1829, Stewart was preoccupied with business in Quebec. On 23 January, Mountain set out on a tour — largely of the Eastern Townships — on the Bishop's behalf. It would occupy him until 1 March.

As G.J. Mountain's son Armine noted in his Memoir of his father, when on his travels the Archdeacon "always kept notes, more or less full … which took the shape of letters to his family." From these he was able

SOCIETY FOR THE PROPAGATION OF THE
GOSPEL IN FOREIGN PARTS.

JANUARY.] QUARTERLY PAPER.—No. LVI. [1851.

CANADIAN MISSIONARY PREACHING IN A LOG-HOUSE.

PLATE 3    *The Church on the Frontier*

to construct a full report which he addressed to the Bishop. The following is an extract from his report of this particular journey:

*Feby 10th* The whole of this day was spent in toiling thro' heavy roads. ... [the Rev.] Mr Johnson, in the spirit of friendly accommodation manifested by all my brethren, was so kind as to bring me [to the Outlet, Lake Memphremagog], and here we parted ... I engaged a cutter or light single-horse American Sleigh, to take me ten or a dozen miles further to Squire Willard's at Stukeley ... Owing to a singular kind of mistake which added 8 miles to our distance, I arrived very late at Squire Willard's. ... Some of the family had retired when we reached the door; but all was soon bustle & cheerful activity in the household; & the wants of man's body, refreshment & repose, were provided for in as plentiful & comfortable a manner as the best among us ought to accept with thankful hearts.

*Feby 11th* The father of this respectable family drove me as far as Frost Village in Shefford, from whence the Rev. Mr Salmon, who had come to meet me, took me on to the Parsonage-house of the Mission, at another little village called Waterloo in the same township, altho' as yet there is no Church at that spot. I preached in the Evening at the School-house.

Not far from Frost Village there was a Church belonging to this Mission which, as was afterwards fully ascertained, was maliciously burnt down. ...The people built another Church in the village itself, but, in the progress of the work their veering sentiments pointed to other quarters, & they have at last come to a conclusion by which the Methodists have the chief right in it, but all others, except I believe Universalists & Unitarians, have admittance to preach.

This is one evidence, my Lord, that Church principles have taken but feeble root in this Mission; and altho' the Missionary who broke the ground & the labourer who received the plough from his hand, are both men of known piety, I may say without hesitation, because I believe that they have become sensible of it themselves, that both of them, with the very best intentions, pursued a system which has contributed to this effect. With the view of rendering their ministrations more acceptable & thence more beneficial to persons unaccustomed to our Church-service, they stretched the spirit of accommodation — a wise and Christian spirit in itself when kept within due limits — farther than I humbly conceive to have been warrantable; & won some of the people no doubt more readily to hear them, but in the mean time, if they did not retard, failed at least to advance the introduction & acceptance of our established & regular forms. ...

*Feby 12th* The remainder of the week was allotted to a visit to the Mission of Yamaska Mountain ... It is about 22 miles from the house of Mr Salmon, who was so kind as to drive me there. We stopped in Granby, at a little village where an appointment had been made for me, at rather short notice, to preach in a most diminutive school-house where I stood in a corner, in close contact with some 25 hearers, with a chair for a [reading] desk. The responses were very well made. It was at that time in the contemplation of some of the people to build a[n Anglican] Church, but the project has since been suspended, and a Minister of another denomination is established in the Village. It was snowing and drifting all this day, but our road lying chiefly thro' the woods, we did not so much feel the effect of the latter. We put up at a most comfortless & dirty tavern at Yamaska Mountain where the Rev. Mr Abbott spent the Evening with us.

*Feby 13th* Many of our Churches in this Diocese are not placed according to rule, their steeples being at the east end & their Communion tables at the west, but in this instance [the church in Yamaska Mountain] it seems to have been resolved to be right in one of the two points, for both are placed together, — the recess for the Altar being in the lower part of the tower, which is at the farther end from the entrance.

I preached in this Church a very plain sermon upon a very simple subject — it was upon prayer in general & the several petitions of the Lord's prayer *seriatim* [that is, in series] — but there was a woman in the Congregation whom Mr Salmon observed to be repeatedly in tears, and we learnt afterwards that she had been one of careless life. A strange Preacher excites attention & this simple circumstance of *novelty* may sometimes cause the word of life itself to strike with a new force upon the heart. — If these tears were like the tears which washed the feet of the Saviour, this is a day which I ought thankfully to note. Alas: how inadequate at best are our feelings in the duty of preaching … when it is considered that upon every single occasion of mounting the pulpit we ought to pray & to hope that we may be rendered instrumental in producing effects, (surely enough to repay the labour of years) which cause JOY IN THE PRESENCE OF THE ANGELS OF GOD!

The entry concludes with a glimpse of Mountain in a lighthearted mood and gives evidence of his influence not only on the planting of missions, but on their very names:

We spent the day at the Parsonage, & I sent off letters in different directions to make all my remaining appointments. My business with the Post Office led to the mention of inconveniences felt from the want of a specific name for this part of the tract called Yamaska Mountain. The title of Yamaska being applicable to so many places as often to cause letters addressed here to get astray. — It appeared that any name once adopted by the Inhabitants would be recognised at the General Post Office & become the established name of the place — As here is a *fordable* river running thro' the Settlement, I made a half playful suggestion to Mr *Abbot* that he should procure it to be called after a highly classical spot at home [as the residence of Sir Walter Scott, on the banks of the river Tweed, Roxburghshire, Scotland] & *Abbotsford* has in consequence actually become its name & will probably belong to it for ever.

Mountain was half right. The post office retains the name as he gave it; the municipality (according to the Commission de toponymie du Québec) has, as of 2000, gone by the name of St-Paul-d'Abbotsford for some forty years.

This account of his travels was written up and transcribed in a hand other than the Archdeacon's some months later (Mountain's own writing is often all but illegible).

Besides descriptions of early missionary activity in the Townships, the account gives insight into the religious pluralism and denominational competition which continued to plague most churches. It discusses, too, the perennial dilemma of the Anglican Church in adapting to the tastes of its would-be congregations, and remarks on the unfamiliarity of the principles of old-country church architecture in new settlements. Above all, however, it captures that momentary awe in a conscientious minister who senses he has touched the heart of one of his listeners.

# A BISHOP
# OF MONTREAL
# 1836–1850

## Clergy Conditions (1836)

In 1832 the government had begun withdrawing the annual grants it had hitherto made to the colonial clergy. Soon after this came the threat of the confiscation of the Clergy Reserves, another source of support for ministry. Consequently, colonial bishops looked with increasing dependence to the SPG to meet their needs.

Bishop Charles James Stewart was tireless in collecting funds, both locally and in England, for the support and expansion of the Church. He also urged the older, more prosperous parishes to strive to support themselves.

In 1836, ill and worn out with his missionary labours, Stewart finally obtained the assistance of a suffragan, George Jehoshaphat Mountain, who had already been Archdeacon of Quebec for fifteen years and had a thorough knowledge of the Diocese. On 14 February of that year Mountain was consecrated in the chapel at Lambeth Palace with the name, style and title of Bishop of Montreal.

Shortly after his consecration, Mountain wrote the following letter to the SPG. The church in Lower Canada had been receiving aid from the Society for some fifty years (since the "adoption" of the Rev. John Doty at Sorel) and it was regarded, he knew, as perhaps less needy than newer places of settlement. Mountain, nevertheless, was prepared to make a strong case for the continued support of missionaries to Lower Canada:

Since the Society has been sometimes reproached with a presumed character of inertness attaching to the Clergy in Canada, and since that bounty, which is so greatly needed from the British public, is proportioned to the estimate formed of its profitable application [Mountain argued], I cannot forbear from adverting to a very few simple facts, as examples of the statements which might be put forth in recommendation of the Canadian Church.

I do not, of course, mean that the labours of *all* the Clergy are in accordance with the picture which I proceed to sketch — some are, from situation, not exposed to any necessity for hardships or severe exertions; and it must be expected to happen that some should be less devoted than others to the cause of Christ; but not to speak of the episcopal labours [of Bishops Jacob Mountain and Charles James Stewart] which ... are of necessity better known, I could mention such occurrences, as that of a Clergyman, upon a circuit of duty, has passed twelve nights in the open air, six in boats upon the water, and six in the depths of the trackless forest with Indian guides; and a Deacon ... when scarcely fledged, as it were, for the more arduous flights of duty, has performed journeys of 120 miles in the midst of winter upon snow-shoes.

I could tell how some of these ill-paid servants of the Gospel have been worn down in strength before their time at remote and laborious stations. I could give many a history of persevering travels in the ordinary exercise of ministerial duty, in defiance of difficulties and accidents, through woods and roads almost impracticable, and in all the severities of weather; or of rivers traversed amid masses of floating ice, when the experienced canoe-men would not have proceeded without being urged.

I have known one minister sleep all night abroad [that is, outside], when there was snow upon the ground. I have known others answer calls to a sick-bed at the distance of fifteen or twenty miles in the wintry woods; and others who have travelled all night to keep a Sunday appointment, after a call of this nature on the Saturday.

These are things which have been done by the Clergy of Lower Canada, and in almost every single instance which has been here given by Missionaries of the Society for the Propagation of the Gospel in Foreign Parts ... yet the chief object of my anxiety is to draw some favourable attention to the unprovided condition of many settlements. ...

In the county of Beauharnois, lying south of the waters of the St. Lawrence, above Montreal, there is a large tract of country inhabited chiefly by Protestants, of whom the members of the Church of England do not form so large a proportion as in most other parts of the province, but are still sufficiently numerous to furnish growing congregations at half a dozen different places, who attend upon the ministrations of two Catechists appointed by the Bishop of Quebec, and paid from the fund placed at his disposal by the Society.

The people lie wholly out of the reach of any of our Clergy; ... they live in a great measure without the sacraments of their religion: the printed sermon read to them is not like the word coming from a teacher, who bears the regular commission to preach it; the relation in which they stand to the teacher is not the same; he has not the weight of one who is clothed with a distinct character of sacredness, and carries the established badge of pastoral authority. ...

I could swell this communication with a mass of details of the same nature, referring to different portions of the province ...

In the township of Kilkenny, lying near to Montreal, I have been assured by one of the principal inhabitants that there are 120 families, and that they all belong to our own Church. I do not think that any of our Clergy have ever penetrated to this settlement; and I have no reason to doubt the melancholy truth of an account given me, that the people hearing of a Protestant minister, whom some circumstance had brought into the adjoining seigneurie, came trooping through the woods with their infants in their arms, to present them for baptism *in the name of the Father, the Son, and the Holy Ghost*, to one who was a preacher of the Unitarian persuasion! ...

I could picture the greetings given to the messenger of Christ by some congregations to whom his visit is a rare occurrence; or I could mention such individual cases as that of a woman who walks three miles to her church, having a river through which she must wade in her way; and of another who comes nearly four times that distance through the woods, to hear the Church Prayers and a printed sermon, at the house of a lady, who assembles the Protestants of the neighbourhood on a Sunday.

In enumerating the trials and sacrifices of missionaries, Mountain was not describing much that he had not done, or was not subsequently to do, himself. He spent nights in open boats, tracked through the wilderness with Native guides and ventured across dangerous rivers to avoid disappointing backwoods congregations.

He paid tribute, too, to the isolated settlers — frequently on the initiative of the women — who, without the hope of a missionary to lead them, drew together in one of the homesteads to read from their Prayer Books and share a printed sermon.

## Proto-Synod (1836)

The year 1836 saw the publication of a remarkably forward-looking anonymous pamphlet, addressed to the "Rt Rev. the Lord Bishop and the Rev. Clergy." It was a modest effort of sixteen pages (thirteen of them actual text) with a typically elaborate nineteenth-century title:

# THOUGHTS
## on
### THE PRESENT STATE AND FUTURE PROSPECTS
## of the
# CHURCH OF ENGLAND IN CANADA
## with
### HINTS FOR SOME IMPROVEMENT IN HER
### ECCLESIASTICAL ARRANGEMENTS
### BY A PRESBYTER OF THE DIOCESE OF QUEBEC

The author, as it turns out, was the Rev. Thomas Brock Fuller, assistant minister at Christ Church, Montreal, with responsibility for the church in Lachine. He was a young SPG missionary — aged twenty-six — and just two years married.

Fuller had been sent to St Stephen's Chapel in 1834 while still a deacon, to be successor to its founder and first rector, the Rev. Brooke Bridges Stevens, who had died that same year. The Bishop addressed was Charles James Stewart, who had raised Fuller to the priesthood in 1835.

Apparently very conscious of his junior status, the young man pleads in his opening paragraph that although he lacks influence or the lustre of an established name, the soundness of his argument and the force of his facts will surely be persuasive to an attentive and fairminded reader:

In presuming to address my venerable and beloved diocesan and my reverend brethren on a subject of such importance as that to which I here call their attention [Fuller begins], I lay claim to no high official station; to no extensive influence, which, of itself, would give weight to any opinions or suggestions I may offer, for none such do I possess. I only claim their forbearance, as one that has facts to state, and arguments to offer, till they have considered those facts, and weighed well those arguments. I wish to call their attention to things, which must *depend entirely* upon *themselves* for weight, and not to opinions, which might derive influence chiefly from the rank or character of him who holds them; and therefore do I regret the less, that I possess not that influence, so desirable under other circumstances, assured, as I am, that my statements and suggestions will, on that very account, not be received, unless they find their own way to every man's judgment, and speak for themselves to every man's heart.

Fuller begins by outlining the problems besetting the Canadian church: the scanty provision for its established parishes, and the many districts of the country — despite advances over the past ten years — where Anglicans were not only without the services of a resident clergyman, but devoid even of the hope of a missionary visit from one year's end to the next. He points also to the impossibility of supplying well educated, locally trained missionaries to serve the people. These were familiar observations often voiced by missionaries in the annual reports to the SPG.

He goes on, however, to point out difficulties in areas less usually touched upon: the vulnerability of the church to government policies and political appointments, the lack of rules binding the conduct of bishops and clergy, the uncertainty of the future.

The solution to all these problems, he believes, is both simple and radical:

To meet all these wants, and to avoid all these difficulties [he argues], I see no other mode, than *a thorough change in our ecclesiastical arrangements.* To changes, in general, I am decidedly averse; but when a change is absolutely necessary to the well being, or rather to the very existence of our church, let us not object to it.

Whilst things remained as they were ten years ago, there was less cause for change.

Fuller refers here to the British Government's withdrawal of the annual grant, amounting to £16,000, which, from the year 1813, it had applied toward the maintenance of the North American clergy. It had pledged continued support to those clergy for whom it had hitherto been responsible, but no new missionaries, or clerical positions would be funded after 1831.

Although the SPG had taken up the slack, it too, in time, it was feared, would grow weary of the burden.

But since our situation itself has been materially changed; ... what was perhaps good under former circumstances, is not so under present. The situation of our church at the present moment, and its probable situation a few years hence (for I contend that we are bound to look to the future), is very different from that of the church in England.

There she makes part of the constitution. The support of her clergy, of her bishops, and of her schools for preparing her youth for the ministry are amply provided for by law. To deprive her of these provisions would require nothing less than a revolution.

But are equally good provisions made for our church in this country? And are even the partial provisions we now have equally well secured to us?

It is difficult to believe that any reader of this pamphlet could answer with full confidence in the affirmative.

Fuller's solution to the problem called for the church in the colony to take its future into its own hands. What he was in fact suggesting was the formation of synodical government:

We *require some change* [he continues]; a change which, under God, will meet our wants, and remove our difficulties. *No change will effect this, less than one by which we may be enabled, together with lay delegates from our parishes, frequently to meet in general council: nothing less than the adoption of a code of laws* [that is, canons], *embraced in a new constitution, can bring order and regularity to our church, nothing short of the admission of the laity in our councils will give us strength and energy.* The laity alone have in their hands what can supply our wants. Before we can avail ourselves of it, we must allow them to have some voice in its disbursement.

He points to the Episcopal Church in the United States which, though left destitute at the time of the Revolution when the support of the SPG was suddenly withdrawn, and much of its property confiscated, was by now in a flourishing state because it had adopted like provisions.

It may again be objected [he points out] that the admission of the laity into the councils of the church is contrary to the practice of the apostolic and primitive church. To this I reply that is not quite so clear as may be imagined. If we look at Acts1:15, 16, 23 and 26, at [Acts] 15:22, 23 and 25, we will find that the councils were not confined to the apostles. Ecclesiastical historians tell us, that the exclusion of the laity, and, soon after, of the inferior clergy from the councils, thence composed of the Bishops, was the beginning of that spirit which afterwards placed all the other Bishops under the feet of him of Rome.

Endeavouring to anticipate other arguments against adopting the American model, he continues:

But still it may be objected that our people are too poor to follow the example set them by their fellow churchmen in the United States. In reply, I would ask the objector to reflect, that nearly all the wealthy in Upper Canada … [and] the majority of the wealthy in Lower Canada, are members of the church.

Let him look at the little diocese of Connecticut, with her eighty well-educated and well-supported clergy, and her flourishing college at Hartford, belonging to the church, and let him remember that the same little state was the chief seat of the Puritans …

Let him look at Pennsylvania, by no means so large or so fertile as Upper Canada, settled, too, chiefly by the Quakers and the Dutch, and in the journal of her last convention he will learn that her parishes are ninety-one, her clergy, including two Bishops, eighty-six; her candidates for orders, twenty-five; that she supports twenty missionaries, has an episcopal fund of several thousand dollars; a fund for the support of widows and orphans of deceased clergymen, amounting to fifty thousand dollars, and a society which has circulated in the last two years eight thousand prayer books, and all this, without monies arising from lands held by the church [that is, Clergy Reserves], and without any assistance from without.

In concluding, Fuller urges the need to act quickly:

Our past opportunities, suffered to glide by unimproved, should warn us to defer not till to-morrow what to-morrow it may be too late to do. The time has been when we might have made much better arrangements than we can make now. But it is probable that we can make much better arrangements now, than we will be able to make a year or two hence. Moreover, as year succeeds year, the numbers of our destitute church people are increased by emigration, whilst they are continually thinned by the accessions made from them to the ranks of dissenters, papists, and infidels. The number[s] of our candidates for orders are each year becoming less and less, whilst our clergy are carried off by that merciless destroyer death, or are rendered unfit for active service by the infirmities of old age; and last, though by no means least, each month of delay brings us nearer to that hour, when, having finished his course, our beloved father [Bishop Stewart] shall be called hence to receive "that crown which the righteous Judge will give him at the last day."

Fuller's apprehension about what could happen to the church on Stewart's death was well-founded. During his episcopate Stewart had expended the bulk of his considerable private fortune in giving direct support to a number of his clergy, in the building of churches, the funding of Lay Readers and catechists serving outlying districts, and in aid to needy pupils — both male and female — allowing them to go to school. He paid personally for his own huge travelling expenses — for he believed profoundly in the importance of knowing his people and overseeing his clergy — and paid the salaries and expenses of his chaplains.

Even as Fuller's pamphlet was coming off the press, however, Stewart was nearing his end. On 27 September of that year the Bishop left Quebec for England where he died.

It is not known whether or not Stewart ever saw the young man's proposal, but similar notions had been stirring in the Diocese since at least 1831 when the Established Clergy Association of Lower Canada was formed. In 1832 the clergy of Shefford, Missisquoi and Rouville met at Philipsburg to form the Missisquoi Association which, like the earlier body, discussed the merits of synodical organization on the American model.

Stewart had great respect for the Protestant Episcopal Church. As his biographer T.R. Millman points out, "from his earliest days in St Armand his services were international and he was delighted to have an opportunity of visiting south of the Border." Stewart and Bishop John Henry Hobart of New York were friends, and from his early days as a missionary Stewart corresponded widely with other American clerics. Had the Bishop lived it is possible that his diocese would have moved more rapidly than it did towards synodical government.

George Jehoshaphat Mountain, Stewart's successor, also made generous use of his personal fortune to support ministry in his diocese, but, unlike Stewart, his interests did not range beyond British models of ecclesiastical organization.

Mountain eventually adopted a means of involving the laity in diocesan affairs. The Church Society of the Diocese of Quebec, incorporated in 1842, was based on the Nova Scotian model and owed little to direct American influences.

Synodical government would not come to what was by then the Diocese of Montreal for another twenty-three years.

The first Anglican synod met in Toronto in 1853 with Bishop John Strachan presiding, but, as Millman pointed out, "the synodical root is to be found in Charles James Stewart's episcopate," and, he might have added, within the territory of the future Diocese of Montreal.

By 1859, the year of Montreal's first synod, Fuller — who was born and raised in Upper Canada — had returned to his native diocese and served as Rector of Thorold in the Diocese of Toronto for nineteen years. In 1861 he was appointed to St George's, Toronto, and, in 1869, named Archdeacon of Niagara by Bishop A.N. Bethune, Strachan's successor.

When duly elected clerical and lay delegates assembled in Hamilton to elect the first bishop of the newly erected Diocese of Niagara, the choice fell upon on Thomas Brock Fuller. He was consecrated on the Feast of Saint Philip and St James in 1875 by the Most Reverend Ashton Oxenden, Bishop of Montreal and Metropolitan of Canada.

## Rebellion (1837)

One of the pitfalls of so-called institutional histories is their frequent failure to establish a connection between their own narrow concerns and the wider world beyond. As far as the Anglican Church in Canada is concerned, 1837 might well be remembered for the death that July of its great missionary bishop, Charles James Stewart, whose legacy was of much greater moment in the history of the church than the short-lived rebellion that broke out in the autumn. Yet the rebellion was certainly part of the Anglican experience, too, particularly in the border areas of the Eastern Townships. To ignore it in favour of purely church matters would be short-sighted indeed.

It had been hoped that the Constitutional Act of 1791 (which had established an elective legislative assembly, an appointive legislative council and an executive each in Upper and Lower Canada) would produce more palatable government in the colonies, but by the fall of 1837 they were both on the verge of rebellion.

In Lower Canada, not surprisingly, the legislative assembly was dominated by French members who, largely uninvolved with the staple trades, opposed measures introduced to advance the interests of the English-dominated merchant class. The English councils favoured building projects, such as the construction of canals along the St Lawrence, whereas the French saw these schemes, from which they derived no direct benefit, as likely to involve increased taxation. "The Anglo-Saxons," as D.C. Masters puts it, "appeared reactionary because they represented control of government by the minority, although in an economic sense they were progressive. ... The struggle assumed the character of a quarrel over finance and was aggravated by the fact that the French Assembly always confronted English councils supported by the governor." There were also the factors of nationalism and culture.

On 23 October, Louis-Joseph Papineau and Dr Wolfred Nelson took prominent part at a meeting at St Charles in the Richelieu valley at which revolutionary resolutions were adopted, constituting an attack on British colonial and economic policies. Seeking to attract conservative rural *habitants*, other proposals included one to reduce church tithes, to which Roman Catholics had continued to be subject. Another sought to abolish some of the fees of the seigneurial system. On the same day, in Montreal, a large demonstration of "loyal and constitutional inhabitants" took place with some 4,000 people in attendance.

The next day, October 24th, Monseigneur Latartigue, Roman Catholic Bishop of Montreal (and first cousin of Papineau), issued a powerful admonition in the form of a pastoral letter, to be read from all pulpits, that revolt against constitutional authority was contrary to the doctrines of the Catholic Church. The opposing parties marched in the streets of Montreal and the Riot Act was read.

On 12 November a proclamation was issued forbidding all public assemblies and processions; volunteer corps of riflemen, artillery and cavalry were then raised by authority of Government. Warrants for the arrest of twenty-six prominent *patriotes* were issued on 16th November, and Papineau fled to join Nelson at St Denis where he lived with his wife and family and operated a distillery. Large rewards were offered for capturing the twenty-six individuals who had been charged with High Treason.

A successful attack by a large party of armed *habitants* under Bonaventure Viger on a body of cavalry escorting prisoners from St Johns to Montreal was a shock to government authorities, as was the news of the strength of rebel forces gathering at St Charles, St Denis and St Ours (in the county of St Hyacinthe).

On the 22nd, a body of troops consisting of four companies of Regulars and a few volunteers from Montreal under Colonel Sir Charles Gore embarked on board the steamer for Sorel from which to march on St Denis. In the face of steady fire from an unassailable position, Gore was forced to retreat, however, which included abandoning several wounded men as well as a howitzer, clogged with mud and frozen solid. On Gore's return on 2 December, St Denis was pacified, and Nelson's property, together with much of the town, was burnt. Gore then proceeded to deal with St Hyacinthe. Meanwhile, rebel forces at St Charles had been defeated by troops under Lieutenant Colonel George Augustus Wetherall, and many — including Papineau and Thomas Storrow Brown — fled south through the Townships.

A last stand by the rebel forces was made near Philipsburg close to the United States border. It was to be a long-remembered event in this Loyalist stronghold, and materials are at hand to recall it in detail.

The first hint of trouble in the village was the noise, at daybreak on 6 December, "of a turbulent mob of fifty or sixty men, boisterously parading its streets." As Charles O. Jones described the event some seventy years later:

Very soon the men of the town appeared [Jones remembered], but their enquiries were answered by shouts of derision and threats of bodily harm. Here, and there, the bolder ones of the intruders, were throwing stones and other missiles, smashing windows and doing any other damage to property that might be easily accomplished. Ralph Taylor, who in some way was supposed to represent the royal authorities, ordered the rioters to desist and disband. Their leader promptly knocked Taylor down, and told him to mind his own business ... After terrorizing the town for an hour or so, the half-drunken band passed on, taking the west road leading to Swanton, Vermont, but, before departing, they declared loudly their intention to return before night and burn the town.

As soon as the invaders — described by Jones as disaffected *patriotes* from the Richelieu valley — had disappeared in the direction of the border, the townspeople hastily prepared to defend themselves against the threatened return:

Surprise and dismay soon gave way to activity [Jones continued] ... The women and children were removed to a place of safety, and messengers sent out in every direction to arouse the countryside. Teams, accompanied by a small escort, were immediately dispatched to the nearest military post for a supply of muskets and ammunition, as there were no military supplies then stored at Missisquoi Bay. Small parties of citizens volunteered to guard the different roads leading to the village and every man was welcome to enter, but none were allowed to leave the town. ... Bands of men arrived during the early afternoon from Bedford, Pigeon Hill and Frelighsburg, until almost three hundred men had assembled in the little village all looking anxiously toward the north end of the lake, where the road from the west skirts the shore, for the teams laden with arms and ammunition. A light snow lay on the ground and late in the afternoon their gaze was rewarded by seeing the little cavalcade crawling along the north shore, showing plainly against the white of the snow.

Contemporary accounts of events take up the narrative in the form of an official dispatch to Sir John Colborne, Commander of the Forces, written on the following day by Captain Oren Jocelin Kemp, Captain of the Missisquoi Volunteers, who arrived on the scene on the afternoon of the 6th:

Sir, —

I have the honour to report for your Excellency's information that yesterday morning I left this place, by a previous arrangement with Col. Knoulton [sic], of Brome, in company with Capt. Henry Baker, of St. Armand, having under my command a company of volunteers to the number of about fifty men, armed with such guns as could be collected, to form an escort to wagons for conveying the arms and ammunition of Col. Knoulton's battalion from Philipsburg. I had proceeded only a few miles on my way when an express from Philipsburg met me with the information that a considerable body of rebels had passed through that village early in the morning to the state of Vermont and were expected to return to burn it the same night.

I immediately despatched expresses in different directions to raise men, armed or unarmed, and bring them to Philipsburg where I had directions from Col. Knoulton to deal out arms intended for his battalion, if necessary.

In consequence of receiving certain information, I left the wagons 4 miles east of Philipsburg and struck through the woods so as to meet the loaded wagons at the head of Missisquoi Bay, in order to strengthen the escort from Caldwell's Manor and St. Armand West. We then proceeded to Philipsburg and reached it at half past four p.m., where I found men assembling from different points and that scouts had come from Swanton, Vermont, with the information that a large body of men ... had taken up their line of march for this province.

Jones mentions that a temporary arsenal had been set up in the Methodist chapel, "a very substantial stone building," its windows barricaded with heavy timbers.

In the emergency [Kemp continued], orders were issued to supply the men with muskets and ammunition from the wagons and, at six o'clock, a position was taken a half mile south of the village on the west road leading to Swanton. We had occupied this position nearly two hours in expectation of the enemy, when positive information came in that they had taken the west road ... and that they were within three miles of the Bay village.

I instantly ordered a strong guard to remain on the west road and marched to a position two miles and a half east of the village, and drew up my men on a height to the left, commanding the highway ... where I found pickets and advanced guard [of the defenders] had retired unperceived before the enemy, who were two hundred strong.

The invaders appeared to be well armed and equipped, and were hauling two small field pieces with horses taken from the Miller and Sixby homesteads, "the first farms they had passed after crossing the international boundary." The spot chosen by Kemp was Moore's Corner (later known as St Armand Station), named after Hiram Moore whose farmhouse was situated at the intersection of the roads in a narrow valley through which Rock River flows:

The force under my command [Kemp continued] amounted to about three hundred men (of whom not one hundred were engaged [that is, were with him at the moment]), but, before it was possible for me to reduce them to order, the van of my line commenced firing without command.

Colonel Knowlton, who also filed a report to Colborne, arrived at Philipsburg the following day. He did not mention the premature fire which, Jones suggests, was the exasperated response of one of the volunteers to the taunts and insults of the advancing *patriotes* whose numbers had been considerably swelled in Swanton.

To a commander of experience [Kemp confided] I need hardly apologize for the impetuosity of an undisciplined body, hastily taken away from their farming operations and placed in sight of an enemy only a few hours after arms had been placed in their hands. This premature fire was instantly returned by the rebels and ... was kept up on both sides for about 10 to 15 minutes when the enemy retreated back toward the State of Vermont, leaving behind one dead, two wounded and three prisoners.

The rebels' retreat, by the same road they had come, was a costly affair, for, as Jones recounts, "Some zealous volunteers had removed a portion of the planking from the bridge which the retreating patriots must recross, and they were unable to take the small field pieces with them."

Kemp concluded with further particulars about the prisoners and the rebels' abandoned arms and equipment:

One of the wounded is Robert Shore Milnes Bouchette [named after a former Lieutenant-Governor of Lower Canada], who led the advance guard of the rebels and is severely hurt. The other is slightly wounded and reports himself to be a nephew of Julien Gagnon, of St. Valentin, in l'Acadie, habitant, leader of the party. They left also two pieces of cannon mounted on carriages, five kegs of gunpowder, six boxes of ball cartridges, seventy muskets, part of them in boxes, and two standards.

From the undisciplined state of the Loyalists, the darkness of the night, it being nine o'clock [in December], and the vicinity to the woods, the rest of the party made their escape.

Besides Bouchette and Gagnon, three other *patriotes* were reported wounded, and one (Hubert Patenaude of Grande-Ligne) killed.

Jones takes up the narrative of the aftermath of the engagement:

The little army now returned to the "Bay" in triumph carrying with them their spoils and the prisoners that had been taken — … The waning excitement, and chill of the night air, soon recalled to many that they had had no food since morning … It was a serious problem to feed three hundred men in a small town. They were pleasantly surprised to find on reaching the old Methodist Church, however, that the pastor, the Rev. William Squires, an ultra-loyal Englishman, had prepared food for the returning loyalists by boiling in large kettles in the rear of the church, a bountiful supply of potatoes and salt pork.

The prisoners seem to have been humanely dealt with. Bouchette, in particular, took pains to pay tribute to the kindness of Harriet Moore, whose husband, Philip H. Moore had played a prominent part in the action. Bouchette had taken refuge in Hiram Moore's farmhouse and was captured there. Mrs Moore, who must have been anxious during the day for the welfare of her three sons — aged 11, 13 and 15 — and unsettled by the recent rebel occupation of family property, took pains to dress Bouchette's wound before he was moved to Philipsburg by his captors.

The Moores were prominent members of St Paul's Church, Philipsburg, and Kemp was churchwarden at Trinity Church, Frelighsburg, a position he would continue to hold until 1853. Paul Holland Knowlton was largely responsible for building the St Paul's Church, Knowlton, in 1843. Denominational affiliation probably played no role in the hospitality enjoyed at the Methodist church on the evening of 6 December.

The Report for 1838 of the SPG reflects the unsettled state of many missions in the Diocese. The Rev. Andrew Balfour, who was on his way to take up a new mission at Waterloo, for example, was within hearing-distance of gunfire in the Richelieu valley. His family was then in Upper Canada near rebel-occupied Navy Island and, with his bishop's permission, he spent four days hard travelling to reach them and bring them out. The clergy on the frontier of Vermont (Richard Whitwell and James Reid) wrote of the 'constant state of uneasy alarm' throughout the previous winter among their people. From Clarenceville, the Rev. Micajah Townsend spoke in glowing terms of the conduct of his "border population" in the face of the recent troubles:

Our border population, mostly from the United States originally, though comparatively few in number, have constituted an impenetrable cordon of loyalty [he reported] — an effectual barrier between the rebels within, and their sympathising friends without, the province. Placed thus between Scylla and Charybdis, constantly threatened, and twice invaded, ... my parishioners have stood nobly for their country; and though drawn by common danger from their families, to assume, during an inclement winter, the duties of soldiers, they have suffered but slightly from those moral evils which usually attend public commotions unrestrained by the civil power. The commander of the forces has repeatedly commended their loyalty; and, on my part, I am happy to acknowledge, that my congregations have been larger, their attention to services more marked, and their devotional feeling apparently more deep, than in former years.

It is worth noting, by contrast, that Dr Wolfred Nelson during his formative years had been a parishioner at Christ Church, Sorel, where his father kept a school. He began his career with all the attitudes of his class and upbringing, but life among the *habitants* of the Richelieu valley where he practiced medicine on being demobilized after the war of 1812, led him to sympathize with their aspirations as a people. His own adverse experience of patronage and the misuse of government authority — especially after his election as member of the Legislative Assembly for the royal borough of William Henry in 1827 — led him eventually to take up the *patriote* cause as one of its most forceful leaders. His commitment to the rebel cause was one of personal conviction. As Montreal historian William Henry Atherton has put it:

A man like Dr Wolfred Nelson who had lived with the French habitants at St Denis, spoke their language and understood their grievances, a man of uprightness, sincerity and disinterestedness, would never have resisted authority and risked his reputation and fortune unless the irksomeness of the situation had become intolerable. Writing from jail at Montreal on the 18th of June, 1838, to Lord Durham, he said on behalf of his fellow prisoners: "We rebelled neither against Her Majesty's person nor her government, but against colonial misgovernment. ... We remonstrated; we were derided. The press assailed us with calumny and contumely; invective was exhausted; we were goaded on to madness and were compelled to show we had the spirit of resistance to repel injuries or to be deemed a captive, degraded and recreant people. We took up arms not to attack others but to defend ourselves."

In the conflict of 1837, the Church in this Diocese, through its adherents, may claim kinship with either side.

# Coping with Scandal (1840)

When Bishop Charles Inglis assembled his Canadian clergy at his primary (and only) Visitation, he delivered to them fourteen 'Injunctions' to guide them in their ministry when they returned to their various far-flung stations. The first and last are of particular interest in connection with the passages that follow:

Ist  That the clergy be exemplary in their lives; and that by a diligent discharge of the duties of their functions, they endeavour to promote the spiritual welfare of their respective flocks.

14th  That the clerk [cleric] be extremely cautious in employing strangers who appear in the character of clergymen to do anything for them, before they have seen the letters of Orders of such strangers, and are also well satisfied about the regularity of their lives and good moral character.

Although most clergy were "exemplary in their lives," laboured faithfully, and set a high standard of duty and devotion to their flocks, there were — from the beginning — individuals who passed themselves off as clergymen (such as John Bryan who in 1787 was receiving £50 from government to minister at New Johnstown [Cornwall], but later turned out to be an impostor). Others seemed to have proper credentials, but appeared on further enquiry, or by their behaviour, to be undesirable. When this happened, they had to be removed.

With new settlements opening up and a great demand for missionaries, the SPG was not able to fill the need, and bishops were forced to draw on clergy who arrived in their dioceses on speculation, so to speak. Many of these men were very worthy and, given the opportunity, rewarded the confidence shown in them. Others were clearly adventurers. It was one of the bishop's many tasks to determine which was which.

In this particular case, Bishop G.J. Mountain had appointed the Rev. Edmund Burke, recently arrived with what appeared to be excellent testimonials from overseas, to the mission of Bedford in Stanbridge. At the time of Burke's arrival, the little community was still rocked by the scandal caused by the previous incumbent, the Rev. Robert P. Balfe, who had fled the area after having seduced the wife of one of his parishioners.

After Burke had taken up his duties (pending the arrival of letters confirming his letters of introduction), Mountain began receiving disquieting news. He therefore instructed one of his trusted local clergy (the Rev. James Reid of St Armand) to report to him on the situation in

Bedford. The mails were slow and local travel difficult, but Reid kept Mountain informed of what he could learn of Burke's behaviour and character. By good fortune, both sides of the resulting correspondence have survived and make fascinating reading. Besides the interest of the case itself, it illustrates the difficulties of episcopal supervision at a distance and at a time when all communication was by an exchange of letters.

Montreal, 6 Nov 1840

My dear Sir [Mountain writes to Reid],

Reports of a [word illegible] nature have reached me respecting the Rev Mr Burke whom I have sent to Stanbridge. That gentleman exhibited to me a series of testimonials of the very highest order; & he spent five days here with Major Christie (a person of known piety & engaged in various religious undertakings) who was exceedingly pleased with him & most favourably impressed respecting his character. — I thought myself safe in allowing him to officiate, pro tempore, at Stanbridge — & I wrote to the Bishop of Chester & to a clergyman in Manchester to whom Mr B had given references, proposing, in the event of a favourable result, to licence him to some permanent charge.

He then asks Reid to report on Burke's deportment

...& [see] if there are grounds for the unpleasant rumours which are afloat, ... I am grieved beyond measure to think that I should have sent a person to fill Mr Balfe's place, ... respecting whom any such suspicions as I now find exist; & I am earnestly desirous to save the Church from further scandal. Your intervention may possibly effect this by putting him upon his guard. It will be my advice to him, however, to leave the place at once if he feels that he cannot meet the charges which I shall communicate to him.

Meanwhile, other reports came in. In a letter dated 31 October 1840, the Rev. George Mackie (a trusted friend and advisor who would later become Bishop's Official and Archdeacon of Quebec) wrote to Mountain that

Dr Marsden called upon me on Wednesday last, to put me on my guard agst this gentleman [Burke]; who had then left Quebec. He informed me that many reports were in circulation to his prejudice — as that he was a drunkard & lent "blackguard books" to some of his fellow passengers while on board ship — & moreover that the lady who travelled with him as his wife, was suspected to stand in a very different relation to him! —

On 1 December Mountain wrote to Reid, "I desire to thank you for acceding to my desire respecting the *surveillance* of this gentleman" and (probably in the hope of avoiding another unpleasant scandal) that he planned to give Burke "his congé ... as civilly as such a thing can be done." Reid took some time to reply, but furnished a full report to the Bishop on 31 December in which he confirmed that, although Burke had initially made a good impression, many reports of his scandalous behaviour had begun to circulate in the community:

He is a gone man [Reid's letter concluded] ... His conduct is notorious but I need not enter on particulars as I do not apprehend that you have any investigation to institute. On my way home one of the Magistrates told me that he and C. Vaughan Esquire had agreed that they would take depositions, and wished to know if they should have any effect with your Lordship. I told him what I thought your Lordship had already done, but urged him to proceed and do what he had intended, as it would be a solemn justification on the spot of your Episcopal act. The people are ashamed of having suffered his predecessor to riot in wickedness which is the reason that they have been so free with me in the present lamentable case. Though I knew that Mr Balf[e] was not esteemed I never knew what was against him till the beginning of winter; now all that I know against his successor was given me of their own accord without being asked. I hope Mr Balf[e] will never come to any part of this Diocese. I never heard of so beastly a man in the country ... Brandy, and the *effects* of being *high*, are the misfortune of poor Burke ...

Reid obviously knew nothing of Mackie's suspicions about Mrs Burke.

Meanwhile, diocesan business took Mountain away from Quebec, but further news on the subject of Burke caught up with him at Leeds, in Megantic. On 3 January 1841 he brought Reid up to date on the result of his enquiries. He had obviously not received Reid's letter of 31 December.

My dear Sir [wrote Mountain],
I am here on a Visitation of the Churches in this tract of country, & have received a letter from Mrs Mountain in which she mentions that among five & twenty letters delivered to my house ... some of which she has examined, there is one from the Bishop of Chester, giving such an account of Mr Burke that I cannot desire him to be an hour longer in the Diocese than is necessary. As I have not heard from you in answer to my letter of 1st Dec, I do not know whether that gentleman may not still be in Stanbridge. If so, I should wish that the letter which I then enclosed to you for him & placed at your discretion, shall be passed to his hands without delay — & not only

so, but that you should *ascertain* that that he *does not officiate there any more*. If, however, he has caused no scandal by his deportment while there, there will, of course be no occasion to blaze abroad the reproach of the Church in his person. But that matter is safe in such hands as yours. Let him, at any rate, go.

I learn, to my great surprise, that Mr Balfe is coming back; & expected to be at his post before the end of the year. If this be so, (& he writes to say so himself) I cannot help hoping that the Reports to his disadvantage will turn out to be calumnious.

On January 7th, Mountain wrote again, briefly, to Reid, enclosing in it an afterthought he had written the next day:

8 Jany [18]41

I am sorry to be so troublesome to you on the subject of Mr Burke: but it has occurred to me, since I wrote yesterday, that, if he is in difficulty as to the means of getting away, it would be better for me to sacrifice £5, if I pay it myself, than to let him hang on in the place. If, therefore, you find that, after your first endeavouring to settle with him by the payment of the £10 remitted to you (which it is the utmost to which he is entitled) for there are obstacles to his removal, be pleased to advance any sum not exceeding £5, & I will D.V., send it you upon receiving information of your having done it. ...

Mountain's anxiety to get Burke out of the Diocese was obviously fuelled by the slowness of communications and the distances involved. Reid, however, once his dealings with Burke were recounted, showed a much greater preoccupation with Balfe and the threat of his return.

St Armand 14th Jany 1841

My Lord [wrote Reid]

I trust you have by this time received my letter giving an account of the delivery to Mr Burke of the letter for him you had inclosed to me about the 1st Decr.

On the 12th Inst[ant] I received your letter, dated at Leeds, together with that which inclosed £10.. 0..0 for Mr Burke. I went yesterday to Bedford — delivered the money — took his receipt here inclosed. He started some difficulties because he was not paid in sterling currency. You will see what he wrote on the back. He says he will insist on getting his expences covered. He said at once he would quit — he would stay on no account. He never was satisfied with the place.

When I was there yesterday ... [p]erceiving that he was mystifying me [that is, trying to deceive me about the contents of the letter], and that there should be no mistake, I read to him both the short Note, containing the money, and also the Letter [you had written to me] from the beginning to the end of the sentence by which you had directed me to ascertain that he should not perform any more duty. I did this because he was labouring to make me believe that the whole difficulty stood in his unwillingness to remain in such a place as Stanbridge.

Hearing that you had a Letter from the Bishop of Chester, he observed that if his Lordship was induced to write an unkind Letter about him, he could shew others from the same Bishop of the most kind description. Every thing, in short, is wrong but himself. He will go home and represent your Lordship, and the state of the Diocese, to the Archbishop of Canterbury and the Societies!!!

I am very sorry to hear that Mr Balf[e] has the face to think of coming out again. Is it not possible, my Lord, to keep him away? The wife of Steinhower has acknowledged her guilt to her husband. Another case still worse than an illicit commerce with a worthless woman has within the last week come to my knowledge. He boarded at the house of Capt. W. Davies on the Ridge. Davies is a quiet, good, honest man. I have known him since he was a boy. In the dead of the night when all the family were asleep, this man, viperlike, left his bed — crawled to the apartment of Mr Davies's daughter — her cries roused the family and brought her father to rescue his child from the grasp of a viper that he had to turn out of his house. The man being very quiet, he proceded no farther, and whether, since his daughter sustained no other injury than the insult and fright, he would be willing to make a deposition on oath of the fact I do not know. He never told it to me, but those who had it from Davies's own mouth told it to me.

The fact is believed. The character in question is unquestionably bad. If such be allowed to remain we shall be run down without remedy. May God shield his Church from wolves in sheep's clothing and support, guide and comfort your Lordship in your arduous responsible office!

It would appear that the people of Stanbridge were determined that the Rev. Mr Balfe would not return "to his post." He, too, had come to the Diocese on his own. A former Roman Catholic priest, he had embraced the Anglican ministry and come to Quebec from the United States, with seemingly good credentials. In 1838 a letter of his written to the Bishop was printed in the annual report of the SPG which gives no hint that anything was amiss. It reads in part:

For the information of the Venerable Society for Propagating the Gospel, I beg leave to submit the following particulars connected with my mission: — I perform, on Sundays, morning-service at Bedford, and evening-service at Stanbridge Upper-Mills, on alternate Sundays; there is a third service at the Lower-Falls, four miles west of Bedford ... At the Lower-Falls there is an interesting little congregation of from 60 to 80 persons, who seem anxious to profit by the means of grace which the divine mercy leaves within their reach. There are two Sabbath schools in my mission; one at Bedford, attended by about 50 children; the other at the Lower-Falls, at which 40 children attend. I superintend both the schools, and explain the Church catechism to the children of one of them every Sunday, alternately. This is certainly one of my most pleasing and consolatory duties, for I consider it of transcendent importance to the future welfare of religion, not only to give the youthful mind clear views of our doctrines, but also to impress the youthful heart with a love and reverence for our apostolic Church.

There were 21 baptisms, 6 marriages, and 8 burials, during the last 15 months. I trust in God that my next report will tell of more extensive improvement in those committed to my charge.

In the April Term of 1841 Balfe was summoned to appear before the Court of King's Bench, Montreal, the Hon. Jean Roch Rolland presiding. The charge was alienation of affection, William F. Stinehour [sic], plaintiff. Among the eight witnesses subpœnaed were William Davies of Stanbridge and the Rev. James Reid of St Armand. The indictment included depriving the plaintiff of "the fellowship, comfort, society and assistance" of his wife, Eliza Amanda Wehr, of debauching her repeatedly and of assaulting and ill-treating her as well. Balfe pleaded not guilty and was tried "by special jury." On 2 July 1841 he was found guilty and condemned to pay damages of £50 to Stinehour, plus an additional £51/ 10/9 for costs. He then appears to have left the country. The case had dragged on from March to July and had heaped the sort of scandal upon the Church that Mountain had been at such pains to avoid. Such were the perils of "employing strangers."

In January 1842, Bedford was finally to receive a "devout, zealous, energetic" minister, in the person of the Rev. James Jones, the next to be appointed to this mission. Jones, who came under the auspices of the SPG, did much to build up the shattered fortunes of the Church and to repair the damage done by his unfortunate predecessors. He continued to serve Bedford until his retirement in 1863, having given two sons to follow him into the ministry.

# Involving the Laity (1842)

The first step toward self-regulation in the colonial church was achieved through the formation of Church Societies. Bishop John Inglis (Charles Inglis's son) was the pioneer-founder of Church Societies in Nova Scotia and New Brunswick in 1836 and 1837, respectively. In 1842 the Dioceses of Toronto and Quebec followed suit, the two Societies being incorporated by a single Act of the Legislative Assembly in that year.

The Constitution of the Church Society of the Diocese of Quebec, was adopted at a General Meeting of the Society, duly convened at Montreal, on 21st July 1842.

From the beginning, the importance of Montreal as equal to that of the City of Quebec was recognized by the Society. In the sixteen articles adopted, provision was made for the alternation of annual meetings between Quebec and Montreal "whereof not less than fifteen days notice shall be given by the Secretary, in at least one of the leading newspapers in Quebec and Montreal." The article governing treasurers (Article V) was modified in 1844 to provide that accounts be opened in the name of the Society in the Bank of Montreal as well as the Bank of Quebec for the deposit of "all subscriptions, donations, rents, issues, and profits, payable to the Society." The Annual Report for 1844 shows that the Society had two treasurers, one for Montreal (T.B. Anderson) and one for Quebec (H. Jessop). Prominent in financial circles, Anderson had been a director of the Bank of Montreal since 1830; he became vice president of the Bank in 1847, and president in 1860. He continued to be treasurer of Church Society until it was merged with the Synod of the Diocese of Montreal.

One of the most important provisions in the Constitution of Church Society was the institution of a Lay Committee, which, it was hoped, would place the church on a firm financial footing through the involvement, and by means of the management, of prominent, well-to-do laymen.

The Committee was to consist of the twenty-five members appointed before the incorporation of the Society (all of them men of wealth and influence) and be subject to the sanction of the Bishop. The objects of the Committee — as revised in 1844 — show the thoroughness with which the founders of Church Society wished to tackle the planting of churches and the support of ministry in the Diocese. As the "General By-Laws" state:

The Objects of this Committee shall be:

*First* — The placing the Clergymen, now resident and doing duty in the Province, upon a just footing as regards the sufficiency and permanency of their incomes.

*Secondly* —The providing for the permanent and adequate support of an increased number of Clergymen, so that, with the least possible delay, the members of the Church in every portion of the Diocese may have the means of access to a Church within a practicable distance.

*Thirdly* — The building in every place where it may be required [of] a Church of stone or brick, upon a well considered plan, as to dimensions, external form, and internal arrangement, keeping in view the probability of its requiring enlargement.

*Fourthly* — The building, in a good situation, convenient to the Church, [of] a comfortable Parsonage of brick or stone, upon an uniform plan, which should be carefully considered, with reference to size, and internal arrangement, and should admit of additions being made, with the sanction of the Bishop.

*Fifthly* — The insuring [of] such Churches or Parsonages against losses by fire.

*Sixthly* — The procuring [of] an adequate and permanent support for all the Institutions [such as the Cathedral, church schools, seminaries, etc.], authorities [archdeacons and travelling missionaries], and functionaries [such as the secretary of Church Society], suitable and appertaining to the Establishment of the Church of England in this Diocese.

*Seventhly* — the investing [of] all life subscriptions (unless so far as the application of these may be otherwise limited by the contributor) in a permanent and accumulating Fund, of which the interest only shall be applied to the general purposes of the Society. [At this time a life membership was £12/10; annual membership was 25s.]

*Eighthly* — The encouraging [of] the formation of a local endowment Fund at every station or place having a Church or Clergyman, by special contributions, or by setting apart a portion of the Pew rents, to form an accumulating fund until the net income shall in each case amount to £50 per annum; for the more effectual promotion of which object the Society will engage, whenever such fund shall be formed and shall amount to £100, invested in Bank stock, or other public securities, to add thereto a corresponding amount of £100; provided always that such investment shall stand in the name of the President of the Society [the Bishop].

A glance at this outline underscores the optimistic, expansionist view of the Church at this period. Despite the slender means provided, and the threat of the withdrawal of SPG support, the stipulation of "keeping in view the probability ... of enlargement" of church facilities reveals a confident and forward-looking mentality that sought only the building materials to establish a firm and lasting foundation.

## Ministry to the Marginalized (1846)

Work among Montreal's outcasts and unfortunates is not well documented before the 1850s, especially those efforts outside the sphere of Roman Catholic ministry and social services. William Henry Atherton, in his history of Montreal (1535-1914), has a chapter on "Movements for the 'Unfortunates'" in which he lists the Hôpital La Miséricorde, founded by Mgr Ignace Bourget, and the Hospice Ste Pélagie, a home for "fallen girls," instituted under his direction by Madame Jetté in 1845. In January 1848, the little group of women who cared for them

was erected into a canonical body under the title of 'Sœurs de Miséricorde' (Sisters of Mercy). Madame Jetté, the foundress, became Sister de la Nativité, and Madame Galipeau, Sister St. Jeanne Chantal, was appointed superior. In 1848 the number of penitents reached eighty-seven and in 1851 it increased to ninety-seven. During the first six years the institution saved the lives of 390 new born infants.

According to Atherton, the next "important development for fallen women was the founding of the Sheltering Home for Protestants." He places the earliest efforts as "late in the '50s, perhaps about 1858," which were those by "some of the officers of the regiments stationed here, and by prominent men of the city, for fallen girls, mostly maternity cases ..."

This home [he writes] was called the "Magdalene" and continued for a number of years, disbanding, however, after the regiments left Montreal. On the 2nd of March, 1868, the home on Seigneurs Street, a direct outgrowth of the previous disbanded Magdalene, was established for the reception of destitute and fallen girls.

Well before the suggested founding of the "Magdalene" there was a refuge for such women, served by an Anglican chaplain, the Rev. David Bernard Parnther, who was born in the West Indies, educated in England and ordained (as both deacon and priest) by G.J. Mountain for service in the diocese of Quebec. Parnther first served within the present boundaries of the Diocese of Montreal in Huntingdon as a missionary of the SPG, but was posted to the city of Montreal in 1843. In 1846, the year he left the Diocese, he was attached to Trinity Chapel.

The following passage appeared in a printed pamphlet containing the current report of the Magdalene Asylum of Montreal and was reprinted in the *Montreal Witness:*

MAGDALENE ASYLUM: The Rev. Mr. Parnther, while residing in Montreal, showed a zeal and assiduity in behalf of the institution which extended [that is, attracted] notice. He visited it every Thursday for the purpose of holding religious services, and conversing with the inmates about their spiritual interests, and his visits were felt to be peculiarly acceptable and profitable. When leaving the city, he endeavoured to find some minister to take his place, but did not succeed. The Great Shepherd of the sheep will raise up successors to him.

The number of houses of ill-fame in the city is at least sixty, averaging about nine inmates each, which gives a wretched population of 540 young females in Montreal living on the wages of infamy, besides the still more degraded women who keep these houses, and the houseless host of street-walkers, vagrants and prisoners of the same sex; all of whom are victims of lust and intemperance. Is it not right that an effort should be made to reclaim all that is possible of this mass of human guilt and woe?

Work continued with vicissitudes until the the Sheltering Home was incorporated in 1898 with a number of prominent Anglicans (such as Mrs M.H. Gault, Mrs E.E. Shelton, Mrs R.W. Shepherd, and George Hague) among "the incorporators." By this time, as Atherton specifies, "the classes of inmates assisted" had been broadened to include

1. Discharged prisoners and those whom the Recorder wishes to be placed in a home rather than imprisoned.
2. Inebriates, many of whom apply for shelter while others are placed by friends.
3. Girls from the streets and houses of infamy.
4. Maternity cases, many of whom are more sinned against than sinning.
5. What is called the 'floating' class — patients discharged from hospitals before strong enough to work; the weak in body and mind; incompetent, idle girls, who, not vicious, would, however, if allowed, sink to the abandoned class.

May 1994 marked the tenth anniversary of the opening of the Auberge

Madeleine which continues to serve all manner of women in difficulty. The Synod report for 1995 states the activities of the 1993-94 fiscal year:

[W]e housed 352 women for an average of 18 days each. We have learned over the years that a large number of the womem we welcome arrive at the Auberge as the end of a terrible life journey: negligence and abuse in child-hood, limited education or training, poverty and violence in their adult lives, etc. We are therefore not surprised to learn that 44% of our residents had mental health problems, and 37% had substance abuse problems. 64% talked about their experiences (past or present) as victims of violence, and 28% cited violence as their principal reason for needing shelter. This year the 18 to 30 age group represented 37% of residents, the same as last year. 31 to 40 year-olds accounted for 35%, and 41 to 50 year-olds for 19% and those 51 or over for 9%. ...

Increasing fund-raising has continued to be a top priority. We finished off last year with a small surplus, due to an additional grant from the Ministry of Health and Social Services ... Our grants from the Diocese and from the United Church are important in ensuring some stability in funding from non-governmental sources and credibility with potential new donors.

Although there is obviously no historical link between the Auberge Madeleine and the Magdalene Asylum of Parnther's day, the pressing need for a ministry to women at risk continues to assert itself and to be met with willing but precarious support.

## Typhus (1847)

Already in February of 1847, news ot the widespread destitution in Ireland and the Highlands and Islands of Scotland had reached the Canadas. Collections for the sufferers were made and sent, Protestants and Catholics alike joining in the effort. As spring approached, the colony braced itself for another sort of involvement: the arrival of immigrants in unprecedented numbers. They were — many of them — impover-ished, malnourished, and worn out by the long voyage below decks. Many of them arrived infected with "Ship Fever" — that is, typhus.

Since the cholera epidemic of 1832, all steerage passengers, sick or well, were obliged to disembark at the Quarantine Station at Grosse Isle some thirty miles downstream from Quebec. They were to carry all their possessions ashore where they washed their clothes and bedding, and remained there until they were pronounced fit to proceed up river by the the resident physician (or until they died and were buried on the island). A battery of three guns (still in place), insured that no inbound vessel would escape inspection; it was manned by a company of soldiers, and commanded the passage between Grosse Isle and the southern shore of the St Lawrence River.

In 1847 the breakup on the ice in the Gulf of St Lawrence was later than usual. The *Cambria*, of Glasgow, the first to reach the island, arrived May 9th but, because she carried cabin passengers only, was not detained. The *Ocean Queen*, of Bristol, the earliest ship with passengers in steerage, arrived on 18 May. She carried 83 (82 in steerage) of whom one died in the Quarantine hospital. On the following day, with the arrival of the *Syria* of Liverpool, bound for Montreal, there were hints of what the season held in store for the colony. Of the *Syria's* 242 passengers (all but one in steerage), nine had died before reaching the island and been buried at sea. Forty more would die at the Quarantine Station.

On May 24th Dr George Mellis Douglas, medical superintendent on the island, stated to the Governor General that since his last report seventeen vessels had arrived with Irish passengers from Cork, Liverpool, Sligo, Limerick, Londonderry and New Ross:

The number of passengers with which these vessels left port [Douglas wrote] was 5,607; out of these the large number of 260 have died on the passage, and upwards of 700 have been admitted to hospital, or are being treated on board their vessels, waiting vacancies to be landed.

Since the establishment of the Quarantine Station, the churches had supplied Protestant and Roman Catholic chaplains to minister to the immigrants landed at Grosse Isle. The Protestants, regardless of denomination, had always been served by a Travelling Missionary, based on the island and supplied by the Anglican Diocese of Quebec. On or immediately before May 25th, the Rev. Charles Forest had arrived on the island to take up this position.

Forest, who was to serve long and faithfully as a missionary in the Diocese of Montreal, had only recently been ordained deacon. He occupied his post alone. By the end of the first week of June he found himself overwhelmed by ministering in the hospital and in the ships at anchor (too numerous to disembark their passengers), as well as in the newly-erected tents, all containing sick and dying immigrants. On June 9th he appealed to Bishop G.J. Mountain that no one man could perform this duty.

In response to Forest's plea for assistance, Mountain acted swiftly, setting up a roster of clergy volunteers to serve in pairs for brief periods so that no one man would be overcome by exhaustion and, it was thought, be less prone to succumb to disease. As his biographer put it:

The Bishop suggested it to such of the clergy of the diocese as seemed to be most able for the work, to offer themselves for the service, each taking a week. He took the first in the turn himself ...

Of the seventeen Anglican clergy (besides the Bishop) who ministered on the island that summer, eight came from (or would later serve in) the subsequently erected Diocese of Montreal: Charles Forest, Narcisse Guerout, Richard Lonsdell, Charles Morice, Charles Peter Reid, Charles Rollitt, Edward George Sutton, John S. Torrance, and Andrew Trew Whitten. Of these, Forest, Lonsdell, Reid and Torrance "caught the fever," but recovered. The others were unaffected. All those who died as a result of their service at the Quarantine Station — Richard Anderson of Upper Ireland, William Chaderton of St. Peter's, Quebec, and Charles J. Morris of Portneuf — were from the Quebec portion of the Diocese. At Montreal and St Johns, two further priests and one layman (Travelling Agent and Assistant Secretary of the Church Society) also lost their lives to "Emigrant Fever."

Turning to the city of Montreal itself, perhaps the best index of conditions there comes from contemporary newspapers. On Saturday, 19 June, the *Montreal Transcript* reported as follows:

With respect to the state of things in Montreal, it is difficult to obtain accurate information from an unwillingness on the part of those in office to divulge particulars. Against this concealment we must offer our decided protest. Surmises, formed on an unwillingness to disclose facts, will have a more wide-spread and pernicious influence than the truth, however startling. — From sources, however, on which we can rely, we learn that 30 corpses were buried on Saturday, and 27 on the Sabbath, and that the average number of deaths is about 25 per day.

Many cases of extreme distress came to our knowledge during a recent visit to the sheds [temporary shelters]. We met with one poor broken-hearted man, whose children were in hospital at Grosse Isle, and whose wife was uttering her last sigh in the sheds. ... Numbers were lying about on their wet bedding and boxes, the subjects of excessive weakness, generally brought on by violent dysentery. They manifested a state of apathy and indifference to personal cleanliness, ever the result of great and protracted suffering. Pitiable in the extreme is their situation during the present rains.

The most serious cases are, of course, found in the hospitals. Rows of roughly constructed beds, each containing two patients, line the narrow sides of the sheds. Dysentery and fever are evidently doing their fearful work with many. We are glad to find several persons serving out medicines to the sick, and attending to their wants. Many nuns and priests were rendering their aid. We understand that ten or twelve, mostly nuns, are present night and day. ... The healthy are rapidly departing towards the west.

So far as we can ascertain, there is at present little cause for alarm in Montreal, on the ground of contagion. —

The rising mortality decimated immigrant families and left many orphaned children of all ages. Existing institutions were quickly filled to capacity, and desperate measures were taken to make some provision for increasing numbers of orphans. The following notice, which appeared in the *Montreal Transcript* of Thursday, 1 July, offered one solution which — by today's standards, at least — seems far from humane:

EMIGRANT ORPHANS — We are authorised to say that any application (post paid) made to Lieut. Lloyd, Church Society's Office, Montreal, by parties who are charitably disposed to receive Orphan Children, male or female, into their employment, stating their [desired] sex, age and requirements, suiting them to the probable occupation, will be promptly attended to. Applicants should also state whether Protestant or Catholic children would be preferred. Direct as above, putting the word *Orphan* in the corner. Editors, both in Canada and in the neighbouring States, may serve the cause of humanity, by copying the above.

Lieutenant Lloyd, R.N., also fell victim to typhus due to his contact with immigrants. As more immigrant accommodations were hastily put up and deaths began to occur among Montreal's citizenry, the press expressed increasing alarm. On 5 July, the *Montreal Witness* ran the following article titled "PUBLIC HEALTH":

Great efforts continue to be made to provide accommodation for sick emigrants. Since our last, a new shed of great length has been completed, and immediately filled with the convalescent cases from other hospitals. This makes 12 extensive sheds or buildings ... The number of patients is not, therefore, decreasing, though many are dead and many discharged or convalescent.

There are one or two additional sheds in process of erection, and this immense lazaretto will soon have the appearance of a considerable village.

We cannot help suggesting, in this connexion, the liability of these dry wooden houses to take fire, more especially as straw for bedding is necessarily used to a great extent, and is in many cases lying loose about the ground, whilst many of the emigrants are addicted to smoking. The effect of a fire sweeping over wooden hospitals containing thirteen or fourteen thousand patients ... besides, perhaps, two or three hundred children ... would be horrible beyond description. ...

There is no doubt now that the fever ... is highly contagious. ... Mr Yarwood's death has been already mentioned [he was the Emigrant Agent for Montreal, and died "of fever"], and we are sorry to add that two or three of the doctors are ill, including Dr Liddell, the chief *emigrant physician*. Nineteen of the nuns are said to be more or less sufferers from the prevailing malady. ...

The disease is spreading also through the city ... Such a state of things demands great caution; and though it should by no means deter any who are urged by religious or benevolent motives to minister to these poor sufferers, yet it should effectually check all [contact] ... merely prompted by idle curiosity.

Despite the danger of contagion, there were those among the public who visited the immigrant sheds. The following letter, which appeared under "Communications and Original Articles," in the *Montreal Witness* was dated 6 July:

Sir, — Perhaps it would be the duty of some more qualified person to write to you on a subject which has for some days occupied my mind. ... All that I know, was learnt by a few visits to the emigrant sheds, and to that of the orphans in particular. ...

I have seen these poor children, lying or sitting, six or seven in a bed, most of them very thin, some sick, and even a few on the point of death. On every side I saw suffering frames and heard pitiful moans. ... I retired from this place of suffering with a heart deeply impressed, asking the Lord ... to help ... these unfortunates, by raising up in Montreal, and elsewhere, generous hearts ...

One of the first steps to be taken in regard to these poor orphans ... would be to have all those whose state of health or convalescence would permit, removed from the sheds to a more healthy part of the town, and kept there under efficient superintendence. In this way they would be better protected from the infection, which, on account of the excessive heat of the summer, will not fail to manifest itself in these sheds, where they are miserably crowded together and mixed with the sick and dying.

Then these poor little ones being more easily reached by the public, who are afraid to visit the sheds for fear of infection, would be more easily given into the hands of people charitable and worthy of confidence. ...

And as Christians, no matter of what denomination, have we not here, on the part of God, the finest occasion to place under the blessed influence of the Gospel, and to train for the Lord, these poor little ones who, without that, will certainly fall into the hands of the wicked.

One feels that this correspondent's attitude is at once more practical and more humane than that expressed in the notice published under the auspices of the Church Society that same week.

The letter in the *Witness* speaks with great praise of the "touching love" and "devotedness, truly worthy of the name of Christian" bestowed upon these orphans by the nuns "and some [French] Canadian females with them" who had them in their care. Although unsigned, the communication appears to be written by a Protestant clergyman. Indeed, it seems to have been widely believed that the Roman Catholics, both priests and nuns, were ministering to the sick with greater tenderness and zeal than were Protestant clergy to their co-religionists. On Thursday, 8 July, in an effort to deny these accusations, the *Montreal Transcript* printed the following:

Having frequently heard that the Protestant Clergy neglect the sick of their persuasion at the Emigrant sheds, we feel it right to state that the case is not so.

We have seen proof that the following clergymen attend thus. — On Monday, Rev. Dr [Daniel] Fal[l]oon [of St Ann's Chapel]; Tuesday, Rev. Mr [Mark] Willoughby [of Trinity Chapel]; Wednesday, Rev. Mr [Charles] Bancroft [of St Thomas's]; Thursday, Rev. Mr Willoughby; Friday, Rev. Mr [William Agar] Adamson [assistant at Christ Church]; Saturday, Rev. Dr [John] Bethune [of Christ Church]. The Rev. Mr [John] Fletcher [assistant at Christ Church] is constantly in attendance at the English Hospital.

Meanwhile, public confidence in the Board of Health began to waver. On Saturday, 10 July, the *Montreal Transcript* reported:

… mortality continues to increase. The return [that is, the report] of deaths for the week ending Friday last, shows that 275 emigrants died within that short period; and from a report made by Dr McCulloch, we learn that subsequently — in the twenty-four hours ending Sunday afternoon — no less than fifty-four died in the emigrant sheds. On that same afternoon (Sunday) there were also 30 deaths among emigrants in the city, so that the total number … for the dead that day was upwards of 80!

This is dreadful, indeed, and shows the necessity of other measures to meet so terrible a crisis. … [I]t is very evident that [the efforts of the Board of Health and the Immigrant Committee] ... are no longer adequate to the occasion, and that the danger has gone beyond them. ...

Another article of the same date but from the *Montreal Gazette* adds to the melancholy picture:

... we regret to say that ... the new Emigrant Commissioners, recently appointed, have decided to continue the sheds where they are, and to erect additional ones at Wind-Mill Point, and on Point St Charles, rather than adopt the views so strongly expressed in favour of Boucherville Island ... There are good accommodations there for about 2,000 souls, *now all ready*, and available in forty-eight hours, so that in that short space of time the plague which is now carrying off many of our valuable citizens, might be so checked as to restore public confidence and bring back the cheerful appearance of business and travel which, from the present state of things, has entirely disappeared from our streets.

On 19 July, the *Montreal Witness* reported that "Immigrant, or typhus fever of the most malignant kind, is now said to be in every street in Montreal, and in one or two localities almost in every house."

Among the severest losses to the Montreal Anglican community was the death, earlier that week, of the Rev. Mark Willoughby of Trinity Chapel. The funeral service — such ceremonies, like all public gatherings, more frequently avoided in these times of contagion — was described in the *Montreal Witness*:

The interment of the Rev. Mark Willoughby, whose lamented decease [on July 15th], has been announced, took place on Friday the 16th instant, in the Old Burying Ground. The funeral ... was attended by a large number of the most respectable inhabitants of Montreal, including the whole of the Clergy of the City [probably the Protestant clergy of various denominations is intended], excepting those who were prevented by illness from being present; the Revs W[illiam Bennett] Bond and W[illiam] Dawes officiated. There were also present many of the poor of the district, attached to Trinity Chapel ... And not a few of the Sunday scholars connected with the Chapel, established and constantly superintended by the late incumbent: an institution which he ever regarded with the most watchful care ... He was removed from us whilst actively engaged ... in a large and extending sphere of usefulness, after a few days' illness, the latter part of which were passed in a state of unconsciousness. The disease under which he fell, was contracted while zealously prosecuting his self-denying labours at the Emigrant Hospital and sheds, where ... he attended very frequently ...

On this one day — 26 July — the *Montreal Witness* reported the recent deaths of three priests as the result of ministering to sick immigrants: Willoughby, the Rev. William Chaderton (of Quebec) and Father John Richards of the Seminary of St Sulpice (the eighth priest of the Seminary to have fallen victim to "the Fever" to date). The Rev. William Dawes, who officiated at Willoughby's funeral, would later fall a victim to typhus while ministering to immigrants who had made their way down the valley of the Richelieu to St Johns, hoping to gain admittance the United States.

The last deaths on Grosse Isle in 1847 were recorded on 20 October by Roman Catholic Father Bernard McGauran; the Rev. Charles Morice, of Lacolle, performed the last Protestant burial on the Island for that terrible year on 11 October.

## Finding Books for Sale (1848)

On the subject of study and private reading among the clergy, William Bennett Bond's biographer recalled that at a public meeting he had heard the future bishop burst out, "Books! I have not time to read books!" Bond was far from typical in this respect, however, and many clergy complained of the obstacles to building up a modest personal library.

Access to books, especially of a specialized nature, was difficult in the Canadas. Although it was possible to obtain books and tracts from the United States (through the Repository of the New York tract society, for example) the Quebec clergy tended to rely on their contacts with the Society for the Promotion of Christian Knowledge (SPCK) in London. A branch of the Society was established in the See city with a "Depository" for publications on order or for sale, but there was no direct provision for other districts in the Diocese.

Shipments of books from abroad were slow and unsure at the best of times, as the Annual Report of the SPCK for 1834 makes clear:

The stock of the Repository [at Quebec] is very low indeed, more particularly of the Books required for Sunday Schools [it observed]; this is chiefly owing to the loss of the *Helen*. — The Committee regret to say that that vessel, by which they had expected to receive Books to the value of £95 sterling, was wrecked last fall, near the entrance of *Miramichi* River: the vessel and cargo have been since sold. Fortunately the Books were insured, and the Committee will lose no time in instructing their agent in *London* to recover under the policy.

It was not until 1847 that provision was made for a book depository for the Montreal clergy, temporarily placed under the direction of the Assistant Secretary of the Church Society at the Society's offices, 57 Champ-de-Mars, Montreal. A more satisfactory arrangement was made in November of that year when the Depository was placed in the hands of a capable laywoman, Mrs Catherine Walton, whose premises were located at Odd Fellows' Hall, Great St James Street. As the Annual Report of the Church Society for 1848 records:

It was also mentioned ... that a Depository for Books and Tracts had been established in Montreal. The books which were ordered last Autumn, from England, did not arrive till May last, so that the stock, and consequently the sales, have hitherto been extremely small. But the Depository being now on a more permanent footing, it is trusted that its usefulness may be widely extended. It is proposed to publish, in an Appendix to this Report, a list of the Books and Tracts in the Depository, which is in charge of Mrs. Walton at her establishment in Great St. James Street, Montreal.

At the last meeting of the Central Board, the Book and Tract Committee presented a Report, which was adopted by the Board, and in which it was recommended that Prayer Books be supplied to the Clergy who are at a distance from Montreal, to be disposed of by them, and accounted for to the Board — and that tracts be gratuitously distributed throughout the Diocese. — The prices of all the Books were also reduced — and it is confidently hoped that the present arrangements will give such satisfaction to the Clergy and Laity in general that the stock on hand will be speedily diminished to a considerable extent.

A "List of Books for Sale at the Depository of the Church Society," dated 1 July 1848, furnishes thirty-nine titles (in addition to various formats of Prayer Books and Testaments), ranging in price from £3 (Mosheim's *Ecclesiastical History* in four volumes) to nine pence (Andrewes' *Devotions*). Many of the titles offered were standard works, such as Burnet's *Thirty-nine Articles*, Pearson on the Creed, Paley's *Evidences*, and Prideaux's *Connexion*. Other works of interest were Heber's *Journal* (in two volumes), a *Life of Cranmer* (in two volumes), *Easy Methods with Deists*, Leslie's *Method with the Jews*, and Russell's *Church of Scotland*. The tracts available were not listed by title; they were supplied both by the SPCK and the Bristol Tract Society.

Catherine Walton had been in business since 1844 as an "Importer and Dealer in English, French and German Fancy Goods," particularly in Berlin wool and notions for fancy work. Taking on the Depository, which she operated in the same premises as her shop, was probably a sound move, for country clergy often went to the city with commissions to purchase items for their local sewing societies. The Montreal *Directory* for 1849 prints the following advertisement:

Mrs Walton, Importer of, and Wholesale and Retail dealer in Berlin Wool … has now on hand a very complete assortment of BERLIN WOOLS, in every variety of colour, which she offers upon most favorable terms. N.B. — Particular attention paid to Country orders, which will be strictly complied with.

The arrangement proved successful. Not only were books ordered and sold through the Depository, but bulk mailings from the SPG and the Church Society were sent there to await pick up by chairmen of the various District Associations. With the erection of the Diocese of Montreal in the following year, and the reorganization of arrangements along local lines, Mrs Walton continued in her dual role. The Annual Report of the Church Society of the Diocese of Montreal for 1852 notes that "Mrs Walton continues her efficient management of the Depository" — high praise indeed from that laconic chronicler of church affairs.

The Diocesan Book Room, established in 1929 under the Diocesan Board of Religious Education might be regarded as a relative — if not a lineal descendant — of the Book and Tract Depository. It, too, was founded because regular book stores did not stock theological books, especially those from England and Scotland. As an informal history of the Book Room points out:

The Anglican and Presbyterian communions have always been noted for a scholarly ministry, producing very important theological works according to the scholarly trend of the times. It was difficult for the regular book stores to keep in touch with that literature, for the English publishers were not too well aware of a Canadian market.

The Book Room was at first installed in the old Synod Building:

The chairman of the [first] Committee of Management was the Rev. Douglas Wiswell [the Book Room's anonymous historian continues]. For a few months there was no manager or salesman; the stock of books was left on display and a box was available to receive cash in payment.

After a short period under the honour system, a regular manager — Kingsley Symonds — was appointed and continued in this position until his death ten years later. He managed to make ends meet throughout these years, but the enterprise "had its anxious times." When Mrs. Dora M. Jones was appointed in his place, the Book Room had "practically no capital." Like Mrs Walton of the Depository days, Mrs Jones brought the business into a prosperous state of operations. She served as manager for more than twenty years.

## The Future Diocese on View (1849)

In 1849 the Rev. Ernest Hawkins, Secretary of the SPG, made an extended visit to America.

Throughout his journey, which began in the United States, he kept a careful journal which shows how thorough he was in visiting the various parishes and seeking acquaintance with both clergy and laity wherever he went.

At 6:30 in the morning on 7 August, Hawkins had his first taste of the Canadian field of labour experienced by numerous missionaries with whom he had been corresponding for many years on behalf of the SPG. Plans were afoot to subdivide the vast territory of the Diocese of Quebec, and the Secretary of the Society had been sent to see at first hand the state and progress of the Church in the Canadas.

He entered Lower Canada by way of Lake Champlain (which he later referred to as "the lake of beautiful sunsets"), went through customs at St John's, and was taken in hand by the Rev. Charles Bancroft, the incumbent there. Bancroft showed Hawkins the church, the churchyard and the monument erected to his predecessor the Rev. Mr Dawes. After breakfast, Bancroft accompanied Hawkins "by Rail R[oad] to La Prairie 15 m., and then by the Steam Ferry to Montreal," where he was taken to lodgings at Donnegana's Hotel on Notre Dame Street (a well appointed establishment with six "bathing rooms" and a billiard room).

This was the beginning of what must have seemed like a whirlwind tour of cities, towns, villages and and raw settlements throughout the Canadas, as well as a blur of dignitaries, members of the colonial elite, missionaries and ordinary people. The journal he kept of this journey, hurried and sketchy as it is, gives a vivid glimpse of what an intelligent, observant outsider made of the Canadian church:

*Sept 21 ...* 7 o'cl[ock a.m.] hired Buggy — crossed Ferry to Longueuil — Large French Church — plank road all the way to Chambly — call on Mr Isaac White & dined with him — a very nice fellow — & a conscientious miss[ionar]y — He has overcome quite an organised opposition. The People have built him a house and contribute £50 a year to him. He has only £50 from SPG & perhaps half as much for service to the Military [garrison at Chambly] —

Called on [the Rev.] Mr [Joseph] Braithwaite — he is now retired & keeps a small school — a man about 45 — looks strong — but has I understand a nervous disorder. [Later] on passed a fine covered bridge over *"the Richelieu"* & on to Rougemont, a church above par of the Country (recently consecrated) which had been built by the untiring Exertions of [the Rev.] Mr [Thomas] Johnson. Thence to Abbotsford over good Plank and Macadamised roads. — Mr Johnson not at home — but [the Rev.] Mr [Frederick] Robinson his son-in-law took me in most kindly — his wife is daughter of Mr Johnson.

*Septr 22* Off at 7 to Farnham in the hope of catching Mr Johnson — did in point of fact meet him — It became very wet. — Saw the new Church [St James] which had been built by [the Rev.] Mr [James] Jones's beggings in England — whi[ch] is sufficient for the Place — round-headed windows —

Hawkins had an interest in architecture and he often makes comments on the churches that he sees. He found Montreal's Place d'Armes "really handsome," but pronounced the large Roman Catholic church off it as "somewhat imposing but fitted up without taste." He judged the Rev. Joseph Abbott's Christ Church in St Andrew's East "a vile Church," probably due to its being "deeply galleried all around." St James, Vaudreuil he thought "pretty" and "well-arranged."

About 12 — it cleared — & Mr Johnson drove me to Dunham where we dined with — or rather — at the house of — Revd Mr Scott — for they had done dinner — Mrs Scott prepared the dinner — & put it on the table. They have no female servant — She gave us tea with it — After dinner to Frelighsburg — The country very pretty from its hills & wood — This parish of B[isho]p Stewart has at least the advantage of being beautifully situated in a circle of wooded heights — but owing to the heavy clouds & rain it did not show to advantage during my stay there.

At Dunham a good stone Ch[urch] is just finished — at Frelighsburg the Church is the first built in "the Townships" — it is of wood — but sufficiently capacious — It has a bell and tower — no font.

Hawkins remained in Frelighsburg over Sunday where he preached in Trinity Church in the morning and read prayers in the schoolhouse at Cook's Corner in the afternoon.

*Monday 24 — Very wet morning* — could not start till near 10. They all … persuaded me to give up the notion of going to Georgeville & [instead] to accompany Mr Johnson back to Granby. This I did — the road was very pretty — & the autumnal tints added much to the beauty of the forests. We dined at Shefford on fowl & *tea* — Mr Slack not at home — I was disappointed. However Mrs Slack — another daughter of Johnsons received & housed us — the Church a very tolerable one — wooden — in the usual style with a kind of sham gothic window & tower & spire.

It is evident that Hawkins was not used to having tea served with dinner, for he draws attention to this North American practice several times (as he does to the curious habit of driving on the right, "à la Française").

Many among the clergy thought that Hawkins himself might become bishop of the rumoured new Diocese of Montreal. Even Bishop G.J. Mountain asked him point blank why his name was not the one supplied as the likeliest candidate. Hawkins was adamant, however. He had no ambitions in that direction. He had come to look and to report. His journey, first and last, provided the Society with a first-hand assessment of the prospects for growth and independence in the fledgling colonial church, and a greater understanding of the conditions under which their missionaries laboured.

# Who Will Be Bishop? (1849)

The prospect of the erection of the Diocese of Montreal had long been the cherished hope of Bishop G.J. Mountain.

On succeeding as diocesan bishop of Quebec on Stewart's death in 1837, Mountain had retained his title Bishop of Montreal, to keep the need for a further division of his vast diocese in the minds of the authorities in England. The Diocese of Toronto had been erected in 1839, making provision for the territory west of the Ottawa River as far as the Lakehead, but the area remaining was still overwhelmingly large.

The British authorities did nothing for a decade, but after the Rev. Ernest Hawkins paid an extended visit to the Canadas in 1849, news of the division of the Diocese of Quebec and the appointment of a new Bishop of Montreal was expected momentarily.

Rumours were rife as to who the new bishop would be when the division was decided upon. One Montreal clergyman went so far as trying to influence the choice.

In October of 1849, the Rev. John Bethune of Christ Church, Montreal, paid a visit to some of the senior clergy in the Townships. As the Rev. James Reid of Frelighsburg confided to his diary on 6 October 1849:

On our arrival at home, we found just lighting at our door [the Rev.] Mr. Whitwell [of Philipsburg] and Dr. Bethune of Montreal, my old and very particular friend. He came out to see some of the Clergy, and this part of the Country which he [had] never seen before.

In the course of conversation, he said, that he has ascertained that a new Diocese of Montreal is to be erected, and that the appointment, or selection of a new Bishop for the same rests with the Governor of this Province.

Had this been so, it would have been viewed with great consternation. The Governor in question was Lord Elgin who had recently enraged Lower Canadian Tories (who included most of the Anglican clergy) for signing the Rebellion Losses Bill. This Act, in the view of most Tories, paid compensation to those who had fought against the Government in the Rebellion of 1837, and the Governor's consent to it had earned him an attack by an egg-pelting mob, not to mention the burning of Parliament, then situated in Montreal. The suggestion that the choice of the new bishop would rest with Elgin — Bethune obviously hoped — would act as a rallying cry to the clergy concerned and Anglican laypeople throughout the country. The diary continues:

He wishes therefore that a meeting of the Clergy of the District of Montreal should be called and assembled forthwith to take the subject into consideration as it affects them more than any.

The Doctor meant to go as far as Lennoxville, at least he said so, but made no attempt. True, the rain prevented, when one was not very urgent. The time was spent very agreeably indeed. He is a very pleasant companion. ...

[A]t Breakfast talking about the new Bishoprick, Mrs. [Reid] asked him who was to be the new Bishop. He said, "perhaps your own husband." I said, speaking through my nose, like a Yankee, "I swear I will not be Bishop." He also said that he would answer her as I did.

He said that [the Rev. William Agar] Adamson told him, that in the event the choice would [fall] on him (Doctor Bethune) he would like to succeed him as Rector of Christ's Church.

I carried the Doctor last night to Stanbridge, where he would get the Stage for Montreal next morning. I suppose he got to his own home next day for dinner. I like the man very much, but I suppose he had more in his mind than he disclosed to me.

Reid's suspicions about what was really at the bottom of Bethune's visit were amply borne out in a short time. On his return to Montreal, Bethune printed and circulated an invitation to the clergy of the district to assemble in Montreal on 25th October "for the purpose of selecting a Clergyman to be recommended for the new Bishopric." It was quite obvious that as the senior clergyman in the Diocese he thought the choice should fall on him. Bethune had used Reid's name and that of the Rev. Micajah Townsend, as senior clergy, to issue the invitation. Reid was furious and immediately took action — as his diary records:

When it came out in this form [Reid wrote on 19th November] I felt indignation at the thought that I was circumvented and involved in a foolish ambitious project in which I felt no interest.

I then began immediately to draw up papers, and mature a plan of operations with a view to defeat the movement. Messers Whitwell, Jones, Scott, and Johnson fell in with my plan, and united with the help of a circular from the Bishop, we succeeded in putting down the meeting, and quashed the pretensions of the real movers.

Reid called a meeting of the Missisquoi District Association of the Church Society on 20 October, at which a Resolution, a Protest, and a Memorial to the SPG, all prepared by himself, were adopted unanimously. A second resolution empowered the Chairman of the District Association (Reid) to act upon this expression of its "decided opinion" at the Montreal meeting "in any way that he may judge necessary, to counteract the object for which it is invited to meet."

The Bishop's Circular, dated 17 October at Quebec, was a direct response to Bethune's invitation. It pointed out that "Colonial Bishops are always appointed by 'the Home Government,' that it was not appropriate for the clergy to nominate the bishop, and that the present communication, although not amounting to a censure, was intended to put the clergy *on [their] guard.*'"

Reid takes up the story, not in his diary, but in his letterbook where he transcribed the Circular, Resolutions, Protest and Memorial:

On my arrival in Montreal [he recounts], I did not call on Dr. Bethune, nor attend the preliminary meeting as he wished I would, to help preparing matter to be brought forward at the meeting. Greatly disappointed he was.

From that meeting he hastened to my Hotel, he and [the Rev.] Mr. Abbott [either Joseph or William]. I was at dinner. He sent up his card. I left my dinner and went down. He attacked me for not attending the preliminary meeting. I told him I had nothing to do there, and attacked him for putting my name ... on the list ... when he knew that he had found me so far from having expressed any desire on the subject, that I had neither thought nor knew any thing about it.

He then declared  on his honour that he had followed merely the order of seniority. I asked him if he had seen the Bishop's Circular. He said he had, but that did neither censure nor forbid their proceeding ... I differed from him entirely ... I told him that since we had received the Circular we could *not hold* a Meeting, and that it was absolutely necessary to consider how it was to be got over.

Bethune obviously still hoped to win Reid over and relied on his knowledge of his old friend's love of food and convivial gatherings with his peers. He was, however, mistaken that Reid would be deflected from his principles:

He rather yielded [Reid continues], and insisted that I should dine with him at five of the clock that evening. He said that a number of the Clergy would be there and that matters would be talked over. The fact was, he flattered himself that the Clergy generally would be brought over to second his ambitious views, and had a great dinner prepared for them.

With great reluctance I consented. There were not however many of the Clergy. Only the two Abbotts, [the Rev. William Turnbull] Leach, Townsend and myself.

After a time, the subject nigh his heart was introduced by himself, with the absurd statement, that the Governor General was vested with power to select the Bishop for the New Diocese of Montreal.

Then followed what must have been a most unpleasant exchange:

I took him up at once, by asserting that His Excellency had no more power to select a Bishop than I had. Thereupon a warm debate ensued, in which the whole subject was argued. None took part in the debate but our selves. I felt more animated and strong than usual. He got no advantage over me.

The result of the whole was that he despaired of doing any thing at the meeting which was to be held the next day; and I felt perfectly sure that he would be willing to withdraw ...

Accordingly, next day when we assembled at the National School House, he stood up with us, who had signed the Requisition with him [that is, the clergy whose names he had listed on the invitation to the meeting], and withdrew it, in consequence, he said, of the Bishop's Circular, but in reality because he found that only the two Abbotts would support him. When this was done, he and the Abbotts and Leach and [the Rev. William Bennett] Bond went away. I took the Memorial which was in my pocket, and those present signed it.

It is clear that Bethune's supporters were proportionally few in number, for there were sixteen clergy who signed the Memorial: Reid himself, Micajah Townsend (Caldwell Manor); Thomas Johnson (Abbottsford); Joseph Scott (Dunham); Isaac White (Chambly); George Slack (Granby); Charles Bancroft, and William C. Merrick (St Johns); Richard Lonsdell (Laprairie); Charles Morice (Lacolle); Alexander Digby Campbell (Trinity Church, Montreal); Jacob J.S. Mountain (Coteau du Lac); Richard Whitwell (St Armand West); Frederick Robinson (Rougemont); James Jones (Stanbridge); and William Jones (Farnham).

In a letter to Bishop Mountain describing the proceedings, Reid hastens to say that he had presented the Memorial "not as to members [of] a Meeting, but as individuals, and as many as were present signed it." He concludes his letter, in which he enclosed the Memorial, by saying:

As it is, I believe that all such unauthorised Meetings have got their death blow for the future. As for myself I have no hesitation in declaring in a meeting or out of a meeting my disapproval of an Episcopal selection to be made by the Provincial Civil Government.

At my time of life in particular [he was within a few weeks of his 69th birthday] I wish to keep out of all such troubles, but unintentionally, while off my guard I got into this ugly scrape, but I hope I shall keep clear from all such snares and scrapes for the future.

It would seem likely that after this acrimonious exchange and the blow administered to Bethune's ambitions, all cordiality between the two old friends might cease. It is pleasant to read in a subsequent diary that on a visit to Montreal on 18 April 1851, for a gathering of the clergy to see their new bishop off on his first trip to England since his arrival in Canada, Reid took a cab "to Dr. Bethune's, where I staid all night, and was honourably treated."

As far as the notion of the clergy having a voice in the selection of their bishop was concerned, Bethune was only a little ahead of his time. On 8

July 1857, Benjamin Cronyn was elected bishop by the clerical and lay representatives of the new Diocese of Huron in session at London, Ontario, in what was to be the first Episcopal election in Canada.

## A Laywoman's Initiative (1850)

Significant contributions were made by women to the Canadian church in the nineteenth century, but they are usually thought to have been necessarily restricted to fund raising through sewing societies and bazaars, or, in the case of the well-to-do, through benefactions and legacies. It is clear, however, that women took upon themselves a wider role than this. The Sunday School of Trinity Church, Frelighsburg, for example, was founded, not by the rector, the Rev. James Reid, but by his daughter Nancy and a group of women-friends.

It is evident from the following brief entry in her father's diary that a good deal of thought and effort had gone into the Sunday School plan, and that the needs of the children of disadvantaged settlers had not been neglected.

At the time of writing, Reid was seventy years old and Nancy twenty-one:

13th April 1850 … Nancy is very much engaged in getting up a Sunday School. She has got Almira [Chamberlin] and Patience Kemp to join her. They have gone round to every house, where children are, to ascertain who would come. They are to make clothes for two poor children, in order to fit them out for coming. I gave them money to make the purchase. …

On 12 April, as the Churchwardens' accounts for 1850 show, seven shillings one penny ha'penny was laid out toward this clothing. Books were ordered, too, at six shillings ten pence, as well as two pounds ten shillings paid toward a Sunday School library.

Many years before this, there had been a Juvenile Library Society at Trinity Church — founded as early as 1823. Perhaps Nancy and her friends consulted some of the books then purchased (such as "Mrs Sherwood on the catechism," "Fenelon on the education of daughters" or "the Youth's Magazine") for it is clear that they were left very much to their own devices on how to proceed. The rector was becoming increasingly deaf which hampered him in communicating with children:

22d April 1850 … Yesterday the young Ladies began their Sunday School.

They had 31 children to begin with. I addressed the teachers and the pupils, but I cannot undertake to teach a class, on account of the dulness of my hearing; and the children all without exception speaking so low as they all do without exception when they read in School. I have promised to meet the Teachers once a week to expound unto them a chapter, or part of a chapter. They are to meet me tomorrow evening at half past 7 — an hour much too late. ...

The initiative prospered:

5th May 1850 Sunday. The day cold, rainy and very windy. The Sunday School was well attended, but there came not more than 30 or so grown persons to Church. I know not how the School is taught. The teachers are mostly all young and inexperienced. I cannot undertake to teach myself, because I am so dull of hearing that I cannot possibly understand them. Indeed the teachers and the Scholars are to me incomprehensible, as I cannot hear one or the other. I stay there all the time, but I do nothing. ...

Once the Sunday School had been well established, although it continued to be managed entirely by Nancy and her fellow teachers, the rector began to think of the School as his own. On 22 May he copied into his diary a letter that he had written to the Rev. Ernest Hawkins, Secretary of the SPG, in which the extent to which he had appropriated his daughter's initiative becomes strikingly evident

My Congregations keep up very regular. ... I have a good Sunday School, and a Bible class of young exemplary persons, to whom I expound a Chapter of the New Testament &c every Tuesday evening. In this exercise we take much pleasure, and find it very profitable.

Although he does not allude to the Sunday School again until 8 December, the work went on, for on that date Reid obseves that he "was very much pleased with both the attendance and manifest improvement of the children" when he looked in on them.

Six years later Almira and Patience had married and moved away; Nancy Reid had died of a painful, lingering illness, but the Sunday School was firmly established, and, as her father noted in his diary, a new generation of volunteers had taken their place: "Our young lady Teachers of our Sunday School are every day hard at work, preparing a Christmas tree, to be hung with presents and toys for all their scholars; and next week the Church is to be adorned with green boughs and festoons." He was not in favour of this particular development in Sunday School tradition, and voiced his misgivings in the privacy of his journal:

I wish they were half as Zealous for the increase of faith, hope and charity to abound in themselves and in the members of the Church, and in the increase of the Congregation! But the carnal mind will still be carnal and its religion will be, and must comport with what the world loves; the gratification & pleasures of the world. … The vast many pretty things they have ready for the tree to be given to the Sunday School Children on Christmas Eve, is truly wonderful.

In his 84th year, Nancy's father wrote again to Hawkins (still in his capacity as secretary of the SPG) that the Rev. James Burrows Davidson, had succeeded to superintending the Sunday School:

The Rev. Mr Davidson, my assistant, is doing his duty faithfully … and takes charge of our Sunday School consisting of about 45 steady pupils and six teachers. They are instructed in the Church Catechism, the Collects, Epistles, Gospels, and Church Singing, and have a tolerably good Sunday School Library of approved books for further reading.

The Nancys, Patiences and Almiras seldom receive credit — or even support — for their devotion and application to such labour-intensive causes as Sunday School, but the results of their efforts are no less enduring.

## A Country Cleric Meets His Future Bishop (1850)

In the spring of 1850, when the St Lawrence was just free from ice and open for shipping, the Rev. George Slack set off for Quebec to board a ship for England. Back home in Milton (in Shefford County in the Eastern Townships) was his young wife Isabella, their three sons — aged four, three, and a year-and-a-half — together with three children from his first marriage, two sons and a daughter, all under ten years of age. The Slacks had moved to Milton from Granby that very spring when the mission was divided into two, and the family had hardly settled in before the planned voyage to England had to be undertaken.

Never, my dearest wife [Slack wrote to Isabella from Quebec] did I know your value till of late — never did I love you as I do now — I trust in the Lord's mercy to be restored to you and permitted by affection & kindness to endeavour to make you some amends for the anxiety and pain I have caused you.

Mrs Slack seems to have been fearful about the voyage, and his in-laws, too, had been full of cautionary advice. It was no wonder that this should be so, for, as an account of his life written almost a decade later asserts, every ship except one in which Slack had crossed the Atlantic had foundered on its next voyage!

On May 31st he continued the letter begun on the 28th to give Isabella an account of his enforced stay in Quebec due to unfavourable weather. He had acquaintance there, both among the clergy and the port authorities, and took the opportunity to call on G.J. Mountain and on an old friend from his days in the British Navy:

May 31st — Today finds us still at Quebec owing to the prevalence of easterly winds — I went on shore yesterday and called on the Bishop and spent some time with my old friend Captn Boxer — The Bishop told me that the question of the division of the diocese is finally settled — Mr Fulford is to be the new Bishop and will probably come out about the same time with my self. The Bishop wished me to call and see him while in London, which I shall certainly do — Captn Boxer promises to take *one of my boys* when ever he gets his flag, which he expects to do shortly so that you see there will be a berth *ready for Tom* —

The identity of the new Bishop of Montreal had long been a matter of speculation. Slack must have been one of the earliest in Canadian circles to know of Fulford's selection. News of the appointment did not appear in the Montreal press until August.

Captain Edward Boxer had commanded the Man of War *Hussar*, a 46-gun frigate on which Slack had served for three years, signing on in 1827 at age 16 when he was just out of school. Slack had come to the ministry relatively late in life and had only been ordained for seven years, following extensive service both in the Royal Navy and in the service of Her Majesty Doña Maria II of Spain.

It may well be that Slack is expressing some doubt that Captain Boxer is likely to get his flag (that is, become an admiral) very shortly for their son Tom was only four!

In a further letter to Isabella, written 16 July, Slack described meeting with Fulford, as Mountain had asked him to do, and the introductions to clerical society that this had produced. He refers to Fulford as "Dr" as he had not as yet been consecrated bishop.

Dr Fulford behaves to me in the kindest and most friendly manner. I went with him this morning to Lambeth Palace to visit the good old Archbishop of Canterbury, who received [us] with the most unaffected simplicity & conversed with me for 20 minutes upon the state of the Church in Canada. —

The Archbishop, John Bird Sumner, was then 70 years of age, but had only been in office since 1848 and in consequence would have had little dealing with overseas matters. His predecessor, William Howley, had served for twenty years, and had seen — at a considerable distance — remarkable expansion in the Canadian church.

This introduction was not to be the full extent of Slack's London contact with Fulford, however. The letter continues:

I dined to day with Mr Howarth the Rector of St George's, Hanover Square, to meet Dr Fulford and a party of 14 other clergy of that parish. It was a farewell entertainment to Dr F. (whose chapel was in that parish) & in consequence "neat & appropriate speeches" were made by Mr H: — Dr F: — your humble servt & Mr Hawkins — I was received in the most cordial manner by all the clergy & spent a very pleasant evening — They were all clergy rather of the old fashioned school — but not in the least degree tinctured with Puseyism, indeed they ridiculed the absurd proceedings of the Tractarians — But in all my enjoyment it is, I assure you my dear, a constant drawback that I have not you with me to share my pleasure — I felt this more especially in Farnham [Surrey] where you would have enjoyed much the sweet flowers — the pleasant drives thro' the green leaves and the cheerful society of kind old aunt Melly, who altho' upwards of 70, gallops her poney like a girl of 17 — I preached in Farnham Church last Sunday. How little could I have thought that I should have done so the last time that I was in that church —

Talk along party lines would have been of particular interest, as the new bishop's churchmanship was to be a matter of special concern. Was he a High Churchman or Low? This was a matter that would be broached on the day of Fulford's arrival in his new diocese, and one that he would dodge adroitly.

Nothing that Slack heard at this intimate party seems to have alarmed him, whereas he had found Ernest Hawkins, when he visited the Townships, too High Church for his taste, and spoke slightingly of Armine Mountain as a Tractarian. Slack himself was an Evangelical, but that did not stop him from expressing consternation, years later, at the treatment meted out to Father Edmund Wood by a then ascendant Low Church party.

Following the excitement of meeting his future bishop and being introduced to a circle that would normally have been closed to him, Slack turned his attention to family visiting. It is possible that the Rev. Mr Haworth of St George's, Hanover Square, was a relative of his first wife, Emma Coulson's, for their marriage had been delayed for five years while she was obliged to care for an aunt, Miss Haworth, who finally died aged 92.

Isabella may well have feared her husband's recollections of this former attachment which could not fail to return as he revisited the scenes of his former courtship and marriage, so long delayed and so short-lived. Emma was suddenly taken ill of "a spasmodic attack" while Slack was away at a funeral and, although "everything was done for her that experience could suggest," she died the next day. She was 34. They had been married for four and a half years. Slack had three small children to bring up, and the founder of his first mission at Granby, the Rev. Thomas Johnson, had several daughers of whom Isabella Ann was the eldest. A year and a half later she and Slack were married. It is therefore touching that in his letters to his wife Slack takes such pains to bring Isabella into the scene that he describes and to say how much he feels she would enjoy it.

Slack also shares with his wife the intimacy of his response to his return to Farnham Church: the strangeness and awe that he felt to find himself preaching in a church that he had last attended — most likely — as a Naval officer with no thought of the priesthood.

# ERECTION AND CONSOLIDTION
## 1850–1868

## Fulford Arrives (1850)

According to his private journal — a sort of scrapbook of newspaper clippings with scrawled marginal notes — Bishop Francis Fulford first set foot in his newly-erected Diocese "at St Johns on Lake Champlain, or rather, [the] Richelieu River about 7 o'clock on Wednesday morning 11 Sept."

The transatlantic voyage from Liverpool to Boston on the Cunard Line's steamship *Hibernia* had been rough at the outset. The Bishop, his wife Mary and the two children "were all very ill for a day or two — Mary did not get over it for several days — but on the whole we had a favourable voyage, & pleasant companions."

They disembarked briefly at Halifax:

We all landed, and called on the Bp of Nova Scotia [John] Inglis — saw him and his family & Archdeacon Willis — the Bp sent his carriage to meet us — we staid about an hour — he is very ill — failing rapidly, I think.

Inglis, who was then in his 73rd year, died on 27 October. He had served his diocese as deacon, priest, commissary and bishop since 1801.

The Fulfords spent several days in Boston and met with kindness and hospitality from "clergy & others," but the Bishop was on visitation and not able to greet them. Fulford preached at St Paul's on the Sunday, and on Tuesday the family travelled by rail to Burlington where they met the Bishop of Vermont and Mrs Hopkins before boarding the steamer for St Johns. Armine Wale Mountain, Bishop Mountain's son, had crossed over to accompany them.

Fulford pasted the *Montreal Herald*'s account of his arrival into his journal:

The Lord Bishop of Montreal arrived at St John's yesterday morning in the steamer Burlington. At half-past seven he was met by the Bishop of Quebec and a number of the Clergy and Laity of the Diocese of Montreal.

The party breakfasted at the Rectory, after which Divine Service was held in the Church [St James']. Prayers were read by the Rector of the Parish [the Rev. Charles Bancroft], and the lessons by the Rev. A.W. Mountain, Chaplain to the Bishop of Quebec, who also read the Epistle. The Litany was said by the Rev. M. Townsend, and the Holy Communion was afterwards administered by the two prelates to the Clergy present and a large number of the Laity.

In 2000, on the 150th anniversary of Fulford's arrival, there was a commemorative recreation of this event in St-Jean-sur-Richelieu. Care was taken to select the Psalm, Epistle and Gospel that would have been used. The Order of Service was fully bilingual and featured special music and liturgical dancing.

The arrival of the Bishop and Mrs Hutchison — by boat from Ile-aux-Noix — was more conveniently timed for 3 p.m. As was Fulford, they were greeted by the Bishop of Quebec, the Rt Rev. Bruce Stavert. The party was then accompanied by Black Watch pipers to St James' Church where a brief ceremony took place to formally open the 141st Annual Synod of the Diocese whose delegates were all on hand. An address of welcome from the clergy of the Richelieu District, recalling the one delivered 150 years earlier by Micajah Townsend, was read by the Rev. Linda Chalk.

As the church was not big enough to accommodate all delegates and guests, a litany carried the procession to the Centre des Aînés Johannais, where the opening Eucharist of Synod was celebrated, followed by a reception.

It was a beautiful day and the festivities were a great success.

In 1850, after Divine Service had been celebrated and Townsend's Address presented, the whole party "partook of a sumptuous luncheon" at the home of J.C. Pierce, Esq.

Fennings Taylor, an early biographer, has recounted an incident which, he admits, may or may not have taken place on this first day, following luncheon, but claims with certainty did occur.

The churchmanship of the new Bishop was as yet unclear, although there had been rumours in the press prior to his arrival. Members of the Evangelical party, prominent in the Richelieu district according to Taylor, were determined to discover whether the Bishop was of like mind or not.

When the banquet was over and the ladies had witdrawn, an unnamed cleric, identified only as "Mr Blank," approached his diocesan as directly as he thought proper:

Seating himself opposite to, and at the same time addressing the Bishop [Taylor recounts], he is reported to have said: 'In the first place, my lord, I shall frankly make a confession with respect to myself, and then I shall as frankly ask a question with respect to your lordship.'

Taylor's account, written within a few years of Fulford's death, presupposed that many readers would remember the Bishop's appearance and manner, but that, fortunately, did not deter him from furnishing a vivid and engaging description of the man himself:

Now the Bishop [he continues] was one of those calm Englishmen whom it was difficult to surprise and not easy to perplex. Those who knew him will easily recall his massive expression and imperturbable manner, his calm, earnest, untroubled eyes, with their steel and bronze tints. They will remember, too, the suppressed humour, the ill-concealed mirthfulness that lodged mischievously near his eyebrows, or lingered patiently in the lines of his mouth.

Neither will they forget the courtly attitude of high bred attention which he habitually wore, but which he more pointedly assumed when anyone addressed him. They will probably fill up for themselves the outline picture which we have attempted to give ... as, without preface or circumlocution, he heard himself addressed by the excited rector somewhat in the following words:

'I am a low churchman, my lord, a very low churchman I may say!' but before the declaration was supplemented with the threatened question, the Bishop broke the thread of the inquiry by observing, in words of measured gravity:

'By which I hope you mean, Mr. Blank, that you are a very humble churchman!' Then turning to his host after the manner of one who knew how to direct as well as how to rebuke, added: 'I think we had better join the ladies.'

The identity of Mr Blank is a matter for conjecture. Robert Black argues that he was probably the Rev. William Anderson of Sorel, since he was "secure as a Crown rector and could not be removed or any way harmed by the Bishop." There were, however, a number of Evangelical clergy in the Diocese who might have been present, including Charles Bancroft, the incumbent of St James', and his assistant C.L.F. Haensl.

At 1:45 p.m. many of those present left for Montreal. The steamboat from Laprairie was met by a number of Montreal clergy, led by the Rev. John Bethune, and, after the bustle attendant on the debarcation of Roman Catholic Bishop, Count de Charbonnel of Toronto, had subsided, they boarded the vessel and were presented to Bishop Fulford:

This done [as the *Herald* reported], Dr Bethune gave his arm to Mrs. Fulford, and led her to the carriage in waiting for the party. The Rev. W. Bond followed with Miss Fulford, then came Mr. Fulford, Jr, a gentleman apparently twenty years of age, and next the Bishops. ...

The new Bishop and his family appeared in excellent health. They proceeded from the wharf to Hall's Ottawa Hotel, and were escorted by a considerable number of the gentlemen who had met them on the wharf.

When the company had dispersed and Fulford finally had a few moments for private reflection in his rooms at the hotel after this day of introductions, he would have proceeded to do what anyone in Anglican orders at that time would routinely have done: read through the Service of Evening Prayer, either by himself or with his family.

The second lesson appointed for the evening on 11 September, according to the Table of Lessons in the Book of Common Prayer, is the twelfth chapter of the Epistle to the Romans. It must have seemed especially appropriate. The chapter begins:

I beseech you therefore, brethren, by the mercies of God, that ye present your bodies a living sacrifice, holy, acceptable unto God, which is your reasonable service.

And be not conformed to this world: but be ye transformed by the renewing of your mind, that ye may prove what is that good, and acceptable, and perfect, will of God.

For I say, through the grace given unto me, to every man that is among you, not to think of himself more highly than he ought to think; but to think soberly, according as God hath dealt to every man the measure of faith.

On the following Sunday, 15 September, Francis Fulford was enthroned (to use the term of the day) in the the old Christ Church on Notre-Dame Street before a congregation of 2000 people. The usual oaths were administered by the Rev. John Bethune.

It was hoped that more suitable accommodations would soon be provided for the Fulfords, who continued to live at the Ottawa Hotel on St

James Street for several weeks. On 21 September, they moved to 16 Bellevue Terrace.

Although the SPG had insisted that the episcopate be endowed before the new Diocese of Montreal could be erected, initial provision for Fulford was far from generous. As of 31 July 1855, for example, his salary was a mere £800, while Mountain received £1,990 and Strachan £1,250. "It was found afterwards," wrote Fulford in his private journal, "that the funds for providing a See House were not so large as had been anticipated, and so I paid my own rent: and continued to reside in Bellevue Terrace, until April 1853."

## Power Struggles at the Outset (1851)

A special relationship existed between the SPG and its missionaries which often predated and even outweighed diocesan loyalties. As it might be expected, the contact between them, at least on the missionaries' part, often provided a safety valve to vent anxieties and misgivings about the mission field. The correspondence sometimes reveals the role that personalities and party interests played in diocesan life. The following letter to an unspecified recipient at the SPG (probably the Rev. William Thomas Bullock) from the missionary at Milton (the Rev. George Slack) is dated 9 Dec. 1851, at Milton Parsonage, and opens "Dear Friend & Brother." It begins with excuses for a delay in responding to a previous communication, and then launches into an account of local affairs.

My delay has arisen partly from a desire to send you a contribution [to the Society's publication] … wh[ich] I have never found leisure to write — my subject would have been a visit paid by our excellent Bishop [Fulford] in Co[mpany] with myself to a new settlement where he preached in a *grist mill* — And while I am mentioning the Bishop I must say that I think we ought to regard it as a special Providence that such a man has been sent to us — I do not know that I ever saw so many opposite qualities of mind and disposition meeting in the same person and tempering each other — It is little to say that he deserves the warmest esteem & most cordial support of all his clergy — He is to us as a brother and his kind considerate conduct alone has won many hearts. And yet alas! There are those … who desire to have a preeminence — The introduction of the Col[onial] Ch[urch] & School Soc[iet]y amongst us at this moment is a most unhappy circumstance — You will have seen, by this time, the Bishop's admirable Pastoral Letter — knowing as I have done for many years — the spirit & temper of the Col. Ch Socy and being well acquainted with some of the Committee — my own mind was perfectly decided and my opinion expressed long before the Pastoral Letter appeared — I stated without hesitation that, putting all *opinions* out of the question, no man of integrity ... could give any countenance to such a movement — Added to this the grievances alleged by the supporters of the Col Ch Socy are altogether fictitious & imaginary. I should never hesitate to state my conviction that it would be difficult to find in the same number of clergymen in England taken in any district more faithful ministrations of the Gospel than those afforded by the Missionaries of the Ven[era]ble Soc[iet]y.

The London-based Colonial Church and School Society was a recent amalgamation of two missionary societies: The Newfoundland and British North American School Society, and the Colonial Church Society. With characteristic hybrid vitality, it had drafted a vigorous program of evangelization, and sent a Rev. Mr. Dunn, from Newfoundland to call on Bishop Fulford in April of 1851 to outline their plans for Montreal. Although Dunn seems to have received no encouragement from the Bishop, he returned again in October (as Fulford notes in his Pastoral Letter) to inform him of "what had been decided upon for this Diocese, viz:— that seven schoolmasters, of a missionary spirit, were at once to be sent out here; that one of them (who has since arrived) was to be stationed in this city, to assist [the Rev.] Mr. Bond, the Society's agent here, to act as a Scripture Reader, and have the care of the Hospital. I foresaw at once that much difficulty and trouble for the Church must ensue ..." Fulford, not surprisingly, objected to such activities and, rather than brook a source of division and independence, refused the aid of the Society.

The mail this evening [Slack continued] brought me a pamphlet — being a report of the proceedings at the meeting held to establish a Branch [of the CCSS] also in Montreal — It is really lamentable to see how men deceive themselves in calling themselves "sound churchmen" while they are deliberately flying in the face of their own Diocesan and violating all fundamental principles of order & discipline. Is it not painfule [*sic*] to see such a state of things in a city like Montreal — Virtually there are two Bishops — Bishop Fulford of the diocese — and *Bishop Bond* of St George's —

Bond, of course, did become bishop (and eventually Primate), but it is unlikely that the comment is meant to be prophetic. Like Bond, Slack regarded himself as an evangelical, so it was Bond's insubordination, not his churchmanship that was at issue here. In his Pastoral Letter, Fulford had written with moderation "on the evil of controversy and the difficulties of contending"; Slack obviously endorsed both his actions and his judgment.

Poor Bond has been always an esteemed friend of mine [Slack adds] — & I cannot but deeply lament his grievous errors — I fear that Satan's choice of weapon — *pride*: spiritual pride — has been mainly the cause of his most unseemly conduct — Flattered & caressed by his congregation he has forgotten himself —

Slack then turns to the state of the church outside the city about which he feels no less distressed.

Indeed I must say that the state of our Church throughout this country is most painful & my mind is full of sad forebodings — oh if you could but see the materials, with wh[ich] we have to work you would soon see that there was but a very faint prospect of the Society's [that is, the SPG's] expectations being realized of any well sustained effort at self support being put forth by our people — The great bulk are Irish of the low class — who have scraped together what they have — who have been accustomed to live *upon* the clergy — not support them — and from whom it is about as easy to extract a dollar as to draw blood from a stone — Then again ... the Socy says to the people — you must raise so much [for the support of a clergyman]. The people reply — we want to know, who is the man you are going to send us before we can subscribe — and after all the most that can be done is a subscription for *one year* — pledges beyond that time are valueless in most instances — and even as to the yearly subscription — there are to[o] many who if they take offence, will repudiate — What clergyman with a family can feel safer [sic] resting upon such ground for their support —? Look at my self for example — with a family of six young children — £90 my sole support excepting what I can raise by the sweat of my brow from the glebe farm — How should I be situated if that income instead of being certain were precarious — I fear that the Church will be called upon to pass thro' a period of severe reverse here, from wh[ich] she will doubtless arise again in renewed strength. Whether we shall see that is another question: — Let it be our part to labor faithfully each in our several vocation[s] — And tho' we see no fruit to our labors yet are we assured of the approval of the great Shepherd of the flock under whom we serve —

# Anglican Standards (1852)

Anglican historians of the pioneer period are quick to point out the constraints and difficulties imposed by an episcopal form of church government on spreading the gospel in a new and unbroken country. With a few notable exceptions, saddlebag missionaries and circuit riders like the Methodists did better at evangelizing new settlements than did the Anglicans.

Greater mobility and a readier supply of missionaries certainly helped in the rapid growth of Nonconformist congregations as new settlements were opened. Livelier music and more participatory services were attractions, too, but the intrenched attitudes held by Anglican clergy toward what they would or would not do in rendering their services was undoubtedly a factor as well. The following passage, from the diary of the rector of St Armand East (the Rev. James Reid), provides a good example:

19th Nov. 1852: Today a man of the name of Deming from the north side of the Pinnacle came to ask me to the funeral of Shubal Smith's eldest son.

The arrangement was that I should attend at the house at 10 of the clock tomorrow, have prayers, and bury the corps[e] at their burying place, and then all in a body go about $2^1/_2$ Miles to the Methodist chapel at Abbott's Corner and preach the funeral Sermon.

The proposition appeared to me to be of such a character as that a Church [that is, Anglican] clergyman should not comply with it. I said I was ready to go to the funeral and do my duty as a Church Minister, but that this Arrangement asked me to perform a Service which the Church did not authorise.

I would go to the house and perform the Service and bury the corpse, if the man was a baptized person ... But if he was not baptized, I had no duty to perform at the grave; I would meet them at the Chapel and preach the Gospel to them.

If he was baptized, I would go to the house, and preach there, and bury the corpse, but would not afterwards go to the Chapel, that to do so appeared to me as an exhibition merely, to please men, that if this arrangement suited, it was understood that I should meet them at the Methodist Chapel, without any further notice. If it did not suit, they were to give me notice. In the evening notice was given me that I need not go.

Reid was obviously upset that his lecture to Deming had produced this result, but it is hardly surprising that the family would prefer to look for someone more sympathetic to their wishes.

The strange proposition of having two services was the difficulty [Reid argues]. These people care nothing about the Burial Service. It is the parade and the funeral *Sarmant* they want [he is imitating folksy speech here] and I ought not to please them to go and act a *Dissenter*.

Although discipline was strictly enforced when Anglican clergy stepped outside the prescribed boundaries of their office — as episcopal correspondence amply confirms — some sense of the feelings and pastoral needs of the bereaved, even in the case of unbaptized persons, was usually encouraged.

The Rev. Charles Caleb Cotton of Dunham had caused serious damage to the reputation of the Church some thirty years earlier. Unlike Reid, who was very conscientious in visiting the people, especially the sick — even highly contagious cases such as consumption — Cotton had been sometimes neglectful. The following passage — penned by the future Bishop Stewart while still a travelling missionary in the Diocese — displays Cotton's crowning failure in the performance of his pastoral duties in his insistence on strict 'Anglican standards' in performing funerals:

I advise you [wrote Stewart] to state that you feel it to be your duty to yourselves, your families, & the Church, to represent to his Lordship [Bishop Jacob Mountain] the low estate of the interests of the Church in this township [Dunham] in consequence of the Reverend Mr Cotton's inattention to the performance of his duties: that his remissness in visiting the people in general & the sick in particular, & in affording them spiritual comfort, & advice, … that his refusal to bury the corpse of a young woman, in November last, after it was brought to the Church, he being in the immediate vicinity of the Church, on the plea that she had been baptized by a Minister of the Dissenters & not in the Church, alleging that he had orders from your Lord[shi]p not to bury persons so baptized, had hurt the feelings of everyone who attended the funeral, & caused most of the people, since that time, to absent themselves from Public Worship: … that you are sorry to trouble his Lordp, or to injure the character or the feelings of Mr Cotton, but that your concern for the Church, & your own interests, oblige you to make the above statement to throw yourselves on his Lordp's candour & mercy, and that you humbly request his Lordp to take your memorial into consideration, & to do what to him in his wisdom seems meet to be done.

If the people of Dunham sent such a memorial or the Bishop responded to it, no record of either has been found. Certainly Cotton continued to serve the parish of Dunham until his death in 1848. He had been the incumbent for forty years.

There is no doubt that the Anglican Church suffered in the eyes of many onlookers for what was regarded as haughtiness and exclusiveness.

Although less divisive an issue in Lower Canada than in her sister province, the Clergy Reserves caused much bitterness among the denominations excluded from a share in their revenues.

The refusal by Anglican clergy to allow their churches to be used by other denominations (for funerals, for example) when free use and access was given to them seemed uncharitable to many. When the Methodist Chapel in Griffintown — a struggling, working class district in east end Montreal — was destroyed by fire in 1845 and neighbouring St Ann's Chapel welcomed the homeless congregation to use its facilities temporarily for worship, Bishop G.J. Mountain reversed the offer and condemned such practices in a Pastoral Letter. Although the Bishop maintained that it was not in his power to sanction such use of Anglican premises, the court of public opinion and the press found him guilty of uncharitableness.

Sadly, such actions over a long period of years have tended to confirm the belief that Anglicans — far from being an outward-looking, compassionate missionary people — were elitist establishmentarians, standing on their own dignity and preoccupied with their own concerns.

## The Bishop in Request (1855)

As Francis Fulford had a fine voice, graceful manner and excellent delivery, it is not surprising that he was often in request as a speaker, on secular as well as on religious occasions. The invitations he received to speak in the city of Montreal alone ranged from the Church of England Association for Young Men of Montreal, to the Mechanics' Institute. Among his few lectures to have survived in print, some concern history (both ancient and modern), literature, and science. His subjects ranged from "The State and Prospects of Science and Literature in Montreal" (delivered on 5 April 1859, in the Lecture Room of the Natural History Society) to "Recollections of a Visit to Abbotsford, and of Sir Walter Scott and his Contemporaries" (presented at Bonaventure Hall on 10 January of the same year).

One of the Bishop's lectures is of particular interest, for it shows him in sympathy with the powerful self-help movement which had inspired the establishment in 1823 of the London Mechanics' Institution. Such liberal-minded Britons as Lord Brougham, Jeremy Bentham and Dr. George Birkbeck, as well as engineering employers who wanted a better-educated workforce, had supported the institution, but its radical, working-class origins were still well known. On December 1855, Fulford was invited to deliver the opening lecture of the Montreal Branch of Mechanics' Institute's Winter Evening Program.

For his subject on that occasion the Bishop chose to give "Some Remarks on Colonial Institutions," and after a brief discussion of political institutions turned his attention to the advance in wealth and independence of the colonies:

But while there is a rapid and acknowledged growth in the general material wealth and prosperity of this country — while there seems a natural aptitude in her population for developing her varied resources in connection therewith — there are in other departments great difficulties to overcome. The cultivation of the intellect, the promotion of scientific knowledge, and the higher branches of learning are not marked by the same manifest progress. But still in these departments, I maintain that it is our duty to work in hope of better things; seeing that, from the very nature of our position, this must naturally have been the case for many years.

The settlers attracted to this country, he pointed out, were not "the men of leisure and highly cultivated minds, devoted to the pursuits of science and the quiet pursuits of literature." The Mechanics' Institute, however, incorporated ten years earlier, with its Library, Reading-Room and Lecture Hall, he judged as an one of several evidences of progress.

With respect, however, to the advantages to be derived from attendance on any public Lectures, which are now so common, on every conceivable subject, I would remind you, that in order to be really useful, they must not be taken as a substitute for all personal study and intellectual labour on the part of those who attend them; but rather as affording useful hints and assistance. In the first place knowledge cannot be truly ours, till we have appropriated it by some operation of our own minds. ...

Any specific branch of science or art is interesting to a certain extent, and for particular objects, and may be essentially useful to this or that particular person in his particular line of life. But the training of the mind, and developing of the intellect, and forming the opinions, through a particular course of study, in proportion as this is effectually carried out, prepares a man to take a high place in his intercourse with his fellows, enlarges the range of his own ideas, and puts him in possession of the experience and the thoughts of men of genius of every age, which, becoming often unconsciously mixed up with the working of his own mind, give additional power and activity to his own natural endowments, when called into exercise on any particular objects.

Like any good teacher, Fulford illustrates his argument with examples suited to his audience. Important scientific discoveries, he points out, were often the result of the observation of everyday incidents open to the experience of ordinary individuals. Intellectual curiosity was the key:

Slight circumstances are the texts of science. Pascal heard a common dinner-plate ring, and wrote a tract on sound. While Galileo studied medicine in the University of Pisa, the regular oscillation of a lamp, suspended from the roof of the Cathedral, attracted his observation, and led him to consider the vibrations of the pendulum. A sheet of paper sent from the press, with the letters accidentally raised, suggests the embossed alphabet for the blind; and a physician lying awake and listening to the beating of his heart, contributes the most learned book upon the diseases of that organ.

How, then, should those who had not had the benefit of much education proceed to educate themselves? Although it was common to encourage abstracts and abridgments of important books, Fulford urges against this for the very reason that such works, although they may contain useful information, lack the wealth of detail that kindles the imagination:

General abridgments of entire works of eminent writers, though they may give us a sufficient acquaintance with certain dry hard facts, are for the most part always heavy, dull and disappointing. And just so in proportion to the excellence of the original work.

What we yearn after are the graphic details, the minute incidents, the reality, that enables us to bring the scene, as it were, all before us, and secure our warm interest on behalf of those engaged. We shall for ever find all this in translations; but it is next to impossible in mere abridgments.

Good translations are like good engravings from the pictures of great masters; they cannot give us all the richness of the colouring, but they may give us the beauty of the design, and all the minute incidents of the piece.

Right-thinking Victorian that he was, Fulford emphasized that the benefits to be derived from a course of study or a course of lectures would necessarily depend on the earnestness and effort of those who followed them:

I was much interested the other day [he remarked] with reading, in the *Illustrated London News*, an account of the third festival of the St Martin's-in-the-Field's Library and Reading Room for the working classes.

There were 400 working men and their wives present; besides many of the London Clergy and other friends of the Institution. ... Many speeches, on topics connected with the Institution and its objects, were delivered; but the most striking one of the evening was by a Mr Parker, a working man, in a coach factory in the parish, who astonished the company by quoting Aristophanes, Æschylus, and Sophocles; and then, as he expressed himself, stripped himself of his plumes by saying, 'that he had learnt all he knew of them, by first attending a Lecture of Professor Browne at that Library on Attic Tragedy: and then by obtaining translations of these Greek poets, which he had read with delight and avidity.'

Here the Lecture-room and the Library were brought into due and proper connection, and by after study, the teaching of the passing hour was carried on. ... Such Lectures should be a help to many who are really anxious to obtain information, but have not had full opportunities for regular training at college or school — should give them hints; and often, as in the case of the working man referred to in the report of the St Martin's Institution, be perhaps the happy accidental means of directing the individual to a particular line of thought or study, that will, in the pursuit of them, open up new fields, not only for pleasure of a high and pure kind, but for the exercise of talent, the cultivation of the intellect, and the discipline of the mind to a greater extent, than, perhaps, he was himself aware that he was capable of. And this, after all, is bringing us nearer to the great end of education; and this is one of the great rewards for studying the best authors in every department of literature.

Fulford's interest in all classes of society and his insistence on mixing socially with those outside his own Communion occasioned grumblings among his clergy, but his broad interests and wide sympathies brought honour and respect from members of the community who never would have given a kind thought to a bishop or a church.

## A Ministry to Native People (1858)

Except for the period immediately following the Conquest, the Anglican clergy of Montreal have had little experience in ministering to Native People. In 1862, however, a small group of Protestant Abenaki — largely French-speaking — were brought into the Anglican fold. They had been settled at Odenak (otherwise known as St Francis Village) near Pierreville, on the estuary of the St Francis River for many generations, and had followed their own ways. In 1858, however, members of their community presented themselves to the Anglican minister of nearby Sorel requesting that he officiate at the forthcoming marriage of a French-speaking man and an Abenaki woman.

The assistant minister at Sorel, a young Channel Islander named Joseph de Mouilpied, was able to conduct the ceremony in French. The bride spoke only her own language, however, and de Mouilpied "was obliged to deviate from our usual form and employ an interpreter to make it intelligible to her, by being rendered in her native dialect." The members of her village, who had accompanied the couple for the ceremony, were so impressed by the young man's proceedings that, before they left, they arranged with him to visit them on the Sunday following to preach to them in French.

A number of Native People at Odenak had become Congregationalists through the influence of a young man from the area, Peter Paul Wzokhilain. While attending a charity school in New Hampshire, he had become a convert, returned to his village as a schoolmaster, and shared his faith at meetings which he organized. When his proselytizing among the local Roman Catholics lost him his position, he petitioned the American Board of Commissioners for Foreign Missions. In 1836, he was licenced to preach by the Champlain Presbytery of New York and Vermont. Despite heavy opposition from the local priest, by 1838 he had gathered a congregation of sixty, 75% of whom were Native People. He preached, wrote, served as a translator from English and French, and composed and printed psalms and tunes in Abenaki. His insistence on Total Abstinence among his adherents put a great strain on the community, however, and in 1858, the year of de Mouilpied's first invitation, Wzokhilain was released by the Board and left St Francis.

In the 1859 *Report of the Colonial Church and School Society*, de Mouilpied described his visit and the new mission field he believed it had promised:

I remained during three days with a Mr Master [probably Masta], half-brother to the Indian Minister who, for many years, had preached to them in their native language, but who has now left them ...

On the Sabbath I held three services in their little church, as their particular wish was that the whole day should be devoted to religious services, and the following Monday I also held another service, all of which were in French. For the first time in their life, they listened to the services of our Church, and evinced much delight as the impressive and solemn words of our Liturgy fell upon their ears.

In the forenoon, about 50 Protestant Indians attended; about 70 persons in the afternoon, many of whom were [French] Canadians [as opposed to Native People]; but in the evening, the news having spread about in the village that a service in French was to be held, there was a large attendance of Canadians, and the number of Roman Catholic Indians was nearly as large as that of the Protestant.

During the services I baptized two of their children, having first explained to those who brought them the nature of the responsibilities that devolved upon them. ...

I am persuaded that there are many more who are anxious to receive further Christian instruction, and am convinced that this is a most interesting spot for Missionary efforts. ...

He then went on to decribe the people and something of their way of life:

Almost all own a little piece of land, which they cultivate with the help of their squaws. The men were making preparation to leave soon for their winter hunt. Their hunting grounds embrace all the boundless forests of Quebec, Maine and New Brunswick. The females make gloves and mocassins, of which latter more than 6,000 pair from the village are sold annually.

Many ... go from here to Saratoga Springs and other parts of New York every summer with baskets, of which they also sell great quantities. The people are sadly destitute of suitable means of education. The number that can read and write is very small indeed.

The Indian village is separated from the Canadian, and is composed of Protestant and R.C. in equal proportion. It has a church for the use of the R.C. Indians.

The building appropriated to the Protestant worship is an unfinished, yet substantial wood-built chapel, and can accommodate, conveniently, about 70 persons.

The St Francis Mission was duly constituted within the next three years, with the Rev. Octave Fortin as its first resident missionary.

On 29 September 1883, the Rt Rev. William Bennett Bond paid a visit to Odenak. On his departure, Chief H.L. Masta presented an address in which he thanked the Bishop on behalf of his people for the benefits they had received from the Church:

We have a school of our own, where our children are taught to read. We have the Great Book, the Bible both in French & English & are allowed — yea recommended to read it & those who are able do read it. We pray God that we may ere long have it in our own language. We have a Church where we can meet together to pray & thank God, & to hear his word read & explained. We have a good man [the Rev. Louis-Vitalien Larivière] who does all he can to make us understand & learn the will of God & live accordingly. His wife is a perfect lady, esteemed by us all. My Lord, we know that you in the hands of God have obtained most of these favors for us. We cannot pay you, but we pray the Great Spirit to reward you with the fulness of his Grace. We thank you once more & bid you good bye.

On Sunday, 5 September 1982 the Diocese of Montreal joined with the United Church Board for World Ministries in the dedication of a memorial to Peter Paul Wzokhilain at Odenak. At this ceremony there were prayers of thanks for "those whose spiritual vision in centuries past nurtured awe and worship among the Abenakis," for the Jesuit Fathers who first preached the Gospel, for native leadership encouraged by the American Board and the Congregationalists, and for "the clergy and lay pioneers" of the Diocese of Montreal. Among those present at the ceremony from the Mission itself, the name of Masta was still in evidence.

## Montreal's First Synod (1859)

On Tuesday, June 7th 1859, the Bishop, clergy and laity of the Diocese of Montreal met in Synod for the first time. There were present on this historic occasion 43 clergy and 99 lay delegates, duly elected from the parishes. As the Cathedral had been destroyed by fire in December 1856, the meeting took place at St John's Chapel on Gosford Street, which ran from Craig Street to Notre Dame on the east side of the Champs de Mars.

Prior to opening proceedings, Morning Service was read by the Ven. Samuel Gilson, Dean John Bethune read the Lessons, and the Rev. William Bennett Bond, who had been one of the chief opponents to forming a synod when the matter had first come up three years earlier, preached the sermon. He took for his text 1 Corinthians 3:10: 'For other foundation can no man lay than that is laid, which is Jesus Christ.'

While enabling legislation was being passed by the Legislature of the Province of Canada — which had jurisdiction over Quebec and Ontario — to allow "Members of the United Church of England and Ireland to meet in Synod," Bishop Fulford had summoned his clergy and lay delegates, elected at the parish level, to meet with him in Montreal on Wednesday, 16 January 1856, "to take into consideration the necessity or propriety of establishing a Diocesan Synod for this Diocese."

The consultation (begun at 10:30 a.m. with Morning Prayer at the Cathedral) soon took a turn for the worse.

PLATE 4 *Christ Church Cathedral, opened for services 1859*

Shortly after the clergy and lay delegates had reassembled for business at the National School House, and had heard the Bishop's explanation of the current situation and its remedy, a friendly motion was presented by Judge J.S. McCord, to the effect that a Synod was necessary, that the Bishop, clergy and laity there assembled should regard themselves as such, and that they then proceed to consider the Report of the Sub-Committee on a proposed Declaration and Constitution. The motion was seconded by the Rev. Canon Micajah Townsend, senior member of the country clergy attending.

Response was swift and devastating. A determined and well-prepared opposition was led by a number of the clergy: the Rev. Alexander Digby Campbell of Trinity Church, the Rev. Canon Charles Bancroft of St John's, and the Rev. William Bennett Bond of St George's. There were several equally-outspoken laymen who assailed the whole notion of forming a Synod. Judge McCord was induced to reduce his motion simply to resolve "That there is a necessity for the establishment of a Diocesan Synod within this Diocese," with no provision for doing so.

Discussion went on for two days, the opposition insisting that meeting in Synod would foment party strife in the church, that half the clergy would refuse to attend, that forming a Synod was contrary to British law and contravened the Bishop's oath of loyalty to the Queen.

At the end of the second day, with a series of obstructionist amendments finally defeated, the emasculated motion received the assent of both clergy and laity. Fulford, however, had had enough. He was a man who sought consensus and disliked the brand of factionalism exhibited by the Diocesan Evangelicals on this occasion. Although he expressed his disappointment to the assembly on the outcome of their discussions, he had resolved to go no further for the present. A contemporary report on the meeting summarizes his remarks:

He felt a deep responsibility rested upon himself in this matter [he said], but his first wish had been to have [the formation of a Synod] so brought before the Clergy and Laity of his Diocese as to enable them to understand fully the real state of the question.

They had had something substantive before them which had awakened feelings of interest and called forth the opinions of both Clergy and Laity. But he did not desire to have the constitution and rules for the government of a Synod hastily adopted. He wished them to be duly considered and intelligently discussed. ...

He had never wished to force Synods upon his people. They had been demanded from him repeatedly by both Clergymen and laymen, and he saw there was a need of some such organization.

Rev. Mr. Campbell [had] said he had his Cathedral chapter as a Council. But he (the Bishop) asked if it was not notorious, that the greatest jealousy and ill-feeling would prevail if that body, of his own appointment, were given the government of the Diocese.

He had had but one wish in this proceeding, as in the remodelling of the Church Society, to call in to aid and counsel him in the government of his Diocese the Clergy and representatives of the Laity.

Those who had acted with him in that Society knew that he had sought to place the representation of the Laity upon the broadest basis ... In all his proceedings, since he came into the Diocese, this had been the principle on which he had acted.

In taking steps for assembling a Synod he was not of opinion he had shown himself disloyal to his Queen.... He recognized the supremacy of the Queen and of the law, here as in England: here as there, all writs run in the Queen's name. But other bodies met under the authority of the Queen and of the law, why should not they? ...

Those who supported [the Rev.] Mr Campbell in his opposition to the Synod had exerted themselves to the utmost, he believed — and he by no means blamed him for doing so. Yet, notwithstanding these exertions, a vast majority had declared themselves favourable to a Synod.

He did not wish to hurry the matter on unfairly. He had thought it best to send out the draft of "Constitutions and Rules" framed by the Sub-Committee for their consideration. Had he not done so, he did not think they would have had a tithe of the interesting discussion of the matter which had now been drawn out. But he had communicated to several of his Clergy the fact that he hardly expected to carry anything into execution now, and he was quite willing to adjourn to give more time to those who desired it.

He desired, as their Bishop, to thank those brethren of the laity who had come to the meeting, at so much trouble, and expense, he doubted not to many of them, for their assistance and advice; and to express his gratification that the subject had been discussed in that full, frank, free manner, and in such a tone that they need not be ashamed to have their debates go forth to the world.

When the Diocese finally assembled its first Synod, the Imperial Parliament had sanctioned the enabling legislation and no doubts could remain as to the legality of such bodies. The Diocese of Toronto had formed a Synod in 1854, Nova Scotia in 1856 and the newly-erected Diocese of Huron in 1858.

At 2 p.m., when the assembly reconvened after the opening Services, the Bishop addressed the members. As always, he did his best to promote a spirit of harmony and mutual respect in alluding to previous attempts to meet in Synod:

Rev. Brethren and Brethren of the Laity — We are met on an important and interesting occasion — one that has brought together a large proportion of the Clergy, so large, indeed, that there are but two clergymen of the Diocese, now in Canada, who are not here this day, and nearly every Church is represented by one or more Lay Delegates

It will be recollected that this is not the first occasion of our meeting together to take into consideration the subject now before us. … But there were scruples entertained by certain members who believed that we could not then legally proceed … Our previous meetings, however, were not, I think, thrown away. None who were then present can regret that we met, and that the subject was discussed so fully in debate, which reflected credit on all who took part in it, and which caused respect to be felt for the Church to which we belong.

Perhaps predictably, in spite of the Bishop's generous introductory remarks, the forces of opposition were still in evidence, although the Rev. Alexander Digby Campbell had left the Diocese in the intervening period. Canon Bancroft, the Rev. John Flanagan, the Rev. John Irwin, and the Rev. William Bennett Bond, with the help of a few laymen, while endorsing the principle of Synod, did their best to deprive the Bishop of his power of veto. They failed. The proceedings of the following day were equally contentious, but the business in hand was finally got through and the articles of the Constitution adopted.

Such difficulties as those experienced in the Diocese of Montreal over the formation of Synod were far from unique. Fulford's brother bishop George Jehoshaphat Mountain of Quebec had much the same experience, in the same year and from the same quarter.

## Isolation (1863)

A recurring theme among the clergy who served in country districts was their sense of isolation — the lack of contact with anyone of similar background and interests with whom to spend an evening or discuss a problem. Yet a clergyman in the 1860s would seldom have thought of refusing such a mission field should his bishop propose it.

The following passage describes the mixed feelings — recalled many years later — of a young man on the brink of such a challenge. The speaker, the Rev. Thomas W. Fyles (who would later become the first rector of Nelsonville), is seen here addressing a large group of friends and wellwishers at the three-day Jubilee celebration of the Parish of Nelsonville.

It was forty-two years ago [that is 1862, Fyles recalled] that I, a young Montrealer, went over to the Cote des Neiges, to visit a dear friend of mine … On my return-journey over the mountain, I looked down upon the vast city spread at my feet, — upon its domes and towers, — and gazed at the wide expanse of flat French country out beyond, dotted here and there by the occasional peaks and mountains. In the distance, I saw a large cluster of mountains, and I remember wondering whether they were situated in the United States or within the boundaries of Canada.

Before he had thought to satisfy this momentary curiosity, Fyles remembered, he was summoned by Bishop Fulford to visit a newly-opened mission in Brome Township:

I finally came out from Montreal to this section of what was then known as Col. Foster's Road to Waterloo [Fyles continued]. By stage we came over to Knowlton, where I spent the night at the Rectory. The Rev. John Smith, Master of the Academy, drove me to West Brome, … On that trip, we drove to Brome Woods … into what was known as the Cutting neighbourhood, which was to be my future headquarters. There we had tea with Mr. and Mrs. John Shufelt, and after tea, I stood in the doorway, and looked up at the dark mountain sides, gazed at the lofty, woody peaks, listened to the myriad voices of the night, and I must confess that my heart sank when I thought of my young wife and her first baby in Montreal.

The occasion was nostalgic and warm, and his tone affectionate, but that apprehensiveness, so bravely acknowledged, was very real.

In a brief memoir, written in 1907, Fyles describes moving his young family to their new home:

It was on the 30th day of September A.D. 1863, that I, the Reverend Thomas W. Fyles, who had been for some time Missionary at Laprairie and Longue[u]il, set out for my new Mission of Iron Hill and West Brome.

   I took with me my wife [Mary Myers "then 21 years of age, bright and active"] and child [an infant daughter, Mary], a servant-maid and my household belongings. Our point of debarkation was Ketzbach's Station on the Colonial Forest Road from St. Johns to Waterloo.

   I had engaged a small block house in "the Cutting neighbourhood," Iron Hill, from Mr. Joseph Benham, at a rental of sixty dollars per annum. From Ketzbach's Station to this dwelling was a distance of six miles.

At the station, as Fyles recounts, the pleasant surprise of finding seven local men with their teams awaited the family, so they and their belongings were carried to their new home in neighbourly style. A mile from the station, at a turn of the road, Fyles recalled catching sight of the white wooden church at West Shefford, on a bluff overlooking the road. He had not known that there would be a fellow clergyman — the Rev. A. T. Whitten "and his kind wife" — not too far from his mission, with whom he and Mary would become "true friends."

On arriving at our destination, late at night [Fyles continued], another agreeable surprise awaited us. The wives and daughters of the good men who had met us at the station had provided a feast of welcome, to which ample justice was done by all present.

A short address, prayer, and the benediction closed a fatiguing but happy day.

Within two months Fyles would set about building a church, in aid of which he provided plans "given to me by Messrs Lawford and Nelson, eminent Montreal architects." After actively seeking subscriptions in the immediate area, he visited the towns on the north shore of the St Lawrence (Sorel, Three Rivers and Quebec), and finally "went from place to place along the Grand Trunk Railway as far as Chatham, Ontario, soliciting aid." Individual contributions, Fyles noted, usually amounted to "a dollar or fifty cents at a house," but he managed to collect $1,368.27 in this painstaking manner. The expense of $205 incurred on these tours was borne by Fyles himself. The Sewing Society earned $18.42 which they contributed, and several "festivals" were held to raise funds, including a particularly successful  blackberry festival.

It will readily be believed that building a church under such circumstances was an arduous task [Fyles wrote]. I paid workmen as they went on, and incurred no debts. My own money went as fast as it came in.

To raise funds I sold my bookcase, and gave lectures around the country; and by one means or another, I was able to meet all claims.

The frame of the church was raised on 24 May 1864. Mr. William Hill, colour merchant of Montreal, gave the paint, but, it being "a busy time on the land" for his parishioners, Fyles painted the building himself, inside and out. The altar, communion service, altar cloth and fair linen, together with many other furnishings were presented as gifts from various individuals in Montreal. The SPCK provided a Bible, Prayer Book and Book of Offices.

The church bell came from the Troy Bell Foundry [Fyles recalled]. I drove to Frelighsburg, paid the custom house dues upon it, and brought it home in my wagon. It was rung for the first time on Christmas Eve, 1865.

A disaffected female of the neighbourhood, as the people were coming to church, stood in the middle of the road and rang a rival peal with a cow bell. But an old countryman, advanced in years, said to me, while the tears came to his eyes, "Sir, I little expected ever to hear a church bell ring in Brome Woods."

## Church Music (1867)

The sermon is a special literary genre, and there was a time when sermons were published widely, and read like any other type of literature. The following example was preached in Christ Church Cathedral on Sunday evening, January 27th 1867, by the Rev. Canon Philip Wood Loosemore, and subsequently "printed by request of the Organist and Choir, and several Members of the Congregation." It was originally composed, as the preface states, "with a view to support an endeavour, on the part of the Cathedral Authorities, to render the Singing more Congregational in its character than has hitherto been the case.

To give an idea of what sermons at this period were like, it is necessary to quote at length, for sermons, to be regarded with any degree of seriousness, were intentionally ample, carefully reasoned, and copiously illustrated from Scripture as well as from the fathers and doctors of the Church.

The sermon opens with a text from St Paul:

SPEAKING TO YOURSELVES IN PSALMS AND HYMNS AND SPIRITUAL SONGS,
SINGING AND MAKING MELODY IN YOUR HEART TO THE LORD
[EPHESIANS 5: 19]

The Apostle is exhorting the Ephesians to wait on God in every appointed means of grace, for larger communications of the Holy Spirit, Whose sacred influences would fill their souls with satisfying consolation under every present circumstance, and tend to the happiest consequences in future [Loosemore begins]. Of such joyous influences they might seek a full supply without any danger of excess.

In order to [do] this, he exhorts them to substitute, in place of the loose songs of the Gentiles, or other frivolous melodies, the "psalms and hymns" of the Sacred Scriptures, and such "spiritual songs" as godly men had composed, embodying the subjects of the Gospel, and teaching according to the doctrine of truth. In these they were to speak to one another, paying at the same time particular regard to the affections of their hearts, that the *inward* melody and gratitude of the heart unto the Lord might accompany the *outward* melody of poetry and singing, when they used their psalms and spiritual songs either in private, social, or public worship.

We seem to have here a picture of the psalmody of the Early Christians. The moral harmony and spiritual music of the Apostle's own Christian life and conversation found their exposition to the Church and to the world in the utterance of sweet sounds of praise and thankfulness to God, by example as well as by precept. For when bound in an inner prison at Philippi with their feet fast in the "stocks, at midnight Paul and Silas prayed, and sang praises unto God: and the prisoners heard them."

The same strain of praise he enjoins on the Colossians, "Let the word of Christ dwell in you richly in all wisdom; teaching and admonishing one another in psalms and hymns and spiritual songs, singing with grace in your hearts to the Lord."

Bingham, in his *Antiquities of the Christian Church*, shows us, in an interesting manner, how the Early Church continued to act upon the Scriptural and Apostolic practice here laid down. The Service usually began with reading or singing Psalms. Quoting Jerome, he says, "They meet at nine o'clock, and then the psalms are sung, and the Scriptures are read, and after prayers they all sit down, and the father preaches a sermon to them." ...

Alluding to the different ways in which the psalms were sung, sometimes by one person alone, sometimes by the whole assembly, joining all together, sometimes alternately by the congregation divided into distinct choirs, the one part repeating one verse, and the other another, sometimes one person repeating the first part of the verse, and the rest joining all together at the close of it, he says, "Sometimes the whole assembly joined together: men, women, and children, united with one mouth and one mind in singing psalms and praises to God. This was the most ancient and general practice, till the way of alternate psalmody was brought into the Church." Quoting from St Chrysostom, he says, "Women and men, old men and children, differ in sex and age, but they differ not in the harmony of singing hymns: for the Spirit tempers all their voices together, making one melody of them all." ...

Now the *responsive* system of music ... in the citations from early Christian writers, which is in use in the Cathedrals of England, and, indeed, generally throughout Christendom, has been supposed to come down to us from the time of St. Ignatius, who is said first to have taught the Christian Church at Antioch to sing alternate verses of Psalms in responsive strains. … The custom is traced by the prophet Isaiah to the blessed angels themselves, who are described as singing the praises of Jehovah in alternate choirs [Isaiah 6: 1-3] … From this example of the highest authority, then, we may say that responsive singing fulfils the apparent intention of the heavenly mind, agrees also with the practice of the Jewish and the Primitive Church, and certainly brings out more satisfactorily than any other method the sense of Holy Scripture itself.

In addressing you on this subject in this place I do not forget, and would have you also remember, that the more *scientific* and *professional* part belongs to others, the *practical* it is my special prerogative to guard and exemplify. This embraces that *Sacred Music* which is used in the service of Almighty God: for the science of music is infinite in its range, divine in its origin, a special gift of God to man. …

God gave the human voice, and endowed it with the gift of exerting a powerful influence over the mind and heart. It can stir in a moment all the passions and affections of man's rough nature. Joy, grief, loyalty, patriotism will spring into being and active exercise at its bidding. But in this place we have only to do with its power of creating and stimulating religious devotion. …

I may now say a few words as to the *kind* of Music which should be heard in the House of God.

We shall all feel that this is best decided by the character of the words which are to be sung. Surely no light and operatic music can be consistent with the solemn words of men "who spake as they were moved by the Holy Ghost." … Devotional music, whether jubilant or plaintive, should have a character of its own. It should be sober, dignified, chaste, severe. The strains which may lawfully delight the ear in places not specially hallowed by the promised presence of God are alien to the church, and should be banished from its sacred walls. The Bible and its simple severe grandeur are different from any other book and its colloquial phraseology. *Church Music*, the music specially chosen and adapted for the *Lord's House*, should be similarly distinct in its style and character.

And I suppose all will agree that the abundant works of the old Masters are not obsolete, but still singularly adapted to our ideas and perhaps eminently superior to any other. And as our Blessed Lord Himself, to show that He is the author of whatever is good and true in every age and in every country, quoted old parables, proverbs, maxims current among the people, so we may here adopt the language of one which He used for another purpose, and say, with reference to the style and genius of the Church Music which has so long reverberated throughout the time-honoured Cathedrals of the old country and been more or less adopted in our own,

"No man having drunk old wine, straightway desireth new: for he saith, The old is better." ...

There may be parts of the service in the morning and afternoon, which the choir sing by themselves, according to the arrangement of a Cathedral service, in which the congregation are invited to join "in spirit and under-standing" if not in voice, as the service for the "Te Deum" in the morning and the Anthem in the afternoon. But in addition to these two services, we have the third in the evening, a service more simple as to its music, in which the congregation are earnestly invited to take an *active responsive* part, and yet a service diversified in its very simplicity.

I feel strongly that if we here, and our brethren in all the Churches of our Communion in the city can only bring the attendants on the public worship of the Church, to feel a personal interest in, and take an indi-vidual part in the service, which is intended for *all*, there would be little fear of that most reprehensible practice of our young people and others, from whom we might expect better things, violating the principles of consistency before God and the Church, and wandering off to strange pastures, or gratifying the lust of the ear for melodious strains or alien pul-pit oratory ...

We deprecate the mere luxury of hearing. We would desire to do away with the mere lust of the ear. We would that the concord of sweet sounds, in whatever degree produced and developed, should serve the purpose of devotion, of drawing out the highest efforts of the really spiritual mind. ...

And as for us, brethren, while the happy system of chanting and singing one to another, of "speaking to one another in psalms and hymns, and spiritual songs," should make us beware of offering the unacceptable serv-ice of the lips only, it should also make us "joyful in the house of prayer."

What solemn associations are here, though our Cathedral is not yet eight years old! What inspiring thoughts may surround us as we worship! The songs we are invited to sing, the hymns we use, are the songs of angels, the songs of just spirits before the throne of God. Our services, however imper-fect, are intended to render us meet for the perfect services of the Church Triumphant, to join the chorus of the sky with those whose record is on high, whose names are written in the Lamb's Book of Life ... And "ten thousand times ten thousand and thousands of thousands" shall prolong the notes of the lofty anthem, "as the voice of a great multitude, and as the voice of many waters, and as the voice of mighty thunderings, saying, Alleluia: for the Lord God Omnipotent reigneth." [Amen]

In the history of the Cathedral, little is recorded of the Rev. Philip Loosemore, beyond the controversy that surrounded his churchmanship and that of another assistant minister brought in at about the time the above sermon was preached. In the words of Frank Dawson Adams:

In 1867 and 1868 an unfortunate incident, known as the Balch and Loosemore Controversy, for a time disturbed the congregation. After the new Cathedral was completed there was of course a heavy debt upon the church and Bishop Fulford thought that this might be, in part at least, removed if some assistant minister could be secured who was a good preacher and could attract a larger congregation.

He found such a man in Baltimore — the Reverend Dr. Balch — who was [in 1867] accordingly invited to come to Montreal. He accepted the invitation and was appointed as Assistant Minister in the Cathedral.

He was an excellent preacher, a veritable "Silver Tongued Orator" who amply fulfilled the Bishop's desire. At the same time there was another Assistant Minister, the Rev. Mr. Loosemore [appointed in 1864] — who was also an excellent minister but of an entirely different type.

There can be no doubt that Adams is referring to the factionalism in churchmanship that was very bitter in the nineteenth-century church on both sides of the Atlantic.

[Loosemore's] appearance and the manner in which he dressed led many of the congregation to consider him as a very high churchman, and as such they did not approve of him. Two factions accordingly developed in the congregation and for a time the feeling between the two ran high.

It is not necessary to enlarge upon this regrettable incident [Adams concluded blandly]. Both clergymen retired from the Cathedral shortly after.

Loosemore's printed sermon shows him to have been a preacher of some persuasiveness, and the request to have it printed suggests widespread sympathy for his ideas. His emphasis here on music and the solemnity of worship was certainly typical of the High Church position. Fulford, however, was a man who sought to smooth away all controversy, especially in matters of factionalism in the church. Although temperamentally a High Churchman himself, he strove throughout his episcopate for unity and peace. It is therefore not surprising that both Balch and Loosemore had to leave.

Loosemore's sermon on "Church Music" is all that remains from his few years at the Cathedral, unless, that is, the awareness of a "Music Ministry" still vibrantly present in the Cathedral today, can be traced through his incumbency.

# Church Debt (1868)

A first step in attracting a minister of any denomination to serve a community was usually the building of a church. Subscription lists were drawn up and promises of materials and labour were recorded. When the building was finally raised, however, there was almost invariably a debt to be cleared.

This was a year of great uncertainty. Bishop Fulford had died unexpectedly on 9 September and the episcopate was vacant. The next bishop would be elected, not appointed by the Crown as Fulford had been. Who would he be? What effect would this have on small rural parishes struggling to pay for their hard-won church buildings?

The following, which concerns the problem of debt, is a Memo, dated at Abercorn on 22 December 1868, from the Proceedings of the Abercorn Church Building Committee.

Notwithstanding the many efforts of our people — coupled with the liberality of friends at a distance, All Saints Church was not completed without having a debt upon the building which at this date has become a source of much anxiety to its members, who are making every exertion to liquidate the debt.

The Revd Mr Smith has applied to the ladies generally who have subscribed $10 each — viz Mrs Seaton, Mrs Spencer, Mrs Nield, Mrs Fay, Mrs Willey, Mrs T. O'Brien, Mrs Richard Shepard — and Mrs Simpson of Montreal — making in all the sum of $80.00 — The debt is $225. — so that it leaves a balance still due in the sum of $145. We must hope sincerely that this balance will soon be paid off —

[signed] B. Seaton

At a meeting called at Richard Spencer's home on 20 July 1864 it had been proposed that "a church should be erected in the neighbourhood." A Building Committee was then struck with Spencer as chairman and Dr Benjamin Seaton as Secretary.

Already, a month earlier, the ladies had organized "a sewing Society to aid in procuring the interior furnishings for the proposed new church to be erected at Abercorn in connexion with the Church of England and Ireland." The founding meeting, on 2 June, was held at the Seaton's home, and thirteen operating rules were adopted. Regular meetings were to take place every alternate Thursday at 1:30 p.m. at the houses of the members, "a plain Tea to be provided by the Hostess [and] at each meeting of the Society a portion of Scripture shall be read with prayer immediately before tea."

Mrs Smith, the clergyman's wife, was elected Matron; Mrs Spencer, Vice Matron; Mrs Seaton, Secretary-Treasurer; and Mrs Nield, Directress. A Committee of five was also named. None of the funds collected as membership fees, contributions, or donations were "to be disposed of without the consent of the majority of the Committee present at any meeting convened for that purpose — the Presiding member to have the casting vote." In this first year, twenty women signed up, of whom nineteen joined and paid the initial twenty-five cent membership fee from which operating expenses could be laid out.

The Society's record book shows purchases of materials to support the purposes of the Society: bleached cotton, brown holland, alpaca and silk; spools of thread, bunches of braid, as well as wool, beads and sundries. The proceeds of their work, carefully recorded, was modest: $1.45 for knitting three pairs of socks, forty cents for "double mittens" and twenty-five cents for making "summer Pants for Willie Seaton." Similar amounts came in for shirts, collars, dresses and aprons, with socks by far the most popular items. Besides this, through bazaars and bees, the ladies raised $122.12 in February 1865. An Oyster Supper brought in more than fifty-two dollars as one of their activities in 1866.

The Society paid for construction material, as well as lumber for the "church pewing," for lamps and a dozen spare chimneys, "asphaltum stain," and paint; for double windows, as well as drain spouts, labour, customs duty, and freight. They probably made their minister's surplice, too, for the accounts list "Cash Paid for Linen for Surplice $7.50." With all this outlay there were still modest sums for Sunday School expenses: "presents for children for Xmas" ($5.42 in 1875) and ninety cents for "Sweeties & raisins for Candy bags" in 1878.

The final memo in the book containing the Proceedings of the Abercorn Church Building Committee reads:

By a resolution which was passed at the Annual Vestry Meeting at Easter on the 18th day of May 1871, it was proposed that an effort should be made to raise an amount sufficient to discharge the debt on our church. That effort was made, and the debt was discharged by a subscription … collected from A. Nield, B. Seaton, R. Spencer, Saml Robinson, Stephen Newton [and] R.E. Fay.

This had been the first church erected in Abercorn, but in 1870, a year before All Saints' debt was cleared, a disgruntled group who had originally adhered to the Anglican fold, broke away from the congregation — perhaps finding the 'Linen Surplice' *un peu de trop* — and constructed a Union Church across the street thus throwing the support of the original church on a smaller group of people. Interestingly, it is that second church which now houses Abercorn's Anglican congregation under their old dedication of All Saints'. The original All Saints was sold to the Roman Catholics in 1924 as a mission church attached to Sutton. In 1941 the growing French population warranted the erection of a separate Roman Catholic parish centred in the old church under the new designation of St Simon. By 1949, the Union Church, which had served several denominations including the Anglicans, was purchased for exclusive Anglican use and became the new All Saints.

On 8 March 1866 an Anniversary meeting of the Sewing Society, its second, was held at the Parsonage. There were fourteen ladies and at least five of their husbands present, besides the incumbent, John Smith. A record of the event was duly kept by the Secretary:

The success which had crowned the efforts of the Society aided by the Bees was fully discussed by the members, and one and all appeared to feel encouraged for the future — a determination was expressed by all present to do their utmost to forward the pewing of the Church — much interest was felt — the old officers were again chosen to serve — after Tea and Prayer from the Revd Mr Smith, the Society separated having spent a very pleasant anniversary afternoon —
signed R[achel] M. Seaton, Secy Treas

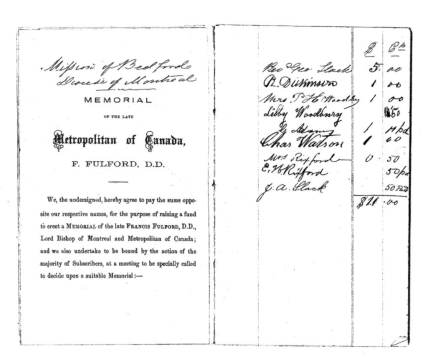

PLATE 5 *A Local subscription List for Bishop Fulford's Monument*
*(Photo Credit:* MDA*)*

# AN ELECTIVE
# EPISCOPATE
# 1868–1895

## Oxenden up the Ottawa (1869)

In the first year of his episcopate, Ashton Oxenden did a phenomenal amount of travelling, getting to know his diocese and the country itself. There had been a long interregnum because of Diocesan Synod's refusal (at first) to elect a successor to Bishop Fulford. A confirmation tour was long due, and churches awaited consecration. Although never robust, and of a finicky disposition, Oxenden did his best to accustom himself to the rougher modes of transport he was subjected to during his nine-year term of office. In 1871 he published a slender volume, *My First Year in Canada*. It gives a useful account of the place as he found it. Although quite positive, he identified all persons mentioned by their initials only.

My first purely episcopal act [he writes] was the consecration of the pretty little church at Como, a hamlet on the south bank of the Ottawa. This took place [on 13 September] just a fortnight after our arrival in Canada.

The morning was lovely, though somewhat hazy. Our party, which numbered eight or ten, consisted of my wife and myself, my chaplain [the Rev.] Mr. [William Turnbull] L[each], two other clergymen, their wives, and the Archdeacon of Ontario, who joined us on the way. We left Montreal by train for Lachine, where we took the steamer, and at twelve o'clock arrived at Como. We had been detained for nearly two hours by a river fog, and found the congregation waiting for us. The church is small, but very pretty, and in good taste. It is situated in a picturesque and peaceful spot near the river. The congregation was not large, but devout and orderly; and all seemed to enter warmly into our simple but beautiful Consecration Service. ...

... on Monday, October 11th, I left home with my wife on another expedition up the Ottawa, with a view of going higher up the river this time, and visiting three stations at the further extent of my Diocese to the north-east.

The day was delightful, the tints most lovely, and the steamer very comfortable. My good friend, [the Rev.] Mr. [Richard] L[onsdell], the rural dean, joined us at Carillon, and remained with us for four days. We reached Ottawa in the evening, but pushed on to Aylmer, where we slept, as the Upper Ottawa boat starts from thence.

Tuesday, October 12th, we left at seven for Onslow; but to our dismay, instead of finding a nice, clean, comfortable vessel, we had to put up with a dirty little tug-boat, rigged out for the occasion, as the regular packet was undergoing a thorough refitting for Prince Arthur, who was expected in these parts in a day or two. [He had arrived in Montreal on 9 October.] This detracted somewhat from the comfort of our voyage.

When on the Ottawa the scene is often enlivened by the appearance of a huge raft which comes in sight. These rafts bring down the sawn timber from the mills at Ottawa and elsewhere, which is eventually shipped either for England or for the United States. They are of an enormous size, and are composed of timber bound together by clamps of wood into a solid stage, and generally so constructed as to be subdivided into two or three compartments, in case of a storm. On one of these rafts are sometimes erected four or five wooden houses, the dwellings of the raftsmen. These floating islands drop down the stream, and are guided by long oars. The lumber of which they are composed has probably travelled some hundred miles from the forest in the interior.

The life of the shanty-men, who fell the timber, is a very peculiar one. Being engaged by the lumber merchants, they go up in the month of October or November in regular gangs to certain localities in the Bush, previously untrodden by the feet of men. ...

These hardy men meet with many privations; but they live well, having plenty of good beef and pork to supply them. They are restricted, however, from the use of spirits, and indulge in no stronger drink than tea ...

The shanties are temporary wooden buildings, each one holding from twenty to thirty persons. They are divided into two compartments — the one for cooking, and the other for eating and sleeping; the latter being usually furnished with two tiers of berths.

An occasional Missionary visits these shanties, attracted there by a desire to carry the glad and welcome tidings of the Gospel; and if he comes in a right spirit, he is pretty sure to meet with a kind and warm reception. Three of our Clergy have volunteered to devote a week or two to this self-denying service in the coming year. But I hope the time will come when our Church will be able to employ two regular travelling Missionaries, whose time shall be entirely occupied in going from shanty to shanty during the winter months. ...

We landed at Onslow about ten o'clock, a pretty missionary station amidst the woods. ... Service was at three o'clock, but rain had come on, and greatly thinned our congregation. There were only five candidates [for confirmation]. On the same evening we had a Missionary Meeting at seven o'clock.

These missionary meetings are very unlike ours in England. In the first place, they are usually held in the Churches, for want of room elsewhere. And then the object is not so much missionary work among the heathen, as the support of the Church in the Diocese. ... I cannot but think that our Church in Canada, needy as she is, would not have a larger blessing if she did more for our brethren in distant lands.

We left next morning early, October 13th, in [the Rev.] Mr. [George C.] R[obinson]'s waggon for Clarendon, a distance of sixteen miles. The drive interested us a good deal, as the scene was new to us, the country through which we passed being only half cleared. ... The clearances are made either by cutting down the trees, or, more commonly, by burning them. But the stumps are allowed to remain about three feet above the ground, presenting the appearance of a huge graveyard. The custom is to leave these stumps for several years till they are fairly rotted, as the expense of grubbing them in their sound state would be ruinous. My wife much enjoyed the drive, and I should have enjoyed it too, for our friends were very pleasant and agreeable, and we had two good horses which carried us along famously, but I was a little out of order, and the morning was chilly. Halfway however we got my indian-rubber foot-warmer [obviously a hotwater bottle] filled at a cottage, which nearly set me right again.

Another recollection of one of the Bishop's journeys up the Ottawa, this time from the Rev. George Abbott-Smith, adds to the picture of Oxenden on the road:

Bishop Oxenden was somewhat under average height and slightly built and his health was not robust [Abbott-Smith recalled]. He seemed more fitted for a scholar's life in rural England than for that of a Canadian bishop, but he devoted himself with earnest zeal to the arduous work which devolved upon him in the extensive diocese of Montreal. ...

I remember seeing Bishop Oxenden on one of his early visits to the upper Ottawa valley, when I was eight years old. I drove with the parishioner who had volunteered to meet him at the steamboat landing. When he came ashore, we saw that he was accompanied by Archdeacon Lonsdell, a tall and dignified Irishman whom our friend supposed to be the bishop. As the Archdeacon began to take the small seat at the back of the vehicle, he remonstrated, saying, "No, no, my Lord, you sit in front with me; the little man can get in behind!"

These events must have occurred on a later confirmation tour than that outlined in Oxenden's memoirs; George Abbott-Smith would have been eight years old three years later, in 1872, the same year in which Lonsdell was made Archdeacon of St Andrew's.

Abbott-Smith would receive deacon's orders at the hands of Bishop Bond in 1887 and would pursue a distinguished career as Principal of Diocesan Theological College and Professor of Hellenistic Greek at McGill University, serving the Diocese for fifty-two years.

In 1965, the stations of Aylmer, Onslow and Clarendon, together with some twenty-five others, were transferred from the Diocese of Montreal to the Diocese of Ottawa by Act of the Legislative Assembly of the Province of Quebec. The Deanery of Clarendon, as the region was called, had been carved out of the Deanery of St Andrews in 1882, well into the episcopate of William Bennett Bond.

## Setting the Tone at Synod (1870)

In the summer of 1870, Ashton Oxenden addressed his clergy and laity assembled in synod for the first time.

There had been an interval of nine months between Bishop Fulford's death and his successor's election — with two acrimonious synods at which candidates were offered and discarded. The complicating factor had been the Bishop of Montreal's automatically succeeding as Metropolitan of the Ecclesiastical Province of Canada. A canon of the Provincial Synod had established the principle that the bishops of the Province were to make nominations to the Montreal Synod from which the new bishop would be chosen. As no Montreal clergy were included among the nominees and the names offered were unpalatable for one reason or another, Synod refused to elect anyone. Both the House of Bishops and the Montreal Synod adjourned until the following May.

When both bodies met again, the threat of deadlock was transferred to the Synod itself where the clergy and laity could not agree. Churchmanship seems to have been a factor; the prominent laymen favoured the more Evangelical candidates whereas the clergy were more evenly divided. It was necessary, however, for a successful candidate to receive a substantial majority in both houses.

"At last," as one historian puts it, "after four exhausting days, and the taking of eleven ballots, the House of Bishops nominated the Rev. Ashton Oxenden, Rector of Pluckley in the Province of Canterbury [England]. He received immediately a decisive majority of the votes of both orders. On the motion of L.S. Huntingdon, one of the great lay figures of the Synod, the decision was made unanimous."

In addressing his first Synod, Oxenden was well aware of these difficulties. A man of deep personal piety, well-known for his authorship of numerous religious tracts, he was an eloquent and forceful preacher. He was also, however, somewhat rigid in temperament, "with an intense dislike for any ornate service in any shape or form":

My Brethren of the Clergy and Laity [the Bishop began], — in presiding for the first time over this your Annual Synod, I must ask you to bear with me, if I begin with a few remarks personal to myself.

Having been summoned by the unanimous vote of the Clerical and Lay representatives of the Church in this Diocese, when solemnly assembled in Synod, I felt that I had no alternative but to leave my quiet retreat in England, where I had watched over a simple and affectionate people for one and twenty years, to obey at once your call, and to come among you as your elected Bishop.

I felt that under such circumstances your call was the echo, as it were, of a higher summon[s] from above; and I regarded the expression of your wishes as indicative of the will of God. I came out therefore to fill my allotted post, not without misgivings, but at the same time with a strongly impressed conviction, and I may also say with an assured confidence, that He, who seemed so plainly to have marked out my path, and who Himself knew all my deficiencies, would give me the needed strength, the requisite wisdom, and the grace to fit me for my new and unexpected work.

During the ten months that I have exercised my episcopal office among you, I may truly say that I have never once regretted the step which I have taken. The kind and generous reception which I met with on my first arrival ... the cordial and affectionate desire shewn by the Clergy to carry out my wishes; and the very hearty cooperation of the Laity, who have evinced a zeal for the Church's welfare, as well as a respect for my office, which at once endears them to me — these would of themselves be sufficient to call forth my thankfulness ... But I have yet further cause for gratitude from the marked way in which God has ... been graciously pleased to endue me with bodily strength, such as I have not experienced for years past ... To Him I desire thus publicly to give the praise.

After outlining his own chief priorities, such as sustaining country missions and opening new ones: appealing for funds more vigorously from "the richer Laity of the Church, in this city and elsewhere," improving the management of endowments and mission funds, and discouraging the use of church bazaars — "a spurious and worldly system of liberality" — as a means of fund-raising, the Bishop turned his attention to regulating religious practice within his diocese:

I cannot but speak with much thankfulness of the general harmony of views which exists among us [he continued], and of the soundness, faithfulness, and moderation, which for the most part mark the preaching from our pulpits. There will ever be some few whose opinions reach the extreme line of what the church permits, but I am not aware of any within my Diocese who are so decidedly overstepping that line as to call for my interference. Still there are some, whom I would gladly see conforming more heartily to the general feeling and spirit of the Church in which they serve. And I am extremely anxious that by a little modification of practice, and by the exercise of a conciliatory spirit, there may be brought about a more entire conformity throughout the Diocese, especially in the ordinary mode of conducting our Services.

In the short period that he had spent in his new diocese, Oxenden had realized that the prominent and well-to-do among the laity, particularly in the city of Montreal, were probably more in sympathy with his own views than were a significant number of his clergy. Perhaps with that in view, he made the unprecedented suggestion of democratizing Synod by limiting the practice of voting by orders:

I am inclined to think that in all mixed gatherings of Churchmen there is some little danger, lest a feeling of clanship should be allowed to spring up between the Clergy and Laity. This should be especially guarded against; for surely the interests of the one body are the interests also of the other; and the moment those interests are divided, the well-being of the Church is in peril of being weakened.

It is for this reason that I would venture to recommend a very sparing use of our privilege of *voting by orders*. It is important for both parties that the privilege exists; but we should resort to it only on very exceptional occasions.

Even at this early date, Oxenden had already determined to establish a theological college of his own where, as he put it, "I could gather my candidates for the sacred Ministry around me here at Montreal, where I could watch their characters and conduct, and superintend their preparation for the Ministry ..."

In concluding his address, and therefore giving his remarks great prominence, he reverted to the subject of churchmanship and conformity among the clergy:

And may I not also express a hope, an earnest hope, that the *Clerical* members of this Synod may have come here prepared to lay aside their sectional differences — that from the tone that prevails within these walls it may be happily apparent that the spirit of party is speedily dying out, and that the spirit of union is taking its place.

Try to forget, my Reverend Brethren, any little specialties either of doctrine or practice, which have in days past ranged you on separate sides; and think only of the greatness of those matters on which you are sent here to deliberate, and of His honour which should be dearer to you than all else. ...

Oxenden's apparently conciliatory tone in promoting harmony did not prevent his entering into an "acrimonious correspondence and acrimonious interviews" with the Rev. Edmund Wood, founder of the Free Seat Chapel of St John the Evangelist and of St John's School (later to become Lower Canada College). At age forty, Father Wood was in his prime. Both a Tractarian and a Ritualist, he had introduced weekly eucharists, and choral celebrations every Sunday well before Oxenden's arrival. The use of "eucharistic vestments, altar cross, and altar lights" at St John's — used for the first time in Montreal — dated from 1868.

As Wood was unwilling to relinquish any "little specialties," as Oxenden had put it, the Bishop placed St John's under a ban, refusing to visit the Chapel, or to administer confirmation on Father Wood's candidates. Under such pressures, as Father Wood wrote, "[Altar] Lights, the Legal Eucharistic vestments, the stole, the sign of the cross, &c., &c., &c., were relinquished," and Oxenden continued to crush the signs of Tractarianism throughout his episcopate.

Among the papers of the Church of St John the Evangelist is a barely legible page, undated and unsigned, in Father Wood's hand. It obviously bears on his relationship with Oxenden and shows his struggle to reconcile his sense of duty to his diocesan with his principles:

When tempted to think uncharitably of the Bishop Let me remember [Father Wood wrote]: —

That he came to the Episcopate an old man: having been Educated and brought up in the old school of Evangelicalism,
    that he did not seek the office: but rather had the office forced upon him:
    that, beyond a doubt, he tries earnestly to fulfil the duties of his office, and prays constantly for a right judgement i[n] discharging them:
    that I myself, having held aloof from him, little wonder if he misjudged me, and my opinions, practice & devotion

that he is entirely, & has all along been in the hands of the Low Church Clergy who (without forcibly meaning to do any harm) have yet warped his judgements, possibly hopelessly so …

that no one is absolutely perfect: — i[n] spite of great personal holiness some inherent faults … lead the Bishop to act [unguardedly (?)], to say the least, at times

that he may sincerely believe the Catholics in the Church of God to be traitors to the Church: in [which] case his action is, of course, not to be regarded as a matter of surprise …

In 1878, at age seventy, Bishop Oxenden resigned the See of Montreal and returned to England — where he resided four months of each year, and spent from seven to eight months at Biarritz, France, "where he gave valuable assistance to the English chaplain." He died at Biarritz in 1892.

Father Wood survived until 1909. Of him Bishop Farthing (the fourth Canadian bishop under whom he had served) has written:

In the death of Mr Wood, the Canadian church lost one of her best known and most honoured priests. Such a life as his is a witness to the fact that 'sacrifice alone is fruitful.' His unselfish service to others, his conscientious discharge of duty, his fidelity to his principles, made his life alike beautiful, attractive and fruitful. His death stirred the whole Anglican Church, and from all parts came the testimony of the value of his life and ministry. … His life has enriched the Church in this Diocese, and his memory will be one of our most sacred treasures.

# Some Founding Mothers (1875)

Women, over the years, have played a major role in establishing and maintaining the institutions and organizations that have formed an important part of Diocesan life.

Laura Mudge, sister of the better-known Anglican layman H.J. Mudge, was the leading figure in setting up the Girls' Friendly Society — an organization for young women parallel to the YMCA. Introduced into the Diocese in 1885, it quickly spread through the city parishes and into the larger towns. According to John Irwin Cooper's *The Blessed Communion*, "the GFS epitomised the social service work of that day. It was deeply religious and entirely personal." Of particular usefulness was the assistance it offered to young immigrant women as they passed through the city on the way to their eventual destinations.

Also in the 1880s, two Montreal Methodist women, Mina Douglas and Eva Findlay founded a soup kitchen for homeless and destitute men that would later become the Old Brewery Mission.

Nina May Nesbitt's bequest of Lismore, her spacious family home in Cowansville, gave rise to the Nesbitt Anglican Residence for the care of the elderly, both men and women, opened in November 1957. Although it has since been sold and turned into doctors' offices, during the period of its vocation the Home provided years of dedicated, personal care, as the detailed record of its daybooks shows.

The earliest social service institution established since the erection of the Diocese, however, is probably the Fulford Residence, or Church Home as it was called at the time of its incorporation in 1875.

It had been founded twenty years earlier, in 1855, by Mary Fulford, née Drummond. The wife of Bishop Francis Fulford, she and her projects received considerable attention, but she was in her own right a person of influence and good family, being the niece of the Right Honourable Spencer Percival, a former Prime Minister of Great Britain, and grand-daughter of the earl of Egmont.

The various histories of the Residence differ somewhat as to Mrs Fulford's initial intention. The most reliable suggests that "her first aim was to provide for young immigrant and friendless women and give them temporary shelter," but that "her sympathy was also aroused for school teachers who, at that time, were trained by the Church," and, if their homes were at a distance, were in need of a respectable place to stay.

A description of the past activities of the Home, drawn up on the basis of its Annual Reports in 1889, shows that over the years it had received nine categories of residents: "Strangers, i.e. Immigrants, Friend-less Persons, Aged & Infirm Females, Boarders for Pay, Students in the Normal or Other City Schools, Needlewomen, Servants out of Place, Young Females out of Health, and Aged Persons in Reduced Circum-stances," but by 1888 it was described as "an Institution for the benefit, mainly, of aged and infirm gentlewomen."

The Home enjoyed the support of the Cathedral and continued as a project of Mrs Fulford's for thirteen years. After her husband's death, and her subsequent return to England, however, the leadership of her successors faltered, and the Cathedral "found itself unable to retain sole charge of the Charity." Bishop Oxenden and the city clergy decided to "adopt" the Home, but the adoption did not come with funds:

The members of the Committee were not of one accord as to what type the

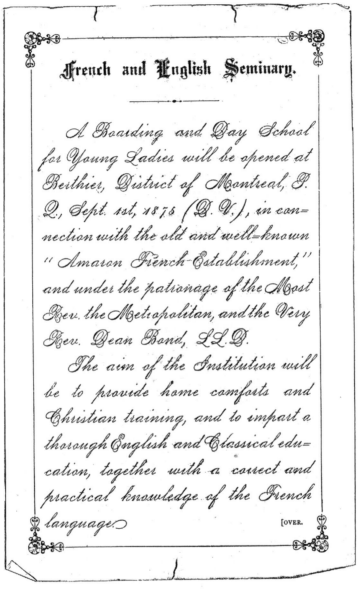

### French and English Seminary.

A Boarding and Day School for Young Ladies will be opened at Berthier, District of Montreal, P. Q., Sept. 1st, 1875 (D. V.), in con=nection with the old and well=known "Amaron French-Establishment," and under the patronage of the Most Rev. the Metropolitan, and the Very Rev. Dean Bond, LL.D.

The aim of the Institution will be to provide home comforts and Christian training, and to impart a thorough English and Classical edu=cation, together with a correct and practical knowledge of the French language.

[OVER.

PLATE 6    *Flyer for young ladies' Church-affiliated boarding school at Berthier-en-Haut  (Photo Credit:* MDA*)*

recipients of the charity should be [the 100th Anniversary History recounts]. Convalescents from the Montreal General Hospital were admitted, and different classes were entertained side by side in the Home …

In 1874 two donors came forward with money to help in the purchase of a home 'for ladies in reduced circumstances.' With the acceptance of this, the policy was decided, and the Church Home was incorporated, enabling it to accept further endowments and legacies.

Premises were purchased on University Street and the Home was transferred from its quarters on Aylmer Street. The first person to be admitted there was "an aged and sick governess, Miss Munson," and from then on "others of the same social group were given hospitality."

We read in the records of its first committee [following incorporation] that 'in the interests of good order and economy and Christian kindness, the Committee of Management use its discretion in the selection of applicants, so that the persons benefitting may be likely to live happily in social equality as members of one family.'

In 1890 the present red brick house with the green trim at 1221 Guy Street (then number 403) was purchased for $19,250 from the heirs of James Major, prosperous government inspector of potashes, who had built it as "Erin Cottage" some four decades earlier. On 17 September of that year the new Church Home was dedicated by Bishop Bond. Miss Munson, the first resident, was still living at that time.

*Montreal Gazette* feature writer Eve McBride described the Home in 1994, its "unobtrusive elegance" and the women who lived there.

The average age at that time was 91 (in 2001 it was 92) and the 38 residents ranged in age from 72 to 103. In its early days, the Home was intended for Anglican use, but now accommodates women from a variety of backgrounds and religious denominations. "One woman once had a large house in Westmount, another was the wife of a mechanic. Several have spent their entire lives as single women, supporting themselves as bookkeepers, nurses and teachers."

The Home continues to operate under a Committee of Management consisting almost exclusively of women. In 1890, just before the move to Guy Street, the Directresses were Mrs G.W. Simpson, Mrs Reford and Mrs M.H. Gault, working with a Committee of 31, all of them women.

There have been a number of changes over the years. To comply with Provincial legislation, on 23 October 1982 the name of the Church Home was changed to La Résidence Fulford Residence. As one of the

**Cathedral Church Auxiliary.**

SOCIAL MEETING

IN THE

NATURAL HISTORY SOCIETY ROOMS,

**Thursday Evening, Dec. 1st,**

AT EIGHT O'CLOCK.

ALL CORDIALLY INVITED.            ADMISSION FREE.

The Museum will be thrown open during the Evening.

*CATHEDRAL*

YOUNG MEN'S CHRISTIAN ASSOCIATION,

**Musical and Literary Entertainment,**

SYNOD HALL,

*Monday Evening, April 20th, 1874.*

### PROGRAMME.

| | | | |
|---|---|---|---|
| 1. DUO, | - | Overture, "Egmont," - - - | *Beethoven.* |

DR. MACLAGAN, Melodeon ; MR. EVANS, Piano.

2. SONG, - - - "Truth in Absence, - - *E. B. Harper.*
MR MACDOUGALL.

3. DUO, - - - "Si la Stanchezza," (Trovatore,) - *Verdi.*
MISS LINDSAY AND MR. MILLS.

4. SONG, - - - "Watching," - - - - *Millard.*
MRS. CALDICOTT.

5. TRIO, - - - "Ave Maria." - - - *Gounod.*
MR. McCULLOCH, Violin ; FRÄULEIN GEORG, Piano ; MR. BETHUNE, Melodeon.

6. READING, - - - - - - - -
REV. JAMES CARMICHAEL.

7. SONG, - - "Regnava nel Silenzio," - - - *Bellini.*
MISS IDLER.

8. SONG, - "Take then these Flowers," (Lalla Rook,) *Maclagan.*
MR. MILLS.

9. PIANO SOLO, - "Fantaisie sur la Sonnambula," - *Leybach.*
FRAULEIN GEORG.

10. SONG, - - - - - - - -
A LADY.

11. SONG, - - - - - - - - -
MR. MALTBY.

12. TRIO, - - "Der Lützerjäger," - - - *Weber.*
MESSRS. MALTBY, MACDOUGALL AND MILLS.

Proceeds to go towards the erection of a Building on Upper St. Lawrence Main
St., for the use of the Cathedral Y. M. C. A. Mission, Estab'd Feb., 1873.

COMMITTEE OF MANAGEMENT.
R. W. SPRINGER.        |        R. C. PINKERTON.
WM. MOREWOOD CROSS.

PLATE 7    *Cathedral activities*
*(Photo Credit:* MDA*)*

informal "histories" of the Home points out, there are also many constants:

The Bishop of Montreal [as specified in a bequest to the Home in 1894] still presides as President of the Corporation, the Committee of Management boasts a First, Second and Third Directress, and Mrs Fulford in her bonnet keeps a watchful gaze [from her portrait in its oval frame] on all who pass through the doors at 1221 Guy Street.


## Relations with Rome (1877)

For many years the Roman Catholic Church in Lower Canada — like the Anglican Church — was a strong supporter of the Government.

Initial assurances of non-interference and the continued right to tithe their people, coupled with fears of revolution and Godless republicanism — of both the American and the European variety — had for many years fostered the loyalty of the Roman Catholic hierarchy.

In times of unrest such as the Rebellions of 1837 and 1838, its priests had urged the importance of obedience to civil authorities, and denounced insurgency among their countrymen and co-religionists.

With the rise of ultramontanism, however, things changed. In centres such as Montreal and Three Rivers, both with ardently ultramontane bishops, a new brand of Catholic nationalism arose that proved most alarming to liberal Roman Catholics and non-Roman Catholics alike. The ultramontanists maintained that the state should be linked to and dominated by the church. Their liberal opponents demanded separation of church and state, and the exclusion of the clergy from politics.

As there was a considerable amount of liberal thinking, both politically and philosophically, among the Québécois, this move on the part of the church hierarchy produced both consternation and alarm. The Institut Canadien, a foundation of the anti-clerical *Rouges*, had been attacked by Bishop Bourget as early as 1858, but the concerted actions of the Quebec bishops after 1870 — the year of the promulgation of the dogma of Papal Infallibility — brought the conflict to a new level, one which would affect every resident of the province regardless of creed or religious affiliation.

On 22 September 1875, the eight Roman Catholic Bishops of Quebec issued a joint pastoral letter. It covered a wide area of concern, but the aspect receiving the most attention was its mobilization of the clergy to advise the faithful on their duty as electors.

The Montreal Diocesan Archives contains a book entitled *Rome in Canada: The Ultramontane Struggle for Supremacy Over the Civil Authority* by Charles Lindsay, published in Toronto in 1877. It gives a notion of attitudes toward ultramontane claims and reflects the anxiety of those who valued the notions of free elections and civil liberties.

The book attempts to trace the growth of ultramontanism in Quebec and the influence of Bishops Ignace Bourget of Montreal and Louis Laflèche of Three Rivers, bringing the account up to 1876.

Two chapters, titled "The Bishops Claiming Political Control" and "Spiritual Terrorism at Elections" are of particular interest. The following passage provides a brief sample:

The united Roman Catholic Episcopate of Quebec instructed the clergy, in a joint pastoral letter, dated September 22, 1875, how to proceed in obtaining control of Parliamentary elections, and thus practically make the State subordinate to the Church, and coerce it into obeying her behests.

The joint letter assumes that the Church is a society perfect in itself, distinct and independent of civil society, having legislators, judges, and power to enforce its laws. But, the pastoral proceeds, "not only is the Church independent of civil society, she is superior by her origin, her extent and her object." "A civil society embraces only a single people; the Church has received for her domain the entire world," with the mission to teach all nations. "The State is therefore in the Church, and not the Church in the State." ...

It is the priest ... who must carry out the instructions of his ecclesiastical superiors, by reading and explaining circulars and pastorals at the altar, and by enforcing the instructions they contain through the confessional.

The refusal of the sacrament to a disobedient elector would, Ultramontane writers tell us, be announced in the secrecy of the confessional. ...

The list of those whom the electors are forbidden to vote for includes: all who affirm that the Church has nothing to do with political questions; all who "criticise and censure the mandates and circulars of the bishops and the instructions of pastors relative to elections, and who, in spite of their protestations in favour of religion, effectually and openly favour journals, books, [and] societies which the Church condemns; all who dare to say that the priests ought to confine themselves to the Church and the sacristy, and who form part of any organization which aims to prevent them from teaching ... the principles of sound politics, as the Church herself teaches."

A sense of increasing powerlessness and frustration felt especially by those outside the Roman Catholic fold is evident here, and one which is important to grasp in trying to capture one aspect of the Anglican ethos in Quebec.

It was partly the change in political stance that appeared so disturbing:

Bishop Langevin [of Rimouski] is a two-sided man [Lindsay continues]. What he now commands, he not long since interdicted. The Bishop Langevin of 1875 and the Bishop Langevin of 1867 are wide as poles apart. At the latter epoch he condemned the abuse of the pulpit in political matters, and absolutely interdicted the priests of his diocese ... to name or designate the candidates in the pulpit, or to pronounce on their respective merits [or] to counsel or order the faithful to vote for one candidate in preference to another.

Six years after the time when Bishop Langevin issued this interdiction to the clergy of Rimouski, no layman could repeat his affirmations except at the expense of being denounced as impious, an enemy of religion and the clergy. ...

Even Bishop Bourget has made almost as great an advance. At the election of 1867 he instructed the clergy to "remain neutral in questions which in no way touched religious principles," for he added, "there is a great difference between the direction, "vote or do not vote for such a candidate," and this other, "vote for him who in your soul and conscience appears to you qualified to sustain the interests of religion and of the country." This was, in effect, a notice to the clergy not to name or express a preference for any candidate ... He is now completely at the opposite side of the circle.

These pastorals produced the effect that was expected from them; they caused the parish priests everywhere to take sides, in elections, in favour of one party and against another.

When the Bishops' actions in framing the joint pastoral letter drew criticism from within the church, Lindsay points out, the matter was adjudicated in Rome. Mgr Laflèche presented their case in person.

The brief of Pope Pius IX, dated September 13, 1876, and addressed to the Bishop of Three Rivers, shows what might from the first have been foreseen, that the victory remains with the Ultramontanes. ... "We rejoice chiefly," the Pope says, "at the care you take to inculcate among the Canadian people sound doctrine, and to explain to them what regards the nature, the constitution, and the rights of the Church ... and we have had to praise the zeal with which you have striven to forewarn the same people against the crafty errors of *libéralisme* called *Catholique*, the more dangerous that, under an exterior appearance of piety, they deceive many honest men, and that, tending to lead men away from the true doctrine, especially on questions which at first sight seem to concern rather the civil than the ecclesiastical power ... We therefore congratulate you, and we hope that you will always labour to unveil their snares and instruct the people with a similar ardour, a like discernment, and with that concord which shows to all your mutual charity, and proves that each of you thinks and teaches only the same thing. This will naturally happen if you carefully nourish in you that devotion to the Chair of St. Peter, mistress of the truth, which you profess in terms so strong and so affectionate."

Thus began a long period of conflict within Quebec society between the ultramontane and liberal forces, a struggle for power that affected every citizen in the province. It exacerbated interdenominational tensions and exaggerated the extremities of nationalistic feeling among the two dominant cultures.

Ignace Bourget retired as Bishop of Montreal in 1876. Although "current historiography is increasingly critical of his religious and political views," writes Philippe Sylvain, "despite his shortcomings, his achievements make him one of the great architects of Québec society" such as it is.

# La communauté du Rédempteur (1882)

In 1997 the Rev. Gérard Lavallée wrote a brief, but extremely useful pamphlet entitled *Petite Histoire de l'anglicanisme dans la société francophone de Montréal et des environs*. It sets out a chronology of the evolution of Anglican ministry in French from the appointment of David Chabrand Delisle in 1766 to his own installation as "pasteur de la communauté du Rédempteur" in 1997.

Drawing a single thread from the other efforts to establish and maintain French ministry, it is worthwhile to trace the history of this single community from its foundation in 1882. To quote from Fr Lavallée's outline of events:

1880    Le Collège de Sabrevois [dating back to 1830] est transféré à Montréal (Petite Bourgogne). ...

1882    En mai, inauguration de l'église du Rédempteur, située rue Chatham, à côté du Collège.

1904    Lors de la célébration du 50e anniversaire de la Mission [de Sabrevois], l'évêque Bond est heureux de souligner que plus de 3000 enfants ont été éduqués dans les écoles de la Mission et que plusieurs d'entre eux sont devenus ministres du culte.

1905    Le Révérend Dollard La Rivière, pasteur de l'église du Rédempteur et principal du Collège, résigne ses functions. Un différent l'oppose à l'évêque. La Rivière pensait que l'éducation était le premier but de la Mission, tandis que l'évêque croyait que c'était l'évangélisation. ...

1910    Depuis le retour du Collège à Sabrevois et l'implantation de plusieurs industries dans l'environnement de l'église du Rédempteur, ce qui avait eu pour conséquences de faire fuir plusieurs fidèles, le ministère francophone dans ce quartier semble voué à un échec. Le nouvel évêque de Montréal, John Cragg Farthing, décide alors de vendre toutes les propriétés et d'acquérir un autre site pour l'église, dans l'est de la ville, à l'angle des rues Sherbrooke et Cartier.

1912    Inauguration, le jour de Noël, de la nouvelle église du Rédempteur. Au cours de son sermon, donné en français, le Doyen Lewis Evans s'écrie: "Ce serait bien pour l'église de cette province ... si tout son clergé parlait les deux langues et les jeunes hommes qui se préparent pour le ministère seraient bien avisés s'ils cultivaient l'usage de la langue française."

1930    L'appel du Révérend Evans ne fut pas entendu. Seules les églises du Rédempteur à Montréal, l'église du Messie à Sabrevois et la desserte de Pierreville continueront à offrir un culte en français. ...

1931    Le Révérend Victor Rahard (un ancien moine) devient le pasteur du Rédempteur. Il occupera ce poste jusqu'en 1940. Son l'église provoque des grandes controverses, car elle attire plusieurs personnes de l'entourage catholique romain.

1960    Vente de l'église du Rédempteur. La communauté paroissiale est logée dans l'Anglican House, située derrière la cathédrale Christ Church. L'autel, le retable, les stalles du chœur et le lutrin en forme d'aigle sont transportés ailleurs.

A great step forward was taken in the late 1970s with the formation of the Comité pour la pastorale en français which was responsible to the Program Committee, but had direct access to the Bishop.

1978    Création du Comité de la pastorale francophone et début de la publication de la revue *La rencontre*. Une équipe enthousiaste, composée de pasteurs et de laïcs, se donne comme tâche de répondre aux besoins pastoraux et communautaires des francophones du Québec, de mieux faire connaître les particularités de l'anglicanisme, de tisser des liens avec les autres confessions chrétiennes et d'établir des contacts avec tous les francophones de la Communion anglicane tant au Canada que dans les autres pays.

1981    Le Révérend Mark Gudwin, vicaire à la cathédral, réalise le projet d'établir une communauté de base dans sa maison d'Outremont — la Communauté chrétienne du Saint-Rédempteur. Son but est de regrouper quelques paroissiens du Rédempteur et des chrétiens désireux de partager une expérience spirituelle dans une Église moins institutionelle, plus œcoménique et plus soucieuse de répondre aux besoins et aux questions de ses membres.

After Mark Gudwin's departure in 1988, the community did its best to carry on with a number of faithful adherents, moving from place to place and occupying in turn St Luke's Chapel at the Theological College, St Anselm's Chapel at the Diocesan Offices, and the Cathedral. St John the Evangelist and St George's Church also provided facilities to the community on occasion.

In 1992 the Rev. Marc-Philippe Vincent, then their priest-in-charge, attempted to install the parish at the Church of the Advent in Westmount, but without success because of the community's slender financial resources.

As Fr Lavallée notes laconically, a further blow to franancophone ministry was to fall that year:

1992    Dissolution du Comité de la pastorale francophone et disparition de la revue *La rencontre*.

The anomalous situation of the community within the Diocese was brought briefly to the fore in October 1994 when the priest-in-charge was interviewed by the *Canadian Anglican* on the subject of the results of the recent provincial election and the prospective referendum:

I'm glad. I'm thrilled [the Rev. Marc-Philippe Vincent enthused]. My only disappointment is that the popular vote was so close. I would have liked the Liberals to have been wiped off the map, just like the [federal] Conservatives were.

My parish is very politically-minded, and we're the only French community [in the Montreal Anglican church] that is basically Québécois by birth.

The divisions that are conflicting between us and the rest of Canada can't be put together [that is, reconciled].

My message is don't fear. Have confidence in your capacities to build a wonderful country [a Canada without Quebec]. I think Canada will discover more and more what a wonderful culture it has by itself.

This attitude was sharply at odds with that of most Quebec Anglicans. Strong disagreement, aimed directly at these views, appeared among the letters to the editor in the November issue.

My word to Rev. Marc-Philippe Vincent in the "Anglicans react to P.Q. election" article is this [wrote another Anglican priest from the Diocese of Montreal]:

"Moi, je suis un vrai Québécois. J'ai reçu mon éducation ici, au Québec, et, comme M. Parizeau, en Angleterre. Je suis né ici. Je reste ici. Je suis Canadien."

Marc-Philippe, get off the "basically Québécois by birth" stuff. It is high and heady ground, but it is only a verbal step or two away from the deep pit of racism.

Continuing his chronology of la communauté du Rédempteur, Fr Lavallée writes:

1995    La communauté issue du Rédempteur est accueillie à la cathédral qui lui offre la chapelle Saint-Jean-de-Jérusalem pour ses célébrations liturgiques et les services de ses bureaux. Le doyen ... et curé de la paroisse-cathédrale, le Très Révérend Michael Pitts, en devient le prêtre titulaire. Mais, en 1996, la communauté perd son statut juridique de paroisse.

1997    Un prêtre francophone, le Révérend Gérard Lavallée, récemment reçu dans l'Église anglicane, est particulièrement désigné comme pasteur de la communauté du Rédempteur en qualité de vicaire.

The loss of parochial status was clearly a serious blow to the community's morale, and with the dissolution of the pastoral committee four years earlier conditions were far from favourable for growth. As Fr Lavallée notes in a memo entitled "Observations sur le ministère dans la ville et le diocèse de Montréal":

Cependant, il faut reconnaître que, hormis la communauté haïtienne, les francophones n'ont pas pu ou n'ont pas su répondre à l'ouverture de l'Église. Cela tient particulièrement aux lois scolaires du Québec et au fait que les catholiques insatisfaits de leur Église se sont tout simplement devenus indifférents à toute forme d'engagement religieuse ou n'ont pas trouvé le chemin vers une Église qui aurait pu les accuellir.

Fr Lavallée was received into the Anglican Church in 1996 and ordained to the priesthood the following year. In 1999, in a personal letter he observed:

Quant à moi, j'ai dû me retirer récemment de mon ministère régulier à la Cathédral. Toutefois je demeure au service des francophones du diocèse et je réponds occasionnellement à des confrères qui réclament mon aide.

# Smallpox (1885)

In the 1880s and 1890s, health conditions throughout the city of Montreal were deplorable. No attempt was made to clear away the piles of winter snow that accumulated in lanes and narrow streets. Consequently, well into summer, the garbage, offal and worse that had collected in them over many months continued to lie there. Outbreaks of typhoid and smallpox, the one in the spring, the other particularly in the autumn, were common occurrences.

Contagion was not confined to the city, however. In May 1874, for example, Francis John Shepherd, while studying medicine in London, England, was disquieted to hear from his father, a resident of Como, of an outbreak of smallpox there:

It is extraordinary how smallpox hangs about a country place like Como [the young man wrote]. Do the people get vaccinated? If they had done so when the disease first broke out it would have been stamped out by this time. It will be a great pity if it prevents your going to Como [from Montreal], but I think if you get well vaccinated and are very careful about coming in contact with contagion, that there would be very little, if any, danger.

In 1879, when a particularly virulent smallpox epidemic threatened the city, the Board of Trade embarked on a campaign of public education, but the Department of Health was ill-paid and undermanned. The widespread fatalism of those most most at risk and the infrequent use of vaccination — despite its proven benefits — made matters worse.

In 1885, after a lull, smallpox broke out in epidemic proportions, raging throughout the summer and into the autumn. As John Irwin Cooper describes it,

[t]he first cases, brought into the city by railway travellers, were reported in February. They were promptly isolated, and this measure appeared to be effective. Unfortunately, some of the early victims were released prematurely and so carried the disease into Montreal.

Although by June the outbreak seemed again under control, the disease reasserted itself in July in a more virulent form. By autumn it had claimed more than 2,500 victims.

In the accompanying panic that seized the city, there was resistance to measures to isolate victims and vaccinate the population which Public Health authorities tried to enforce. Montreal troops returning from the Saskatchewan Rebellion found themselves drafted as sanitary police.

In the autumn, Bishop Bond ordered that the clergy adopt a special form of prayer for the removal of the smallpox which he had printed and distributed under the title:

A SPECIAL

FORM OF PRAYER

TO

**ALMIGHTY GOD;**

TO BE READ IMMEDIATELY AFTER THE THIRD

COLLECT IN THE MORNING AND

EVENING SERVICES,

**On Sunday, the Twentieth Day of September, 1885**

AND FOLLOWING SUNDAYS DURING THE PREVALENCE OF

SMALL-POX IN THE CITY OF MONTREAL

This was not an unusual course of action in time of crisis. For example, Bishop G.J. Mountain had appointed a day of fasting and prayer on 17 August 1849 on account of the cholera epidemic.

Let us pray to Almighty God for deliverance from the disease which is now afflicting the City of Montreal [Bond's special prayer began]. O Almighty God and Merciful Father, our only refuge in the time of need, we approach Thee under a deep sense of our sinfulness, and our dependence on Thee, in Whom we live and move and have our being. We desire to humble ourselves under Thy mighty hand, confessing our iniquities which have justly provoked Thy wrath against us. Correct us, O Lord, but not in Thine anger; and withdraw from us, in Thine own good time, the scourge with which Thou hast visited us. Give us an heart to comfort and succour all who are stricken by it; incline us to aid in ministering to their wants, and assuaging their sufferings.

And in the presence of the great mortality around us, may we be reminded that in the midst of life we are in death. Give us grace to turn from our evil ways, and seek the Lord our Saviour, while He may be found, with hearty repentance and true faith; so shall we in quietness and confidence await Thy Holy Will, and be ready, shouldst Thou call us, to yield up our souls to Thee, O gracious Father, in the blessed hope of everlasting life, through the mediation, and for the merits of Thy Son Jesus Christ our Lord. Amen.

During this terrible time a number of clergy, at considerable personal risk, made tireless rounds among the sick and gave comfort to the dying and the bereaved. One of these among the Anglican clergy was the Rev. George Rogers of St Luke's Church.

His sympathies for the victims led him to devote a large portion of his time to visiting them [wrote the anonymous historian of St Luke's]. Fearless of contagion he went into their homes, conversed and prayed with them, and brought consolation to many a dying patient. He was a broadminded and liberal-spirited man, and visited victims of all denominations alike, relieving the ministers of other churches of a very dangerous task.

Rogers, who had come to the parish only two years earlier, escaped the disease and continued to minister to his own congregation until 1890.

Perhaps the best known among the Anglican clergy for his devotion during the epidemic, however, was Father Edmund Wood of the Church of St John the Evangelist. The following tribute by a prominent (though unfortunately unidentified) Montreal doctor, paid at the time of Father Wood's death in 1909, furnishes a vivid picture of those labouring to minister to the sufferers during the epidemic:

It will be recalled [the Doctor remarked] that the scourge swept the city with little or no warning. Of course vaccination was not as generally practiced as it is now. ... St. Roch's Hospital, situated at the base of the mountain behind the Golf Club House, Fletcher's Field [as well as the Montreal General Hospital], soon became filled with patients. The authorities then took the building on the Exhibition Ground and used that as a hospital, the premises being separated for the two nationalities and creeds, the Protestant side being known as St. Saviour's Hospital. The interior management of the Protestant section, apart, of course, from the medical side, was under the direction of the Sisters of St Margaret, and the two Sisters, Elizabeth and Sarah, who were untiring in their devotion, have since passed away. Father Wood held devotional services in their quarters, but it was in visiting from house to house in his parish that most of his energies were expended. He was a man of large sympathetic nature and there are many who will remember the solace he imparted to them in those dark hours.

After the Great Epidemic, as it came to be called, the City Council named a commission to choose a site for the erection of a civic small-pox hospital, purchased a property in the Hochelaga Ward, north of Moreau Street in May of that year, and began construction.

The devoted and tireless labours of the Sisters of St Margaret and members of the clergy such as Father Wood lived long in the city's memory among people of all denominations.


# The Woman's Auxiliary (1886)

Before the Provincial Synod had instituted the Domestic and Foreign Missionary Society in 1883, there was no organized missionary society in Canada. Money raised for "foreign missions" was channeled through the British societies, which circulated publications and pamphlets describing their work throughout the world.

Parochial Women's Missionary Societies already existed in a few parishes (in Montreal, Toronto and London, Ontario). This kind of organization often drew its membership from three or four parishes. It was in Ottawa, however, under the dynamic leadership Roberta Elizabeth Tilton — the American-born wife of a Deputy Minister in the Canadian government — that mission-work for women on a nation-wide scale would finally get under way.

On a visit to friends in New York during the winter of 1885, Mrs Tilton had been invited to accompany a member to a meeting of the Woman's Auxiliary to the Missionary Society of the Protestant Episcopal Church. Impressed by what she saw, she managed to interest a small group of devoted Ottawa churchwomen in setting up a Canadian organization along similar lines. On April 16th Mrs Tilton headed a

*Church of the Ascension, West Brome, 1885*

*Trinity Church, Lakefield, 1900*

<small>PLATE 8</small>   *Country Churches, summer and winter*

deputation of seven women to place before a meeting of the Domestic and Foreign Bible Society a plan for a Woman's Auxiliary. Bishop John Travers Lewis, who was in the chair, gave her permission to read the following address to the meeting:

My Lord, Reverend Fathers in Christ, and Members of the Domestic and Foreign Board of Missions:

We come before you as a small deputation of Church Women of Ottawa, to ask your consideration of woman's work, in connection with your Board.

There are in the Church to-day Marys who have chosen the better part; there are the restless serving Marthas, who only want the opportunity to do something for Jesus; the Magdalens, who tell the story of our blessed Lord's resurrection; the Phoebes, who convey messages of love and Christian greeting; the Tryphenas and Tryphosas, Dorcases, who are never weary in well doing; Priscillas, who are occupied in shewing the way of the Lord more perfectly; yes, in the Church of Canada — from Victoria to Sydney — there are women longing to labor more abundantly, to consecrate all their talents to the Lord's work. And, knowing this, we ask that as the Apostles of old recognized the women of their day, as laborers with them, you, our beloved Fathers in Christ, may recognize the women of the Church in Canada, and give your hearty and earnest consent that there should be established, in connection with your Board, a Woman's Auxiliary. That you will consider, before separating [that is, before the end of this series of meetings], the best and most practical method of work, in every way facilitating the formation of Branch Auxiliaries in the different Dioceses and Parishes.

We are assured that the women of the Church of England are prepared to accept whatever plan your Board may consider the wisest, for the promotion of Missionary effort, and the advancement of our Master's Kingdom.

The chairman replied to this address on behalf of the Board in a very positive manner, and after the delegation had withdrawn, a resolution was passed that the Board welcomed "the cooperation of all our Christian Sisters in the Church of the Ecclesiastical Province in carrying out the noble object of our Missionary Society," and expressed its "unfeigned gratitude to God" that the offer had been made. A sub-committee consisting of two bishops, an archdeacon, one priest and one layman was set up to confer with the deputation and draw up a constitution.

The first real meeting of the Provincial Board of the Woman's Auxiliary took place in Montreal, on September 9th and 10th, 1886, at the Diocesan Theological College.

The notices that had been sent out had invited "All Churchwomen desirous of joining in the movement to attend," so — in the words of Emily Willoughby Cummings, the WA's first historian, "it is decidedly disappointing" that only about thirty women responded.

There were seven from the Diocese of Quebec, six from Ontario, two from Huron, one ("who was staying with relatives in Montreal") from Toronto, and one from Algoma, as well as one each from Niagara, Fredericton and Nova Scotia. Not surprisingly, Montreal had the largest number in attendance. They were Mrs Henderson, Mrs Leach, Mrs Norton, Mrs R[obert] Lindsay, Mrs D[avid] Lindsay, Mrs H[enry] J[ames] Evans, Mrs Holden, Miss Gamble "and several other members of the Montreal Society."

During the course of the meeting, reports were read of what was being done already in the various dioceses. Here follows the summary of Montreal's activities as printed in the report of the Provisional Committee, put out in 1886:

Mrs Henderson, the President of the Diocesan Woman's Missionary Association, gave the report of work in this Diocese. It was not yet formally incorporated with the Auxiliary, but had a Diocesan Society, with five Parishes assisting it in the town and four in the country. It had held a most successful meeting with the Bishop of Algoma, and had sent several boxes [of clothing] to the North-West. A great deal of interest was being aroused in the city and country, which would no doubt bear rich fruit in the future. The Bishop [W.B. Bond] took a most hearty interest in the work [whereas at least one Canadian bishop steadfastly refused to allow the Auxiliary to be formed in his diocese], and was most anxious to meet the wishes of its promoters; and the Society would doubtless be made a Branch of the Auxiliary when time had been given to mature arrangements.

The Tenth Provincial Synod was meeting in Montreal at the same time. After the Provisional Committee of the Woman's Auxiliary had met and unanimously adopted the plan of proceeding, the Provincial Synod was only too happy to recognize the new organization and adopt it as the official "Auxiliary" to the Domestic and Foreign Missionary Society.

There were, however, some serious flaws in the constitution that caused difficulties from the start. The bishop's wife was to be diocesan president regardless of her talents or inclinations. The delegates from the dioceses to the Triennial meetings were to be these same diocesan presidents plus two delegates appointed by the bishop. Furthermore, there was no provision for Dorcas work (sewing and providing garments), for work among girls or juniors, or for the study and discussion of missionary activities.

Cummings' early history points out that the expectations of the Society's board and of the women themselves were very different:

It was most unfortunate [she remarked] that at the very beginning of our work, what proved to be a serious misunderstanding arose, which caused much confusion and even differences of opinion at times between the Board of Management of the Domestic and Foreign Society and ourselves for several years, the cause of which however did not become clear for a long time.

That Board quite understood that it was the intention of the women in offering to be their Auxiliary to undertake to collect the money required by the Board from house to house in the Parishes, while of course the women never had such a thought in mind, nor indeed would ever have been willing to work in that way.

As time passed on, and this was not done, it is not surprising that members of that Board were heard to say, "the W.A. do work hard, but they are no real Auxiliary to us," nor did that Board in the least realize how much they owed the increase in their funds to the work of the Woman's Auxiliary in spreading Missionary information and interest.

The members of the Auxiliary shaped the framework they had been given, at least to some extent, to suit their own needs and interests. The proviso in the constitution that the diocesan president be the bishop's wife was dropped and the office, like all the others, was made elective. By 1928 only in the Diocese of Huron was the president appointed by the bishop.

Within the first years of the Auxiliary, particular branches wished to have some say in the uses made of the money they raised. They read missionary publications and developed a lively interest in particular mission fields, but the Board insisted that all their funds be forwarded undesignated.

In 1897, included in the undesignated offerings, was a request from the Board for an annual sum of $15,000, besides $5,000 to support a missionary in Japan.

The feeling of dissatisfaction and of the impossibility of complying with the wishes of the Domestic and Foreign Missions Board [Cummings recorded] caused the meeting later on to vote that we cease to be an auxiliary to the Board of Domestic and Foreign Missions, but become instead a separate Women's Missionary Society. However, before the conclusion of the sessions it was decided unanimously to rescind this resolution.

In her 1995 study on Montreal's Anglican Church and the Quiet Revolution, Joan Marshall expressed surprise at the functioning of women's groups in the particular parishes on which she focussed her research:

One interesting aspect of women's groups in all the churches is that they tend to retain complete control of their finances; their funds often do not appear in the audited financial reports and are contributed to the total church revenue at the discretion of individual executives. This issue is one of the most delicate ones for any rector to address.

It would seem that the same misunderstanding of the role of women's contributions to the support of the church lies behind this observation as underlay the expectations of the Board of Domestic and Foreign Missions. Women's organizations do not now, nor have they ever, seen themselves as a mere collection agency for the church. Present-day women's organizations' insistence on "the independence of their budgets, in order to protect their 'domain,'" as Marshall puts it — rather than reflecting the marginalized position of women in the church, as she implies — is more likely the result of long-established experience dating from the foundation of the WA.

In 1902 the Board of Domestic and Foreign Missions, by resolution of the newly formed General Synod, ceased to exist, and the enlarged Missionary Society of the Canadian Church (MSCC), to which the WA would then become attached, came into existence. The Woman's Auxiliary, according to Carrington, had the distinction of being "the first nation-wide organization for women in Canada."

In 1968, again by resolution of General Synod, the WA itself ceased to exist and Anglican Church Women (ACW) emerged to replace it. Less oriented towards missionary work, the new body continues to furnish valuable support to the church in a variety of ways. Even in its more evolved state, however, the advice of Miss Emery of New York, chairman of the parallel American body, still has relevance. It was she who addressed the founding members gathered in Montreal in September 1886:

Always try and employ those who seem to be interested ... Never let your officers be figure heads. ... In order to keep up the interest ... have constant communication with the points to which effort is being directed. ... Appeal to the working classes, and [do] not pass them by ... In conclusion, I would say the fewer rules and the more elastic the better for a working society such as this.

# Domestic Missions (1887)

*The Canadian Church Magazine and Mission News*, the official organ of the Domestic and Foreign Missionary Society of the Church of England in Canada, first issued in July of 1886, gave encouragement to fledgling parochial missionary societies. The news it provided of missionary activity at home and abroad aroused considerable interest. Its profiles of pioneer bishops and clergy, the line drawings of life in distant lands, the descriptions of outposts in the north and west, all tended to draw readers towards a stimulating and inspiring cause.

It was true that there had been earlier publications of this kind — notably *The Colonial Church Chronicle*, of which Francis Fulford had been editor before taking up his episcopal duties in Montreal, but the *Mission News* was Canadian, and as such could take up local concerns more directly.

In the February 1887 issue, for example, there was an appeal to Canadian clergy to encourage the establishment of parochial branches of the newly-founded Woman's Auxiliary — for these organizations required not only the sanction of the bishop (for any branch to be formed in his diocese) but also the support of the parish priest. The following item suggests how modest were the early plans for the establishment of local WAs, and how far we have fallen away from this early ideal of the numbers of participants needed to carry on a viable organization:

We wish we could persuade every clergyman to form a Woman's Auxiliary in each of his congregations or stations. No congregation, however small, can fail to have amongst them at least two or three devout women — quite sufficient, if rightly directed and favorably placed, to leaven the community in which they live. Let them meet and organize as a Woman's Auxiliary by appointing officers, etc.

From the first, as the following item shows, women took an interest in mission needs of a particular, as well as a general kind. They met to discuss missionary activities in different parts of the world and circulated information about what was being done. Efforts were made to provide assistance on a variety of levels. The following article, on the needs of congregations in the Laurentians west of Montreal was written by Mrs H.J. Evans of that city for the June issue.

In the summer of 1885 the mission being vacant ... Mr. [William] S[anders], of the Theological College was sent out as Lay Reader, and was afterwards ordained deacon, and appointed to the full charge of the Mission. ... There is a total of 95 Church families in the Mission, distributed as follows: — Wentworth, 20; Arundel, 30; Lachute, 45. Besides this the congregation of course includes some in each of these and other places in the Mission, who, although not actual members, attend the services and will probably eventually be drawn in. ...

Now, what is most wanted of outside help? In Lachute there is no communion service [no chalice or paten], for the service used is an old one belonging to St. Andrew's, which the church kindly lends; and the altar linen is always lent for the occasion by some parishioner. Sunday School papers too would be most acceptable, either a yearly club of, say 25 copies, which would come direct from the book seller or office of publication and would alternate with the club taken by the school itself, and surplus of old copies which might be saved from any of our city Sunday schools. Subscriptions also towards the building of the Parsonage are needed. ...

As for Arundel, it is still poorer. ... Books, papers, reward cards, and Sunday school literature of every description are here required, also a surplice and communion service and linen, a reading cushion and carpet for the chancel, and furniture for the vestry.

It is for our Society to take up the cause of struggling parishes such as this and many others. To bear them in our hearts in prayer and to succor them with our gladly-given material help is a duty clearly laid upon us as Christian women.

Such efforts, modest examples of saving, sharing and recycling are typical of the missionary activities of the period. Writing, by women, on missionary subjects was further encouraged by the Literature Standing Committee of the Woman's Auxiliary, which was made "a regular department of work, and its Convenor an officer of the Board," in 1908.

# The Unique Style of Bishop Bond (1889)

William Bennett Bond was a man of humble birth with few advantages in early life. Through hard work, singleminded devotion and great energy he had been enthroned (ten years earlier in 1879) as third Lord Bishop of Montreal, after having been elected on the first ballot, a rare event in episcopal elections. The ballot itself was a decisive one. Bond received twice as many votes as his nearest competitor in the clergy vote and more than three times as many from the laity. Yet Bond was far from a popular figure, having neither urbanity — such as Fulford's — nor charm, nor wit — such as Carmichael's or Maguire's — to draw people to him.

According to one commentator Bond was "an austere person, reticent in conversation, brusque in manner, unemotional and matter-of-fact in temperament," but "he was said by those closest to him to be of a kindly nature." Both sides of his pesonality are apparent in the following letter, written in Bond's characteristic style — point-by-point  and telegraphic.

The recipient was the Rev. William Herbert Naylor, Rural Dean of Clarendon, someone for whom Bond obviously felt a gruff affection:

𝕭𝖎𝖘𝖍𝖔𝖕'𝖘 𝕮𝖔𝖚𝖗𝖙, 𝕸𝖔𝖓𝖙𝖗𝖊𝖆𝖑,

42 Union Avenue

My Dear Naylor                                                    29 Oct. 1889

1    Yr letter of 26th reached me today.
2    I am glad to know that you are in the parsonage, however incomplete.
3    Painting is not healthy — be careful. I do pray that you will all be preserved f[ro]m sickness.
4    I am now in the war of settling up past duties, put off by my absence — & preparing for winter duties — things seem satisfactory — tho' I have 10 vacancies — wh[ich] I hope to fill
5    I regret to hear about typhoid — Do not "rush" — Take yr time — (that is easily written) nevertheless. "Be careful for nothing &c &c" — It is Divine Wisdom —
6    I am pleased to hear good of Harry — I, D[eo] V[olente], begin my lectures next Thursday
7    The last journies to Rawdon &c "took it out of me" (that place means a great deal.)
8    Let Harry or yrself be frank in dealing with us, when he wants any-thing.
9    I feel yr home duties come before Alleyne & I do not see how you can get there with the roads I have experienced.
10   Write to Empson or myself if you want to say anything to the Ex[ecutive] Com[mitt]ee.
11   Fyles is to be married in the Cathedral on the 6th.

With warm regards to all
                    W[illiam] B[ennett] Montreal

Scriptural asides were very typical of Bond's letters and conversation. An earlier message to Naylor dated 31 May 1882 at Waterloo (which, surprisingly, does not have numbered paragraphs) reads — in part — as follows:

I have your letter of 26 May received last night.

Do not be discouraged nor cast down — my message from God to you is Isaiah XII:10 — "Fear thou not, etc." Trust God, test Him, commit thy way to Him. I sympathize with you in your conflict but you shall be more than conqueror — only be of good courage — read Joshua 1 Chap. vs 5, 6, 7, 9, 10 — and tell God you lean on his arm.

Can we not send you additional help? Tell me — if we can —

Do not be surprised — the Devil always does his work with craft and deceit … Go on patiently — steadily — prayerfully.

Both letters suggest that the Bishop answered his letters promptly.

After such a lapse of time, Bond's flurry of references is not easy to sort out. Alleyne was one of the smaller stations which would be served by whoever among the neighbouring clergy could be expected to reach it. Naylor was already doing regular duty at Starke's school house as well as his own morning and evening service every Sunday.

Canon John Empson had been appointed clerical secretary to the Diocesan Synod in 1872 and was also a member of the Executive Committee. A native of Kilkenny, Ireland, Empson had come to Canada in 1858. He served in North Gore before becoming rector of St Matthias, Westmount, from which charge he had retired in 1883.

There were two Fyleses, father and son, who served the Diocese of Montreal. William Adolphus Fyles, who was ordained Deacon and appointed to Chelsea that same year, married Ann Manning of Rougemont on 6 November in Christ Church Cathedral. The Rev. Thomas W. Fyles signed as a witness. Chelsea was not far from Naylor's charge, so news of Fyles' forthcoming marriage would be of particular interest to him.

As to Bond's comments on his correspondent's living quarters, Naylor's daybook of church work for the year 1889 provides some useful information on the progress of the new parsonage. The Daybook does much more than this, however. It is a meticulously kept ledger listing distances travelled, numbers of parishioners visited, services held, types of services, numbers attending, numbers of communicants and so forth — and gives insight into the wide round of visits and activities expected of a conscientious country clergyman. The Ladies' Auxiliary Social was held at the old parsonage on 5 February, for example, and on 11 March a vestry meeting was convened to discuss the new parsonage.

Over a period of four days during the second week in April, the brick veneering on the old parsonage was removed (probably to conserve the bricks for reuse), and on 24 April the family moved out of the building.

The old parsonage was then taken down on 20 May, but the frame of the new one did not start going up until 2 July. There is no indication of where the Naylors were living in the intervening period, however.

Bond visited Clarendon on Sunday, 25 August and the daybook records that 400 people attended Morning Prayer that day (the usual congregation being from 115 to 125).

Snow and heavy rain in October must have made the move into the new parsonage more difficult. The family spent its first night in their new home on 10 October.

One of a bishop's chief episcopal duties is to be a pastor to his clergy. Brusque as he may have been, there is no doubt that Bond was prompt, attentive and conscientious in performing it.


## Sisters of St Margaret (1890)

Practically all Anglican sisterhoods originated in works of mercy. The earliest of all, the Park Village Community, was established in England in 1845 to minister to the poor population of St Pancras, London. Their Rule was compiled by Dr Edward Bouverie Pusey whose sermon, "National Apostacy," delivered on 14 July 1833 in St Mary's Church, Oxford, had launched the Tractarian Movement.

The Society of Saint Margaret, centred at East Grinstead in Sussex was founded in 1855 by John Mason Neale, a member of the Cambridge manifestation of Anglican longings for a return to its shapelier medieval roots, the antiquarian Camden Society.

"As the Oxford Tractarians dwelt upon the Catholic doctrines of the Church of England in the seventeenth century," explains church historian Owen Chadwick, "so the Camdenians nursed the ritual solemnities which survived the Reformation." Nunneries from both these directions were at first generally regarded as "medieval toys and fancy-dress," but some suffered public onslaughts. The sisters of St Margaret, for example, were assaulted by a mob at the funeral of one of their number, whose father accused their founder "of forcing her to leave money to the sisterhood and then to nurse a patient with scarlet fever," but such attacks on religious communities for women were unusual.

PLATE 9    *The second reredos of the Church of St John the Evangelist, Montreal*

When the Sisters of St Margaret began their ministry in Montreal some twenty-five years later, it was from the United States, and not from England that they came. In 1890 — when the Order applied to the Provincial Legislature for an Act of Incorporation by means of a Private Bill — the preamble stated that

... there has existed, since the sixth day of May, 1885, in the city of Montreal, in the Province of Quebec, a branch of the community of the Sisters of St. Margaret, of the city of Boston, in the State of Massachusetts ... whose members aim at devoting themselves in common to works of piety and charity consistent with the contemplative life led by them, and particularly of providing a home for the incurable and the infirm; ...

Individual sisters had been at work in the city before that date, however.

In 1881, Sister Sarah, a native of Montreal and parishioner at the Church of St John the Evangelist, returned from Boston where she had been professed to the sisterhood, and began work in the Diocese of Montreal.

The following year found Sister Sarah and Sister Josephine Margaret operating a small home for incurables at 240 St Urbain Street. It should be noted that at this time — apart from the Montreal General Hospital — there was no provision for the non-Roman Catholic sick in the city of Montreal.

In 1883 the Sisters moved to 835 Ontario Street and the year after that to 666 Sherbrooke, still caring for a small number of patients in what was by then called St Margaret's Home for Incurables.

Later that same year, during the great smallpox epidemic, two additional Sisters — Sister Elisabeth and Sister Alice — were sent from the Convent in Boston to help with the work which continued until the epidemic was over in March 1886.

Although quiet and unassuming, the Sisters' work did not pass unnoticed. When it became known that they were seriously considering establishing a branch of the Society on a more permanent basis, a letter of encouragement in the form of a petition was presented to Sister Sarah at St Margaret's Home. It was dated 27 October 1886 and reads as follows:

The undersigned having learnt of your intention to separate yourself from the sisterhood of St. Margaret's Home, Boston, Mass., believing that the establishment of an active Sisterhood in Montreal, independent of any outside organization would be of great benefit to the City, respectfully ask your kind consideration of the proposal to establish such an institution, for which your work during the past year with the late small-pox epidemic has pointed you out as especially fitted, agreeing if you consent to take up the work among the poor of our own and other towns and cities of the Dominion, in so far as we can to assist you in making it successful.

One hundred and one of Montreal's prominent citizens subscribed their names, the first being Honoré Beaugrand, the mayor.

Among the signatories were Sir Donald Smith, the Hon. J.J.C. Abbott, Senator John Hamilton, F.G. Johnson, Superior Court Judge, Henry R. Grey, Chairman of the Board of Health, James F.D. Black, City Treasurer, William Robb, City Auditor, and Charles Glackmeyer, City Clerk. Thirty-five were medical doctors, both English and French. Familiar names of Montreal's well-known merchant families, the Gaults and the Molsons for example, are also there. Conspicuous by their absence are the signatures of the Anglican ecclesiastical hierarchy.

When, four years later, the Sisters attempted to obtain an Act of Incorporation, the Diocese of Montreal does not appear to have been supportive. A handwritten opinion among Bishop Bond's papers — although apparently not in the Bishop's hand — seems openly hostile to the Bill:

I have carefully read the copy of … "An Act to incorporate the Sisters of St Margaret," and it seems to me, on the face of it, a rather surprising document.

The Sisters do not claim to be of any church, but describe themselves as persons given to contemplation and works of piety and charity.

They ask for all the "rights, powers, and privileges of Corporations" whose objects are moral, spiritual or religious in clause 7; and in clause 6 they repudiate all individual responsibility.

I do not understand who will be responsible for the Corporation's debts & liabilities, or is it any concern of mine provided it is well understood that the Sisters of St Margaret have no part in the Corporate existence of the Church of England in the Diocese of Montreal. It is necessary that this should be quite clear in order that their irresponsibility may not bring trouble or scandal into this Diocese.

These were hard words indeed, particularly after the city-wide recognition the Sisters had so recently received.

Already, by the papers I have seen that a Charity calling itself St Margaret's Nursery has been abandoned by the Sisters with a debt upon it [the commentator continues]. I know nothing of the circumstances but as these Ladies claim generally to belong to the Church of England I wish to make it quite plain that they are not entitled as a body to the Corporate privileges of our Church even though they should use our form of worship.

The Bill was passed, nevertheless, receiving Royal Assent on 30 December 1890.

St Margaret's Nursery, which was operated by the Sisters in conjunction with the Associated Charities of Montreal between 1887 and 1892, was founded to combat the high mortality among foundling infants. It accommodated about twenty women and forty children. When the Sisters were forced, by the poverty of their Order, to give up this work, it was taken over by a Committee. Later, it was moved to a new building on St Urbain Street, and became known as the Montreal Foundling and Baby Hospital.

Meanwhile, St Margaret's Home for Incurables continued, moving again in 1888 to 660 Sherbrooke Street. A brief history of the institution, produced by the Sisters in 1958, indicates the extreme economy with which they were compelled to function:

Here [on Sherbrooke Street] there was room to accommodate 18 inmates — some were free patients, others paid from four dollars a month upwards, according to their ability, and by dint of most careful management the home was maintained on the modest sum of two hundred dollars per month, inclusive of rent!

In spite of these good works — and perhaps because of them — the Sisters continued to be viewed with suspicion by the upper echelons of their church. One objection seems to have centred on the Sisters' nun-like garments. Their Anglo-Catholic churchmanship would, no doubt, have been a further cause for distaste among those dominant in the Diocese at that time. A correspondent signing himself (or herself) "another Episcopalian," penned a furious letter to the Editor of the *Montreal Star* in defense of the Sisters:

Sir, — The Very Reverend Dean [James] Carmichael does not like sisterhoods and does not care to be even suspected of favoring them. ... I don't like the dress they wear myself. Possibly I might object to the outfit of some of our most orthodox clergy, but I don't dislike the whole body on that account. As regards ecclesiastical millinery generally I am not particular, having arrived at the conclusion that the most elaborate and gayest of college hoods [in which the clergy officiated] fails sometimes to secure eloquent or even logical sermons, and the addition of a stole, of a cope or a biretta, or even a mitre, has been known to prove inadequate to secure to the wearer

Christian charity or common sense. But as to the dress of these women much more can be said than for that of the males. Any of the former can, in pursuit of duty, go anywhere by day or night, safe from insult or interference even from the lowest and most degraded — an immunity scarcely to be hoped for by the wearer of a Paris bonnet with a stuffed bird on it ... so there is some sense in the very ugly costume of these women after all. I am, however, sorry that the Dean distrusts them and the Bishop and the Synod of Montreal do not countenance them, for to my mind they deserve better treatment. I have seen something of their work and can truly say that I do not know, and cannot conceive of a higher example of Christian devotion. ... I am sorry that the opposition to the Sisters should come from a section of their own church, and should affect the public sympathy for a noble charity ...

Still the Sisters' work was growing steadily, but after a further move to accommodate more patients in 1891, it became clear that it would be necessary to receive some outside support to sustain the Home. As the Society's seventy-fifth anniversary history records:

An appeal was sent out and in 1893 all anxiety concerning a permanent St. Margaret's Home was allayed by the kindness and liberality of the Hon. Sir George A. Drummond, who purchased for this purpose the very desirable estate of the late William Notman, Esq., ... on the north side of Sherbrooke Street, just west of St Lawrence Boulevard. ...

Sir George and Lady Drummond continued their benevolence toward the Home throughout the remainder of their lifetime, and this same generosity was then continued by Mr. Huntley R. Drummond. Love inspired by God Himself has been manifested in their kindness.

Not a word of the obstacles thrust in their way forms part of the Sisters' own account.

In 1920, St Margaret's Home became a nursing home for women only and continued to operate under the Sisters' care until 1975 at which time they withdrew from the management of the Home and returned to Boston. Later that year, however, a number of Sisters were induced to return to Montreal by newly-elected bishop Reginald Hollis to operate Pilgrim House at 1 Weredale Park, Westmount, a retreat house for the Diocese.

On Sunday, 24 May 1981, a special Thanksgiving Evensong was held at the Cathedral in observance of the Centenary of the work of the Sisters of St Margaret in Montreal.

Pilgrim House continued to function as such into the mid-nineteen-eighties. As of 2000 the premises served as office space for St Stephen's church, Westmount, and the sisters had returned, long since, to Boston.

## Christieville (1892)

Parish endowments, whether painstakingly built up over many years or the result of lump-sum benefactions by individuals, have been of great benefit to a number of parishes in the Diocese.

Trinity Church, Christieville, was founded — virtually singlehandedly — by Major William Plenderleath Christie in 1841. He set apart four acres of land "on which he caused to be erected ... [a] rectory, Church and school at the rear to be used also as a vestry." To this he added a generous yearly sum, in perpetuity, to provide a clergyman's stipend for the church and a grant for the school. As an article on Christieville in a Canadian missionary publication describes it:

The provision made for the maintenance of the church and school, in perpetuity, will scarcely, I think, find a parallel in this country. By Major Christie's Will he endowed the church with $600 for the clergyman's salary, and the school with $200 annually, chargeable on the seigniory of Bleury ...

Christie encouraged settlement on his undeveloped lands, apparently favouring English-speaking Protestants but, time and again "tried to secure bilingual and Evangelical schoolteachers" for the schools he founded in the region. He also brought in a number of French-speaking Protestants from the Channel Islands and from Switzerland, by which means he hoped to assimilate local French-speaking Roman Catholics.

Time was against Christieville — present-day Iberville — however, and already in 1892 the parish showed signs of population shift which would not be commonplace in country parishes for decades. The article continues:

This is, however, one of those English parishes in the Province of Quebec, which have suffered much through emigration. Forty years ago there were about eighty families worshipping chiefly in Trinity Church; now there are left about twenty-five families or 105 souls.

The Annual Report of the Church Society for 1852 shows that there were forty-eight named contributors to the Society in the previous year, half of whom gave less than three shillings. Forty years later, the parish was probably heavily dependent on Christie's provisions for it. In 1892,

with the exception of four families these all reside in the town of Iberville, of which the whole population is a little over 1,700. From this will be seen the relative strength of the French and English population of the place.

There is some hope, however, that the decrease of numbers has reached its lowest ebb; and it is pleasing to note that, while the parish has suffered so much in this respect, the church and school privileges remain permanent, through the endowments provided therefor. There is a prospect of an increasing number of Montreal families settling permanently in the parish.

The rector, besides his work in Trinity Church and school, is able to reach and minister to some twenty families in adjoining parishes, also to a few French Protestants. The parish school is open, of course, to all, and there are a few French Roman Catholics who attend.

The first incumbent of Trinity Church was the Rev. William Dawes of the Newfoundland and British North American School Society who would become the first secretary of the Church Society of the Diocese. He and his friend Mark Willoughby were ordained together and Willoughby was appointed first rector of Trinity Church, Montreal, also a foundation of Christie's. Both men, like their patron, were of strong Evangelical sentiments.

Trinity Church, Iberville, celebrated its centenary in 1941 and was able to make "a very worthy contribution to the Mission Fund of the Diocese" from which it had received an annual grant of $500 "for many years."

Demographics were not on the side of Trinity Church, however. Although it ceased to function as a parish church, it served, for a time as a retreat centre under the name Epiphany House. Its "warm, friendly atmosphere," offering "quietness and time for spiritual renewal," gave a new vocation to the cluster of old buildings.

In 1995, it was reported to the 136th Annual Synod of the Diocese of Montreal (held across the river from Iberville in Saint-Jean-sur-Richelieu) that "the very picturesque Retreat Centre," that was Trinity Church, had closed officially on December 31, 1994, "because of its continuing financial losses which the Diocese could no longer sustain." The Report, as printed in the Synod Journal, concludes:

The Trinity Church building and the original rectory building along with all the land has been declared an historical site. This has complicated the possibility of subdividing the land into a number of separate lots which would increase the value of the property. This is still being examined. The whole property has been surveyed and is now up for sale. Arrangements have been made to reduce the remaining expense to an absolute minimum.

The economic realities of the 1990s left only this shadow of regret on relinquishing the fruits of Major Christie's benefaction.

## "Women's Work" (1895)

Among the papers of St George's Church, Montreal, is a slender pamphlet entitled *Woman's Work*. Although it covers a single year — 1895–6 — it pays tribute to the good work done by the women of the congregation "for more than forty years."

Women have banded together to work for the church from the earliest period of parish life in the Canadas. Often a Sewing Society was formed when a congregation came into existence. Some of the older parishes are not able to date the earliest women's groups that served them.

When churches were being built, it was the women who traditionally found the money for furnishings. In 1849, for example, the ladies of Vaudreuil "were very active raising funds to get the church ready for consecration"; two sales of fancy work netted £21.3.6½.

In Sutton, the Sutton Church Sewing Society (founded in 1855) not only provided small comforts for the parsonage — such as "a complete bedroom set with water-bottle and glass, seven pieces in all" for $4.20, "2 chairs and a Towel-horse" for the spare bedroom for $2.00, and "for the kitchen in the parsonage — A Pump" for $3.00 — all purchased in 1860. They also took on some of the cost of building and repairs, such as $19.97 for shingling the parsonage in 1865.

In the 1880s the Women's Guild of St James Church, Hull (then part of the Diocese of Montreal) "laboured for eleven successive years at the Central Canada Exhibition in Ottawa, where they catered to the staff and general public" in order to raise funds to rebuild the church and rectory after their destruction in a disastrous fire.

In 1892-3, the Young Ladies' Industrial Society of St Paul's Church, Knowlton, offered "to provide the seating for the nave." Through entertainments and sales, featuring homemade candy, dolls and needlework, they managed to raise the requisite amount, "over $400, for the beautiful oaken pews in the new church."

In Valleyfield, following the fire of 10 January 1961 that destroyed St Mark's Church, the Women's Reconstruction Group "besides replacing the dishes, cutlery, linens, etc." was able to raise $4,500 for the building fund. The twice-monthly rummage sales, described in the mid-1990s as run by "about twenty faithful workers" at Grace Church, Montreal, provided "needed coats or shoes or skates or slacks" to local people "at prices ranging from fifty cents to a couple of dollars."

Records of a Ladies Association at Grace Church go back to 1871, the year of the church's first vestry meeting. On 4 October of that year, at such a meeting,

a vote of thanks was tendered to Mrs. Brydges and the Ladies Association for their arduous efforts in connection with the Bazaar held in the Victoria Skating Rink — from which Grace Church was entirely freed from debt.

A Ladies' Accumulating Fund was launched in Frelighsburg in January 1860. The minute book sets out its aims and origins in what 140-odd years later would be regarded as a mission statement:

We the undersigned Ladies of Frelighsburg & Vicinity, Members of Trinity Church and Others, wellwishers, & friendly to the same, being desirous of providing for the Interior decoration & adornment of a new Church which we hope to see erected by the Gentlemen, in the course of a few years, and wishing to make the burden light & pleasant to everyone, do agree to subscribe a small sum to be put in a Note on Interest as an Accumulating Fund.

The money so collected shall be used for Curtaining (if necessary), Cushioning, Carpeting, Dressing Pulpit, Desk, Chancel — & all other necessary arrangements — and for no other purpose whatever without the unanimous consent of the Subscribers or their Representatives —

The Note shall be drawn payable to the Secty Treasurer of the Ladies Accumulating Fund, & shall be renewed year by year, with the Interest and other Subscriptions added thereto.

And may the Almighty bless the undertaking & incline our hearts to give without grudging to His House of Prayer a portion of the substance with which He has blessed each & every one of us —

Parish histories and parish papers go some way toward recording the importance of women's work in building up the church community and contributing materially to its maintenance, but the slender pamphlet printed for St George's, Montreal, seems to be unique in singling it out for recognition. *Woman's Work* lists seven distinct women's organizations at St George's Church: the District Visiting Society (for visiting and assisting the poor in the district), the Mothers' Meeting (which seemed to provide a means of gathering needy mothers of the district together for fellowship and Bible Study), the Dorcas Society (for providing clothing for the poor), the Young Ladies' Missionary Association (which, among other activities collected and sent bales of clothing to missionaries), the Industrial School (a day school for poor children "instil[ling] into the minds of its members, habits of usefulness, neatness and cleanliness, which will influence for good their future lives"), a branch of the Band of Hope (a temperance society for children also providing music and gymnastic exercises), and, finally, a Girl's Friendly Society — for bringing girls together for sewing, knitting, reading, singing and, during this particular year, lessons in French. They also contributed to the Deep Sea Mission to the fishermen of Labrador to which they sent a bale of clothing through Dr Grenfell.

The Young Ladies' Missionary Society, to select one organization as an example, listed more than forty-seven names. The precise number is unclear as it includes "the Misses Galt" and "the Misses Williams" as well as the names of individuals. The report of the secretary-treasurer, Miss M.E. Bacon, gives an idea of the young ladies' activities:

We have several new members this year [the report begins], but as some of our former ones have resigned, the numbers remain the same. Eighteen meetings have been held from Nov. 5th, 1895, until Mar. 23rd, 1896, with average attendance of twenty.

Since our opening in November we have sent off six bales to Missionaries in our own diocese and one bale of second hand clothing, containing 46 articles to the Rev. Mr. Hutchins at Arundale for the poor settlers in his parish, and a supply of ready made clothing to the Washakada Home.

At Christmas time a box of toys was sent to the Rev. Mr. Dilworth for a Christmas tree, the members being most generous in their donations.

A few books have been added to the Library in the Montreal General Hospital, and two of our members go down as usual every Monday to distribute them to the patients.

When the late extensive alterations were made in the Hospital, it was necessary to have a new book-case in keeping with the surroundings. An appeal was made to the governors of the Hospital and they very generously provided a suitable one. It is felt that the contents ought to be in harmony with the book-case, and we appeal to our many friends for new and second-hand books to fill our rather empty shelves.

Before closing our report we thank Dean Carmichael [the Rector of St George's] for helping us so materially, and the members for being so faithful in their attendance.

The financial report shows receipts and disbursements for the year balanced at $145.07. The balance sheet makes clear that the group was an affiliate of the Woman's Auxiliary for it paid fees to the WA of $3.10 and sent a thank offering of $5.00. Express charges on missionary bales came to $4.10 and they paid a substantial $89.35 on materials.

As is apparent from the reports in *Woman's Work*, these organizations performed much-needed social work in the area — which had become an economically disadvantaged one by the 1890s. They provided education and what amounted to vocational training for local children, a meeting place and some employment opportunities through the "Mothers' Meeting," and engaged in missionary outreach. In a time when there was little relief for the poor and destitute they aided pensioners, and arranged for bread, coal or wood during a particularly hard winter. Eighty-four families received Christmas dinners "which were distributed at the school-house on the day before Christmas."

In this work, the ladies of St George's received the full support of their rector. This was not invariably the case, however.

When the ladies of Dunham prepared a two-day tea and sale on 29 August 1850, the neighbouring rector — who believed that parishioners should contribute to the support of their church directly and not indulge in frivolities — was induced to preach a sermon before the festivities opened. As his diary records with some disgust:

Yesterday I preached in the Church of Dunham, to the Ladies Sewing Society. I took great pains to prepare a Sermon for them on this text: Oh, how amiable are thy Tabernacles O Lord! ... the Sermon was followed by a great tea party and a bazaar of their fancy work, in the Basement of the Church. [The Rev.] Mr [Joseph] Scott at the Tea proposed toasts ... Then Joel Baker commenced auctioneering the Ladies' trinkets, on the which occasion the [latter] proved himself the greatest blathering humbug I ever heard. ... Had I known how it was to be conducted, I would neither have given a sermon, nor be[en] there at all.

Catch me there again if you can. The same farce is there repeated again today, a Sermon and Tea party for the Sunday Scholars. [The Rev.] Mr [Robert] Lindsay was expected to preach. I would have been glad to hear him, but I had so much farce and profanation yesterday, that I would not go.

Some one hundred and forty years later the ladies of Dunham received a similar rebuff for their efforts in fund raising, this time from the rector of a neighbouring church who had been asked to publicize an upcoming event to his congregation:

Dear Mrs Patterson [he wrote],

This is just to inform you that I did not advertize your Christmas Social and Sale.

We live in a very secularized society which tends to think of Sunday in the same way as of any other day of the week.

The Christian Church thinks of Sunday as the Lord's Day in thoughtful remembrance of His glorious Resurrection on that Day. It is the duty of Christians to abstain from unnecessary work and to worship God with His people on that Day.

It would be the hope [*sic*] that in the future your organization would refrain from holding fund raising public events on the Lord's Day.

A copy of the letter was sent to the Bishop and to the Rector of All Saints, Dunham.

At about the same time, as Joan Marshall reports on her research at St Paul's, Knowlton, the newly arrived rector suggested to the ACW that rummage sales and bazaars "did not meet his criteria for 'Christian action.'"

The first issue of the *Montreal Churchman*, begun under the highly patriarchal Bishop Farthing in 1912, reported triumphantly that there had been a recent groundswell in the men's groups of the church. The editorial went on to state that

[t]he Church needs to-day as seldom before the force of Christian manliness, and the parish priest needs the virile touch of the men in the parish whom it is his privilege and responsibility to lead in the work of the parish.

Yet even here in this most confident period a tribute to women's work had grudgingly to be be paid:

Through the long day of masculine apathy and inactivity [the editorial continues] the Priscillas of the Church have ever been active workers, and Women's Guilds and Auxiliaries have flourished and abounded. This work will ever be held in high esteem.

We may not forget that the Apostolic age had its Phoebe and Priscilla and that when St Paul is making appreciative mention of his fellow-workers he does sometimes rank the wife before the husband. But we must also insist that Aquila [which is a man's name] is also in the list, that the husband should also be, with the wife, a fellow helper in Christ Jesus.

# PROSPERITY AND OPTIMISM
## 1896–1914

## Parochial Expectations (1897)

It was usual for congregations in search of their first minister to receive a list of responsibilities they must fulfill before their needs would be considered. In the days when the SPG furnished missionaries, congregations were expected to build a church and a parsonage, provide a glebe, and pledge their continued financial support to whatever missionary the Society might choose to send. It is, therefore, something of a novelty finding a congregation setting out a series of stipulations regarding the ministry they expected to receive. The following passage comes from the Vestry Book of Trinity Church, Beauharnois, dated 18 January 1897:

A special vestry meeting of the mission was held in the Dissentient-School-house this evening at 8 o'clock. … The chairman [James Dunsmore, in the absence of the William Bertal Heeney, Lay Reader-in-charge] … stated that one of the objects in calling the present meeting was to come to a decision on the proposition made by the Revd R.Y. Overing of Valleyfield that the Mission amalgamate with the Parish of Valleyfield about to be founded out of part of the Parish of Ormstown.

In August 1895, Robert Young Overing, Divinity student and Lay Reader at Valleyfield, had heard that there were a number of Anglicans at nearby Beauharnois, and came to suggest that they form a mission. According to an unpublished parish history, "He found about ten families, nearly all lately arrived, and nearly all Yorkshire folk employed in the mills of the Dominion Blanket and Fibre Co., Ltd." Week-night services were begun, a building scheme was soon under way and the foundation for what was to be "a remarkably sturdy building" was laid in the spring of 1897.

The Chairman invited a full discussion of the matter and explained the principal points which would have to be considered ... After the Chairman had named Mr Titus Berry as vestry Clerk pro-tem it was moved by J.G. Kammerer, seconded by J.A. Goodfellow

That whereas it is desirable for the more effectual carrying on of the work of this Mission that it should be under the supervision and form part of the parish of some duly ordained Clergyman and whereas the Revd R.Y. Overing [ordained priest in 1896] has suggested that this congregation consent to the Mission forming part of the proposed Parish of Valleyfield of which he is to be the first Incumbent, It is therefore resolved

That this congregation agrees to amalgamate with and become part of the Parish of Valleyfield and be under the supervision of its Incumbent on the following conditions — viz: —

(a)  That the said Incumbent maintains a fit and proper person as his assistant at Beauharnois for the carrying on of the regular Sunday Services and ordinary parochial work there, the assistant to reside in Beauharnois continuously during at least four months in the year.
(b)  That the Incumbent celebrates the Holy Communion in the Mission once a month. Holy Communion to be celebrated on the Sundays next after Easter, Whit-Sunday and Christmas Day and to count as being the regular monthly celebration for the month in which these days shall fall.
(c)  That the Incumbent visit the members of the congregation at their homes once in every two months as nearly as possible.
(d)  That for the carrying out of the duties mentioned in sections (b) an (c) he shall pay his own travelling and other expenses except maintenance.
(e)  That Revd Mr Overing acknowledge by letter his acceptance of the conditions of this resolution on the same being conveyed to him by the vestry clerk pro-tem.

This Mission on its own part agrees

(1)  To guarantee to the Incumbent from the Mission Funds the sum of $280 per annum for salary, and expenses of his assistant here.
(2)  So long as the income of the mission shall remain at its present rate (about $400 per annum) to guarantee to the Incumbent the sum of $50 per annum in addition to the $280 above mentioned.
(3)  In the case of any extra duties performed by the Incumbent — such as Baptisms, Visitation of the Sick, Burials &c except when occurring on some one of his ordinary visits, his expenses in connection with the same to be paid out of the funds of the Mission.

(4)  To refer to him matters of complaint in re the carrying on of the work.
Resolved also That the conditions set forth herein shall take effect from
the day on  which Valleyfield shall be constituted by the proper
authorities a separate parish from that of Ormstown
　　Resolved also That the vestry clerk pro-tem be instructed to write
Revd Mr Overing and convey to him a copy of this resolution.

After discussion the above resolution was carried unanimously.

Perhaps it was the shrewd Yorkshire background of the vestrymen that
moved them to set out their conditions so clearly and to do so in writing.

By March, the Diocesan authorities had still  not constituted Valleyfield
as a separate parish and the people of Beauharnois, impatient that their
agreement should take effect, called another meeting at which it was
resolved

that clauses (b), (c), (d) [and] (2) (down to and including the words "per
annum" where they occur the second time in the said clause, (3) and all
other parts of the resolution of this vestry relating to this matter ... which do
not in any way conflict with the ordinary rules of the diocese for the gov-
ernance of Missions shall be considered as in force from this date until
such time as the union of  Valleyfield and Beauharnois by the proper
authorities shall give the said resolution full effect. Carried.

Meanwhile building went on, and later that  same year, on Saturday, 18
December, Trinity Church, Beauharnois, was dedicated, with two arch-
deacons, several other clergy and numerous dignitaries present. For the
occasion, handsome pasteboard invitations had been sent out. In the expectation that a number of visitors would attend from Montreal, and, as
usual leaving nothing unspecified, the reverse side of the invitation  read:

TRAIN LEAVES
**Windsor Station**
SATURDAY MORNING 9:30 O'CLOCK
AND RETURNS LEAVING BEAUHARNOIS AT 8:28 PM.
Round Trip, 95 Cts.
LUNCH AND DINNER WILL BE FURNISHED

# The Evolution Controversy (1898)

For the first half of the nineteenth century, religious belief in England was comparatively little disturbed by new discoveries in the natural sciences although they would soon enough be regarded by many as inconsistent with the Christian view of the universe.

According to Alec R. Vidler's *The Church in an Age of Revolution*, until well into the 1850s, religious controversy concerned such questions as the apostolic succession, the claims of the papacy, baptismal regeneration, and the relations of Church and State, rather than the fundamentals of belief.

The anonymously published *Vestiges of the Natural History of Creation*, which postulated that "the introduction of species into the world must have been brought about in the manner of [natural] law," caused a minor sensation when it first appeared in 1844, but, as Vidler points out, "It was not even necessary for the theologians to refute the book, since the scientists did so for them." The crisis in belief was postponed until 1859 with the publication of Charles Darwin's *The Origin of Species by Means of Natural Selection*. As Vidler sums up the impact of Darwin's theory:

[t]he whole scheme of Christian belief, which was based on the supposition that man had all at once been created with a fully formed capacity for communion with God, a capacity that the human race had lost through the disobedience of the first human pair, was thrown into disarray. The work of Christ had been to redress this primordial catastrophe. ... As Dr Pusey put it: 'It lies as the basis of our faith that man was created in the perfection of our nature, endowed with supernatural grace, with a full freedom of choice such as man, until restored by Christ, has not had since.'

Initially, and not surprisingly, churchmen such as Bishop Samuel Wilberforce spearheaded attacks on Darwin's theory. The English Roman Catholic Archbishop Henry Edward Manning also denounced the new view as "a brutal philosophy" where there was no God and the ape was "our Adam."

Gradually, however, there developed among believers the notion "that there might well have been a natural process of evolution." Many began to suppose "that the creative action of God should be seen in the gaps or lacunae, especially the gap between inorganic matter and life," and, above all, the gap between rational man and irrational animals.

By the 1890s, British theologians — in the universities at least — were no longer making reluctant concessions to advances in the natural sciences, but, according to Vidler, "claiming them almost as a godsend." Almost simultaneously, however, it was necessary for believers to come to terms not only with advances in scientific thought but with those in Biblical criticism as well.

Controversies centred on Evolution appeared rather later and caused less ferment in Canada than they had in Britain, but their impact was felt nonetheless. In 1898, for example, the Very Rev. James Carmichael, Dean of Montreal, published a forty-eight page pamphlet defending the belief in creation as an intentional and divine act. It was modestly titled *Why Some Fairly Intelligent Persons Do Not Endorse the Hypothesis of Evolution: A Plea for Divine Intention in Creation.*

The pamphlet reveals that Dean Carmichael, for a churchman of his time, was remarkably liberal in his views and familiar with the debate on both sides. Besides citing passages from Darwin's *Origin of Species*, he refers to specific works by bioligist Thomas Henry Huxley, naturalists Ernst Haeckel, Karl Vogt and Jean Louis Armand de Quatrefages de Bréau, as well as Canadian geologist Sir James William Dawson, and American geologist, mineralogist and zoologist James Dwight Dana. The pamphlet also makes general reference to Welsh naturalist Alfred Russel Wallace and Scottish physicist James Clerk Maxwell.

The substance of Carmichael's argument is presented as an appeal to reason — that the gradual evolution of the eye, for example, would not make any sense as an advantage until it could actually convey useful information —

One could understand how a partially developed eye in the head of a sightless creature would have certain limited advantages, and how an advanced eye would have greater advantages [he argues]; but the inflamed nerve, the initial eye state, cannot produce one solitary advantage, and consequently would not be likely [in terms of Natural Selection] to be passed on. Mr. Darwin spreads the process of eye evolution over 'millions of years,' so that we may allow at least a thousand years for the inflamed nerve period, during which a succession of animals would be born with inflamed nerves in their heads that would be perfectly objectless and useless, for the simple reason that in this initial stage it would not tend to produce an image.

On this basis he argues for intention in nature rather than "unintelligent cause." Observation and reason rather than scriptural authority form the basis of his argument:

As a rule things seem to be made with a purpose; the earth appears to have been intended to enfold and mature seed, the sun appears to have been intended to give light and heat; air appears to have been so mixed as to be useful for breathing, and the function of respiration appears to have been so ordered as to permit oxygen to penetrate the substance of living organisms; in short, there appears to run through all nature a dependence of things upon each other which implies a planned system of Nature. But according to Evolution there never has been anything approaching a plan. Nothing was intended to be what it is, for all forms arise from profitable variations in original forms, and the original favorable point in the variation was never an intentional point; consequently all this seeming order was never ordered, and this seeming dependence of things upon each other was never intended; but things in earth and sea, and air, are what they are under the action of dead, senseless laws, without mind behind them.

Now thousands of intelligent people cannot believe this. They find no analogy for such a hypothesis in other things. They know that their business will go to pieces if mind is not behind it, and in it; that home will never arrange its order without mentality; that chaos, and chaos only, can be the result of mindlessness. And what strikes them primarily here is, that notwithstanding this evidence, or that, in favor of Evolution, the universe as a whole seems ordered, and they cannot believe that such order as exists was never thought of until the mind of man realized its wide-reaching evidence.

Carmichael's view of Darwin's work is not entirely negative. His pamphlet shows clearly that he regarded some elements of the evolutionary theory as fully consistent with Christian notions of creation:

Nature itself is full of diversity, and why should it be thought unlikely that a wide diversity of operations should have been active in creating that general object and order, which the Creator had in view from the beginning? Thus there is nothing to debar us from believing that amongst other agents of creation something akin to Natural Selection and heredity, etc., may have been used as agents, for the agents of creation are not described in the general scheme of Revelation.

He argues that the laws of Natural Selection are not mirrored in society at its best, but are frustrated and reversed by the advance of civilization:

Then explain it also how you will: as civilization and education advance, the irresistible working of Natural Selection is driven out before them everywhere. Even in lowest life, the hungry cry of a starving child gives energy to the foot of a strong-made father in his hunt for food, and many a war path has been tracked through lonely forests, as the strong came to the rescue of the weak, to win back a stolen child, or save unharmed a timid girl. The weak would always go to the wall, save for the law which brings the strength of love, or the strength of muscle, or both combined, to the rescue of the weak ...

And this is still more apparent under the highest teaching of education and civilization. There is a mighty power in the world, ever increasing which only lives to protect the weak. A power that tends the sick, and builds the hospital, and trains the nurse, furnishes the free medicine, and provides the ablest skill. ... A power that teaches us that evil is to be remedied by love and gentleness and pity; that the weak are not of necessity to die of weakness, or the poverty-stricken to die in a ditch, because of poverty, or climate, or want of food; or through uncared for debility and wretchedness. This power may be called Judaism, Christianity, Morality — anything; but it exists and works, and the wider its area and the stronger its strength, the less room remains for the working of Natural Selection, which only exists to crush out the weak and enable the hand of a man to snatch from the hand of a woman the last crust, that fairly divided might preserve the lives of both.

A reader of Carmichael's pamphlet cannot help but be struck by the interest he displays in the world of nature. There are many references to plants, animals and insects.

Speaking of adaptation he mentions "the yellow leaf that is made the home of the yellow insect ... the soft, green leaf, the home of the soft, green caterpillar ... the leaf so like a butterfly that you cannot tell, in passing, which is leaf and which is fly ... the brown, rusty, bare twig that has sticking to it the brown, rusty, living creature, that looks at you as you pass, and that, if it could, might laugh at you, for the success of its mimicry which preserves it from your touch." It is not surprising, therefore, to learn that Carmichael, in the words of a contemporary, "was as expert with the microscope as with the pen," and had "made a special study of ant hills and was thoroughly conversant with the habits of their busy occupants."

Carmichael did not shrink from controversial subjects. Another example of his public involvement with an issue of current debate is his paper *The Stone of Destiny*, an Archeological Study presented in 1881 before the Hamilton Association in Montreal.

The British-Israelites and others had argued that the Stone of Scone, or Coronation Stone preserved in Westminster Abbey, was "the stone on which Jacob laid his wearied head at Bethel, and which, previous to the age of Moses, was brought to Egypt by some Hebrews," thence to Spain, to the hill of Tara in Ireland, to the island of Iona off Scotland, and finally to Scone.

Using geological evidence, Carmichael points out that the Coronation Stone is a type of red sandstone similar to that around Scone (from whence the stone was brought to England by Edward I). He further notes that the rocks of Iona consist of "a flaggy micaceous grit," that those of Tara are of the carboniferous age, and that "geology denies that there is any sandstone about Bethel." He then proceeds to dispose of the notion that "the throne of England is a perpetuation of the throne of David ... and that the throne of England is fulfilling the promises given to the royal house of Judah." It is an entertaining and well argued presentation, but certainly a piece of fluff compared to the pamphlet on Darwinism.

In 1898 an optimistic belief in progress was still the norm. Men like Carmichael felt sure that truth would triumph and that it would be a truth with which they would feel at home:

Hypothesis after hypothesis might perish [he concludes his pamphlet on Evolution], but there has scarce ever been one that did not contribute something to the great advance, as calm, peaceful and undisturbed the Truth went on its way. And so it will ever be. There are few questions that have not two sides to them; time alone can settle on which the weight of truth lies. Give time, and truth must come. And when it comes, it will come as a fact that all will receive, though stripped it may be of a thousand fancies that heralded its birth.

How chagrined such men would be at the nature and status of this debate more than one hundred years later.


# Diocesan Jubilee (1900)

The Fiftieth anniversary of the erection of the Diocese of Montreal, and the coming of its first bishop was celebrated by the publication of a history prepared by the Rev. J. Douglas Borthwick, a priest of thirty-five years service in the Diocese, who had been ordained both to the diaconate and the priesthood at the hands of Bishop Fulford.

In his preface, Borthwick remarks on the great and happy change among church leadership, both clergy and lay, in the Diocese at the present time. All seemed to him so young and energetic:

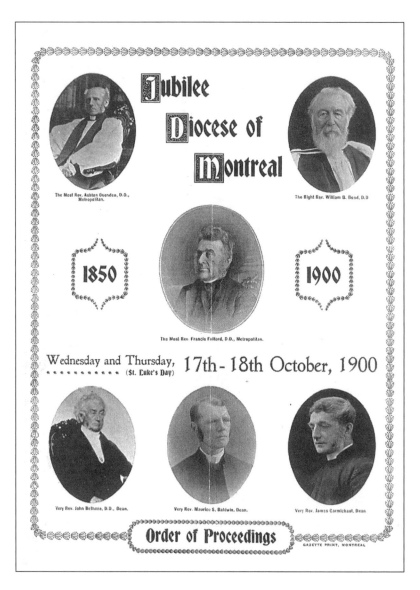

PLATE 10    *The First Diocesan Jubilee, 1900*
            *(Photo Credit:* MDA*)*

Nothing struck me more than this [Borthwick exclaimed], at the last meeting of the Synod in February, 1909, when I scanned the members of the Synod, Clerical and Lay Delegates, I saw so few white haired men present.

My eye rested then on a host of young athletic Clergy and Laymen 'all eager for the fray'...

Elsewhere in the *History* Borthwick quotes Bishop Bond, who had presided over the Fiftieth Anniversay celebrations:

A service of jubilee thanksgiving was held October 1900 [Bond recalled], in which we offered praise, feeble and halting, as all such human effort must be, but heartfelt, humble and true, nothwithstanding shortcomings, to the Author and Giver of all good things. What man can feel self-satisfied who realizes the Divine Presence? We did what we could: we offered willingly of our best, in music, in praise; and we prayed that it might be accepted of God, that God in whose sight the heavens are not clean, accepted not for its merit, but for the merit of our Lord Jesus Christ. Congratulatory letters were received from several quarters, including a very kind letter from the Primate of all Canada [the Most Rev. Robert Machray], and one from Mr. Francis Fulford [Bishop Fulford's son]. Two days in October were set apart for the celebration of the joyous event.

Although he was remarkably energetic for his age, the Bishop sounded old and tired — out of harmony with the optimism of the age. The remarks of Rev. W.P.R. Lewis of Nelsonville, made at the celebrations of his own parish jubilee in 1904, illustrate more accurately the spirit of the day:

We, who are living now in the vigor of life, appreciate, I trust, the work done by those who have gone before ... But we must not stop at appreciation; we must perfect, enlarge and expand the great religious heritage we have received. We must improve our opportunities, and increase the spiritual and moral power bequeathed from the past. ... We must buckle on our armour, keep our tools burnished and sharpened for the important work of the golden day yet to come.

This was a time of energy and expansion, felt as much in the church as the secular world. The Jubilee history bears its stamp.

# Montreal's First General Synod (1902)

At 4:30 p.m. on Wednesday, 3 September 1902, Archbishop William Bennett Bond. Metropolitan of the Ecclesiastical Province of Canada, opened the Third General Synod of the Church of England in the Dominion of Canada, the first of such gatherings to take place in Montreal.

The Primate, the Most Rev. Robert Machray, was ill and had been unable to make the journey from Rupertsland, and Bond would serve not only as host, but also — by resolution of the assembly — as President of the Synod.

Bond's first act was to read aloud the Primate's Address. It urged the members that by far the most important question before them was "the establishment of a Missionary Society for the whole Dominion." Being a priest whose missionary fervour had been the hallmark of his entire career, Bond concluded his delivery with an endorsement of his own:

Beloved [he began], suffer a very few further remarks. God has called our Church in this Dominion to a glorious work. God has placed before us a grand opportunity of glorifying Him in spreading the Gospel of Christ. Consider the magnitude of our portion of the field. Consider its destiny. Consider the prospect that even now meets your mental vision — its grand harvest safely gathered, its varied industries *not* bounded by the three oceans that break upon its shores, nor the vast country that stretches away beyond its present range. Consider, moreover, the spiritual aspect whitening for harvest from almost every quarter of the globe, thousands of souls for whom Jesus died waiting only for spiritual labourers. ... Surely this General Synod of the Church of England will avail itself of this opportunity of cheering the hearts and strengthening the hands of those men and women already in the field, and give an earnest that in entire dependence upon God they will go on occupying until Christ comes. Have faith in God.

At this point the members of the Upper House retired to their own chamber. Still on the opening day, the Upper House sent down (as Message number two) its proposal for Canon II, the Missionary Society. In the afternoon session of the second day, after lively debate and some amendments, the Lower House adopted the resolution and sent it back to the Upper House for concurrence.

Among those taking an active part in the debate was the Rev. John Cragg Farthing who was then serving a parish in Woodstock, Ontario, in the Diocese of Huron.

Before the next Synod, Bond was to succeed Machray as Primate. He filled the office for a mere two years, until his death in 1906.

Although he was a man of strong party affiliation, Bond made a powerful effort — in his opening sermon to this Synod and on other occasions — to urge a spirit of unity and mutual forbearance within the church. It forms an interesting contrast to Oxenden's earlier appeal to his first Diocesan Synod:

Beloved ... let us go to our work in the true spirit of charity, that Charity which is tolerant, rejoicing in the truth. I do not mean by toleration a mere putting up with differences of opinion, I do not mean a polite tolerance of doctrines untenable within the Church of England, I do not mean a blindness of policy to things actually wrong, things wanting in truth or righteousness. ... [W]e must cultivate that spirit of charity which will anxiously weigh the words of all who seem to differ from us; we must honestly strive to learn from the experience of others and add thereby to our own Christian knowledge; we must remember that we may know well the needs and circumstances of our own portion of the Mission Field, and yet have little apprehension of other parts of the Field. By impatience of detail, or irritation of temper we may defeat the very object for which many of us have come so far. Such a unity of spirits as I have in view, such spiritual unity, will educate us concerning the needs of others, will point out their wants, so that the strong will help the weak, the older Churches bear up the younger, till they, in their turn, carry on the missionary work, so that from Atlantic to Pacific and Arctic all shall know the Lord.

Since that time, to date, the Diocese of Montreal has hosted General Synod on three further occasions: in 1934, 1959 and 1998.

## Prisoners' Aid (1905)

The Prisoners' Aid Association of Montreal was originally a lay initiative of the Anglican Church, an outgrowth of a subcommittee of the Lay Helpers' Association of the Church of England. As a subcommittee, the members had visited the jails (with the sanction of the prison chaplain) and furnished assistance to discharged prisoners on their release. The work grew until, in December of 1892, a separate association was formed.

Up to that time and since [the thirteenth annual report of the Association claimed], no other organized effort had or has been made to reach and reform the unhappy victims of their own evil propensities who have been compelled to undergo the discipline of the Montreal Jail and the

Penitentiary of St. Vincent de Paul up to the appointment last year of an official by the Dominion Government to visit penitentiaries.

The Association's annual report for 1905, printed in the Forty-seventh Annual Journal of Synod, gives some idea of the scope of its work:

A little timely help to a discharged prisoner who has expressed a desire and shown a disposition to reform, is absolutely necessary to make it possible for him to carry out his good purposes. The Officers of the Association are in constant touch with many reformed prisoners who are now doing well, some of them holding responsible positions. The following are a few instances out of many which might be cited. The facts are stated, but for obvious reasons the names are withheld.

(1)     [For] young man from Penitentiary. Purchased suitable clothing to go to work and paid three weeks' board and lodging for him at his boarding house. Got work.

(2)     [To] man from Penitentiary. Given an outfit of clothes to commence work with, and one month's board and lodging paid to boarding house. Got work.

(3)     Rent of room paid and meals given to a teacher until he obtained all his old pupils back again.

(4)     Fare paid to town in Ontario for man on parole from Penitentiary who had obtained work.

(5)     Man from Jail with respectable out of town connections, given board and lodging until he could get money to take him home.

(6)     Young man from Penitentiary. Hat and overcoat purchased and helped at intervals. Has occupied his present situation steadily for five months.

(7)     Redeemed prisoner's clothes and tools out of pawn and sent them by express to place where he had secured work.

(8)     Paid funeral expenses of young man who died shortly after release.

(9)     Paid fare home to Lower Provinces for young man from Penitentiary in delicate health.

(10)    Two stowaways, from Jail, had two offers of work before noon on day of release. Commenced work at once and worked until after 6 p.m. without anything to eat. Guaranteed their board and lodging for one week, at the end of which time they paid it themselves.

(11)    Fare paid home to Michigan for man from Penitentiary.

(12)    Man in Jail for not supporting family. Got work day after release and housekeeping again. Provided for until first pay day.

Second hand clothing and good reading matter for the use of the prisoners will be thankfully acknowledged if sent to 26 Kent Street.

The contrast between the Association's total financial dependence on its subscribers and the provisions made at the time for similar groups elsewhere does not place Montreal or the province in a flattering light:

Each year the Association has endeavoured to put into practice the lessons it has learned from experience, and thus to enlarge effectively the sphere of its usefulness. It does not profess to have reformed all, or even a large percentage of those whom it has materially benefitted, but the many whom it has restored to law-abiding and respectable citizenship, have, the Association is convinced, placed the Civic and Provincial Authorities under obligations to it. ... The expenditures in consequence of the increased number of cases needing assistance during the past year, compels us to ask for larger contributions from our friends, as the Association receives no Civic or Government grants, although our sister Society of Toronto receives grants from the Provincial Government, the City of Toronto, and the counties adjacent.

The remainder of the report consists of acknowledgements to particular individuals for donations of clothing and boots, as well as to the *Montreal Daily Witness*, the *Herald*, the *Gazette* and the *Star* "for gratuitous insertion in their respective papers of items referring to our work."

Anyone reading the foregoing report today would be struck by the absence of any reference to female prisoners. It appears that provision for such women, whether in jail or recently released, fell to another branch, a Woman's Auxiliary of the Association.

In 1905 it consisted of at least ten members who probably met bi-monthly. Attendance was fairly small — according to their report that year it averaged six per meeting — but the Auxiliary strove to provide help of the same standard as that afforded to the men. In cooperation with the Sheltering Home, the Salvation Army Home, the House of Refuge and the Verdun Asylum, the Auxiliary bore the initial expense of lodging women in need of it on their release from prison. It provided clothing, food, "and money for fares."

This was by no means an arms-length charitable activity for the ladies of the Auxiliary; there was direct, personal contact with inmates. In its "Summary of the Work Done," the Auxiliary's report announced that "a new branch" had been added that year (since April) "to the work of this mission which seems very encouraging, that of visiting the prisoners in their cells before and after sentence is passed."

A statistical breakdown shows that during the year 150 prisoners were "visited in the cells," and four visits received, probably from former prisoners. In addition, there were six "extra visits to the jail," by members of the Auxiliary, perhaps because, as the report states,

Not having a telephone for our Jail, the work is much hindered. All our communications now have to pass through the men's Jail.

'Our jail' at this period was the Fullum Street Female Prison. Special provision for women under legal sentence was then relatively recent in Montreal. Until 1876, men and women shared the same jail. The Rev. J. Douglas Borthwick, who served as prison chaplain for some twenty years, was among those who campaigned for a separate women's prison. Although the care of the convicts, once this dream was realized, was placed in the hands of the Sisters of the Good Shepherd (a Roman Catholic order of nuns) Protestant prisoners were accommodated as well. As Borthwick describes it in his *History of the Montreal Prison*:

The liberality of the Government was greatly taxed [in funding the construction of the Fullum Street Female Prison] and the loan of $25,000 from the City of Montreal needed before the building was an accomplished fact. Nevertheless only the Roman Catholic women were its inmates for the first eight months on account of some misunderstanding between the Government and others. All the women are now [in 1886], and have been for some years past, sent to the female prison in Fullum Street and so vast has been the success and change in every thing connected with them that it is a subject of wonder to all.

The Prisoners' Aid Association of Montreal worked with inmates of all denominations and for this reason, in 1908, it was decided that it should become interdenominational. During the sixteen years of its existence as an Anglican institution, Borthwick estimated that "3,495 men ha[d] been definitely helped."

From 1915, the official voice on social issues of the Anglican Church of Canada was the Council for Social Service. In 1944, the Council's Montreal Branch was much concerned with conditions at the Fullum Street Prison as part of the field of inquiry of the Committee on Juvenile Delinquency and Penal Reform. An undated report from about the same period reviewed the changing philosophy of punishment and rehabilitation, as well as the problems faced by released prisoners re-entering society. It concludes:

Prisoners' Welfare work in Montreal is at present in the care of the Prisoners' Aid & Welfare Association, but this work, already understaffed, has recently been seriously handicapped by partial withdrawal from the Federated Charities. The Salvation Army provide police Court Officers. It will be seen from the foregoing summary of the problem that there is need for a much more adequately organized undertaking if the problem is to receive the attention it deserves.

Eighty years after the thirteenth Annual Report of the Prisoners' Aid Association of Montreal was presented to Synod, the comparable report in the Proceedings of Synod of 1996 was that of "Chaplains in Correctional Services." As it happens, one of these chaplains also served as incumbent of the parish of Arundel, Rockway and Weir.

As was the case in 1905, at the level of the inmates themselves, much important work seems to have been shouldered by volunteers. In the words of the report,

Visits of volunteers from the P2 Programme, linking long sentence inmates with permanent visitors, are continuing through the Visits and Correspondence Department. Unlike many penitentiaries, LaMacaza has the Inmates' Visits facility open only on Wednesday to Friday afternoons and weekends. This greatly reduces the ability of family and friends and volunteers from making contact with those who are residents here. Since the P2 volunteers have such a long way to travel, and so many inmates to visit, they occasionally come for a full day, spending the morning in the chapel facilities in contact with residents. ...

Visits from parishioners of Arundel and Weir continue for Thanksgiving, Christmas and Easter celebrations. As with other volunteers, the residents are always eager to share and meet with those who can make it out to see them.

Your prayers are requested for the residents, volunteers and myself as we continue to seek and find God in the difficulties and joys experienced by those "inside" and "marginalized" by society.

Although Borthwick speaks from his perspective in 1886 of "the unhappy victims of their own evil propensities," and the chaplain at LaMacaza in 1995 of the "marginalized position" of "residents," one traces in these accounts a common thread of commitment to and personal involvement

PLATE 11A *19th century Sunday School library book*

PLATE 11B *Early 20th century Sunday School certificate*

with individuals. Prison chaplaincies continue to draw momentum from a supportive body of lay people.

## Bishop Carmichael's Itinerary (1906)

Sandwiched between Montreal's two longest episcopates is the shortest in its history, that of James Carmichael. As Coadjutor Bishop of Montreal, he succeeded automatically in 1906 on the death of Archbishop William Bennett Bond. John Cragg Farthing, who was elected to follow Carmichael, held the office for 30 years, Bond for 27. Carmichael, by contrast, served for two short years, until his death in 1908.

A list of episcopal acts seldom makes interesting reading, but Carmichael's, kept in a telegraphic diary-form in a ledger written in his own hand, gives a ready notion of the multiplicity of his activities and the complexity of his concerns without the least touch of tediousness. A glance at the month of June alone, in his account of the year 1906 astonishes the reader at his energy and stamina.

Although Carmichael was at this time only Bond's assistant and coadjutor, more and more episcopal duties had fallen upon him of late. At 92 Bond was remarkably hearty, and could still engage in correspondence and consultaion, but for some months had been suffering from "a paralytic disease" which prevented him from the tours of visitation and confirmation so central to a bishop's duties.

There were many scheduled duties, of course: fourteen separate confirmation services to be held in the Deaneries of Shefford, Brome, Bedford and Clarendon, all of them to be reached by train. There were two ordinations, one at the Cathedral at which two candidates for the diaconate and one for the priesthood were to be presented, and another in Shawville, of a priest and a deacon. There were two meetings of the Educational Council of the Diocesan Theological College, and examination papers submitted by two of the ordinands to be looked over, not to mention commencement exercises at Dunham Ladies' College. Carmichael managed all of these.

Then there were the unexpected duties. His entry for the month of June opened, for example, with two pages devoted to what Carmichael titled "the Nye business." It seems that twenty-three years earlier, unknown to anyone, the incumbent at Bedford had "loaned himself" the capital of the parish endowments amounting to $2,000. Since that time he had paid the interest of 5½% into the parish stipend fund, but the capital — and the incumbent, too, by this time — were gone. The Church Advocate L.H. Davidson had thrown up his hands in disgust saying it was the negligence of the Wardens that had allowed this to happen in the first place and that the money had better be written off. Carmichael, with great patience, wrote to the incumbent, then living in Emporia, Kansas, and persuaded him to sign over his superannuation allowance in Trust for Bedford, to the Executive Committee of Synod, until such time as the $2,000 was paid off. Davidson was brought around, too, and drafted a letter of agreement for all the parties to sign, which Carmichael sent to Nye on June 1st.

Before the round of confirmations in more distant quarters began, Archdeacon Ker of Grace Church, Montreal presented his well-filled class of fifty-one on June 3. There were "20 males and 31 females," ranging in age from 12 to 20, with 4 adults in addition.

On the day following, Carmichael took the train to spend two days in South Stukely and Eastman (Shefford Deanery) to confirm the Rev. Charles Ireland's candidates. His brief account of the visit shows his interest in the churches themselves:

June 4: Preached on "What shall it profit" etc in South Stukely Church [St Matthew's]. Train hour & ¼ late, but Rev. C. Ireland kept the congregation some-way till I came. The Church was filled. The Church has been lately very tastily colonaded, & a very beautiful Chancel Memorial Window put in, in memory of Knowlton family & Archdeacon [David] Lindsay ...

Carmichael had officiated at Lindsay's funeral in 1900.

June 5: Confirmation in St John's Church, Eastman, Rev. C. Ireland, BA. Wonderful Good Congregation for week day at 10:30. Jim, Ireland, Miss Ireland, Allan Davis & self dined at Easty's. After doze visited old Sparling & Mrs Sparling. Used to live in Bolton. S[parling] was lay delegate for yrs from Bolton. As Emmet had met with accident his confir[mation] postponed till Sep[tember] so I came back into town [that is, Montreal] from Eastman at 4:15.

On the following day he was back on the train for a day-trip to Granby where he confirmed a class of five. Then, on the 7th he attended a meeting of the Educational Council of the Theological College, and on the 8th dealt with matters of licencing. With an Ordination coming up on the 10th he familiarized himself with the preparedness of each of the candidates:

June 9: Went over Exam papers of H. Coffin & Boyce [he remarked]. Coffin's papers admirable, Boyce's on the whole poor. He has a strange general kind of knowledge but fails in coming down to particulars. Dawson had sent in his papers ... to the Board, but as we rec[eive]d word today that the Board has postponed its meeting I told Horsey [Bond's Examining Chaplain] to put him through a viva voce [that is, an oral] exam on the paper given to Boyce.

The ordination took place the next day — Sunday — with the Rev. George Abbott-Smith, professor at Diocesan Theological College, preaching and the Rev. Herbert Edward Horsey presenting the candidates. Ernest Edward Dawson and Samuel Joseph Boyce were made deacons and Hubert Coffin priested.

Carmichael seems to have had two days' respite; then, on the 13th attended a second Educational Council meeting at the College.

The next day he embarked on a more extended tour in the Townships, confirming three candidates at St Paul's Church, Mansonville, on the evening of the 14th. After the service he called privately on the incumbent, the Rev. Edward H. Croly, and arranged that he take on additional partial duty in Bolton until a regular appointment could be made. "The willing way he agreed to this [was] commendatory," the Bishop added.

At Carmichael's next stop — Trinity Church, South Bolton, the parish had recently become vacant because the incumbent, the Rev. Thomas Everett — who had been serving in the Diocese for thirty-three years — was not well enough to carry on the work:

*June 15:* Everett having resigned, Croly presented the [three] candidates Everett had prepared. There was three times as large a congregation than [on] my last visit. Everett has done a wonderful & fully appreciated work. It is delightful to hear the way the people speak of him. The wardens asked that no app[ointmen]t be made until Everett's restored health might enable him to return. They were consequently quite ready to receive the services of Croly. Drove to Knowlton with Jim where I stopped for the night.

On the 16th Carmichael confirmed three more candidates at St John's Church, Brome, and five more on the following morning, a Sunday, at Grace Church, Sutton. In the afternoon it poured rain as he drove over to Abercorn where he preached at an evening service at All Saints' Church. The 18th seems to have been a day off.

He made special mention of the drive to his next stop, Dunham:

Mr Wyatt of Sutton drove Bell, Miss Mercer and myself from Sutton to Dunham in an automobile — a delightful mode of locomotion when all goes well as it did with us. Had a delightful time at Plaisted's.

On Tuesday the 19th the Rector of Dunham, the Rev. Henry A. Plaisted, presented five of his six candidates for confirmation at All Saints' Church. The sixth, Carmichael noted, was "a young man dying of cancer." After the ceremony he went privately to the young man's home and confirmed him there.

The next day was a taxing one:

*June 20:* Closing [that is, Graduation Day] of Dunham Ladies College. Service at 10:30. I preached. Small attend[an]ce outside of School, but School Closing crammed. It was an awful hot day & I felt clean fagged out. Jim was unable to be over thro' sad drowning accident, but Arch[deacon] Davidson [of Frelighsburg], Bell [of Sutton], Judge [of Brome], Lewis [of Cowansville], Overing [of Stanbridge East], Harris [of Farnham], etc., were present. College plainly in good condition.

On the evening of the 21st , a Thursday, he met with "a splendid congregation" at Trinity Church, Cowansville, where he confirmed 14, including three adults. As usual he marks in the margin beside the names of those who had formerly belonged to other denominations. Two of the adults were former Roman Catholics, the third a Universalist.

June 22nd saw an even larger group of candidates at St James' Church, Farnham — "8 males 11 females" of whom five were adults: two of them former Methodists and one Roman Catholic.

Following a day without a schedule, Carmichael was at St James Church, Bedford, on the 24th where the Rev. W.C. Bernard presented 11 candidates. On the same day — a Sunday — the Rev. R.Y. Overing presented 19 candidates, among them five adults, in the Church of St James the Apostle at Stanbridge East.

Thus ended Carmichael's circuit of this part of the Townships and he returned to Montreal for a few days' respite before setting off again on June 28th for the Deanery of Clarendon, and St George's Church, Portage du Fort.

St George's had five candidates, prepared by Deacon-in-Charge William Jesse Palmer Baugh, who had been appointed the previous year, and on Friday the 29th, in St Paul's Church, Shawville, Baugh was raised to the priesthood. It was expected that there would be two candidates presented that day, but William David Armitage, who had expected to be ordained deacon was "unable to be presented through dangerous illness."

Carmichael's last recorded episcopal act for the month was the confirmation of Archdeacon William H. Naylor's thirteen candidates in St Paul's, Shawville on the 29th.

During the latter part of the month of July, when the Bishop was touring the St Andrews Deanery, his record includes a summary of his impressions as well as a day-to-day journal. His delight in the flourishing condition of the church in the entire region is a pleasure to read and offers a fitting conclusion to this brief glimpse of Carmichael's round of episcopal duties:

This tour for Confirmations lasted from 18th July to 25th. Arundel-Ponsonby is really splendidly worked by Rev. H[enry] A[lford] Naylor. Everyone likes him. ...

*Mille Isles:* I stopped at Mille Isles for dinner & preached to a very good Congregation. Everyone pleased with [the Rev. Hubert] Coffin & Mrs C.
*Lakefield:* [the Rev. Allen Edgar] Mount is working hard & is greatly liked. The Church is being wholly renovated & the parsonage improved. ...
*St Andrews:* [the Rev. Thomas William] Ball & Mrs [Ball] successes. Ball wonderfully improved. Lives in the old Rectory which is renovated & made most comfortable.
*Hudson:* The new Rectory here which is practically out of debt, is a beauty & the new grounds equally so. [The Rev. Henry] Bancroft deserves credit for the quiet way he has worked this ticklish business.
*Grenville:* [the Rev. Augustus Clifford] Ascah another success. I confirmed his wife.
*Buckingham:* [the Rev. James Ellis] Ireland has waked up his parish wonderfully. The Church has only a debt of $100 on it & has rec[eive]d many gifts. Buckingham becomes a Self Supporting Rectory 1st Jan.

It struck me that no Deanery could be better manned. Every parish is satisfied, no grumbling or complaints. The Congregations every where were large, in Grenville, Lachute & St Andrews crowded. ...

The circuit had taken eight days and Carmichael had confirmed only fifteen candidates among the seven stations visited, but the Bishop saw the work's potential and the successful efforts being made by his people to build their congregations from within.

# Requiescat and After (1908)

On September 20th 1908, Bishop Carmichael was to preach his first sermon in the Cathedral since his return from attending the fifth Lambeth Conference and the first Pan-Anglican Congress. "The service," an article published in the *Standard* stated, "was much the same as the ordinary Sunday service of Morning Prayer. The congregation was a large one, and the music was well up to the standard of excellence for which the Cathedral is noted. The chief feature, apart from that of worship, was the sermon of His Lordship."

The sermon, as expected, was a forceful one and masterfully delivered. The text was Genesis 49:10: "Unto Him shall the gathering of the people be," and the subject "the Anglican Communion as seen in the light of the two great meetings lately held in London."

When the sermon was concluded he pronounced the ascription, slowly left the pulpit, and "wended his way over the marble flags of the choir pavement ... to the sanctuary." At that moment he seemed quite well. "There was not the faintest premonition that the music of his eloquent voice would soon be stilled ..."

After the presentation of the alms and the reading of a prayer on behalf of the General Synod, now in session at Ottawa [the article continued], the Rev. Dr. [Herbert] Symonds [Vicar of Christ Church Cathedral] left the Holy Table and His Lordship ascended the marble steps leading thereto. As he took his position [before the altar] a shaft of sunshine from one of the clerestory windows bathed his figure from head to foot in a golden flood of light, imparting to it an almost supernatural appearance. ...

With hands clasped ... he began that which proved to be, in the all-wise ordering of Divine Providence, his final blessing. ...

For a brief interval thereafter he stood, with hands again clasped, awaiting the conclusion of the Sevenfold Amen. In that short interval it is believed the finger of God touched him. Quickly he made his way to the kneeling stool at the end of the altar, on which he sank, at the same time pillowing his face on his right arm which rested on the edge of the altar. In that reverend and lowly attitude he awaited the ending of the "Amen."

Under ordinary circumstances the Bishop would have remained standing in front of the altar until the final note had died away, and this deviation from his usual practice "was quickly noted by those who had been closely watching him. But no one realized its significance at the moment."

The "Amen" finished, he turned to the Vicar and, looking in the direction of the mass-door leading from the choir to the clerk's vestry, said: "Can I get out by that door? I think I am going to faint."

With those whispered words, the Bishop was assisted by Dr Symonds through the low carved archway into the vestry. He was given a glass of water which seemed to revive him, and was then helped by the verger to an armchair in the nearby chapter house. There he awaited the coming of the choir and clergy as the recessional hymn swelled to its close:

Onward, therefore, pilgrim brothers,
Onward with the cross our aid;
Bear its shame, and fight its battle,
Till we rest beneath its shade.

Soon shall come the great awakening,
Soon the rending of the tomb;
Then the scattering of the shadows,
And the end of toil and gloom.    Amen.

On their arrival, Carmichael took his accustomed place at the head of the table, dismissed the choir with the prescribed collect, signed the preachers' register and made his way to Bishopscourt — in those days located just behind the Cathedral.

Shortly after reaching home, he was seized by a second spasm of angina pectoris. A few hours later he lapsed into unconsciousness and, at 7:10 on the following morning, he died.

Tributes flooded in from all parts of Canada. One of the most heartfelt was written by John Philip DuMoulin, Bishop of Niagara. He, Carmichael and Edward Sullivan had all been recruited for the Canadian church while still divinity students by Benjamin Cronyn, bishop elect of the newly-erected Diocese of Huron. Cronyn had travelled to Britain for consecration and, on a visit to his native Ireland, had delivered several addresses about the needs of his bishopric. All three responded to his appeal, crossed the Atlantic and were ordained by his hands. In their early days in Canada they were known as the 'three musketeers.' All three would become close friends and supporters of each others' ministry. Each served in Montreal churches for a time, and all became bishops. Sullivan, Lord Bishop of Algoma, had died in 1899.

Little wonder is it if I feel the death of my dear old friend, the late Bishop of Montreal, very deeply [DuMoulin wrote]. For the 47 years of my clerical life in Canada he was my friend all along and without interruption. ...

We met [most recently] in old England at the Pan-Anglican Congress [in June], walked in the same procession at the great closing service in St. Paul's, stayed together under the Bishop of London's hospitable roof at

Fulham, met at the Marlborough House garden party, sat together in the Lambeth Conference [in July], were photographed side by side in the historic picture of that memorable assembly, walked and talked in the lovely grounds at Lambeth Palace, and finally met at the London and North-Western Hotel, Liverpool, drove from thence in the same cab to the steamer the "Empress of Ireland" for our homeward passage. The journey was a fine one, giving opportunity for daily happy intercourse, ever bright and cheerful — his presence secured all that — till we reached Quebec, where, with cordial words, we parted ...

On Sunday, September the 20th, I held a confirmation at Chippewa; on Monday morning I took train for home. At Niagara Falls, in the train, I bought a newspaper and therein read of the sudden and serious illness of the Bishop of Montreal. On reaching home I learned from a tearful face, that met me at my door, how his soul was delivered from the burden of the flesh into joy and felicity.

Recalling the events of Carmichael's last service in Christ Church Cathedral, the writer of the *Standard* article directed the minds of his readers back to the Bishop's final sermon, capturing that moving quality that was the hallmark of his usual delivery:

The Bishop's voice was sonorous and strong, and he preached with his accustomed vigour and eloquence. At times that wonderful right hand of his was used to emphasize his points with splendid dramatic effect. And at others the voice rang out with magnetic power, riveting on the speaker every eye in the vast congregation.

In a tribute published in the October issue of the *Canadian Churchman*, the Rev. Oswald W. Howard, Professor of Church History and Apologetics at the Montreal Diocesan Theological College touched upon this particular gift:

Of Bishop Carmichael's eloquence it is almost unnecessary to speak. Privileged as he was for so many years to occupy the chief Anglican pulpit of Canada, as rector of St. George's, Montreal, his inimitable public ability was known not only in the city of Montreal but to visitors from all parts of Canada and the United States.

His rich Irish voice, his perfect mastery of that voice for purposes of pleasantry or pathos, his dignity of bearing, his remarkably handsome face surrounded by an abundance of silvery hair, his unerring use of pauses that were often more eloquent than words, made him one of the most attractive public speakers that any country has ever produced.

His smile, his ready wit, his humour, his histrionic power, added to his other oratorical gifts, made him nothing short of a genius before the public. He was the master of every occasion. As preacher, lecturer, after-dinner speaker, he always said the right thing, and when he had finished, the listener felt that there was no need for any one else to say more. ...

He was also particularly gifted in enabling others to express themselves publicly:

No attempt to give an appreciation of the Bishop's abilities can omit a reference to his admirable power in presiding over great public gatherings [Howard continued]. For years he was Prolocutor of the General and Provincial Synods, and in those great Councils of the Church he showed the masterly power of his personality. ... Not only was he the master of all parliamentary procedure, but he was also able to see in advance the turn that many a complicated debate was likely to take, and was thus ready with his ruling when the crucial moment came.

His ready wit, thrust in at the proper time, saved him many a difficulty in the management of such gatherings. He turned difficulty aside and softened the acrimony of heated opponents by pleasantries that would convulse the whole assembly with laughter. This wit was never caustic but, like himself, always refined and kindly. ...

He ruled with a strong and masterly judgment, but was never overbearing or inconsiderate. For the timorous speaker he always had encouragement, while for the brow-beater who would break rules and disregard order he had a strong reserve of sledge-hammer discipline.

The suddenness of Carmichael's death, its dramatic circumstances, and the affection in which he was held made the prospect of meeting in synod to choose a successor seem almost unthinkable. Although his enthronement as bishop was less than two years past, he had served the Diocese for thirty-six years — as curate, rector, dean and and first coadjutor bishop. Who would succeed him?

On 29 October of that year, Synod elected a 44-year-old Scot, then Bishop of Stepney in England, as the new bishop of Montreal, and informed him of his election by cable that same day. The reply, dated 30 October and directed to The Very Reverend Thomas Frye Lewis Evans, Dean of the Cathedral, was brief:

Deeply appreciate honour — regret cannot accept, Stepney

The cable was confirmed by letter that same day:

In 1909, the Rt Rev. Cosmo Gordon Lang was translated from Stepney to York, and in 1928 was appointed Archbishop of Canterbury, an office he would hold until his retirement in 1942. Meanwhile, a second electoral Synod met in Montreal in November and on the 24th of that month elected John Cragg Farthing, then Dean of Ontario, as their fifth diocesan bishop.

Farthing was American-born, raised and educated in England, and ordained in Canada. He was well-suited to the challenge and quite willing to take it on.

On 6 January 1909 he was consecrated and enthroned. His episcopate, which would extend for thirty years, concluded with his retirement in 1939.


# A Legend in the Musical World (1908)

The Diocese has nurtured a number of great organists who have served its churches before moving into the international spotlight. William Reed, for example, whose musical talent was first recognized by Father Wood at St John the Evangelist, went on to win the open organ scholarship at Keble College, Oxford, in 1878. He had served as a choirboy at St John's and, according to its historian, it is certain that the keys of the little harmonium (made by Mason & Hamlin), used by Father Wood for the week-day choirboys' practices, "were the first ones touched musically" by the youthful Reed.

The best-known organist to come out of the Diocese, however, was doubtless Lynnwood Farnam. Born in the small rural community of Sutton in 1885, Farnam moved with his family to Dunham when he was four years old and grew up on a farm. The Farnams were all musical and Lynnwood received his earliest training on the piano from his mother. His talent was such that, at an early age he was allowed to take lessons from a Mr Cornish, "an exceptionally fine musical instructor at Dunham Ladies' College." It was the organ, however that captured his interest. "Let's finish our chores, Ernie, so we can go down to the English Church [that is, the Church of England] and listen to the organ," he would frequently urge Ernest Turner, the young Englishman who boarded with his family to learn farming. The two (neither of them Anglicans) would slip into All Saints' Church, Dunham, to listen to the strains of the small pipe organ which had been presented to the church in 1854. Mr Cornish encouraged Farnam to enter a competition for a scholarship. Lynnwood won.

The Lord Strathcona Scholarship, which was awarded to Farnam in 1900, paid three years' tuition at the Royal Academy of Music in London, England, after which the College granted him an additional year's tuition for excellence. In 1903 he became an Associate of the Royal College of Music, and in 1904 of the Royal College of Organists.

On his return to Canada Farnam spent a year as organist at St James Methodist Church, Montreal, and then served from 1905 to 1908 at the Church of St James the Apostle. In 1908 began his tenure as organist-choirmaster at the Cathedral which would continue until 1913 when he left Montreal to fill positions at Emmanuel Church, Boston, and the Church of the Holy Communion, New York. During his Cathedral years, Farnam gave many recitals, prefiguring the notable series of dazzling recitals for the American Guild of Organists that consolidated his reputation among his colleagues.

According to the *Encyclopedia of Music in Canada*, "Farnam has become a legend in the organ world. He did no improvising, and his only composition, a French-style *Toccata* on the Easter Hymn 'O filii et filiae,' was published posthumously … But he was counted among the great interpreters, attracting to his performances not only organists, but other leading musicians and a wide listening public."

Among the New York critics, Richard Aldrich of the *Times* praised Farnam's executive power, artistic sense, and comprehensive knowledge of organ literature. Lawrence Gilman of the *Herald Tribune* wrote that he "had whole-hearted dedication kindled by genius, intensity of vision, sincerity, and excelling craft."

Farnam played his last recital at the Church of the Holy Communion in New York on 12 October1930 "in great distress" and was rushed to hospital immediately afterwards. He was diagnosed with terminal liver cancer and died a month later. He was 45.

The suddenness of Farnam's death caught everyone by surprise, and there was no time to organize any sort of tribute at the time. His friends and colleagues were determined, however, that proper tribute should be paid to the great musician in the city where he had begun his professional career. The *Montreal Churchman* carried the following description of the memorial service held in the Cathedral on the anniversary of his death:

A solemn and impressive service was held in Christ Church Cathedral on Monday evening, November 23rd, the first anniversary of the death of Lynnwood Farnam, when a memorial bust of the great organist was dedicated.

The service opened with the Finale of the Fifth Symphony, dedicated to Farnam by Louis Vierne, organist of Notre Dame in Paris. It was very fitting that this should be played by Mlle Renée Nizan, one of the most gifted young organists in France, since she was not only a pupil of Vierne, but a personal friend of Farnam, who was a guest at her mother's home on his last visit to France.

This was followed by Bach's "Prelude & Fugue in E flat," one of Farnam's favourites ... during which the solemn procession of Clergy and Choirs took their places in the stalls. The opening hymn was, "O God, our help in ages past" — followed by a brief service; after which the Motet, "Jesu, the very thought of Thee," dedicated to Farnam by the composer, Dr Alfred Whitehead, organist of the Cathedral, and which was in press at the time of Farnam's death, was sung by the massed choirs ...

This was followed by three organ numbers by Widor, Brahms, and Karg-Elert; played by Arthur Egerton, successor to Farnam at the Cathedral, and now of Wells College, Aurora. ...

The dedication of the Memorial was made by the Lord Bishop [Farthing], after which Dr Healey Willan, as Orator, gave a brief sketch of the life of Lynnwood Farnam, and voiced the tribute of himself and his brother artists.

Dr Willan's Motet, "O King, to whom all things do live," specially written for this service, was then sung by the massed choirs. This was conducted by Mr Stanley Oliver, organist of St James United Church [where Farnam first served as organist in Montreal]; and was so beautifully sung that at the request of the composer the choirs returned to the church after the service and repeated it; in order that he might have the opportunity of hearing it from a proper distance. ...

Carl Weinrich, successor of Lynnwood Farnam at the Church of the Holy Communion, New York, gave a wonderful rendition of three Bach Preludes and Bach's Allegro from the Fifth Sonata ...

The closing hymn, "Now thank we all our God," sung in unison by the massed choirs, with a magnificent organ accompaniment by Dr Whitehead, was tremendously impressive, and made a glorious finale for the singers.

Before and during the Choir recessional, Mr J.E.F. Martin, organist of the Church of St James the Apostle [where Farnam had served as organist-choir master from 1905 to 1908], made a beautiful conclusion to the service in an Elegy by Bairstow, and one of Bach's Choral Preludes. ...

Records of this Memorial Service, press notices, letters from musicians, &c., will be preserved for posterity in the pedestal of the bust of Lynnwood Farnam.

Although Farnam left Montreal for the United States in 1913, his connection with the city did not end there. He returned periodically to give recitals, and maintained an interest in the Cathedral.

In 1920, Arthur Egerton ("Mr Egg"), Farnam's successor at the Cathedral, felt no qualms about sending Farnam a copy of his report to the wardens on the state of the organ, in hopes that his predecessor's opinion would urge them to have the instrument rebuilt. Farnam's reply served Egerton's turn and reflected the value he set on the organ's quality:

I feel it almost superfluous [Farnam wrote] to give my opinions regarding the Christ Church Cathedral organ, as its needs have been so much dwelt on by me in the past.

As I have, however, during the last few years watched its growing state of delapidation and absolute unreliability, I have marvelled that any work approaching the standard that obtains at Christ Church Cathedral should be attempted on it. On the last three occasions I have tried the organ I have been filled with dismay and wondered how long it could continue.

Without going into detail I can wholeheartedly endorse and second the remarks made by you in your report of November 11, 1920, and express the hope, long cherished, that the organ may be rebuilt with its parts more effectively disposed, while retaining those beautiful qualities that make it tonally famous.

In his will Farnam left a generous bequest of $2,000 (a large sum in 1930) to Christ Church Cathedral, designated for the Organ Fund.

In 1999, the Organ Historical Society decided to hold its national convention in Montreal, with recitals — which were a large part of the convention — on the great organs of large city churches of which three were Anglican: Christ Church Cathedral, St Matthias, and St John the Evangelist. Also included, however, were performances "in small rural churches" with "particularly unique organs." It is worth noting that All Saints', Dunham, scene of Lynnwood Farnam's first dreams of being an organist, was one of those chosen.

# A Spirit of Confidence (1910)

After the turn of the century, and prior to World War I, Montreal's English-speaking business community enjoyed an unparalleled sense of confidence and general well-being. Those who had lived in the city for some years and seen the improvements in its institutions, facilities and commercial prospects looked forward to unlimited expansion in the future. In his "Jubilee Sketch of the Diocese of Montreal," published in 1910, the Rev. J. Douglas Borthwick expressed the optimism — and what in late twentieth-century terms would be called the triumphalism — of his day:

Living as I have done for years in Montreal before the opening of the Synod in 1859, I have seen not only the wonderful increase of population of the city, but also the wonderful increase of our own dear old Church of England [Borthwick claimed].

In the Census returns of the year 1851, a year after the formation of our Diocese, we find that out of a total population of the City of Montreal, viz., 57,725, there were 3,903 adherents of the Church of England.

In the Census of 1861, and eleven years after Bishop Fulford's arrival, we find the population of Montreal had increased to 90,320, out of whom there were 9,739 Episcopalians, more than double the last census.

Montreal's population in 1871 was 107,225 out of which no less than 11,573 were of the Church of England, an increase of 1,834 since the last census in 1861, but the great increases begin from the times of Bishop Bond and in the census of 1881 and that of 1891 we mark a wonderful progress which culminated in the census of 1901.

We find then that the Church of England population of the City of Montreal, *outnumbered* that of both the Presbyterians and Methodists put together, and I doubt not when the next Census of 1911 arrives, we will see and be astonished at the results.

There is no doubt that our Church of the present day exceeds any other Protestant denomination in the Diocese, in building churches and chapels throughout the city, its environs and the country at large.

From the perspective of the latter part of the century, and the devastating out-migration among English-speaking inhabitants from the entire province, such enthusiasm comes as a surprise.

Present-day Anglicans have become familiar with figures showing the opposite tendency. Anglican membership within the territory of the Diocese of Montreal dropped from 95,000 in 1961 to 25,000 in 1991, for example. According to a report on inter-provincial migration, from 1976 to 1981, 131,530 English-speaking people moved out of the province; 94,000 left between 1971 and 1976, and from 1966 to 1971 there were 99,000 more who relocated. With such massive losses of population — a significant portion of it likely to be Anglican — Borthwick's image of the Montreal church forms a sharp contrast with projections for 2010.

# Housing the Poor (1911)

The period before World War I was one of rapid growth for the city of Montreal, and the increasing population, swelled by immigration, was seen as a cause for concern.

The following sermon, preached at St George's Church, Montreal, on 29 October 1911, makes a powerful plea for proper housing for the city's poor. It also reveals a pronounced anxiety among the established population that alien forces were threatening their way of life, a degree of xenophobia — despite a spirit of concern — which is disquieting to a reader at the turn of the twenty-first century.

The preacher was the Rev. John Paterson Smyth, who had been appointed Rector of St George's in 1909. He had come directly from Trinity College, Dublin, where as Professor of Pastoral Theology, and Rector of St Ann's Church, he had established a fine reputation as a preacher and interpreter of the Bible.

The sermon, titled "Housing the Poor," was afterwards printed in the parish magazine, *St George's Monthly*, and appears with frequent italics, to suggest the special emphasis which, no doubt, would have been conveyed in delivery.

The text was drawn from the parable of the marriage of the king's son (Matthew 22: 1-14) which described the guests that would not come, and the servants who "went out into the highways, and gathered together all as many as they found, both bad and good" to furnish the wedding with guests.

After an analysis of the text, and a discussion of the marriage customs of the East, the preacher draws a parallel with contemporary conditions:

That is what the Church must do to-day — she must go down into the highways of the city and strive to gather into the Kingdom of Christ all who are to be found therein, both bad and good. *We must learn to care more for those in the highways.*

Oh, I have been overwhelmed with the sense of responsibility lately when I have thought of the great numbers who are coming into our city to make their homes among us. So many of them are without the ideals of life which we hold before ourselves, and then so many are among the "bad," judging by the records of our Police Courts.

The deeds of violence and secret organizations for evil, which have been shown to exist, are warning us that we have coming into our midst men who will not stop at anything. They will be a menace to our very civilization unless we can win them to Christ.

There are many difficulties, for they speak different languages, and yet we must, if we are to be Catholic in anything but name, be able to minister to them. We surely cannot leave them to go on in their evil without at least an effort being made to save them.

Then, too, we have so many things to avoid. There is the housing problem, which must be dealt with. We cannot expect children to learn to live decently when they are huddled together in such a way as to make it impossible for the very decencies of life to be observed. Is it any wonder if immorality is on the increase?

Is it to be wondered at if crime is on the increase, as some assert it is? **We shall be veritably guilty if we neglect these people**, and our city does not care whether they are properly housed or not. ...

The recent census shows that Montreal is increasing at the *rate of 81% in ten years*, and if this increase should continue as it has been for the last ten years, then in 1921 we shall have a population of 950,000, or nearly one million. It will be far harder then to deal with this housing question, and it will be far more expensive too. Now is the time to deal with it, and the responsibility is ours if we do not.

Are we not wise enough to discern the times? *Can we not read the signs? Socialism is a growing force*, and if we neglect the plain duty of the hour, *and allow the conditions which breed Socialism to exist, and crime to flourish*, then we must not be surprised if these forces come down upon us and *compel us to recognize them.* It may be too late to give them justice then.

It is far more important that we should have good houses for our people where they can be taught to live as true men and women should than that we should spend millions in building magnificent halls for our civic offices. It will be time enough when we have our people housed properly to then consider the question of civic grandeur.

Let us have a proper pride and proper ideals and let it be our ambition to have the best housed people in the world. We have lots of land here — there is no need to huddle our people together, two families or even one, in a room. ...

I know that it would not be considered wise to do this by civic owner-ship, but private enterprise must enter into it. ... [T]here must be a *spirit of philanthropy and not of greed.* A fair return, *not a fabulous interest on the investment* should be looked for. I say that the *Church must stir up people to consider these things* that the poor may have a fair chance and that *these beautiful children* of the poor may have an opportunity to know how to live ...

It has been said that "the duty of the Church is not to build better houses for the people, but to make better people to put into the houses." That is true, but it must also be borne in mind that the Church is terribly handi-capped in making good people to put into the houses by the condition in which many of the people have to live. ...

The Church must not stop there. She must be striving to bring these people to the only power that can make them good citizens — she must bring them to Christ — to the wedding feast.

"Go out into the highways and byways and compel them to come in that My house may be filled," is the command that is ringing in our ears. Gather in the good and the bad to the Table of the Christ. There He offers them the wedding garment of righteousness ... The servants in the parable did not discover the man who had not the garment of righteousness on him, but the King did. When the King offered to His guests the wedding garment, and the invited one did not have on that robe, then he showed that he slighted the King, because he refused the offer of the King's present.

Christ gives us his righteousness — divine righteousness — and clothed in that we are able to sit at the King's Table.

# The Diocesan Paper (1912)

The *Christian Sentinel and Anglo-Canadian Churchman's Magazine* was the first Anglican periodical produced within the boundaries of the Diocese of Montreal. It first appeared in 1827 under the editorship of the Rev. B.B. Stevens. As T.R. Millman, in an article on early Canadian Anglican journalism phrased it, "A high subscription rate of ten shillings for six issues, and a lack of supporting pens" caused the paper to give up "after two and one half years of untiring effort." After a year's interval it was revived briefly, but outside the boundries of this diocese, in Three Rivers.

With the erection of the Diocese of Montreal, Bishop Francis Fulford, who had edited the London-based SPG publication *The Colonial Churchman*, was eager to start a diocesan paper. This finally materialized as the *Church Chronicle of the Diocese of Montreal* in 1860. It ran until 1862. Thereafter at least six Montreal Anglican publications appeared and disappeared in the course of the century.

The *Montreal Churchman* (ancestor of the *Montreal Anglican*) began publication "under the sanction of the Bishop," in November 1912.

When it first appeared, a subscription (if paid in advance) was fifty cents per annum or five cents a copy. As the publication appeared monthly, the charge of one dollar for arrears of subscription was a real penalty. Although there was no charge for postage, subscribers paying by cheque drawn on banks outside the city of Montreal were asked to add fifteen cents to cover the charge of exchange.

The paper was first edited by the Rev. Arthur Henry Moore of St Johns. John Campbell of Montreal acted as manager. The following is a brief excerpt from the initial editorial which outlines the genesis of the publication:

In introducing ourselves to our readers [the editor confided] we wish to tell them as briefly as possible of the circumstances which have brought our diocesan paper into existence.

PLATE 12   *Sample front page of the* Montreal Churchman, *1917*

On the first day of this year of grace the Lord Bishop of the Diocese, in a circular letter to his clergy, wrote as follows: — "In the near future I hope to have a small paper to keep before the Church people the needs of the diocese and I would be grateful if you would kindly send to me the names of those of your parishes to whom such a paper could be sent."

There was no immediate response to this request, but some of the clergy discussed the matter among themselves and agreed that so large an under-taking should not devolve wholly upon the Bishop of the Diocese.

The question was submitted to the Diocesan Synod following, and a resolution was adopted unanimously endorsing the idea of such a publication and urging the Bishop to appoint a committee to proceed. The committee consulted the diocesan clergy who responded with enthusiasm.

The initial editorial then goes on to outline the conception of the paper as a whole and some of the needs to be served by it:

It is now a matter of common experience in the Church, both in England and in the United States, that the diocesan magazine is an invaluable ... means whereby the Bishop of the Diocese may communicate with his peo-ple. Pronouncements and announcements, pastorals and instructions are in this way given to the entire diocese ... Then, in addition to direct episco-pal guidance, the diocesan magazine is becoming more and more a means of instructing Church people in the faith and practice of the Church. ... Furthermore the diocesan paper supplies the necessary information con-cerning the work and life of the Church in the entire diocese to enable Church people to take an intelligent and sympathetic interest in diocesan life and to realize that the Diocese is after all one family ... In this immense diocese ... having the great commercial metropolis of Montreal at its cen-tre, with its problems and conditions so widely different from rural church work, there is apparently a crying need of some means whereby each may keep informed of what is going on elsewhere in our household of faith. ... We shall also attempt to keep our readers in touch with the work of our whole Canadian Church in its efforts to grapple with and solve the problems pre-sented by our unequalled missionary opportunities both at home and abroad ... It is only by means of this larger vision of our life and its prospect that the Church can be saved from a narrow and paralyzing parochialism. ...

One parish priest in commenting on the diocesan paper idea has written thus: — "I would suggest that the paper be prepared for the people and not for the Clergy, as is so often the case with Church Magazines of like nature. The lay folk are not always interested in the things that appeal to the Clergy."

We accept the advice as most timely and exceedingly wise. We wish to speak to the lay folk of the Church. We believe that the future success of the Church is going to be determined by the extent to which the lay folk rise or fail to rise to the growing opportunity that the conditions of modern life are giving to the laity.

It is made clear from the outset that the paper was not intended as a medium for discussion or exchange. Letters to the editor were not to be excluded, but they would be carefully vetted before publication:

We have received several inquiries concerning the policy of this paper in the matter of a correspondence column [the editor remarked]. We frankly admit that in our opinion a vast amount of valuable space in church papers is wasted in this way. We have no intention of presiding over controversies or of making these columns a place in which to exploit novelties or ride hobbies. The Editor will gladly receive suggestions or criticisms from every quarter, but no letter will be published save over the name of the writer, and we shall welcome ... criticism, suggestions and instructions ... designed to have constructive value. We hope to give our readers much helpful material under this head.

As it was hinted in the Bishop's early reference to publicizing "the needs of the diocese," financial considerations were high on the list of benefits to be derived from publishing a diocesan paper. Indeed one could argue that the hopes of its founders were pinned chiefly on its usefulness as a means of attracting financial support at all levels of diocesan activity.

A strong plea was made in this first issue for raising a Permanent Endowment Fund, launched in the previous summer and to be taken up again that same month, for a variety of purposes, including mission work and pensions for clergy and their widows and orphans.

We are publishing on another page of this issue [the editorial continues] a contributed article ... It will be seen from that admirable statement ... that we are facing a crisis in our work ... In short, we have either to increase our diocesan income or abandon some of our weakest missions, be content to leave others vacant for a long period because of the difficulty which the Bishop finds in securing clergymen to take charge of them at a stipend which is less than a living wage and we must also endure the sad spectacle of seeing our best young men shrinking back from entering the ministry because of the sheer poverty into which they must be content to go.

The sad state of stipends is made clear in the Bishop's Charge to Synod, printed in the February issue:

I want to see the Mission clergy paid $1,000 a year instead of the $800 paid ten years ago [the Bishop stated]; and I want to see our superannuated men getting $600 according to length of service, instead of $400 as now; and our widows getting at least $400 instead of the $300 [that is, less than a dollar a day] they receive now. This is what I have set before myself to try to achieve. It is possible of attainment, and we can see at least another step towards it.

Farthing was far from planning to make entering the priesthood financially attractive, however. It may be a shock to the modern reader to realize that at this period it was assumed that enduring a degree of material hardship and sacrifice was part of a clergyman's vocation. An ordination sermon, preached at the Cathedral by Archdeacon William Herbert Naylor and printed in the December issue, makes this clear:

The sacred office would lose its glory — a large measure of it — if it were robbed of its hardness. What could take the place of hardness, trial, privation, affliction in some form, to give the Christian ministry the stamp and character of Christ's ministry — ... What I urge is that a large measure of the glory of the ministry is its hardness, the truth contained in the homely saying, "*no cross, no crown.*"...

When we reach the end of our ministry it will not be the material rewards of our labours or the temporal comforts we have experienced which will give us satisfaction, but the faithfulness with which we stood up against injustice and wrong, the patience with which we endured want, the diligence with which we pursued our work with the means at our command — these are the things which will comfort us in that day. ...

How many a priest of God, poor in the world's goods, but rich in faith and strong in devotion and love toward this old historic church of Christ, has laid its foundations deep and built them firmly in the lives of this generation and others yet to come?

I think of them often — those saints of the days that are past, a Falloon, a Neve, a Johnson, a Robinson, a DuVernet, a Henderson and others, whose wealth was their faith, their works and their character, whose spiritual sons and daughters are spread over the face of this continent for the up-building and ennobling of both the church and the nation.

To gain some perspective on the standard of living a clergyman was expected to aspire to — according to the norms of the time — one must return to the initial editorial. It asks that a young man entering the ministry not be asked to work for "less than the ordinary skilled labourer in his congregation," or for "less than a living wage."

Quite possibly a large proportion of Anglican laypeople might not have been aware of the degree of poverty in which their ministers expected and were expected to live. The *Churchman* was able to make this clear; it could also inform the whole Diocese at a stroke of the gifts of appreciation offered, for example, to the Rev. Cornwallis Lummis of "a new driving sleigh" by the two congregations of Boscobel and North Ely, while the people of the Nixon Mission "added their gift to the equipment in the form of a beautiful set of bells for the sleigh."

A few days before Christmas [began another account], when the annual treat was being held for the children, Mr. J.M. Nelson, lay reader, acting on behalf of the people, presented [the Rev.] Mr. [Cyrus W.] Baugh with a beautiful fur-lined coat and a fur cap, and Mrs Baugh with a handsome muff, while a purse of money, the unexpended balance of that raised for the purpose, amounting to $16.30, was also handed to Mr. Baugh. ... We heartily congratulate the Incumbent of Arundel and his good wife on this so cheering token of sincere appreciation of hard and faithful work.

Such descriptions would, no doubt, encourage other parishes to follow suit.

The *Montreal Churchman* has been, since its inception, an excellent means of communication for the Diocese as well as an invaluable historical resource.

Its own history is far from straightforward, however. From 1912 the paper carried on without a break until 1946 when publication lapsed until 1959 after which it recommenced for ten more years.

In 1969 it was replaced by *The Anglican Newsletter* which continued until 1975. The *Churchman* then resumed. These fits and starts have been unfortunate from the historical perspective. The neighbouring Diocese of Quebec, for example, has had an unbroken run in its diocesan paper — from January 1894 to the present day.

In December 1992, in an attempt to divest itself of colonial vestiges, the publication's name was changed to the *Montreal Anglican* under which banner it continues to provide valuable insight into the life of the Diocese.

# IN WAR AND DEPRESSION
## 1914–1933

## Controversies and Confrontations (1914)

In the year 2000, with its hypersensitivity to political correctness and the responsibilities of living in a pluralistic society, it is difficult to imagine the Anglican church embroiling itself in controversy over the evangelization of another communion, but such was the case as the New Year opened in 1914. As an article in the January issue of the *Montreal Churchman* puts it:

The recent correspondence in the *Montreal Gazette* on "Jewish Missions" has excited a good deal of interest in different quarters, in the question of the evangelization of the Jews.

This correspondence was occasioned by Rabbi de Sola's criticism on and allegations against Jewish Missions and their methods generally, with strong insinuations against th[e] Montreal Jewish Mission [an Anglican initiative], but especially attacking Bishop Farthing for the active interest his Lordship has taken in the Mission to the Jews.

Earlier evidence of such proselytization had appeared in June 1913 when the *Churchman* reported that the MSCC "had decided to take up work among the Jews in Canada" directly, rather than through the London Society for Promoting Christianity Among the Jews.

The background to this reawakened interest in evangelizing the Jews is worth examining. In May of 1882, several thousand Jewish refugees, fleeing from a wave of anti-Jewish pogroms in Russia, had made their way to Montreal, Toronto and other large cities, more than doubling the small Jewish communities of each.

Montreal was now becoming a multicultural city — no longer merely French or English — but the newcomers would not, on the face of it, be likely to swell the ranks of the Anglican communion. The Rev. D.J. Neugewirtz and his staff in Montreal from the London Society had elected "to remain with us for the next few years at least" and the Canadian Church was to take over responsibility for the stipends of those engaged in the work:

During the coming summer [an article in the March issue of the Churchman reported], we hope a hall will be built, which will give much needed relief to the present congestion. We should have on our staff a lady who can speak Yiddish, to assist in the work among women and girls.

I bespeak your enthusiastic support of this important work and your careful consideration in choosing the best possible committee to direct this mission [the members to be elected at Synod], which is now so peculiarly our own.

The coming summer was to bring other concerns, however.

Canon Frederick George Scott — a Montrealer by birth, and one-time curate of St John the Evangelist Church — recalled his reaction to events in Europe in the summer of 1914 in his book, *The Great War as I Saw It*:

It was on the evening of the 31st of July, 1914, that I went down to a newspaper office in Quebec to stand amid the crowd and watch the bulletins which were posted up every now and then, and to hear the news of the war. One after another the reports were given, and at last there flashed upon the board the words, "General Hughes offers a force of twenty thousand men to England in case war is declared against Germany." I turned to a friend and said, "That means that I have got to go to the war." Cold shivers went up and down my spine as I thought of it, and my friend replied, "Of course it does not mean that you should go. You have a parish and duties at home." I said, "No, I am Chaplain of the 8th Royal Rifles. I must volunteer, and if I am accepted, I will go."

Scott was at this time fifty-three years old.

On 28th September, the 14th Battalion, to which Scott had been attached, and several other units, marched off from Camp Valcartier, north of Quebec City, to the entraining point and thence overseas aboard the *Andania*.

Bishop Farthing, too, had recollections of the opening of hostilities, and of a visit to the same camp:

Though expecting the declaration of war [the Bishop recalled], I had gone to Muskoka for my holiday. I hastened back to Montreal as soon as it was declared, to do what I could to help in the necessary war activities. In a marvellously short time 35,000 men had been assembled at Valcartier, to prepare to go to England for training. About 70% of these were Anglicans. Practically all the regiments had chaplains. The Minister of Militia, Col. Sam Hughes, asked me to visit Valcartier to address the men at their service on a Sunday just shortly before they were to sail, and I gladly accepted his invitation. I then heard that he intended to send one Anglican chaplain, one Roman Catholic, and six Salvation Army chaplains. At once I wrote a very courteous note in which I contended that chaplains should be sent in proportion to the number of each Communion enlisting, so that every man should have the ministration of his own Church.

I went to Valcartier as the guest of Sir William Price in Quebec, who motored me out on Sunday morning. ...

After service I said to Archdeacon Almond, one of my Montreal clergy who was a chaplain ... "I hear the Minister is in camp; come along, let us go and pay our respects to him." As soon as we entered his room at Head-quarters, he broke out in an angry and insulting attack on me and our Church. ... He emphatically declared that he would only send one Angli-can, one Roman Catholic, and six Salvation Army chaplains. "You want all the chaplains to be Anglicans [Hughes said]." I said, "No, Sir, in my letter to you I said I wanted the number to be proportionate to the men of each Communion enlisting, and that is what we are determined to have. We Anglicans could not accept the ministrations of the Salvation Army." He exclaimed, "Why not?" I did not answer his question. ... "Well," he said, "the Salvation Army men will wash dishes and do any kind of work, and your men are no good." I replied, "I do not think washing dishes is a chaplain's work." He completely lost his temper, and his language was most offensive and abusive. ... When Sir William Price heard what had taken place he telephoned Sir Robert Borden, the Prime Minister ... The next day Sir Robert telephoned me and ... apologized for his Minister, and wanted me to send a written account of what had taken place. This I did. During that week Sir Robert Borden and Sir George Foster, a member of the Cabinet, both went to Valcartier and decided to send every chaplain in camp overseas, and even added to the number! Col. Samuel Hughes was furious with me!

In his memoir, Scott mentions the uncertainty felt by the chaplains as they waited for orders in Valcartier "because rumour had it it that [Hughes] did not believe in chaplains, and no one could find out whether he was going to take us or not." Scott was "most punctilious in the matter of saluting General Hughes" as he "rode about with his aides-de-camp in great splendour like Napoleon." In Farthing, Hughes had apparently met his Waterloo.

Scott probably owed his opportunity for service overseas to Bishop Farthing's intervention. He would serve with distinction as Senior Chaplain, First Canadian Division, Canadian Expeditionary Force. He was awarded the Companion of St Michael and St George in 1916 and the Distinguished Service Order in 1918.

## In the Midst of War (1916)

During the course of the Great War — as it was called until other twentieth-century wars made the term seem less appropriate — attitudes and expectations altered dramatically. In 1915, for example, Bishop Farthing's New Year's Message placed emphasis on the underlying brotherhood of the opposing forces:

My Dear Brethren,
  It is hard, in our peaceful land to realize that never did the world endure greater physical, and mental suffering than now. Hundreds of thousands of homes throughout ten nations of the world are plunged in sorrow.
  The Father loves all men. The Eternal Son took Humanity into His Godhead, and He died for the world. The Germans, Austrians, and Turks, are as much the objects of His love and care as are the Allies. These are self-evident truths, but they are in danger of being forgotten. ...
  We are all, the foe as well as the ally, being purified by suffering; we are all equally suffering, and we all need the purification which suffering brings.

One year later the tone of the Bishop's Message for the New Year was considerably altered. The Allies were doing badly and the United States had not yet entered the war. Anglican enlistment had continued to be high and losses had been heavy The prospect of defeat was very real and the Bishop's evident anxiety could not have been cheering for his people:

The year 1916 will probably be one of the most eventful years in history [it began], for the destinies of mighty Empires will be determined. Though the war may drag on (which God forbid), yet the issues of this great and awful war will be made clear by the events of this year. ... The conviction grows on many of us that if we are defeated, Canada will become a German possession. It is idle to say that the United States would not permit it. A victorious Germany would compel the States to fight for their own freedom, and they would have all they could do to look after themselves.

Farthing then quotes from the Swiss correspondent of a London paper who had reported on the role of German religious leaders in the war effort:

German Roman Catholic priests have approved the unspeakable outrages perpetrated on the Catholic population of Belgium; German Protestant pastors have proclaimed the righteousnesess of military terrorism; German rabbis have glorified the crimes of Germany's rulers.

Specific examples follow:

In a sermon preached in Berlin by the Rev. Fritz Philippe ... occur these words [the message continues] — 'Just as the Almighty caused His Son to be crucified for Redemption, so Germany is destined to crucify humanity for the renewed salvation of mankind. Humanity must be redeemed by blood, by fire and by the sword. German warriors do not willingly shed the blood of other nations, but they do it as a sacred duty, which they dare not neglect without committing sin.' ...

Dr Lobel, the leading Lutheran Pastor in Leipzig, says that Heaven has blessed the Germans by appointing them as the chosen people; that Germany is carrying out the Divine wishes ... Professor Seeberg, Professor of Theology in Berlin University preaching in Berlin Cathedral, says, "when we kill, when we inflict untold suffering on them, when we burn their homes and overrun their territories, we are performing a labour of love ... German armies are overcoming the hosts of organized evil."

Dr Scholz, preaching at Halle says, 'After Germany's final triumph over her enemies the way will be made clear for a truly German Christianity.' ...

"Yes," Farthing continues, "That is the moral issue":

'A new Christianity [the Bishop exclaimed],' a 'truly German Christianity,' the spirit of which has animated the German people during the war! This is to be forced upon the world by victorious Germany. Because I want you to realize what is involved in the issues of war, I have given these extracts. ... Do not let us live in any fool's Paradise. With such a spirit ruling in the governing class, we would have untold misery and persecution, and would be the slaves of the German spirit. May God deliver us!

Such pronouncements, which seem today both inflamatory and defeatist, can hardly have been helpful on the homefront.

News from chaplains serving overseas appear in the *Montreal Churchman* from time to time. A letter from Captain, the Rev. A.P. Shatford, Rector of St James the Apostle, Montreal, but now Chaplain of the 5th Infantry Brigade, 2nd Canadian Division — dated the previous November 22nd — described conditions at the front. It appeared in the January issue:

When the men are in the trenches we manage to visit them and speak the cheering word but conditions make services there practically impossible. The advance dressing stations and the Field Ambulances are, of course, our grave concern and there the Chaplains are ever in evidence. Most touching scenes are witnessed and often the heart is deeply moved by the sense of the Divine Presence. Perhaps the saddest of all our duties is the burial of the dead. Often amid the roar of the guns and the screaming shells we lay them tenderly away, wrapped in a simple blanket.

By 1917, according to the Canadian Associated Press, there were 276 Canadian chaplains serving overseas. The largest denomination represented, whether Protestant or Catholic, was Church of England with 102 padres overseas. Then came the Presbyterians with 58, closely followed by the Roman Catholics with 53. Thus 45.7% of all Protestant chaplains and 37% of all chaplains together, serving with Canada's Overseas Forces, were supplied from the ranks of the Anglican Church.

Every day there were reminders of the losses sustained throughout the Diocese. Returning to May 1916, the *Montreal Churchman* carried an article titled "Honour Rolls Unveiled":

On the evening of April 17th the Officer Commanding the 4th Division, Brigadier General Wilson, unveiled the longest of these lists at St Clement's, Verdun. A military service was held and General Wilson complimented the men on the valour they have shown and the wives and mothers for the willing sacrifice they are making.

The Honour Roll contains 361 names and it is a great credit to this parish and a fine tribute to the patriotic spirit of the Rev. F.L. Whitley its zealous rector.

St Clement's Church, through the efforts of its military pastor, has been for years the centre of military life in the city of Verdun. The boys who now form the major portion of the Verdun Squadron of the Scottish Dragoons, received their first military training as members of a signalling corps formed by the pastor of St Clement's from the youngsters of the parish. ...

A further Honour Roll, containing fifty-six names, "including several young ladies, who have gone as nurses," was unveiled on the evening of Easter Sunday by Bishop Farthing at St Martin's Church. The article goes on to give numbers of the men and women serving overseas from other parishes: 200 each from St Jude's and Grace Church; 187 from St George's; 170 from St Mary's Hochelaga; 60 each from St Matthias and St Barnabas in St Lambert; and more than 50 each from St Cyprian's and St Luke's — and no mention here is made of enlistment figures and heavy losses for the rural portions of the Diocese.

In his annual Charge to Synod, delivered on 13 February 1917, Bishop Farthing was outspoken in his call to duty, urging every able-bodied man in the Diocese to present himself for service:

Every man should be at the disposal of the Government [he maintained]. And those who are of military age who are not indispensable in home work, should enlist in some branch of the services on land or sea or air. If the Government can feel free to use each man where his service will count for most, then we will get the best results for winning the war. We should all heartily advocate, and by example strengthen the appeal for National Service made by our Premier, Sir Robert Borden, whom we are fortunate to have at the head of affairs at this time, a man in whose integrity and patriotism we can all so confidently trust.

Conscription became a burning issue throughout Canada, but especially in Quebec where there was much bitterness which often erupted along linguistic and religious lines. Farthing's September Message addressed this issue with an appeal for understanding:

Amidst the world crisis, Canada is facing a great crisis of her own, a consequence of the war. Never was there need for wiser statesmanship in our leaders, and cooler heads on our people. While this applies to all Canadians, it particularly applies here in the Province of Quebec, which will be the storm centre. We who live here must be especially careful.

Unfortunately many are seeking to make the struggle a question of race and religion.

Nothing will be gained by denouncing the French race, or the Roman Catholic Church. Many French Canadians, many Roman Catholics are fighting with us. Let us show that while we are out and out for conscription, we are fighting the battle for a principle, in the spirit of our God. ... Facts must be stated, but they can be stated in a gentle and manly spirit, not in clamouring denunciation.

Other attitudes on the homefront were a source of unease. A letter from the Rev. A.P. Shatford — now promoted to the rank of Major — written to his parishioners, refers to Canadian newspapers that had reached him overseas and the demoralizing impression they had made:

When one sees daily the straitened circumstances of our lads who fight to save our country, and then read of crowded picture halls and immense throngs at baseball and horse races at home, the heart grows sick with fear, of a people enervated and degenerate. Count over the columns and pages in our big daily papers devoted to flaming advertisements of cinema attractions and sporting pleasure — then ask if our people really have entered into the spirit of support for our brave men on the battlefield?

The letter was dated the Feast of St James the Apostle, the patronal festival of Shatford's church in Montreal. On that day in the previous year, as he reminded his parishioners, he had written "from the stricken fields of Belgium." The present letter was composed 'in a broken, devastated village in France, within sound of the roaring guns.' It was the third year that he had been away:

Forgive me, my beloved congregation, for writing so tensely upon these matters [he concluded a lengthy description of life at the Front], but the time is critical and I must ease my own conscience of its burden. I yearn to see a whole Canada in this war. I want to be assured that my comrades out here are not fighting and dying for an unworthy nation. God help us all to learn something more of the Spirit of our Divine Master.

## Influenza (1918)

The November issue of the *Montreal Churchman* was in press when news of the Armistice broke on a world weary of sacrifice and privation.

Montreal had benefited from war production — manufacturing munitions and building submarines — but the conscription issue had produced bitter internal divisions throughout the province. The weekly wage of unskilled workers in Montreal was about two dollars less than the going rate elsewhere and morale was low.

To make matters worse, the Spanish Influenza, a worldwide epidemic, was decimating the province, while the unabated news of war dead and wounded had brought grief or bereavement to almost every Anglican family in the nation.

The Central Board of Health of the Province had ordered that all churches be closed to minimize contagion and the Bishop was determined that the regulations should be complied with.

It is not surprising, therefore, that Bishop Farthing's Message for November printed in the *Churchman* struck a solemn note.

My dear brethren [he began]:—

Never surely did a darker cloud of sorrow hang over the world! Millions of hearts are heavy and sad. Some sorrow for those who have passed over into the Great Unseen; while countless ones are filled with sickening anxiety for those who hourly face danger and death for us all. Many homes of our Church people have been bereaved during the past few months. It is the price of victory. ... With war slaying our youth in France, and Pestilence slaying them here, it is levying a double toll ... Sorrow fills our hearts. Then to make it worse, kind Science comes and tells us that we must not foregather, because this dread Pestilence lurks in the very breath of our nostrils, and by breathing we may pass it on, though we ourselves escape. ... To avoid even the possibility of this we have consented to the closing of our churches for four Sundays. It has been a terrible loss and trial; it came too, just when we needed most the ministry of His Word and Sacrament ...

Though we cannot meet together to pray, let us all pray earnestly, that our prayers may ascend to God as one, though we pray separately. Then when we can once more meet to worship, let it be a great thanksgiving, that He purified us through suffering.

As the *Churchman's* November editorial makes clear, there was some bitterness among Anglicans that while their churches were closed in accordance with health regulations, others had refused to conform and had suffered no penalty for it.

From observations it appears that our churches throughout the Province have accepted these orders and loyally kept to them. We cannot say this of many Roman Catholic churches. ... Some have disregarded it altogether while others have done violence to it in many respects.

A most interesting question grows out of this consideration, viz:— Is the observance of laws and regulations in this Province only obligatory upon those who are law-abiding and law-respecting? Why has nothing been done to bring transgressors of the order to book? It is not because Church of England people do not love their church and prize its privilege as much as anybody else that they have kept the law but it is because they also respect the civil law and desire to co-operate with the civil authorities in every possible particular. ... A longsuffering public cannot be expected to allow such a thing to pass unremarked and we only try to state a question that seems to be very serious and vital to our civic well-being and leave it with our readers.

Contributing to this frustration, too, was a series of regulations which closed churches, but allowed "pool halls and big stores" to open their doors as usual.

According to Montreal historian John Irwin Cooper,

there were said to be over sixteen thousand cases [of influenza] in the city alone, of which nearly three thousand were fatal. ... The anxieties and hardships of four years exacted their toll. The lowered vitality that made Montrealers easy victims of influenza had its counterpart in a lowered morale and lowered morality that rendered them complacent under misgovernment for many years to come.

# Episcopal Dress (1919)

The Great War finally ended in November 1918. Food and fuel shortages had been felt throughout the country, and Montreal wages "had failed to match the rapid rise of wartime living." Relief at the news of the Armistice had been tempered by the most virulent epidemic of influenza to strike the world in the twentieth century. Finally, Montreal had marked the last weeks of the year by a firemen's and policemen's strike.

It is against this background — although not with this in mind — that Bishop Farthing recalled a particular event of the year 1919 in his episodic, chatty memoirs:

MY TENTH EPISCOPAL ANNIVERSARY — 1919

Mr George E. Drummond gave a dinner party for me at the Mount Royal Club, on the 6th January 1919, Dean Evans and the Ven. Archdeacon Paterson Smyth being the only two clergy present, with thirty to forty laymen. It was a very happy gathering. In the speeches constant jocular remarks were made about the Bishop's official dress — his hat, gaiters, apron, crosses, etc. I told them that when I came to Montreal [on being elected Bishop] I was very doubtful what to do regarding the official dress.

Here he reminisces about the decision he came to at that time:

I consulted a number of laymen about it. I did not go to the ecclesiastical laymen like my honoured Chancellor. I knew what they would say. I went to the more radical laymen. Every one advised me to wear the official dress and not give up anything in this Roman Catholic city, as it would lower the status of the Anglican Church in the eyes of the Roman Catholics. So I have always continued to wear the uniform within the diocese and when on church work; but when I go to the lake for my holiday, I wear flannels. Now you laymen joke about it; tell me frankly, do you think that I should continue to wear it or not?" [The gentlemen at the dinner] were unanimously in favour of my continuing to wear it, as it upheld the dignity of the Bishop's office. I am sure they are right. The Bishop is always on duty in his diocese, and should, I think, always wear his official uniform, whatever it is understood to be. An officer in the army when on duty always wears the uniform of his rank. So should it be in the army of Christ.

A glance through Owsley Robert Rowley's collection of formal portraits in *The Anglican Episcopate of Canada and Newfoundland* (published in 1928), shows remarkable changes in attitude toward episcopal dress since the first bishop was appointed to the New World in 1787. Early bishops wore a surplice with lawn sleeves, a rochet — a full-length black sleeveless garment open at the front — and bands at the neck. This appears to have been invariable until 1859 when George Hills, first Bishop of British Columbia, dispensed with bands. Thomas Brock Fuller, consecrated Bishop of Niagara in 1875, may have been the last to wear them.

In the meantime, the pectoral cross had appeared with the consecration of John Travers Lewis as Bishop of Ontario in 1862.

Coloured stoles appear later still, and Charles Hamilton, consecrated Bishop of Niagara in 1885, may well have been the first Canadian Diocesan to pose for his episcopal portrait in mitre with crosier.

Bishop Fulford, who was not insistent on episcopal garb, had one of the first episcopal staffs in Canada, made for him as Metropolitan under the direction Father Edmund Wood. It was used on one occasion only and that in Quebec City. After Fulford's death it was entirely disused until Farthing pressed it into service for his consecration. "As far as I know, I was the first Bishop of Montreal to use the old staff, or any other, in the diocese," Farthing remarked.

Farthing enjoyed the trappings of episcopacy, and had the bearing to carry them off. His predecessor, Bishop Bond, a man of great presence — over six feet tall, bearded and massively built, "with a deep booming voice that would easily penetrate the recesses of church or cathedral, however large" — was simple in his tastes and abhorred display.

Farthing has been referred to as Montreal's 'last great prince of the Church'; in demeanour Oxenden may well have been the first. Fulford, a fine and commanding figure, equally at home on ceremonial as on informal occasions, is perhaps better described as 'a Christian Gentleman.'

A charming anecdote concerning Bishop Fulford was recounted years after the event by W.S. Humphreys, a Montreal layman, who was a choirboy at the consecration of the new Cathedral in 1859:

One little incident I remember well [he recounted]. It happened when I was in my tenth year. It was New Year's morning and I was about to enter the Cathedral when I noticed the Bishop approaching. I waited, and as he neared me, I took off my cap and said: "I wish you a very happy New Year, Sir." Then I remembered that I was addressing a bishop, and I hastened to add: "I beg pardon — my Lord." The Bishop took my hand in his right hand, and raising the other aloft, he said: "Willie, my boy, there is but one Lord, and He is above." Then he wished me all the happiness of the New Year.

In the year 2000, day-to-day episcopal garb has changed from black to purple, and richly brocaded copes, stoles and mitres are constantly in ceremonial use. Yet day-to-day events and even parish and diocesan meetings allow great informality in most parts of the Canadian church, so that it may be difficult at times to distinguish priests and bishops from the laity. As Montreal continues to invoke a dress code for its clergy — at least for Synod — the following limmerick, penned in Bishop Farthing's time by the Ven. John Paterson Smyth, still has some relevance:

> There was an Archdeacon who said
> May I take off my gaiters in bed?
> But his Bishop said, No,
> Wherever you go
> You must wear them until you are dead.

# Prayer Book Revision (1921)

As early as 1902 there was a resolution passed in General Synod that an adaptation of the Book of Common Prayer be prepared for Canadian use. At first it was thought that an appendix to the Prayer book would be sufficient which, according to Philip Carrington, would contain such supplementary prayers and services as had been put out from time to time by Bishops or by Provincial Synods; a Harvest Thanksgiving for instance, the Consecration of a Church, or the Institution of a Clergyman in a parish.

Although there was support for the project in many quarters, when the appendix (prepared under the chairmanship of Fredericton's Bishop Kingdon) came before General Synod in 1905, it was rejected. In 1908 another committee, for the Enrichment and Adaptation of the Prayer Book, was struck, for at this stage "no one wanted to see the old services changed in character or doctrine."

In the work that followed, three men of marked literary ability stood out: Archdeacon Paterson Smyth of St George's, Montreal, Canon F.G. Scott of St Matthew's, Quebec, and Professor George Abbott-Smith of Diocesan College.

Bishop Farthing of Montreal had been among "the earliest friends of revision," as W.J. Armitage, one of those involved in the work, remembered:

Dr Farthing brought to the Committee a devout spirit, and a highly trained mind. His wise discrimination and sound judgment were of great value, and as chairman of the Special Services Committee his work was of the highest importance.

The work brought together what Carrington termed "a galaxy of talent, high-church and low-church, clerical and lay, eastern and western, all working together in high spirits and good humour. A snatch of verse, penned by J. Paterson Smyth, recalls something of this mood:

> Day by day in St. George's Hall,
> From morning till late moonrise,
> They worked till the text of 'The Book Annexed'
> Went swimming before their eyes.
> And still their Taskmaster urged them on,
> 'Revise! Revise! Revise!'

The draft books were ready for the next General Synod in 1915, but a bomb-shell was thrown into proceedings when Chancellor Davidson read a memorial from "Communicants and others in the Diocese of Ottawa" asking that the Book of Common Prayer should not be changed in any way, at least during the War. It was further stated that there were sixty-two such memorials.

The New Prayer Book was finally adopted by General Synod in 1918 and ratified in 1921.

It left the old services very much as they were [Carrington noted], but provided for shortening when necessary and for a few alternatives, and made them more adaptable to Canadian needs and conditions. It provided many new prayers, and new services for various causes and occasions ... it had required assiduous labour on the part of the various committees, but it did not make any dramatic changes.

Forty years later this book, in turn, was replaced by a revision that had taken sixteen years of solid work. This time the Diocese of Montreal seems to have been less obvious in its contributions, although Archdeacon Kenneth Naylor formed an important part of the team. This second Prayer Book is closely associated with Montreal for other reasons, however; the book's final form — which was adopted unanimously "after less than an hour of discussion" — took place at the twentieth General Synod, held at Macdonald College in Ste-Anne-de-Bellevue in 1959. It received final ratification in Kingston three years later.

The aim of the revision, according to Colin Cuttell, was "to preserve the essential beauty and splendour of the English prose of 1662." Carrington, who was the driving force behind the work, saw the proposed new book "as a stronger and simpler form of the old."

I am more and more convinced [Carrington wrote in a Pastoral Letter at the close of 1959] that it is by God's good grace that the Anglican Church preserves in its Prayer Book and Liturgy the great truths and traditions of the ancient Church which are in danger of being lost in the modern world.

In 1983, yet another volume was placed in the hands of Canadian Anglicans. The Book of Alternative Services (BAS) was given qualified approval by Gereral Synod and instituted on an experimental basis. It, too, had been the result of many years of work, this time under the ecumenical influence of the Liturgical Movement and Vatican II. Experimental liturgies had preceded it in many Canadian Dioceses, Montreal being one.

In 1966, Bishop Kenneth Maguire set up a Liturgical Commission that, as he stated in a Pastoral Letter, "has accepted as a basic liturgical principle that there should be more than one authorized form of the Services found in the Prayer Book.

In Montreal there was a real effort to get "a genuine cross-section of parish opinion, and not only those likely to favor the liturgy." As the

Bishop was quoted in the lead article of the *Montreal Churchman* in the January issue:

If your parish would like to assist in testing one of these forms, I ask you to write to the Chairman of the Liturgy Commission …

I remind you once again that the General Synod on Prayer Book Revision is attempting a tremendous task, which will be formative of the Church of the future.

Everyone must take seriously the need to re-examine what we do Sunday by Sunday in our churches.

Your participation is urgently sought.

When the new book was printed and ready for distribution it was Bishop Reginald Hollis who determined how the introduction would be handled in the Diocese. Unlike many Canadian bishops (who literally forced parishes within their dioceses to adopt the new book and abandon the old) Bishop Hollis left the choice of Service Books to individual parishes.

In his 1987 Address the Bishop announced that the opening Eucharist at Synod would alternate annually between books. Joan Marshall, in her study of the Diocese, describes his support of the BAS as "consistently cautious," although he "underlined the need for parishes to give the book a 'healthy trial' so that they might provide useful feedback to the national liturgical commission."

It had been predicted that the introduction of the BAS would attract young people to the Church and reverse the alarming downward spiral of church membership. In 1961, shortly after the introduction of the second Canadian revision of the BCP, there were 95,000 Anglicans in the Diocese of Montreal. In 1981, five years before the BAS was available in parishes, membership had fallen to 38,000.

At the 1986 Youth Synod four motions were presented, including one "calling for the encouragement of the use of the Book of Alternative Services," but to the surprise of the organizers it was defeated, "due largely," a report in the *Montreal Churchman* claimed, "to misinterpretation and lack of information concerning the content of the new orders of service." The other three motions — one requesting a section of the *Montreal Churchman* to be set aside for youth news, a second condemning the use and manufacture of nuclear weapons, and a third calling for a condemnation of the practice of abortion on demand — all passed.

The *Churchman* report, explaining the defeat of the BAS endorsement, brought at least one angry response from a participant at Youth Synod:

I am writing to clarify a statement made by myself in the Youth Synod article dated June 1986 [replied the article's author in the October issue]. The motion concerning the encouragement by the youth to use the Book of Alternative Services was defeated. The reasons why this motion was defeated are variant [sic], depending upon the perspective one delves into. Miss Katherine Hume (St. James the Apostle) pointed out quite correctly that according to the vote, the youth do not want to encourage the use of the B.A.S. Period. End of debate. I earnestly believe that the youth defeated the motion due to the nature of the presentation and the experience of the youth with the B.A.S. at that particular time.

It is still to be demonstrated that the introduction of the BAS is of itself a drawing card to the church. Although it has found wide acceptance, particularly among the clergy in the Diocese of Montreal and elsewhere, there has been considerable resistance as well. In fact an attachment to the liturgy of the Prayer Book is more typical of the whole eastern portion of the country than of central Canada or the West. The Prayer Book Society of Canada, founded in 1986, is firmly established in the Maritime provinces and the Diocese of Montreal. The Society has made little inroads in the neighbouring Diocese of Quebec, but the Prayer Book iself, as of 2000, is largely the service book of choice.

Writing in 1995, Joan Marshall theorized that the substantially lower rate of acceptance of the BAS in the Diocese of Montreal than in Toronto is attributable

not to an eastern regional conservatism but to a need for the kind of stability and rootedness that can be found in the tradition of the prayer book. If the socio-political situation in Quebec had not been so threatening, and had there been higher rates of in-migration of young families over the past thirty years, there might have been greater acceptance of the new prayer book in Montreal.

The 450th Anniversary of the Book of Common Prayer was celebrated at a special evensong held at the Church of St James the Apostle on 16 May 1999. In addition, Bishop Andrew Hutchison gave his permission to use the Holy Communion Liturgy of the 1549 Prayer Book, on Sunday 13 June in churches throughout the Diocese. The Book of Alternative Services had by then been in use for thirteen years.

Adherence to one or the other of the service books has been polarized from the beginning, but fortunately Montreal has continued to permit the use of either or both books. Where a priest has been particularly insistent on a form not favoured by some members of a congregation, they have generally tended to go elsewhere or nowhere.

In June 2000, representatives from the Maritimes, Quebec, Montreal and Newfoundland were assembled in Renforth, New Brunswick, for one of a series of four Liturgical Consultations by General Synod. A Montreal delegate among those attending observed:

> As always happens, some people (of all age groups) felt strongly that the Book of Common Prayer was their choice, with its beautiful language and sonorous phrases. Others, also of all age groups, liked the alternatives offered and the more modern language of the Book of Alternative Services. We had many a discussion on BCP versus BAS. It was agreed, too, that both these books are in need of revision ... We felt that perhaps the best option would be to continue to use both books for several more years, giving us more time to consider revisions and look at the needs of the future.

## Who Was Welcome? (1923)

In 1923 Susan Kathleen Daley left her home in Kinsale Village on the Island of Montserrat and set out by ship for Montreal to join her sister Mary who had gone to Canada three years earlier. Mary Daley (or Nellie, as the family called her) had already secured a position in service for her sister Susan — she herself was working as a cook — and there was at least one other family member, a cousin, to meet her on arrival.

The journey was a long one and she was alone. She sailed on the *SS Chaleur* to Saint John, New Brunswick, and then travelled by train the rest of the way:

> On that run [from Saint John to Montreal] she was bothered by one of the porters [recalled Richard Lord], but she didn't pay any attention because she'd been told by her family before she left not to talk to any strangers. But when the train arrived in Montreal and she was met by her cousin Robert Hussey at the Windsor Station she was surprised to see him greet the porter as an old friend. His name was James Levi Theophilus Lord. Robert Hussey introduced them. That's how my mother met my father.

James Lord was the son of a fisherman, and had come to Canada from St Philip's, in Barbados. On arrival, he had first found employment working in the mines in Northern Quebec, but with the outbreak of hostilities in Europe he volunteered for the army — presenting himself at the recruiting station across from the Champ de Mars in Montreal. He served overseas in the trenches, was wounded in action — shot through the jawbone — but patched up and returned to battle before his eventual demobilization and return to Canada.

Once back in civilian life, Lord found employment with the Canadian Pacific Railway as a Pullman porter, a position he was to hold for forty years. At the time he met Miss Susan Daley he was living on Desrivières Street, behind the old Queen's Hotel between St James and St Antoine, near the Windsor Station.

Nellie Daley "lived in," but her employers, in offering her sister a place in their Westmount home as well, did not require that she be on the spot at all times. Consequently she was expected to arrange for her own accommodations elsewhere.

On a Sunday morning, soon after her arrival, Susan Daley set off by herself to walk to St George's Church near her new lodgings.

After the service [her son recounts] the Rector, Mr Paterson Smyth, spoke to her and told her that she should be attending the Union Church which was "the coloured church." But the Union Church was not Anglican. The next Sunday she went back to church at St George's, carrying her baptismal certificate and her confirmation certificate that she had brought with her from Montserrat. When she showed them to Mr Paterson Smyth to prove that she belonged to the Anglican Church, he accepted that and didn't try to send her away any more. The next year my parents were married at St George's by Mr. Paterson Smyth.

The initial check to Susan Daley's attempt to worship in the Anglican Church was removed because of her spirit and determination, and after she became a member of the congregation others followed, but, as Canon Anthony Jemmott pointed out in a lecture delivered at the Montreal Diocesan Theological College, others fared differently:

Many Caribbean Anglicans in this Diocese [he observed] have the sad story to tell that on their arrival, far from finding a warm welcome in a sister church, they were directed to the Black Church — Union United, where many continue to this day. ... Sometimes the closest they came to an Anglican church was in the attendance at various meetings of Island groups in the Halls and basements of our churches.

It is obvious that this situation continued well into the sixties and seventies.

Although his work-schedule of twenty-two days a month aboard the train did not permit James Lord an opportunity to attend St George's very often, his wife, four sons and two daughters were regularly present. All the children were baptized and confirmed there, and all attended Sunday School. Years later, their son Richard would serve St George's as a Synod delegate and be elected People's Warden.

After the Rev. John Paterson Smyth's retirement, he was succeeded in 1927 by the Rev. Canon Albert Gower-Rees who seems to have been much more open in his attitudes. When the Lords' son Richard was admitted to Michigan State University, Gower-Rees provided him with letters of introduction to the Episcopal Church in East Lansing, and gave encouragement and moral support.

He wrote me a reference for my first job, too [Lord remembered]. After he died his daughter gave me his Bible, the one he always used to write his sermons — containing a dictionary and concordance. He was my mentor. His daughter said that he had left it especially to me. She gave it to me in St George's.

At Michigan State, Lord was the only Black student in Chemical Engineering, but then he had been the only Black in his class throughout his primary and secondary schooling. An outgoing and popular student, he became head of his dormitory, captain of the NCAA [National Collegiate Athletics Association] Hockey Team, Secretary of his Fraternity, President of the Varsity Club, and founder and first President of the Canadian Club on campus.

My parents both believed in education [Lord recalled]. My Dad finished school, but there was no high school in my mother's village. She just had an elementary school education, but before I went to school I had learned my twelve-times-tables at home. My mother kept moving house so that all of us could attend good schools. We finally moved to the first street in Lower Westmount. I was the only Black in Westmount High at that time. After I graduated in 1948, I took senior matric. When I was accepted at Michigan State in 1949 I had a real advantage over a lot of students because of the good preparation I had had in high school and grade twelve.

The necessary preparation went back further than high school, however. Recalling the formative experiences of his childhood, Lord pointed to the discipline insisted upon at home, the importance of responsibilities, the significance of Sunday:

We weren't allowed to play in the park on Sunday. Sunday was a day of respect. We always went to Sunday School and we had excellent teachers all through, like the three Brennans, the two Percivals and Miss Wheeler. They were wonderful teachers. They taught us good values. When I went to Michigan State and sometimes had some prejudice to deal with I was well prepared to deal with that.

When Susan Daley died, a lamp on the Intercession Desk at St George's Church was dedicated in her memory. A small brass plaque on the side of the desk gives her name and dates together with a brief inscription — "Let there be Light."

## Finding Furnishings (1928)

Many small parishes throughout the Diocese have depended on the women of the larger city churches for help in obtaining proper church furnishings. Decent altar linens, frontals, and so forth, would have been out of reach for many a struggling congregation without the efforts of such organizations as the Woman's Auxiliary, forerunner of the ACW, but always more missionary-minded in outlook.

The Annual report of the Senior Branch of the WA of Montreal's Church of St John the Evangelist, printed in the Lenten issue of the Parish Review, 1929, gives an idea of the scope of this group's involvement in practical outreach:

Completing the fortieth year of its history, the Senior (afternoon) Branch of the Woman's Auxiliary reported another excellent year's work when the twelve months, ending December 31st, 1928, were reviewed at the annual meeting in January. One of the most outstanding features of the year's programme was the report on Dorcas work, which, besides the provision of outfits for Indian school girls and a bale [of supplies] for white settlers, included aid in the furnishing of three mission churches in the Diocese [at Papineauville, Avoca and St-Amadée].

… Each church was in need of altar furnishings, and, in the case of the first one, repairs to the fabric. During the early part of the autumn a cheque for $50 was forwarded [to Papineauville] … as an anonymous gift from a member of St. John's … [with the request] that it be used in the restoration of the interior and furnishings of the Papineauville Church. When the student-in-charge of the Church was interviewed by the corresponding secretary … it was found that he had two other churches in his charge and that each needed attention. After consent was given that each church should receive aid, the branch, with the assistance of Miss Evans, of the Church

Furnishing Guild of the Cathedral, and a member of St. John's, set about to make or renovate altar frontals and superfrontals for each church.

St John's has long been known for needlework. As early as the 1870s the Church Embroidery Society, which was renamed the Guild of St Luke, was providing furnishings for the church. In 1928, the Jubilee history of the parish stated that, apart from vestments which have been private gifts or purchased by the Guild of St Anne, "all the chausibles, maniples, stoles, albs, surplices and cottas and many of the cassocks have been made by the Guild."

As the corresponding secretary told the meeting in her report "the altar frontal of the Papineauville Church was brought down, and as it was of good material it was found that it could be dyed. It was a sorry looking object when we opened the parcel to look at it. The original crimson only remained in patches on a surface faded almost white. This dyed beautifully to a rich crimson, and a new fringe was put on, with an altar cover to match. This will go to Avoca where the church has been without an altar frontal, the altar being merely a table with a white cloth spread over it for celebrations of the Eucharist."

The churches at Papineauville and St Amedie [sic] each have new frontals and superfrontals with covers to match. With money collected from various sources, altar missals and rests, chalice veils and purificators have been procured for each church. ...

Another piece of work in which the branch was instrumental was the renovation of the church at Papineauville. The walls were broken in many places and the surface was very soiled and faded. The Church could pay for the mending of the walls, but found it impossible to bear the cost of tinting. From a paint company in Montreal the necessary material was procured gratis, and the men of the congregation did the work. The result is that the church fabric and furnishings are now in a thoroughly good condition.

On 28 June 1968 St Mary's, Avoca, and St John's, St-Amadée, were both deconsecrated. Three years later, on 8 July 1973, St Stephen's, Papineauville, met the same fate.

# The Fellowship of the West (1929)

This year saw the formation in Montreal of a movement called the Fellowship of the West. As Philip Carrington describes the Fellowship, "It had in view the needs of the Diocese of Athabasca, especially in the valleys of the Peace River. An increasing amount of immigration was flowing into this part of Alberta, and it was [later] accelerated by the years of depression and drought which came to the prairies in the thirties." The Caravan Sunday School Mission undertaken by Eva Hasell and Iris Sayle, first broke the ground in this mission. They made their initial journey up the Peace River on foot. Miss Hasell appealed to the Diocese of Montreal for help. To the publicity surrounding the heroic efforts of these two women was added the impact of a huge rally at the Montreal Forum held on 6th May 1928, and attended by 12,000 people, at which the Rt Rev. Malcolm Taylor McAdam Harding, Bishop of Qu'Appelle, and the Ven. Robert B. McElheran, Archdeacon of Winnipeg, spoke more generally of the needs and development of the west. The rally was, as Bishop Farthing put it, "a magnificent demonstration of Anglican unity, enthusiasm and strength; and manifested the triumph of modern science. The instalment of amplifiers enabled the vast assembly to join in the singing, to follow the prayers, and to hear every word."

The sparkplugs of the movement, however, were priests: Geoffrey Guiton, Elton Scott and R.K. Naylor, who determined to start summer work immediately until more permanent arrangements could be made. The following item in the July number of the *Montreal Churchman* illustrates the rapidity of the Fellowship's progress:

After seven months of preparation [the article stated] the Fellowship has gone into action by sending out its Missioners.

On June 2nd … Rev. Elton Scott and Mr. William Springer, Rev. Kenneth Naylor and Mr. Selwyn Willis were commissioned in the Cathedral at Evensong by the Dean of Montreal [the Very Rev. Arthur Carlisle], acting for the Bishop of Montreal. … The short service of commission took place after the sermon. …

On Wednesday, June 5th, the Fellowship held a supper in the Herbert Symonds Parish House to send off the Missioners. … About sixty members of the Fellowship attended.

Mr. Scott and Mr. Springer left for Edmonton the same evening. They secured a Ford car and bought necessary equipment in Edmonton and left for the north on July 12th. They spent the following day with Archdeacon Little at Arthabasca and then went on to Grande Prairie, where they arrived on the 15th. From Grande Prairie they will work their way into the Peace River block.

Mr. Naylor and Mr. Willis left for the West on June 25th, and will follow the same route to Arthabasca, and then go north and west to Peace River, and thence to the Whitesand Hills.

In 1930 three teams were sent out: Geoffrey Guiton and Richard Haviland, W. C. Eccleston and Henry T. Holden, and Kenneth Naylor and Mary, his wife of two months. They had been married in St Matthew's Church, Quebec, on April 25th.

As had been the case in the previous year, the first leg of the journey was travelled by train and continued by secondhand car picked up on arrival. Camping supplies and groceries were purchased on the spot. Emergency equipment included a block and tackle and 100 feet of rope. The following excerpts from Naylor's hastily scribbled diary give a lively picture of the varied challenges of this mission field:

*[June] 27 [1930]* Completed shopping, loaded & started for Arthabasca at 3 p.m. Began to rain at Clyd 50 miles north, but we kept on and reached Arthabasca at 10 p.m. Warm welcome from [Archdeacon] Little. Left Little a good part of S[unday] S[chool] supplies from St Matthew['s].

*[June] 28* Left Arthabasca at 3 p.m. for Smith, roads fair but tricky. Slid off road just about where we saw our first trouble last year. Worked two hours and built up a platform & five men came along in a car & helped us out. Ten miles farther on we slid into another ditch. Made camp on good ground. Another car came along & helped us out but we kept to our camp for the night.

*[June] 29* Drove on to Smith ... and then crossed the river by ferry and went in to Moose Portage. Changes in highway made it hard to identify the road. Called at the houses along the trail and arranged for service in the evening. ... We drove into a lake on the road ... and had to be pulled out twice. It affected our gears and they ground badly for the rest of the day. Held service in the evening with 16 present. ...

*[June] 30* Drove back to Smith for gas and then went on to Moose River, visited Grant Knapp and Earnie Roe but missed Petrovitch on account of change of road. ... Last year's camp ground completely covered by water. Road dry but yards filled with water. ...

Road conditions were a constant challenge, and, as visiting with the people in their homesteads seems to have been a priority, much time was spent on unmarked, unmapped roads and trails, with consequent impact on their vehicle.

*[July] 23* Spent the day visiting Alf Thompson ... Left camp at 11, bought gas in Notikewin and asked directions. ... After one wrong turn we were

halted by a morass … were shown a way round and got to Le Foy's. He told us we could go no further … We went back to Notikewin and had lunch and tried again. We could not find a way round an ugly looking muskeg so we put on chains and tackled it in low [gear]. We made it but took a five mile detour to avoid it on the way back. When we got to Thompson's we found we had broken the rear spring again. We had tea with Thompson & helped him get out a few stumps. Called on the Parkers on the way back & had supper at 10.

[July] 24 Packed up … Drove South, stopped at Dixon's for a few minutes and reached Pullins about 6. Got tea ready for the family and camped in the bunkhouse.

[July] 25 Called on Russell's and arranged to baptize the four children on Sunday. Went west as far as Tom Gibbons, first car to make the trip this year, Stuck on one stump and had to build one bridge; lunched on wild strawberries. … Left Mary with Mrs Gibbons and helped Dan Todd pull willow roots. Had tea at Mrs Gibbons and drove back …

[July] 26 Mary took car to Fairview for repair,  We had broken the rear spring twice. Bruce Pullin went with her. I went almost to the highway with them and then went north to Smith's saw mill — six miles from the grade — longest six miles I have ever seen or walked.  Visited Smith, Hughes and Mrs Warden. Prepared part of address for Wednesday. … Called on Hall and Earnie Adams and got home half an hour before Mary who had a very bad road where the roadmakers had been at work. The spring had been pretty badly broken.

[July] 27 Celebration at the Pullins at 8:30 a.m. Took Mary to the Russell's where I baptized the four children. Had lunch with the Pullins and held service in the school — 40 present. Took Earl Pullin and drove to Battle River.  Heavy rain and greasy road. Took trail straight east to Dixon's and nearly got stuck. We picked up three men and took them three miles, then another and took them to Notikewin. Slid off the road 8 miles north of Dixon's and spent an hour getting back with the help of six men. Met Droler, brother of Mrs Baldry of Clear Prairie who recognized me from snapshot taken last year. Reached Notikewin one hour late. Held service … and drove back to camp. …

As the entries show, Naylor got from place to place in all manner of ways, often by himself, while Mary stayed at the camp, herself engaged in visiting locally, or managing car repairs and shopping. He travelled on foot, on horseback, in an acquired democrat — a wagon with several seats and no top — and even by raft.

[August] 6 Celebration ... at 9 a.m.. Only the old people. Drove west to Chester Raspberry's and had very late lunch. Trails changed from last year and very bad in spots. Met Byron Groves trying to drive an old Ford truck to Fairview. Called on 'Windy' Brown at the old Blake place ... Arrived at George Webster's about 9. No one home, so we camped and got supper ready — soup, bacon, prairie chicken. Oregon Jack came by on horseback with a bear skin & part of the bear. He came back later with part of the leg & we had steak.

[August] 7 Breakfast of bacon & bear. Tired of the democrat, decided to walk to Clear Prairie. Carried knapsack with cassock & surplice & communion vessels. ... Took four hours to walk to Wes Morgan's — 13 miles — no water to drink on the way. Went on to Harry Robertson's. They have a wonderful crop of hay, but it rains a little every day and keeps it out. They have built a kitchen. Held communion for Mrs Robertson and Harry Bartholomew. Robertson returned from town before we left. They lent us Harry B. and two horses to go to the Baldry's and we rode half way home. The second half was a long walk. Camped again at Websters. ...

[August] 21 ... Called on Jim Beattie, who lost a leg by amputation last fall, and broke his wrist in Calgary a couple of months ago. Has five children but would not let me baptize them because he had too much religion as a boy. Stayed two hours and got back to Portage at 5:20. Left at 6 and arrived at 8:40 at [Hudson] Hope. Had magnificent supper & then prayers with the Fergussons and walked to the MacDougalls and woke up Mr McD & slept in the bunk house. ... My right foot has rather played out. I wish I could have stayed a few days in [Hudson] Hope.

[August] 22 Slept like a log. Had breakfast with MacDougall. After Mr MacD had got the cows I had celebration at 10 for the two. Then Mr MacD and I went out for logs to make a raft. Built a raft with seven small spruce & poplar logs, two slabs, eight six inch and about as many four inch nails, paddle eight feet long. Left Lynx Creek at 3, passed Tomkins ... at 4 and reached Halfway at 9 and put raft in a very muddy bay.

[August] 23 Slept at Tomkins and had celebration at 7 a.m. for Mrs T., Mr & Mrs Giles. After breakfast held service for children, sent word to Mary to meet me at 4 at Old Fort St John and got started at 9:10. Found water pretty fast at Cache Creek and Deep Creek, but very fast just before the Old Fort.

Got in just before 6. Mary met me ... and reported our car gone to pieces — axle, crown gear, drive pinion, spider, and some of the parts not in yet. Mary had been staying with Nurse Roberts so we had tea there and then came to Hotel.

Naylor made his last entry for that summer's work on 26 August at Peace River where the couple were to take the train on the following day for their return to Montreal. "Turned in car on a car for next year," he wrote, "and got $425." In 1930, Naylor was 45. His commitment to the Fellowship in a variety of capacities would continue actively for more than 25 years.

# Happy New Year? (1931)

During the depths of the Depression the sense of hoplessness about the prevailing economic situation felt by many members of the Montreal clergy and laity seems often to have gone unrecorded. People just tried to muddle through somehow. Now and then, however, a flash of indignation would appear in the Diocesan paper. The following is the *Montreal Churchman's* January Editorial:

"A New Year — A New Age?
"Hope springs eternal in the human breast" and every year we hope that things will be better than in the past. Experience warns us of disappointments in store, but still we start the year with hopes. It were ill for us if we did not.

The past year has seen much that we call disastrous. We have seen a disastrous crash in the stock market, due to the rapid growth of gambling in stocks; a disastrous fall in the price of wheat and most other commodities, due to an over supply; a disastrous curtailment of work in our factories, due to an over production in every line.

There was a time when great numbers of business men would have rejoiced in the lower price of stocks and shares because they would have had an opportunity to invest, but not so now. ...

Very few people rejoice in the reduction in the prices of raw or manufactured foodstuffs and other commodities, because we fancy that it is only when prices are high that the country is prosperous. To-day, as a matter of simple fact, we know that the reduction in the price of grain makes living conditions almost intolerably hard in the Canadian West, and also far harder than usual in the East.

There never have been so many unemployed men and hungry families in Canada as there are to-day, and the same condition is found all over the world. Yet material conditions have never been so good. What does man require for bodily welfare? Food, clothing, housing and fuel.

What are the facts about these things? Wheat, the basic article of food, the raw material of the staff of life, is cheaper to-day than it has been since the Winnipeg grain exchange was opened. And yet we never have had so many men unable to buy food for themselves. Does it seem natural and right? Wool, one of the basic materials of clothing, is so cheap that it is hardly worth while shearing a sheep. Yet we have never had so many men unable to clothe themselves.

Housing and fuel are not affected in the same way, because there is a greater spread between the producer and the consumer; but there are many manufactured articles that are being dumped on the market because there is an over supply, and yet there are more people than ever who are not able to buy.

Almost every day some business man prophesies through the papers the return of prosperity, by which he means a return to the conditions of two or three years ago, high wages, high prices for commodities, and a chance to gamble on the market, with factories running full time.

But there never can be a return of prosperity in the right sense of the word until we adjust ourselves to conditions of modern life. Modern life will never be healthy and Christian and decent till we have solved the problem of unemployment. Every man who will work is entitled to work enough to buy his daily food and maintain his family in some degree of comfort and security.

Our life will be diseased and cancerous as long as we have twenty thousand men, with fifteen thousand families, homeless or hungry or both, while another twenty thousand citizens in the same city carouse their way into the New Year. That, of course, is in itself a small thing, but it is symptomatic of the whole situation.

The city of Montreal has not freed itself from the responsibility by contributing a million dollars to organized charity. Neither has the Dominion of Canada solved its problems by voting twenty or thirty million dollars to relieve the unemployment situation.

There must be sooner or later a revision of the whole of the industrial and economic situation. We can never go back to the day of rapidly expanding trade to meet the need of rapidly expanding markets, for every nation is becoming industrialized and will soon supply its own needs except in specialties. The day when China or even Africa would take up the over production of America is about over. ...

There are not many solutions to the industrial problems. There may be an industrial war in which one group of nations will try to seize the right to provide goods for the rest of the world — fantastic and horrible, but not impossible. There may be such a success of the Russian method that the rest of the world will be compelled to adopt it, and an industrial war is almost sure to follow.

Or there may yet be time for Industry and Business to realize the folly of selfishness and to apply to themselves the principles of Christianity and labour not for the enrichment and luxury of the few, but for the safety and well-being of all.

# Economies (1932)

The Depression brought cutbacks in church work throughout the country:

In order to save expense [the *Montreal Churchman* announced in June 1932] the Provincial Synods of Canada, Rupert's Land and Ontario have been postponed *sine die* [that is, indefinitely]. The three Executives have decided not to call the Board of Management of the M.S.C.C., the General Board of Religious Education, and the Council of Social Service to meet this year. The Primate has decided not to call the Executive Council of the General Synod either. These economies were decided on unanimously in order to save as much expenditure as possible in this year of great depression. The whole Church, we feel sure, will approve most heartily of the action taken.

Earlier in the year, Bishop Farthing announced local measures to conserve diocesan resources:

In order to balance our Diocesan Budget, it was necessary to make economies in our mission work [it was noted in April], and, after consulting with the Deanery of Brome-Shefford, the Bishop has made the following changes, which will be effective for one year, in order to try them out.

1    South Roxton and North Shefford have been attached to Boscobel and North Ely, and will be under the Rev. A.W. Smith.
2    Iron Hill and West Shefford will be made into one parish, under the Rev. Eric Almond.
3    East Farnham and Adamsville will be attached to the Rectory of Dunham, under the Rev. Hubert Coffin, who has self-denyingly consented to try the arrangement for one year.
4    There will be only one Hospital Chaplain, and only one Church Extension Missionary. The latter will be assisted by Students and Lay Readers.

The arrangement in the Deanery of Shefford will effect a saving of $1,220 and one man.

The changes in Montreal will save $4,200 per annum in clerical stipends, but will cost about $600 for students ...

It will be seen that by this arrangement we will [save] approximately $4,820, and there will be three men less in the field. It is not contended that these changes strengthen our work, but they are regarded as necessary temporary changes which, we hope, will not be required for any length of time. These men, especially the two in the city, are required, and should be reappointed as soon as possible.

In his Charge to Synod in June, the Bishop referred to "other economies" that could be effected, but added that he felt he "must not abolish all our smaller parishes by these reorganizations, or else we will have no places in which we can put our older men."

Churches of various denominations contributed to the relief effort in the city. The United Church and the Anglican Church in Montreal each contributed $1,000 toward the establishment of a Rest House in premises contributed free of charge by the Montreal Tramways Company where unemployed men could meet, be kept off the street and maintain morale. The Rev. Geoffrey Guiton was the Anglican representative in this work, and the head of the organizing committee was Dr Frank D. Adams, then a member of Synod. There were other efforts as well:

The Andrews Home has been utilized during the past winter entirely for relief work [the Bishop's Charge announced]. $75.00 a week has been provided from the funds of the Andrews Home augmented by subscriptions from the Central Anglican Churches to assist our Anglican young men and boys. ... The work there is not duplicating but augments the work of the other organizations ...

The central place of relief for the white collar men is not able, having only a small sum weekly allotted, to provide for the relief of all, and the Andrews Home has helped those whom the central organization has referred to them. It has also looked after Anglican young homeless men who are sick (but no one is given sick relief without a medical certificate), and all those under 18 years of age, for it has been felt that the influence of the mixed gathering at Vitre Street — where the general relief for the homeless is given — would not be in the best moral interest of these young boys.

The Anglican Council of Emergency Relief and Social Service, which endeavoured to supply the needs of "those families in the Industrial Parishes who would not normally come upon the regular organized charities," was run and staffed by the women of the church, hardpressed to find sufficient funds to carry on. The Council had been formed at the call of the Bishop in the early twenties and was initially composed of two women-delegates from each central city parish and two associate members from each industrial parish appointed by their respective clergymen. These women collected and distributed clothing, bedding and furnishings, furnished groceries, and made out orders for fuel. Some ran soup kitchens. They visited families to determine their needs, and, in some cases provided "home-made jam, jelly, soap, cough mixture, and dripping."

While all this was going on the Anglican communion throughout the world was marking the centenary of the Oxford Movement. The *Montreal Churchman* ran four laudatory essays on the Movement's contribution to the church, to the extent that Bishop Farthing felt he must devote his December Message to disclaiming any sympathy with the "Roman element" that still existed in the Movement and had recently surfaced in the form of a manifesto issued by fifty clergy active in England:

We are comprehensive, and we have our "Schools of Thought," [he acknowledged sternly], but we all hold the Historic Faith that has been handed down to us from Apostolic times, and we are striving to express that Faith in worship and in life. The expression of it may differ according to the temperament of our people, but we are all, I trust, absolutely loyal to the Anglican tradition, and there is no thought of our working toward reunion with the great Roman Church until that Church by reformation has cleansed herself from those things which the Church of England cannot sanction, and which are contrary to Catholic and primitive practice.

That the annulment of mixed marriages by the Quebec Superior Court (in this case of a Protestant woman and a Roman Catholic man — married by an Anglican priest at St Stephen's Church, Lachine — had been in the news again that summer no doubt had added to the Bishop's desire to correct the *Churchman's* enthusiasm. There was urgency, it appeared, on every front.

# THE
# DUPLESSIS YEARS
# 1933–1959

## St Michael's Mission (1935)

True to its Ritualist origins, the parish of St John the Evangelist, Montreal, had always reached out to the poor and disadvantaged. St Michael's Mission, which continues to form part of its parish work, was opened as a formal mission in 1927, but its roots can be traced to Father Wood and his earliest congregation. The first permanent mission house was located at 127 Dorchester Street West (today Boulevard René-Lévesque) and was placed under the care of the Sisters of St John the Divine. Sister Laura, who took over from Sister Lucina as Sister-in-Charge in 1937 may well have written the following report:

As everyone knows there are two sides to the work at St. Michael's Mission. There is the evangelistic effort: and there is that which for want of a better term we call "social service." It is important, however, that no person should imagine that they are two distinct, separate departments. They are different expressions of the one thing — our belief in the religion of the Incarnation.

It is comparatively easy to report on social service. Statistics can be given. The following is a report of work done from December 1935 to December 1936, which was compiled to accompany an appeal which the Rector [Fr W.H. Davison] sent out before Christmas: …

On the Mission Register there are 15 families, and 420 individuals. The Mission Staff keeps in close touch with all persons on the Register and many others. Individual interviews have averaged 30 per day. Medical treatment has been arranged and paid for in 12 cases; milk has been supplied to 16 families; 165 families have been assisted with food; 47 families supplied with fuel; 21 families assisted to obtain relief through other agencies; 10 families supplied with furniture, stoves, etc.; 72 young men out of employment have been assisted; transportation or assistance to homes or jobs has been provided for 25; 1,080 parcels of clothing have been given out; shoes were repaired for 38 persons; 119 Christmas baskets were distributed. These figures speak for themselves; and no comment is needed, except to add that, in the distribution of relief, our constant aim is ultimately to bring those to whom it is given into the life and fellowship of the Church.

Figures can be given also in connection with our evangelistic endeavour, although of course in a matter of this kind they can never be a true pointer of either success or failure. There are 140 children on the Sunday School Roll: of whom about 70 are in the Primary Department, and 11 in a senior class for girls which meets on Sunday mornings. The Girls' Guild which meets on Thursday has an enrollment of 12. An important branch of the work is the Mothers' Meeting on Wednesdays, which has a registration of 54, with an average attendance of 35. There are also the Sunday Evening Services, at which the capacity of the chapel is severely tested.

It is by no means easy to speak of the love of God to people living, as many of our people have to, in houses which a really Christian public opinion would not tolerate, and with inadequate food, fuel and clothing; but it is done, and there are signs that it is not altogether in vain. Every year a number of adults and children come forward for Confirmation; and a small, but on the whole faithful number are finding their way to Communion at the Altars of the Parish Church.

We thank all our kind helpers, both within and without the Congregation, for their continued interest in our work and their generous support.

The Sisters continued to operate the mission until the heyday of slum clearance when the city of Montreal expropriated their property. "It was required," as one historian puts it, "for civic improvement, space for luxury motor cars and luxury buildings. In this way, the present affluent society seeks to obliterate the squalor that is at its base."

The present St Michael's Mission is housed adjacent to St John's. The Annual Report for 1996 reflects its continuing vocation. Only the language has changed:

Last year St Michael's Mission received a much needed face-lift. Major renovations were completed at a cost of over $240,000. Improvements were made throughout the Mission. ... We now have an entirely new set-up including a much needed commercial kitchen and a fantastic washroom.

The attitude within the Mission has changed. Clients seem to feel some investment in the Centre. Low self-esteem and low self-worth are common problems facing the poor and destitute. I believe the positive and comfortable environment of the Mission helps these people. "The Red Roof," as we are known on the street, is home to many of our regular clients. We are a much needed and very dependable resource. Our numbers are still high. We serve between 90 to 120 individuals every day, five days a week.

# The Padlock Law (1937)

Premier Maurice Duplessis's first three years in office put the stamp of his autonomist, nationalistic, and staunchly conservative style on Quebec politics, and few, if any, would suggest that a concern for basic human rights was one of his priorities.

In 1937, "urged on by many among his own people and by strong pressure, it may be assumed, from certain circles in the [Roman Catholic] church, and nothing loath himself," Duplessis enacted the notorious 'Padlock Law' under which the Attorney-General could, without court action, close for one year the premises of anyone suspected of using them to propagate communism.

Although it has been suggested by noted Canadian historian A.R.M. Lower that "few of the English people of the province showed concern," and that "the satisfaction of 'business' and its satellites in seeing 'Communists' persecuted exceeded solicitude over abstract questions of liberty," it is clear that the *Montreal Churchman* spoke out unequivocally against these measures:

We do not often comment on a situation that is purely political [states the April editorial in 1937] … There are times, however, when political measures affect life as a whole so closely that to avoid comment would be a neglect of duty. The present seems to be such an occasion.

The Quebec Government has rushed through a bill designed to curb the spread of Communism in the province. Special legislation aimed at a particular group is generally bad legislation, and this is a particularly bad specimen of the whole class.

We wish to make it perfectly clear that we loathe Communism. The only worse form of political and social organization is Fascism. But while we are as strongly opposed to Communism as Mr. Duplessis, we are convinced that he has added to our statutes a law which will prove a greater danger than any Communism which can develop in this province.

In the first place there was no need for the haste which the Premier displayed. The bill appeared on March 17 and passed the Lower House on the following day, without any time for public comment. Six days later it passed the Council, three readings in one day.

A very objectionable feature of the bill is that it fails to define the evil at

# Old Fashioned
# Garden Fete

## *StanbridgeEast*
## *Parish Lawn*

# Thursday, July 22, $\frac{1}{3}\frac{9}{7}$

6.00 p. m. D.S.T.

## PROGRAMME

### SUPPER

**GAMES** | Guessing Contests
Popularity Contest
Racing, etc.

**MELODRAMA** | "Love Triumphs Over Fate"
CAST:
Horatio, the Hero.....................T. BROWN
Belinda, the Ingenue..........MISS J. BULLARD
Father, the Keeper of the Lighthouse..G. BULLARD
The Villain, (Sylvester Bullit)..........J. CHEEK

**COMMUNITY SINGING** ---- Old Fashioned Songs

**DANCING** -- G.Cochrane and a StringOrchestra

In case of bad weather the Fete will be postponed to the following Saturday

General Admission to Grounds 10 cts.

Supper 25 cts. - Dancing Free

PLATE 13 *Advertisement for a local parish fête*

which it aims. Both in the Lower and Upper Houses the Government leaders were asked to define Communism and they declined. The Premier declared that there would be little difficulty in making decisions, for Communism could be felt, and it would not be advisable to have a definition. ...

An equally objectionable feature is that action lies with one man — the Attorney-General — who has already shown himself prejudiced. ...

Worse still, when action is initiated and the case comes before a judge of the Superior Court the burden of proof rests on the accused. He must show that his house was not used for propaganda purposes. ... [T]he owner has no recourse in law to secure damages. Nor has he any appeal against the decision.

If the unquestioned rule of one man is dictatorship, then we have travelled a long way towards dictatorship in Quebec in the last month.

A disquieting feature of the whole situation is that the Premier can see only one danger. When he was asked to include Fascism as well as Communism in this drastic 'padlock' law he refused, on the ground that there was no danger of Fascism in Quebec, for the people have had a parliamentary system which they would maintain. Curious, that democracy can resist Fascism but not Communism! It has not proved so in Germany and Italy.

The editorial also acknowledged its distress that both parties, and English as well as French-speaking members, had failed to voice their opposition when it came to a vote:

An amazing feature of the passage of this law [the editorial concluded] was the fact that while many members objected in the course of the debate, not one voted against it. It is a strange thing to see French-Canadian Liberals forgetting the whole of their Liberal tradition, and English Conservatives equally careless of the inestimable privilege of British freedom of speech without a struggle to the imposition of dictatorship.

It is hard to imagine an editorial in a similar paper speaking out more fearlessly over a breach of human rights by government some sixty-odd years later.

## War Again (1939)

On 31 August 1939, at 10:24 a.m. — "right on time" — the Rev. David Victor Warner pulled into Montreal following an interval away from home. It was fine and warm all day, as he noted in his diary; the temperature in the city in the early afternoon was 87°.

Warner, who was a Nova Scotian by birth, had come to Montreal as an assistant to the rector of St Matthias' Church in Westmount after serving overseas with the First Canadian Contingent in World War I. By this time, besides his theological training, he had received a Master's Degree in Political Science from Columbia University, New York, had published, *The Church and Modern Socialism* — "a treatise which aroused considerable favourable comment" — had taken a special course in psychology and philosophy at the University of London following the war, and, in recognition of his wartime services, had been awarded the Order of the British Empire.

Warner had seen action in Flanders and France before being posted to England for two years as senior chaplain to the Canadian forces in the London area. After the Armistice, he was appointed Senior Chaplain to the Canadian Forces, succeeding Col. Canon John McPherson Almond, also of Montreal.

In 1922 he took up his duties as rector of St Cyprian's, Montreal, which was still under construction at the time.

Warner's diary — which by the time of his death ran to at least 36 volumes — is both detailed and succinct. He lists purchases, expenses, appointments, things accomplished, and usually comments on the weather. He notes the time he rose and breakfasted, and the time he retired for the night, but does not indulge in long meditations or descriptions. His observations on the news and world events are terse, but reveal his deepening concern nonetheless. His entry for August 31 concludes:

[W]as home [after errands, shopping, and calls] at about 10:55 p.m. War news at 11 p.m. Looks more like war than at any time since August 1st 1914 [the day Germany had declared war on Russia]. Poland stands firm against Germany & Russia & Italy. G[reat] B[ritain] & France support her. God knows what will happen next.

It was Warner's habit to rise at 6 or 7 a.m., read the *Gazette* before beginning the day's activities, and listen to the news before he went to bed. On 2 September, for example, he wrote

Radio News 11 p.m.. Bed about 11:45 p.m. GB and France have not yet actually declared war but may do so within 48 hours. Or it may come about by lapse of time as happened in 1914. God help us.

The next day he noted simply:

War declared against Germany by GB and France to-day. Chamberlain, King George and Roosevelt spoke.

There is no doubt where Warner stood about the war. On 7 September, for example, he writes:

Hitler may propose separate peace with Poland, but that will not stop the war. He must be wiped out, and all his gang.

Still, the life of the parish went on. Warner was planning a boys' Bible Class and had collected the names of 70 or so, whose families he planned to visit in order to encourage the boys to attend.

He was, moreover, in the midst of collecting for the Golden Jubilee Fund, and canvassing potential donors by mail. On 12 September, he notes in his diary that he had that day addressed 300 envelopes "most of them before lunch. It was a moderately good start."

Warner was no stranger to such campaigns. In the mid 1920s he had been successful in raising $10,000 for the Children's Memorial Jubilee Chimes at St Cyprian's, formally dedicated in December 1927 to mark the 60th anniversary of Confederation.

On Sunday, 10 September he recorded that there were 18 present at early Communion at 8 a.m., and that the collection was "$1.30 plus a few envelopes." Of the 51 families he had visited the previous week, only eight appeared for Bible Study. The 11 a.m. service was more cheering, with a congregation of about 110. His text for the sermon was taken from Exodus 14:14, "The Lord will fight for you."

In 1939 Warner was 60 years old, so there was no question of his leaving St Cyprian's and his position of Rural Dean of Montreal East to serve his country a second time. His Bishop, however, summoned him to a meeting on 11 September for war work at home:

… to Synod Office. Meeting of ex-chaplains and others under direction of Almond — first meeting of a series probably, at 2:30 p.m. Some 17 or 18 men there. Com[mittee] to be appt by Bp, to consist of Almond, Gower-Rees & myself.

Arthur Carlisle, who, following Bishop Farthing's resignation and the convocation of an electoral synod, had been consecrated bishop in April of that year, had himself served overseas as chaplain to the 18th Battalion of the 4th Infantry Brigade, Canadian Expeditionary Force. He had kept up his military connection after the war and, as chaplain to the Canadian

Grenadier Guards in Montreal, frequently officiated at military church parades and other functions. Until his early death in 1943 he was a steadfast supporter of the war effort on the homefront.

Almond called Warner the day following their meeting about preparatory work for the Chaplains' Department.

By 15 September, in spite of other duties, Warner had addressed 996 campaign letters and purchased an even 1000 one cent stamps to mail them. Six young people came that evening to help prepare the envelopes, and worked until after midnight. "Glad to have their fine help, as I hadn't time to do the work alone."

This was a time, too, of many weddings — two on Saturday, 9 September. After he had returned home from performing a marriage ceremony on the afternoon of 16 September, he was called upon by a second couple:

Bessie M— and a young officer came in re Marriage. Asked them to see me early next week. No time to-day. They may go elsewhere. I am not keen on the case anyway. Both are mere kids.

This was, of course, just the beginning of a very long haul. Warner remained at his post at St Cyprian's until his retirement in 1945. He continued, too, as Rural Dean until 1942 in which year he was appointed a canon of Christ Church Cathedral.

In a tribute in the *Montreal Star*, on 15 September 1949 at the time of his death, it was noted that, when he took up his first post at St Matthias, Warner had

brought to his position 'unique experience, unusual executive powers, and a gifted mind. In theology he is said to be a broad churchman of wide sympathies and constructive mind. His coming to Montreal is considered a distinct acquisition to the Diocese.'

St Cyprian's closed in 1986.

# Financial Crunch (1941)

The Anglican church in Montreal has had a long history of assistance from abroad for the support of its clergy, and, in the same spirit, has in turn extended its ministry into newly settled regions beyond its borders.

Such organizations as the Fellowship of the West served this end. Much of the work, however, continued to be funded by the old missionary societies overseas. The war necessarily changed all this. Suddenly the Canadian dioceses found themselves morally bound to step in and replace these missionary grants with funds of their own. Although frail in health — he would suffer a heart attack during the course of the year — Bishop Carlisle worked manfully and persistently to meet these obligations on behalf of his diocese. Throughout 1941, his monthly "Bishop's Message" in the *Montreal Churchman* reiterated the urgency of the situation — virtually to the exclusion of all but perfunctory reference to the Canadian war effort or to servicemen and women overseas. The November issue carried the following example of his efforts:

My dear friends,

The very special prominence which has been given to our missionary effort this year by reason of the critical nature of the situation in our own Diocese, and also the very special effort which is being put forth as a result of the relinquishing of English grants [that is, grants from missionary organizations in Britain], is my excuse for bringing this matter once again to the attention of all readers of "The Montreal Churchman."

It is not necessary for me to go over all the ground once more. By this time everyone in our Diocese ought to know something at least of the urgency of the present situation. The Diocese of Montreal must pay its way, that is, it must balance its budget. We cannot keep on drawing from capital funds without very serious consequences.

We are all most anxious that the stipends of our missionary clergy shall not be reduced; in fact most of us feel that with the increased cost of living and the special war taxes, they ought to be increased. To maintain them at their present level, it is absolutely essential that our missionary receipts should be considerably higher than they ever have been.

Every right-minded churchman must feel that it is our duty to bear our share of the increased burden laid upon the whole Church in consequence of our relinquishing of the block grants made by the English Societies for so many years to our Western dioceses. $60,000 of our 1941 contributions, and a similar amount from our contributions in subsequent years, must be allocated to take the place of the very generous grants received from overseas.

Everyone has hailed this determination on the part of our Canadian Church. Most of us feel that it is a step which ought to have been taken long ago out of gratitude for all that the churchmen of the Old Land have done for us, and as an extension of our sympathy with them and pride in them in bearing heroically the burden of war. Surely every one of us will want to do his share in making up this additional amount required for our Western missionary areas.

Carlisle's first message of the new year had made clear that the $60,000 burden was to be divided among financially independent dioceses throughout Canada. For the Diocese of Montreal it would mean raising $42,777.77 for extra-Diocesan work (which included projects other than missionary work in the West) — this amounted to $12,000 more than had been collected in 1939. The actual Diocesan budget was to rise from $60,000 to $84,000.

Since its formation in 1885, the Woman's Auxiliary had turned its considerable energies to the support of missionary work of all kinds. It is not surprising that Carlisle's next appeal was to Anglican women. In February, his "Message" was urgent and direct:

On Wednesday, February 5th and following days [he wrote], there will be held the Annual Meetings of the Montreal Diocesan Woman's Auxiliary. These meetings will open with a Public Service and Corporate Communion in the Cathedral at half past ten on Wednesday morning. They will consider all phases of the present-day missionary problem and responsibility, and particularly that part which has been so generously assumed and so efficiently administered by the Woman's Auxiliary.

In view of the present national crisis and the new financial objective of the Canadian Church for its missionary endeavours, these meetings are bound to be of very great importance. I cannot help feeling that the spirit generated by them may have a lot to do with the success of our diocesan effort for this year.

I have, therefore, issued an appeal through the Presidents of the various Branches to do all that they can to make these gatherings memorable ones. I have particularly requested that an invitation be sent to all the women of our Churches to be present in a spirit of faith and devotion at the Opening Service, and to make it one of Witness, Thanksgiving, Intercession and Dedication.

The oft-proved enthusiasm of Auxiliary members, backed up by the prayers and efforts of the rest of us, ought to have a very helpful effect upon all our Christian service.

It was not often that the crucial contribution to the church made by women was as publicly and as handsomely acknowledged.

Conditions in Canada, as well as pressures (due to the war) on the overseas missionary societies, had depleted Diocesan funds. As the Bishop's January message had made clear:

Owing to a decline in interest rates, our income from endowments has been steadily declining also. The result has been that we have had to draw on reserve funds to balance our Diocesan Budget for the past five years. That reserve is now almost exhausted, and if we are to pay our way in the Diocese we shall have to get a substantial increase in Diocesan Missionary contributions from our people.

We are making a very serious effort to reduce our Diocesan Missionary needs. Earnest appeals are being made to all our Mission congregations (and every possible pressure put upon them) with a view to securing at least a 25% increase in their stipend Guarantees as well as a small increase in their missionary contributions. ...

Population shifts and the exodus from many of the rural areas of much of the English-speaking population had been a factor in placing churches on the mission rolls.

"The Lenten Pastoral" in March refers to the many "beautiful little churches in our own diocese erected at the cost of great sacrifice in districts where the English-speaking population is now declining" that "would have been closed long ago, had it not been for the generous missionary spirit of our people."

He points, at the same time, to the continuing needs of "thousands of our fellow-Canadians in the Western part of our land" who "would have been without the ministrations of the Church" without missionary support — through Montreal funds and Montreal manpower.

Then came news of nation-wide price control "to save the people of Canada from the evils of inflation and high prices," and the Primate's statement that "we should endeavour, through the clergy and laity, to help in every way we can to make this new effort work smoothly."

When the diocesan books closed at the end of the year, Carlisle directed that the following letter, reporting on "the outcome of our Missionary effort for the year 1941" be read from the pulpit by the clergy to each of their congregations:

My dear Friends,

It is with a very full heart that I write to tell you what we have been able to accomplish with respect to our missionary task during the past year. In January last we asked the Diocese to contribute $86,000.00 towards our general Missionary Budget. We received on this account just over $83,000.00. This has enabled us to pay our apportionments to M.S.C.C., G.B.R.E., and the Council for Social Service in full (a thing that we have never done before) and to meet all our Diocesan obligations with a deficit of less than $500.00. The loyal co-operation of the clergy in presenting our needs to their people and the splendid response of our congregations, which has sometimes meant great effort and great sacrifice, have combined to make this remarkable achievement possible, and I want to thank you all from the bottom of my heart for the part that you have played and the support that you have given to this very necessary work.

I feel that what we have been able to do is so wonderful that we ought not to fail to lift up our hearts to God in praise and thanksgiving for His grace and help in achieving this end. I am therefore asking that Sunday, February 8th, be marked by special thanksgivings to God for all His mercies and particularly for what He has done for our Diocese, and by special prayers for a continuance of His help and blessing on all our efforts.

Local matters paled in the context of the international situation, however. With the bombing of Pearl Harbour in December, the war had entered a new phase. Carlisle's message for the new year following, reflects the nation's sombre mood:

The dawning of the year 1942 [he wrote] is marked by the most widespread chaos and confusion that we have ever known. There seems to be hardly a part of the world which is not now involved in this tremendous struggle, the issues of which are of such great importance to us, to our civilization, and to our Christian way of life. The most recent happenings in the Far East have brought the threat of attack by sea and air more closely to our shores. This will probably arouse the citizens of our two great North American countries to a new sense of their dangers and a new resolve to throw themselves wholeheartedly into the conflict, whatever the cost may be.

One can only hope that amidst the excitement of organizing for war men will not forget that the greatest bulwark of any nation is the character of its people, and the one source of real strength there is religion. Never was the church more needed than it is today. Never was the Church's function more clear and definite than it is now. Amidst all the other things that may be demanded and expected of us, let us strive always to remember how necessary the Church is, and how much it depends for its effectiveness in these days upon the kind of support and help that we can give it. Stand by the church to which you belong, support it by your presence, your help and your generous offerings, aid it in all its endeavours on behalf of children, the under-privileged and the Christless everywhere.

Whatever else the present war situation may mean, it certainly is a call to all of us to a new faith in God and new loyalty to His Church.

May I conclude by extending to you all my most earnest wishes for a happy, prosperous, and peaceful New Year.

# Chaplains Overseas (1942)

During the war, the opening phrase, 'This is London calling North America,' became a familiar one to radio listeners anxious for overseas news. The BBC also issued a printed overseas journal entitled *London Calling*, containing commentary and background on broadcasts thought to be of particular interest. The following article comes from that journal, and was reprinted in the August issue of the *Montreal Churchman* in 1943.

On Easter Sunday a BBC recording car visited the village of South Merstham, in Surrey, where a very touching ceremony was taking place. This was the dedication of the new church of All Saints, which was to take the place of the old parish church destroyed by German bombs. It was a significant occasion, for the entire building of this new church was the voluntary work of eighteen Canadian sappers.

Two and a half years ago [in 1941], a private serving in a field ambulance unit of the Royal Canadian Army Medical Corps arrived at the old church to find that it had just been completely destroyed by bombs. The Vicar's sister had been killed and the Vicar himself sent to hospital for six months.

The private's name was Hedley Wolfendale. Only after he had signed up did he reveal the fact that he was the Reverend Hedley Wolfendale, an Anglican clergyman. There was a waiting list for chaplains, so he volunteered as an ordinary soldier. ...

When his ambulance unit arrived in the village, South Merstham had no church and no vicar. So Private Wolfendale took on the parish in the intervals of soldiering. His commanding officer helped, and so did his comrades; they did some work so that he could get away on Sundays.

Once he was due for guard duty and at the same time due to conduct a Sunday service. He worked all day cleaning his equipment and managed to be chosen as 'stick man,' the smartest man on guard. That exempted him from duty. He uses the incident as a text to prove that besides having faith, you must work if you want results.

But this was not enough for Wolfendale. He had a plan for rebuilding South Merstham church, a beautiful and unconventional plan.

When he got his commission [once appointed to the chaplaincy, in 1942, Wolfendale was promoted captain] he began to agitate for funds for the church. The army hesitated to give permission; it might seem like intruding on an English domestic matter. For this padre wanted more than funds; he wanted Canadian soldiers to rebuild that church with their own hands.

Eventually, after the big manoeuvres held last March, the OK was given and the Royal Canadian Engineers, of whom Wolfendale was now padre, started work. In five weeks, with only eighteen men working on it in their precious spare time, that little church was rebuilt by loving, willing, and expert labour.

Padre Wolfendale told some of the story in a recent BBC broadcast [presumably also using recorded material made at the time of the dedication].

Speaking to his 'men' he said: "Five weeks ago, you remember, we gathered together just on this spot here, and I told you what you were up against, and what you were going to do. I said, here's an opportunity to do something which will be lasting, something which will live long afterwards. And I asked you all to bear in mind that you were building a church, and you all have done. Only in the barber's shop last night they said: "My, I don't know how it is, but all those chaps are so keen about this job you'd think it was their own church in their own town they were building." Well, that's a marvellous spirit, and I want to say just one thing more to you: that you just pass by once. Well, you have passed by once, and you've done your job. It's the finest thing that anyone could do, to have the opportunity of building a church."

The article goes on to discuss the complexity of the task as well as the technical problems surmounted in accomplishing it. The men had not merely replaced the church, but truly reconstructed it:

Technically, this resurrecting of a church from its ruins in a mere five weeks was a wonderful piece of work. All the material, except cement and sand, was salvaged from the wreckage of the old All Saints'. The salvaging itself was a tremendous labour; piecing together window frames and bits of shattered glass, restoring damaged panelling and doorways, removing the scars of enemy action from the church furniture. Bricklayers and plasterers worked at top speed (they laid eight hundred bricks a day!); carpenters did a tremendous job; painters completed their task in six days and used a good deal of paint and a lot more elbow grease.

All Saints' where the Canadian and British flags now hang together by the altar, is a symbol and an inspiration.

The Bishop of Southwark, when the church was appropriately dedicated on the Feast of the Resurrection, aptly compared it with the altar built by the three tribes on the other side of the river they had crossed. "Because they thought the river was a barrier between themselves and the tribes they had left, they built an altar on the river brink in order that future generations might understand that, whichever side of the river they were on, the altar was the testimony of a common faith. ... This church, this spontaneous gift ... is going to stand for generations, I hope, as a symbol of the link between our two peoples."

Indeed the bond between Montreal Anglicans and the people of Great Britain, if such things can be reflected in enlistment figures, was a strong one.Honour rolls in churches throughout the Diocese attest to it as well. The handsome brass tablet in St George's Church, Granby, said to be the first honour roll in the Diocese to be dedicated by the Bishop to those who served in World War II, contained ninety-two names from the parish:

The Rev. I.M. Lidstone, who presided, remarked that of the 92 names on the tablet, 3 were killed, 4 were mentioned in dispatches, and 2 received the D.F.C. [Distinguished Flying Cross]. There were five brothers from one family and a father and three sons from another.

Of the eight men who formed the procession at St George's, five had served as chaplains overseas and two were war veterans. Of these, two had recently received decorations: Major the Rev. Harry Andrews was on the King's 1945 Honours List and made a member of the Order of the British Empire. Also in December, the Netherlands conferred the Order of Orange-Nassau with Swords upon Major the Rev. Gordon R. Addie for his part in the action at Bergen op Zoom during which he had repeatedly retrieved wounded men by wading into a marsh under enemy fire, saving many of them from drowning.

Captain the Rev. Hedley Wolfendale was also on the King's Honours List — in December 1944 — as a Member of the British Empire "for outstanding service." It was not until after the war that it was learned that this honour had been posthumously awarded. As it was reported in the September issue of the *Churchman*:

It is with deep regret that we have to record the death of Capt. Wolfendale, one of the outstanding younger priests of this Diocese. It was only after the defeat of Germany that all the records of "Prisoners of War" fell into our hands and it is recorded that — "Capt. Wolfendale was taken prisoner in May 1944 severely wounded, and that he died in a German Hospital in June 1944." No information is available at this time as to the date of his passing or where he is buried.

George Hedley Wolfendale was educated at Diocesan Theological College and elevated to the diaconate by Bishop Farthing in 1931. His first appointment was as Rector of Fort St John in the Peace River, under the auspices of the Fellowship of the West, and he was ordained to the priesthood by the Bishop of Caledonia. When he returned to the

Diocese of Montreal in 1935 he was first appointed incumbent of Arundel and later of Aylwyn. He joined the Royal Canadian Army Medical Corps on 15 November 1939.

## A Voice Against Discrimination (1944)

Over the years the Church had has a rather mixed record in speaking out on human rights, especially in politically sensitive times. An opportunity to take a stand arose at a meeting of the Executive Council of General Synod in September 1944, held in Ste-Anne-de-Bellevue at the western tip of the Island of Montreal.

Describing the proceedings in the *Montreal Churchman*, the Rev. S.L. Pollard — who was well-known for his outspokenness on matters of social and political concern — reported on a number of issues under discussion at the various sessions. Of particular interest is one concerned with measures taken by some Canadian institutions against citizens of a particular ethnic origin:

Wide support was given to an immediate problem in social justice [Pollard wrote] — the disfranchisement of loyal Canadian citizens of Japanese origin.

The Archbishop of Kootenay, the Right Reverend W.R. Adams appealed for generosity of treatment to the loyal Japanese Canadians, and was well supported in his resolution on this point.

The Archbishop would have been in a better position to know the extent of this discriminatory treatment than would many Eastern members of the Executive Council since the vast majority of Japanese-Canadians lived on Canada's West Coast. By 1944 most of them had been removed from their homes, and many had been living in internment camps for two years.

There were other forms of restrictions for those with freedom of movement. Pollard's account continues:

The Reverend Canon P.[S.]C. Powles pointed out that some institutions of learning had been closed to Japanese students who had attempted to enroll.

Canon Powles was a knowledgeable spokesman; he had served as an MSCC missionary at Takata, Mid-Japan from 1916 to 1941, but was forced to return to Canada during the War. He was currently Immigration Chaplain in Montreal. In 1948 he would return to the Far East where he would be consecrated Assistant Bishop of Mid-Japan.

Although the Archbishop of Kootenay's appeal on behalf of a disenfranchised ethnic minority may well have been "well supported," and Canon Powles' remarks about "some institutions" quite pointed, the resolution arising from the discussion was lukewarm indeed. No target group was mentioned; no institution was specified:

Thereupon [the article continues], a resolution was passed expressing "the hope that institutions of learning which share with the church great traditions of freedom, continue to open their doors to the public of all races."

A few weeks later the opportunity presented itself for another group in the Diocese to speak out against such discriminatory action. The occasion was the Annual Meeting of Alumni of Montreal Diocesan Theological College. The following item appeared on the editorial page of the *Churchman*, also in the October issue, under an uncompromising heading:

RESOLUTION CONDEMNING ACTION OF THE SENATE OF MCGILL UNIVERSITY — BARRING JAPANESE OF CANADIAN BIRTH — PASSED AT ALUMNI MEETING OF DIOCESAN COLLEGE

During the Annual Meeting of the Diocesan College Alumni held on Oct. 19th and 20th in the Synod Building the following resolution was proposed by the Rev. N.E. Peterson, B.A., L.Th. (arts 1920 McGill), seconded by the Rev. S.L. Pollard, M.A., L.Th. (arts 1929) and passed unanimously — "This Annual Meeting of the Montreal Diocesan Theological College Alumni Assn, many of whose officers enjoy the privileges of McGill University, and as graduates take a pride in their Alma Mater, view with serious concern the decision of the Senate of McGill University to exclude from study Canadian Students of Japanese origin who after matriculation wish to pursue regular studies at McGill."

This resolution was forwarded to the Board of Governors and Senate of McGill University.

As the Diocesan Theological College had been affiliated in one way or another with McGill University since 1880 this protest was a bold one.

# Conference on Post-War Problems (1944)

Although the War was far from over, there was great concern about returning servicemen and women in the Diocese and how they would view the society they had left behind when they finally came home.

A conference to discuss the question was organized by the Bishop's Committee on a Christian Social Order — a branch of a committee of the national Church — and held in Montreal on the 7th, 8th and 9th November 1944. Canon W.H. Davison was committee chairman and handled the planning, but the event itself was led by the Rev. Joseph B. Fletcher, Professor of Practical Theology and Social Studies at the Episcopal Theological School, Harvard University.

The meetings were held in the Synod Hall and the Montreal High School. According to an editorial in the *Montreal Churchman*, staging the conference was "rather a bold venture for even a Bishop's Committee as the agenda called for nine lengthy meetings in three days." It was bold, too, in being (according to the General Secretary of the Council of Social Service) "a gathering unique in the annals of this Diocese — in fact … the first of its kind in the whole of the Canadian Church."

A summary of the conference, "written specially for the *Montreal Churchman* by the Findings Committee of the Bishop's Committee on a Christian Social Order," appeared in the December issue under the title:

THE MONTREAL DIOCESAN CONFERENCE ON THE FIRST POST-WAR PROBLEM

THE CHURCH'S WELCOME TO RETURNING SERVICEMEN AND WOMEN

The account of proceedings is of particular interest not only for the scope and breadth of the conference, but also for the social and political attitudes implicit in it.

The Anglican Church in this old-fashioned Diocese of Montreal has set the lead and the pace for the Church of Christ in Canada. We ought to offer a 'Te Deum' and a prayer that having put our hand to the plough we may never turn back.

AN EXPERIMENT IN SOCIAL FELLOWSHIP

It was a great experiment in social fellowship with 79 [of a possible 105] parishes officially represented at the Conference … from these parishes, 239 lay representatives registered, and 89 clergy.

It was an experiment in the practical expression of the brotherhood we preach about in that all expenses were shared equally by the parishes, thus enabling distant places like Noranda and Campbell's Bay to have a full lay representation present (which probably never occurs at any synod of the diocese as so many country congregations have to be represented by prominent city churchmen).

The serving of buffet suppers both to the clergy and the lay people in the Herbert Symonds Parish House also served to break down reserve and barriers, and to make for greater fellowship among the delegates — to which may be coupled the generous offers of hospitality from our city church people to our country delegates.

It was also unique in that women were invited as delegates — not to represent some organization — but as representative parishioners whose voices were of equal value with those of menfolk in a diocesan gathering of the Church. [Women would have to wait more than twenty years to be admitted as delegates to Diocesan Synod. They first took their seats at the 107th Synod, held in 1966] ...

### Free Discussion on Vital Issues

No doubt a contributing factor to the general feeling of the Conference was that people could come together to raise and discuss the vital issues of the day under the leadership of the Church. The people must be allowed to express themselves and to decide on which side they will range themselves in the tremendous issues that face the world in these days — and to do so in the light of Christian teaching and judgment. This Conference was undoubtedly helpful in clarifying the real issues that we have to meet as Christians in an unredeemed world order.

### Representative Types of Speakers

The Conference also showed what could be done in bringing together such a wide array of speakers who were 'representative types.' We had the armed services, the chaplaincy, the medical profession, the parish priest, the farmer, industry, finance, management and labour — all represented under the missionary, educational and social service aspects of the Church's work.

We were able to hear questions discussed from all sides — to notice how people overcome the personal angle and discuss the broad underlying issues. The problems of the rural community became the problems of the town, and vice versa. People realized how closely we are interrelated, and yet found out how things divide us!

### Returning Men Not the Problem — Problem Is Ours and the Community's

The general consensus of opinion in the Conference about the welcome to returning servicemen and women appeared to be that the problem is ours and the community's.

The big task that confronts us all is to make the kind of society that will avoid such wars in the future and that will not be based on competitive trade wars that go on in the days of so-called peace. ... The really big job is to remould society, not just to put patches on an old garment — our Lord said this latter will not do. The Church has its duties both on the pastoral and prophetic sides — but at present it is so inadequately equipped that it has slipped into the eddies and side-streams of human life. Unfortunately it is still the hope of some people that it may remain aloof from the relevant human situation and confine itself to being a refuge.

## Vital Questions

A number of vital questions were raised — we hope not to be lightly forgotten — ... How the returning servicemen and women feel towards the community they left behind — the medical and pastoral approach to them: the importance of holding on to our work in the rural community, even though it does not pay dividends in the accepted sense: the need of adequate pastoral care in so many of our large city parishes: the division between industrial enterprise and labour, between finance and needs: the banker and his 'sound money' theories in a century of deficit spending: the great problem of 'full employment' as it is euphemistically called — these are just a few of the questions raised.

With all the criteria of social decay evident around us in a pagan world, our basic problem is can we win the peace — can we make a world fit for our men to return to, for they will be interested in performance and not in words —

## Can We Win the Peace?

There are many individual problems, there are many irrelevancies — but underneath it all there is this realization that there can hardly be any comparison between the pre-war and the post-war world — returning men and women will be different as a result of the experiences they have gone through ... They will come back into a world of growing irrelevancy of the human personality to modern industrial capitalism. There is a great danger that we at home may experience moral fatigue as men have experienced battle fatigue. ... Twenty-five years ago we failed to win the peace — are we going to repeat our mistakes of yesteryear?

## The Christian Problem

Our Christian problem is the relationship between theory and practice, between belief and action. If psychology tells us anything, it teaches us that these two are not separate, nor even separable. ... Belief has no claims until it is translated into operational terms ... The weakness of the Church today is that what we do speaks so loud that what we say cannot be heard. ...

## The Choice Before Us

With regard to the immediate post-war world and the return of men and women from serving in His Majesty's Forces, there is a choice before the world — and the Church cannot stand aloof. We may strive to return to the status quo ante bellum ... we may adopt a fascist structure, which we are defeating militarily but may yet succumb to here at home: we may adopt a planned economy in the interests of the people and through the people's representatives ...

These are great days of opportunity, great days in which to be alive if we will only rid ourselves of our inhibitions and fears. The Church, cooperatively and individually, prophetically and pastorally, has an opportunity to do — not merely to say — the right thing within the next few years that may never recur in a disintegrating Western Society in five hundred years.

Implicit throughout this summary of proceedings is the desire to transform the existing social order. 'The choice' offered, a thinly veiled call for Social Democracy, was very much in tune with the deep sense of commitment to justice issues that had surfaced elsewhere in the Diocese — in the formation of the Arundel Group — and in the sympathies of recently elected Bishop Dixon.

# A Portable Altar (1945)

The brief account — in the February issue of the *Montreal Churchman* — of the dedication of a new altar at the Ste Agathe sanatorium in the Laurentians seems, at first glance, hardly worthy of more than passing note. This particular altar was portable, however — a rather ingenious device invented and used by one of the Diocesan clergy.

A picture of such an altar, both assembled and folded up, had appeared in the May issue of the *Montreal Churchman*. The inventor was not identified by name, but parishioners in the Ottawa valley and the Laurentians would easily have recognized the Rev. Edward Geoffrey May standing beside it, for he had laboured among them for many years. The altar was fully described and offered for sale for a modest charge through the *Churchman* office.

The sanatorium did not buy the "ready made kit of altar, case and one set of hangings," however. The inventor-priest had allowed the use of his plans for what appears to have been a happy collaborative effort between patients and staff:

A new altar, designed by Rev. E. Geoffrey May, of Trinity Church, Ste. Agathe des Monts, for use at services held in other than church buildings, has been built through the co-operation of staff and patients at the Royal Edward Laurentian Hospital at Ste. Agathe. The materials were supplied by the hospital and purchased from contributions made by the patients, one of whom, Fred Riley, assisted by Fred West of the hospital staff, [was able] to build the altar. Mrs. N. Orr, also of the hospital staff, made the white hangings of rayon silk.

When in use for service, the altar has a width of about eight feet. The front is ornamented with a gilt Canterbury cross, behind which hangs the white frontal ... a three-panelled reredos forming the back. ... When not in use, the altar may be folded up.

The altar is for use in the services of all denominations and stands in the assembly room of the hospital. It was used for the first time at the Communion service on Christmas Eve.

Mrs. Orr is in charge of the Linen Room, and the Engineer shared in the work by fitting up the electric candles. The altar is a great improvement and creates a devotional atmosphere previously lacking — it has also created great interest among the patients.

The initial article about the altar gives specifications and suggests a wide range of usefulness. Although not apparent in the promotional description, May had obviously named his invention in honour of his current parish of Ste Agathe des Monts:

The 'Ste. Agathe' Folding, Portable Altar [the article begins], the invention of a clergyman of the Church of England, is the result of careful thought as to Portability, Stability in use, as well as Suitability for its sacred purpose, to provide a religious, devotional atmosphere, an atmosphere which is only too often lacking when an Altar has to be improvised by use of a bedside table, or the corner of a bureau littered with toilet articles and photographs.

When set up, the Ste. Agathe Altar stands about 30 inches high, it measures $32^1/_2$ inches across, has a surface depth of $11^1/_2$ with the addition of a low retable $3^1/_2$ inches deep, surmounted by a reredos $10^1/_2$ inches [high].

The Altar can be "Set up" in one minute, or folded away in as short a time; when folded it can be as easily carried as a Bridge Table, the weight is from $11^1/_2$ to 18 lbs. According to the wood used in construction.

In Church circles, amongst the Clergy, the Ste. Agathe Altar should be welcomed, providing as it does something suitable for use in the administration of Holy Communion in Private homes, or by those whose duties take them into Hospital wards, or Charitable Homes for the Aged or Infirm. Missionary Clergy, in the Foreign, or Domestic Fields, would find this Altar invaluable; and in many parishes where Religious Services have to be held in Buildings, or Rooms used at other times for Secular purposes, such an Altar would be most serviceable.

It would be a very great convenience if Railway or other Summer Hotels had such an Altar to place at the disposal of any Clergy who are asked to hold Service in such places during the Visitor Season. Passenger Steamship Companies who would install one on every ship carrying passengers in their Line would find them greatly appreciated by those clergy who are so often asked to hold Service, or by regularly appointed Chaplains for Emigrants.

Army Chaplains would in all probability be grateful if the Government would supply these Altars for their use and would find them easier to take on the field, and of a more Devotional nature than Biscuit or Ammunition Boxes.

The Ste. Agathe Folding, Portable Altar may be Obtained on order from Mr A. Whitchurch Little, Montreal Churchman Office, 1461 University Street, Montreal, P.Q. Price Complete with Waterproof case and one set of coloured hangings $40.

A.W. Little was the *Churchman*'s Business Manager.

One would expect that the unconditional surrender of all German fighting forces on May 7th would have transformed the staid pages of the *Montreal Churchman* to reflect some measure of the widespread relief and rejoicing that swept the North American Continent. Although the June cover displays a photograph of "The British Prime Minister and Mrs. Winston Churchill leav[ing] St Paul's Cathedral, London, after the national thanksgiving for the defeat of Germany," as far as the rest of the issue is concerned, it was business as usual. The second part of Bishop Dixon's Charge, begun the previous month, is continued; a Summary of Synod Reports receives prominence; there are four full columns dealing with "Human Relations in Industry and Commerce." An award-winning entry in the 1941 Churchill Essay Competition by Harcourt Fuller, a former Montrealer in the Seaforth Highlanders of Canada, killed on active service, is also featured.

The second topic in the Editorial (following a description of "the fiery discussion of Sunday Schools ... in Synod") is titled "V-E and After." It is the briefest of the three items covered:

The crowded churches during and after V-E Day were a moving sight. The black cloud in the East was forgotten in the light of Victory in the West. Mass movements like this are always of interest, good ones as well as bad. Those of us who had lost the sense of crusade in the war in Europe regained it when the veil was lifted from the degradation in Germany, and people turned with a natural and spontaneous desire to be in Church during some of the hours of Victory. The most vivid language of the liturgy as to the evil in human nature, (something treated lightly by certain forms of modern thought), has been found true. Serious people on all sides have been made to realize that this problem of evil in the world is after all so big as to be God's problem — so many-sided — so beyond human reason to find a cure.

Perhaps war weariness was the cause. Perhaps the more frenetic coverage in the daily press and on the radio had made further commentary in a monthly publication seem superfluous.

The two part editorial in the *Churchman's* September issue, alluding to V-J Day, is even more low key. The first part is titled "Christian Ethics and the Bomb":

There is only one bomb now that matters, apparently. The blockbusters shrank over night — the night we heard of the first atom bomb.

The civilized world seemed to hold its breath when that explosion nearly wiped out a large city. The Allied Peoples were like the soldier when he holds his first mills bomb [a type of hand grenade] in his hand; pin released; fearful of the power compressed between his fingers, with only a few seconds between destruction of self or an enemy.

The Christian conscience sensitively drew back from it as if some new unholy thing had come into the midst of the human family. But the heart of the Allied Peoples, sick of years of toil and tears eased at the knowledge that now was the end reached at last. Only time and the womb of the future has the answer to the ethical problem raised by this product of modern alchemy.

### THE KING'S ENGLISH

Coming after such exciting announcements as were featured in radio broadcasts while the war was coming to an end, the King's address fell upon rather dulled ears. Its true value was not appreciated by many. We were glad to read it next day in the Press for that very reason. Then we realized better how suited to the occasion was this homely one-way conversation of a democratic king with his people, — the one remaining living symbol of a mighty union of free nations.

His were simple phrases fitting a time when our feelings were of an elemental nature — "From the bottom of my heart I thank my peoples for all they have done, not only for themselves but for mankind." — "We have spent fully of all that we had; now we shall have to labour and work hard to restore what has been lost." — "I doubt if anything in all that has gone before has matched the enduring courage and the quiet determination which you have shown during these last six years." These are not historical sentences. Just ones that a person might write to a friend in the unguarded moment of intimacy, and like the character of the man, as we sense that he is, was the quality of his words.

Perhaps the small triumph of the installation of one of the Rev. Mr May's Portable, Folding Altars by the patients and staff of a Laurentian sanatorium is not such an inappropriate way to mark the year after all.

# A Mission to Poland (1946)

Relief work in Europe following the war was less of a priority, perhaps, than reintegrating returned servicemen and women into Canadian society, and — for many — transforming that society to embody the principles of justice and responsibility. One priest of the Diocese, however, believed that his duty lay in ministry in post-war Poland.

Adolph Louis Sergent came to Canada in 1927 under the aegis of the Missionary Society of the Church of England, and joined the staff of the Montreal Jewish Mission. Sergent was Polish by birth and a convert to Christianity. In 1931 he enrolled for study at the Montreal Diocesan Theological College and served as a layreader until his ordination to the diaconate in 1943. Following the outbreak of the war he became involved in assisting "numberless refugees from his own and other European countries." His knowledge of languages made him a valuable teacher at the Jewish Mission where many refugees had their first English lessons. On 31 December 1944 he was ordained to the priesthood, and a year and a half later his dream of assisting his former compatriots, formed shortly after the onset of the war, was fulfilled. The circumstances are recounted in an article in the June issue of the *Montreal Churchman*, 1946:

A year after the war broke out, Mr. Sergent met the Secretary of the Friends of Israel Missionary and Relief Society of Warsaw, and made up his mind to serve his native land when the war was over.

Now, a year after V-E Day, the way is open. Mr. Sergent has obtained a year's leave of absence from the Lord Bishop of Montreal. For that year he continues on the strength of the Diocese of Montreal [that is, on the Diocesan clergy list], but is under the jurisdiction of the [British] Bishop of Fulham, who is also Bishop of Northern and Central Europe.

He has obtained leave to enter and remain in Poland for one year to do relief work which is supported entirely by the Friends of Israel of Canada and the United States. At the same time he will be the first non-Roman, non-Orthodox priest to be admitted to Poland. And will be closely connected with the small Protestant community of Poland. ...

When it became certain that Mr. Sergent would be able to go to Poland and would be allowed to take supplies with him, the response to the need was remarkable. He has received about three tons of food and of good new and used clothing. His apartment has been a wonderful scene of activity and crowding.

As the cases have been packed, largely by Mrs. Sergent, The T. Eaton Company has removed them for the final baling, and they will be shipped at once.

Mr. Sergent goes as the agent of the interdenominational Friends of Israel, with an inter-church committee [chaired by the Secretary of the Montreal Branch of the Bible Society] behind him, but he is also a priest of the Anglican Communion under the jurisdiction of an English bishop, requiring the prayers of his own Church here in Montreal.

On May 6th, at the Annual Meeting of the Jewish Mission, Sergent received a well-wishers send off, and on June 1st, boarded the freighter S.S. *John Bakke* together with his wife Rachel and daughter Madeleine. The July issue of the *Churchman* was able to report their safe arrival in Poland.

The Continuation Committee, formed shortly before the Sergents left Montreal, consisted of twenty members, thirteen of them women. Their names, addresses and telephone numbers were printed in the September issue of the *Churchman* to facilitate the collection of food, clothing and cash donations.

Mr A. Whitchurch Little received correspondence from the Sergents and did his best to keep their work in the minds of *Churchman* readers. He inserted the following piece in the November issue.

Now that Church Organizations have started up their Fall Activities we hope that they will keep in mind the Missionary Work being accomplished by the Rev. A.L. Sergent and his family amongst the people in Poland.

Before they sailed from Montreal, a Special Committee of an inter-denominational character was formed to carry on the work of supplying them with — NEW AND USED CLOTHING [and] CANNED AND DEHYDRATED FOODS.

These should be sent to the Bible House, 1450 Union Ave., Montreal, where the Rev. W. M[aynard]. Booth (who is Chairman of the Committee) has placed the basement at our disposal; here the ladies on the Committee have undertaken to sort and pack the goods — donated — for shipment to Poland. ...

I am quoting from a letter recently received from the Rev. and Mrs. Sergent [dated 30 July at Warsaw], which will give to our readers a good picture of both their needs and an outline of their work:

Dear Mr. And Mrs. Little,

We have already been a month in Warsaw. Due to conditions and lack of adequate lodging we are living outside the city about 7 miles, but we are hoping to get a larger flat in the same building, about the end of August. It is very hot here, perhaps not hotter than in Montreal.

Our work of relief is going on very nicely. Day by day we are finding out former members of our congregation [presumably from his previous residence in Warsaw] and the new contacts made will add to the number.

So far we have not been able to have regular services in English as our former building is totally destroyed. People from England who own the place will not be able to rebuild it under the present monetary regulations. Only money from America could help us to see the Church or at least a small chapel rebuilt. I am hoping however to start soon "English Services" in the U.N.R.A.A. building [probably a misreading of UNRRA: United Nations Relief and Rehabilitation Administration] where I am hoping to obtain a temporary room. Many English speaking people have asked me to start religious worship. Of course we hold small Communion services in our own home from time to time.

As far as Polish Services are concerned, I had the privilege to conduct a Morning Worship for the members of the Evangelical Reformed Church (Presb[yterian]) who are "ecumenical in outlook and broadminded in Christian spirit." I wore, of course, my liturgical robes and as far as I could gather people were happy and thought my way of conducting the service was very acceptable.

The above mentioned Church has no building. The Church was destroyed during the Insurrection of Warsaw, and the whole Protestant cemetery, in which so many foreigners were buried, reveals a sight "Beyond human description." War marauders opened the graves in search of gold teeth, and many tombs are still open. My heart's desire is to see that the cemetery is put in order. I wish our Church and the Presbyterian Church could help me accomplish this. … I wish to suggest that the matter be brought to the attention of our little Committee and see what they can do to interest their parishioners. The people here would never forget it.

Of course there is some relief work going on in the Churches of the Council in Geneva, but as far as I can see it tends only to give material help at present. …

Due to prejudices still prevailing in Poland, we had as a Local Committee, even to change our name of the Relief Society. Not Friends of Israel etc., but "The Philadelphian Relief Society for Poland," which is a chartered member of the Foreign Voluntary Agencies in Poland …

Our aim as a Relief Society is to help all the needy regardless of race, creed or political belief. But we make some slight preference in this regard — First come the Jews of Christian persuasion; then the needy friends of the Jews from all Protestant Churches; then the needy Jews who due to persecution, even now prevailing, ... must hide themselves under false Slav names; finally we are seeking out Poles of all denominations who, out of their Christian conviction and love, were ready to stick out their heads to hide Jews from Hitler's extermination. ... Many of those whom I found alive would not have survived if it had not been for those fearless Christians. Of course anyone who I find in need of material things is being helped immediately. ...

Our stock of food and clothing is gradually diminishing, but we are confident that our friends in Canada will not forget us and those unto whom we minister, and will answer to our Mission call. We hear that the U.N.R.A.A. is pulling out at the end of the year. If it is so, our needs will still be greater and only God knows what will happen to many Protestants in Poland. The Roman Catholics have great support from the U.S.A. and I know they will look after their people. No doubt our Committee in Montreal is planning to do something for us soon. ...

We would appreciate it if you could put in some of the cases — if you send them — some items for us personally, such as sugar, condensed milk, butter. The foreigners find Warsaw very expensive due to monetary exchange restrictions.

We are so hungry for news. Could you send us some daily papers? Madeleine is asking for funnies from the *Standard* and different comics.

Forgive me for writing so much, but I wanted you to know what our needs are. I trust Mr. Booth received the letter I wrote him some time ago. I am writing to him again today.

We are yours very gratefully and fraternally,
Adolph and Rachel Sergent

P.S. Next week I will probably baptize two children: an infant and a boy 2 years old. What a joy! Mrs. Sergent asks a personal favour. Send her Eaton's Catalogue. Thank you for the *Churchman*. ...

From the earliest days of the Diocese of Montreal, the prayer "to be used at all meetings of the [Church] Society" made particular petition for the conversion of the Jews:

O merciful God, who hast made all men, and hatest nothing that Thou hast made, nor wouldest the death of a sinner, but rather that he should be converted and live; Have mercy upon all Jews, Turks, Infidels, and Hereticks, and take from them all ignorance, hardness of heart, and contempt of thy Word; and so fetch them home, blessed Lord, to thy flock, that they may be saved among the remnant of the true Israelites, and be one fold under one Shepherd.

Although the need for relief in impoverished areas has changed little, the attitude toward missionary activity has been radically transformed — in the Anglican Church in Canada and probably throughout the Anglican communion. A good illustration of more recent views appears in the *Montreal Anglican*'s Bishop's Message of May 2000, in which Bishop Hutchison describes a visit to Montreal's then Companion Diocese, the Episcopal Anglican Church of Brazil:

Here is a little Easter story from our recent visit. At the parish church in Erechim, the parish priest became aware of frequent visits to the food bank from aboriginal people. He asked them where they were from, but could never get an answer. Eventually, he followed them home to a camp in the hills several miles from the town. They lived in the most primitive conditions, and suffered high levels of poor health. Soon the parish was in motion. Under the leadership of its priest, and a lay volunteer who owns a mechanic shop, they worked alongside this fragile community of about 40 families. A water tower was installed, and running water is now in every home. A health diet was developed for children, and the infant mortality rate has dropped to zero. The project under way during our visit was the completion of a fish farm to allow the villagers to provide food for themselves. Other churches had tried working with them, but all had abandoned them once it was clear to the natives that the primary interest of the church had been to change their beliefs. Our mission is trusted because it is the first one that has simply responded to their obvious need, and been willing to work alongside them respecting their traditions. There are no church services on the reserve, and no specific Christian teaching is done. The natives still practise their ancient traditional ceremonies. The Christian witness is in the work itself … Yet, as we left, a beautiful crucifix of wood and woven grasses made by one of the villagers was presented to me. It was clear that something of the good news of the Christ who suffers in the afflictions of his people had been communicated.

## The Arundel Group (1947)

There has been a long tradition of 'social concern' in the Diocese of Montreal, a thrust at times towards what might be regarded as left-wing thinking. Perhaps the period of its greatest flowering coincided with the early years of the episcopate of John Harkness Dixon.

In an interview with the Montreal *Standard* on his election as bishop in 1943 he was quoted as stating that "church leaders are vitally interested in a new and better world. They study, discuss and preach the

subject constantly, they are alert to the possibilities of post-war developments." In the same article he spoke warmly (and with surprising naiveté)
of the example set by the Soviet Union:

I am sure a better mutual understanding between Russia and other nations
will follow as a result of this terrible conflict [the Bishop-elect remarked].
We must admit that in the past, there has been fault on both sides. For
many years we stayed suspicious of the Soviets fearing their economic and
social doctrines. ... Certainly we have something to learn from Russia. The
efficient way they are doing things now, the success of their military
campaigns and their industrial progress, the devotion of the people and
their willingness to make sacrifices for the state must surely have some
lessons for us.

Social concerns came immediately to the forefront. In June of that year
began a series of long articles in the *Montreal Churchman* on the activities
of the diocesan Social Service Committee. In August the first Arundel
Conference was held from which would be born the Anglican Fellowship for Social Action which would soon have branches in other dioceses. As Philip Carrington remarked of the AFSA:

It awoke the social conscience of church people. It exercised a strong influence in the Diocesan Synods, and stirred the General Synod and its
Department of Social Service ... It even criticised the economic order of
the Church itself ...

The first Arundel Conference was held during the last week in August at
the invitation of Dr J. Cyril Flanagan at the Flanagan home on the shore
of Bevan's Lake, near Arundel. He was the chairman of the Social
Service Committee, and together with A.E.M. Warner, had signed the
June report. Most of the 22 clergy and three laymen attending were
billetted at the Doctor's, and the WA of Grace Church, Arundel, served
"three hearty meals to the whole assembly" for four days. The first of a
three-part article in the *Montreal Churchman* describes the event:

The main subjects covered at the conference were: The recommendations
for social reconstruction championed by Archbishop Temple; The Christian Doctrine of Man, and the Christian View of Democracy; The Gospel
Bases of Christian Sociology; The Christian Interpretation of History; and
the Christian social teachings with regard to property, labour, trade and
money.

Among those attending were the Bishop, Canon P.S.C. Powles, and the Revs Ernest S. Reed, John Peacock and S.L. Pollard. The conference was conducted "on a socialistic basis," travelling expenses being pooled and shared equally.

At the second conference, also held at Bevan Lake, membership was up to 28 and this time included representatives from the Dioceses of Nova Scotia, Ottawa and Quebec, as well as a member of the sisterhood of St John the Divine. An editorial in the December issue of the Churchman spoke encouragingly about the group:

There is something healthy and happy in the initial grouping of men of goodwill for better attainment of some ideal. One turns to the early story of some of the greater movements in and out of the Church to illustrate this. The stimulus to think harder and more clearly and sincerely in living and immediate problems, both intellectual and practical, is apparently one objective of this group who gather for a few days' study each summer at Arundel under a capable leader. ... If, as is apparent, the informal gatherings at Arundel are a clearing house for ideas on religious questions and an encouragement for Christian Social Action then someone deserves a pat on the back for launching this, as yet, somewhat amorphous group.

Soon several of the prime movers of the Arundel Group were making their views known on the floor of Synod and through articles in the press. The following excerpt from "Church Trends," by the Rev. S.L. Pollard in the April 1946 issue of the *Churchman*, is a good example:

Three years ago [Pollard reminds his readers] the Social Service Committee put forward the following recommendation, which was adopted by Synod — 'that in order to secure a wider representation of our church population on the Boards of the Church, steps be taken by the Executive Committee to make possible the payment of the expenses of lay as well as clerical members to Diocesan, Provincial and General Synods.'

The implementation of this recommendation would radically change the lay membership of synod. *At present it is still a truism to say that 'the Church is administered and officiated by the [monied] classes; her influential laity belong almost wholly to the [monied] classes.*

The essential unfairness in the comparative influence of the different classes of the laity is further exemplified in the lay control of the ministry 'through the power of the purse'; religious equality cannot obtain in the church when the possession of property (movable or immovable) enables the rich to dictate who shall look after their souls, while the poor man has no such choice. *Let us be truthful and admit that 'it is ultimately money alone that sits enthroned.'*

Such control is still further exercised by the maintenance of the private appropriation of seats in the House of God on a basis of pew rents.

The evidence clearly points to the fact that the church is still largely organized on a class basis.

The high-pressure tactics in Montreal and elsewhere became rather wearing, however. As Andrew Wetmore points out his study of the AFSA, although there were many sympathizers and like-minded people throughout this clergy-based movement, others became "wearied by constant opposition from their brother clergy."

In his Charge to Synod in 1947, Bishop Dixon, who started off as a proponent of the movement, expressed his growing irritation with clamourings from the Social Service Committee and the Arundel Group to engage the church in direct social action. Quoting Archbishop Temple he stated that "it is of crucial importance that the Church acting corporately should not commit itself to any particular policy":

With great reluctance [Dixon continued] I express my disappointment that our Social Services report again ignores such distinctions [as developing in parishioners "a sensitive and educated Christian conscience" as opposed to making "official pronouncements"] and continues to attempt to make Synod a debating ground on political and economic techniques and highly controversial theories. Few of us could vote on them intelligently even if such a course were proper. …

I deplore the unnecessary irritation which it causes. I view with deep concern the weakening of our diocesan unity when the challenge of the times calls for utmost good will and cooperation. It of course creates great difficulties for me as Bishop and unpleasant situations for me as President of Synod, but I grudge most of all the wastage of our great reservoir of interest and support which could be at our disposal. … In corporate Diocesan action we are not planning or doing much social service. It calls for much more sacrifice than reading books and telling other people what they should do. The sick, the poor, the lonely, the prisoner are not items in reports. They are people next door. An actual hand is required, to hold out the cup of water.

Quoting Archbishop Temple again, he reminded the Synod that "Nine-tenths of the work of the Church is done by Christian people fulfilling responsibilities and performing tasks which in themselves are not part of the official system of the Church at all."

The Very Rev. John Harkness Dixon had succeeded Arthur Carlisle as Bishop of Montreal in 1943, and moved from a position in which Carlisle himself had preceded him as Dean of the Cathedral. Before that, the two men had succeeded one another as rectors of Grace-Church-on-the-Hill in Toronto.

Carlisle's death at age 61, after an episcopate of less than four years, had come as an added blow to a diocese in the midst of war and political unrest.

Bishop Carlisle's funeral had been an elaborate and solemn occasion in January of 1943, with the Bishop lying in state in the sanctuary of the Cathedral for two days, flanked by lighted candles and attended by pairs of "Clerical and Lay watchers" through the night. Yet Carlisle had been a man who spoke simply and quietly, one who had chosen to remain in his own house and turn over Bishopscourt, the episcopal residence, to serve as additional office space.

The bishop-elect and Mrs Dixon, at the time of the consecration and enthronement, decided to forego the usual festivities surrounding such events:

The Committee discussed with the Dean and Mrs Dixon its proposal to hold a public reception in their honour [it was announced in the May issue of the *Montreal Churchman*]. They would have welcomed the opportunity to meet both the people of the Diocese and our friends of other communions, many of whom have shown a cordial and generous interest and good will. Two considerations have led them to decline the suggestion. They share the deep sense of loss in the passing of Bishop Carlisle of which we are all so keenly conscious. They also feel that the utmost simplicity seems fitting under the stress and strain of these anxious days.

## Men For All Seasons (1951)

In 1951, the Rev. Horace G. Baugh had just entered the second year of his fully-ordained ministry in the Diocese, but he represented a long line of clergy who had served Montreal for generations.

His father had set (and at this time was still setting) a formidable example, both in energy and longevity. The Rev. Canon Cyrus W.P. Baugh, was described in 1966 as "the oldest practicing Anglican rector in Canada." He retired at age 93. Over the years his career included service in parishes at Portage du Fort, Valleyfield, Park Extension, Arundel, Papineau, Morin Heights, Lakefield, Shrewsbury, Dunany and Louisa.

A history of Holy Trinity Church, Lakefield, compiled in the 1980s, describes the early days of his ministry, starting in 1906, when he travelled by horse and buggy in summer and by cutter in winter:

Getting around to ... preaching stations [at Lakefield, Shrewsbury, Dunany and Louisa] originally required that he drive horse and buggy an average of 30 miles. He kept this up year after year and now his parishioners estimate he has travelled more than 100,000 miles on Sundays alone. This does not take into account parochial visiting during the week. ...

Recalling his past activities, Canon Baugh said his first horse which took him from Pontiac to Arundel was called 'Lady' and from then on all the other horses he used in his pastoral duties also bore the name 'Lady' although some were not mares.

"Some of them did not behave like gentle ladies since several bolted and left me stranded on lonely country roads miles away from home. On such occasions 'Lady' would arrive home hours before me," he said. ...

During his sixty years of service he recalled only two occasions on which he was unable to officiate because of illness, and, during that time, never took a vacation:

Smiling, he said: 'How could I, earning only $54 a month for the 14 first years of my service?'

The Canon credits his long service to plenty of fresh air and good home food.

Equally a legend in his own time, his son Horace, as of 2000, has served the church for much the same interval, having had an early start by managing "to neatly sidestep" Montreal Diocesan Theological College's age requirements.

In the course of a long career, son Horace (who, like his father was eventually made canon) has been instrumental in the building of four churches, four church halls, three rectories and six mission halls. Particularly close to his heart was the construction in 1951 of the pine-log "skiers' church" of St Francis of the Birds in St-Sauveur-des-Monts, built with the generous support of John Molson (other members of whose family in previous generations had built and sustained two successive churches dedicated to St Thomas in Montreal).

Unique in the Diocese in its form and style, St Francis was "constructed from some 600 local pine logs by a crew of artisans headed by Victor Nymark following the Scandinavian tradition."

The windows of the church are particularly beautiful, depicting the four seasons, and also night and day. The main window portrays St Francis of Assisi surrounded by twenty-one species of birds native to the Laurentians. Another window represents the Holy Spirit descending upon earth and bringing order to the formless void.

In addition to his parish ministry, Horace Baugh has served as non-stipendiary chaplain at Montreal's two airports (when Mirabel still catered to passenger travel). Numerous passengers fearful of flying, among other problems, have received his comfort and counsel.

Perhaps best known in the Diocese-at-large for holding the annual blessing of the pets each fall at Beaver Lake, Canon Baugh has striven actively to promote kindness to animals. Since 1960 he has blessed "all kinds of creatures — from poodles to turtles."

Speaking of the changes he had seen in the church over the years, he noted that clergy are less involved in the community than they were in his younger days. They often seem to shrink from joining service clubs and similar organizations, he believed:

I consider it part of the ministerial mandate [he remarked]. Priests don't do it now. They say they don't want to be in conflict with the congregation. I think that's a red herring. I wanted to be part of anything that came along.

He similarly expressed disapproval of priests who prefer to appear in public 'out of uniform':

Clergy today don't wear their collars. My attitude is: you're a priest, you should identify yourself in public. There might be someone who needs you. The duty of a priest is mostly to be a spiritual comfort for his people.

Not surprisingly, personal contact with parishioners is an indispensable part of Canon Baugh's ministry, and even in his eighty-first year he made a point of undertaking "regular home visits" throughout his rural parish. When asked about his chief concern for parish ministry in the Diocese on the eve of the twenty-first century, he listed "the neglect of training young clergy in caring for the aged."

On 22 December 1996, Canon Baugh's little church in New Glasgow was ravaged by fire, but the blow to the 156-year-old Laurentian village church of St John's was twofold. Shortly after the fire in which the interior of church was gutted and only the pale blue altar was saved from destruction, the parish's indefatigable priest suffered a heart attack. There

*A class for boys, St Mark's, Longueuil*

*Confirmation of adults at the Lasalle Mission*

PLATE 14   *Sundy School and Confirmation (Photo Credit:* MDA*)*

was no other Anglican church in the whole area and it looked as if the thirty or so parishioners would be left without a place of worship indefinitely.

Thanks to the parish's $135,000 insurance policy, however, as well as some donated furnishings and the determined efforts of the people themselves, a fully–recovered Canon Baugh was able to celebrate at the old altar in St John's on Easter Sunday of the following year.

A photograph printed in the 1999 June issue of the *Montreal Anglican* reflects the continued vigour of Canon Baugh. Sitting very upright in a group of three dignitaries is an energetic-looking, white-moustached gentleman in clerical dress, hands on knees and looking squarely at the camera. The caption reads:

Canon Horace G. Baugh is shown with the Lieutenant-Governor, the Hon. Lise Thibault ... on a recent visit to Maison Emmanuel, in Val Morin Quebec, for handicapped children. Also seated ... is the founder, Inge Sell. Canon Baugh blessed this institution on its opening several years ago.

Although St John's, New Glasgow, rose from the ashes in 1996, its continued existence, like that of so many other small outlying parishes, hangs by a thread. Even the Canon has expressed the opinion that, once he retires, the church would 'most probably' become a mission post. Parishioners leave. Others lose heart. 'Professionalism' among the clergy and a move away from parish visiting, which the old Canon has so deplored, are nonetheless symptomatic of the times. Fire might be a less destructive force than these.

## "Her Gift of Music" (1952)

Devoted active laypeople with gifts to share in their parishes are not easy to come by, and they sometimes present themselves in unexpected ways.

In 1952, Archdeacon Kenneth Naylor, then Rector of Trinity Memorial Church, was asked for an appointment by one of his small number of West Indian parishioners. Although she attended services only occasionally, he remembered her and received her warmly. She brought with her a young music teacher from Barbados who had recently completed her Associate of Music in piano at the McGill Conservatory and had gathered a number of promising private pupils. The children had made such good progress that their parents were anxious to hear them perform at a recital, and the Archdeacon's parishioner was one such parent. The children were ready to perform and Marita Archer, their teacher, was eager to give them that opportunity, but renting a hall for a recital seemed to be an insurmountable obstacle. She could not afford it. Perhaps some arrangement could be made for Trinity Church Hall, one parent had suggested.

Archdeacon Naylor listened sympathetically to the young teacher and readily offered her the use of the hall free of charge. "You are doing a great work, Miss Archer," she remembers him saying, "just give the sexton a tip."

Although Marita Archer had then been living in Montreal for less than five years, her connection with the city had begun long before. When she was a child of six or seven, she recalls, her father left home in Barbados to find the sort of regular employment that would support his family. He found it in Canada working for the Canadian Pacific Railway.

My mother would never go to live in Canada [Miss Archer remembered]. She said it was too cold! We three girls were brought up in Barbados and had our schooling there.

My father wrote to us regularly every month, and of course we all wrote to him. He always wanted to hear about our school reports and all the things we were doing. He came home for visits — not every year, because it took fourteen days by boat in those days — but he came as often as he could.

After completing her education, Miss Archer studied music extramurally through the Royal School of Music in London, England, through private tutoring and accredited examination.

By 1947, when she arrived in Montreal to study music at McGill, she had already received her Licentiate in Music (LRSM) and her father was nearing the end of his working life:

I was a small child when he left home to work in Canada and he served the railway for perhaps thirty years. When I came to Montreal, his run was from Winnipeg to Saskatoon, but in his younger days he went right through the Rockies.

While I was at the Conservatory I boarded with friends of his in Montreal. We spent his holidays together.

Although her father's friends provided a network of support to the young teacher she clearly had many obstacles to overcome before she could hope to establish herself in a strange country. The opportunity of giving a recital, she felt, was a turning point, and here began her long and faithful association with Trinity Memorial Church.

When Miss Archer had first come to Montreal she had become a member of Union United — "the Coloured Church" as it was called — near Delisle and Atwater. The friends with whom she was boarding were members there and she herself had been raised a Methodist.

After the sympathetic treatment she had received at Trinity Memorial, however, she became a member there. She was asked to play there on a number of occasions and was soon involved in the Sunday School, teaching them children's hymns to her accompaniment. She would fill this role for more than twenty years.

At that time, Miss Archer recalled, there were few Black members of the congregation, but one stood out particularly in her memory: a Mr Harris — also a musician — who sang in the choir.

He had a beautiful tenor voice, and he was very faithful. He was there every Sunday, from January to December. Archdeacon Naylor thought very highly of him.

Music had long been emphasised at Trinity Memorial and there was then a fine men and boys' choir. Later — but not for many years — it became a mixed choir with women's voices introduced.

During Miss Archer's membership at Trinity Memorial, great changes have taken place:

After the War many members of the white congregation moved out of NDG, northward to the upper part of Côte-St-Luc, and attended other churches. The economy was booming and you could buy a house with a small downpayment. At the same time a number of young women from the Islands were coming into the area and joined the congregation. After Archdeacon Naylor retired, Canon [Gordon R.] Addie came. He was very welcoming and outgoing. His wife, who had a beautiful voice, used to come to recitals. They were both very friendly.

As of 2000, Trinity Memorial was in the care of the Rev. Canon Anthony Jemmott, an energetic Barbadian priest who had rebuilt the parish after a period of decline which set in some time after Canon Addie's departure. "It really went down," Miss Archer recalled, "but our Canon Jemmott brought it back. We are very proud of him and his whole family." Once again the church had a large, active Sunday school, but Miss Archer was no longer able to be involved with it. At 89, she had difficulty getting out — although in the year 2000 she still had three pupils who came to her home for their lessons. And she continued to support her Church.

In a lecture delivered at Montreal Diocesan Theological College on 21 November 2000, Canon Jemmott described the struggles and sacrifices made by Montreal's Caribbean community to establish themselves in Quebec society, and paid tribute to the values that enabled them to do so:

Many came with a higher education for the jobs they ended up doing [he pointed out]. They were schooled in the belief that any honest paying job would suffice if it did permit the next generation to escape the hardships of the present one.

He mentioned two such new Canadians who had made outstanding contributions to their communities. One was Marita Archer who, as he put it, offered "her gift of music in the church."

# Deconsecrations (1954)

Generally speaking, the 1950s were years of growth and expansion in the number and size of congregations in the Diocese, but shifts in population, particularly among English-speaking Quebecers in some rural areas, were causing church closures and deconsecrations even then.

The deconsecration of a church, like any human death, usually involves the disposal of property. Such certainly was the case of St James Church, Berthierville, whose sentence of deconsecration was passed on 12 September 1954. Even before this took place, however, the building had been stripped, and the furnishings — accumulated over more than a hundred years — packed up for removal from the site. Although there does not seem to have been any ceremony of leave-taking, or any closing service as such, someone locally took pains to draw up a careful inventory.

In the Diocesan Archives is a letter from Archdeacon J.F. Morris, Clerical Secretary, thanking a Miss Kitson for her involvement in closing the church, and reassuring her with tact and kindness that St James's furnishings would bring help and new life to existing or emerging congregations. His letter is dated September 21st 1954:

Thank you so much for all you have done with details of the moving.

I am very glad to have your list of things and their present location, so that we can keep track of them.

Since our telephone conversation last week the Bishop and I have come to a solution of the disposition of the Altar, Prayer Desk, Pulpit, Lectern, Bell and Iron Cross [from the steeple], which we hope may meet your approval.

Only last week a decision was taken by Rosemere to build a new Church (They are now worshipping in a Community Hall). Mr. Thomas Havill is one of the leaders. He has just undertaken to store these items and others that may become available.

Mr. Havill has given me particulars of the best way to reach his address. These I have put on another sheet so as to give you two extra copies for Mr. Goulet and his carter.

I am so happy to hear that you have found a place for the Memorial Windows.

My apologies for the delay in sending this letter. I went out of town on Wednesday afternoon but failed to reach the office before it closed on Friday afternoon.

Gratefully yours

Even earlier than this, as the Rev. E.E. Dawson records, a very different congregation — a long established parish in the Eastern Townships — had received a windfall gift from Berthierville:

On Monday, August 30th 1954, there arrived at St. George's Church, Clarenceville … a Truck Load of the contents of St. James Church, Berthier … The chief items were

1   The Pipe organ, carefully taken down and packed under the supervision of Mr. Wm J. Selwood, sometime organist at St. Peter's Church, Mount Royal, and now a Divinity Student and Lay Reader, stationed at Clarenceville. This organ was installed in St. George's Church. It was reported that … the pews had been taken to Kilkenny, Que. for use there.
2   A small organ [actually a harmonium], in good order, had been presented to Mr. Selwood, himself, who presented it to St. George's Church.
3   A brass Lectern
4   Presentation Copies of Bible and the Prayer-book, Hymn-boards and a Notice-board.
5   The Aisle-Carpet and the Seat-cushions.
6   Electric fixtures, lamp-shades, a box of prayer and hymn-books, several hassocks, twelve plain chairs, in good order, and the coal scuttles.

Annotations on the inventory show that some of the Clarenceville items actually went to Noyan. In addition to the pews, already itemized, Kilkenny received a "black wooden coffin rest" and two palls — one "silk and velvet," one "black cloth" — kneeling benches, and a second notice board.

St Cuthbert's Church, in Park Extension, Montreal, was presented with two chancel chairs and the altar frontal.

Not everything was useable. Beside the inventoried items "pew cushions," and "door mat" appears the assessment "no good" written in another hand.

Eight framed photographs of clergy who had served Berthier had hung in St James's vestry; by 1954, two could no longer be identified. All were deposited with the Archives Committee. A note by the Rev. A.R. Kelley dated 21 July 1955, records that the mural tablets "formerly on the walls of Berthierville" had been placed in the Sorel rectory.

The Rev. E.E. Dawson, who endeavoured to trace the disposition of St James's furnishings, had a strong attachment to "the old wooden Church at Lake Maskinongé." As a deacon he had ministered at Kildare, DeRamsay and Brandon in 1906; he had taken services at St James, and knew a number of the former pupils of the school — the French and English Seminary — at Berthier. On Sunday, 17 October 1954, when the choir of St Peter's, Mount Royal, "came to Clarenceville and sang Evensong, while the accompaniment from the sweet toned old Berthier Organ played by Mr. Selwood, filled the church with music," Dawson took pains to be a member of the congregation. If St James's Church lacked a proper send off, at least one of the many who had served there saw the symbolic continuity of its vocation in that choral evensong.

In 1999 the national convention of the Organ Historical Society, held that year in Montreal, took pains to include Berthierville's 1875 Scudmore organ, now in St George's Church, Clarenceville, in its round of recitals on unique instruments.

# New Congregations (1954)

Each year the Proceedings of Synod contain a table of parish and diocesan "vital statistics" which include, among other things, the founding year of each still-existing parish in the diocese. This date may have no relation to the age, or even the location of the current church building, or, in some cases, to any building at all. It is usually an effort to show how long a recognizable body of faithful people in a present-day parish has been formed into a self-sustaining or assisted worship community. Sometimes, however, these dates can be misleading and even cause the record of earlier efforts to be neglected and lost.

The parish of Roxboro-Pierrefonds, according to the statistical table, was established in 1958, but this dating entirely ignores the remarkable story of the ancestry of the current St Barnabas Church: a story of faith, determination and remarkable leadership by an initially small group of young families, recent residents of a new development which had no church.

On 29 April 1953, Betty and Cliff Howes, together with their four-month-old baby son, moved into their first house, "full of hopes and dreams." Roxboro was a new development then and everything seemed to be in the process of construction, including the Howes' house which was only partly finished. Many of the roads were not yet paved. Although there were institutions such as churches and schools serving the long-established French-speaking community nearby, the largely English-speaking and Protestant new-arrivals had not had time to see to their own needs, and the lack of a church to the church-going Howes made a gap in their lives in this new setting.

The following is the first-hand account of what happened next: the story of leadership provided by a young father — employed full-time during the day, taking courses at night — and his energetic wife (a stay-at-home mother) in the establishment of a community church, and, as it turned out, against all odds:

One day in early 1954 [Mrs Howes recalled], I took my baby down the dirt road and met three other young mothers, Betty Skare, Becky White, and June Curwood. As we chatted over cups of tea, I told them I felt lost without a church close by. In the evening, over supper, Cliff and I talked about our day. When the subject of church came up, we looked at each other and said, "why not!!"

Cliff felt the only way it could be done was to find out how many persons were interested. As we didn't have a car, Cliff started by asking our new friends how they felt about a church — the answer was yes, a good idea — so the following weekends Cliff walked all over Roxboro to find out who would be interested. He found 68 families, one of whom was Captain James of the Salvation Army, who volunteered to hold the first service and start a Sunday School when we were ready. The Captain had already begun an informal Sunday School among the neighbourhood children.

Clearly the interest was there, but what then?

"Where could we meet? Why not our livingroom," was what came to us. I had my piano and hymnbook.

The news spread that the first service would be held in our home on Nov. 7th for an Armistice Day service. Would anyone come?

The Howes' home was not large and was still in the process of being finished. Until people started to arrive they had no idea that thirty-six people would come, many very sensibly bringing their own chairs, a practice that would be repeated:

Those who hadn't brought their own chairs used our livingroom furniture and some even sat on our bed across the hall. It was a lovely service of hope and I'm sure the Spirit of God was amongst us. I played the hymns, but during one interval I had to leave and feed a crying baby in his room, then back to play the last hymn.

Someone asked for a collection plate and, if memory serves me, we received 10 dollars in total: the first bit towards starting a Church.

Every other Sunday a service was held, until there were too many people to continue meeting at the Howes.

Our friends, Olaf and Betty Skare (also in the midst of building) offered their larger, unfinished livingroom for [use] every Sunday.

By now, news of this local effort had spread, even into the neighbouring French-speaking community. In an ecumenical spirit rare for the period, Father Valois, priest of the Roman Catholic Church of Mary Queen of Peace, contacted Cliff Howes and offered him space in the church itself to hold a public meeting.

The speakers for the evening were from the Community Church on Isle Bigras who told [us] interesting and pertinent details about the building of a community church. The Rev. R. De Witt brought best wishes from the United Theological College.

Particularly significant here was the ecumenical nature of the gathering — an element which was fully appreciated at the time.

This event was history making in the sense that it brought Anglicans, Presbyterians, United, Baptist, Lutheran and Salvation Army together, meeting as guests of the Roman Catholics. During the evening a Committee was formed and Cliff was elected as President. ...

To the delight of everyone at that meeting Fr Valois offered the assembly room at Lalonde School to hold our services for a small fee to be given to the janitor for putting up and taking down chairs. We were on our way!!

Appeals for basic furnishings went out over radio stations CFCF and CKVL and, in response, a pump pedal organ from Beaurepaire and a font from Valois United Church were donated.

On 16 March 1955 the first service at Lalonde School was held with Mrs Howes playing the organ. As she was expecting another child (twins as it turned out) the men had decided that the pedal pump had become too difficult for her and had considerably installed an electrolux motor. This new arrangement, however, lent an unexpectedly dramatic touch to the service, for the motor immediately overheated and, as the first hymn was played, emitted clouds of smoke from underneath the instrument:

Cliff ran with the fire extinguisher. Someone opened up the piano and led me across to it to finish playing the hymn.

One of Cliff Howes' duties as President of the Community Church Committee was to set up a rota of ministers to take services:

Cliff had quite a time contacting the heads of each denomination for services every week [Mrs Howes recalled] and of course our old friend Captain James [of the Salvation Army] was there every fifth Sunday — he had other commitments in town. It was quite a job making sure someone was either picked up or met off the train.

In the meantime our twin daughters were born (the first twins in Roxboro). Our home still wasn't finished, we were all working at trying to have a Church building. We always called Deborah and Dorothy "the ecumenical twins" because they were baptized by an Anglican priest (the Rev. Roland Bodger) using a United Church font in a Roman Catholic school.

Besides sympathy and material assistance from the local Roman Catholics, the new Community Church received a remarkable degree of support from municipal authorities:

Mayor Roland Bigras called and met with the committee to tell them he was donating a piece of land at the corner of Gouin Blvd and 6th Ave for the purpose of building a Church.

Fundraising began in earnest:

One of our members had a connection with Belmont Park in Cartierville. He was able to loan us a big tent in which to have a huge Bazaar.

The congregation had grown to over 150 families and was increasing. We would soon be able to dig the foundation.

Work was begun, but finances were tight and every effort was made to keep expenses down:

The foundation was dug and foundation walls were in place, but it was going to cost more money to place girders across to support the building. Twenty-five men volunteered to hoist those girders on their shoulders and put them in place on the base. I can assure you they all came home aching but happy that at last we would have our Church building. The conrnerstone was laid by Rev. R. Fricker from the Presbyterian Church on Sept 5, 1956.

The first service in the new church was held on Christmas Eve, 1956.

People trudged through wet, sloppy snow carrying kitchen chairs, stools, and deck chairs on their way to the Church service. The Rev. Roland Bodger and a young assistant, Reginald Hollis, conducted an Anglican Eucharist.

As with the first service at Lalonde School, however, it was not uneventful:

There had been freezing rain that of course froze on the wooden, unfrozen roof, but the builders were determined the roof would be finished for the service so on went the roofing tiles. Unfortunately there was a thaw Christmas Eve and the ice melted under the roofing material causing water to leak through the ceiling.

Someone found an umbrella and held it over me at the organ. Perhaps it was to save the electrolux motor that finally worked.

Fearful for the safety of the ceiling in the still-unfinished entryway, Cliff Howes and the Treasurer, Tom Amberly, "climbed ladders and literally held up the ceiling in the vestibule" for part of the evening.

It was, however, "a wonderful service of faith," for everyone who was present.

The spirit of enterprise and self-reliance continued unabated. During the next few months each family donated chairs — "a quite interesting assortment" — but by now the populations in Roxboro and Pierrefonds had increased to such an extent that the possibility of denominational churches seemed a reality. The United Church members were the first to withdraw to begin the organization of a church of their own.

Within the Community Church, the largest denominational representations remaining were the Anglicans and the Presbyterians. It was decided the congregation seek formal affiliation with one or the other. A vote was taken to decide the matter, and, as Mrs Howes put it:

As there were more Anglicans than Presbyterians the church became St Barnabas. It had been quite a struggle for this to come about. Mostly due to the fact that we were on our own for so long. [Then] no Church Session or Synod would help us. Each denomination didn't think the area would grow so quickly and therefore there wouldn't be enough money available to be worth [their while] helping us. I'll always remember Cliff feeling so depressed when, after meeting with each Church head, we were told we were on our own.

The new congregation took care that the Presbyterians were not to be left homeless, however:

As we had now become an Anglican Church, we made sure that the Presbyterians could use the building for their services as well. So every Sunday after our service the altar would be cleared and the lectern moved from the side to the middle.

Under the aegis of the Anglican communion, the newly renamed St Barnabas Church was put under the care of the Rev. A.M. Reid of the Church of the Good Shepherd in Cartierville. However, as Mrs Howes recalled, this was not always a workable arrangement for that busy rector:

It was difficult for him to run from one church to the other so we used to have students and new graduates from the [Theological] College: Barry Valentine, Murray Magor, Ian Stuchberry, Allen Goodings, and finally our own Rector — the Rev. Bill McCarthy. Archdeacon Morris made Cliff the first Rector's Warden.

Thus Cliff Howes, who had organized transport for a rota of ministers, was back to managing the funds for defraying the travel costs of a succession of student clergy, often digging into his own pocket "to help pay the students' fare home on the train." Money was so tight that he and another member of the congregation "decided they would look after the furnace and clean the church to save having a caretaker."

From the beginning fundraising had been a priority, but even with the breakup of the original Community Church a strong community spirit continued to prevail:

We had all kinds of bazaars, bake sales, dances, and flea markets in which the whole community joined forces. It didn't matter whether one was English or French, Catholic, Protestant, Anglican: we all came together to help each other's churches. When the United Church congregation started their own everyone supported their fund raising efforts. The same when Mary Queen of Peace built their new church; we were there remembering how we had been helped. When the Presbyterians started their church, again everyone supported them.

Time moves on! Bill McCarthy went on to head the Old Brewery Mission and the Rev. Reginald Hollis was appointed as our new Rector. During his time it was decided the church was too small, so a new St Barnabas was built in Pierrefonds. It was sad to see our old Church sold, but we had outgrown the walls.

The spirit which built this first church, and which had led neighbours to gather for worship in each other's homes is traceable to the earliest days in the territory which forms the Diocese of Montreal today.

In the backwoods where there was no clergyman people gathered with their Prayer Books and their Bibles. Perhaps someone read a printed sermon aloud or led in the singing of a psalm. People walked or drove their sleighs or wagons many miles for such a service. Once or twice a year a travelling missionary or circuit rider might pass their way and baptize the children. It was the people themselves who were what church there was.

Such stories of faithfulness should be remembered.

As Mrs Howes concludes her memoir of the early days of St Barnabas Church:

Unfortunately those struggling years have been forgotten and few people know how hard we all worked as a community for our various churches.

Happily for the post-pioneer church in this Diocese, such a spirit of faithfulness and enterprise among its lay people was not unique to St Barnabas. In 1962, for example, when Connie Bridgeman and her husband Allan moved to the new development of Brossard, the two of them immediately recognized a local need and started a Sunday School in their home. They had both been active in the Sunday School in their previous parish and it seemed to be the natural thing to do. "As it grew," she recalled, "our neighbour opened his home for [regular] worship services the next year." A sizeable congregation soon formed, "and," she concluded, "in 1965 Bishop Maguire built our church [St Joseph of Nazareth] where we still worship." This is a modest oversimplification of what had really happened, however. As with the Howes, surely, it was the Bridgemans and their neighbours, drawn together in faith, who had built the community that built the church.

## Exchange Scholarships to Diocesan College (1957)

In 1951 the Rev. R.H.L. Slater succeeded the Rev W.A. Ferguson as Principal of Montreal Diocesan Theological College.

Slater seems to have been a remarkable man. In the words of the College's historian Oswald Howard, he was "courageous, scholarly, enthusiastic, broad-minded, devoutly religious, and [what seems still more remarkable] he performed his onerous duties with the full confidence of the Board of Governors and Corporation, the loyalty of the Alumni, and generous support of the Diocese at large."

At the time of his appointment he was already a member of the Faculty of Divinity at McGill University as well as a member of the Faculty of the Diocesan College.

Born in Newcastle-upon-Tyne in the north of England, Slater served first in a Tyneside parish after taking first-class honours in Theology at Cambridge. Seventeen years in the Orient, serving first as Chaplain and Lecturer at Rangoon University, then as Senior Chaplain in charge of the Cathedral of the Holy Trinity, Rangoon, and finally as Senior Chaplain with the British Forces in Burma, India, and Ceylon during the Second World War, further expanded his horizons.

In 1946 he was appointed Visiting Lecturer in Comparative Religion at Union Theological Seminary, New York, and thence to Huron College, London, Ontario, as Professor of Church History and Apologetics, until his appointment to the Chair of Systematic Theology at McGill.

Upon his appointment as Principal [Howard writes], Dr Slater threw himself enthusiastically into the work of the College. With an interest in every phase of its life and work he made a conspicuous success of his position as Principal. The financial position of the College improved, the attendance of students showed a steady growth, the high standard of scholarship and the strong emphasis upon the spiritual life and development were maintained, and every effort was made to produce men of deeply religious character for the ministry of the Church.

Among Slater's initiatives — that of offering scholarships to allow promising theological students from the Caribbean to study at the College —

one was to have a far-reaching impact on future multicultural ministry in Montreal, for one of the recipients of these scholarships was John McNab:

Regarding my association with the diocese [writes Dr McNab in a personal letter] this is the story. In 1957 the late Principal Slater offered the late Bishop Percival Gibson two scholarships at Montreal Diocesan Theological College for clergy in the diocese of Jamaica.

The hope was expressed at the time that this would develop into a regular student exchange between St Peter's College in Jamaica and Montreal Diocesan. The Bishop sent Orland Lindsay (now the retired Archbishop of the West Indies) and myself. I was completing the B.D. degree of London University as an external student.

On the successful completion of that degree, Dr Slater recommended that I continue towards an S.T.M. at McGill. I completed the required postgraduate courses and returned to Jamaica.

In 1963 I returned to McGill for three months to complete and present my thesis on *The Social Thought of William Temple* — and was awarded the S.T.M. During this time I held the Bishop's [John Dixon's] licence and served as Sunday assistant for two years at St Stephen's, Lachine.

In 1969 I was awarded a fellowship by the Theological Education Fund of the World Council of Churches which enabled me to return to McGill (1969-72) to pursue doctoral studies. On the completion of my thesis, *Towards a Theology for Social Concern,* a comparative study of the thought of F.D. Maurice and Walter Rauschenbusch, I was awarded the Ph.D. ...

In 1978 Bishop Reginald Hollis invited me to be the Rector of St Paul's in the Côte des Neiges district.

In 1958 Dr Slater was invited to join the Faculty at Harvard University to be the first to hold the new Chair of World Religions recently established there. After much hesitation he accepted, but obviously continued his interest in the students he had taken such pains to bring to the College. Though his successor expressed the hope that the exchange would continue, a regular exchange did not in fact develop.

At the same time, however, the number of students from the Caribbean studying at Canadian colleges and universities was rising. From a mere 450 in all of Canada in 1955, the number grew to 3,000 ten years later, "with particularly large contingents," according to Robin Winks, "at Queen's, McGill, Sir George Williams, Mount Allison, and Dalhousie universities, at Macdonald College and the School of Agriculture at Guelph ... and at the universities of British Columbia, Manitoba and Toronto. Few attended the French-speaking universities, although a handful of Haitians did so."

In 1984, Dr McNab was appointed Director of Pastoral Studies at Diocesan College. On his retirement in 2000, an article in the *Montreal Anglican*, paid tribute to his distinguished career as a teacher and mentor:

Dr McNab, as Director of Pastoral Studies, has helped to form, guide, nurture and inspire the theological reflections and ministries of dozens of Dio graduates. Through them his influence is felt not only across this country, but within schools, parishes and Diocesan Administrations in several lands. ...

One of his ministries at Dio has been to organize trips for final year students to such places as Cuba, Mexico and Jamaica — as well as to Kahnawake on the South Shore.

He reports, "I have not encountered a student that has been on one of the trips to a poorer part of the world who has not remarked, upon returning to Canada, 'I never knew it was like that.'"

There is no doubt that Dr Slater's initiative — brief as it was — in broadening the horizons of his theological students through establishing intercultural contacts has borne a rich harvest.

# THE QUIET
# REVOLUTION AND
# VATICAN II
## 1960–1976

## Choir Camp (1961)

A new venture in the support of church music in the Diocese was taken up in 1961 with the launching of a week-long choir camp for boys, held at Camp Gleneagle in Vermont. Marcia Hollis's article in the Montreal *Gazette* of 2 September gives an excellent idea of the initiative and its organization:

NEWPORT, Vermont — "Has anyone seen my ruff?" yelled a tanned little boy in camp shorts and sneakers. A few moments later he was robed and in procession with 40 other boys in cassocks of blue, purple, black and red — representing choirs of nine Anglican churches in the Diocese of Montreal.

The youngsters, who range in age from eight to 14, are taking part in a new venture — the first Montreal Diocesan Choir School ...

"I hope this will become an annual affair," said Norman Hurrle, musical director of the choir school.

Hurrle, at that time organist and choirmaster of St. Matthias' Church, Westmount, was particularly well qualified for the task. He had formerly been on the staff of two similar schools — one run by the Royal School of Church Music in England, and the other under the auspices of the Diocese of Toronto at Trinity College School.

The aim of the week-long school [the article continues] is "to extend and amplify the tradition of boys in choirs, and of all-male choirs in particular," Mr. Hurrle explained. ... "We are not trying to do anything outstandingly difficult, ... just standard things — hymns, some selections from Merbecke and Willan — to help them do a better job in their own choirs."

Two hours in the morning and an hour in the evening were devoted to practice. The large camp recreation hall was converted into a practice room with the boys seated facing each other in traditional choir formation.

For services such as the Choral Communion held at the camp on Wednesday morning, the boys wore traditional cassocks with white surplices and finely pleated ruffs. The high point of the school's practice was performing at the camp's closing Evensong, held at St Mark's Episcopal Church, Newport.

While all of the 41 boys have treble voices, some small measure of balance is lent by four older 'prefects' from Mr. Hurrle's own choir who sing alto, tenor and bass. ...

Despite the heavy practice schedule [the article hastens to add], the boys live a full camp life. Swimming instruction usually takes up what's left of the morning after choir practice. But the afternoon is clear with plenty of time for more swimming, water-skiing, canoeing, tennis and football. Also on the schedule are outdoor barbecues, treasure hunts and a trip to nearby Jay Peak and a ride on the chairlift.

The camp and the choir school were a great success and the boys threw themselves into the opportunities afforded there:

Certainly the boys sing for pleasure as well as practice [the writer observed]. Even after the heavy morning, three or four can usually be found grouped around the grand piano in the practice hall trying out new hymn tunes or going over favorite anthems.

With the cost of attending the camp at $50 for the week, many of the boys were sponsored by their churches to allow the most promising choristers to participate regardless of their means.

Among the churches represented at the school that first year were St Andrew's, Strathmore; St Mark's, Dorval; St Margaret's, Mascouche; St John the Divine, Verdun; Trinity Memorial, NDG; St Matthias, Westmount; St Cuthbert's, Park Extension; Church of the Advent, Westmount; and St Barnabas, St Lambert.

Hurrle's hopes that the choir school camp would become an annual affair were not disappointed. By 1972 the camp was being held in the Diocese, at Lake Macdonald, near Weir. The chaplain's report, which appeared in the Synod journal of the year following, shows how the program had evolved since 1961. There were now three musical directors:

Gerald Wheeler (of the Cathedral), Stephen Crisp (St Matthias), and Dr
Derek Holman, a guest-director, who was the organist and choirmaster
of Grace Church-on-the-Hill, Toronto.

Last year's camp was as bi-national and bi-racial as ever [the report stated],
drawing boys from as far away as Florida. It was also the largest camp we
have held, with 72 boys, and a staff of 20 involved in music, recreation and
general superintendence. What was most noteworthy was that our own
diocesan boys this year came from a far greater number of parishes — a
hopeful sign for the future both of the camp, and of church music in the
diocese. ... Up to now, most of the boys at the camp, as well as most of the
financial backing for it, have come from the three parishes of the Cathedral, St Matthias' and St Philip's.

The following year, applications for the camp were so numerous that
some boys had to be turned away.

In 1995 the Montreal Boys' Choir Course celebrated its 35th anniversary. Camp that year, still at Lake Macdonald, welcomed fifty campers (just ten more than the earliest group), under the direction of Dr
Barry Rose, Organist and Master of the Music of the Cathedral and
Abbey Church of St Alban, England. Campers and the staff of ten
represented parishes in Quebec, Ontario, Manitoba, New York, Indi-
ana, Michigan, North Carolina, Ohio, and the District of Columbia.

Choristers followed an extremely busy schedule [reads the report in the
Synod Journal] alternating three-and-a-half hours of daily rehearsal with
competitive sports, crafts and swimming. One of the week's highlights was
the celebration of the Eucharist by Choir Course Patron and Bishop of
Montreal, Andrew Hutchison.

The closing Evensong on August 27 saw Trinity Memorial Church filled
to capacity. The music, chosen primarily by Dr. Rose, focussed on our
offering of worship to God: from the Processional Hymn, "Ye Watchers
and Ye Holy Ones," through the Introit, "Truly the Lord Is in This Place"
(Peter Hurford), the Preces & Responses (Leighton), Psalm 138 ("I will give
thanks unto Thee, O Lord, with my whole heart") and the Magnificat and
Nunc Dimittis (Edgar Day). The musical highlight of the service was Henry
Purcell's magnificent "Te Deum in D," with alto soloists Brian Davies and
Jimmy Schultz (Grand Rapids Choir of Men & Boys), bass Andrew Vivian,
chorus, and duo-organists Patrick Wedd and John Stephenson. The Ven.
Peter Hannen, Archdeacon of Montreal, spoke engagingly and eloquently
on music and its effect on the community of worshippers of whom this
course is a part. The service ended with two anthems, "Prevent us, O Lord"
(Ridout) and "O Lord our governor" (Rose).

In concluding her report to the 1996 Synod on this 35th anniversary program, Cynthia Hawkins, a member of the staff of musical directors, paid tribute to "those musicians and administrators who paved the way before us; from the late Norman Hurrle, founder of the course, through the directors of music of Christ Church Cathedral Montreal, St. Matthias, Westmount, and our American counterparts."

By 1996, the Fulford Trust, the Anglican Foundation, and the Diocese of Montreal were providing much of the funding for the program. In 1961 the organizers had begun with little more than vision and determination, the blessing of the Archdeaconry of Montreal, and the backing of a few parishes who valued choral music and were willing to invest in the lasting impact of a week of camping.

# The Old Brewery Mission (1963)

In 1963 the Rev. Bill McCarthy was asked to take over the management of Montreal's Old Brewery Mission.

A product of "a scrappy Montreal neighbourhood known as Mile End," he had enlisted in the infantry at age 18 and served for two years in the Korean War. On his return to Montreal he entered Diocesan Theological College, was ordained in 1960 and served St Barnabas, Roxboro, building it up to 600 families in three short years. The ideal candidate to run the OBM, he served it with grit, faith and Irish good nature for a full thirty years.

In his book, *The Rev: Memoirs of Montreal's Old Brewery Mission*, McCarthy describes the world of the down and out, the homeless and the destitute, giving them faces and telling their stories with humour and affection. A large part of his narrative deals with finding the means to feed, clothe and otherwise provide for the hundreds of men who presented themselves at the Mission for assistance:

At the Brewery Mission, clothing was distributed according to three categories. Ordinary, functional clothes would be issued to fellows who appeared not to care much about their personal appearance. It would serve no purpose to give them a good suit (actually, we never gave anyone a whole suit as they would sell it for sure). However, if a man was really trying, he would get better quality clothing. Finally, if someone was really progressing — perhaps even looking for a job — he would be given the best we had to offer. It was remarkable to see the rehab workers all dressed up on special occasions. We used to kiddingly call them bank managers. Chances are, they were wearing some bank executive's suit!

P<small>LATE</small> 15A  *Ground-breaking ceremony in Ste-Agathe-des-Monts
(Photo Credit:* Barcus Salmon*)*

P<small>LATE</small> 15B  *French language courses become a priority after the Quiet
Revolution  (Photo Credit:* Mac Juster*)*

Many well-known Montrealers brought their used clothing to the Mission with no fanfare. Donald Gordon, my old boss at the CNR [who had become Chairman, President and Director of the Canadian National Railways in 1950], was a Scottish immigrant who had fought his way to the top, all the while remembering just how difficult life could be. He didn't forget those he passed on the way up.

After he passed away, as per his request, we received his whole wardrobe. He was a very big man physically and we could always find someone who badly needed an oversized pair of shoes, pants or jacket. But what to do with the ten-gallon hat that had been presented to Donald Gordon by the City of Calgary? It took me two years [Donald Gordon died in Montreal in early May, 1969] to find a man with a head size big enough to appreciate it. When I finally did, old Nick [pseudonym of one of the men in the Rehabilitation Program at the Mission's Camp Chapleau] proudly paraded around the streets of old Montreal with that stetson; in the summer, he wore it around camp, often wearing very little else. What a sight!

McCarthy had a way of beguiling the media — not for nothing was he voted Montreal's Irishman of the Year in 1984 — and the OBM's drive for clothing reached mammoth proportions with media help:

By far the largest clothing collection we ever had came one winter weekend through a special event organized by CBC staffers. George Springate headed the campaign, along with David Bronstetter and Kathy Keefler. Pick up points were arranged at several major shopping centres, all staffed by CBC personalities.

We ended up with approximately twelve tons of new and used clothing, which was great, but we had no obvious way to deal with it. Talk about being all dressed up with no place to go! ...

One of my Legion contacts told me that the Church of the Redeemer in Côte St. Paul was up for sale, so off we went to the synod office to convince a charitable Bishop's Executive Officer to look favourably upon our borrowing a deconsecrated church. Our request was a little out of the ordinary and some people might have been uneasy that we were going to fill the church with homeless people. However, the Reverend Canon Sandilands, the Executive Officer, was more than cooperative and Bishop Hollis, too, had no doubts about the issue and granted our request. Instead of paying any rent, we simply paid the heating and carried the liability insurance until they sold the church [in 1984].

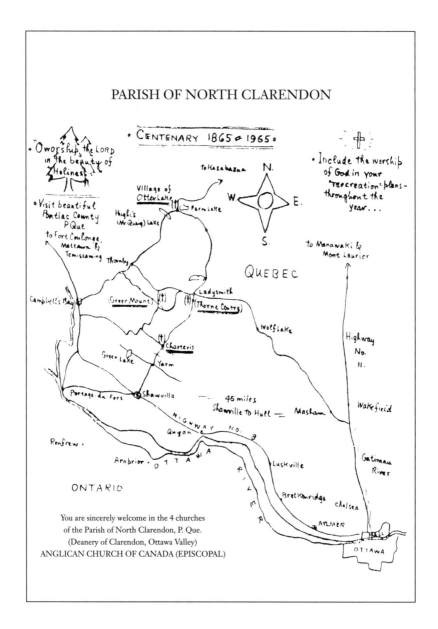

PARISH OF NORTH CLARENDON

• CENTENARY 1865 ⚬ 1965 ⚬

• O worship the LORD in the beauty of Holiness

• Include the worship of God in your "recreation" plans – throughout the year...

• Visit beautiful Pontiac County P.Que.

to Fort Coulonge, Mattawa & Temiscaming

to Kazabazua

N.
W. E.
S.

Village of Otter Lake

Farm Lake

Hughi's (Mr. Quang) Lake

Thornby

QUEBEC

to Manawaki & Mont Laurier

Campbell's Bay

Greer Mount

Ladysmith (Thorne Centre)

Wolf Lake

Highway No. 11.

Charteris

Green Lake

Yarm

Portage du Fort

Shawville

45 miles Shawville to Hull —

Masham

Wakefield

HIGHWAY NO. 8

Quyon

Renfrew

Arnprior

OTTAWA

Luskville

Gatineau River

ONTARIO

Breckenridge

Chelsea

AYLMER

OTTAWA

You are sincerely welcome in the 4 churches
of the Parish of North Clarendon, P. Que.
(Deanery of Clarendon, Ottawa Valley)
ANGLICAN CHURCH OF CANADA (EPISCOPAL)

PLATE 16    *The multi-point parish of North Clarendon, 1965*

We had a work crew at the church every day for four or five months and two watchmen to ensure no one would break in or cause any damage. My wife Colette worked there four or five days a week helping with the sorting.

In the 1980's, the City of Montreal and the Quebec government chose the Old Brewery Mission as "the agency best suited to meet the needs of the homeless and needy of Montreal." It was also singled out by the latter to bring its name, dating from the 1880s, into conformity with Bill 101, the province's Language Law. As McCarthy describes it:

One of the things we had to deal with was the challenge to the organization's name by l'Office de la langue française. I must admit that the person handling the complaint was very gracious when I noted that the word "brasserie" today means drinking establishment, not a brewery, and that "mission" is in any case the same in both languages. We came to a verbal agreement that henceforward, signs in front of the building would read "Mission Old Brewery Mission." We were open to everyone and in fact, there was no Francophone mission at that time, la Maison du Père [the first Francophone mission to the homeless in Montreal] not having been opened.

There was never any question as to how, what or who motivated the work of the Mission [wrote McCarthy in his introductory chapter]. It was always a Christian mission serving the children of God regardless of race, religion or colour. Our Blessed Lord could, would and did sustain it.

## Reinstitution of the Cathedral Men and Boys Choir (1966)

Most of the city churches with a strong tradition of music have had a long history of choirs composed exclusively of men and boys — St. Matthias, Trinity Memorial and St John the Evangelist, to name a few — but maintaining such choirs has always been difficult for a variety of reasons. For a time the difficulty concerned the composition of the choir; later, added to this was the question of choir members' safety in the city at night.

Some years before St Martin's closed in 1954, for example, it became clear that the choir needed strengthening, and some members of the congregation "advocated a radical change by giving up the men and boys and having a mixed Choir of ladies and gentlemen." The matter was finally settled by raising a special subscription to "engage four boys and two men" as leading members of the choir. Some thirty-five years later, the possibility of rethinking the men-and-boys-only composition of the choir of St Matthias, Westmount, was met with similar hostility. The Men and Boys Choir at the Cathedral, by contrast, was allowed to disappear for a time, but was revived soon after the appointment of Gerald Wheeler as Director of Music in 1965.

A "Report on the State of the Choirs of Christ Church Cathedral," presented by Wheeler in September 1985 traces the state of affairs at the time of his reinstitution of the Men and Boys Choir:

In 1965, when I was appointed director of music, there were three services each Sunday; 9:15 a.m. (Eucharist), 11:00 a.m. (alternately Mattins and Eucharist) and 7:00 p.m. (Evensong). A temporary choir of mixed voices was formed at that time to sing the 11:00 a.m. services, whilst the singing at the 9:15 a.m. service was led by a voluntary choir of men. It should be mentioned that in 1965, all three services used the 1959 Prayer Book rites.

The Choir of Men and Boys was formed in September, 1966 and gradually took over the singing of the 11 a.m. service, and one Evensong each month. The voluntary choir of mixed voices sang the remaining Evensongs and became known as the Cathedral Singers, thereby resurrecting the name of the former cathedral choral society.

Over the years, there have been changes to the number of services, and to the order of liturgy. Also the Cathedral Singers now [in 1985] sing the 10 a.m. service on the last Sunday of each month, and the two choirs divide duties at major festivals and diocesan services.

When the Men and Boys Choir was formed in 1966, Wheeler notes, twenty-four boys were enrolled in it. In 1985, there were twelve. At the same time, and in this diminished state, it was serving as the principal choir at the Cathedral.

At the present time [the report continues] the choir activities cost the Cathedral approx. $12,000 per year; the boys' choir spending a high proportion of this amount by means of Choir Scholarships, choir camp subsidies, lunches on the first Sunday of the month, travelling expenses, and maintenance of choir robes. Of the $7^1/_2$ hours of rehearsals each week, two are spent with the boys alone, $1^1/_2$ with the men who sing with the boys, and one hour before the Sunday service with the full choir — a total of $4^1/_2$ hours or 60% of the total rehearsal time. Therefore, the question should be asked as to whether the money, time and energy spent on this choir produces a worthwhile standard of choral music. It should be noted that in my opinion, at the present time, the Cathedral Singers produce a more satisfactory standard of singing for a considerably smaller expense of time, money and energy.

There were other problems as well. Construction on the Cathedral site made noise a factor at the traditional 4:30 practice time, and that time period itself — although the authorities seemed slow to recognize it — had become a factor in discouraging boys from signing up for the choir.

The small number of the boys, and the continuing decline in numbers [the report continues] are my great concern at the present time. One of the most active recruitment campaign[s] ever held for new boys has been carried out during the past summer, which has resulted in the addition of only two new boys. However, six boys left during the past year due to change of voice. The recruitment campaign consisted of wide distribution of a new professionally printed folder, coverage of the choir's activities in the *Gazette* and on CBC-TV, personal letters to principals of the P[rotestant] S[chool] B[oard of] G[reater] M[ontreal] schools in the area with follow-up 'phone calls, and paid advertisements in the *Gazette*. ... Only one reply was received in response to the *Gazette* advertisements, and in this case the mother involved said she would not let the child travel alone on the bus or métro system. In talking to parents of present boys, I do hear a general concern regarding travelling to the cathedral in downtown Montreal, especially on dark winter nights.

Travel conditions in the city, especially for young boys, was apparently a major difficulty in recruitment for the choir, as one letter in the Cathedral archives attests. It is dated 9 October 1985:

Dear Mr. Wheeler:
    I decided not to pursue my suggestion of alternative evening choir prectises at your Sunday, October 6 meeting because it appeared I was walking on very sensitive ground with respect to other parents present. Parents of children unable to join the choir because of the practise time were not present. In as brief a form as possible, I would like now to respond ....

*Concerns*
Without becoming melodramatic, a number of children have been murdered in the Montreal area over the past 3 years and newspapers warn us that the perpetrator(s) are still at large. The young boy living near us was beaten up by a gang in the metro on his way to school. I am now a member of a silent majority called "paranoid parents."

Not only will I not let my children take the metro alone, I would not let them take a taxi alone. Not before they are 21, anyway.

*Current Situation*
I consider myself (and [my son] too) very fortunate that I have a 16 year-old brother-in-law. I pay him $10 to spend 1½ hours fighting rush hour traffic to drive [my son] to choir practise. Luckily I work 3 blocks away from the Cathedral and pick [him] up after practise. Few families have this luxury. If the husband uses the car for work, if the wife wishes to make supper, if the wife hates driving in traffic, if there are other children with needs to be fulfilled, the child cannot join the choir.

*Experience with other Programs*
As a director of Les Loisirs de Saint Simon l'Apôtre, I am involved in almost every recreational activity in our region in Montreal. We have learned, from experience, not to schedule cubs, soccer, badminton, etc., before 6:30 p.m. Our best attendance is for activities at 7 p.m. …
    Your work and your patience with [my son] is very much appreciated. [He], for his part, adores his teacher, a feeling, I am beginning to learn, is universal.

One of Wheeler's suggestions to meet the crisis in the Men and Boys Choir was to engage a number of professional singers to bring the voices up to strength. The proposed music budget listed "Choir salaries $10,000" as a major item in the total budget of $23,947. This figure was up to $10,500 the following year, but other items related to transportation show that the men and boys had not been dispensed with.

In 1993, Wheeler led a tour of the choir whose very continuance less than ten years before had been in doubt. They travelled to Washington DC, were received by the Canadian Ambassador, John de Chastelain, and sang at the National Cathedral:

The first impression of the National Cathedral would be 'awesome' for any-one's first visit [wrote Wheeler in an article for *Cathedral Script*], but for the entire choir, first impressions on the Sunday morning were stunning. After a short rehearsal, the choir sang their 25-minute recital on the chancel steps as a prelude to the main 11 a.m. service. Again it was pleasing for me to have the choir in top form, and the echoing silences after the "alleluias" in Barstow's 'Let All Mortal Flesh Keep Silence' were simply thrilling. For the service which followed, the choir was placed in a section of the choir stalls adjacent to the communion rail. As a bonus, we heard an excellent sermon from Lord Coggan, the retired 101st Archbishop of Canterbury, who preached on the second best-known prayer in the Christian liturgy — "The Grace of our Lord Jesus Christ ..." and the three gifts of Grace, Love and Fellowship. ...

As one of our newest trebles fervently remarked, "I had a great time and will remember it always."

By the year 2000 the Men and Boys Choir had become Men and Trebles (with two girls enrolled in it) and continued to include a number of professional singers. The Cathedral Singers, the largest of the Cathedral choirs with some twenty-five members, has a varied and extensive repertoire. There is now also a flourishing Girls' Choir, and music at the Cathedral has expanded to include the teaching and performance of liturgical dancing.

# Expo '67 (1967)

In the year of Canada's Centennial Celebrations, the Diocese of Montreal made an all-out effort to welcome visitors from across the country, and its choice for an Expo Motto (coined by Archdeacon Barry Valentine) was "The Friendly Diocese — Host to the World."

In the June issue of the *Montreal Churchman* for that year, Bishop Kenneth Maguire addressed all "Anglicans at the Fair" with the following message:

Dear Visitors: —

This issue of our *Montreal Churchman* is intended especially for you, and on behalf of my Anglican people in this diocese, which has at its centre and as its See City the City of Montreal, I extend with real pleasure a warm welcome to you.

Everybody in Canada is undertaking Centennial projects this year: our diocese has as its special projects participation in the Christian Pavilion at Expo '67 and also a Hospitality and Information Centre.

The Centre, at Anglican House, immediately behind Christ Church Cathedral, our official Expo Church, is being staffed throughout the six months of Expo by members of many parishes. We hope that we may look forward to welcoming you there.

We shall feel privileged if we can help and serve you in any way.

This Expo-Centennial issue will give you a thumbnail sketch of our diocese, and serve as a modest guide and be a memento of your visit. ...

PLATE 17    *The Hospitality and Information Centre, Expo '67*
            *(Photo Credit:* MDA*)*

The Hospitality Centre was a mammoth undertaking, requiring a slate of volunteers for twenty-six weeks from 10 a.m. to 4 p.m., seven days a week. In addition, there were four young full-time staff members — all university students — jauntily dressed in kilts and jackets.

Other Anglican initiatives in the city had visiting students in mind:

The Anglican Chaplaincy at McGill [a brief notice in the *Montreal Churchman* reported] will be hosting University students throughout the summer, providing not only cheap accommodation but also an open-air coffee house.

The Chaplain, Rev. Glenn Pritchard, has planned the coffee house as a meeting place for all students in Montreal during Centennial summer. In addition to coffee and companionship, [the] Canterbury [Club] will also be providing entertainment on Friday and Saturday evenings.

The Chaplain explained that many of the attractions of the World Festival will be beyond the financial reach of students and after a long day touring the exhibition itself, a relaxing evening 'under the stars' to the accompaniment of folk singers and dramatic productions would be a welcome change of pace.

In 1965, General Synod had authorized a campaign to raise $175,000 for the Anglican Church's share of the Christian Pavilion. Expo officials had donated a site to the participating churches in a central location, and the cost of the Pavilion would be shared by the Roman Catholics, the Anglicans, the United Church, the Presbyterians, Lutherans, Baptists, and the Greek-Orthodox Church. The maximum budget for the building, the exhibits, the operation and the general administration of the pavilion had been estimated at $1,300,000:

While there was obviously much soul-searching among delegates about the cost involved [an article in the *Montreal Churchman* observed], most of them agreed with the view that the situation was not unlike the one in the Gospel where Jesus commended a woman for a 'holy waste' in anointing him with expensive perfume.

The motion to raise the required funds was introduced by Bishop Maguire who noted that "it would take twenty-five years for a church seating 1,000 people every Sunday to reach as many people as it is expected will enter the Christian Pavilion at Expo '67." The Dean of Montreal, the Very Rev. William Bothwell, told the Synod that the Roman Catholic Church "had given up plans to build its own pavilion in order to join with the six other churches in presenting a common Christian witness."

It was an unprecedented opportunity, and the Diocese of Montreal seized it with energy and verve. The Bishop — whose signature tune, it was affectionately suggested on at least one occasion, ought to have been "Lord of the Dance" — was the ideal host. It is difficult to imagine a better place for Anglicans to have celebrated the nation's hundredth birthday.

## Closures and Amalgamations (1968)

In the early days of the diocese, rapid expansion was the chief policy. In 1864, for example, Bishop Fulford announced to the annual meeting of Church Society with evident satisfaction that, since his arrival in 1850, the number of clergy in the diocese had increased from 49 to 70. Church building was encouraged, assisted by grants from a variety of sources, and many communities took pride in having a church for their own, even if another of the same denomination (and perhaps even served by the same clergyman) was within an easy drive. Such a practice was bound to meet with a reverse once populations began to decline.

The following letter, addressed to Bishop Maguire and dated 1 April, 1968, is typical of this situation, and reflects the hard reality for those parishioners who continued to live in dwindling rural parishes:

I am writing to inform you of a decision made by the Vestry of the Church of the Good Shepherd, Bondville.

A duly constituted meeting of the above Vestry was held on Wednesday, February 28th, 1968, at 2 p.m. ... The meeting was requested by the members of the Vestry to discuss the rapidly changing situation within the area, and its relation to the church in resources, manpower, money and facilities available to cope with the deteriorating situation.

Discussion included:

1   The significant lack of families necessary to keep the church solvent and discharge its responsibilities.
2   The breakdown in the development of future leadership by young people, due to there being no young people available.
3   The impediment to the witness of the church and its structures, due to lack of manpower.
4   Cooperation with the Vestry of St. James, Foster.
5   Worship at St. James, Foster.
6   Integration with or into St. James Church congregation.

Finally it was resolved unanimously that: "The Church of the Good Shepherd, Bondville, regretfully close its doors, and that the Synod be petitioned to this effect, and a request [be] made for one service annually."

It was suggested that present families would maintain the fabric of the church in good repair.

As you are aware, My Lord, the distance between Bondville and Foster is only 4 miles. Some of the Members of Bondville are already attending St. James, Foster.

Attendance at Bondville last summer averaged two per service. Although Bondville is a small summer resort, the influx of visitors is Roman Catholic and French.

Fulford Church is having the same difficulties, and will ask for the same conditions, pending the decision on Bondville.

Bondville and Fulford, ironically, were the only two communities in the Diocese to have taken their names from Anglican bishops — as Charleston (Hatley) in the Diocese of Quebec, for example, was named for Bishop Charles James Stewart.

Bondville, which took its name in 1888 when Bishop Bond consecrated the church, had the further distinction of being memorialized in a special music-box, made by the German toymaker, Gerhardt Brinkmann: "While visiting Bondville ... he saw the little white church with the green painted roof and decided to use that as his model. ... It is an exact replica of the Bondville church and when the church door is opened the music-box plays 'Silent Night' ..."

The Wardens of St. James, Foster [the letter continues], are aware [of] and in agreement with the Bondville resolution, as far as it concerns them.

Regarding the annual service which has been requested, I do not believe this will constitute a great barrier to closure. In my estimation, it was purely an emotional and nostalgic wish, and not out of context at the time of the resolution. I do believe they will realize this. The wish was also strengthened by the fact of the Ladies' Guild having approx[imately] $900 in Bonds which led them to believe this would be sufficient to keep the church in constant repair.

At the meeting I did not consider it was an appropriate time for me to remark upon this, but in actual fact, it is insufficient to carry out repairs required at the present time. I am sure they will be wise enough to see this as time goes on, and in discussion. ...

On Saturday, April 6th, I am meeting at Foster with the Wardens of Foster, Bondville, Fulford, and Bromont churches ... The question of the future for our churches will be brought up for consideration. ...

I will let the matter rest with you, my Lord, and await your suggestions.

It is not surprising that even a tiny congregation will wish to try to preserve its church, nor is it unusual for churches to retain their status as consecrated buildings by holding a single service per year. Such celebrations, it might be reasonable to suppose, could coincide with homecomings and gatherings of friends and family. Usually the clergy, not the people, press to close such churches.

On 8 April, following the wardens' meeting held two days before, a second letter to the Bishop makes it clear that the purely "emotional and nostalgic wish" of the parishioners had been talked out. There was now "agreement and realization that [Bondville and Fulford] should close without requesting one annual service, as long as there was a church within a reasonable distance (8-10 miles). No further services would be held, pending a decision."

# The Impact of Provincial Politics (1969)

The following is a a sample of the impact of social and political changes in Quebec, not only on church membership, but on the clergy.

"The Rt. Rev. R. K. Maguire,
1444 Union Avenue,
Montreal, P.Q.

December 30, 1969

Rt. Rev. and Dear Sir:

I assume it is in order for me to write an official letter of resignation from this Parish and Diocese.

Accordingly, let me say, it is with mixed emotions that I do submit notice of my resignation here to be effective January 31, 1970.

My reasons for this course of action are purely due to the political and social situation in this Province at the present time. Concerning both the Diocese and this Parish, I have only the deepest gratitude for all that it has been my pleasure to experience here.

I realize that I owe a debt of gratitude to yourself and the Diocese for the way in which I have been received here and for the opportunities that I have been given during my time with you.

Concerning the Parish, it has been a labour of love and has carried its own reward to me. I have not served without having made some mistakes but I have served with my whole heart.

It is with a heavy heart that I say goodbye to many wonderful friends in both the Diocesan Family, because I really feel the sense of family within the Diocese, and in the Parish. But, at the same time, I must be honest and admit it is with a light heart that I prepare to return to my native Province and those things and ways that are and always will be, near and dear to both myself and my family.

From the bottom of my heart, let me say thanks to you and the Diocese for all.

The year 1969 saw the passage of Bill 63 in which the Provincial Government affirmed its right to determine the language of education for children in the school system. In the previous year there had been riots in the Italian district of St-Léonard when the school board eliminated English as the language of education. In the year following, Quebecers would experience the kidnapping of James Cross, the murder of Pierre Laporte, and the invocation of the War Measures Act.

# The French Fact (1970)

The English-speaking community in Quebec, and the Anglican Church in particular, have been accused in many quarters of being out of sympathy and out of touch with the French-speaking society within which they have functioned for so many years. According to Joan Marshall, in her study of the Diocese of Montreal and the Quiet Revolution, published in 1995:

All of the documentation [Bishop's Charges, Synod Proceedings and articles in the Diocesan paper] prior to the election of the Parti Québécois in 1976 shows a church that is essentially unresponsive to the society within which it is located. It took the challenge of a separatist government, the passage of restrictive education bills, and the reality of out-migration of anglophones to force the church into a pro-active position. Even so, despite calls for a French ministry and bilingual priests, the concrete actions of the church have been cautious. The reasons are open to debate. Some people have pointed to the leadership ...

A brief examination of the *Proceedings of Synod* from 1963 on — the year of Kenneth Maguire's election to the episcopate, shows that — whatever the views of the individual in the pew might be — the new bishop wanted his priests to become more fully integrated into Quebec society by becoming functionally bilingual.

He inaugurated French language training for the clergy and set up study groups to facilitate French ministry. This, of course, showed little immediate result, but the intention was clear to those within the system.

Maguire's Charge to Synod in 1970 was outspoken in its sympathy for the growing aspirations of nationalist French-speaking Quebecers to be *maîtres chez soi*. To increase an awareness and sensitivity among the clergy he had invited one of the most articulate of French-speaking Quebecers to address a clergy conference. He also took pains to project this open and positive attitude through the media.

The Charge to Synod makes his views quite clear:

In a rapidly changing world society, Quebec is no exception. There is no doubt that, in the midst of these changes, some English-speaking Quebecers feel threatened, and wonder about their future here. This may well be a natural reaction of those who know themselves to be a minority. What often fails to be appreciated with sufficient sensitivity is the very real threat which our French-speaking brothers see to their language and culture in the vast North American continent. Their fears are not without foundation and I know that all of the clergy deeply appreciated hearing Monsieur Claude Ryan, the editor of *Le Devoir*, when he gave generously of his time to speak to us at a two-day Conference last Fall on the French Fact.

In an interview being taped for radio some months ago, I finally found myself saying to a charming young interviewer that she was asking the wrong questions — for, in fact, the questions were questions which would lead one to speak defensively or aggressively from an "English" standpoint rather than as a Quebecer. So to speak can lead to a divisive polarization and to the assuming of stances which you do not wish to assume.

This polarization ought not to be inevitable, for the two cultures can be enrichingly complementary. Much as we treasure our own culture, nevertheless if it so happened that the influence of French culture in our society declined sharply, I believe that we would be the first to recognize that our Quebec style of life had been sadly impoverished. But that belief must be made sympathetically evident, and therefore I welcome the fact that, in setting its targets for the Seventies, the Board of Programming urges that priority in the field of continued education be given to French language and culture.

The Policy and Programming Report, under the heading Personnel Training, item 4, stated that "a goal of the Diocese should be the provision of a working knowledge of French for individuals involved in ministry," and noted that "a step towards this goal was the recent French Course at Macdonald College on a shared cost basis between the individual, the parish, the Diocese and the National Church."

In an address to Synod in 1972 — under the heading, "The Bishop Looks at the Future" — Maguire noted that in the course of the past year a group of clergy had begun to discuss "such questions as What is

Quebec's Future? In What Direction Is It Moving? and to study initiatives which might be taken by individuals and the diocese to involve us more with the French-speaking community. ... [T]hese are questions we must face."

He goes on to state:

In the past we of the Anglican Church of Canada here in Quebec, by accidents of our history have been known as the Church of, by and for "les Anglais," but in reality we are not, and cannot be just this and no more, no matter how many of our people speak English as their first language. We, as Anglicans, but primarily as Christians, must come to an appreciation of the legitimate cultural and linguistic aims of all people who are our neighbours in this city and province, and in doing so we cannot but take note of the fact that this is primarily a French province and a French city. As Christians it would be fitting for us to want to understand their legitimate aspirations, their fears and hopes.

None of this smacks of unresponsiveness.

Although other matters were discussed as well, the church's role in Quebec society was a constant theme at Synod. In the "Bishop's Address" to Synod in 1973, Maguire reminded those present:

Last year in Synod I spoke at some length about the role and future of our Anglican Church in the Province of Quebec. Words in themselves are of singularly little value and can lead to frustration if nothing happens. I am therefore happy that a number of people worked at this area of concern and the recent memorandum "towards a bilingual image," prepared for me by Canon Turpin, is full of sound, practical suggestions of ways of moving forward.

The following year he stated once again that "our Diocese has made a firm commitment to bilingualism."

On his election to the episcopate, Maguire had stated that he would serve the diocese as its bishop for twelve years and, true to this commitment, resigned the office in 1975. Reginald Hollis, therefore was the presiding bishop at Montreal's 116th Annual Synod, held in the year of his election. Hollis's initial Charge to Synod stated unequivocally his intention of continuing Maguire's program of pursuing a bilingual image, but with a telling extension which would mark the rest of his episcopate: that of evangelism:

At last year's Synod, Bishop Maguire announced that he would submit a brief on Bill 22. This he did. It was a very moderate statement which both recognised the priority of the French language in the Province and also called for a safeguard of basic human rights. Recognising our French setting, we have continued to develop a bilingual image and we have been grateful to the Government, through the Catholic School Commission, for providing French immersion courses for some of our Clergy. It is my hope, however, that we develop more than a bilingual image. I am concerned that we have a French ministry which can reach out to the increasing number of French-speaking people in the Province who no longer have active ties with any Church. Here is our mission field. We have small beginnings. Église du Rédempteur, the weekly Eucharist in French here in the Cathedral, and a new congregation of Haitians who worship in French in St Hilda's Church. But these congregations must be only the beginning of an enlarging ministry.

In her comments on what she sees as the failure of the church to seek integration into Quebec life, Joan Marshall points a finger straight at the top. To backtrack slightly in resuming her assessment:

… despite calls for a French ministry and bilingual priests, the concrete actions of the church have been cautious. The reasons are open to debate. Some people have pointed to the leadership, noting that the bishop [Hollis] continued, throughout his sixteen-year tenure, to import clergy from Britain, and that despite his announced intent that the church become more bilingual and in closer touch with the realities of Quebec, his actions spoke of continuing links with the Church of England. Others have said that the bishop was intentionally, and wisely perhaps, cautious about bilingualism because so many parishes were extremely apprehensive about French in their churches.

Such criticism fails to take into account two important considerations.

Until the end of the 1950s Hugh MacLennan's portrayal of French and English-speaking Quebecers as two solitudes was a shrewd and accurate one — based no doubt on his long-time residence in Montreal teaching at McGill University. Until that time the cultural integrity of French-speaking Roman Catholic Quebec was virtually impenetrable to English-speaking Protestants. Schools were separate and strictly based on religious affiliation. No Roman Catholic, by law, could teach in a Protestant school and vice versa. No Roman Catholic girl could join the Guides, no boy the Scouts, without a reprimand from the parish priest. Should a Roman Catholic student seek to receive training beyond the curriculum of a Catholic university — in Engineering, perhaps — his family would receive a pastoral visit. Until Vatican II the power of the Roman Catholic Church within Quebec society would be difficult to overestimate.

As Canon Reginald M. Turpin put it in his report on French-English relations and the church in Quebec, presented to General Synod in 1977:

This may be an appropriate point to suggest that in trying to understand how the "Two Solitudes" came about, it is an oversimplification to blame it all on British economic power. On the one hand, in its singleminded commitment to developing French-Canadian identity, preserv[ing] the French language, and foster[ing] the Catholic ethos, values, and Faith, the Roman Catholic Church of the past in Quebec feared the Protestant ethos, values and Faith. It was both a religious duty and practical wisdom, therefore, not to mix the two. On the other hand, the general reluctance of Anglican Church leaders (to speak only of our own family) to proselytize, and the gradual development, in a French milieu, of an Anglicanism which has been largely a chaplaincy to a unilingual Anglo-Saxon-Celtic population, has not helped to promote dialogue.

Canon Turpin had for some time been involved in efforts to extend French ministry in the Diocese of Montreal and to encourage bilingualism among the clergy.

The second consideration touches Marshall's judgment against "imported clergy."

With attitudes of separateness and social disengagement from their French-speaking neighbours — especially in matters of religion — ingrained in many native-born English-speaking Quebecers, bringing in clergy from outside the province to break the cycle of this mindset was probably a good idea. Drawing upon Britain in the 1960s for priests willing to come to the Diocese was a far cry from returning to the colonialism of Bishop Mountain's days. It seems more likely that Hollis was looking for clergy with particular qualities and was willing to seek them far afield, whether in Britain or the Caribbean.

Following its presentation to General Synod, Bishop Hollis circulated Canon Turpin's report to his parish clergy, urging them to "share it with your Wardens and key laity." Extra copies were available from Synod Office. It contained ten recommendations to equip the Anglican communion in Canada, as well as that in Quebec, to function and minister in a largely French-speaking society. Far from a mere handbook for survival, however, the report pointed out the opportunity afforded by the current challenge to ministry:

Whether you are among those who find it difficult to consider the future of the Church apart from the future of the Country, or are among those who feel that the Church should not be overly concerned about the particular form of government and organization of society, you can unite in one thing. You can fight intolerance, ignorance, selfishness, and fear; you can expose ethnocentricity, racism, and domination. At the same time you can contribute to a new climate of trust by entering into dialogue with other Canadians, by encouraging identity, understanding the issues, seeking justice for all, and learning patience with your opponents.

# A Laywoman's Many-faceted Involvement (1972)

Pamela McBeth came to Canada in the early seventies. Previous postings in Puerto Rico, the Dominican Republic and Venezuela had exposed her to the poverty and hopelessness of people in these latter countries, and there she had been caught up in the spirit of the theology of liberation. She felt called to spread the Gospel and to be instrumental in providing assistance to those in need. By the time the McBeths came to Montreal she was keenly sensitized to the disparities in any community in which she might find herself and was prepared to use her gifts and energies wherever they were needed. She was to become, in the words of the Rev. Dr John McNab, "one of the most prominent persons in the Church from the Caribbean to come to Canada in the Seventies."

Paying tribute to the scope of her activities in the eulogy he delivered at the time of her death, a friend gave the following glimpses of Pamela's many-faceted involvements, initially with immigrants and refugees, later with her church community, always "in the front lines" :

In 1972, she and [her husband] John were transferred by the Bank [of Montreal] from Venezuela to its Head Office in Montreal. She quickly started being on the lookout for used furniture and household articles that could be provided for those less fortunate. Many of these people had to leave their countries with just the clothes on their backs to escape political persecution. She would promote the sale of works of art among those that came to Canada and helped them find jobs. She drafted many letters and petitions to assist those caught up in the bureaucratic maze of government, judicial, and other bodies.

Pamela went "garage saling" nearly every Saturday morning, from early spring to late fall, buying collectibles that would be sold for the benefit of St. Mark [Dorval]'s projects or put up for sale at her home to raise funds for her own charities in South America.

She became a parishioner af St Mark's in 1972. She sang in the choir from then until 1980 and served on the Administrative Committee from 1974, and as Warden from 1976 to 1984. She was an area representative for Mission and Evangelism, active in stewardship visitations and fund-raising activities. She was also a Lay Assistant at St. Mark's. She frequently filled in when the Church organist was away, both here and at other Churches, including Delson.

For many years she was responsible for producing and directing "Christmas around the World" every December, with a completely different and well-researched performance each time. Besides their educational and entertainment qualities [these productions] involved many people from the congregation. She was instrumental in having the Jubilation Gospel choir perform at St. Mark's, and the driving force of the annual International Food Festival. All these events raised money for missions. I need not tell you she herself sold many tickets far beyond the parish.

Over the years Pamela served in a wide variety of positions at the Diocesan level, as well as in the arenas of the Ecclesiastical Province of Canada and the national Church. Locally, she was Diocesan coordinator for Anglicans in Mission, and chaired the Partners in World Mission and the Companion Diocese relationship with the South-western Diocese of Brazil. She co-chaired the Mission Allocations Committee and sat on many others, including those concerned with Program, Refugees and Race Relations, as well as the World Mission Unit and the Montreal Unit for Social Action.

She sat on the Board of Governors of the Montreal Diocesan Theological College and the Board of Tyndale-St. George.

In the Ecclesiastical Province of Canada she was a member of Provincial Synod and Deputy Prolocutor from 1986 to 1989.

In the national Church, she served for six years on the Program Committee and the National Executive Council. Of the nine years she spent on the Partners in World Mission Committee, three were served as vice-chair and three more as chair. She also sat on the Inter Church, Inter Faith Relations and Centennial Committees of General Synod.

In the ecumenical field Pamela was a member of the Board of the Canadian Bible Society. She served for six years on the General Board of the Canadian Council of Churches, and for three years as Vice-Chair of the Board of the Canadian Centre for Ecumenism, the first woman to hold that office.

When Pamela McBeth was in full stride she was serving on about 25 committees, Units or Boards of the Church at the same time. She was the official translator of all Spanish and Portuguese correspondence to the Diocese. She and John regularly provided accommodation and meals for visiting clergy and lay people from overseas, often at short notice.

Being an able administrator, a veteran of committee work and a dependable organizer is one thing; being a friend-in-need to countless individuals is another. It is through the recollections of those who witnessed her day-to-day concern for others that her spirit is best captured. In the words of Gloria Augustus, whose life was touched by Pamela's gift for helping others:

she was a warm, caring, loving person who would go out of her way to help others in need, no matter who the person in need was. Who you were did not matter to Pam — what mattered most was that she could help. Pamela believed each and every one of us is God's child and we should try our best in whatever way we can to help those less fortunate than ourselves. If Pamela received a call that someone was in need, whatever need that was: a bed, clothes, food, etc. — Pamela telephoned people that she thought able to help her to meet that person's need. That's the kind of person Pamela was. Even though she did not drive, her husband John was always willing to drive her wherever she had to go. Pamela was also very outspoken, not afraid to speak up for what she believed in, and she always encouraged you to go further — could be in Ministry or whatever gifts the Lord has called you to be. She was a very trustworthy person — one could look up to her as an inspiration. Her Faith and trust in the Lord was very strong.

At a special service at St Mark's on Sunday, 16 February 1992, the Most Rev. Michael Peers presented Pamela with the Anglican Award of Merit, an honour which she valued highly.

She died on 27 October 2000 and was buried from St Mark's Church, Dorval, of which she had been a faithful member for twenty-eight years.

# La Nativité (1975)

The founding of l'Église de La Nativité dates from meetings first held in a private home in Rivière des Prairies in October 1974 under the leadership of Fr Lafond Lapointe, a Haitian priest. In November, the small group began to hold services in a hotel room — rented for that purpose at $35 a week.

The high rent indicates the seriousness with which the people pursued their goal [an article in the Montreal Churchman affirmed], and the fact that our Diocese only had to help them once indicates their success in achieving it.

From December 1974, the Diocese and St Hilda's Parish arranged that the congregation could worship in St Hilda's church.

By the following spring there were more than 30 families comprising well over 70 members. A good relationship developed between the English and French-speaking congregations, and in August 1975 the Haitian congregation's organist, Franz Casseus, was playing for the English congregation as well.

Official licensing for Fr Lapointe had caused some difficulty, however, and, in March 1975, the Rev. C.P. Carr was appointed as "le premier titulaire de la paroisse" by Bishop Reginald Hollis. On the face of things, Carr might not seem an ideal choice, being both white and English-speaking. However, according to Joan Marshall, who made the parish part of her study of the Diocese during the Quiet Revolution, "during his eight-year tenure he became a loyal friend to many recently arrived Haitians and the trusted spiritual leader of the Haitian church."

In June of 1980, La Nativité, among other parishes, furnished responses to the Partners in Mission Consultation for Anglicans in the Province of Quebec (Consultation des "Associés dans la mission" à l'intention des épiscopaliens québécois). Together with other French-speaking Anglicans, they responded to the question, "Qu'est-ce qui pourrait aider les francophones montréalais à s'approfondir leur foi crétienne?"

[Réponse] Les relations interpersonnelles. Le travail en petits groupes de base. L'identification à la collectivité québécoise.

Their response to the second question: "Quels changements la collectivité francophone de Montréal a-t-elle connus pendant les années soixante-dix?" was quite different from that of French-Canadian Anglicans.

[Réponse] (Canadiens-français) Volonté toujours croissante d'être 'maîtres chez eux'. Accès au monde d'affaires. Francisation du milieu. Une société de plus en plus éloignée de la foi, mais ouverte aux nouveaux idées. Pluralisme.

[Réponse] (Haïtiens) Chomage. Pauvreté. Un peu de racisme. Sentiment d'isolement. Solidarité de leur parenté et du diocèse du Haïti. Parlent souvent créole plutôt que français.

The two groups agreed that the changes experienced in their churches over the past ten years were not changes at all, but a continuation of a frustrating dearth of human, financial and logistical resources:

[Réponse] Nombres croissants mais toujours très petits. Pas de clergé à temps plein. Pas de ressources fiscales. Partage insatisfaisant de bâtiments. Sentiment de non-appartenance au diocèse. Une situation chargée de possibilités.

To the final question, "Quelles doivent être les préoccupations principales des épiscopaliens québécois qui songent à l'avenir?" the Haitian respondents added "Establish Food Cooperatives" to the other concerns:

[Réponse] Bilinguiser clergé existant. Sensibiliser notre église aux besoins. Co-operative alimentaire. Régler question des bâtiments. Organisation — palier d'autorité francophone? Chercher candidats francophones au sacerdoce. Relations avec église catholique romaine. Formation des leaders. Finance. Publications.

In 1985 the Rev. Yves-Eugène Joseph, a Black Haitian priest was appointed to serve the congregation of l'Église de La Nativité. Interestingly, there was at first some anxiety that a priest from Haiti would assume the more authoritarian style of the parent church. What many hoped for was someone who would "help integrate them into North American life." The job description prepared by the search committee, for example, included someone skilled in counselling, helping with problems related to immigration and unemployment, someone to facilitate the formation of self-help groups for families or the elderly. The congregation wanted someone to help strengthen its existing community and improve its security in Canada. Although, on his own admission, these were not Father Joseph's chief concerns, following an interview by members of the congregation he was accepted as their priest.

On moving on to another sphere of ministry, Carr wrote hopefully of La Nativité's prospects, and pointed out that "although weak financially" the parish had "the biggest attendance in the deanery." In addition to Fr Joseph, Ogé Beauvoir was "going full steam ahead with his plans for ordination, and Emmanuel Duplessis has been a big help recently attending several important events, preaching a quiet day for us, helping in the interim."

[Father Joseph, Joan Marshall suggests] sees a need for the Haitian community to reach out to and become engaged in the society around it. He has tried, unsuccessfully, to involve the congregation in such current issues as free trade, refugee policy, and the goods and services tax (GST). ... His objective is to encourage ... more active engagement in social action.

His efforts in this direction she judged to have met with little success.

He has expressed disappointment [Marshall continues] in the congregation's lack of interest in issues not directly related to their situation. At the annual vestry meeting in 1989 he introduced a motion to oppose the expulsion of illegal Haitian immigrants from Canada. To his dismay it was unanimously defeated.

There have been several attempts to start other Haitian congregations in different parts of the city, with varying success, but La Nativité remains the focus of the Anglican Haitian community. The Baptist and Pentecostal Churches often attract Haitian Anglicans for regular services (as opposed to the major festivals of Christmas and Easter) for these other denominations appear to be "moins rigides et fermées."

La Nativité has its own distinctive cultural flavour. Services are performed in a mixture of French and Creole and the atmosphere is more relaxed than in most Anglican churches. In parish matters, on the other hand, although 90 to 95% of the regular participants at worship services are women, the men of the congregation expect that committee work and positions of authority should naturally fall to them.

There has been some frustration expressed that the community, no matter how numerous or vibrant, is operating on the fringes of the Diocese, that it has little impact on decision-making bodies, and is not at home in a largely English-speaking mind-set.

For its part, Synod Office has attempted to introduce some French into Synod proceedings, and to pay tribute to the distinctive nature of its Haitian parishioners.

In 1978, four students from the Diocesan Theological College went to Haiti for several weeks, with part of their time spent living with Haitian priests and sharing in their life and ministry. The project was "an effort to allow the future leaders of the Church to experience the Church's expression of the Gospel in a Third World and francophone nation." There have been other contacts as well.

In his Charge to Synod in 1994, Bishop Hutchison expressed his concern for the Haitian people:

A year ago, I was privileged to go with the Reverend Yves-Eugène Joseph of the Diocese of Haiti for the consecration of the new Bishop, Mgr Zaché Duracin. We presented vestments to the Bishop, our Primate preached the sermon, and we were able to visit with the Rev. Ogé Beauvoir and his family. Our many links with Haiti prompt us to pray for an early resolution of their distress. …

Also that year, it was reported at the same event, Christ Church Cathedral established a companion parish relationship with a parish in Haiti. In 1999, the Diocese participated in an international SOMA (Sharing of Ministries Abroad) mission to lead an Episcopal Clergy Retreat in Haiti. These initiatives may go but a short way toward the full integration of the people of La Nativité into Diocesan life, but they have at least tended toward a wider recognition of Diocesan diversities.

# PARTI QUÉBÉCOIS
# VICTORY AT THE
# POLLS AND AFTER
## 1976–2000

## The Turpin Report (1977)

Following the Parti Québécois victory in 1976, the future of English-language institutions in the province — including churches of various denominations — at first seemed very much in doubt. At the General Synod held the following year, Canon Reginald M. Turpin presented a report entitled *The Church in Quebec*. In doing so he drew on his wide experience within the Diocese of Montreal where he was currently working towards French ministry and a bilingual clergy, as well as on his recent contacts with key figures in the Roman Catholic Church and a variety of francophone groups within the province.

It was a thoughtful, perceptive report: realistic about the prevailing situation, sympathetic to the aspirations of French-speaking Quebecers, and open to the need for a positive change in the church's mode of doing things.

For the benefit of members of General Synod not familiar with developments in the province he explained the impact of recent legislation:

A clue to understanding what is happening in Quebec lies in the word "francization." What does it mean? In oversimplified terms it means to convert and modify as many aspects of life as possible so that they will have a French look and expression. In practice the policy and process is aimed at all structures, organizations, and institutions which directly involve the public. Its impact will vary in the different parts of our Church in Quebec.

The report goes on to explain the differences from region to region — the bilingual Arctic Anglicans (speaking the Inuit language and English),

*Theology students take a break, 1975 (Photo Credit:* MDA)

*The ordination of the first woman to the priesthood in the Diocese of Montreal, 1978*
*(Photo Credit:* Journal de Montréal)

PLATE 18   *The vocation of women to the priesthood*

the more fully francized Anglicans in the Diocese of Quebec, and the Montreal region with its larger English-speaking communities incorporating a variety of ethnic groups "where the economic and political 'power struggle' is really taking place," the Ottawa Valley, living in the dual world of everyday French "all the while being part of a unilingual English church-world on the other side of the bridge," and finally the church members in Temiscamingue [still part of the Diocese at that time] who, being close to North Bay could "provide us with valuable insights about the feelings of their French-minority neighbours who live in a mixture of bilingual and unilingual settings."

Earlier I mentioned the the word "francization" [the Report continues]. Taking into account the different conditions in each diocese [Montreal, Quebec, and parts of Moosonee and the Arctic], the Anglican Church in Quebec now has to come to grips with this process.

Some measures will be forced on it, at least where it is seen to be an institution serving the public. But as a sign of its "change of heart," it should adopt others voluntarily and as quickly as possible.

The dictates of strategy and the wise use of human and material resources in the light of this "new day" in Quebec make imperative a more meaningful collaboration and cooperation among our dioceses, while on the broader Christian front there is a new chance to prove whether Anglicans in Quebec take the Lund principle seriously.

The Lund principle is so named from a meeting in Lund, Sweden, of the World Council of Churches in 1952, at which it was laid down that churches should do everything together except those things which their consciences forbid.

Among the items which, it is suggested, will equip the Church to act more effectively are the following —

1    find a French equivalent for the name "Anglican Church";
2    provide intensive French language training for clergy and ordinands, with personnel to replace temporarily those undertaking such studies;
3    provide and have access to adequate translation services for the needs of the Dioceses and the National Office;
4    provide and organize the necessary help to deal with Government Agencies and communications in French;
5    provide Liturgies, the Church Offices, and Hymns, etc., in French;

6   set a policy to have Press Releases in English and French from the National Office and Diocesan Headquarters;

7   related to the *Canadian Churchman* [now the *Anglican Journal*] and any Diocesan Paper in Quebec, provide Church news and information sheets in French and, at times, where helpful, in other languages;

8   make use of our Church network across Canada to encourage people-visits and exchanges with French, English, Ethnic, Cree, and Inuit Christians in Quebec;

9   produce pamphlets in French describing the Anglican Church;

10  produce a history of the Anglican Church of Canada, and in collaboration with other interested people, produce a social history of anglophone, ethnic and Native People's contribution to the life of Quebec, which can be added to histories plentifully available about the French-Canadian majority.

In his concluding comments, Canon Turpin suggested that recent events, and the challenges posed by them for the church in Quebec, should be viewed in a positive spirit:

My friends, we are not a generation which sits easily with rhetoric. But would it be misleading to observe that he must be dull indeed who cannot sense that these very issues raise our horizons? Futurologists in North America and Europe are watching what is happening in Quebec with great interest. For, it may have something to teach about modern societies seeking identity, at grips with conflicting values where the urge for economic development and political experiment meet head on with an equally compelling desire, and look inwards for spiritual direction. As Christians we do need to pause and ask if, in this concrete situation, God is saying something new and creative to us. Surely, it is material for theological reflexion.

Although — in the year 2000 — much remains to be done, there have been tremendous changes in attitude among Quebec Anglicans. On the one hand, more priests have a working knowledge of French. More efforts to establish communications with the French-speaking community are being made. On the other hand, French ministry is being established more slowly than many could wish, and unilingually French-speaking congregations such as those established for the Haitian population are not able — for reasons of language — to participate fully in such consultative bodies as Diocesan Synod. Flexibility and adaptation appear to be crucial to survival as the Church enters the twenty-first century in Quebec.

# Multi-Ethnic Ministry (1978)

Prior to 1950 few West Indians immigrated to Canada, but there was already a Black population in Montreal of about 3,000 by 1930, some of whom had been living there for generations. In the 1850s, for example, when one of the missionary societies was looking for a suitable setting for a 'free coloured mission' for the benefit of settled fugitive slaves, Montreal was given serious consideration. Work had begun in connection with Trinity Church and St George's, but London, Ontario, was settled upon as the society's principal establishment. According to historian Daniel G. Hill, a contemporary map indicating "major routes to freedom taken by runaway slaves," shows Montreal as a major destination for freedom-seekers from New York state, crossing into Canada through the Vermont border.

In the 1880s Montreal became the general employment centre of porters for the Canadian Pacific Railway, and by tbe early twentieth century Blacks largely controlled the profession for both major railways. In fact, in 1918, the porters of the Canadian National Railways' transcontinental service organized Canada's first Black union. The community was concentrated in the St Antoine street area near the railway terminals. The opportunity for steady and relatively well-paid employment ($95 a month after three year's service in 1928) fostered a conservatism in the community that was in sharp contrast to the "sporting crowd" attached to the Nemderoloc Club and the two other Black cabarets in the district — what Robin W. Winks, in *The Blacks in Canada*, has referred to as "the flitting element" coming north from Harlem to escape Prohibition or more briefly for the races.

During the 1920s Montreal Blacks formed a number of local self-help societies: the Porters' Mutual Benefit Association, the Little Mothers League, and the Phyllis Wheatley Art Club. The Women's Club, the oldest Black organization in the city, had been formed as early as 1902, and the Woman's Charitable Benevolent Association in 1919.

Late in 1955, the Canadian government agreed to admit one hundred female domestics each year from Jamaica and Barbados, and by 1960 the number was increased to nearly three hundred. Under these regulations some of the new arrivals were able to have their fiancés or close relatives join them, and the domestics could take out citizenship after five years. According to Winks, "the effect of this regulation, though it supplied upper-class homes in Montreal, Toronto, and Ottawa with badly needed household help, could well have been harmful to the West Indian community as a whole, for it brought into Canada a class of people calculated to foster White notions of superiority ... In fact, however, some of the domestics were relatively well-educated young women who chose this means of gaining entry to Canada ..."

The Rev. Dr John McNab, who first came to Montreal in the late fifties as a student from Jamaica, describes the impact of this sudden shift in Canadian immigration policy:

Prior to 1960 migrants to Canada were predominantly from the British Isles and Europe. ... There was a change in the source countries in the 1960s. This shift to Asia, Africa, Latin America and the Caribbean presented new challenges — ethnic, cultural diversity, inter-faith rather than inter-church challenges.

In the Nineteen sixties persons from many parts of the world who were not part of the earlier migrants began to arrive in Canada. Many of us who came had been active in the life of our churches in India, in Hong Kong, in the West Indies and Caribbean region generally. Attempts were made by the newcomers to draw the attention of the Church to the presence of Anglicans among the new wave of immigrants from Asia, Africa and the Caribbean.

There were stresses and strains manifested in the majority population, however, and the new society which would, of necessity, emerge as a result of so diverse an infusion of racial, cultural and linguistic elements, was — and continues to be    the fruit of a slow and frustrating transition:

Migration and changing demographics [McNab continues] are altering the face of today's urban environment in Canada. People from diverse cultures encounter one another daily, with both satisfying and frustrating outcomes.

Misunderstanding, miscommunication, and racial stereotyping contribute to the development of conflict groups, between the dominant and minority groups and among minority groups themselves.

Part of my personal story coincides with the story of attempts at ministry in a multi-cultural context in the diocese of Montreal.

In 1978 I was invited by Bishop Reginald Hollis to minister at St. Paul's Church in the Côte des Neiges district in Montreal, a parish that had become predominantly West Indian. I had first known that parish when I was a student at Diocesan College in 1957. At that time there were two or three West Indian members of the congregation. In 1969 I returned to McGill and noticed that there had been a noticeable change in the composition of the congregation at St. Paul's. It was now 60% West Indian. Nine years later in 1978, when I was appointed Rector, there were about ten white persons remaining: six of whom were regular worshippers. Four were persons to whom I administered the sacrament of Holy Communion at home regularly. I was never quite sure why at least two of these four never came out to church services. They seemed healthy and were able to go to other public places.

I learned later that this shift in the composition of St. Paul's congregation corresponded to the shift in the composition of migrants to Canada in the Sixties. A scheme of bringing women from the West Indies to work as household helpers along with some loosening of immigration laws enabled West Indians to come to Canada in significant numbers. Many of these settled in the Côte des Neiges district.

St Paul's Côte des Neiges was the first parish to have the designation as "West Indian." In 2000, 99% of its parishioners are of Caribbean origin. Canon Anthony Jemmott has paid tribute to Dr McNab's work there "as a pastor and enabler." McNab himself has pointed to the gifts of those who were already part of the congregation when he arrived, merely waiting for a catalyst to release them:

Bishop Hollis did much to welcome and integrate the newcomers into the life of the diocese. Archbishop Ted Scott extended the same welcome at the national level. Both bishops appointed members of the parish to diocesan and national committees and so exposed them to the wider church. Among the appointees by Archbishop Ted Scott was Miss Euline Arthur from Barbados who had worshipped at St Paul's for over twenty years unnoticed. Her appointment to attend an A[nglican] C[ouncil of] N[orth] A[merica and the] C[aribbean] meeting in Ottawa released great leadership potential. Feeling accepted and affirmed she returned to the parish ready to undertake every challenge that presented itself and to inspire others. A lasting tribute to her service is the Seniors Club at St Paul's which she founded and led for many years.

In an article entitled "St. Paul's Makes History," published in the Montreal periodical *Afro-Can* in 1981, Margot Blackman points to the remarkable growth experienced in the parish since the 1970s:

Within the last five years, and especially since 1978, St. Paul's has experienced great spiritual and population growth, coupled with greater participation of members and the discovery of long-dormant leadership ability. The vibrancy of the church is evident. Its bright future is reflected in the Sunday School — 70 on the roll, average attendance 50 — and in the young people who are well represented in terms of participation and the general life of the church. ...

The spiritual growth and Christian fellowship existing at St. Paul's are undoubtedly due to the dynamic leadership, sincerity of purpose, and religious convictions of rector Dr. [John] McNab ... [who] came to St. Paul's in October 1978 from Kingston College, Jamaica, where he had been headmaster for three years.

McNab's pastoring influence at St Paul's and beyond, and his roles as Director of Pastoral Studies at the Montreal Diocesan Theological College have had a profound effect on the Montreal church. His interest in and contribution to the first series of multicultural symposia held in the mid 1980s were the natural outgrowth of the subject he had chosen for his doctoral thesis: *Towards a Theology for Social Concern.*

Significant West Indian membership is found in several Montreal parishes today. Chief among these are St Paul's, Côte des Neiges; Trinity Memorial, NDG; St. Lawrence, LaSalle; the Church of St James the Apostle; and St Barnabas, Pierrefonds.

Besides Dr McNab, others whose abilities have been honoured in the diocese are Anthony Jemmott as a Canon of the Cathedral and the Ven. Jim Bennett, the first West Indian from the Black community to be appointed Archdeacon. There can be little doubt that this branch of the Montreal diocesan family has become one of the most vibrant and vigorous elements in urban parish life today.

# The Ordination of Women to the Priesthood (1978)

In November 1976 the first women in Canada were ordained to the priesthood, but the road to that landmark in the history of the church had been far from smooth.

Indeed, until quite recently, women had not been permitted to exercise a significant role in the church at all — beyond fund-raising projects and menial service — despite the resolution adopted at the Lambeth Conference of 1920 that "women should be admitted to those Councils of the Church to which Laymen are admitted, and on equal terms. Diocesan, Provincial or National Synods may decide when or how this principle is to be brought into effect." The first woman took her seat at General Synod more than a quarter of a century later, in 1946. In the Diocese of Montreal, women were not admitted to sit as elected members of Synod until 1966 — during the episcopate of Kenneth Maguire — despite the introduction of motions to admit them as early as 1921.

Discussion of the ordination issue had been surfacing in the Canadian church since the worldwide Anglican Congress held in Toronto in 1963. With the 1970s, pressure became increasingly insistent, and speakers on both sides of the question argued their positions eloquently and with considerable passion. The "principle of the Ordination of Women to the Priesthood" was accepted at the 26th session of General Synod held in Regina and would be ratified or rejected at the 27th session in Quebec City in 1975. As approval at two consecutive sessions was necessary to effect the change, and rejection would set the whole process back for at least six years, the stakes were high for both parties.

In the Diocese of Montreal, a widespread airing of the subject was initially encouraged. As Bishop Maguire stated in his Charge to Synod in 1974:

I propose that the theme for study in Lent '75 be the ordination of Women to the Priesthood. Again I hope that the issue can be studied against the broader background of the nature of 'Ministry.' For that study, the Anglican-Roman Catholic joint statement on Ministry will be a useful resource … I ask all of you, clergy and laity, to support fully this Lenten study so that we may, in our next Annual Synod, be in a position to make known to General Synod, where we stand.

In March 1975, Dr Lettie James delivered an address at Christ Church Cathedral entitled "The Ordination of Women to the Priesthood." It presented a carefully reasoned argument, examining the Gospels and the various attitudes of St Paul. It dealt in turn with such issues as the maleness of the persons of the Trinity and of the Apostles. In her discussion of the nature of the priesthood she argued that

[as] Alister McKinnon has pointed out … the real issue is not 'whether women are competent to exercise a role traditionally associated, and even historically defined by the male,' but rather 'it is the nature of that to which [they are] to be admitted.'

The main argument advanced concerning the nature of the priesthood is that — the priest represents Christ, and Christ is male, therefore a woman cannot represent Him. …

Perhaps, however, we might enter into a deeper understanding of the nature of the ordained priesthood if we very briefly consider the Eucharist.

People have argued that in the Eucharist, the priest represents Christ as the spouse, consummating the marriage, the spiritual union that is betwixt Christ and His Church, therefore the priest has to be a man. But they have never concluded also that the congregation must be entirely female, which is surely a logical progression of that hypothesis. ... When the priest stands at the altar, he represents at the same time both Christ and the people of God. To quote the famous sentence of St Augustine, 'When Peter does it, when Judas does it, it is always Christ himself who does it.'

And this is precisely the meaning of ordination. And here we see how close is the connection between the commission given at ordination to administer the sacraments, and the commission to preach the Word. Can a woman represent Christ? It must be noted that the nature of the priesthood is one which is held independently of the personal worthiness of those ordained. The grace bestowed at ordination through the Imposition of Hands is a gift of the Holy Spirit, which if we understand grace, is received independently of such factors as worth or sex. For women as for men, ordination will be a day of dread as well as joy, for no one can live up to it except by the grace of the Holy Spirit.

...We are all androgenous beings. In every man there is some female-ness and in every woman there is some masculinity. Only when we recognize this can we become whole persons with acceptably different parts of our natures. Only then can the priesthood reach its full dimension.

Dr James then goes on to tackle the question of tradition, doing so more from an inborn sense of rightness than from outward evidence:

It is not surprising that women within the Church have found in our history a depressing litany of theological justifications for the oppressive customs of patriarchial societies. Yet, my historical judgment and my theological understanding tells me that it is highly unlikely that the Christian tradition has been unrelievedly destructive of one half of humanity. I turned away from the popes, Patristic fathers, Church Councils and Synods, and I turned to the Church at prayer — the Church experiencing, listening, seeking and witnessing. It was in the world of spirituality that women were found — ...

It is not difficult to imagine a woman celebrating the Eucharist or giving absolution [she concludes], a woman deeply united to Christ, a woman indwelt by the Holy Spirit. ... It is not her womanhood that qualifies her for, or disqualifies her from the priesthood, it is the grace that abounds, the call, the vocation. Paul writes to the Corinthians, 'Not that we are sufficient of ourselves, to claim everything as coming from us; our sufficiency is from God, who has qualified us to be ministers of a new covenant, not in a written code, but in the Spirit; for the written code kills, but the Spirit gives life.' ...

This is where it must begin, this is what counts; in any case it will be the only justification for the Ordination of Women to the Priesthood in the Anglican Church.

Church Union would also be an issue at the 1975 General Synod. Many Anglican clerics were more fearful of prejudicing eventual union with the Roman Catholic Church than they were enthusiastic about uniting with the United Church of Canada, with whom there had been talks for some years. This would be one of the strongest arguments against the ordination of women to the priesthood.

Discussion of the ordination issue took place in the parishes as proposed, but with the election in December of 1974 of a new diocesan bishop, the position on its debate in synod was totally changed.

You have been discussing the Ordination of Women in your parishes [Bishop Hollis remarked in his Charge to Synod in 1975]. We had the 'opinion form' with its multiple-choice [questions] circulated through the parishes, and again tomorrow we will fill out the same questionnaire. We are not voting on this issue because I do not think it is our role to vote and make a decision. The decision level is General Synod [which had not yet taken place], but I am concerned that our delegates to General Synod know what is being said by the membership of the Church.

This course of action was rather different from that followed in Montreal's sister diocese of Quebec where there had been a formal two-and-a-half hour debate of the issue at Synod in 1974. At the request of the Quebec diocesan clergy the vote which followed was taken by orders and was defeated 14 to 9. Although the resolution was automatically lost, a vote was taken in the House of the Laity nonetheless; it supported female ordination 34 to 20.

Bishop Timothy Matthews of the Diocese of Quebec was a well-known champion of the ordination of women. No doubt it was his hope that General Synod, under favourable circumstances, could accomplish what conservative diocesan synods could not. His role of host to the delegates who would make this decision may well have been a critical factor in the ratification of Regina's approval in principle.

When the General Synod vote was about to occur, there was a request by six members that it be taken by Orders. The main motion was nonetheless carried by comfortable margins in all three. No doubt to underscore this point, it was then requested that the vote on the resolution be recorded. It broke down as follows:

| | In Favour | Against |
| --- | --- | --- |
| Laity | 88 | 18 |
| Clergy | 75 | 30 |
| Bishops | 26 | 8 |
| Total | 189 | 56 |

Even so, it looked as if the ordination of women might still take some time, for another resolution passed at Regina had stipulated "that implementation was not to take place until the House of Bishops had worked out a pattern for the Canadian Church" that would include "an educational process for the Church." It was this proviso and the temporary 'conscience clause' (whereby a bishop or a priest who opposed the ordination of women could refuse to recognize the validity of such orders) that allowed a significant number of clerics and some laypeople to behave as if the vote at General Synod had never been taken. The conscience clause remained operative until 1986.

Some diocesan bishops proceeded to ordain women to the priesthood within the next year, for there were women across the country who had prepared themselves as fully as they could — as far as training and acadamic qualifications were concerned — to be ready if and when the moment arrived.

In Montreal, Bishop Hollis made his intentions clear in his Charge to Synod in 1976:

Our Canadian Church at General Synod last year approved both the principle of the ordination of women and the immediate implementation of this principle. Nine of our diocesan Bishops have given notice that they will ordain women to the priesthood in November.

There has been considerable discussion as to whether our church should be moving ahead on its own in this way. I regret that we did not await the wider consultation that the Lambeth Conference would have afforded.

In accepting a woman for ordination to the diaconate in June, I have made it clear that I think it might be to the advantage of our life as a diocese to wait for ordination to the priesthood until after the Lambeth Conference in 1978.

Yet we will be enriched by the contribution our first woman deacon can make, for Dr Lettie James is a trained and experienced pastoral counsellor and the holder of two doctorates, including one in Theology.

Bishop Hollis was as good as his word. In the autumn of 1978 a printed invitation announced that

*Through the invocation of the Holy Spirit*
*and the imposition of hands,*
*Lettie James*
*will be ordained to the priesthood*
*by the Right Reverend Reginald Hollis*
*Anglican Bishop of Montreal*
*in Christ Church Cathedral, Montreal*
*at 4:30 p.m.*
*Sunday, the first of October,*
*nineteen-hundred and seventy-eight.*

*As you have shared in my preparation for ministry by your friendship, encouragement and prayers, so you are invited to share in the joy and happiness of this day and to join me in celebrating the Eucharist on Saturday, October the eighth at 12:20 p.m. at Christ Church Cathedral, Montreal ...*
*Deo Gratias*

For Lettie James, whose sense of calling had announced itself twenty-seven years before, this was the fulfilment of a long period of patient faithfulness. For about one-third of the diocesan clergy it was a travesty, an event they had promised to oppose and disrupt. Twenty-six priests signed a document protesting the ordination.

When, as part of the Service for the ordering of priests, the Bishop addressed the congregation from the Prayer Book

Good people, these are they whom we propose, God willing, to receive this day into the holy office of Priesthood ... But yet if there be any of you who knoweth any impediment or notable crime in any of them ... let him come forth in the Name of God, and show what the crime or impediment is

a formal objection was raised by a spokesman from this group. When the Bishop announced that he would proceed despite the objection, their leader and fifty of his supporters rose in a body and walked out of the Cathedral. The headline in the Montreal *Gazette* read "Protest fails: Montreal Has Female Priest":

James, 53, the first woman priest in the diocese of Montreal [the article stated], was ordained along with Philip Carr-Harris, 24, by Bishop Reginald Hollis in front of 500 people.

'I'm bursting with joy,' said James immediately afterwards. 'I feel like I'm coming apart with joy.'

In the *Montreal Churchman* for the month following, the Bishop devoted his monthly Letter to the event:

Thank God the ordination did not turn into a major confrontation [he remarked]. There is more than enough schism in the church. We are not here to be fighting among ourselves, but to proclaim the good news of Jesus Christ. We are to find reconciliation between the churches so that we can speak of peace to the world.

Another article in the same issue took a rather different tack:

From a cold, grey, and wet sky painted somberly by an evening sun, a flash of brilliant forked lightning pointed down [it began]. And from the perspective of the hall at St. John the Evangelist, it seemed to point down to the cathedral. There was a great crash. Someone murmured 'judgment,' and there were quiet smiles.

Lettie James was the twelfth woman to be ordained to the priesthood in Canada.

Following the delivery of her paper at the Cathedral stating her case for the ordination of women in 1975, James had asked if there were any questions. One laywoman asked, "What can we do?" The speaker recalls that at that moment she had nothing to suggest, but that the answer had come to the questioner. It led, shortly thereafter, to the formation of the Support Group for Women in Priesthood, co-convened by Frances Sheppard and Ted Parkman. It met every Tuesday for a noon-time Eucharist, and offered prayers naming each candidate as well as one for those opposed. In addition its members "wrote to and prayed daily by name for" every woman theological student in Canada, and followed them right to ordination.

In 1994 Bishop Hutchison, turning from a rather bleak financial review, gave a brief outline in his Charge to Synod of the progress made in the whole ordination issue:

On the brighter side [he remarked] the Church of England has now joined the other churches of the Communion who ordain women. Since 1976 our Primate and most Canadian bishops have declined to celebrate the

Eucharist in England because of England's refusal to accept women priests from other parts of the Communion. This year Archbishop Peers was happy at last to accept an invitation to celebrate. ... On November 1st, I was present with our Primate for the ordination of Bishop Mary McLeod of Vermont, North America's first diocesan woman bishop. Then in February this year, I assisted at the ordination of Victoria Matthews as Suffragan Bishop of Toronto, Canada's first woman bishop. In October, most of our clergy met Bishop Barbara Harris who celebrated and preached at our clergy conference, and who has the distinction of being the first woman bishop in the world.

It seems wonderfully appropriate that as we approach the mid point in the ecumenical decade of the churches in solidarity with women, we should at last reach this stage of our own maturity as a Church.

By the year 2000, there were at least fifteen women on the list of active clergy serving the Diocese of Montreal, more than half of whom were engaged in full-time parish ministry.

## Helping the Boat-People (1979)

In the late 1970s and early 80s, many parishes in the Diocese saw the plight of South East Asian refugees as a call to supply humanitarian aid of a personal and immediate sort. The parish newsletter of St Mary's, Beaconsfield, for example, carried the following challenge in its September 1979 issue:

*Vietnamese Refugees: What Shall We Do?*
There are three possibilities which our Parish might consider as we try to decide what, as a Parish, we can do in assisting the Vietnamese refugee problem.
1   Sponsor a family. This of course would be the most effective way, and many Parishes have already undertaken to do this. It would involve maintaining and supporting a family in this country for one year. It would include finding and equipping housing, providing food, clothing and some medical help, helping with school enrolment and adaptation to our culture, approximate cost $10,000.
2   Sharing with another group or Parish in sponsoring a family.
3   Establishing a "Parish Refugee Fund" which may be used in a positive and effective way to aid refugee families.

In the same issue, the "The Rector's Letter," a regular feature, urged the same theme:

My dear People:

During the past two months, I am sure we have all become aware of the tragic plight of the so-called 'Boat-people' or those refugees fleeing from Viet Nam. We have been heartily reassured by the warm and compassionate response of many countries, including our own, and many individual groups of Christians across the land in their readiness to reach out to sponsor so many of these homeless people.

It is normal, perhaps, that we stop and think of our own problems, national and personal and to reasonably state all the many reasons why, as a people, we should not admit more refugees into this country. Some of you may wish to argue the point, but, in the eyes of most people, this is a moment of crying need, to which genuine compassion is the response of the Christian.

What are we going to do, here, at St. Mary's, as our response to this tragic need? I hope we shall be able to have an answer to that question in early September. I propose to have an early meeting of the Wardens, followed by a Parish Council meeting on September 11th, after which I hope we shall have suggestions and proposition[s] to place before the congregation. Whatever we may decide to do, we shall need the help of all of you. In the meantime, please give it much thought and offer it daily in your prayers, that, as a Parish, we may be led to do His will.

Sincerely,

Your friend and Rector

Frank M. Toope

The parish responded to the urgency of their rector's appeal and applied to sponsor a family. Subsequent newsletters trace various events in the lives of the four-member Cambodian family whom they adopted — the COFI French classes for immigrants, attended by the 22-year-old young woman, who would become the breadwinner when the family was on its own, the grandmother's need for hospitalization for the extraction of her teeth, and the enrolment of the two grandchildren, aged seven and eight, in school. The February 1982 newsletter describes the family as on the brink of independence:

*our refugee family:* On January 13th, 1982 D— began working for the Sheraton-Mount Royal Hotel, Montreal. She is earning $5.25 an hour as a chamber-maid. The apartment lease at 506 St John's Road expires as of May 31st, 1982 at which time D— wishes to move the family of four downtown nearer her job and their Cambodian friends and family. Her take-home pay at this time is approximately $600 a month and their rent each month (now) is $230, Hydro and telephone approximately $30. The rest is spent on food and transportation costs and any other expenses. It will be quite a challenge for D— (22) to provide for the needs of all four of them ...

Before the ... family left Thailand's Refugee Camp, the Canadian Government extended ... a transportation loan in the amount of $1,500 to [the grandmother] to fly herself and her two grandchildren to Canada. A loan in the amount of $750 was also granted to D— for her passage. These outstanding loans totalling $2,250 are interest free and are to be repaid in appropriate amounts according to their earnings each month. It was the feeling at Parish Council, February 8th, that it would be going that 'extra mile' with [our family] if we endeavoured as a Parish to raise an additional $1000 which when combined with the balance of our Refugee account would give D— a sense of security knowing that these loans have been provided for. All contributions may be marked "ST MARY'S REFUGEE FUND" and as such are tax deductible (in a plain white envelope, so marked).

We thank God for you and for your response to Him as seen in [our adopted family] and offer to you these words from Matthew 25 — 'For I was hungry, and you gave me to eat: I was thirsty, and you gave me to drink: I was a stranger, and you gathered me in ...'

There is a tragic postscript to this story which has nothing to do with St Mary's or its support of refugees. About 1 a.m. on Sunday morning, 2 April 1995, three local boys, aged 13, 14 and 15, entered the Toope home and brutally murdered Frank Toope and his wife Jocelyn. The Toopes were then retired, but still living in Beaconsfield, having served the parish for 22 years. He was 75 years old and his wife 70. They were bludgeoned to death in their beds with a baseball bat and a beer bottle in what was described as a thrill-killing. In 2001 the killers' identities are still protected under the Young Offenders' Act; the case continues to be cited as an example of mindless violence.

Outreach to refugees has continued in the Diocese. As Action Réfugiés Montréal reported to Synod in 1995:

The number of persons suffering has increased worldwide with the continuing tragedies unfolding in Somalia, Haiti, Rwanda. And the options available for these folk have decreased with more restrictions and obstacles in their search for a safe haven. ... The Anglican Diocese of Montreal [the report adds proudly] is the second largest group involved in the private sponsorship of refugees in Montreal.

# Staying On (1981)

In 1980, the ruling Parti Québécois staged and narrowly lost its first Referendum on sovereignty-association. It was a time of great uncertainty for the diminished and, it seemed, ever-diminishing English-speaking population in the province. Many young families and professional people who had waited out the péquiste victory to "see what would happen" now judged that it was time to leave. An unpublished report drawn up in 1983 on the subject of language and inter-provincial as well as international migration from the province indicated that there was an outflow of 156,496 people from Quebec between 1976 and 1981. Of these 131,530 were English-speaking, the balance being made up of "others."

Yet life for those who remained did not change dramatically. In 1981, for example, St Peter's Church, Town of Mount Royal, produced a new parish history as part of its sixtieth anniversary celebrations, in which its changed circumstances over the years were recorded with philosophical good humour:

What more can be said? Without a doubt the nominal roll at St Peter's shows many fewer names than it did in the late 1950's [the post-war years which saw increased church attendance throughout North America]. Many very likely would blame the political situation in Quebec or the current government for this and, furthermore, would point to the flight of English firms and capital to the West. This is part of an explanation. But only part. The Town of Mount Royal has slowly been catching up with some very general trends in Northern Europe and other parts of North America, where church-going for many years has not been the done thing. So those that take an active part in the work and activities of the church increasingly do so because they feel that they have important business there. ... Therefore, if we are to look to numbers and statistics, we can easily see that church attendance has kept up very well ... Bible-study groups have prospered in recent years as never before; the choir has been strong and has increasingly attracted new members ...

So St Peter's is not quite what it used to be a couple of decades ago. But as that recently professed Christian, Bob Dylan, used to sing, 'the times they are a-changin.' So they are. ... Just as St Peter's nominal role grew dramatically with the post-war housing boom, so it has recently decreased with new shifts in population.

Eighteen years later, in commenting on life at St Peter's, one of the authors of the 60th anniversary parish history and still an active parishioner gave the following thumbnail sketch of its current activities and organizations. It shows a shift away from traditional women's groups to more pastorally-centred and wider-community-oriented concerns:

**ACW** Over many years the ACW has been a source of Christian fellowship for women of St Peter's, and its members have engaged in community projects. One of the most notable was the 'Observation Nursery' in the 1950s which provided an opportunity for mothers to observe how their children interacted with others and to discuss with experienced women how to improve unsuitable behaviour.

Membership has been steadily declining over the years and the group will probably soon cease to exist. In recent years their main function has been fund-raising, and since most of their members are over 75, these activities are becoming increasingly difficult.

**Pastoral Care Team** Under the leadership of our Pastoral Assistant, this group provides physical and emotional support to the sick, the bereaved and the elderly. Members drive parishioners to medical appointments, visit in homes or hospital, provide meals in case of sudden emergencies, and generally offer a helping hand.

**Ministry of Prayer Team** Members of this team offer constant prayerful support to the parish. Some lead the prayer in our services, some are available during services for personal prayer with or for parishioners, and all are part of a prayer link which provides long-term, continued prayers for the concerns of parishioners.

**Outreach Group** This group of community-minded people identifies needs in the Montreal area and raises funds to support these needs by offering various kinds of lunches or suppers (most notably 'Casa San Pietro' which has the best spaghetti in town). Their activities have provided funds recently for Mile End Mission, Tyndale-St George's Community Centre & the Côte-des-Neiges Council of Churches.

**Lunch Club Team** This group plans, prepares and serves a lunch, mostly from September through June, to seniors living in the Town of Mount Royal or members of the Parish regardless of where they live. It is a festive occasion with table linen, china, silver, floral centrepieces, hot main course, salad, dessert, tea / coffee and mints, followed by a programme of sorts.

Besides these groups, "the monthly gathering of clergy and laity [known as the 'Tuesday Fellowship'] has met at St Peter's since its inception" in the 1970s, and since the mid-1990s the parish has hosted an Essentials yearly gathering. Events sponsored by the Diocesan Evangelism and Congregational Development Units have also taken place here.

When we came to St Peter's from an English parish in 1979 [writes parishioner Catherine Hughes] we found a congregation that was mainly from affluent Town of Mount Royal, with women who were home full time. Twenty years later that has all changed. While we still have a faithful core group of 'Townies,' more and more members are coming to us from the surrounding areas of Greater Montreal. ... Very few of the 'below 60' women are at home now [she continues] and so most of the daytime volunteering is done by younger seniors.

A mixture of cultures and races have been drawn to worship at St Peter's, she adds, so that on an average Sunday morning (as of 1999) fully one-third of the congregation will be of non-European origin, "and they have greatly enriched our parish life."

## Cathedral Place (1983)

The 1980s was a period of high inflation and political uncertainty in Montreal. Many churches were 'feeling the twin pinches of pressing financial needs and underused facilities,' as Kathe Lieber put it in 1988 in an article on Christ Church Cathedral in Montreal's bilingual magazine *En Ville*, but the Diocese of Montreal had found a spectacular solution to the constraints of the times:

The Anglican diocese of Montreal has managed to ensure its financial future without losing control of what happens to land surrounding the cathedral.

In partnership with an insurance company and two real estate developers, the church has masterminded a highrise and underground retail and office complex, known as Les Promenades de la Cathédral.

The new tower, a 34-storey building located behind the cathedral, was completed in the spring of 1988, and the 400,000 [square]-foot underground complex, which will shore up the foundations of the cathedral and connect it to the department stores and the metro, has just been completed.

The diocese has given the developers a 99-year lease for the land, after which the church will repossess it all. ...

What pleases the Dean most about the cathedral project? Everything is based on the premise that the church is here to stay. In more ways than one the cathedral is now on a very solid foundation.

In June 1983, W.T. Duncan Shaddick — Cathedral parishioner, professional engineer and Church Group Project Manager — presented a series of five principles "to be recognised in any proposal for use of Diocesan and Cathedral Land":

1   The Church does not wish to sell its land outright; ideally the land would be leased under an emphyteutic lease. ...
2   Any agreement must provide the Church with a minimum guaranteed gross annual payment to reflect in some agreed way, the continuing inflation (or deflation). ...
3   Any agreement must recognise the value of underground access to the main site from Ste. Catherine, Union and University Streets, and of the air rights to the extent that any proposal may use the air rights.
4   The Church will incur additional space costs during construction phase of the project. The developer should recognise this in his proposal.
5   The Cathedral and Diocese are heated from the same boiler house located in Anglican House. Any proposal should provide for the supply of heat for the Cathedral during and after completion of, construction.

To these was added the critical buy-back principle that the church would buy back the land for $1.00 after entering into an agreement and then lease it to the developers.

Architecturally, structurally and logistically the project was a challenging one. As an article in *RSIC / IAAC*, a publication of the Reinforcing Steel Institute of Canada, put it:

As part of the $85 million development project, room had to be made underneath the stone walls of historic Christ Church Cathedral for Les Promenades de la Cathédral, two levels of shopping and one level of parking.

Structural engineers, Quinn Dressel Associates, devised a method of transferring the load of the 16 345 tonne cathedral, built in 1859, to a series of concrete filled steel caissons; thus avoiding any damage to the heritage structure and any interruption to daily service[s] during the eight-month construction schedule.

Reinforced concrete was chosen for its constructability, given the restricted headroom under the church's timber floor and also to avoid deflection, which was closely monitored throughout the carefully staged project.

An article by George A. Peer, engineering editor of *Heavy Construction News*, adds further details:

Despite the unusual nature of the job, there have been few surprises. But the tremendous strength of the 127-year-old stone walls came as a shock when it came time to carving out entrances for workers and equipment to get beneath the church for the caissons and concrete beams. ...

[The walls] were so strong, in fact, that after trying in vain to break through with a hammer and chisel and then a hand-held air hammer, Magil [Construction Ltd, general contractor of the Maison des Coopérants] had to take a drastic step. 'Our initial plan had been to make one opening, pour a beam and then make the next opening [Jossi] Gutstadt [Magil's vice-President] says. ...

Success was finally met by using a hydraulic hammer held by a backhoe. 'Everybody thought we were crazy,' Gutstadt says. The heavy-duty combination worked so well that as many as five openings were made in one day, thus abandoning the earlier, more cautious approach.

Except for one broken stained-glass window, the church has not suffered any damage.

Harmonizing the new and old structures that shared Cathedral and Diocesan land was also a factor to be considered among other features. A publicity brochure furnished by Magil Construction Limited describes the new office tower:

Pointed arches and porticoes with mullions and columns resting on grey limestone bases associate the Maison des Coopérants with the scale and aesthetics of the Cathedral. Accent mullions, etched in black, subtly define the image of the Cathedral spire.

The form of the tower, which also responds to the Cathedral, gracefully transforms to smaller floors as it rises ...

Clad with a curtain wall of reflective copper glass of a pink tint and aluminum, the building is ever-changing against the skyline through the interplay of sunlight and cloud on the sculptured form.

A distinctive, ecclesiastically-inspited, twin-peaked roof surmounts the building, assuring its recognition from many parts of Montréal.

Along de Maisonneuve Boulevard — Montréal's undisputed new business centre — the Maison des Coopérants dominates the row of office buildings.

Some response to the development of Cathedral and Diocesan land along these lines was sharply critical:

There is no real concern for architecture and urbanism here at all. It is all merchandising pure and simple [wrote Derek Drummond, professor of architecture at McGill University].

How else can one explain the church becoming merely one of the attractive anchors in an urban shopping centre while at the same time being dwarfed by the massive commercial tower behind it? Being seduced by the financial comfort provided by the transaction resulting from this development is one thing, but allowing the church to become so blatantly commercialized by its ongoing relationship with the development, its developers and the tower's major tenant is degrading. ...

The mere naming of the retail portion of the development Promenades de la Cathédral (it opens [for the first time] on Wednesday), must turn the stomach of many parishioners. They must agonize over the symbolism of the stone-clad umbilical cord joining the chapter house of the cathedral with the commercial tower that firmly cements the relationship between the triumvirate in perpetuity.

G.M. Elbourne, lay reader and chairman of the mission committee of Christ Church Cathedral, took issue with these and other objections to the project:

There is indeed a conscious relationship between the tower architecture and that of the cathedral [he admitted]. We do not see this as surrender on our part, but rather as a rare and welcome recognition by the business community that the church has a place in the centre of its life.

The more people who are led by the name Promenades de la Cathédral to visit the church, the better. We logged 750 visitors on a recent Sunday over and above those attending services — and we rejoice in it.

That a Roman Catholic insurance company, a Jewish property developer and an Anglican religious community can work together for the benefit of God's people seems to us wonderful, and a great improvement on attitudes that have been prevalent in the past.

Revenue from this development — which has been kept separate from the regular diocesan budget — has in fact given the diocese the where-withal to engage in new initiatives in ministry and outreach, invest more heavily in social services and community concerns, earmark more funds for outreach beyond the diocese, provide for clergy development and assistance, and care for diocesan and parish buildings.

'More and more of our resources were poured into survival, propping up the fabric. That's not what the church is about. The income from [the development] will enable us to rise again in our new role' [Dean Andrew Hutchison remarked in an interview in his temporary office in Place Ville Marie while work was still in progress].

'The Church and commercial interests are very different in their time frames. Business interests are extremely short term. The church's interests are long term. What interests me is what's going to happen 800 or 900 years from now.'

## A Native Son for Bishop (1984)

Since the appointment of its first bishop by the Crown in 1850, the Diocese of Montreal seems to have found it natural to draw upon clerics from faraway places to supply its chief pastors. Of its ten diocesan bishops, whether appointed or elected, seven were born in England or Ireland, and one in the United States. The two remaining, albeit Canadian born, had entered the Diocese to fill senior positions as Deans of the Cathedral.

In the autumn of 1984, following his election as Suffragan Bishop in June, James Aubrey MacLean was consecrated on the Feast of St Simon and St Jude, October 28th, the first native-born Quebecer to hold the office of bishop in this diocese. He was also the first, and to date, only Suffragan Bishop to be appointed or elected here.

MacLean rose to this position from humble beginnings and, with a deep sense of vocation, procured the necessary qualifications for ordination long after a seminarian would in the natural course of things have completed his prerequisites for entering theological college. The son of a fisherman, MacLean received his elementary schooling at Grosse Isle, on the Magdalen Islands. His love of reading and interest in study led an uncle in New Glasgow, Nova Scotia, to enroll him in high school there, and provide him with a home while he completed his schooling. There was no high school on the Islands then, and most boys would naturally proceed no further with their education, but follow their fathers to the fishing grounds.

In 1942 MacLean enlisted in the Royal Canadian Navy as a medical assistant, having been turned down by the Air Force because of poor eyesight. While in the service he received further training as an X-ray technician.

In a tribute at the time of his death, Monica Kirby — a co-worker-volunteer, and member of many diocesan committees — described the sequence of events that had led MacLean to seek holy orders. His father had been a churchwarden, she pointed out, and he 'grew up familiar with the three-times-a-Sunday services of those days.' He had himself been churchwarden at Holy Trinity, Grosse Isle, from 1940 to 1942, so the church had long been a prominent part of his life:

In 1946 Jim came to Montreal and worked at the Chest Hospital as chief radiographer. His parish was St. Martin's on St. Urbain street, where he threw himself wholeheartedly into youth work, becoming the Sunday School superintendent and eventually a lay reader. For several years he tried to find a way to get theological training so that he might apply for ordination. This was made more difficult because he lacked an arts degree, then a pre-requisite for theology. But finally, in 1950, Archbishop Dixon recommended him for entry into the Diocesan College, and he graduated with an L.Th. in '53, was made deacon, and became the assistant at St. Peter's, T[own of] M[ount] R[oyal].

Also unique for a bishop in this diocese, all of MacLean's ministry was spent in Montreal. After St Peter's he was sent to the parish of St Ignatius and St Hilda, then to the Church of the Good Shepherd in Cartierville and, finally, to St George's, Ste-Anne-de-Bellevue. Prior to his consecration as Suffragan, to which were added the responsibilities of Administrative Officer of the Diocese, he had served as Rural Dean of Royalmount, Regional Dean of Ste Anne's, Archdeacon of St Andrew's and Archdeacon of St Lawrence.

In a brief address to Synod [wrote Kirby], Jim said, "I do not have great gifts, but I do have a heart which can love, hands which with God's help can be instruments of his grace, and feet which can carry me in the steps of the Master. I ask your prayers that I may serve well and faithfully as Suffragan Bishop" — and so indeed he did.

During his five-year tenure MacLean's administrative duties coincided with what Bishop Hutchison has described as "the turbulent years of development": the demolition of the former Synod building, the temporary occupancy of offices in Place Ville Marie and finally the move to fine new facilities in the Maison des Coopérants.

On his retirement, he admitted that the administrative tasks had sometimes interfered with what he had hoped to accomplish in his episcopal role:

I'm not the world's worst administrator nor the best [MacLean remarked self-deprecatingly]. But it sometimes irritates me, having to make gobs of decisions. It takes away from the things you are supposed to be doing. ...

A bishop is supposed to teach, preach and lead clergy in matters of faith. ...

One of the things I'd hoped to have done a lot more of was the pastoring of clergy. It's important in this day and age, when a lot of priests are sometimes unclear where they ought to be going. A pastor needs a pastor.

As a colleague pointed out, MacLean cared deeply about the individual. He "believed in visiting his people, at a time when visiting had begun to go out of favour with the clergy."

MacLean feared that people were in danger of being left behind in the changes made in liturgy, music and the structures of the church, and that pastoral care was ceasing to be a priority in parishes.

To the question, put to him at the time of his retirement: "Do you have something to say to the Diocese as a Whole?" he responded:

I'm concerned about the quality of pastoral care ... amazed that priests don't have personal knowledge of their parishioners; and that people don't know their Rector ... What's happening here?

Ministry required a special kind of man — or woman — he believed:

I don't think you can paint the ministry as some sort of escape from the realities of life [he observed in an interview]. It's a life of service to people, a gruelling kind of life.
The cornerstone of the priesthood is a love of God and a love of people. If people annoy you, don't go into the ministry, because there are annoying people everywhere, especially in parishes.

MacLean's sense of committed involvement, in part, led him to produce a regular column in the *Montreal Churchman* — at a time of revolution in hymnody — on old, loved hymns in the Anglican tradition. His last writing was devoted to one of Frances Ridley Havergal's, "Take My Life and Let it Be." Another article in the series suggests that his preference for these familiar hymns — like his attachment to the Book of Common Prayer — came from a deep understanding of the need in many people for spiritual resources that are so deeply infused with memory that neither sickness nor the inability to read or meditate can diminish them:

I am dictating this article from my hospital room [he wrote], so if it is not as comprehensive as usual, I am sure you will forgive me. Papers have deadlines and they wait for no man!
Of all the hymns in the English language, "O God, Our Help In Ages Past" probably enjoys the widest acceptance of any hymn written. It was written by a Nonconformist but has found its way into the hymn book of every single denomination. It is the hymn that is most sung at great assemblies and on very solemn public occasions.
I have chosen this particular hymn not only because it is a great hymn and loved by all, but because it kept coming back to me at a very critical

point in my recent illness. As I was battling a high fever and the bodily discomfort that it brought, I remembered the several times that, along with the help of medical science and technology, God had brought me through other serious illnesses. I discovered anew the precious gift of memory, for when I was unable to say prayers or to read, I could recite from memory this famous hymn and prayers that I knew so well.

He died of leukemia on 18 May 1992, one month short of his seventieth birthday.

## Parish Newsletters (1985)

Parish Newsletters have a long tradition in the Diocese. Some are modest affairs involving a couple of mimeographed sheets stapled together, others (like *The Parish Review of the Church of St John the Evangelist* or *St George's Monthly*) are professionally printed and sometimes bound. Whatever the format, however, parish newsletters provide a means of contact between the incumbent and parishioners, and can convey a whole spectrum of information and subtext.

The following newsletter — serving the three-point parish of Grace Church, Arundel, Church of the Redeemer, Weir, and St George's, Rockway — radiates a sense of engagement and sympathy with the people both as parishioners with responsibilities toward their church and as individuals in need of pastoral care. It covers recent summer activities and brings parishioners up to date on repairs and finances. Most important, it allows a newly-settled minister to voice his priorities and concerns, as well as to reassure and encourage his people, in a direct and informal way. Simply titled "Newsletter," and dated 27 August 1985, it begins as follows:

Dear Friends,

Many thanks to all who supported the Anglican Summer Camp in July. 'Crosstalk' the organization which supplies our leaders for these camps, is short of funds at the moment. It was accordingly a real joy to be able to send them $50 from this parish toward their costs of training future teams.

43 children from 29 families in Arundel, Bark Lake, Mont Tremblant, St. Jovite and Weir, were at day-camp this year, plus 8 of our own teen-age assistant trainers. It seems more than worthwhile to try to keep this group together. Accordingly, I hope that these same families may be able to join our Family Thanksgiving Service at Grace Church, Arundel, on Sunday, October 13th, at 11.00 AM —

The camp had concluded with a special "Closing Children's Service" in Grace Church, designed for the occasion. It included a Bible quiz, a play ("The Kind Soldier"), and songs with guitar accompaniment.

The Newsletter continues:

Sometimes, I worry about missing a phone call when Anne and I are both away. Accordingly, I will be plugging in an answering machine here sometimes which I used in business. If you should be answered by a 'recording,' will you please just leave your name [or] number. I'll call back, of course, as quickly as possible. ...

Back in the parish, with the excellent renovations done on the rectory, our costs have been heavy. However, the Federal Government will be paying our diocese $6-7,000 annually for the chaplaincy services which I am providing at La Macaza. As you should know, the total cost of clergy ministry in this parish (salary + travel allowance, pension and insurance) runs about $18,000 annually. In recent years, the parishes have contributed $6-7000 towards this, with the Diocese picking up around $12,000. The prison chaplaincy should reduce our shortfall here ... It would be wonderful if we could manage a 'balanced budget' by say 1986/1987.

In the past three weeks, I have had the joy of baptizing two little boys at Grace Church. A wedding is being planned for September 7th. This is a trend which I naturally hope will continue!

In the odd home on my 'rounds' I have encountered some discouragement about the future, which is quite natural. As a community, you have obviously come through some drastic changes, particularly in the last thirty years. The point though is, to me, that you have come through them.

One of the many attractive things which I have already noticed about this part of the country, is the marvellous way in which most people, of different churches and languages, do get along. This could be an example to our province, and to our country as a whole.

You have developed a marvelous school locally, which is fast becoming a focal point for a much wider area around. With the tolls coming off the autoroutes, it seems natural for this region to develop further, and perhaps comparatively, as a tourist resort area.

As a newcomer, I accordingly find it difficult to be anything but optimistic about the *future* here, even if the average age locally may, for a while at least, be closer to 50 than 30.

All this brings me real hope that whatever I may be able to bring to you of the Lord's Word and Love, within the next 4-5 years, it may bear abundant fruit 25, 35 or 50 years from now ...:

[signed] Your friend and pastor

As an important means of communication and community building, newsletters can be particularly important when the minister is not only new to a parish but, as is the case here, new to the ministry itself. The writer, who was Deacon-in-charge, had been ordained as recently as June 2nd and, although he had served for many years as a lay reader, it was largely in a suburban parish on the West Island, a far cry from a struggling rural parish in the Laurentians. This newsletter, one of the modest, inexpensive variety, is a fine illustration of a newcomer's sensitive and thoughtful beginning in a new parish.

# "The Nature of Youth Work" (1986)

Organizations specifically for young people have taken a variety of directions in the Diocese over the years. Besides Sunday School, one of the earliest aimed equally at both sexes was the Anglican Young People's Association, or AYPA. The earliest branch in the Diocese, and the first in the Ecclesiastical Province of Canada, was established at Grace Church, Sutton, in 1913.

Beginning in the 1970s, but traceable to the 1950s, Crosstalks started its series of Youth Camps — first for a long weekend, later for a week — "to provide a Christ-centred camp within the Anglican family for evangelism and discipleship." A parallel series of day camps followed in 1979. Meanwhile, in another direction, the first Youth Synod in the Diocese was held in 1975 under the chairmanship of Bishop Hollis. It gave 100 young people, representing all its Deaneries, a taste of the issues being debated in the Church at that time, and allowed them to voice their staunch support (75%) for the ordination of women. Votes were taken and five delegates were chosen "to represent Youth" at Diocesan Synod to be held later that year.

By the end of the century, Montreal's young people had won the right to a seat with full voting privileges on the Diocesan Council, but even before this, Youth Synod had managed to secure for its interests some concessions from "regular Synod."

At the March 1984 Youth Synod, for example, a motion was presented and passed "that a committee be formed to investigate the possibilities of establishing a drop-in centre for Youth in the downtown area." Diocesan Synod endorsed it. A committee was formed and held its first meeting on 27 February 1985 to discuss the idea.

The Resource Person throughout was the Bishop's Youth Chaplain, Quentin Robinson:

The Drop-In was seen as an alternative meeting place for young people [the Minutes of the first meeting recorded], particularly those in their early teens, which would encourage them to stay off the streets and out of shopping malls, etc. on the weekend. It would serve as a kind of focal point for Youth Groups and would help establish links between groups. It would have an educational function since it might sponsor discussion groups and would advertise other Diocesan and interdenominational events. The Drop-In itself, although run by Anglicans initially, would be interdenominational. It would be a very valuable form of Community outreach since it might make it easier for non-Christian kids to get involved in the church.

The Minutes of this first meeting show that its organizers had high hopes that a variety of needs could be met by such a project:

The idea of incorporating a service for destitutes into the plans was discussed at length. This would give kids involved in the Centre a chance to serve others and would enhance the outreach aspects of the Drop-In. [The Rev.] Brett [Cane] pointed out that the Cathedral provides a service for the elderly and St. Michael's mission provides help for street people, but there is not much aimed specifically at transient young people. It was thought that perhaps a Soup Kitchen providing a low-cost meal might attract teens from all walks of life and would thus discourage stereotyping. The Soup Kitchen and the actual Drop-In would function at different times. A Fall opening date is envisioned, with the centre functioning on the weekends only at first.

By the second meeting, held in May, the people of St George's had agreed to make their church hall available for the project if the young people involved "[would] be willing to help with the two events held in the hall, the Christmas Bazaar and Rummage Sale, as a condition of … using the facilities the rest of the year." The dates of these events were 31 October and 12 March.

On 3 June, 110 copies of a letter were sent out to Youth Leaders in the Diocese signed by two of the organizers, announcing the projected Drop-In and asking for volunteers for "Program planning, Refreshments (possibly Soup Kitchen), Setting-up & decor, Prayer Support and Counsellors/bouncers." Ideas and furniture were also solicited.

At the committee's third meeting, the opening date for the centre was set for Saturday, 7 September and tentative programs were suggested to include a special event each week, such as a coffee house, dance, dramatic presentation, comedy night, movie or special speaker. (Records show that at least one film — *The Hiding Place* — was rented for an evening.) They hoped to stage weekly rotating workshops on "Drama, Music, Art and perhaps writing."

As the opening date drew closer, meetings were more frequent. On 20 June the Soup Kitchen idea was abandoned, partly because of inadequate cooking and washing facilities, partly because "it was felt that this is too much to plan for just now." The Program Committee announced the schedule for the first two months which was to be the trial period. Robinson stressed that "all staff, no matter what their responsibilities in the Centre, should be trained and well informed of the way the Centre will run":

It is essential to define roles and create a job description for every position [he stressed]. It was thought also [the Minutes continued] that there should be a team of relief staff ... that another woman ... be asked to join the training team, and that, when the Centre is operating, there should be a constant balance of male/female counsellors on duty.

The Minutes of the fifth meeting confirmed that training sessions for youth volunteers at the Centre would be mandatory and begin on 27 August.

The opening took place as scheduled on 28 September at 3 p.m., with a service of dedication at 5, and a dance from 8 to 11 o'clock. There were by then sixteen names on the Committee phone list, but the Drop-In's days were numbered. By the end of October its fate was sealed.

On 14 January 1986, Robinson informed the Corporation of St George's Church, Montreal that the contemplated Drop-In Centre project for which they had provided facilities was to be abandoned. After thanking the parishioners for supporting the project, he made the following observations:

As you are aware, even though you agreed to a two-month trial run, we closed the Drop-In Centre after only one month.

The month that the Drop-In Centre was open was a good time. The generosity of so many people who provided furniture and other items was an encouragement to everyone involved. ... While we weren't swamped with people attending, we did see a number of new faces and we know now that some significant friendships were formed.

As I worked on this project, the vision for it became clearer. I also gained more insight into our current work with youth. It became evident that, while we sought to minister to younger teens, our real ministry was to the committee members. ... So there was a need to bring in more adults, not only to be counsellors, but also to set an example for the young people by their work in running the Centre. We had not set up the Centre to be run by the counsellors, rather we had anticipated that it would be run by the committee.

I started to realize that we were on the wrong track the weekend that the young people were to assist the people of St. George's in setting up for the Christmas Bazaar. I was disappointed by the inadequate participation of the committee members in this task and it was then that I realized that either a radical change was to be undertaken or the project would have to be suspended before anyone got hurt or taken advantage of.

So, at this time, the Drop-In Centre remains a dream for the future. I would like to see the dream become a reality, but it will certainly require many adults and young people who are deeply committed to the project as their own ministry.

A variety of youth ministries have made their appearance in the Diocese over the years. The Church of England Association for Young Men of Montreal, for example, predated the formation of the AYPA (in London, Ontario) by forty-six years. The Montreal Association was formed on 4 December 1856 at a meeting chaired by Bishop Fulford in the Diocesan Library. Its Minute Book, now in the Diocesan Archives, shows it to have been — quite in keeping with the times — a thoroughly clergy-driven organization. The president, it was decided, was to be the Dean of Montreal, with the clergy of the city serving as vice presidents. The Bishop was named patron.

A committee was struck to draw up "Bylaws & Regulations." At the next meeting, held two weeks later, there were thirty-five members on the rolls, and twelve more elected (not counting honorary members). There was to be a Reading Room, for which newspapers and periodicals were to be purchased, as well as Bibles for the use of the projected Bible classes. A course of lectures was planned for the winter.

On 5 February, forty new members were elected to the Society, and the Lecture Committee reported that six lectures — the first to be given by the Lord Bishop — would be presented from 16 February to 23 March with such titles as "The Primitive Church" (by the Rev. W.B. Bond), "Wycliffe and the Lollards" (by the Rev. Canon William Turnbull Leach), and "The Present Condition of the Church"(by the Very Rev. John Bethune). Members could attend the lectures free of charge and the general public were admitted at 1/3 for one evening or 5/- for the season.

The records of the Society continue until 1860. On 6 April 1865 the St George's Young Men's Christian Association was formed and carried on the work. Added to the "readings, recitations, debates, essays, &c.," that enlivened their meetings, the Association sponsored an afternoon mission Sunday School, and its members "undertook the arduous duty of visiting the sick, reading, and praying with them, and spreading the Word of Truth in the homes of the poor of the congregation [of St George's Church]."

Although young women, and even girls, were often included in parochial sewing societies, not much attention was paid to this group until the formation of a Junior Department — with Junior Branches — of the Woman's Auxiliary in 1890. In 1921, a secretary for the Girl's Department of the Dominion WA was elected in the person of Mrs Willis James of Calgary, and there was a name change from "Babies Branch" to "Little Helpers."

Shortly after World War II, in 1946, there was a surge of interest in what was termed "girls' work," spearheaded by Gwendolyn Carrington, National Secretary of the GA, and manifested in "a tremendous Conference in Toronto for Youth Leaders for six weeks," as one of the participants described it. Hitherto girls had been expected to follow along with the same sort of activities as the WA, but this initiative sought to offer something more to girls joining the organization, and to demonstrate to potential leaders what this might be:

This Conference was terrific [recalled Mercia Church more than fifty years later] — Each week we were given a different handicraft to learn (quite complicated things — I've forgotten them now) — & a different clergyman spoke daily — I only remember Archbishop Carrington — We had swimming lessons, & folk dancing & singing — & a lecturer from England gave us lectures on how to run a group of young people … Her name was Miss Marindin … at the end of the course some of us were interviewed as possible 'Regional supervisors' for the teen-age girls' work in the church. This, of course, was at the back of Mrs Carrington's mind when she organized this whole conference — I remember being completely captivated by Miss Marindin in her lectures —

Jean Marindin, who held a diploma in Political and Economic Sciences from Oxford University, was Organizer of Training for the National Association of Girls' Clubs in England; she was also a member of the Imperial Girl Guide Headquarters Committee and served on the executive of the British Junior Red Cross. Her lectures at the conference centred on the "Methods and Principles of Youth Work" and the "Needs of the Individual," but she also held a number of tutorial classes where the methods and skills learned were "adapted to the needs of the various types of Girls' Groups," and each student received individual instruction.

At the time, this conference was hailed as "making history." The emphasis given to physical and health education, personal counselling, and courses on group work and the needs of the individual show a real departure from the conventional attitude to the GA leadership.

After the conference, Mercia Tibbs (as she was then) was in fact asked to be Regional Supervisor for the Dioceses of Montreal, Quebec and Nova Scotia with her headquarters in the Synod Office building behind Christ Church Cathedral, Montreal. Like a number of the young women targeted for this work, she had recently been demobilized from the Canadian Forces, and her modest fees and accommodations at the conference in Toronto had been paid for by the Department of Veterans Affairs. It was assumed, probably correctly, that such leaders would have wider experience and serve as more interesting role models than traditional GA organizers.

As part of her work Miss Tibbs spent the summer of 1947 at Quebec Lodge Camp (at the old site on the other side of Lake Massawippi) near North Hatley. There she met her future husband, the Rev. W.H.M. Church, of the Diocese of Quebec, and was consequently lost to youth work in the Diocese of Montreal.

It is interesting to note that Quentin Robinson, Youth Chaplain to Bishops Maguire and Hollis, would later become the Director of the new Quebec Lodge in the mid-1990s. This camp, in the picturesque Eastern Townships, had been the setting in 1972 of the first Anglican Provincial Youth Camp, the initiative of Crosstalk Ministries.

When asked about his recollections of the Drop-In Centre experiment some sixteen years after the fact, Robinson described the short-lived project as a useful learning experience for all concerned. "But that's the nature of youth work," he added. "Some things work out and some don't."

Crosstalk Ministries, on the other hand, have grown and prospered. One of the follow-ups emerging from Youth Camp was a monthly Crossroads Youth Service. It originally met at the Church of the Ascension in the early 1980s, but moved to St. George's in 1983. In the first year attendance ranged between 106 and 158; by the third and fourth years, according to Canon Robin Guinness, "approximately 400 young people (and some adults) came out for the opening meetings."

Significantly, too, between 1970 and 1990 at least thirteen men and one woman who had come up through the ranks of Crosstalk-related activities entered the ordained ministry in the Diocese of Montreal, thus doubling their impact on youth work here.

# Acknowledging Multicultural Needs (1987)

Although the church has been slow to respond, for several decades it has been clear that the Anglican Church of Canada embraces in its mission and ministry people of every race and culture.

In 1992, General Synod adopted a policy statement and a series of principles on multiculturalism, and recommended the same to each of its component dioceses.

The work which had led to General Synod's endorsement of multiculturalism in mission and ministry came largely out of two National Symposia, one held at Aurora, Ontario from the 21st to the 24th October 1985, and the second, at Toronto, from the 19th to the 22nd of February, 1987.

A priest from the Diocese of Montreal, the Rev. Dr John McNab, was one of the driving forces behind the organization and evolution of these events.

The first Symposium sent a message to the national Church titled "Varieties of Gifts But the Same Spirit: A Long Way to Go." Its opening statement presents the Symposium's initial aims:

As a representative of the multicultural society that is the Anglican Church of Canada, and its people of many colours, many languages, many traditions, and one faith, we have met together for the following purposes:

1 To draw the attention of the Church at large to its responsibilities for ministry and evangelism in a multicultural society;
2 To help the Church recognise the gifts brought to it by the richness of a multicultural society;
3 To promote awareness and recognition among congregations of different racial origins of the specific contributions they have to offer and to provide encouragement in their efforts;
4 To recommend strategies at all church levels (parochial, diocesan and national) for achieving these aims.

Among the concerns expressed — and these ranged from consciousness-raising to "the need to create access to the decision-making bodies of the Church for Anglicans of all races and cultures" — was one concerned with liturgy:

Because there are many people in our parishes [the section on liturgy begins] whose culture is not reflected by the dominant Canadian Liturgical tradition, there should be opportunities from time to time to express these

PLATE 19A *Race Relations Day, 1997 (Photo Credit: Joan Shanks)*

PLATE 19B *Youth Synod, 1999 (Photo Credit: Joan Shanks)*

different cultural traditions in liturgy. This is especially appropriate in the case of personal offices (such as marriages, baptisms, and funerals). However, since liturgical texts are set and authorised, and because of their common source in the Church of England, there are real difficulties in adjusting our liturgies (both text and ceremony) for our people. We therefore propose the following measures to ameliorate this situation:

1  to include a favourite prayer (in translation, if necessary) at an appropriate place in the liturgy or to include some liturgical practices that are meaningful to particular groups within the congregation;
2  to encourage people of all ethnic origins to take a visible part in the liturgy;
3  to encourage musicians and composers to provide liturgical music that reflects the music of different cultures;
4  to celebrate an inter-cultural service, at least annually, in parishes where there are a large number of different ethnic groups.

Finally, we acknowledge the need for clergy and laity to develop sensitivity to the unique meanings of words and symbols for different ethnic groups in the congregation.

Among other concerns expressed were "Ministry among Immigrants," "Ethnically and Linguistically Distinct Congregations," the "Francophone Fact," and "Indigenous Peoples." The report was presented to Archbishop Edward W. Scott at a public meeting held in the Church of St Michael and All Angels, Toronto.

In a paper entitled *Ministry in a Multi-Ethnic Context*, presented at the invitation of Dr. Don Wiebe, Dean of Trinity College, Toronto, on 28 October 1998, McNab comments on some of the other findings that came out of the Symposium:

We learnt some significant things:

1  People from Asia and the Caribbean had experienced similar feelings of rejection in the society and in the church; the rejection in the church was a surprise to many.
2  Aboriginal People who attended the Symposium reported that they had had similar experiences. The Aboriginal People welcomed our efforts, told their story and gave their moral support; but they told the Symposium that their participation in the multicultural movement would only cloud their already complicated agenda of issues.

3   Very few white persons accepted the invitation to attend the Symposium.
4   The term "Ethnic" was understood to mean minority groups and did not include Anglo-Saxons and Francophones.
5   French participation was minimal. There was a delegate from the Diocese of Quebec.

The Second National Symposium, held in 1987, was, in Dr McNab's words, "really a continuation of the work of the first Symposium. There was some despondency. Nothing seemed to be happening." It also sent a message to the national Church, this one was entitled "Called to Be Leaven." It began with a mission statement which reads as follows:

We are all equally chosen people and therefore our church must now recognize and respect our racial and cultural diversity in such a way as to ensure that this richness is incorporated as a reality that is central to both its substance and organization.

This report — in the form it was presented — gives more of an idea of the flavour of the Symposium than did the previous one. It appears that its text follows closely the discussions and workshops of the event itself, so that the aims, energies and frustrations of the participants come through quite clearly. Section III, for example, titled "The Contemporary Church Situation," presents a vivid impression in telegraphic style:

Look at the major images the Church presents to us [in 1987]

(a)   Diocesan Synods: A sea of white bald heads and blue rinse
(b)   The House of Bishops: No visible minorities, no Native Canadians [Charles Arthurson, a Cree, was elected Suffragan Bishop of Saskatchewan in 1988, the first Native Canadian to be elected bishop.]
(c)   Church House: Visible minorities in secretarial positions, but none in staff and executive positions.
(d)   Bishop's office (in Toronto) has no secretarial or staff person who is [of] a visible minority.

Here follow two searching questions

(e)   Clergy: Are minority clergy acceptable into mainline parishes?
(f)   The paradigm: Look at the life in any large parish. Then, look at the life of the church congregation. Compare the community with the congregation. Do they match, or is there dissonance?

General Synod met in Ottawa in 1992, and adopted a Policy Statement and Principles on multiculturalism that had been prepared by the third Symposium. These principles were three in number and are remarkably faithful to the aims and objects put forward in the first Symposium:

... this General Synod endorses the following principles:

1   That in the activities pertaining to partnership in mission our connection with the world-wide Anglican communion be used to promote the multicultural nature of our church at both local and global levels; [that] connections be made between the call to partnership with Anglicans overseas and the call to partnership with these same people when they emigrate to Canada.
2   That in the activities pertaining to evangelism and social action in Canadian society we actively invite and welcome people from all cultures and races into our church fellowships; [that] we encourage cross-cultural learning and relationships within congregations; [that] we address issues that divide and oppress people due to cultural misunderstanding or racism in both church and society.
3   That we actively promote an identity which is culturally rich, diverse and inclusive by seeking ways to honour the gifts and the heritage of ethnically distinct congregations and to encourage their sharing with the wider church; by encouraging worship which is expressive in its music, words and symbols of the activity of God in many cultures; by seeking leaders, both lay and clergy, who collectively represent the cultural diversity of our church and bring gifts that will enhance the church's life; by ensuring that educational resources, continuing education programs, and educators promote sensitivity to the multicultural nature of the Anglican Church of Canada and Canadian society; [and] by encouraging theological schools to address issues of ethnocentrism and racism.

Arising out of General Synod, the National Multicultural Parishes Project — chaired by Dr McNab — was established. This Committee was based in Montreal with representatives from Toronto. Two parishes of a significantly multicultural character were chosen to provide the membership of the committee: St Lawrence in LaSalle and St Barnabas in Pierrefonds. A Conference of the sixteen parishes which formed part of the Project was held in Montreal, and there were activities in Toronto and Vancouver as well. Financial cutbacks eliminated the implementation of plans for the future, but the Toronto group of the project has continued to publish a Newsletter.

Plate 20  *Christmas party at Tyndale-St George's Community Centre
(Photo Credit:* Joan Shanks)

At its 1997 Annual Diocesan Synod, the Diocese of Montreal endorsed both the Policy Statement and the Principles on Multiculturalism as adopted by General Synod in 1992. The mover of the resolution was the Rev. Canon Dr John McNab, the seconder was Linden Rogers.

## Women's Plainsong (1991)

The Cathedral retreat planned for early April 1992 was to be held in the quiet, meditative setting of Epiphany House, Iberville, and one of its organizers approached Elizabeth Rowlinson, then at the Montreal Diocesan Theological College, to lend her knowledge of plainsong, and her experience as a member of several plainsong choirs as part of the devotional program. She and a small group of women had been singing Evensong together informally for a few months, and Dr Archibald Malloch's invitation to sing at the retreat consolidated the group. Thus began the Women's Plainsong Choir. When the retreat was over, the group began to sing Evensong regularly at the Cathedral. Their weekly plainsong Service would continue to be sung for a period of ten years.

Describing the choir's history, the Rev. Dr Rowlinson recalled:

It started during the winter of 1991-92, when a group of women began to gather informally to sing a simple BAS Evensong, using plainsong settings, on Thursdays at 5:15 pm.

We assembled at 4:30 in the vestry, and went over the day's music before the service; the number [of singers] fluctuated, but was usually between 5 and 10. We sang only plainsong, accumulated from various sources. In the later years we used handbells during the psalms, but apart from that there was no accompaniment.

It was a very egalitarian group; everybody took some part in the services, either officiating, or reading a lesson, or singing as cantor for a psalm or canticle. There was no director; all decisions were made by the group.

We wore academic gowns instead of choir robes. And there were no guilt trips — you came if you could, and if you couldn't, nobody complained. We didn't have auditions; any woman was welcome. Sometimes the singing was a little shaky, but it was sufficiently simple that everybody picked it up after a while.

Occasionally we sang at special services, or learned some rather more ambitious music. It was a very meaningful time of worship for us all, and we have fond memories of those Thursday afternoons.

The much more elaborate Sunday Choral Evensong continues to be broadcast live from the Cathedral on Radio Ville Marie (91.3 FM) and also on the Internet via the Cathedral website. On 12 March 2000 (Lent I), for example, the "Trebles, Girls and Adults," together with participants in "Kids in the City," sang the Prayer Book Service with hymns from the Book of Common Praise. The organ Prelude and Postlude were by J.S. Bach, the Preces and Responses, Plainsong, with other settings by Vincenzo Ruffo and Thomas Leighton. By way of introduction, the Service Bulletin reads:

Cathedral Choral Evensong in the Anglican Church is a musical offering, joining in the worship of the saints and angels in Heaven. The music sung by the choir is a time for you to join in meditation on the greatness and beauty of God, and of his presence in our lives and to reflect on the passages of Scripture which have been read. The congregation is invited to join heartily in the singing of the two hymns of the service and in the recitation of the Creed.

As you pray this service, please lift up to God your fellow worshippers, not only those who are present in the Cathedral, but the several thousand who will be taking part through the radio broadcast.

Many who will be listening will have French as their first language, and part of the service will be in French. A translation of the reading in French is provided on the back page.

Sadly, the modest, though equally reverential Thursday plainsong service came to an end in August 2000. The numbers in the Women's Plainsong Choir had dwindled and, "there weren't enough of us to keep it going." During its lifespan, however, the choir made a rich, distinctive contribution to the spiritual life of the Cathedral.

## "Under the Influence of the Liturgical Movement" (1992)

The Catholic tradition in the Diocese in its most fully elaborated form is found at the church of St John the Evangelist, Montreal. The following reflections first appeared as part of the "weekly notes" prepared under the aegis of the Liturgy and Music Committee of the parish, published in the parish bulletin between Michaelmas 1991 an Eastertide 1992, and "meant to inform fellow-parishioners on the construction of the building and the historical background which gives it meaning," but quite naturally strayed into the field of liturgy and furnishings:

The Roman influence manifested itself only moderately in our parish and apparently only from the 1950s. We have a few usages and decorations which are of Roman and even post-Tridentine inspiration: laced albs, cottas, birettas (now discarded), pink vestments, representations of the Sacred Hearts of Jesus and Mary (St. Anne's Chapel), the (St. Sulpice style) plaster statue of St. John, votive lights, stations of the Cross, holy water stoups, … In ritual, there is Benediction, Roman ceremonial at Evensong, increased use of incense … But we were spared the excesses of the movement, and our church has kept its typically Anglican character, borrowing moderately, and generally wisely, from Roman usage.

There was finally the influence of the Roman Liturgical Reform which began with the new Order for Holy Week in 1957 and culminated in the New Roman Missal of 1971. The effects of the former were important for us and they generally improved our Holy Week services. The influence of the latter was felt in the Anglican Church generally and it led to the production of our Book of Alternative Services in 1985.

Unlike many Anglo-Catholic parishes, we have not adopted this new book, even for occasional use. This is due no doubt to the relative poverty of language of the BAS, its poor sense of liturgy, and its unenthusiastic "Catholic" character. … We have been content with the 1959 (1962) Canadian Book, which, though extremely conservative, allows a Catholic interpretation. It, in particular, supports a liturgy which is compatible with the architecture of our church, itself a reflection of our Tractarian devotion and theology.

Modern liturgies, with their priest-president, direct congregation participation, and community awareness require radially arranged buildings with a central altar. Our linear church with its concentration on the east high altar cannot be transformed adequately or elegantly for these new rites. Indeed, experiments in this direction in the 1960s proved inconclusive and no one appears eager to repeat them.

There is, however, one transformation in the church, done in the 1950s under the influence of the Liturgical Movement, which now seems most regrettable, that is the removal of the ironwork and the great iron gate in the rood screen. … [T]hese structures were of great symbolic importance in the original planning of the church. Their loss has deprived our church of some of its most distinctive traits and architectural peculiarities. Hopefully, a future restoration will consider putting them back.

# The Dilemma of Sexual Orientation (1993)

On 10 November1993, the Rev. Warren Eling, rector of St James the Apostle, Montreal, was found strangled in his rectory. He had missed a meeting with parishioners the evening before and failed to keep an appointment on the following morning. The parish curate and a parish-ioner, concerned by the rector's absence, entered his residence and found him. As an article in the December issue of the *Anglican Journal* described it,

His semi-nude body was in bed, his hands tied behind his head. He had been strangled with a belt.

"The house had been ravaged," said Bishop Andrew Hutchison of Montreal.

A computer, a sound system, Mr. Eling's wallet and car had been stolen. The car was found in Toronto the next day. ...

There is speculation that Mr. Eling was the victim of a homophobic serial killer. Police are refusing to comment.

Roger Leclerc of the Committee of Gays and Lesbians Against Violence said that Mr. Eling was the 14th homosexual slain in Montreal in the last three years. ...

In a statement issued the day after Mr. Eling's body was found, Bishop Hutchison said, "a parish, a wide circle of friends and a whole community are in shock as speculation continues as to the possible motive and the very nature of the crime. ...

If, however, the speculation is correct that this crime is in some way related to sexual orientation we are doubly outraged, for it makes of it not simply a violent crime, but one motivated by hatred."

Speaking to the press, the Bishop affirmed that, following news of Eling's death, representatives of Montreal's gay community had been to see him:

"This is a threat to the well-being of our community and a terror to a large segment of the population in particular, namely, the gay community [Hutchison stated]. ... Regardless of what may have been Fr. Eling's sexual orientation he was a good and caring man. His whole life was lived out in profound commitment to challenging the bigotry of a violent world."

Fr Eling had come to Montreal in January 1992, having served in the Diocese of Toronto for more than twenty years. An article in the Toronto *Globe and Mail* by Douglas Chambers — reprinted in the Advent-Christmas issue of *Integrator*, the newsletter of Integrity, Toronto — pointed to the circumstances of Eling's move to Montreal:

Warren Eling left the diocese of Toronto in the wake of the Jim Ferry case: the case of a priest in a stable and loving relationship who had been "outed" by one of his congregation and, thus, dismissed by his bishop. That case was the *Kristalnacht* for any Anglican priest known to be gay, no matter how "respectable." ... Warren went to Montreal, far from most of his friends and the community he knew, depressed and increasingly desperate — in the literal sense of "without hope."

Chris Ambidge, Co-Convenor of Integrity, Toronto, suggests, however, that Eling clearly "felt comfortable" moving to Montreal, and in the short time that he was there, Bishop Hutchison asserted, Eling "had earned a significant place in the life of the diocese because of his well known skills in liturgy and his social justice concerns." Elings friends and family were also convinced that it was the attractiveness of a new challenge at St James the Apostle rather than anxiety about "exposure in the wake of the ecclesiastical trial of homosexual priest Jim Ferry" that had prompted the move from Toronto to Montreal.

In his Charge to the 141st Synod of the Diocese of Toronto, Bishop Terry Finlay drew attention to the implications of Eling's death:

… this week we mourn the death of a caring, gifted priest who was a victim of the mindless violence that characterises so much of life today. It has been suggested that this is another tragic example of the negative implications of secrecy concerning sexual orientation. If this be true, then I call upon all of us in the Church to stop this charade. Let us build communities based on understanding and acceptance, and work to become honest and trustworthy with one another. Let us make our communities safe places in which to be open about sexual orientation.

A further response in a different setting came from Bishop Hutchison. As Chris Ambidge has pointed out:

Just after the time of Warren's death, the Quebec government was holding hearings on the provincial human rights legislation as part of a regular review. Bishop Hutchison appeared at those hearings, and I remember hearing of his speaking strongly of the need for protection of and equality for homosexuals.

Although liberals as a whole were cheered by Bishop Finlay's words to Synod, many gay priests reacted less positively. One such gay man, signing himself "the Rev. John Doe," made the following observation:

When I heard Bishop Finlay's charge to build understanding and acceptance, my initial reaction was "more words! Will there ever be a serious commitment to change?" My fear is that engaging in dialogue may not ever amount to more than talk, and that as long as we are talking no one can say that the church is not dealing with the issue.

However, I truly believe that Bishop Finlay cares and wants his church to be inclusive of all of us. The question is: "Can we be a prophetic church that will risk and move on accepting gays and lesbians?" To do so will likely be divisive, but it is in such difficult times that we grow. We go nowhere by just being cautious and safe, though it would certainly be the easier route.

In November 1998, following discussion at the previous Diocesan Synod, Bishop Hutchison requested Diocesan Council to establish a Diocesan Sexuality Commission. The previous May, the Council of General Synod had invited the dioceses "to expand and deepen the dialogue concerning human sexuality" through setting up such commissions "to establish a forum where conversation on human sexuality can be carried on in an atmosphere of trust and respect."

The Commission's initial report underscores some of the stumbling blocks that had faced its organization:

Diocesan Council had been especially concerned that the Commission's members be representative of the wide diversity of opinion within the Diocese. As well, participants were nominated with consideration of regional representation, age, gender, and sexual orientation. During the first few months following its establishment the difficulty of implementing this objective became apparent. A significant number of those appointed declined to participate or resigned after attending the initial meetings.

Once the usual difficulties of finding mutually convenient meeting times were worked through, the members pursued a modest, consciously non-confrontational program of discussion:

We have considered such topics as traditional Anglican moral teaching, pastoral responses to changing sexual morality in society at large, and the nature of covenants, celibacy, and marriage [the Report continued]. We have repeatedly struggled with the implications of the often conflicting interpretations of scripture in the area of human sexuality. We have deliberately avoided focusing on topics of contention such as ordination of practicing homosexuals or the blessing of same-sex relationships. Our hope has been that through a broader discussion of the theology of sexual expression we might shed new light on these as well as other contentious moral issues which the Church has and will continue to face.

At one time "the atmosphere for Anglican gays and lesbians in the diocese of Montreal was almost as negative as in the far north," the area of least acceptance throughout Canada. Although there was a Montreal branch of Integrity — an association of "gay and lesbian Anglicans and friends" — in the late 1970s and early 1980s, according to Chris Ambidge "the chapter withered on the vine fairly early ... and it was certainly moribund if not dissolved by 1984." In the mid-1990s efforts were made to start up again; "they actually got going with a revived chapter in 1997 and met for a couple of years [Ambidge noted], but the chapter has since foundered and isn't meeting now [in 2000]."

Two decades ago, the gay community throughout Canada viewed Bishop Reginald Hollis as one of the major forces of opposition to their appeal for greater acceptance within the church. Indeed Hollis's 1979 Charge to Synod spoke out strongly against pressures to moderate the official position of the Anglican Church on the ordination of homosexual clergy and the blessing of same-sex relationships:

It's unfortunate [Hollis noted] that the question of the ordination of homo-sexuals came up in such proximity to the ordination of women. The questions are not related. We are not about to bring this matter to General Synod as though we were making a decision on the ordination of yet a third sex. The bishops' stand at their February meeting was an affirmation of the church's traditional morality. Sexual relationships belong within marriage. ...

The bishops are not prepared to accept a re-interpretation of the Bible to show that the condemnation of homosexual practices is purely a cultural matter. But we are prepared to recognize that a person can have a sense of homosexual orientation. This should not necessarily be a bar to ordination, provided that he or she recognizes the calling in Christ to abstain from sexual relationships outside the marriage bond. That is the calling for every minister, indeed for everyone who would follow Jesus, whatever the person's sexual orientation.

Douglas Chambers' *Globe and Mail* article places much of the blame for Eling's death at the door of the House of Bishops:

It will not do [he maintained] for bishops to deplore the consequences of the hatred — sexual as well as racial — that their own churches have prom-ulgated overtly and covertly. The bishops have had a hand in his death.

In an open letter addressed to the members of Synod of the Diocese of Toronto and distributed to them at the close, Fr Eling's family thanked the hundreds of people from across the diocese who had attended the

Requiem Eucharist for him in St James Cathedral. The letter concludes as follows:

… we believe that Warren could have made a far greater contribution to the life of the church had he not had to wrestle with its policy on sexual orientation.

Warren was not alone. Many other priests find themselves in a similar dilemma …

Bishop Terence Finlay of this diocese and Bishop Andrew Hutchison of Montreal have been of enormous comfort to us during the past week and we thank them for their support and prayers. Their unswerving willingness to deal honestly and openly with the horrible details of Warren's murder was courageous. …

If anything positive is to come from Warren's death, let it be change —…

Let's end the bias, bigotry and ignorance. Let's remove the roadblocks that restrict people like Warren from living their lives within the church in true pride and honesty.

Help us to ensure that Warren's death was not in vain.

On the evening of 21 February 1997, after four days of deliberation, a Montreal jury found thirty-three year old Danny McIlwaine guilty of second-degree murder in the strangling death of Warren Eling. McIlwaine's earlier conviction for premeditated murder in 1994 had been overturned in 1996 by the Quebec Court of Appeal and a new trial ordered on the grounds that the Superior Court Judge in the original case had erred in his instructions to the jury.

McIlwaine's plea, that he was on crack cocaine at the time of his fatal encounter with Warren Eling and that he had not realized what was happening, together with the fact that his presence in the rectory was at Eling's invitation, suggested that the crime had not in fact been homophobically motivated as was originally supposed. Eling may have died during the performance of a consensual act 'by accident.'

Although widely suggested as a footnote to this tragic affair, accidental death, to the minds of many, continues to be an unsatisfactory conclusion. As one spokesperson for the gay community has phrased it,

No, it wasn't a serial-killer-of-homos, as was speculated at the time; but Eling appears to have been participating in risky activities involving sex … This would not have been necessary if the church-as-institution had not been so unforgiving to homosexual priests. … I'm a little uncomfortable with 'Eling may have died by accident.'

During the investigation that followed his death, Warren Eling was described as a gentle, quiet man. His brief incumbency and its aftermath have had a profound impact, not only on the Diocese of Montreal, but on the whole Canadian Church.

## The Essentials Movement (1994)

Early in 1994, an article in the *Anglican Journal* announced that "Canadian Anglicans committed to orthodox Christian faith" were planning "an ambitious national conference" to be held in mid-August at John Abbott College in Ste-Anne-de-Bellevue.

The idea for Essentials '94 was first proposed in the fall of 1992, when Barnabas Anglican Ministries (BAM) suggested that such a conference be held "which would affirm the Biblical roots of the Anglican Church of Canada and the role of the gospel in the contemporary life of our national church." BAM invited the Prayer Book Society of Canada (PBSC) and the Anglican Renewal Movement (ARM) to join with them in this endeavour.

A Steering Committee, under the leadership of the Rt Rev. John R. Sperry, retired Bishop of the Arctic, was established in Toronto which oversaw the work of nine committees, each responsible for a different aspect of the conference. The Rev. Canon Dr Tom Robinson of Halifax chaired the Administration Committee and the Rev. Dr J.I. Packer of Vancouver the Content Committee. The Diocese of Montreal furnished chairpeople for Worship and Arrangements (Rev. Canon Brett Cane and Dr. M. Louise Cornell respectively).

Before the conference opened, registrants received a thick paper-covered binder of twenty of the papers to be presented. This was intended to stimulate and facilitate discussion in the workshops (of which there were two each day). From them, it was hoped, a number of Declarations would flow as the chief achievement of the five-day conference.

The conference featured such respected speakers as Michael Green, Harold Percy, Robin Guinness and Robert Crouse. It was attended by almost one quarter of the Canadian House of Bishops (including Montreal's retired Archbishop Reginald Hollis). The Archbishop of Canterbury George Carey had accepted an invitation to address the assembly. Yet it was thought that the conference would only attract a modest number of participants.

As Louise Cornell remarked in a letter included in each participant's welcome kit, the organizers were astonished at the number of registrants:

We had initially thought that Essentials '94 would attract some 350 people [she wrote]. Just a few months ago, there were some only 250 registrants; now there are close to 650!

By the close of the conference there were over 700. More than two-thirds were laity. Almost ten percent were under the age of thirty. As a report in the *Quebec Diocesan Gazette* described those attending:

Delegates represented every province and territory and a variety of ministries. There were prison, army and hospital chaplains as well as youth, college and camp ministry leaders. The Order of Saint Luke, a Christian healing ministry, and the Mission to Seamen were also involved. The Church Army, an Anglican evangelistic and social services ministry, was out in full force.

With these unexpected numbers, conference facilities were stretched to the utmost. Two sittings had to be arranged for meals, the numbers and sizes of workshops had to be adjusted and accommodated, transportation for events in the city had to be managed somehow.

An added factor which could not have been foreseen was the unprecedented heat. There was no air-conditioning in any of the meeting rooms, residences or the double gymnasium used for plenary sessions. Yet in spite of this — or perhaps because of it — a tremendous sense of community developed. Few complained. No one collapsed. The unexpected numbers continued to be a source of encouragement and surprise.

The article in the *Anglican Journal* announcing the conference had suggested that Essentials '94 would "draw from Anglicans who uphold a Christ-centred, spirit-filled, Trinitarian Christianity," but few participants seemed initially to believe that they occupied more than a minority position in the church at large. Many had been made to feel unwelcome and out of step. To be suddenly surrounded by other deeply concerned Anglicans from all across Canada, every ecclesiastical province, members of First Nations communities, and representatives from all but two dioceses, brought hope and optimism on every side.

Little optimism seemed otherwise to have been in evidence elsewhere in the Canadian Church if the tenor of the *Anglican Journal* for that year is a reliable indicator. News of the national Church seemed regularly centred on its continuing financial woes:

The church spent much of the last half of 1993 cutting spending for 1994 after National Executive Council (NEC) ordered reductions in May [it was reported in the March issue of the *Anglican Journal*]. ... Despite cuts already made, however, further reductions must be made this year and probably in 1995.

The wildly misforecast projections for Anglican Appeal income for 1993 and 1994 are largely responsible for the scrambling to make cuts now.

The article revealed that the $950,000 budget deficit of 1993 and almost $300,000 in that of 1994 would be eliminated by spending funds from the Isabel Johnson bequest:

With a further $867,000 from the bequest already being spent in the budget, these expenditures effectively wipe out the bequest, leaving no remaining funds to cover the new deficit.

In the same issue it was reported that two executives of the World Mission department were leaving their positions. The editorial suggested that the church was apparently reluctant "to make controversial decisions, to take action that may offend," and urged greater social activism, while a report entitled "Priest faces 17 charges," heralded the aftermath of Anglican involvement with residential schools. A further item, titled "Sexuality, the future, top bishops' agenda," hinted darkly that the church might best be purged of the traditional Anglicans still in its pews:

[A presentation to the House of Bishops] discussed the implications of the increased search for a spiritual home among baby boomers and what this will mean for congregations, especially in urban centres.

He noted in particular the conflict that will emerge between newcomers and people in the pews 'who have taken [the] community captive.'

'Where Anglican churches are growing in Canada ... there are people prepared to pay the price to grow,' he stressed.

'Often, paying the price means asking people to leave, and it means being available when people do leave to make sure they have a meaningful exit.'

Among the Letters to the Editor, five wrangle over the relative merits of the Book of Common Prayer (BCP) and the Book of Alternative Services (BAS). Four more are centred on issues of sexuality. Despite the lead article celebrating the consecration of Victoria Matthews as Canada's first woman bishop, the overall impression of the state of the Anglican Church of Canada was dreary indeed. The optimism generated in the sultry, airless halls of John Abbott College was an astonishing contrast and, as it were, a breath of fresh air.

The *PBSC* Newsletter for September contains a presentation to his parish by the Rev W. Michael Birch of St Mark's, Calgary, describing his impressions of the conference:

It was about +2º C in Calgary when two of us from this parish boarded a plane at Calgary International Airport to attend the Essentials '94 conference. We arrived in Montreal in the midst of a heat wave — the temperature, once the humidity was factored in, was 44º C! It was quite a shock ...

But oh! The faith exhibited there! Over seven hundred Anglicans from the Prayer Book tradition, the evangelical tradition and the charismatic tradition gathered for five wonderful days of prayer, praise, addresses, services and workshops.

The practices and vocabularies of some participants were strange to many of those of us who uphold Prayer Book worship — but they believed in the Bible. They believed that Jesus is the Saviour of the world, and the Lord of the Church. They loved the Anglican Church of Canada.

When the Declaration of Essentials, always part of the agenda, was formulated, not all participants at Essentials '94 were equally positive. In an article entitled "Our faith is not reflected here," the Archdeacon of Montreal questioned the consistency of some of the findings. How could the many charismatics present accept the BCP as "the norm for all alternative liturgies?" he asked. He questioned the focus on the family rather than on "the fellowship of those who believe and obey." The issue of gender and ordination, he suggested, remained unresolved:

The basic problem is that the declaration's vision of what is essential is too narrow to carry us beyond 1994. ... Its vision of Anglicanism affirms the [thirty-nine] Articles, the Solemn Declaration and the BCP as 'Anglican foundational documents,' but nothing more recent: no Lambeth Reports, no Anglican Roman Catholic International Commission Agreed Statements (our most up-to-date doctrinal position).

Does the declaration not take seriously its stated belief that the Holy Spirit 'leads God's people and the church's counsels in every age'...

Another dissenting note from within the diocese was sounded in the volume of essays which was published to respond to those presented at the conference itself. *The Challenge of Tradition: Discerning the Future of Anglicanism*, edited by John Simons, Principal of Montreal Diocesan Theological College, itself seeks to challenge the traditional stance of the Montreal Declaration.

The majority of participants in the conference, however (at least 142 of whom came from the Diocese of Montreal), seem to have returned to their parishes with a strong sense of renewal. As the Rev. Michael Birch concluded his report on the conference:

Many of us have been increasingly troubled over the seemingly terminal decline of the Anglican Church. Arbitrary alterations to liturgy, uncertain proclamations of faith, loss of moral courage, and an enforcement of ill-considered changes on a largely unwilling laity have resulted in thousands leaving our church. The Declaration is a sign that what we have been standing for in this parish does not exist in isolation. Thousands believe as we believe, and have spoken through Essentials '94 to the Anglican Church of Canada to say, "Here we stand; we can do no other." We are not alone, and the Faith has not changed. Take heart, for in following the Bible and the guidance of the Prayer Book, you will be shown to be in the right ... Do not even *think* of leaving the church just yet — she has desperate need of you.
By God's grace, we must not let our fire be put out. ...

Seven years later a second national conference, Essentials 2001, was planned to take place at the opposite end of the country at Trinity Western University, Langley, British Columbia, in the Diocese of New Westminster. As was the case in Montreal, the conference was acknowledged to be in, rather than of, the diocese that acted as its host.

The Essentials Movement, as it has been called, has gathered momentum since its first conference in Ste-Anne-de-Bellevue. The Montreal Declaration of Anglican Essentials, the Essentials Coalition claims, "is now [in 2001] being used internationally as a benchmark statement of key Anglican convictions."

## The Ministry of Lay Readers (1995)

Still in the midst of the national Church's undertaking of "the most extensive process of consultation ever," in order to develop "a new sense of its mission and purpose for the 21st century," the Diocese of Montreal turned its eyes increasingly on its own material resources. There was considerable soul searching on methods of consolidating its administration and restructuring its approach to ministry.

Our determination to harness our material resources and redirect them to effective mission continues [stated Bishop Hutchison in his Charge to Synod].

… From this work have emerged a number of alternate models of ministry including part-time and shared ministry, one lay pastorate, and non-stipendiary ministry. In several cases it has resulted in a much deeper sharing of leadership between laity and clergy, and in every case it has revitalized the church.

The LAOS Institute for education and development of Lay Ministry was in its third year, and had been working with the Lay Readers' Association at their regular conferences.

A reliance on lay ministry in the form of Lay Readers is long-established in the Diocese of Montreal, however, and members of the Association have done faithful, unobtrusive service for many years. Elliott Alleyne, a diocesan Lay Reader at St Paul's Côte des Neiges, for example, embarked on his long period of service on 7 March 1964; his 35th anniversary was suitably marked with a tribute in the *Montreal Anglican* in 1999.

Although incumbents may come and incumbents may go, lay workers and parochial Lay Readers often supply the thread of continuity so important in maintaining parish traditions and parish life.

In the parish of St John the Baptist, Pointe Claire, for example, there was an exceptional 'lay reading duo' made up of Frederick Hamilton Hodgson and Frederick Cyril Grant Sheward, which lasted for more than forty years.

Their long, close association and devoted leadership were perhaps unique [observed the March 1993 issue of *The Church of St John the Baptist News*]. Certainly, among the annals of the Lay-readers' Guild — if such an august body exists — it is unlikely that we will find another Fred Primus / Fred Secundus partnership, certainly not one of such stellar quality.

Both men were known for a sense of humour, evidenced by wit both on the stage and in the pulpit. During two interregnums in the mid-seventies, many visiting clergy were guided and encouraged by their lively sense of purpose. On the occasions when the visiting clergy *failed to visit*, Fred and Fred scarcely missed a beat. We were blessed — and probably took our blessings for granted most of the time.

Although Lay Readers are without a doubt supposed to support, assist and follow the lead of the incumbent of their church, there were times, at St John the Baptist at least, when this role was expanded. As an anonymous contributor to the parish *News* reported (long after the fact) of an incident involving Fred Sheward:

In spite of his very dignified and sober manner when on duty, Fred had a mischievous side which none could miss. Some of us who were in the choir during the time of the Rev. Malcolm Hughes will well recall one Christmas midnight service. The choir was assembled … waiting to process into the Church. When Malcolm appeared, he was sporting a somewhat Popish biretta on his head — a new and somewhat startling addition to his robes! Fred [Sheward], a great traditionalist, was aghast. He asked Malcolm if he actually intended to wear it at the Service. When Malcolm affirmed that he did, Fred disappeared for a minute. When he reappeared, he was wearing a bowler hat set at a rakish angle. 'Well,' said Fred, 'if you wear that, I shall wear this!' Strangely enough, I cannot remember whether Malcolm left his stunning biretta behind as we processed a moment later.

Fred Hodgson's name was submitted to the Bishop for a Lay Reader's licence by the Rev. Gordon Phillips in 1941, and he afterwards was licenced as a Diocesan Lay Reader. Canon James R. Allen put forward Fred Sheward's name after the war.

Fred Hodgson predeceased Fred Sheward by five years. At the time of the former's death, the latter paid him the following tribute:

Generous with his talents, always ready to lend a hand, I relished Fred's keen sense of humour and his outstanding skills as a raconteur. A source of parish history, I cannot overstate how much I learned from him. After we had both retired, he once remarked to me, "When you are on pension, every day is Sunday — except Sunday." In his latter years, Sunday became the focal point in his week. His sermons were studiously well prepared and presented.

During his forty-five years in St John the Baptist, he saw many changes in the church — licensed lay-readers reading lessons, handling the chalice, even taking entire services. When he began, congregational participation was unheard of as was the acceptance of women into the priesthood. Fred Hodgson, traditionalist though he may have been, knew that *his* church — God's church — would survive in spite of, or is it because of, these changes.

In 1923, under Bishop Farthing, Lay Readers' work was reorganized and divided into two classes: parochial and diocesan. He outlined his intentions in his annual Charge to Synod:

The Parochial Lay Readers will be licenced to work under the direction of their own rectors. These will he appointed as heretofore on the nomination of the rector, or incumbent, and the conditions will remain the same.

The Diocesan Lay Readers will be licenced to work under the direction of the Bishop. They will be required to satisfy appointed examiners as to

PLATE 21  *Celebrating the Mile-End Mission, 1999*
         *(Photo Credit:* Joan Shanks*)*

their knowledge of Scripture, Church History and Christian Doctrine: and of their ability to conduct public services. As these men go out alone, and are often responsible for the sole conduct of public worship and have to give instruction in congregations, I have felt that it is as necessary that I should be assured of their knowledge of what the Church stands for and teaches, as I am of the clergy I ordain.

In 1923, the need for greater lay involvement in ministry had resulted from insufficient resources in the face of a rapidly expanding Anglican population; in the 1990s declining numbers and diminishing resources were the cause. Bishop Farthing's tribute to Lay Readers in his charge might well have been uttered by all the intervening bishops since his day:

I cannot too strongly express my appreciation of the excellent character of the work done by these Lay Readers in the past. It has been simply invaluable to the Church, and to them it has been a 'labour of love' most cheerfully and devotedly rendered.

In 2000, at the annual Lay Readers' Day, held that year on 11 November at Trinity Memorial Church, forty-three lay readers participated and as many as eight received their first one-year licences.

## The Mile-End Community Mission (1996)

Although the Mile-End Community Mission took on new life and new direction in 1996, it has its roots in the early 1980s when Elaine and the Rev. Michael Pountney (newly appointed to the Church of the Ascension) began an outreach ministry to marginalized people in the community. This included food distribution and the serving of meals.

In 1991, the Church of the Ascension was deconsecrated and then sold for approximately $750,000 to the city of Montreal to be converted into a municipal library. The Rev. John Beach, who had continued the Mission after the Pountneys moved elsewhere, "felt committed to keeping a ministry presence in Mile-End." The Diocese agreed to support the project from the interest generated from the sale of the church, and when its Outremont rectory was sold some five years later, a similar arrangement was made. By the time Beach left this ministry in 1995, as his report to Synod that year attests, the Mission supported "a number of programs and organizations which strive to reach out and lift up those who are not beneficiaries of traditional social, economic, and educational initiatives":

Such initiatives include[d]: the Mile End Anti-Poverty Group, a weekly food bank, a weekly children's reading circle, a weekly open stage coffee house, a collective kitchen, and a clothing bank.

There was also a weekly Thursday morning Eucharist in which many of those involved in the above projects participated, but Beach expressed the opinion that the Mission was not sufficiently pastorally grounded:

A frustration which I have felt over this "experimental" ministry over the past 4 years [his report continues] has been the fact that it has not been formally attached to a parish church. Consequently, it has been difficult to offer the sacramental and pastoral ministry of the church to the many people who have sought it. I am grateful that the Mission will be yoked with St. Hilda's/St. Cuthbert's/St. Luke's/The Ascension and that the Rev'd Roslyn Macgregor will be taking on this ministry starting on the first of May.

At the same time the enlargement of the Mission's space at 87 Bernard ouest was being successfully negotiated. The Bishop came in June to bless the new premises.

"Welcome" was painted on the storefront windows in many languages (with help from the Montreal Children's Hospital) to reflect the cultural diversity of Mile End.

The transition period involved a two-day visioning workshop held in the summer of 1996 under the leadership of a Mile-End resident with expertise in the field:

The workshop was divided into two sections: Current Reality, and Action Plan. Current Reality had us look at

1    External trends that affect the Mission
2    Where we are now (Policies: organisation, practices)
3    Our base of skills, knowledge, attitudes & values we can build on
4    Major concerns that "keep us awake at night"

Out of this we came up with a Statement of Purpose: "To be a safe and welcoming community, where people can come together for mutual support, personal growth, and concrete programmes, and to be part of and serve Mile End."

The group identified four "leverage areas" that formed the Action Plan: Programs, Fund-raising, Church in action, and Organisational development. As a result, by 1997 the Mission had gained control of its finances, had engaged in successful fund-raising, and had applied for grants from the Social Outreach Committee of the Diocese, and the Federal Government's student employment program. In 1998 the Mission was incorporated as a non-profit organization. Active efforts were made to attract partner parishes, and by that same year, links had been forged between the Mission and St Barnabas (St Lambert), St Paul's (Lachine), Christ Church (Rawdon), St George's (Ste-Anne-de-Bellevue), St Peter's (Town of Mount Royal), and the Cathedral. Old programs were rethought; a renewed sense of community emerged.

The spirit of Mile-End may be glimpsed in the mutuality of support which resulted from placing a theological student at the Mission in the year preceding her ordination to the diaconate. As part of her training, she became responsible for community meals at the Mission, assisted with the Thursday Eucharist, and had responsibility for developing a Friday Drop-In "that began to blossom" before her time at Mile-End was completed. She "fit in so well" that strong attachments were formed on both sides. That September,

[a] group from the Mission attended her ordination [the Director reported]. Savanna and Suzanna helped give out the booklets, and Connie, Doris and Lubo carried the bread and wine for communion to the altar ["with dignity and grace." Ros Macgregor preached the sermon]. There have been so many community-building activities, but [this] ordination was a highlight.

Stating her appreciation in her own annual report, the new deacon observed:

I began the year as a student at the Mission. In April, I said my good-byes with a Mexican Fiesta. In May, I graduated from theological college and began to prepare myself for ordination to the diaconate. ...

I cannot begin to express what your support has meant to me. The Mission community has been there for me all the way. ... THANK YOU! This is what community is all about. Sharing the joys and sorrows of each other's lives weaves us together.

Operating in both English and French is one of the realities and challenges of the Mission. This is reflected in its bilingual newsletter *Mission Possible*, which began publication in 1998. Its articles, poems, profiles and recipes are neither duplications nor translations, thus encouraging those who have both languages to read all eight pages. Similarly, the Mission's Annual Reports are written in the language of each writer: the Food Bank and Student Reports (in 1999) in English, the Pause Café and Program Extra Reports in French:

En octobre [reads the latter Report], j'ai commencé un projet extra à la mission communautaire Mile-End. Au début, je ne savais pas à quoi m'attendre mais très vite, j'ai appris à connaître les gens et à travailler avec eux.

Je tiens à remercier toute l'équipe pour l'encouragement et l'aide qu'il m'apporte et plus particulièrement Joyce, Lori et Connie. Elles m'ont acceptée telle que je suis, elles m'ont soutenue dans mes projets et elles ont fait des efforts pour me parler en français. Elles m'ont aussi aider à apprendre l'anglais. ...

[À la mission] on trouve toujours une oreille prête à nous écouter et des gens qui nous accueillent avec le sourire. On est respecté. Avec eux, j'ai retrouvé le goût de retourner sur le marché du travail.

À la mission, on est toujours accepté sans être jugé.

As another contributor to *Mission Possible*, writes:

All types of people involve themselves in the Mission, of various religious, linguistic, and cultural backgrounds. As an offer of hope and help to the community, the Mission plays an important role. Social relations are developed, and bonds of friendship and understanding are established. The Mission is interested in an active community, and the energetic efforts of those who participate find ample reward.

# What Constitutes a Sphere of Mission? (1997)

In his Charge to Synod in 1994, Bishop Hutchison made what might be regarded by some as a startling admission. The old hallmarks of Anglican identity were no longer meaningful. It was high time for Anglicans to see themselves in a new way:

There was a time [the Bishop recalled] when the Anglican Communion was held together by bishops dispatched from England, in communion with the Archbishop of Canterbury, sharing a common language, cultural history and Book of Common Prayer. Most of those features of our common life have long since gone, and one must reasonably ask, 'What is it that now holds us together as a Communion? Archbishop Tutu's answer is *that we meet together because we choose to*. That is the glue that binds us together.

Writing Mission Statements became popular in the 1980s. Individual churches were encouraged to examine their identities and phrase their priorities in clear, pithy terms. Businesses often draw up Mission Statements, too, as do many institutions.

The wording of the following text, the Mission Statement of the Diocese of Montreal, was given final approval at Diocesan Synod, 3 October 1997:

### Our Mission

We are called as members of the Body of Christ to affirm the Lordship of Jesus Christ by the ongoing worship of God and with the guidance of the Holy Spirit to work together in unity and thanksgiving using our diversity of gifts, traditions, cultures and languages, to encourage and equip one another to:

1.  work for reconciliation, healing and renewal;
2.  live and share the Good News at home and abroad;
3.  transform unjust structures in the church and in society;
4.  safeguard the integrity of creation and sustain and renew the life of the earth.

A Mission Statement is, in a way, rather like what used to be termed "the objects" of an organization. The objects of the Church Society of the Diocese of Montreal, established in 1852, were five. They are, of course, much more related to the temporalities of the church than the objects of the Diocese at that period would have been:

The objects of the Society shall be comprehended in the following distinct departments of Christian exertion, viz:

First— The encouragement and support of Missionaries and Clergymen of the United Church of England and Ireland, within the Diocese of Montreal, including the creation of funds toward the Stipends of poor Clergymen, and towards making a provision for those who may be incapacitated by age or infirmity, and for Widows and Orphans of the Clergy of the said Church in the said Diocese.

Second— The encouragement of Education, and the support of day and Sunday Schools in the said Diocese, in conformity with the principles of the said Church.

Third— Granting assistance, where it may be necessary, to those who may be preparing for the Ministry of the Gospel in the said Church within the Diocese.

Fourth— Circulating in the said Diocese the Holy Scriptures, and such publications as have the sanction of the Church, viz: Prayer Books, Homilies, catechisms, Collects, Canons, with the addition of the Tracts circulated by the Society for Promoting Christian Knowledge.

Fifth— Obtaining and granting aid towards the erection, endowment and maintenance of Churches in the said Diocese, the creation and maintenance of Parsonage Houses, and setting apart of Burial Grounds and Church-Yards, the endowment and support of Parsonages and Rectories ... and the management of all matters relating to such endowments.

Many of the objects of the Church Society, such as pensions and education, were managed differently in the 1990s, and the church's conception of its sphere of responsibility had, consequently, changed a good deal. What is striking in the two formulations is the difference in focus, and the contrasting images of what constitutes a sphere of mission.

## The Ice Storm (1998)

The Bishop's Newsletter, written a week and a half into what came to be known simply as "The Ice Storm" opened with an apt quotation from the Gospel according to St John:

The Light shines on in the darkness, And the darkness has never put it out.

It is now *Day 10* of the most punishing ice storm our part of the country has known [he began]. Over 325,000 Quebec households and businesses remain without light, heat and power, along with many more in Eastern Ontario and Western New Brunswick. Until a few days ago, the figure was over a million. Police, firefighters, road crews, municipal workers, Hydro crews, assisted by more than 10,000 Canadian Forces personnel and an army of volunteers, struggle in hostile weather conditions to restore services and provide for the safety and security of citizens. Hospital blood supplies are reduced by as much as 75%. Large numbers of patients ready to be released cannot be returned to frigid homes. Emergency wards are strained to capacity by patients injured on icy streets and sidewalks. The downtown core of Montreal has been shut down for days, not only for reasons of power shortage, but also because of the danger of huge sheets of ice crashing to the ground from tall buildings. Schools and universities remain closed. More than 30,000 trees have been lost in Montreal alone.

As I write, the news is that those living in the darkened triangle on the

South Shore are unlikely to have power restored for another ten days. ...

There is, however, much light shining on in the darkness. It begins with the readiness of people all over the continent to respond. Truckloads of firewood flow into the area from the Lac St-Jean area; Hydro poles, parts, and equipment pour in from outside our borders, as do generators, beds for shelters, and food. Snow and ice clearing equipment are contributed from municipalities near and far. Hydroelectric experts and technicians from Connecticut, Virginia, Long Island and our close neighbours work hand in hand with our own workers under conditions for which they were never prepared. ...

The February issue of the *Montreal Anglican* also contained a survey of a selection of parishes outside the immediate area of the city of Montreal, describing circumstances in a variety of communities.

In an interview with the paper, the Rev. Dawn Barrett outlined recent events in the Granby, Waterloo, Otterburn Park and Rougemont region — the area of her clerical responsibility. She described not only the challenges faced by those inhabiting the "triangle of darkness," but also the surprising number of positive experiences — "blessings" — that had accompanied them:

[P]eople have gotten to know each other and this knowledge has crossed linguistic lines. Relationships have formed between neighbours who have never before spoken to one another.

On a community basis, people have been brought closer together. [Barrett] described the first Sunday of Prayer for Christian Unity. The Mayor arranged for a generator to be brought in to heat the Roman Catholic Church. The Mayor first addressed the people, then Mrs Barrett preached in French, and the French-Canadian Roman Catholic Priest preached the English sermon, and then they concelebrated. After this glorious ecumenical liturgy, the restaurant in Rougemont, Les Quatre Feuilles, invited the whole town for a free lunch. Over 1,000 people attended; local residents, Hydro workers, Bell workers and soldiers were present.

A third result of this storm is the bringing together of families. ... Generally the community has not lacked for anything, for supplies of wood, candles and generators have been sent in from many other areas. ...

Although the Church buildings are too cold to use, the services of worship in the parishes have not ceased. They are now being held in people's homes, followed by a potluck meal. The worshippers gather in a semi-circle around the source of heat, to pray and reflect upon the extraordinary experience they are all sharing. ...

During this time, Dawn has practised a telephone ministry with the people of her four parishes. She and the Wardens keep in contact with everyone, assessing needs, helping where they can and generally giving support and encouragement. She also visits the shelters in the area. ... Relief for this area is expected within the next few days. But for now there is still the sense of loneliness after dark. In a five block area only four houses show any lights. But [because power was restored more quickly in parts of Montreal] one can look and see the city lights in the distance.

The Rev. Dawn Barrett's experiences were similar to those of clergy and laity throughout the affected area of the Diocese. As the Bishop's February letter continues:

Clergy and laity, many of whom are themselves without power, have worked together in parish after parish to call every household on the parish list, and visit all those who might be especially vulnerable. On the first Sunday of the storm, an informal survey of churches that opened to hold services was conducted by a Montreal radio station. Anglican churches topped the list! And several did so without benefit of Hydro. Churches that had power remained open for warmth, coffee, counsel and cooking in the church kitchen. Hot meals were taken to those determined to remain in their homes. ...

In Ste-Anne-de-Bellevue, the Rev. Cedric Cobb's parish decided to open a shelter in the Church basement and use the Church as a Community Centre "where people could come and get warm." Both the Church and Rectory were on the same power line as the Military Hospital and had never lost power. Many of St George's congregation lived in such hard-hit areas as Dorion, Pincourt, St-Lazare and Hudson. Yet even the elderly and infirm tried to stay in their homes as long as they could, and many were unwilling to leave family pets behind.

There were, however, many people with some source of heat who took neighbours into their homes — to stay or just to warm up. Organist, Ed Benton, and his wife Shirley, of the Church of St Margaret in St Hubert, for example, "sheltered a total of twenty-nine persons, two birds and one dog. This in a house consisting of three bedrooms and two bathrooms! ... Shirley made pots of soup and all kinds of food for their guests, who spent the time playing cards, talking and laughing, and generally enjoying themselves under the circumstances."

Others, with wood stoves and wood furnaces — particularly in the Townships — opened their homes to neighbours with thawing provisions from their freezers, enabling them to save provisions by transforming them into large hot meals, to be shared on the spot or carried home.

The devastation, when all was over, is difficult to imagine: toppled telephone poles, twisted power pylons, snapped trees and sheared off branches, woodlots resembling matchwood. The interruption of electrical power was, for some, to be a long one, dragging on far beyond the projected date for the restoration of light, heat and normalcy.

By April the ordeal was a memory. The Bishop's Easter Message, printed in the *Montreal Anglican*, began with the observation that "as part of God's Creation we find ourselves very closely connected to nature." He went on to observe that the challenge posed by "the ice storm of the century" had tested individuals and communities, "both physically and spiritually," in a profoundly communal way:

There were some important learnings for us as we reached for resources within ourselves and connected again to essential values [the Bishop wrote]. As with all important learning, this was not without cost, and some paid more dearly than others. Among other things we learned of our profound interdependence. ... Many discovered the joy of being of service to a neighbour in need, and many knew something of the triumph of the Spirit over very discouraging circumstances.

The Lenten journey into the wilderness reminds us of the ever present temptations to look first to our own comfort ... The long journey of our Lenten observance ends with the sacrifice that brings new life to the world. ... May the new life that bursts forth in the coming days and weeks give music to the stirrings of hope and possibility that are among the precious gifts of Easter.

## Common Praise (1998)

Music has formed an important part of diocesan life in Montreal from its earliest days, and it is no surprise that one of the major figures in the production of the "new blue hymnbook" — Common Praise — should have been a prominent musician from this diocese.

Patrick Wedd, sometime organist of St John the Evangelist, Montreal, and more recently of Christ Church Cathedral, "played a major role in the development of Common Praise," wrote Paul Gibson, Project Manager of the collection, "I cannot imagine that the book would have been the same without him." Wedd was the only full-time member of the new book's Task Force to be recruited from the Diocese, or indeed from the province of Quebec.

As a member through all those years of the Hymnbook Taskforce [wrote Wedd, in an article in the *Montreal Anglican*], I can attest to a process full of discovery and adventure, reflection and probing, frustration and disap-

PLATE 22  *Liturgical dancers  (Photo Credit:* Joan Shanks*)*

pointment. I was privileged to meet at least monthly, often more frequently, with a group of some fifteen theologians, musicians and poets, clergy and lay, every one of whom brought dedication and expertise to the task.

Other contributors from the Diocese, whose arrangements appear among the hymns selected, are Michael Capon, Stephen A. Crisp, and Richard C. Hunt. Wedd himself contributed eighteen.

According to the preface of the new volume, Common Praise is the fourth hymn book authorized by General Synod for Anglican use in Canada. It appeared

following a period of intense change: new translations of the Bible; new forms of worship; new lectionaries; new styles of language and music in worship; shifts in sensitivity to the ways in which language can exclude or include; increased awareness of and contact with other cultures, races, languages, and religious denominations. It also comes after a period of unparalleled creativity in both words and music for congregational song.

The origins of *Common Praise* lay in a proposal made at General Synod in 1983 immediately after the adoption, on an experimental basis, of The Book of Alternative Services:

After three years of discussion and refinement [the Preface continues] a resolution was prepared for presentation in 1986. This resolution, adopted by the National Executive Council, called for a hymn book which would contain material new and old, which would draw on a wide variety of styles and traditions, which would complement the Common Lectionary, and which would be couched in language as inclusive as possible. In 1992 the General Synod extended this mandate to interpret the word "inclusive" in terms of theology, languages, music, and cultural heritage in addition to gender.

Conceived mainly for use in "congregations, homes and conferences," Common Praise is based for the most part on texts in The Book of Alternative Services. Like the red Hymn Book of 1971, produced jointly with the United Church of Canada, the music appears with the words, but this time guitar chords are provided for many hymns as well, and some of the texts are offered in other (including aboriginal) languages.

The new book was not without its detractors, as a sympathetic article in the *Anglican Journal* attests:

Almost immediately, the project was controversial. Many people didn't understand why, in times of financial constraint, the Anglican Church would

PLATE 23   *Service bulletin for the choral Evensong celebrating the 450th annivesary of the Book of Common Prayer, 1999*   *(Photo Credit:* Joan Shanks)

produce a new hymn book. ... More protest came from the conservative sectors in the church that objected to the use of inclusive language, especially when the task force began selecting hymns that made female references to God. ... There were complaints the group was overloaded with liberal-minded people ... There were also complaints not enough evangelical hymns were chosen for the new book.

If a tongue in cheek insert in the *Montreal Anglican* on Anglican-Lutheran relations and the imminent signing of the Waterloo Declaration can be taken at face value, satisfaction with the new book ran high. Second among the "Top Ten Things I like about being Lutheran [and Anglican]" — which included "lots of acronyms" — and "a well-trained taste for single-malt scotch" as "the prerequisite for ordination as a bishop" — was "our attractive Green liturgy book [the BAS], and the new Blue Hymnal."

## A Space Age Diocese (1999)

With science and technology increasingly shaping the values and setting the tone in much of the Western World's cultural life, the role and relevance of the churches is often factored out. For those who regret this tendency, it is a welcome surprise to happen upon a brief feature in the *Montreal Anglican*'s June issue for 1999 describing Christ Church Cathedral's active participation in launching Canada's first female astronaut into space. During preparations for the May 27th launch of the space shuttle *Discovery*, the article reports, an organ fanfare, sent for the occasion from the Cathedral, "resounded through the Crew Quarters at Cape Canaveral."

The Canadian astronaut Julie Payette, as well as having astronautical skills [the article continues], is also an accomplished musician, and has sung in choirs with Cathedral Music Director, Patrick Wedd.
    Dean Michael Pitts of the Cathedral sent a message of prayers and good wishes, along with the fanfare, played by Patrick Wedd, to Cape Canaveral on behalf of Julie's musical friends in Montreal.

That same day, the article informs us, the Dean was delighted to receive the following response from Julie:

Thank you for this 'musical' show of support. We played the fanfare very loud in the Crew Quarters, to give us some spirit before the launch. It was very nice.
    Regards to Patrick Wedd and everyone in Montreal. Ad Astra!

Surely this initiative qualifies Montreal, within the Canadian Church at least, as a space age diocese.

# The Context of the National Church (2000)

As the sesquicentennial year of the Diocese opened, events at the level of the national Church cast a pall of uncertainty over the future of the administrative structures of the Anglican Church of Canada.

The lead article of the February *Anglican Journal* quoted the ACC's general secretary, Archdeacon Jim Boyles, as saying that "the preferred option is for General Synod to continue indefinitely as it is. But mounting bills relating to residential schools could force it into bankruptcy." The April *Journal's* front page urged Anglicans, nation-wide, that the Federal Government's policy of third party suits against the churches, and not the Native People, was threatening the future of the national Church.

In May the *Journal* issued a 16-page supplement devoted to residential schools, and the Primate issued a Pastoral Letter to be read from pulpits throughout the country.

In his June message, printed in the *Montreal Anglican*, Bishop Andrew Hutchison wrote with frankness and candour of the position of the Diocese and of the national Church:

By now most of you may have heard the pastoral letter, written by the Primate, which I directed should be read in all the churches of the Diocese on Sunday, May 28th. ... The letter concerns issues arising from our involvement with the Government of Canada in residential schools for aboriginal Canadians.

In the news media you may have heard or read a variety of articles, some of which indicate that the Anglican Church of Canada may face bankruptcy within a year as a result of a number of lawsuits in which we have been named as vicariously responsible for abuses that took place in the schools. Those reports are correct as far as they go. A generous evaluation of the assets of the General Synod is $10 million, which includes the national headquarters building (Church House) in Toronto, and the assets of the Anglican Book Centre. Only the Pension Fund is guaranteed protection against the litigation. The Primate's World Relief & Development Fund is hoping for similar protection of its funds to be assured. To date approximately 7000 cases have been filed against the Government. The Anglican Church of Canada, and a number of its Dioceses, have been named in nearly 1700 of those.

Of the 26 residential schools run by the Anglican Church under contract from the Federal Government, none ... was located within the diocese of Montreal. As a separate legal entity under the Church Temporalities Act of this Province, therefore, we are not directly exposed legally or financially. That is not to say, however, that the present scenario would not have profound impact upon us. More about that later.

The residential schools were not an Anglican invention. There was a broad Canadian consensus predating Confederation that the best hope for the development of aboriginal peoples lay in assimilation into the new European culture through education. It was legislated through the Indian Act. The Government built the schools, hired and paid staff, rounded up the students, and provided budgets to operate the schools. The Anglican Church, the Roman Catholic Church and the Presbyterian Church entered into contracts with the Government to run the schools. There were dedicated and exemplary Christians among the teachers in the schools, many of whom made enormous positive contributions to the lives of their students. It is clear today, however, that the system itself was fundamentally flawed. We collaborated in depriving the students of their language and traditional family upbringing. It is also clear that among the staff were others who were far from exemplary. Many children were subjected to physical and sexual abuse both by staff and by older students.

The Anglican Church withdrew from the system 31 years ago, and began a new walk with its native constituents. We found a new and better role in advocacy of native land claims and justice issues. ...

In the present crisis, our chief concern is our commitment to the new direction of our walk with native Canadians that began in 1969, and maintaining the capacity to continue the work of healing and reconciliation. The loss of the structures and personnel of the national Church, and of our northern dioceses that are funded from the national Church, would seriously obstruct that. It is at that point that dioceses like ours may be called upon to test our commitment to these vital missions. A secondary concern is for our work overseas through the Partners in Mission programme. The national Church has notified all our overseas personnel and projects that we will meet our obligations for this year, but can make no commitments beyond that.

Discussions are under way with government officials to find a less confrontational way to resolve legitimate complaints than through litigation ... Legal costs to resolve such actions eat significantly into the limited funds we have available to settle with legitimate victims. Alternative Dispute Resolution, we believe, provides a better vehicle.

I ask your prayers for those who are on the front lines of these actions, both at the national Church and in many of our dioceses. I ask your prayers as well for the individual victims of abuse who seek healing and restitution.

PLATE 24A *Bishop Andrew Hutchison and dancers at PWRDF Annual Dinner, 1999*
*(Photo Credit:* Joan Shanks*)*

PLATE 24B *Bishop Jubal Neves and the Partners in World Mission Committee, 2000*
*(Photo Credit:* Joan Shanks*)*

Pray for the staff at Church House and in our northern dioceses facing an uncertain future. Above all pray for the native peoples within the Church and outside us who find themselves at the centre of a controversy not of their own making, and difficult to endure. I remain convinced that God is at work in all this, challenging us to maturity in our commitment to *strive for justice and peace among all people, and respect [for] the dignity of every human being.* We will emerge from this as a stronger, more faithful Church, with a deeper understanding of the Passion of Christ, and the power of his Resurrection.

Yours faithfully,

+ Andrew

# Keeping the Feast (2000)

July 25th — the Feast of St James the Apostle — marked the starting-point of the Diocese, on which day Francis Fulford was consecrated first Lord Bishop of Montreal in Westminster Abbey, the Archbishop of Canterbury, John Bird Sumner, officiating, with the bishops of Salisbury, Chichester, Oxford, Norwich, and Toronto assisting. Not surprisingly, this was the date chosen to launch Montreal's sesquicentennial celebrations.

Montrealers have been known long since for "putting on a good show" and "doing things well." The sesquicentennial year was no exception. In an article in the *Montreal Anglican*, entitled "Therefore Let us Keep the Feast," some events of that summer were outlined with flair and gusto:

Wherefore "therefore"? — because it's the Diocese of Montreal's sesquicentennial (a.k.a. 150th anniversary), and "therefore" there is good reason to feast and celebrate — and so we will. ...

By the time you read this, the first event will probably be over: our farewell to our companion diocese of the South West, Brazil, ... Now we look forward to the events of July 25th — 150 years to the day since Francis Fulford's consecration. It falls on a Tuesday, and at Evensong in Christ Church Cathedral that day at 5:45 p.m. we will duplicate much of the music used in the Abbey 150 years ago (e.g., "The Lord gave the word; great was the company of the preachers" from Handel's "Messiah") New canons will be installed, and the Fulford monument beside the cathedral, currently being restored, will be rededicated by our Metropolitan, Archbishop Arthur Peters. ...

And then, in the courtyard behind the cathedral (now named in honour of Raoul Wallenberg), there will be a Thé Dansant! And what, you ask, is a

Thé Dansant? It is a late afternoon dance, with punch and tea, cucumber and watercress sandwiches, and a string band to dance to. You are invited to wear period costume or some reasonable facsimile (gaiters will be in evidence), and you will certainly want to look your best since a video is being made for our anniversary, and you may be captured on camera.

Other events of our sesquicentennial will be publicized by a special brochure, by notices in church bulletins, and by articles in the Fall issue of the *Montreal Anglican.* ...

All the events of the anniversary are open to the public (not just Synod delegates, for example), and most of them are free. ...

"Therefore let us keep the feast!"


# What Is a Church But the People? (2000)

Sometimes it is easier to trace the history of a church than of a parish. Buildings usually stay in one place. They may be renovated, expanded, turned to other purposes, torn down or burned down, but the narrative thread of their existence can usually be followed without too much difficulty. Parishes, although usually centred in a church, have a more amorphous and evanescent existence.

Since the period of the Quiet Revolution — more obviously still since the Parti Québécois victory at the polls in 1976 and two subsequent Referenda — there has been a steady migration out of the province. Although this trend apparently slowed toward the middle of the last decade, it has had a devastating effect on the English-speaking community and on parish rolls, removing as it has young families and mobile professionals. Churches have closed. Congregations have been amalgamated — once, twice, and more — often leading to feelings of grief and anger among those who have remained. The pastoral needs of such deracinated communities are very great, and decisions have not always been implemented in the most pastoral of ways.

The phenomenon of combined parishes is not new to the Diocese, however. In 1908, for example, churches and congregations at Iron Hill, West Brome and Bondville formed a single parish, as did Bedford and Mystic, Thorne and Leslie, Hemmingford and Hallerton, Huntingdon and Hinchinbrooke, to name a few. Country parishes were particularly subject to such combinations, but city congregations, especially in more recent years, have experienced them as well.

Perhaps the most dramatic among the combinations in the Diocese is that of St Cuthbert's, St Hilda's, and St Luke's. Its recent History, produced in the final months of the year 2000, points out that the parish is in fact "the faithful remnant of twelve-plus Anglican Churches in eastern Montréal":

We came to these parishes over the years from many places [the History begins]: Barbados, England, France, Gaspé, Ghana, Hungary, Ireland, Japan, St Vincent, Scotland, Trinidad, Wales — but our Christian roots go back almost 2000 years. Our faith is what unites us. Church buildings were dear to us, yet God has brought us together into this particular community of faith.

A list of the various churches then follows, together with their locations: All Saints (at St-Denis and Marie-Anne), Church of the Ascension (Park Avenue), St Alban's (at St-Zotique and de Chateaubriand in Amherst Park), St Andrew's (in Ahunsic), St Augustine's (Rosemount), St Basil's (at Racette and Brunet, Arona Park), St Chad's (on Duquesne street, Longue Pointe), St Cuthbert's (Park Extension), St Cyprian's (Morgan Boulevard, Maisonneuve), St Hilda's (de Lorimier Avenue), St Luke's (Holt and 8th Avenue, Rosemount), St Mary's (Sherbrooke and Cartier Streets), and St Thomas (Sherbrooke and de Lorimier Streets).

Not all the remaining parishioners from these churches would have found their way to the new combined parish, however. The History suggests that some members from the former St Chad's and St Basil's would probably have gone to St Margaret of Scotland, Tétreaultville, or St Ignatius, in Montreal North, which were still in existence.

Many of these parent-churches had been closed for a long time — St Mary's was sold in 1947 and disbanded in 1970, St Alban's burned in 1962 and was deconsecrated the following year, St Andrew's was closed and deconsecrated in 1970 — others, such as St Augustine's, took on a new name when the congregation outgrew its old accommodations, and became St Luke's when its new church was built.

The History goes on to trace the final stages of amalgamation:

The Church of the Ascension was sold in 1991 to the City of Montréal for use as a library. The renovation was done in a respectful manner, and the stained-glass windows, wood beams, and large memorials remain as a testimony to those who worshipped there. Many of the Ascension parishioners joined with the Parish of St Cuthbert, north in Park Extension. ...

Shortly after, St Cuthbert's also closed, and many from the combined parish moved to the Parish of St Hilda ... The parish became known as St Cuthbert and St Hilda's. There followed a period of some uncertainty as people from all three parishes adjusted to the changes and challenges of the two closings and moves in such a short time. ...

In January 1995, the congregation from the Parish of St Luke, in Rosemount, moved west and joined the combined parish, becoming the Parish of St Cuthbert, St Hilda and St Luke (St CHL for short!), and the Rev. Roslyn Macgregor was appointed to the parish.

Over these past five years, we have journeyed together through a process of grief and enormous challenge to a place of health, trust, and hope in the future. This is a church which continues to address issues of an aging population, while welcoming and encouraging the involvement of younger members. Most parishioners, young, old, and in-between, must use several stages of public transportation to get to church, yet they faithfully appear, by bicycle, bus, car, metro, and on foot.

Our parishioners are committed to reaching out to others in the congregation in various ways, as well as being committed to outreach in the greater community. In addition, we share our space with a Greek Baptist Church, which holds services every Sunday at 11:30 a.m.

The many moves and re-alignments of the parishes have created a racially and culturally diverse community, representative of the church in the world.

Preaching at the service of deconsecration at the Church of the Ascension in 1991, the Rt Rev. Allen Goodings, retired Bishop of Quebec and a former rector, recalled that even in 1964, when he came to the parish, a difficult change was already taking place:

His four years there were the happiest of his life [he is quoted in the Montreal *Gazette*], and he loved the ethnic diversity characteristic of the neighbourhood, and the *joie de vivre* characteristic of the church. But there was another side.

"It was difficult for the residue of what had been a middle-class congregation to realize that it had become part of a downtown inner-city congregation," Goodings said. But the parish got involved in new issues like confronting city of Montreal officials threatening to evict low-income tenants from their homes, and inviting youths from the area, regardless of faith, to participate in activities at the church.

Sometimes ninety or so young people would appear for a Friday-evening young people's program, Goodings remarked, and discover that —

whether they cared or not about what the church stood for — "the church cared for them."

Marcel Terreau who has held the post of people's warden for several years [the article continued], thinks that it was fellowship that particularly marked the Church of the Ascension. Like Goodings, he recalls the church as particularly rich in its church organizations back in the 1950s and 1960s: groups to help the poor, Scouts and Guides, women's and men's groups, choirs and so on.

St CHL's history project has brought together a wealth of anecdotes, recollections and cameo profiles drawn from its various constituent parish traditions. It suggests that community can be carried over from one place to another, and that fellowship, in part, consists of shared experience, in bad times and in good.

# Afterword

The individual segments of which the bulk of this volume is composed may be seen metaphorically as a pile of fieldstones to which, it is hoped, the reader will supply a shape and, to some extent, a purpose. The materials are there. What is made of them — now, or at some future time — will depend a good deal on the eye that beholds and the hand that shapes them — into a stairway or into a wall.

The founding spirits of this Diocese laboured long and hard when they ventured into the wilderness to build their church. Times have changed, and most of the land has been cleared and developed. For Christians in a pluralistic society, however, the world is still a wilderness. After 240 years in this place the church is still a work in progress. God willing, her people will continue to build it up, in faith, on its historic foundations.

| *Francis Fulford* | *Ashton Oxenden* | *W. B. Bond* |
| *1850–1868* | *1869–1878* | *1879–1906* |

| *James Carmichael* | *John Cragg Farthing* | *Arthur Carlisle* |
| *1906–1908* | *1909–1939* | *1939–1943* |

PLATE 25  *Bishops of the Diocese of Montreal, 1850–1943*
        *(Photo Credit:* MDA and Notman Collection, McCord Musuem)

*John Dixon*
*1943–1962*

*Robert Kenneth Maguire*
*1963–1975*

*Reginald Hollis*
*1975–1990*

*Andrew Sandford Hutchison*
*1990–*

PLATE 26  *Bishops of the Diocese of Montreal, 1943–2000*
(*Photo Credit:* MDA)

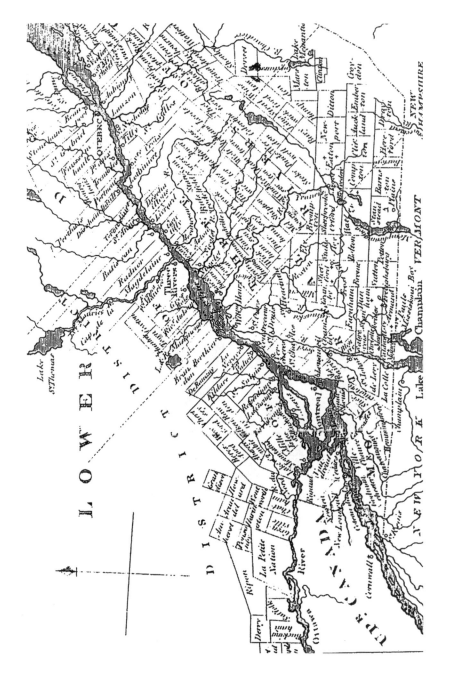

PLATE 27  *Map detail showing the territory of the Diocese of Montreal and a portion of the Diocese of Quebec, 1822*

1. Christ Church Cathedral
2. St. George's
3. St. James the Apostle
4. St. John the Evangelist
5. St. Martin's
6. St. Edward's
7. St. Jude's
8. St. Stephen's
9. The Advent
10. St. Matthias'
11. The Good Shepherd
12. St. Columba's
13. St. Matthew's
14. St. Philip's
15. Grace Church
16. St. Simon's
17. St. Aidan's
18. The Redeemer
19. St. Luke's
20. St. Mary's
21. St. Thomas'
22. L'Eglise du Redempteur
23. St. Cyprian's
24. The Ascension
25. All Saints'
26. St. Alban's
27. St. Cuthbert's
28. St. Hilda's
29. St. Augustine's
30. St. Peter's (site)
31. St. Margaret's
32. St. Chad (no site)
33. St. Clement's
34. St. Andrew's
35. St. Bartholomew's
36. St. Ignatius'
37. Arona Park (site)
38. Cartierville (site)
39. Mt. Royal Heights (site)
40. Rivermere (site)
41. St. Paul's
42. Keystone Park (site)
43. St. Margaret's, St. Lambert Annex
44. St. Saviour's
45. St. Stephen's
46. St. Barnabas'
47. St. Oswald's
48. St. Mark's
49. St. David's

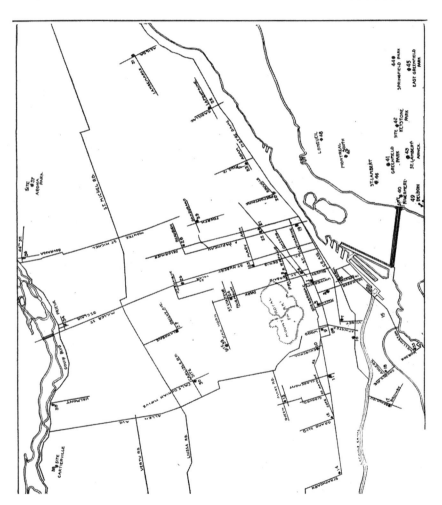

PLATE 28   *Plan of central Montreal showing the location of churches and proposed church sites, 1923*

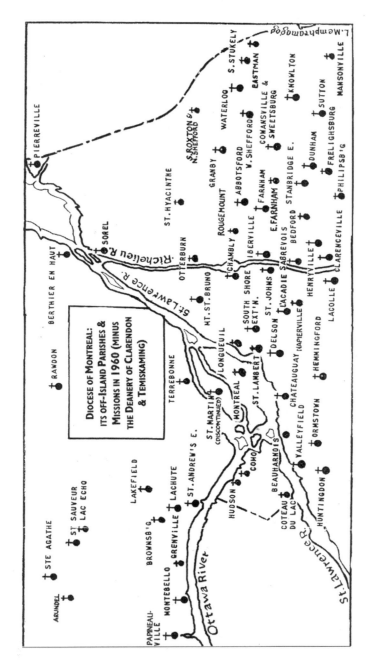

The map contains the following labels:

L. Memphramagog

PIERREVILLE
S. STUKELY
EASTMAN
KNOWLTON
MANSONVILLE
S. ROXTON & N. SHEFFORD
WATERLOO
COMANSVILLE & SWEETSBURG
SUTTON
GRANBY
ABBOTSFORD
W. SHEFFORD
DUNHAM
FRELIGHSB'G
ST. HYACINTHE
ROUGEMOUNT
FARNHAM
STANBRIDGE E.
PHILIPSB'G
CHAMBLY
IBERVILLE
E. FARNHAM
BEDFORD
OTTERBURN
SABREVOIS
CLARENCEVILLE
Richelieu R.
MT. ST. BRUNO
ST. JOHNS
HENRYVILLE
SOREL
SOUTH SHORE
EXT'N.
L'ACADIE
LACOLLE
BERTHIER EN HAUT
St. Lawrence R.
DELSON
NAPERVILLE
HEMMINGFORD
RAWDON
LONGUEUIL
ST. LAMBERT
CHATEAUGUAY
TERREBONNE
MONTREAL
VALLEYFIELD
ORMSTOWN
ST. MARTIN (DISCONTINUED)
COMO
BEAUHARNOIS
HUNTINGDON
HUDSON
COTEAU DU LAC
St. Lawrence
STE AGATHE
ST SAUVEUR
LAC ECHO
LAKEFIELD
LACHUTE
ST. ANDREW'S E.
BROWNSB'G
GRENVILLE
ARUNDEL
MONTEBELLO
PAPINEAU-VILLE
Ottawa River

DIOCESE OF MONTREAL:
ITS OFF-ISLAND PARISHES &
MISSIONS IN 1960 (MINUS
THE DEANERY OF CLARENDON
& TEMISKAMING)

PLATE 29   *Map detail of off-Island parishes in the Diocese of Montreal,*
          *1960*

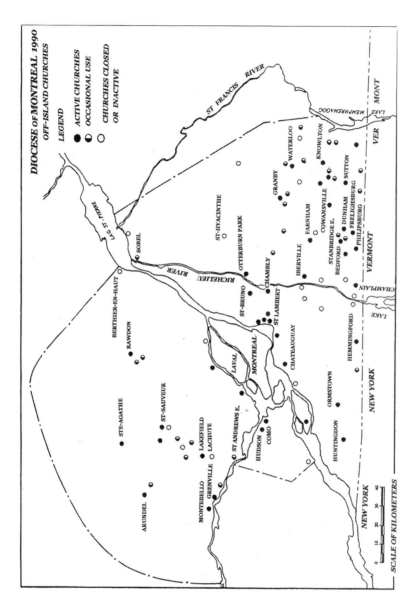

PLATE 30 *Off-Island churches, 1990*

# CLERGY

### Who Have Served Within the Area of
### the Diocese of Montreal

Ordination dates may not be complete, particularly those of the early SPG missionaries. Ordinations taking place within the territory of the Diocese before 1850 are marked with a †; those known to have been performed by bishops of the Diocese of Montreal from 1850 to 2000 are marked with an asterisk.

assoc = associate; asst = assistant; chpl = chaplain; cu = curate; Ext = Extension, as in South Shore Extension; Hts = Heights, as in Morin Heights; Ja$^s$ = James, as in St James the Apostle; J$^n$ = John, as in St John the Divine; (L) = Lachine; Missn = Mission, as in Emmanuel Mission; miss$^y$ = missionary; (M) or Mtl = Montreal; (SPG) = support by the Society for the Propagation of the Gospel; (V) = Verdun; (W) = Westmount

| Name of Cleric | Ordination | | 1st Posting | Date |
|---|---|---|---|---|
| | *Deacon* | *Priest* | *in Diocese* | |
| Abbott, Charles Peter (SPG) | 1859* | 1860* | Clarendon | 1860 |
| Abbott, Joseph (SPG) | 1813 | 1814 | St Andrew's East | 1818 |
| Abbott, William (SPG) | 1824† | 1826† | Abbotsford | 1824 |
| Abbott-Smith, George | 1887* | 1888* | MDTC | 1898 |
| Abraham, Charles John | 1951 | 1952 | cu (M) Trinity | 1952 |
| Acton, Robert | 1880* | 1881* | Lacolle | 1880 |
| Adamson, William Agar | 1824 | 1843 | (M) Christ Church | 1844 |
| Adam, Jack Emmanuel | 1952* | 1953* | Bishop's miss$^y$ | 1952 |
| Addie, Gordon Rennie | 1930* | 1930 | Rouyn | 1930 |
| Albiston, Robert Graham | 1964* | 1965* | Mansonville | 1964 |
| Allan, George | 1873* | 1875* | Bristol | 1874 |
| Allan, John | 1858 | 1859* | Ile-aux-Noix | 1871 |
| Alldis, James Alexander | 1950* | 1951* | Bishop's miss$^y$ | 1950 |
| Allen, Anthony Aaron (SPG) | 1852 | 1853 | Berthier | 1854 |
| Allen, Francis Aaron (SPG) | 1880* | 1881* | Rawdon | 1880 |
| Allen, Frederick Albert | 1908* | 1910* | cu Aylwin | 1908 |
| Allen, Joseph Antisell | 1842† | 1844† | Iberville | 1843 |
| Allen, James Roger | 1928 | 1929 | (L) St Stephen's | 1941 |
| Almon, Herbert Lewis Ashby | 1881 | 1882 | Aylmer | 1891 |

| | Deacon | Priest | in Diocese | |
|---|---|---|---|---|
| Almond, Eric | 1928 | 1929 | (M) Trinity | 1930 |
| Almond, John McPherson | 1896 | 1897 | (M) Trinity | 1905 |
| Anderson, William (SPG) | 1834† | 1835† | Sorel | 1837 |
| Andrews, Clifford | 1938* | 1939* | cu (M) Trinity | 1938 |
| Andrews, Claude Maxwell | 1941 | 1942 | cu (M) St Jas Apostle | 1944 |
| Andrews, Donald | 1932* | 1934* | cu N. Clarendon | 1932 |
| Andrews, Henry | 1925* | 1925* | Clarenceville | 1925 |
| Andrews, Rodney Osborne | 1964 | 1965 | Nelsonville | 1984 |
| Andrews, Stanley | 1927* | 1927* | cu Charteris | 1927 |
| Angioli, Alex | 1987* | | asst (W) St Matthias | 1988 |
| Ansley, Amos (SPG) | 1824† | 1826† | Hull | 1824 |
| Archibald, Edward | 1874* | 1875* | Mille Iles | 1874 |
| Armitage, William David | 1906* | 1907* | Bolton | 1906 |
| Armstrong, J.M. | 18?? | | | |
| Armstrong, Louis Oliver | 1874 | 1875 | Lachute | 1877 |
| Arnold, William (SPG) | 1826† | 1827† | Laprairie | 1840 |
| Asbil, Walter Gordon | 1957* | 1957* | Aylwin | 1957 |
| Asbil, Peter George Frederick | 1967* | 1968* | Clarenceville | 1967 |
| Ascah, Augustus Clifford | 1894* | 1895* | Terrebonne | 1894 |
| Ascah, Robert Gordon | 1905* | 1905* | Valleyfield | 1906 |
| Ashdown, Harold Kirkland | 1929* | 1930* | cu Clarenceville | 1929 |
| Atkinson, Abraham Fuller (SPG) | 1828† | 1829† | asst (M) Christ Ch | 1828 |
| Atkinson, Robert | 1886 | 1887 | Portage du Fort | 1909 |
| Babin, Jeremie | 1864* | 1865* | Buckingham | 1865 |
| Bailey, Gregory Evan | 1982 | 1983 | Rosemere | 1991 |
| Baker, Frank William Charles Elliott | 1909 | 1910 | (M) Andrews Home | 1911 |
| Baker, Lancelot Tagge | 1929 | 1930 | Rawdon | 1932 |
| Baker, Robert Bruce | 1960* | 1960* | (M) St Jn the Divine | 1960 |
| Balch, Lewis W.P. | | | asst (M) Cathedral | 1867 |
| Baldwin, Albert Lawrence | 1938 | 1940* | cu Hampstead | 1940 |
| Baldwin, David Boyd | 1956 | 1957 | (M) St Jn Evangelist | 1958 |
| Baldwin, Francis Morgan | 1885* | 1886* | asst Waterloo | 1886 |
| Baldwin, Maurice Day | 1899* | | Clarendon | 1900 |
| Baldwin, Maurice Scollard | 1860 | 1861 | (M) St Luke's | 1865 |
| Baldwyn, William Devereux (SPG) | | | St Johns | 1817 |
| Balfe, Robert P. (SPG) | | | Stanbridge | 1838 |
| Balfour, Andrew (SPG) | 1832† | 1833† | St Andrews | 1832 |
| Balfour, Philip Harold | 1947* | | asst (V) St Jn Divine | 1947 |
| Ball, Josiah (SPG) | 1878* | 1883* | South Ely | 1878 |
| Ball, Thomas Leander (SPG) | 1865 | 1866 | | |
| Ball, Thomas William | 1893 | 1894* | Milton | 1894 |
| Bancroft, Charles (SPG) | 1843† | 1844† | St Johns | 1847 |
| Bancroft, Charles, Jr (SPG) | 1865 | 1869 | cu (M) Trinity | 1872 |

| Name of Cleric | Ordination | | 1st Posting | Date |
|---|---|---|---|---|
| | *Deacon* | *Priest* | *in Diocese* | |
| Bancroft, Henry | 1897 | 1898 | Vaudreuil | 1902 |
| Bareham, Alfred (SPG) | 1879 | 1880 | Sorel | 1880 |
| Barlow, J. (SPG) | | | Buckingham | 1866 |
| Barnes, Frederick William | 1897* | | miss$^y$ Thorne | 1897 |
| Barnett, Frederick Gavin | 1958* | 1958 | Mascouche | 1963 |
| Barnett, Grahame Ross | 1936 | 1937 | Arundel | 1949 |
| Barnett, James | 1929 | 1930 | Sorel | 1960 |
| Barrett, S. Dawn | 1995 | 1996 | GORA regional ministry | 1997 |
| Bartels, Reginald Cain | 1911 | 1912 | (W) St Matthias | 1914 |
| Bartholomew, R. | | | (M) Cathedral | 1854 |
| Barton, John Stafford | 1957* | 1957* | Ormstown | 1958 |
| Bate, Maurice William | 1976* | 1977* | cu Greenfield Park | 1976 |
| Baugh, Cyrus Wesley Palmer | 1906* | 1907* | cu Thorne | 1906 |
| Baugh, Horace G. | 1943 | 1944 | Morin Hts & Mille Iles | 1950 |
| Baugh, Horace George Leonard | 1910* | 1911* | cu Papineauville | 1911 |
| Baugh, William Jesse Palmer | 1905* | 1906* | Portage du Fort | 1905 |
| Baylis, John Gilbert | 1872 | 1873* | (M) St Jude's | 1872 |
| Beach, George | 1965* | 1966* | Pincourt Mission | 1965 |
| Beale, Frederick Richard | 1952* | 1953* | Clarenceville | 1953 |
| Beattie, Thomas Low Forbes | 1938 | 1939 | Chambly | 1952 |
| Beattie, William James McGahy | 1888* | 1889* | Franklin | 1889 |
| Beaufoy, Mark Raymond | 1936 | 1937 | Montebello | 1952 |
| Beauvoir, Ogé | 1989* | 1990* | (M) St Ignatius & Mascouche | 1989 |
| Belcher, Samuel | 1856 | 1857 | (M) Grace Church | 1871 |
| Bell, C.R. | | | Potton | 1870 |
| Bell, James Henry | | | Alleyne | 1893 |
| Belle, Christopher | 1994 | 1995 | Vaudreuil | 1999 |
| Benedict, E. | | | Bristol | 1878 |
| Bennett, Edwin Francis | 1920* | 1921* | cu (M) Grace Church | 1920 |
| Bennett, James Edward William | 1966 | 1966 | (Pte C) St Augustine | 1986 |
| Bennett, James Winston | 1965 | 1966 | Hampstead | 1999 |
| Bennett, Samuel | | | Montreal | 1764 |
| Bennett, Thomas Edward | 1943 | 1944 | Hemmingford | 1946 |
| Benoit, Henri-Edouard | 1895 | 1896 | (M) du Rédempteur | 1901 |
| Beresford, Eric | 1982 | 1983 | Lachute | 1985 |
| Bernard, Walter Chambers (SPG) | 1884 | 1885 | Adamsville | 1889 |
| Bethune, John | 1814† | 1816† | (M) Christ Church | 1818 |
| Birtch, Robert Sydney (SPG) | 1852* | 1853 | Nelsonville | 1852 |
| Bishop, Walter John | 1943* | 1944* | cu (M) St Luke's | 1943 |
| Black, Robert Merrill | 1979* | 1980* | cu Vaudreuil | 1979 |
| Blackstock, William Henry | 1946* | 1947* | cu (M) St Luke's | 1946 |

| Name of Cleric | Ordination | | 1st Posting | Date |
|---|---|---|---|---|
| | *Deacon* | *Priest* | *in Diocese* | |
| Blasé, Hendrick Willem | 1957* | 1957* | Wakefield | 1957 |
| Blizzard, William Terry | 1975 | 1977 | (w) St Matthias | 1997 |
| Blunt, Peter R. | 1970* | 1970* | cu Greenfield Park, | |
| | | | Brossard & Lafleche | 1970 |
| Bockus, Walter Alfred | 1942* | 1944* | (v) St Clement's | 1943 |
| Bodger, Roland | 1934* | 1935* | (M) St Jas Apostle | 1934 |
| Bolton, Kenneth Charles | 1932 | 1933 | North Clarendon | 1939 |
| Bonathan, John Bertram | 1926 | 1927 | (M) St Jn Evangelist | 1929 |
| Bond, Allan | 1958* | 1959* | cu Hampstead | 1958 |
| Bond, William Bennett | 1840† | 1841† | Russelltown | 1840 |
| Bonsall, Clarence (SPG) | | | Clarendon | 1859 |
| Bonsall, Thomas (SPG) | 1858* | | Portage du Fort | 1860 |
| Booth, Oliver J. (SPG) | 1898* | | Iron Hill | 1898 |
| Booy, Richard Samuel | 1910* | 1912* | cu Campbell's Bay | 1910 |
| Borthwick, John Douglas | 1864* | 1866* | (M) Trinity | 1865 |
| Boswell, Edward Jukes | 1827† | 1829† | (M) Christ Church | 1833 |
| Bothwell, William | | | | |
|    Michael Campbell | 1947 | 1948 | (M) Dean & Rector | 1963 |
| Boulden, Charles Howard | 1913 | 1915 | Mount Royal | 1933 |
| Boulden, Charles John | 1884* | 1885* | cu Sorel | 1884 |
| Bourne, N.A.F. | 1886 | 1887 | Bristol | 1886 |
| Bourne, Rowland Hill (SPG) | 1837† | 1838† | Rawdon | 1837 |
| Bovington, James Gordon | 1949* | 1950* | (M) Ascension | 1949 |
| Boyce, Samuel Joseph | 1906* | 1907 | Pierreville | 1907 |
| Boyd, Charles (SPG) | 1872 | 1872* | Mille Iles | 1871 |
| Boyle, Horatio Temple Stannage | 1900* | 1900* | cu Shawville | 1900 |
| Bradbury, William James | 1914* | 1915* | North Shefford | 1914 |
| Bradley, John Elliott | 1970* | 1970* | cu St Lambert | 1970 |
| Brady, Dean Maurice | 1983* | 1984* | asst Ste-Anne-de- | |
| | | | Bellevue | 1983 |
| Braithwaite, F.G.C. (SPG) | | | Onslow | 1862 |
| Braithwaite, Joseph (SPG) | 1829† | 1830† | Chambly | 1829 |
| Brethour, William (SPG) | 1837† | 1838† | Ormstown | 1837 |
| Brett, John Henry Macklem | 1931 | 1932 | Abbotsford | 1949 |
| Brewer, Robert Center | 1892* | 1894* | cu Rivière Desert | 1893 |
| Bridge, Henry Darley | 1881 | 1882 | Philipsburg | 1881 |
| Bristow, Philip Robert | 1972* | 1972* | cu (L) St Paul | 1972 |
| Britten, Henry | 1904* | 1904* | missy North | |
| | | | Shefford | 1904 |
| Broburg, Anselm | 1946 | 1950 | Shawville | 1950 |
| Brockwell, Charles | | | | |
|    Alexander Brodie | 1902 | 1903 | cu (M) Cathedral | 1909 |
| Brooke, Henry Arthur | 1892 | 1893 | (M) St Jas Apostle | 1903 |
| Broome, Frederick (SPG) | 1840† | 1841† | (M) Christ Church | 1840 |

| Name of Cleric | Ordination | | 1st Posting | Date |
|---|---|---|---|---|
| | *Deacon* | *Priest* | *in Diocese* | |
| Brotherwood, Nicholas Peter | 1983 | 1984 | chpn McGill & asst | |
| | | | (W) St Stephen's | 1989 |
| Brown, James H. | 1905* | 1906* | North Clarendon | 1906 |
| Brown, Robert Walter | 1960 | 1961 | (M) Cathedral | 1963 |
| Brown, Robert Wyndham (SPG) | 1880 | 1881 | Lachute | 1884 |
| Brown, Russel Featherston | 1933* | 1934* | cu (M) Cathedral | 1933 |
| Brown, William Ross (SPG) | 1886* | 1887* | cu Waterloo | 1872 |
| Browne, Herbert William | 1915 | 1916 | cu (M) St Alban's | 1920 |
| Brownlee, George Edward | 1902* | 1905 | miss^y Campbell's Bay | 1902 |
| Bruce, Guy Oliver Theodore | 1903 | 1904 | (W) Advent | 1905 |
| Bruce, Randolph Frederick | 1973 | 1974 | cu Montreal West | 1973 |
| Brueton, Kenneth Noel | 1927* | 1928* | cu (V) St Clement | 1927 |
| Bryant, Augustus Aelfred | 1887 | 1890 | (W) Advent | 1904 |
| Buck, John Martin | 1953* | 1954* | cu (M) St Luke's | 1953 |
| Buckland, Alfred Wellington | 1897 | 1898 | Eastman | 1899 |
| Bulmer, Garth Elliott | 1970* | 1971* | Montreal West | 1970 |
| Burges, Henry (SPG) | 1826 | 1827 | (M) St Mary's | 1864 |
| Burgess, Frank Graham | 1967* | 1968* | cu Chateauguay | 1967 |
| Burke, John Elson | 1957* | 1958 | cu (M) St J^n Evgt | 1965 |
| Burrage, Robert Raby (SPG) | 1819† | 1820† | (M) St Stephen's | 1857 |
| Burt, Frederick (SPG) | 1858* | 1860* | (M) City miss^y | 1859 |
| Burton, Frank Alan | 1955* | 1956* | cu (M) Ascension | 1956 |
| Burton, Joseph | 1916* | 1917* | (V) St Clement's | 1916 |
| Burton, James Edmund (SPG) | 1821 | | Terrebonne | 1820 |
| Burwell, Adam Hood (SPG) | 1827† | 1828† | Hull | 1832 |
| Bushell, Edward | 1886 | 1887 | (W) St Matthias | 1890 |
| Busing, Paul Frederic Wolfgang | 1951* | 1951* | Arundel | 1951 |
| Bussell, Francis Kemp | 1957* | 1957* | Arundel | 1957 |
| Buzzell-Frey, Karen J. | 1990* | 1991* | Farnham, St-Jean, | |
| | | | Sabrevois, Lacadie | 1990 |
| Butler, George Henry | 1880 | 1881 | Chambly | 1891 |
| Butwill, Norman Michael | 1973 | 1974 | (L) St Paul's | 1975 |
| Caldwell, Arthur Bell | 1915* | 1916* | Hemmingford | 1916 |
| Calverley, Joseph William | 1982 | 1983 | asst Montreal West | 1985 |
| Cameron, Alan Lindsay | 1962* | 1963* | Clarenceville & | |
| | | | Lacolle | 1962 |
| Cameron, Alex W. | 1990* | 1991* | | |
| Campbell, A.D. | | | (M) Trinity | 1848 |
| Campbell, Charles Cadogan | 1939 | 1940 | Montreal West | 1954 |
| Campbell, George Latimer III | 1979* | 1980* | Knowlton & | |
| | | | Mansonville | 1979 |
| Campbell, George Latimer, Jr | 1976* | 1977* | cu (W) St Matthias | 1976 |
| Campion, Brian Haddon | 1947 | 1949 | (M) Trinity | 1972 |
| Cane, Geoffrey Brett Salkeld | 1973 | 1980* | Mount Royal | 1975 |

| Name of Cleric | Ordination | | 1st Posting | Date |
| --- | --- | --- | --- | --- |
| | *Deacon* | *Priest* | *in Diocese* | |
| Canton, Carol Ann LaScola | 1984* | 1986* | Bishop's miss^y | 1984 |
| Capel, Edgar Tracy | 1889* | 1891* | asst (M) St Thomas | 1889 |
| Capon, Anthony Charles | 1953 | 1954 | Principal MDTC | 1978 |
| Cariss, Carington Rowe | 1948* | 1949* | cu (W) St Matthias | 1948 |
| Carlisle, Arthur | 1904 | 1905 | Dean (M) Cathedral | 1922 |
| Carmichael, James | 1859 | 1859 | cu (M) St George's | 1868 |
| Carmichael, James Saumarez | 1885* | 1886* | New Glasgow | 1885 |
| Carpendale, John Algernon | 1892 | 1899 | Papineauville | 1904 |
| Carr, Christopher Patten | 1964* | 1965* | cu (M) St Thomas | 1964 |
| Carr, John Joseph | 1964 | 1965 | Stanbridge East | 1975 |
| Carr-Harris, Philip Michael | 1977* | 1978* | cu (M) St Ja^s Apostle | 1977 |
| Carruthers, Christopher | 1903* | 1904* | miss^y N. Clarendon | 1903 |
| Carson, Roy Livingston | 1906 | 1906 | (M) St Jude's | 1910 |
| Cartlidge, James | 1911 | 1912 | Iron Hill | 1915 |
| Cattermole, John | 1875* | | Papineauville | 1876 |
| Chabrand Delisle, David | | 1764 | Montreal | 1766 |
| Chalk, Linda Faith | 1995* | 1996* | asst cu St Lambert | 1995 |
| Chambers, William Percy | 1881* | 1882* | Aylwin | 1881 |
| Chapman, Thomas Shaw (SPG) | 1848† | 1849† | TM destitute settlemts | 1848 |
| Charbonneau, Paul Joseph | 1985* | 1986* | asst Ste-Anne-de-Bellevue | 1985 |
| Charters, Frank | 1888* | 1889* | Iron Hill | 1888 |
| Charters, Herbert | 1902* | 1903* | cu Frelighsburg | 1902 |
| Chatterton, Wayne Leslie | 1965* | 1965 | (W) St Matthias | 1969 |
| Clapham, Harry | 1918* | 1919* | Edwardstown | 1918 |
| Clark, Frederick Patrick | 1932 | 1933* | cu (W) Advent | 1932 |
| Clarke, Barry Bryan | 1978* | 1979* | cu (W) St Matthias | 1978 |
| Clarke, Edwin Kent | 1956 | 1957 | St Lambert | 1966 |
| Clarke, Ronald George | 1987* | 1988* | asst (W) St Stephen | 1987 |
| Clarke, W.C. | | | Buckingham | 1876 |
| Clayton, Frank Henry | 1872* | 1874* | Bolton | 1872 |
| Cleator, Kenneth Irving | 1959 | 1960 | (M) St George's | 1967 |
| Clinton, William de Witt | 1954 | 1955* | (V) St Clement | 1954 |
| Coates, Glenn Curwood | 1979 | 1980 | Lakefield | 1982 |
| Cobb, Charles Cedric | 1984* | 1985* | asst (W) St Matthias | 1984 |
| Cochrane, John (SPG) | 1832† | 1833† | Laprairie | 1834 |
| Codd, Francis (SPG) | 1860* | 1861* | Clarendon | 1861 |
| Coffin, Hubert | 1905* | 1906* | Pierreville | 1906 |
| Coffin, James Moreton | 1892* | 1893* | Leslie | 1893 |
| Cohen, Herbert John | 1962* | 1963* | Grenville | 1962 |
| Coleman, Arthur Edmund | 1927 | 1928 | Church Extension | 1931 |
| Collett-White, Thomas Charles | 1962 | 1963 | Huntingdon-Ormstown | 1976 |
| Collins, Henry Archer | 1905 | 1906 | (W) Advent | 1908 |

| Name of Cleric | Ordination | | 1st Posting | Date |
|---|---|---|---|---|
| | *Deacon* | *Priest* | *in Diocese* | |
| Combe, Charles Eastburn | 1913 | 1914 | Rivière Désert | 1917 |
| Conliffe, David Augustine | 1956* | 1956* | asst Pointe Claire | 1956 |
| Constantine, Isaac (SPG) | 1850† | 1852* | Stanbridge | 1851 |
| Conway, Charles Abbott | 1991* | 1991* | assoc chpl McGill & hon. asst Ste-Anne-de-Bellevue | 1991 |
| Cook, Allen Francis | 1957* | 1959* | St Lambert | 1957 |
| Cook, Reid Stanley | 1970* | 1970* | asst Roxboro | 1970 |
| Coombs, David | 1916* | 1917* | Papineauville | 1916 |
| Coombs, Frank Guy | 1912* | 1913* | cu (M) Trinity | 1912 |
| Cooper, Walter Samuel | 1905 | 1906 | Thorne | 1921 |
| Cornwall, John (SPG) | | | (L) St Stephen | 1849 |
| Cotton, Charles Caleb (SPG) | 1797 | 1804† | St Armand | 1804 |
| Cotton, John Bowman | 1947 | 1948 | asst (M) Advent | 1950 |
| Coulthurst, Percy | 1910 | 1911 | St Johns | 1926 |
| Cowley, Abraham | 1841† | 1844† | Huntingdon | 1841 |
| Cox, Hubert Cecil | 1914 | 1915 | (M) St Jⁿ Evangelist | 1919 |
| Craig, William | 1872 | 1873 | (M) Trinity | 1877 |
| Craig, William Woodham | 1896* | 1897* | (M) St Martin's | 1898 |
| Crewe, John Albert Wright | 1951* | 1952* | Foster & Bondville | 1952 |
| Crisp, Stephen | 1989* | 1990* | asst (M) St George's | 1989 |
| Croft, Reid Lionel | 1975* | | cu Greenfield Park | 1975 |
| Croly, Edward H. | 1902* | 1902* | Mansonville | 1902 |
| Cross, Parnell leBas | 1883* | 1886 | (M) St Luke's | 1883 |
| Crothers, Loring William Foreman | 1922* | 1922* | cu Quyon | 1922 |
| Crummer, William Robert | 1933 | 1934 | cu (M) St Jⁿ Evangelist | 1934 |
| Cunningham, T.E. | 1880* | 1881* | Buckingham | 1880 |
| Curran, William Bannington | 1861* | 1862* | cu (M) Trinity | 1861 |
| Cutts, Montague Fox Gapper | 1953 | 1954 | Dunham | 1960 |
| Daniel, Charles Andrew | 1864 | 1866 | cu (M) St Jⁿ Evangelist | 1866 |
| Dann, Eyre Frederick Morton | 1940 | 1940 | cu (M) St Jⁿ Evangelist | 1945 |
| Darcus, Roy Lionel Heath | 1972* | 1972* | cu (M) St George's | 1972 |
| Darnell, H.F. | | | St Johns | 1862 |
| Dart, William J. | 1867* | 1868* | Laprairie | 1868 |
| Davidson, James Burrows | 1861* | 1862* | asst Cathedral | 1861 |
| Davidson, John Casement (SPG) | 1854* | 1854* | Nelsonville | 1855 |
| Davidson, John Wilmur | 1957* | 1957* | Iron Hill | 1957 |
| Davies, William | 1884* | 1885* | Rawdon | 1884 |
| Davis, Christopher | 1885* | 1986* | Bishop's missʸ | 1985 |

| Name of Cleric | Ordination | | 1st Posting | Date |
|---|---|---|---|---|
| | *Deacon* | *Priest* | *in Diocese* | |
| Davis, Jennifer M. | 1994 | 1995 | Rosemere-Mascouche | 1998 |
| Davison, Peter Wood Asterley | 1961 | 1961* | cu (M) Trinity | 1961 |
| Davison, William Holmes | 1908 | 1909 | (M) St Jⁿ Evangelist | 1917 |
| Dawes, William D. (SPG) | 1838† | 1840† | St Johns | 1842 |
| Dawson, Ernest Edward | 1906* | 1906* | Kildare | 1907 |
| Deane, Norton Arnold William | 1940* | 1941* | cu (V) St Clement | 1941 |
| Dearden, John Coskery | 1895 | 1896 | Immigration chpl | 1910 |
| de Corneille, Roland | 1952 | 1953 | (M) St Jⁿ Evangelist | 1953 |
| de Gruchy, Philip (SPG) | 1869* | 1872* | cu Berthier | 1870 |
| DeHoop, Thomas | 1968 | 1969 | cu Roxboro-Pierrefonds | 1975 |
| De Mouilpied, Joseph (SPG) | 1856* | 1860 | Sorel | 1856 |
| Dennis, John William | 1889* | 1891* | Lacolle | 1889 |
| Derby, William Vinton | 1972 | 1973 | cu St Lambert | 1972 |
| desBrisay, Lestock | 1874 | 1876 | (M) St Luke's | 1878 |
| Devine, James Augustus | 1843† | | Chambly | 1844 |
| Dewdney, Alexander Stratton | 1927 | 1928 | MDTC | 1953 |
| Dickerson, Richard Keith | 1960* | 1960* | cu Hampstead | 1960 |
| Dijkman, Jan Hendrik Leonard | 1963 | 1963 | vicar Cathedral | 1987 |
| Dilworth, William Crawford | 1891 | | Arundel | 1892 |
| Dixon, James Henry | 1870* | 1871* | Mille Iles | 1870 |
| Dixon, John Harkness | 1912 | 1913 | Dean (M) Cathedral | 1940 |
| Dobson, John William | 1912 | 1914 | Campbell's Bay | 1927 |
| Dodd, Ian Neville | 1967* | 1968* | Lakefield | 1967 |
| Dodwell, G.B. | | | Chambly | 1867 |
| Doidge, Jack Nicholls | 1938 | 1939 | (W) St Matthias | 1962 |
| Dossett, Edward James | 1947* | 1948* | Dean of Res. MDTC | 1947 |
| Doty, John (SPG) | | | Sorel | 1783 |
| Douglas, John | 1901 | 1902 | Adamsville | 1902 |
| Doull, Alexander John | 1896 | 1898 | cu (W) Advent | 1899 |
| Dove, John | 1941* | 1942* | cu (M) Cathedral | 1941 |
| Dowker, George Hasted | 1927 | 1927 | Dean (M) Cathedral | 1952 |
| Drainville, Dennis Paul | 1982 | 1982 | chpl McGill & associate Cathedral | 1986 |
| Driscoll, John Campbell (SPG) | | | Berthier | 1830 |
| Dubois, Yves-Marie Alphonse G. | 1963* | 1964* | asst Cathedral | 1963 |
| DuMoulin, John Philip | 1862 | 1863 | (M) Trinity | 1866 |
| Dunbar, William Henry | 1907 | 1907 | Boscobel | 1907 |
| Dungan, Eric | 1948 | 1949 | (M) Advent | 1970 |
| Dunwell, Leslie | 1928* | 1929* | (M) Church Extension | 1928 |
| Dunwoody, Derek Cecil | 1963 | 1964 | cu St Lambert | 1967 |

| Name of Cleric | Ordination | | 1st Posting | Date |
|---|---|---|---|---|
| | *Deacon* | *Priest* | *in Diocese* | |
| Durnford, Roy Charles Henry | 1932 | 1933 | hon. asst Ste-Anne-de-Bellevue | 1959 |
| Duthie, William N. | 1888* | 1889* | North Shefford | 1888 |
| DuVernet, Edward (SPG) | 1852* | | Henryville | 1851 |
| DuVernet, Frederick Herbert | 1883* | 1884* | cu (M) St Jaˢ Apostle | 1883 |
| Dykes, Frederick Alfred | 1953 | 1954 | Ste-Agathe-des-Monts | 1981 |
| Earle, Cyril Wall | 1934* | 1935* | Rivière Désert | 1935 |
| Early, W. Townsend (SPG) | | | Huntingdon | 1866 |
| Earp, Ernest Charles | 1906 | 1906 | cu (M) Trinity | 1918 |
| Eason, Glenn Owen | 1980* | 1981* | cu Montreal West | 1980 |
| Eason, Michelle C.D. | 1995* | 1996* | Ste-Anne-de-Bellevue | 1995 |
| Eastman, F.S. | | | Eastman | 1897 |
| Eccleston, William Charles | 1926* | 1927* | (M) St Alban's | 1926 |
| Edgecumbe, John | 1872 | 1875 | Kildare | 1888 |
| Edmondson, Gerald Paul | 1967* | 1968* | cu Montreal West | 1967 |
| Edwards, Albert Raymond | 1963* | 1964* | asst Campbell's Bay | 1963 |
| Egerton, Norman | 1926* | 1927* | (M) Ascension | 1926 |
| Elcombe, Arthur George | 1940 | 1941 | cu (v) St Jⁿ Divine | 1945 |
| Elcombe, Frederick George | 1951 | | Abbotsford | 1959 |
| Eley, Fred | 1914 | 1915 | (M) All Saints | 1920 |
| Eling, John Warren | 1964 | 1964 | (M) St Jaˢ Apostle | 1992 |
| Ellegood, Jacob (SPG) | 1848† | 1849† | (M) Christ Church | 1848 |
| Elliott, Alex | 1893* | | cu Eardley | 1893 |
| Elliott, James Alfred | 1892ᴬ | 1894* | Mille Iles | 1893 |
| Elliott, Robert George | 1948* | 1949* | cu (v) St Clement | 1948 |
| Ellis, Clarence Douglas | 1947* | 1948* | cu (w) St Matthias | 1951 |
| Ellis, John David | 1918* | 1919* | cu (v) St Clement | 1918 |
| Ellis, McAllister Scott | 1952* | 1953* | cu (M) St Columba | 1952 |
| Ellis, William James | 1912* | 1913* | missʸ Papineauville | 1912 |
| Emmett, Robert | 1894* | 1895* | Papineauville | 1894 |
| Empson, John (SPG) | 1870* | 1871* | (M) Cathedral | 1883 |
| Ereaux, James Samuel | 1897* | 1938* | Longueuil | 1898 |
| Evans, Alan Morewood | 1980 | 1981 | (L) St Paul's | 1988 |
| Evans, Brian Allen | 1967* | 1968* | asst (M) Trinity | 1967 |
| Evans, Henry | 1844† | | cu Dunham | 1844 |
| Evans, Henry James | 1863 | 1865 | Christieville | 1866 |
| Evans, Kenneth Charles | 1930 | 1931 | Dean (M) Cathedral | 1944 |
| Evans, Thomas Frye Lewis | 1869 | 1870 | asst (M) Cathedral | 1871 |
| Everett, Thomas | 1873* | 1873* | Mascouche | 1873 |
| Falloon, Daniel (SPG) | 1841† | 1842† | Clarendon | 1841 |
| Farr, William John | 1915* | 1916* | (M) St Cuthbert | 1915 |
| Farrell, Frederick Richard | 1910* | 1911* | cu Poltimore | 1910 |

| Name of Cleric | Ordination | | 1st Posting | Date |
|---|---|---|---|---|
| | *Deacon* | *Priest* | *in Diocese* | |
| Farrell, Peter Ross | 1937 | 1938 | cu (w) St Matthias | 1950 |
| Farthing, John Cragg | 1885 | 1886 | 5th Lord Bishop | 1909 |
| Farthing, Paul Andrew | 1983* | 1984* | asst Montreal West | 1983 |
| Fee, George Bertram | 1939 | 1940 | (M) St Jaˢ Apostle | 1970 |
| Fee, James Erwin | 1905* | 1905* | St Hyacinthe | 1905 |
| Fenn, N.V. | | | Sabrevois | 1862 |
| Fenty, Peter Decourcy | 1975 | 1975 | LaSalle | 1992 |
| Fenwick, Algernon Clavering | 1911 | 1913 | (M) St George's | 1919 |
| Ferguson, William Aldworth | 1906 | 1907 | Principal MDTC | 1941 |
| Fessenden, Elisha Joseph | 1865* | 1868 | Potton | 1866 |
| Fiander, Richard Goodwin | 1928* | 1929* | cu Lakefield | 1928 |
| Fife, John Ross | 1938 | 1939 | Huntingdon-Ormstown | 1979 |
| Finch, Frederick | 1960 | 1961 | cu Greenfield Park | 1978 |
| Findlay, Eber Alva | 1916* | 1916* | Aylwin | 1916 |
| Fitzgerald, William Frederick | 1888 | 1890 | Onslow | 1899 |
| Flanagan, John (SPG) | 1839† | 1841† | Mascouche | 1846 |
| Flanagan, James Luther | 1891* | 1892* | Thorne | 1891 |
| Fleming, Edward Daniel | 1956 | 1957 | (M) St Thomas | 1970 |
| Fletcher, John | 1846† | | (M) Christ Church | 1846 |
| Flumerfelt, Donald Bruce | 1975* | 1976* | cu Beaconsfield-Kirkland | 1975 |
| Forbes, Malcolm | 1889* | 1894 | cu North Shefford | 1889 |
| Ford, Charles William | 1926* | 1927* | asst South Shore Ext | 1926 |
| Ford, Frank Thomas | 1910 | 1911 | Rouyn | 1928 |
| Forest, Charles (SPG) | 1846† | 1847† | Grenville | 1847 |
| Forneret, George Augustus | 1875* | 1876* | Missʸ to Germans | 1875 |
| Forneret, George Reginald | 1933* | 1934* | cu (w) St Matthias | 1934 |
| Forsey, George | 1886* | 1887* | Chambly | 1886 |
| Forshaw, George | 1912* | 1913* | Alleyne | 1912 |
| Forth, David Selwyn | 1956* | 1957 | Sorel | 1959 |
| Fortin, Alfred | 1864* | 1866* | Ely | 1867 |
| Fortin, Octave (SPG) | 1865* | 1866* | Sorel | 1867 |
| Foulkes, Llewellyn | 1899* | 1900* | Lakefield | 1899 |
| Fox, J. | 1869 | 1873 | Mille Iles | 1873 |
| Freeland, Brian Desmond | 1950 | 1951 | (M) St Jⁿ Evangelist | 1952 |
| French, A. (jr) | | | (M) St Jⁿ Evangelist | 1916 |
| French, Arthur Thomas William | 1876 | 1882* | (M) St Jⁿ Evangelist | 1881 |
| Fricker, Herbert Victor | 1914 | 1915 | asst (M) Cathedral | 1918 |
| Frith, John Griffith | 1947 | 1948 | cu (M) Cathedral | 1959 |
| Fulford, Francis | 1826 | 1828 | 1st Lord Bishop | 1850 |
| Fuller, Hume Samuel (SPG) | 1876* | 1879 | Clarendon | 1876 |
| Fuller, Thomas Brock (SPG) | 1833† | 1835† | Lachine | 1834 |

| Name of Cleric | Ordination | | 1st Posting | Date |
|---|---|---|---|---|
| | *Deacon* | *Priest* | *in Diocese* | |
| Fulton, James | 1848† | 1849† | Russelltown | 1848 |
| Fyles, Thomas W. (SPG) | 1862* | 1864* | (M) City miss^y | 1863 |
| Fyles, William Adolphus | 1889* | 1891* | Chelsea | 1889 |
| Gagnon, George-Henry | 1897* | 1897* | Valleyfield | 1896 |
| Gale, William Henry | 1909* | 1910* | Aylwin | 1909 |
| Gallant, Louis-Marie | 1989* | 1990* | (M) St Rédempteur & asst cu Cathedral | 1989 |
| Garland, John William (SPG) | 1871 | 1873* | Ely & Stukely | 1874 |
| Garner, William | 1905* | 1905* | North Wakefield | 1906 |
| Garrett, John Colquhoun | 1884* | 1885* | Lacolle | 1885 |
| Garth, William Henry | 1891 | | (M) St Stephen's | 1891 |
| Gartrell, Frederick Roy | 1938* | 1939* | cu (M) St J^s Apostle | 1938 |
| Gault, Thomas Solmes | 1924* | 1925* | cu (M) Cathedral | 1924 |
| Gauvin, Joseph Henri Armand | 1963* | 1964* | asst Aylmer | 1964 |
| Gavin, Daniel | 1848† | 1848† | Sabrevois | 1848 |
| Gedye, Frank William | 1904 | 1906 | miss^y Bristol | 1912 |
| Genge, Kenneth Lyle | 1957 | 1958 | St Lambert | 1974 |
| Gibbs, Charles Harold | 1932 | 1932 | (M) St J^n Evangelist | 1939 |
| Gibson, Jonathan Rickey | 1987* | 1988* | asst (M) St George's | 1987 |
| Gibson, Mary Irwin | 1981* | 1982* | Bishop's Miss^y | 1981 |
| Gibson, Paul Saison | 1956 | 1957 | chapl McGill | 1960 |
| Gilbody, Ernest Arthur | 1951* | 1952* | (V) St J^n the Divine | 1951 |
| Gilson, Samuel (SPG) | | | asst (M) Cathedral | 1855 |
| Given, Alexander Boyd | 1883* | 1884* | West Shefford | 1884 |
| Glencross, Bruce Robert | 1980* | 1981* | cu Mount Royal | 1980 |
| Glover, Charles | 1925 | 1926* | cu (M) St J^n Evangelist | 1926 |
| Godard, Harlow | 1907* | 1909* | Portage du Fort | 1907 |
| Godden, John (SPG) | 1854* | 1855* | St Hyacinthe | 1855 |
| Godden, Thomas (SPG) | 1862 | 1863* | Mascouche | 1866 |
| Godsoe, Arnold W. | 1991* | 1992* | asst (M) St George's | 1991 |
| Gomery, Henry | 1884* | 1885* | Onslow | 1884 |
| Goodfellow, Henry Groves | 1924* | 1925 | cu (M) St Columba | 1925 |
| Goodings, Allen | 1959* | 1959* | asst (M) Trinity | 1959 |
| Goodland, Joseph | 1923* | 1924* | cu (M) St Thomas | 1923 |
| Gore, Norman | 1947 | 1948* | (M) Emmanuel Missn | 1948 |
| Goring, Vincent Ingham | 1950* | 1951* | cu (V) St Clement | 1950 |
| Gower-Rees, Albert Philip | 1905 | 1906 | (M) St George's | 1927 |
| Graham, Frederick Helier | 1895* | 1895 | (M) Trinity | 1896 |
| Grainger, Anthony David | 1989* | 1990* | Ste-Anne-de-Bellevue | 1989 |
| Grainger, Philip | | | Kildare | 1905 |
| Grant, Anthony Vivian | 1912 | 1913 | St Lambert | 1918 |
| Grant, Daniel Ian | 1964* | 1965* | (M) Trinity | 1964 |

| Name of Cleric | Ordination | | 1st Posting | Date |
|---|---|---|---|---|
| | *Deacon* | *Priest* | *in Diocese* | |
| Gray, A.Y. | | | (M) Trinity | 1866 |
| Greenbaum, Emmanuel Solomon | 1932* | 1933* | (M) Emmanuel Miss<sup>n</sup> | 1933 |
| Greer, Alfred John | 1882* | 1883* | Thorne | 1881 |
| Gribble, John | 1854* | 1855* | Portage du Fort | 1856 |
| Griffin, Joseph (SPG) | | 1852* | Gore of Chatham | 1851 |
| Groulx, Albert-Benjamin | 1901 | 1901 | Rivière Désert | 1896 |
| Gudwin, Mark Alan | 1975 | 1976 | (M) Cathedral | 1978 |
| Guerout, Narcisse (SPG) | 1839† | 1840† | Berthier | 1849 |
| Guinness, Robin Gordon | 1963 | 1964 | Lakefield | 1972 |
| Guiton, Geoffrey | 1928* | 1929* | cu (M) Cathedral | 1928 |
| Guy, Gordon Ernest Scott | 1965* | 1966* | Mascouche | 1965 |
| Gwen, A.B. | | | West Shefford | 1885 |
| Hackenley, Henry | 1883* | 1884* | Buckingham | 1885 |
| Hackett, Henry Monck Mason | 1875 | 1876 | Principal MDTC | 1899 |
| Haensl, Charles Lewis Frederick | 1826 | 1826 | Iberville | 1848 |
| Hague, Dyson | 1882 | 1883 | (M) St George's | 1901 |
| Hall, George | 1931* | 1932* | Rivière Désert | 1931 |
| Hall, John Buchanan | 1947 | 1949 | Ormstown | 1959 |
| Hamilton, George Alan | 1953 | 1954 | cu (v) St J<sup>n</sup> Divine | 1956 |
| Hamilton, William J. | 1895* | | Onslow | 1896 |
| Han, Sinpoh | 1992* | 1993* | asst cu Ste-Anne-de-Bellevue | 1992 |
| Hancock, Peter Thompson | 1956 | 1957 | Mount Royal | 1980 |
| Hannen, Peter Douglas | 1959 | 1959 | Stanbridge East | 1961 |
| Harding, Kenneth Dennis George | 1983* | 1984* | Mount Royal | 1983 |
| Harris, William | 1887* | 1888* | Arundel | 1887 |
| Harrison, Douglas Bernard | 1938* | 1939* | (v) St Clement | 1938 |
| Harrison, Harold Wilfred Levi | 1924* | 1927* | cu Campbell's Bay | 1924 |
| Harvey, Anthony Peter | 1981 | 1982 | Two Mountains | 1984 |
| Harwood-Jones, John | 1948* | 1949* | Papineauville | 1949 |
| Haslam, Thomas Aitken | 1879 | 1879 | Granby | 1879 |
| Hatcher, William Gordon | 1921* | 1922* | Poltimore | 1921 |
| Hatcher, William Snook Buffett | 1926* | 1926* | Rouyn | 1926 |
| Hatton, George Russell | 1957 | 1958 | Asst Bishop & Archdeacon of Bedford | 1998 |
| Hawes, Albert Emanuel | 1939* | 1940* | Manawaki & Gracefield | 1939 |
| Hawes, Howard John Richard | 1973 | 1974 | Cartierville | 1985 |
| Hawkes, John William | 1924 | 1925 | (M) St Columba | 1926 |
| Hawkins, Edwin | 1912* | 1913* | cu (M) St Stephen | 1912 |
| Haynes, Cecil Douglas | 1954 | 1955 | Grenvelle | 1960 |
| Hazard, Henry (SPG) | 1842† | 1844† | Sherrington | 1843 |
| Heap, Daniel James MacDonell | 1951* | 1952* | Kazabazua | 1951 |
| Heaton, George | | | Mascouche | 1863 |

| Name of Cleric | Ordination | | 1st Posting | Date |
|---|---|---|---|---|
| | *Deacon* | *Priest* | *in Diocese* | |
| Heaven, Cecil Arthur | 1899 | 1900 | Berthier-en-Haut | 1908 |
| Heaven, Edward Gyde | 1910 | 1913 | Poltimore | 1918 |
| Heeney, William Bertal | 1900 | 1901 | Edwardstown | 1901 |
| Henderson, Murray Balfour | 1970 | 1971 | Roxboro | 1972 |
| Henderson, William | 1857 | 1858 | Dunham | 1872 |
| Heniser, Gary D. | 1974 | 1974 | Pierrefonds | 1983 |
| Hepburn, Lionel Galbraith | 1911 | 1912 | cu (M) St Matthias | 1919 |
| Hepburn, G.G. | | | Longueuil | 1876 |
| Heron, Robert | 1920 | 1921 | Bordeaux | 1926 |
| Hertzler, Harold Leopold | 1944 | 1945 | Dean of res. MDTC | 1949 |
| Hewetson, George Benson | 1891* | 1897 | (M) Trinity | 1892 |
| Hewett, Walter Albert | 1934* | 1937* | Bristol | 1934 |
| Hewitt, William Charles | 1937 | 1938 | cu (M) Ascension | 1946 |
| Hewton, Richard W. (SPG) | 1884 | 1885 | (L) St Stephen | 1890 |
| Hibbard, Walter Robert | 1903 | 1906* | Berthier-en-Haut | 1905 |
| Hilchey, Harry St Clair | 1944 | 1945 | (M) St Jaˢ Apostle | 1964 |
| Hill, Henry Gordon | 1948 | 1950 | Asst Bishop | 1981 |
| Hinde, William | 1872* | 1874* | Ormstown | 1872 |
| Hodder, James Gardner | 1946* | 1947* | cu (W) St Matthias | 1946 |
| Hodgkinson, John | 1910* | 1911* | cu (W) St Stephen | 1910 |
| Hodson, John Edward | 1911 | 1912 | (V) St Clement | 1915 |
| Hollis, Reginald | 1956* | 1956* | chpl MDTC & McGill | 1956 |
| Holmes, Henry Forrester | 1873* | 1873* | South Stukely | 1873 |
| Homer, James Lionel | 1904 | 1905 | (M) Ascension | 1918 |
| Hood, Thomas | | | (M) St George's | 1885 |
| Horsey, Herbert Edward | 1890* | 1891* | Abbotsford | 1890 |
| Houghton, Ernest J. | 1877* | 1878* | (L) St Paul's | 1877 |
| Howard, Arthur George | 1923* | 1924* | (M) St Mary's | 1923 |
| Howard, Oswald Walker | 1894 | 1898 | (M) St George's | 1899 |
| Howard, Roger Sharples William | 1891 | 1892 | (M) St Martin | 1919 |
| Howard, William Aylesworth | 1898 | 1899 | North Shefford | 1905 |
| Howells, David | 1981 | 1982* | St Lambert | 1984 |
| Howells, Lucinda Jane Reid | 1981 | 1985* | St Lambert | 1984 |
| Hughes, Donald John Michael | 1962* | 1963* | asst (M) Ascension | 1963 |
| Hughes, Frank Richardson | 1941* | 1941* | asst Rouyn | 1941 |
| Hughes, Malcolm Albert | 1960 | 1961 | Vaudreuil | 1970 |
| Hunt, James Edward | 1962 | 1963 | cu (L) St Paul's | 1965 |
| Hutchings, Richard Frederick | 1893* | 1894* | Arundel | 1893 |
| Hutchinson, Raymond | 1956 | 1958 | Arundel | 1978 |
| Hutchison, Andrew Sandforth | 1969 | 1969 | Dean (M) Cathedral | 1984 |
| Ingram, Gordon Earl | 1958 | 1959 | Granby | 1984 |
| Ireland, Angus Austin | 1901* | 1902* | missʸ Clarendon | 1901 |
| Ireland, Francis Charles | 1904* | 1904* | missʸ South Stukely | 1904 |

| Name of Cleric | Ordination | | 1st Posting | Date |
|---|---|---|---|---|
| | *Deacon* | *Priest* | *in Diocese* | |
| Ireland, James Ellis | 1904* | 1905* | Buckingham | 1905 |
| Irving, Joseph (jr) | 1914* | 1915* | Mille Iles | 1914 |
| Irving, Stanley Herbert | 1952* | 1953* | cu S. Shore Mission | 1952 |
| Irwin, John (SPG) | 1847† | 1848† | (M) Christ Church | 1847 |
| Irwin, Richard David (SPG) | 1870* | 1880 | Clarendon | 1871 |
| Irwin, William Basil | 1927 | 1928 | cu (W) Advent | 1934 |
| Isaacs, Hubert John | 1942 | 1943 | Dunham | 1957 |
| Jackson, John (SPG) | 1800† | 1801† | Sorel | 1811 |
| Jackson, William Ernest | 1933 | 1933 | (M) St Jaˢ Apostle | 1944 |
| James, Charles John | 1883 | 1884 | asst (M) St George's | 1894 |
| James, John Paul | 1960 | 1961 | (W) St Matthias | 1987 |
| James, Lettie | 1976* | 1978* | cu Mtl West & Dio. Councelling Centre | 1976 |
| Jay, Eric George | 1931 | 1932 | Principal MDTC | 1958 |
| Jeakins, Charles Ernest | 1902* | 1902* | Arundel | 1902 |
| Jeakins, Thomas Bentley | 1891* | 1892* | Hemmingford | 1891 |
| Jekill, Henry | 1892* | 1893* | (M) St Mary's | 1892 |
| Jenkyns, Ebenezer Hamilton | | 1868 | Mansonville | 1868 |
| Jemmott, Anthony Gordon Edwin | 1973 | 1975 | asst Cote-des-Neiges | 1982 |
| Jennings, Paul H. | 1991* | 1992* | asst cu Pierrefonds | 1991 |
| Johnson, John C.T. | 1992* | 1992* | Louisa & Mille Iles | 1993 |
| Johnson, George | 1884* | 1885* | Clarendon | 1885 |
| Johnson, Moody Bernard | 1913 | 1914 | asst (M) Cathedral | 1914 |
| Johnson, Thomas (SPG) | 1815 | 1817 | Abbotsford | 1833 |
| Johnson, T. | | | Bristol | 1872 |
| Johnston, John (SPG) | 1838† | 1840† | Clarendon | 1840 |
| Jolly, Leslie Verne | 1922* | 1923* | (M) Ascension | 1922 |
| Jones, Alewyn Sanders | 1903 | 1904 | Church Extension | 1922 |
| Jones, Gilbert Basil | 1918 | 1919 | Ste-Agathe | 1950 |
| Jones, James (SPG) | 1841 | 1842† | Stanbridge | 1842 |
| Jones, Thomas Dale | 1934 | 1935 | Cote-des-Neiges | 1966 |
| Jones, Trevor Glyn | 1978* | 1979* | Mount Royal | 1978 |
| Jones, William (SPG) | 1843† | 1844† | Farnham | 1848 |
| Jones, William Ross Lewis | 1955 | 1956 | asst Mount Royal | 1966 |
| Joseph, Yves-Eugène | 1983 | 1984 | (M) La Nativité | 1986 |
| Joyce, John Edward Lees | 1910* | 1911* | Glen Almond | 1910 |
| Joyce, Keith Roy | 1982 | 1982 | Knowlton | 1987 |
| Judd, Francis Emerson (SPG) | 1850† | 1852* | Chambly | 1850 |
| Judge, Edgar Percival | 1890* | 1891* | Papineauville | 1890 |
| Judge, Patrick Russell | 1955* | 1956* | Mount Royal | 1955 |
| Kaapche, Carl Julius (SPG) | 1865* | 1866* | Bowman | 1866 |
| Kaneen, William Edward | 1892* | 1892* | Aylwin | 1892 |
| Kearns, Raymond Norman | 1991* | 1991* | (M) St Aiden's | 1991 |
| Keefe, Kenneth Bernard | 1940 | 1942* | cu (M) Ascension | 1941 |

| Name of Cleric | Ordination Deacon | Priest | 1st Posting in Diocese | Date |
|---|---|---|---|---|
| Kemp, Dudley Fitch | 1927 | 1929 | (M) St George's | 1956 |
| Kendell, George Douglas Foster | 1940* | 1940* | cu (M) St Matthias | 1940 |
| Kennedy, Walter Howard Frere | 1955 | 1956 | (M) Cathedral | 1961 |
| Kenworthy, James | 1916* | 1917* | (M) St Alban's | 1916 |
| Ker, John | 1876* | 1879* | cu Glen Sutton | 1876 |
| Ker, Robert | 1877 | 1878 | Chelsea | 1877 |
| Kerr, Jonathan Henry James | 1905* | 1905* | Glen Sutton | 1906 |
| Kerr, John Winston | 1937 | 1938 | cu (W) Advent | 1948 |
| Kersey, Lloyd Francis | 1967* | 1968* | Arundel | 1967 |
| Kettleborough, Edward Graham | 1941* | 1942 | (M) St Luke's | 1942 |
| Kidd, Donald Worcester | 1939 | 1940 | Mount Royal | 1960 |
| Kilner, Charles Gibson | 1875 | 1876* | Adamsville | 1875 |
| King, Cecil | 1931* | 1932* | cu (M) Cathedral | 1931 |
| King, Ernest Augustus W. (SPG) | 1870 | 1873 | (W) St Matthias | 1886 |
| King, Jesse Edward | 1915* | 1918* | Kildare | 1915 |
| King, Walter Thomas | 1891 | 1892 | Portland | 1893 |
| Kingston, Peter Bradley | 1951 | 1952 | (M) St Cuthbert's | 1961 |
| Kingston, Thomas Martyn Sibbald | 1964 | 1965* | cu (W) St Matthias | 1964 |
| Kingsford, Maurice Rooke | 1923 | 1924 | cu (W) St Stephen's | 1928 |
| Kirby, John Charles | 1939* | 1940* | cu (M) St Columba | 1940 |
| Kirkpatrick, Francis John | 1904* | 1905* | (M) St Thomas | 1905 |
| Kirkpatrick, Patricia Groten | 1985* | 1986* | asst (M) St Ja$^s$ Apostle | 1985 |
| Kittson, Henry (SPG) | 1871* | 1873* | North Gore | 1872 |
| Klassen, Arthur Michael Lloyd | 1970* | 1970* | cu (M) St Columba | 1970 |
| Knowles, Edward | 1920* | 1920* | West Shefford | 1920 |
| Knox, Thomas Stephen | 1951 | 1952 | (M) St Thomas | 1958 |
| Kohner, Jenö George | 1957 | 1958 | (M) St J$^n$ Evangelist | 1960 |
| Kunkle, Howard Rinker | 1949* | 1950* | cu (M) Trinity | 1949 |
| Lack, Walter Frederick | 1909 | 1911 | cu (M) St J$^n$ Evangelist | 1926 |
| Lackey, Isaac H. | 1892* | 1893* | Glen Sutton | 1892 |
| Lackey, Jacob Albert | 1893* | 1894* | Brome | 1893 |
| Lancaster, Charles Frederick | 1905 | 1906 | Ste-Anne-de-Bellevue | 1909 |
| Lancaster, C.H. | 1864* | 1867* | Thorne | 1865 |
| Lang, Robert Cyrus | 1933* | 1934* | (M) St Luke's | 1933 |
| Larivière, Dollard | 1884* | 1885* | (M) du Rédempteur | 1885 |
| Larivière, Louis-Vitalien | 1880* | 1880* | Pierreville | 1880 |
| Latimer, Ralph Robertson | 1930 | 1931 | (M) St Ja$^s$ Apostle | 1950 |
| Lavallée, Gérard | | 1997* | (M) du Rédempteur | 1997 |
| Lawler, Frank Roberts | 1949* | 1950* | (M) du Rédempteur | 1949 |
| Lawlor, Edward | 1890 | 1893 | Adamsville | 1910 |

| Name of Cleric | Ordination | | 1st Posting | Date |
| --- | --- | --- | --- | --- |
| | *Deacon* | *Priest* | *in Diocese* | |
| Laws, Harold Stewart | 1909 | 1910 | cu (M) Trinity | 1919 |
| Leach, William Turnbull | 1843† | 1844† | (M) St George's | 1843 |
| Leacock, W.T. | | | Chambly | 1865 |
| Leavitt, Ralph T. | 1995* | 1996* | (M) St George's | 1995 |
| Leckie, Edward Percival | 1953* | 1957 | Beauharnois | 1953 |
| LeCras, Winter Charles | 1929* | 1930* | cu Quyon | 1929 |
| Lee, Alfred | | | Abbotsford | 1880 |
| Lee, Kenneth Edward Earle | 1985* | 1986* | Cartierville | 1987 |
| Lee, John Ross | 1956 | 1957 | Director of Program | 1969 |
| Leeds, John (SPG) | | | (M) Christ Church | 1818 |
| Legge, George William | 1918 | 1919 | (M) S. Sh Extension | 1925 |
| Leigh, George Franklin | 1925 | 1926 | (M) Ch Extension | 1930 |
| Lemarquand, Grant Read | 1983* | 1984* | asst Pierrefonds | 1983 |
| LePoidevin, Alfred Leonard | 1950* | 1951* | cu (M) St Luke's | 1950 |
| L'Estrange, Theodore Victor | 1920 | 1921 | cu (M) St Columba | 1922 |
| LeTarte, Pierre-Maurice | 1942* | 1943 | (M) du Rédempteur | 1942 |
| Lewis, Benjamin Papineau | 1860* | 1862* | Sabrevois | 1860 |
| Lewis, William Pheris Ray | 1895* | 1896* | asst Cathedral | 1895 |
| Lidstone, Isaac Malcolm | 1927* | 1927* | (M) Greenfield Park | 1927 |
| Ligget, Thomas John Whiteford | 1933* | 1935* | cu Portage du Fort | 1933 |
| Lightbourne, Francis Gwynne | 1921 | 1922 | (M) St Ja$^s$ Apostle | 1923 |
| Lindsay, David (SPG) | 1851† | 1852* | Frost Village | 1851 |
| Lindsay, Horace | 1910 | 1910 | Bishop's Miss$^y$ | 1918 |
| Lindsay, John | | | asst Vaudreuil | 1883 |
| Lindsay, Robert (SPG) | 1850† | 1851* | Brome | 1850 |
| Lindsay, Sydenham Bagg | 1910* | 1911* | (M) St J$^n$ Evangelist | 1911 |
| Litchfield, Arthur Vincent | 1922* | 1923* | (V) St Clement's | 1922 |
| Little, Henry Marwood | 1894 | 1895 | (W) Advent | 1910 |
| Little, Sidney Charles | 1934* | 1935* | (M) Ch Extension | 1934 |
| Liversuch, Ian Martin | 1983 | 1984 | Hemmingford-Clarenceville | 1992 |
| Lloyd, Bennett William | 1954* | 1955* | cu Rosemount | 1954 |
| Lloyd, Michael John | 1963* | 1964* | cu (L) St Paul | 1963 |
| Lobley, Joseph Albert | 1863 | 1864 | MDTC | 1874 |
| Lockhart, Anthony Dixon (SPG) | 1850† | 1851* | New Glasgow | 1850 |
| Loiselle, Henri-Octave | 1894* | 1895* | Pierreville | 1896 |
| Long, George Alfred | 1967* | 1968* | Grenville | 1967 |
| Longhurst, William Belsey | 1870* | 1871* | Mascouche | 1871 |
| Lonsdell, Richard (SPG) | 1839† | 1840† | Laprairie | 1848 |
| Loosemore, Philip Wood | 1855 | 1856 | asst (M) Cathedral | 1864 |
| Love, Archibald Thomas | 1908 | 1909 | Nelsonville | 1920 |
| Lowe, John Jackson | 1898* | 1898* | cu Shawville | 1898 |
| Lower, Henry Martin | 1845* | 1847* | asst (M) Cathedral | 1854 |
| Lummis, Cornwallis | 1877* | 1880* | Mille Iles | 1877 |

| Name of Cleric | Ordination | | 1st Posting | Date |
| | Deacon | Priest | in Diocese | |
|---|---|---|---|---|
| Lummis, Wallace James Hamilton | 1914* | 1915* | Rivière Désert | 1914 |
| Lundy, Francis James (SPG) | 1837† | 1838† | St Martin | 1843 |
| Lupton, Albert Horner | 1917* | 1918* | cu N. Gore | 1917 |
| McAndrew, William John | 1909* | 1910* | Berthier-en-Haut | 1915 |
| McCann, Walter Ellard | 1910 | | Kildare | 1914 |
| McCarthy, Joseph William | 1960* | 1960* | cu Cartierville & Roxboro | 1961 |
| McColl, Edmund Neil | 1949* | 1950* | Poltimore | 1952 |
| McCormack, George John | 1916* | 1917* | Bondville & Foster | 1917 |
| McCulloch, Robert Lindo | 1956 | 1957 | asst (M) Ascension | 1963 |
| Macdonald, Daniel John | 1912 | 1915 | Huntingdon | 1929 |
| Macduff, Alexander Ramsey | 1869 | 1970 | (M) St Jude's | 1872 |
| McEwan, S.R. | | | Edwardstown | 1896 |
| McFarlane, Percival Alan Rex | 1951* | 1952* | chpl Bordeaux Jail | 1966 |
| Macfarlane, Robert Lindsay | 1883* | 1884* | Eardley | 1884 |
| MacFarlane, W.D. | | | | 1894 |
| Macfarlane, William Gleason | 1927* | 1928* | Glen Sutton | 1927 |
| McGonegal, John Armstrong | 1950 | 1951 | (V) Prot Hospital | 1959 |
| McGreer, Arthur Huffman | 1909 | 1910 | asst (M) Cathedral | 1912 |
| Macgregor, Roslyn Ann | 1991* | 1992* | asst (L) St Paul | 1991 |
| Machin, Charles James | | | Sorel | 1882 |
| Machin, Thomas (SPG) | 1849† | 1849† | St Hyacinthe | 1852 |
| McKeown, John (SPG) | 1848† | | Hemmingford | 1850 |
| McKeown, Lyndon Kenneth | 1960* | 1960* | Hull | 1962 |
| McKibbin, Arthur Gordon Deeves | 1985* | 1986* | Arundel | 1985 |
| Mackie, Robert | 1942 | 1943 | cu (W) St Matthias | 1944 |
| McKinley, Reginald Michael | 1966 | 1967 | Mount Royal | 1968 |
| Macklin, Ernest Francis | 1908 | 1909 | Portage du Fort | 1928 |
| MacLean, James Aubrey | 1953* | 1954* | Mount Royal | 1953 |
| McLeod, James Alexander | | | Iberville | 1854 |
| McManus, Edward | 1872* | 1876* | Berthier-en-Haut | 1872 |
| McMaster, John (SPG) | 1838† | 1839† | The Gore | 1838 |
| McNab, John Ingram | 1956 | 1957 | Cote-des-Neiges | 1978 |
| MacRae, Arthur William Meredith | 1955 | 1956 | asst (M) St Jasᵗ Apostle | 1956 |
| MacTier, Albert Norman | 1900 | 1901 | (M) St Simon's | 1941 |
| Maddocks, Edward Henry | 1918 | 1919 | MDTC | 1941 |
| Magill, Peter George | 1975* | 1976* | cu (W) St Matthias | 1975 |
| Magor, Murray Churchill | 1959* | 1959* | Vicar (M) Cathedral | 1959 |
| Maguire, Robert Kenneth | 1947 | 1948 | (M) St Jasᵗ Apostle | 1949 |

| Name of Cleric | Ordination | | 1st Posting | Date |
|---|---|---|---|---|
| | *Deacon* | *Priest* | *in Diocese* | |
| Majka, John Edwin | 1964 | 1965 | Pincourt | 1966 |
| Major, William Stevenson | 1896 | 1896 | (M) St George's | 1908 |
| Mallinson, S.H. | 1896 | 1897 | (M) Sault-au-Récollet | 1898 |
| Manning, Arthur Herbert | 1889* | 1893 | Bolton | 1889 |
| Marriott, Basil Sterling Talbot | 1893* | 1894* | Buckingham | 1893 |
| Marshall, Arthur Joseph | 1935* | 1936* | cu (V) St Jn Divine | 1935 |
| Marston, James Guy | 1940 | 1940 | cu (M) Cathedral | 1949 |
| Mascarenhas, Lawrence | | 1983* | St-Jean-sur-Richelieu | 1983 |
| Martin, John William | 1884 | 1885 | Boscobel | 1904 |
| Martin, Stuart Morison | 1955* | 1956* | cu (M) Cathedral | 1955 |
| Mason, Frank Hubert | 1923* | 1923* | (M) St George's | 1923 |
| Mason, George Albert | 1895* | 1896* | cu Dunham | 1896 |
| Mason, Peter Ralph | 1967* | 1968* | cu Hampstead | 1967 |
| Massey, Samuel | 1888* | 1888* | (M) St-Henri | 1888 |
| Maxwell, Thomas Winston | 1956 | 1957 | Roxboro Pierrefonds | 1970 |
| May, Edward Geoffrey | 1894 | 1895 | St Andrew's | 1914 |
| Meek, Henry A. | 1887* | 1888* | Glen Sutton | 1887 |
| Mellor, Alexander | 1935 | 1936 | cu (W) Advent | 1952 |
| Meloche, Donald J. | 1984 | 1984 | Dir. Pastoral Services | |
| | | | Mtl Children's Hosp. | 1989 |
| Mercer, Gordon Gladstone | 1940 | 1941 | (M) Trinity | 1944 |
| Mercer, John David | 1967* | 1968* | cu Vaudreuil | 1967 |
| Merrick, Joseph (SPG) | 1862* | 1866* | Brandon | 1859 |
| Merrick, William Chad (SPG) | 1849† | 1850† | Chambly | 1849 |
| Merryweather, Ernest Augustus | 1914* | 1915* | Ville Emard | 1914 |
| Mervyn, W.A. | | | Montreal Junction | 1893 |
| Meyer, John Bleaden | 1902* | 1902* | Portland | 1902 |
| Midlige, Benjamin Angus | 1947* | 1948* | cu (V) St Jn Divine | 1947 |
| Miles, Adèle Alison Rosalind | 1994* | 1995* | asst (M) Cathedral | 1994 |
| Miller, Levi Thomas | 1903* | 1903* | North Gore | 1904 |
| Millman, Thomas Reagh | 1933 | 1934 | MDCT | 1936 |
| Mills, Robert Davies | 1870* | 1872* | Brome Corners | 1870 |
| Mills, Seth Adoniram | 1888* | 1889* | Bristol | 1888 |
| Mills, William Lennox | 1872 | 1873 | St Johns | 1875 |
| Milton, John Lawrence (SPG) | 1833† | | Shefford | 1833 |
| Mitchell, Arthur Samuel | 1918 | 1919 | Ste-Agathe-des | |
| | | | Monts | 1929 |
| Montgomery, Hugh (SPG) | 1854* | 1855* | Sutton | 1855 |
| Moore, Arthur Henry | 1895 | 1896 | St Johns | 1912 |
| Moore, Samuel | 1883* | | Mascouche | 1884 |
| Moorehead, William Henry | 1911 | 1912 | (M) Ascension | 1920 |
| Morice, Charles (SPG) | 1842† | 1843† | Lacolle | 1842 |
| Morrell, John Keith | 1991 | 1992 | Cartierville | 1998 |
| Morrill, Garth R. | 1959 | 1960 | Lachute | 1994 |

| Name of Cleric | Ordination | | 1st Posting | Date |
| --- | --- | --- | --- | --- |
| | *Deacon* | *Priest* | *in Diocese* | |
| Morris, Alexander James Pitman | 1959* | 1959* | (M) St Hilda | 1959 |
| Morris, Charles Franklin | 1985* | 1986* | Mascouche & asst | |
| | | | cu (M) St Ignatius | 1985 |
| Morris, Edward | 1912 | 1913 | cu (M) St Thomas | 1914 |
| Morris, Eustin John | 1967* | 1968* | cu (L) St Paul | 1967 |
| Morris, John Alexander | 1852* | 1853* | asst (M) Cathedral | 1852 |
| Morris, John Frederick | 1914 | 1915 | cu Glen Sutton | 1915 |
| Morris, William (SPG) | 1842† | 1843† | Huntingdon | 1842 |
| Morrison, Ian David | 1964 | 1965 | asst (M) St Ja⁵ | |
| | | | Apostle | 1965 |
| Morrison, James Dow | 1869 | | Hemmingford | 1870 |
| Mortimer, Hugh Augustine | 1940* | 1942 | cu (W) St Matthias | 1940 |
| Motherwell, Thomas (SPG) | 1872* | 1873* | Portage du Fort | 1881 |
| Mount, Allan Edgar | 1894* | 1896* | Lakefield | 1894 |
| Mount, Hector Peart | 1902* | 1903* | Bristol | 1902 |
| Mountain, George Jehoshaphat | 1812† | 1814† | as Bp of Montreal | 1836 |
| Mountain, Jacob | 1774 | 1780 | as Bp of Quebec | 1793 |
| Mountain, Jacob Jehoshaphat Salter (SPG) | 1847† | | Coteau du Lac | 1848 |
| Mountain, Jehoshaphat (SPG) | 1778 | 1779 | (M) Christ Church | 1800 |
| Muller, Adolph Conrad | 1899 | 1900 | asst (M)  St Columba | 1923 |
| Murray, Bertram Spence | 1929* | 1930* | cu Knowlton | 1929 |
| Mussen, Thomas W. (SPG) | 1855* | 1856* | Sherrington | 1856 |
| Mutch, Robert Bruce | 1952* | 1953* | cu (M) Ascension | 1952 |
| Naughton, Michael William | 1911* | 1912* | miss^y Pierreville | 1911 |
| Naylor, Henry Alford | 1896* | 1897 | Chelsea | 1901 |
| Naylor, Reuben Kenneth | 1912* | 1913* | Rawdon | 1912 |
| Naylor, William Herbert | 1873* | 1874* | cu Philipsburg | 1873 |
| Nesbitt, A.C. (SPG) | 1864* | 1865* | Aylwin | 1864 |
| Nesbitt, Andrew Clair Liddon H. | 1920 | 1922 | Campbell's Bay | 1922 |
| Neugewirtz, David John | 1905* | 1905* | Emmanuel Mission | 1904 |
| Neve, Frederick Smith (SPG) | 1843† | 1844† | Clarendon | 1843 |
| New, Walter Gerrard | 1930* | 1931* | asst Ch Extension | 1930 |
| Newell, Alex James | 1948 | 1949 | cu (M) St Ja⁵ Apostle | 1952 |
| Newman, Robert Stevenson | 1942 | 1945 | Warden MDTC | 1958 |
| Newnham, Jervois Arthur (SPG) | 1878* | 1880* | Onslow | 1878 |
| Newton, John David | 1974* | 1974* | cu (M) St Ja⁵ Apostle | 1974 |
| Nicholson, William George | 1910* | 1911 | asst (M) Cathedral | 1910 |
| Nicholson, William Henry | 1904* | 1904* | Mille Iles | 1905 |
| Nicolls, Gustavus George | 1879 | 1881 | (W) Advent | 1909 |
| Nixon, Charles Richard Harris | 1977 | 1978 | Stanbridge East | 1984 |
| Norman, Arthur (SPG) | 1827† | | (M) Christ Church | 1832 |
| Norman, Fred Taylor | 1925* | 1925* | Quyon | 1925 |
| Norman, Richard Whitmore | 1852 | 1853 | (M) St J^n Evangelist | 1868 |

| Name of Cleric | Ordination | | 1st Posting | Date |
| --- | --- | --- | --- | --- |
| | *Deacon* | *Priest* | *in Diocese* | |
| Norquay, Douglas E. | 1988* | 1989* | asst Vaudreuil | 1988 |
| Norris, Gerald Leigh | 1953 | 1954 | Waterloo | 1959 |
| Norton, John George | 1865 | 1866 | Dean (M) Cathedral | 1884 |
| Norwood, Robert Winckworth | 1897 | 1898 | (M) Trinity | 1909 |
| Noseworthy, Nathan | 1930* | 1931* | (V) St Clement | 1930 |
| Noseworthy, Donald Wilbur | 1946* | 1947* | cu Aylwin | 1946 |
| Nurse, Theodore Ernest Roy | 1929* | 1930* | cu Aylwin | 1929 |
| Nye, Henry Wason (SPG) | 1861 | 1870* | Iron Hill | 1872 |
| Ogden, W.M. | | | asst (M) St J<sup>n</sup> Evangelist | 1864 |
| Ogilvie, John (SPG) | 1749 | 1749 | Montreal | 1760 |
| O'Grady, G. DeCourcy (SPG) | 1851* | 1852* | Hemmingford | 1851 |
| Oliver, David Nelson | 1975* | 1976* | cu Montreal West | 1975 |
| Oliver, Gilbert | 1914 | 1919 | (L) St Stephen | 1927 |
| O'Malley, H.R.A. | | | (M) St Jude | 1898 |
| Ormos, Claude Patrick | 1978* | 1979* | cu Montreal West | 1978 |
| Osborne, James Alfred | 1911* | 1912* | cu (M) St Thomas | 1911 |
| O'Sullivan, Richard Benjamin | 1887* | | St Andrew's | 1886 |
| Ottiwell, Arthur Vivian | 1934 | 1935 | cu (M) Cathedral | 1956 |
| Overing, Robert Young | 1896* | 1896* | Valleyfield | 1896 |
| Owen, John Bradley | 1941* | 1941* | cu (W) Advent | 1941 |
| Oxenden, Ashton | 1832 | 1833 | 2nd Lord Bishop | 1869 |
| Page, Richard Eustace | 1907* | 1911* | Pierreville | 1907 |
| Parker, Daniel Thomas | 1904* | 1904* | North Clarendon | 1905 |
| Parker, George William | 1953 | 1954 | St-Agathe-des-Monts | 1978 |
| Parker, George Henry (SPG) | 1863* | 1864* | asst Dunham | 1863 |
| Parkin, Edward (SPG) | 1814 | 1816 | Chambly | 1819 |
| Parks, Robert Henry | 1928 | 1928 | Valleyfield | 1933 |
| Parnther, David Bernard (SPG) | 1840† | 1841† | Huntingdon | 1841 |
| Parrett, Douglas A. | 1989 | 1990 | Mount Royal | 1997 |
| Paterson, Ivor David John | 1973* | 1973* | cu Greenfield Park | 1973 |
| Payne, William Thomas | 1912* | 1913* | Bolton | 1912 |
| Peacock, John Oswald | 1937* | 1938* | Hampstead | 1937 |
| Pearce, Bryan W. | 1964* | 1965* | cu (M) St George's | 1964 |
| Pearce, George Roland | 1960* | 1960* | Rivière Désert | 1960 |
| Pearce, John Gilbert | 1952* | 1953* | (M) St Ignatius | 1952 |
| Pearse, Lewis Blight | 1887* | 1889* | Aylwin | 1887 |
| Peaston, Monroe | 1938 | 1939 | MDTC | 1965 |
| Perron, Odette M.A. | 1980 | 1981 | St Margt of Scotland | 1991 |
| Perry, Alan T. | 1993* | 1994* | cu (M) St Ja<sup>s</sup> Apostle | 1993 |
| Peterson, Norman Edwin | 1922* | 1923* | cu (M) St Alban's | 1922 |
| Petry, Henry James (SPG) | 1854 | 1855 | Chambly | 1864 |
| Phelps, R. | | | Lachine | 1873 |

| Name of Cleric | Ordination | | 1st Posting | Date |
|---|---|---|---|---|
| | *Deacon* | *Priest* | *in Diocese* | |
| Phillips, Alfred Tennyson | 1913* | 1914* | Aylwin | 1914 |
| Phillips, Gordon William | 1929* | 1930* | cu Arundel | 1929 |
| Pilcher, Norman Donald | 1938 | 1939 | asst (M) St Margarets | 1970 |
| Pitts, Michael James | 1969 | 1970 | asst Cathedral | 1988 |
| Plaisted, Henry A. | 1884* | 1885* | Rivière Désert | 1885 |
| Plees, Robert George (SPG) | 1841† | 1842† | Russelltown | 1842 |
| Plumptre, Henry Pemberton | 1895 | 1896 | cu (M) St George's | 1903 |
| Poland, Frederick William | 1884 | 1887 | Ste-Agathe-des-Monts | 1912 |
| Pollard, Samuel Lister | 1934* | 1935* | cu Poltimore | 1934 |
| Poole, Aquilla James | 1937* | 1938* | cu (M) St Alban's | 1938 |
| Postlewaite, Charles Wilson | 1926* | 1927* | Aylwin | 1926 |
| Poston, J.A. | 1898* | | Edwardstown | 1899 |
| Pountney, Michael James | 1982* | 1983* | (M) Ascension | 1982 |
| Powell, Robert Chester Spencer | 1963 | 1964 | asst Mount Royal | 1964 |
| Powles, Cyril Hamilton | 1943* | 1944* | cu Hampstead | 1943 |
| Powles, Percival Samuel Carson | 1914* | 1915* | MDTC | 1914 |
| Pratt, Francis  Armstrong | 1894* | 1895* | cu Dunham | 1894 |
| Prendergast, Ross William | 1962* | 1963* | Hemmingford | 1965 |
| Prideaux, Brian Kenneth | 1968* | 1969* | Mascouche | 1969 |
| Prime, A. | 1868* | | North Onslow | 1869 |
| Pritchard, Owen Pierce | 1941* | 1942* | cu (M) St Jaˢ Apostle | 1941 |
| Prosser, Peter Edward | 1975* | 1976* | cu Hampstead | 1975 |
| Pyke, James W. (SPG) | 1839† | 1841† | Coteau du Lac | 1841 |
| Race, Alfred Ernest | 1904 | 1906 | Leslie | 1922 |
| Radmore, William Robert Arthur | 1925* | 1925* | Campbell's Bay | 1925 |
| Rahard, Victor AndrÈ | 1907 | 1907 | (M) du Rédempteur | 1931 |
| Ramsay, James (SPG) | | | (M) St Mary's | 1838 |
| Ramsey, Thomas Alfred | 1954* | 1955* | cu (M) Trinity | 1954 |
| Randell, Cecil | 1939 | 1940 | Shawville | 1944 |
| Randell, Richard Lawson | 1991* | 1992* | cu (M) St Jaˢ Apostle | 1991 |
| Ratcliffe, Holly Elizabeth | 1986 | 1987 | (L) St Stephen's | 1992 |
| Rattray, John Andrew | 1914* | 1915* | Alleyne | 1914 |
| Raven, Walter | 1889* | 1890* | Eardley | 1889 |
| Rayson, Robert Spencer | 1925 | 1925 | Dorval | 1955 |
| Reade, John (SPG) | 1864* | 1865* | Mascouche | 1865 |
| Reed, Ernest Samuel | 1931 | 1932 | Cowansville | 1934 |
| Reed, Ernest James | 1964 | 1965 | cu St Lambert | 1964 |
| Rees, Archibald Paneton Clement | 1928* | | (V) St Clement | 1928 |
| Rees, Brian Allison | 1980* | 1981* | cu (M) St Jaˢ Apostle | 1980 |
| Reid, Anthony Meredith | 1957* | 1958* | cu Cartierville | 1957 |
| Reid, Charles | 1909* | 1910* | Portland | 1909 |
| Reid, Charles Peter (SPG) | 1835† | 1836† | Rawdon | 1835 |
| Reid, Edward | 1918* | 1919 | Quyon | 1921 |

| Name of Cleric | Ordination | | 1st Posting | Date |
|---|---|---|---|---|
| | *Deacon* | *Priest* | *in Diocese* | |
| Reid, James (SPG) | 1815† | 1816† | St Armand | 1815 |
| Renaud, James Frederick | 1875 | 1876 | (M) Cathedral | 1880 |
| Rexford, Elson Irving | 1876* | 1894* | (M) St Luke's | 1878 |
| Reynolds, Eric Thomas | 1974 | 1975 | Vaudreuil | 1998 |
| Reynolds, Hugh Justus Armiger | 1950 | 1951 | (M) Cathedral | 1953 |
| Rhys, John Howard Winslow | 1941* | 1941* | asst (W) St Stephen's | 1941 |
| Richardson, John Alexander | 1912* | 1913* | Bishop's Miss^y | 1913 |
| Richardson, J.K. | | | Chambly | 1877 |
| Richmond, William (SPG) | 1858 | 1859 | North Gore | 1874 |
| Rider, Stanley Ellis | 1937 | 1938 | cu (M) Cathedral | 1939 |
| Ripper, Stanley Charles | 1919 | 1920 | Glen Sutton | 1922 |
| Ritchie, Lawrence Dudley | 1953 | 1953 | (V) St J^n Divine | 1957 |
| Robbs, Francis Headley | 1927 | 1931* | MDTC | 1930 |
| Roberts, John Lloyd Puleston | 1889* | 1890* | Thorne | 1889 |
| Roberts, Lawrence Graeme Allan | 1888* | 1889* | Vaudreuil | 1888 |
| Robertson, David (SPG) | 1827† | 1830† | Stanbridge | 1832 |
| Robillard, Roger Manuel | 1979* | 1981* | cu Roxboro-Pierrefonds | 1979 |
| Robinson, Bernard Seabury | 1919 | 1920 | cu (M) All Saints | 1923 |
| Robinson, Cuthbert Cooper | 1920 | 1938 | Noranda | 1944 |
| Robinson, Frederick (SPG) | 1847† | 1848† | Rougemont | 1848 |
| Robinson, George C. (SPG) | 1863* | 1864* | Clarendon | 1864 |
| Robinson, William | 1882* | 1883* | Iron Hill | 1883 |
| Robson, John Wingate | 1949* | 1950* | cu Hampstead | 1949 |
| Robson, Michael J. | 1986* | 1987* | Bishop's Miss^y | 1986 |
| Rogers, David Benson | 1908* | 1909* | cu (M) Grace Church | 1908 |
| Rogers, David Handley | 1960* | 1960* | Hemmingford | 1960 |
| Rogers, Edward (SPG) | | | Hochelaga | 1851 |
| Rogers, George | 1883* | 1884* | Lacolle | 1883 |
| Rogers, Isaac W. | | | Kildare | 1883 |
| Rogers, Kenneth Herbert | 1950 | 1951 | MDTC | 1953 |
| Rollitt, Charles (SPG) | 1844† | 1845† | Travelling Miss^y | 1846 |
| Rollit, Archibald Dixon | 1935* | 1936* | cu (M) Trinity | 1935 |
| Rollit, Albert Ernest | 1928* | 1930* | Mansonville | 1928 |
| Rollit, Charles Gore Dixon | 1892* | 1894* | Bolton | 1892 |
| Rollit, John | 1866* | 1868* | Thorne | 1867 |
| Rollit, Percival George | 1905* | 1905* | Campbell's Bay | 1906 |
| Ross, Graham Robert | 1964 | 1965 | (M) St Thomas | 1967 |
| Rowe, John Goring | 1951* | 1952 | cu N. Clarendon | 1951 |
| Rowe, Michael Gordon | 1980* | 1981* | (W) St Matthias | 1980 |
| Rowe, Thomas Desmond | 1952* | 1953 | cu Mount Royal | 1957 |
| Rowlinson, Elizabeth Maud Hunter | 1993* | 1994* | chapl McGill & hon. asst (M) Cathedral | 1993 |

| Name of Cleric | Ordination | | 1st Posting | Date |
|---|---|---|---|---|
| | *Deacon* | *Priest* | *in Diocese* | |
| Roy, Edward | 1868* | 1871* | cu Sabrevois | 1868 |
| Roy, Jean | | | Rawdon | 1876 |
| Roy, Jean-Jacques | 1874* | 1887* | Sabrevois | 1872 |
| Royle, Edward Cecil | 1936 | 1936* | cu (w) St Matthias | 1936 |
| Rudd, James Sutherland (SPG) | | | Sorel | 1803 |
| Russell, Edward Charles | | | (w) St Stephen's | 1913 |
| Rutter, Kenneth George | 1961 | 1952 | (M) Advent | 1966 |
| Ryder, Walter Earl | 1916 | 1919 | Temiskaming | 1920 |
| Sadler, Ralph Trego | 1906 | 1908 | (M) St J$^n$ Evangelist | 1915 |
| Salmon, George (SPG) | 1826† | 1827† | Shefford | 1826 |
| Sanchez, Joyce Mary Warnes | 1998* | 1999* | (M) Cathedral & Mile End Mission | 1999 |
| Sanders, William | 1885* | 1887* | Lachute | 1887 |
| Sandilands, George | 1969* | | cu (L) St Paul's | 1969 |
| Sandilands, G. Andrew | 1986* | 1987* | asst cu Mount Royal | 1986 |
| Santram, Philip James | 1952 | 1954 | Lakefield | 1978 |
| Saphir, Edward John | 1885* | 1891* | North Shefford | 1886 |
| Saunders, E.C. | | | (M) St Jude | 1881 |
| Saunders, William | 1885* | 1887* | Lachute | 1885 |
| Sawers, Frederick John | 1903 | 1905* | cu (M) Cathedral | 1904 |
| Scarth, Archibald Campbell (SPG) | 1857* | 1858* | Adamsville | 1857 |
| Schaffter, Frederick William | 1909 | 1911* | Bristol | 1909 |
| Schippling, Roy Frederick | 1939 | 1940* | cu (M) St J$^n$ Evangelist | 1939 |
| Schmidt, Keith Allan | 1989* | 1990* | Mansonville | 1993 |
| Schulte, J. | | | Iberville | 1878 |
| Scotland, Nigel Adrian Douglas | 1966 | 1967 | Lakefield | 1970 |
| Scott, Ebenezer | 1910* | 1910* | Valleyfield | 1910 |
| Scott, Elton | 1923 | 1924 | cu (M) St J$^n$ Evangelist | 1925 |
| Scott, Joseph (SPG) | 1843† | 1844† | Brome | 1843 |
| Scrimgeour, Charles Ernest | 1912* | 1913* | (M) Ascension | 1912 |
| Scully, John G. (SPG) | 1866 | 1866 | New Glasgow | 1876 |
| Scyner, Lawrence Anthony | 1962* | 1963* | cu (M) Cathedral | 1962 |
| Seaborn, William Minter (SPG) | 1861* | 1861* | Kildare | 1865 |
| Seaman, John (SPG) | 1863* | 1865* | North Wakefield | 1872 |
| Seaman, Justus John Smith | 1903 | 1904 | Clarendon | 1912 |
| Seaver, Donald Vanor | 1976 | 1977 | St Lambert | 1978 |
| Sellwood, William John | 1955* | 1956* | Clarenceville | 1955 |
| Senior, James | 1885* | | Lakefield | 1886 |
| Senkler, H. J. (SPG) | | | Montreal | 1845 |
| Sergeantson, John Cecil Mylles | 1966* | 1967* | cu (w) St Matthias | 1966 |
| Sergent, Adolph Louis | 1943* | 1944* | (M) Emmanuel Missn | 1944 |
| Shanks, Edith Joan | 1989* | 1990* | (M) St Ja$^s$ Apostle | 1990 |

| Name of Cleric | Ordination Deacon | Priest | 1st Posting in Diocese | Date |
|---|---|---|---|---|
| Shand, Alexander (SPG) | | | New Glasgow | 1866 |
| Shatford, Allan Pearson | 1896 | 1897 | cu (M) St Ja$^s$ Apostle | 1906 |
| Sheffield, Arthur Edward | 1978* | 1979* | cu St-Anne-de-Belleview | 1978 |
| Shepherd, Ronald Francis | 1952 | 1953 | Dean (M) Cathedral | 1970 |
| Shepherd, William Harry Edwin | 1981* | 1982* | Pierrefonds | 1981 |
| Shires, Robert John | 1913 | 1914 | (M) St Andrew's | 1916 |
| Shore, Henry Minchin | 1907 | 1908 | (M) St Augustine's | 1922 |
| Short, Robert Quirke (SPG) | 1783 | 1787 | St Armand | 1800 |
| Shortt, Jonathan (SPG) | 1832† | 1834† | Laprairie | 1833 |
| Simons, John MacMillan | 1969 | 1969 | (M) Cathedral | 1973 |
| Sinnamon, Frederick Joseph | 1918 | 1919 | (M) St Thomas | 1932 |
| Sinyard, Boyd Gabriel | 1947 | 1948 | Montreal West | 1956 |
| Skynner, Henry John | 1952 | 1953 | (W) St Matthias | 1954 |
| Slack, George (SPG) | 1843† | 1844† | Granby | 1843 |
| Slater, Christopher Peter Robert Lawson | 1957* | 1958* | Mansonville | 1958 |
| Slater, Robert Henry Lawson | 1924 | 1925 | Principal MDTC | 1951 |
| Slattery, Humphry Oswald | 1951 | 1952 | (M) St J$^n$ Evangelist | 1955 |
| Smart, Timothy, E. | 1987* | 1988* | Mtl Nord & Mascouche | 1987 |
| Smith, Alfred William | 1931* | 1932* | Boscobel | 1931 |
| Smith, Aloha Lee | 1988* | 1989* | asst Chateauguay | 1988 |
| Smith, Buxton Birbeck (SPG) | 1869 | 1871 | Onslow | 1872 |
| Smith, Francis Robert (SPG) | 1875* | 1877* | Chelsea | 1875 |
| Smith, George A. | | | Eardley | 1887 |
| Smith, Gordon Ewen | 1954 | 1955 | Farnham | 1978 |
| Smith, Henry William Frank | 1916* | | Adamsville | 1916 |
| Smith, Jacques | 1963* | 1964* | (M) St Mary's | 1963 |
| Smith, John (SPG) | 1862* | 1864* | cu Knowlton | 1865 |
| Smith, Leonard William | 1911* | 1912* | cu (M) St J$^n$ Evangelist | 1912 |
| Smith, Percy W. (SPG) | 1864* | 1866* | Eardley | 1865 |
| Smith, Roberts Cameron | 1974 | 1975 | Pierrefonds | 1983 |
| Smye, Frank Hazell | 1925* | 1927 | S. Shore Extension | 1925 |
| Smyth, John Paterson | 1880 | 1881 | (M) St George's | 1907 |
| Sparling, James Wallace | 1966* | 1967* | cu Greenfield Park | 1966 |
| Staes, Francis Basil | 1929 | 1932* | cu (M) St Alban's | 1932 |
| Standish, Grenville Nelson | 1942 | 1943 | cu (W) St Stephen's | 1942 |
| Stanway, John David | 1965* | 1966* | Lasalle Mission | 1965 |
| Steacy, Frederick W. | 1897* | 1897* | Papineauville | 1897 |
| Steen, Frederick Julius | | | MDTC | 1897 |
| Stephens, Brooke Bridges (SPG) | | | Montreal | 1824 |
| Stephens, Major Alfred | 1934* | 1935* | (M) St Columba | 1934 |

| Name of Cleric | Ordination | | 1st Posting | Date |
| --- | --- | --- | --- | --- |
| | *Deacon* | *Priest* | *in Diocese* | |
| Stephenson, Francis Henry | 1907 | 1908 | Bondville & Foster | 1912 |
| Stephenson, Richard | | | | |
|    Langford (SPG) | 1850† | 1851* | Travelling Miss$^y$ | 1850 |
| Steven, Peel Othmar | 1973* | 1973* | cu (L) St Paul's | 1973 |
| Stevens, Cecil Gardner | 1911 | 1912 | St Lambert | 1931 |
| Stevenson, Herbert Richard | 1905 | 1906 | (M) St George's | 1907 |
| Stewart, Charles James (SPG) | 1798 | 1799 | St Armand | 1807 |
| Stewart, Reginald Gordon | 1934* | 1935* | cu Lakefield | 1934 |
| Stobart, John | 1925* | | (V) St Clement's | 1925 |
| Stone, Cyril Haynes | 1935* | 1936* | cu Papineauville | 1935 |
| Stone, J.S. | | | (M) St Martin's | 1883 |
| Stote, Philip Raymond | 1937* | 1940* | cu (M) St Luke's | 1937 |
| Stott, Geoffrey Justus Richard | 1928 | 1929 | Rouyn | 1932 |
| Strong, John Irwin | 1893* | 1894* | cu Waterloo | 1893 |
| Strong, Samuel Spratt (SPG) | 1835† | 1836† | Hull | 1837 |
| Strowbridge, Isaac | 1914* | 1915* | Leslie | 1915 |
| Stuart, John (SPG) | | | Montreal | 1780 |
| Stuchbery, Ian | 1960* | 1961 | (M) Cathedral | 1969 |
| Sullivan, Edward | 1858 | 1859 | cu (M) St George's | 1863 |
| Sutton, Edward George (SPG) | 1844† | 1845† | Travelling Miss$^y$ | 1845 |
| Sweeny, James Fielding | 1880* | 1881* | (M) St Luke's | 1881 |
| Swindlehurst, Frederick | 1900 | 1902 | Andrew's Home | 1927 |
| Sydenham, G. | | | (M) St Thomas | 1875 |
| Sykes, James Samuel (SPG) | 1855 | 1855 | Clarendon | 1855 |
| Symonds, Herbert | 1885 | 1887 | Vicar (M) Cathedral | 1903 |
| Tardy, Lorne Randolph | 1979* | 1980* | cu Pierrefonds | 1979 |
| Tate, Francis B. (SPG) | | | (M) St Luke's | 1857 |
| Taylor, Arthur James | 1918* | 1920* | (M) St Alban's | 1918 |
| Taylor, A.O. (SPG) | 1862* | 1866* | St-Hyacinthe | 1862 |
| Taylor, Eustace Lovatt Hebden | 1952 | 1952 | cu (M) Hampstead | 1954 |
| Taylor, Humphrey John | 1943 | 1944 | cu (M) St J$^n$ Evangel$^t$ | 1948 |
| Taylor, Kenneth Elder | 1924* | 1925* | cu (M) Trinity | 1924 |
| Taylor, Linda Gail Borden | 1996* | 1996* | Dorval | 1996 |
| Taylor, Richard Frederick | 1888* | 1889* | Mille Iles | 1888 |
| Taylor, Wilfred | 1917* | 1918* | Bolton | 1917 |
| Temple, John Vincent | 1926* | 1927* | cu Glen Sutton | 1926 |
| Temple-Hill, Lionel Novinger | 1938* | 1939* | cu (V) St J$^n$ Divine | 1938 |
| Thatcher, John Farler | 1964* | 1965* | cu (W) St Matthias | 1964 |
| Thicke, Septimus Cox | 1880* | | Knowlton | 1882 |
| Thomas, John Henry | 1898 | 1900 | cu (W) St Stephen's | 1911 |
| Thompson, Evered Francis Leslie | 1924* | 1925* | (M) St Jude's | 1925 |
| Thompson, George Henry | 1942 | 1943 | cu Valois | 1942 |
| Thompson, James | | | North Shefford | 1895 |
| Thompson, Joseph Henry | 1848 | 1849 | asst (M) Cathedral | 1862 |

| Name of Cleric | Ordination | | 1st Posting | Date |
|---|---|---|---|---|
| | *Deacon* | *Priest* | *in Diocese* | |
| Thompson, William | 1841† | 1841† | Montreal | 1841 |
| Thorndike, Charles Faunce | 1866* | 1867* | Chambly | 1867 |
| Thorne, Oliver | 1912* | 1913* | Bishop's Miss^y | 1912 |
| Thornloe, James | 1866 | 1868 | (M) St Luke's | 1870 |
| Thorpe, Benjamin James | 1930* | 1931* | N Clarendon | 1930 |
| Timmons, Edward Patrick Alfred | 1951 | 1951 | cu (W) St Matthias | 1957 |
| Tiplady, Frederick Thomas | 1968* | 1969* | Arundel | 1970 |
| Tippet, Richard Simonds | 1912* | 1915 | cu (W) Advent | 1912 |
| Toase, Richard Whiteside | 1960 | 1961 | (M) St Thomas | 1962 |
| Todd, William Andrew Hankins | 1955 | 1956 | cu Vaudreuil | 1975 |
| Toope, Frank Morris | 1945 | 1947 | Hampstead | 1956 |
| Torrance, John (SPG) | 1839† | 1840† | Mascouche | 1840 |
| Townsend, Micajah (SPG) | 1815† | 1816† | Clarenceville | 1815 |
| Trebitsch, I.T. | 1902* | | (M) Emmanuel Missn | 1903 |
| Trench, Albert Charles | 1910 | 1912 | Papineauville | 1914 |
| Trickey, Kenneth Wilson | 1958* | 1959* | cu Montreal West | 1958 |
| Trill, Roger Hailey | 1915* | 1916* | cu (M) St Alban's | 1915 |
| Trivett, Wilfred Martyn | 1911 | 1912 | Poltimore | 1924 |
| Troop, George Osborne | 1877 | 1878 | (M) St Martin's | 1886 |
| Troop, George William Hill | 1905* | | asst (M) Cathedral | 1954 |
| Trotman, Charles | | | (M) St George's | 1885 |
| Trueman, George Edgar | 1919 | 1920 | cu (M) Grace Church | 1927 |
| Tucker, Louis Norman | 1876 | 1878* | South Ely | 1876 |
| Tucker, Nevil Francis | 1938 | 1939 | Waterloo | 1974 |
| Tulk, Gerald Andrew | 1959* | 1959* | Mansonville | 1959 |
| Tully, Joseph | 1910 | 1911 | (M) Andrews Home | 1923 |
| Tunstall, James Marmaduke (SPG) | | | (M) Christ Church | 1789 |
| Turney, William Charles | 1915 | 1916 | (M) St Columba | 1920 |
| Turpin, Reginald Matthew | 1942 | 1942 | Buckingham | 1952 |
| Twining, John Sandford | 1943 | 1944 | cu (M) Ascension | 1945 |
| Valentine, Barry | 1951* | 1952* | cu (M) Cathedral | 1952 |
| Vincent, Marc-Phillipe | 1991* | 1991* | (M) St-Rédempteur | 1991 |
| Vokey, Edward Philip | 1956* | 1957* | Sorel | 1956 |
| Vokey, Joseph | 1948* | 1949* | (V) All Saints | 1948 |
| Wagland, John Frederick | 1944 | 1945* | cu (M) Cathedral | 1944 |
| Waller, Charles Cameron | 1892 | 1893 | cu (W) Advent | 1892 |
| Walsh, Henry Charles | 1902* | 1903* | Rivière Désert | 1902 |
| Walsh, Henry Horace | 1923 | 1924 | MDTC | 1946 |
| Walsh, William George | 1902 | 1905 | St Armand East | 1909 |
| Ward, James Edward | | | (M) Trinity | 1918 |
| Warner, David Victor | 1905 | 1906 | (W) St Matthias | 1920 |
| Warner, Gesner Quintin | 1909 | 1910 | cu (M) Trinity | 1912 |
| Warren, Robert James | 1984 | 1985 | (M) St Ignatius & St Margaret's | 1990 |

| Name of Cleric | Ordination | | 1st Posting | Date |
|---|---|---|---|---|
| | *Deacon* | *Priest* | *in Diocese* | |
| Warrington, Robert | 1896* | 1897 | Portage du Fort | 1898 |
| Waters, Edward Henry | 1931* | 1932* | cu (M) St Luke's | 1931 |
| Waters, H. | | | (M) Trinity | 1870 |
| Waterson, William | | | | |
| James Matthew | 1893* | 1894* | Rougemont | 1893 |
| Watson, Cyril Coleridge | 1950* | 1951* | cu Hampstead | 1950 |
| Weaver, William | 1884 | 1885 | Hemmingford | 1884 |
| Webber, Frederick William | 1883* | 1884* | Longueuil | 1883 |
| Webster, Richard Webster Boot | | | Longueuil | 1872 |
| Wells, Gwenda | 1982 | 1983 | chpl McGill | 1996 |
| Westin, Harald | | | | |
| Malcolm Douglas | 1956* | 1956* | Ormstown | 1956 |
| Westin, John Paul | 1986 | 1987 | (M) St Jⁿ Evangelist | 1993 |
| Wetherall, A.F. (SPG) | 1854* | 1854* | Stukely | 1854 |
| Wheeler, Patrick John Elgar | 1999* | | Sorel | 1999 |
| Whitcroft, Thomas Henry | 1959 | 1959 | (M) Cathedral | 1977 |
| Whittall, John Duncan | 1969* | 1969* | St Lambert | 1969 |
| White, Frederick | 1903 | 1903 | North Shefford | 1913 |
| White, Isaac Patrick (SPG) | 1843† | 1844 | cu Chambly | 1848 |
| White, R. | 1873 | | cu (M) St Jaˢ Apostle | 1874 |
| White, Robert Dusautoy | 1866 | 1869 | Chambly | 1869 |
| White, William James | 1942* | 1943* | cu Portage du Fort | 1942 |
| Whitley, Frederick Lewis | 1902* | 1902* | cu (M) Grace Church | 1902 |
| Whitten, Andrew Trew (SPG) | 1843† | 1844† | St Johns | 1843 |
| Whitwell, Richard (SPG) | | 1819 | St Armand West | 1826 |
| Whyte, William Thomas | 1967* | 1968* | cu (M) St Jaˢ Apostle | 1967 |
| Wilkinson, Frederick Hugh | 1924 | 1925 | (M) St Jaˢ Apostle | 1936 |
| Williams, P.S. (SPG) | | | Sorel | 1855 |
| Williamson, C.M. | | | Sabrevois | 1857 |
| Willis, John James | 1900* | 1901* | cu Papineauville | 1900 |
| Willis, Selwyn Thomas | 1936* | 1937* | cu (M) Cathedral | 1936 |
| Willoughby, Mark | 1839† | 1840† | Travelling Missʸ | 1839 |
| Wilson, Arthur Charles | 1894* | | Bolton | 1894 |
| Wilson, Donna Jeanne | 1979* | 1980* | cu (M) Cathedral | 1979 |
| Wilson, F. | 1853* | | Huntingdon | 1854 |
| Wilson, T.J.E. | | | Edwardstown | 1902 |
| Winch, Henry Courtney | 1906 | 1909 | (M) Grace Church | 1911 |
| Windsor, Walter | 1881 | 1884* | (L) St Stephen | 1884 |
| Winter, Thomas Bradbury | 1909 | 1910 | (M) St Jⁿ Evangelist | 1912 |
| Winterbourne, Henry J. | | | (L) St Stephen | 1887 |
| Woehrle, Paul R. | 1992* | 1993* | asst cu St Lambert | 1992 |
| Woeller, David John | 1951 | 1952 | Director religious Ed. | 1961 |
| Wiswell, Douglas Morgan | 1922 | 1923 | cu (M) Cathedral | 1925 |
| Wolfendale, George Hedley | 1931* | 1931 | Arundel | 1935 |

| Name of Cleric | Ordination | | 1st Posting | Date |
|---|---|---|---|---|
| | *Deacon* | *Priest* | *in Diocese* | |
| Wood, Edmund | 1855 | 1861* | asst (M) Cathedral | 1859 |
| Wood, H.L. | 1888* | 1890* | Hemmingford | 1889 |
| Wood, Randolph Scott | 1958 | 1959 | (W) St Matthias | 1985 |
| Wood, Sydney | 1932 | 1932 | Waterloo | 1940 |
| Wray, H. | | | Laprairie | 1861 |
| Wright, Charles | 1892* | 1893* | Arundel | 1893 |
| Wright, George | 1910 | 1912 | (M) St Cuthbert | 1920 |
| Wright, Henry Enoch (SPG) | 1891 | 1892 | (L) St Stephen | 1898 |
| Wright, John van Nostrand | 1969* | 1969* | cu (M) St Jaˢ Apostle | 1969 |
| Wright, William | 1864* | 1871* | cu (M) St Jaˢ Apostle | 1864 |
| Wurtele, Louis Campbell (SPG) | 1859 | 1861 | Upton | 1866 |
| Xavier, Joseph Francis | | | Bishop's Miss˃ | 1986 |
| Yates, Nelson Peter | 1886 | 1887* | Franklin | 1886 |
| Yarrow, David Alexander | 1975 | 1976 | Chomedy-Bordeaux | 1978 |
| Yarrow, Pamela A. | 1988* | 1989* | asst cu St Lambert | 1988 |
| Young, Thomas Ainslie (SPG) | 1848† | 1849† | St Martin | 1848 |

# ANGLICAN CHURCHES

Founded within the Diocese of Montreal

Bold type indicates churches or parishes still listed in diocesan statistical reports as of 2000.

Italic type indicates churches or parishes no longer active or transferred to another diocese by 2000.

*Note: the location and fate of some church buildings, especially in the city of Montreal, cannot now be determined. The following list, therefore, has some unavoidable gaps.*

| Location of Church/Parish | Name of Parish or Congregation | Year established | Remarks |
|---|---|---|---|
| Abbotsford | **St Paul's** | 1822 | |
| Abercorn | **All Saints** | 1861 | |
| Adamsville | *St George's* | 1876 | deconsecrated 1940 |
| Ahunsic | *St Andrew's* | 1887 | deconsecrated 1970 |
| Alleyne | *St James* | 1863 | to Dio of Ottawa 1965 |
| Arntfield | | 1935 | to Moosonee 1947 |
| Arona Park | see St Basil's, Montreal | | |
| Arundel | **Grace Church** | 1873 | |
| Avoca | *St Mary's* | 1901 | deconsecrated 1968 |
| Aylmer | *Christ Church* | 1843 | to Dio of Ottawa 1965 |
| Aylwin | *St John-in-the-Wilderness* | | to Dio of Ottawa 1965 |
| Back River | see Ahunsic | | |
| Beaconsfield | **St Mary's** | 1955 | |
| Beauharnois | *Trinity Church* | 1895 | closed 1979 |
| Beaurepaire | **Christ Church** | 1924 | |
| Bedford | **St James'** | 1832 | |
| Berthier-en-Haut | *St James'* | 1823 | deconsecrated 1954 |
| Bolton Centre | **St Patrick's** | 1869 | |
| Bolton East | *The Atonement* | 1865 | became propery of RC Church by 1937 |
| Bolton Glen | **St Michael and All Angels** | 1892 | |

| | | | |
|---|---|---|---|
| Bolton Pass | *St Andrew's* | 1891 | closed 1993 |
| Bondville | *Good Shepherd* | 1885 | deconsecrated 1969 |
| Bordeaux | **St Bartholomew's** | 1915 | |
| Boscobel | *St John the Divine* | 1863 | deconsecrated 1950 |
| Bristol Corners | *St Thomas'* | 1871 | to Dio of Ottawa 1965 |
| Bristol Mines | *St Barnabas'* | | to Dio of Ottawa 1965 |
| Brome Village | **St John's** | 1859 | |
| Brome West | see West Brome | | |
| Bromont | **St John's** | 1821 | |
| Brookline | *St Aiden's* | 1929 | deconsecrated 1969 |
| Brossard | **St Joseph of** | | |
| | **Nazareth** | 1962 | |
| Brownsburg | *St George's* | 1911 | deconsecrated 1986 |
| Bryson | *St James the Lesser* | 1887 | to Dio of Ottawa 1965 |
| Buckingham | *St Stephen's* | 1845 | to Dio of Ottawa 1965 |
| Caldwell | *St Luke's* | 1886 | to Dio of Ottawa 1965 |
| Caldwell's Manor | see Noyan | | |
| Calumet | **Holy Trinity** | 1886 | |
| Campbell's Bay | *St George's* | 1902 | to Dio of Ottawa 1965 |
| Cartierville | **The Good Shepherd** | 1923 | |
| Cascades | | | to Dio of Ottawa 1965 |
| Cawood | *St Peter's* | | to Dio of Ottawa 1965 |
| Cedars | *(Fraser & Brace* | | |
| | *clubhouse)* | 1891 | closed 1958 |
| Chambly | **St Stephen's** | 1820 | |
| Charteris | *St Matthew's* | 1864 | to Dio of Ottawa 1965 |
| Chateauguay | **St George's** | 1924 | |
| Chelsea | *St Mary Magdalene* | 1876 | to Dio of Ottawa 1965 |
| Chomedy Laval | **St Simon's** | 1961 | |
| Christie's Manor | see Clarenceville | | |
| Christieville | see Sabrevois & Iberville | | |
| Clarendon | see Shawville | | |
| Clarenceville | **St George's** | 1815 | |
| Clarke's | *St John the Evangelist* | 1867 | to Dio of Ottawa 1965 |
| Como | **St Mary's** | 1866 | |
| Coteau du Lac | *St Lawrence* | 1827 | deconsecrated 1959 |
| Coteau Landing | see Coteau du Lac | | |
| Coteau Station | *St Aiden* | 1874 | sold 1946 |
| Cowansville | **Trinity** | 1854 | |
| Croyden | see St Margaret, | | |
| | St-Hubert | | |
| Danford Lake | *Holy Trinity* | 1887 | to Dio of Ottawa 1965 |
| Delson | **St David's** | 1922 | |
| Deux-Montagnes | see Two Mountains | | |
| De Ramsey | **All Saints** | 1825 | |
| Dorval | **St Andrew's** | 1898 | becomes St Andrew's |
| | | | & St Mark's in 1969 |

| Dunany | **St Paul's** | 1840 | |
| Dunham | **All Saints** | 1808 | |
| Duvernay Anglican Mission | | c.1961 | inactive after 1968 |
| Eardley | *St Luke* | 1845 | to Dio of Ottawa 1965 |
| East Farnham | *St Augustine's* | 1874 | deconsecrated 1984 |
| East Greenfield | see St Stephen's, St-Hubert | | |
| Eastman | *St John's* | 1888 | deconsecrated 1967 |
| Echo Lake | *The Redeemer* | 1921 | dismantled c.1970 and destroyed c.1971 |
| Edwardstown | **St Matthew's** | 1847 | |
| Farmborough | | c.1937 | to Moosonee 1947 |
| Farnham | **St James's** | 1847 | |
| Flats, The | see Lacolle | | |
| Foster | **St James'/ Bishop Carmichael Memorial** | 1910 | |
| Franklin Centre | *Christ Church* | 1847 | sold 1948 |
| Frelighsburg | **Holy Trinity / Bishop Stewart Memorial** | 1807 | |
| Frost Village | *Christ Church* | 1821 | sold 1979 |
| Fulford | *St Stephen's* | 1862 | sold 1971 |
| Gatineau | *St George's* | 1929 | to Dio of Ottawa 1965 |
| Gatineau Mills | see Gatineau | | |
| Glen, The | *St John the Divine* | 1900 | deconsecrated 1986 |
| Glen Almond | *St John's* | 1856 | to Dio of Ottawa 1965 |
| Glen of Harrington | see The Glen | | |
| Glen Sutton | *Good Shepherd* | 1831 | deconsecrated 1999 |
| Gore, The | see Lachute | | |
| Granby | **St George's** | 1843 | |
| Greenfield Park | **St Paul's** | 1910 | |
| Greermount | *St Stephen's* | 1864 | to Dio of Ottawa 1965 |
| Grenville | **St Matthew's** | 1831 | |
| Griffintown | see St Ann's Chapel, St Stephen & St Edward, Montreal | | |
| Hallerton | *St John the Baptist* | 1860 | sold 1964 |
| Hampstead | **St Matthew's** | 1911 | |
| Havelock | **Trinity** | 1856 | |
| Hemmingford | **St Luke's** | 1855 | |
| Henryville | *St Mark's* | 1843 | sold 1891 |
| Herdman | *St Paul's* | 1841 | |
| Hinchinbrooke | *St Paul's* | 1842 | |
| Hudson Heights | see Vaudreuil | | |
| Hull | *St James* | 1823 | to Dio of Ottawa 1965 |

| Huntingdon | **St John's** | 1842 | |
| Iberville | *Trinity* | 1841 | sold 1996 |
| Iron Hill | **Holy Trinity** | 1864 | |
| Joseph's Farm | *St Barnabas'* | 1936 | to Dio of Ottawa 1965 |
| Kazabazua | *St Stephen's* | 1892 | to Dio of Ottawa 1965 |
| Kildare | *St John's* | 1820 | closed c.1953 and rededicated 1960 |
| Kilkenny | **St John the Baptist** | 1840 | |
| Kilmar | *(mission)* | 1943 | last service 1960 |
| Kirkland | see Beaconsfield | | |
| Kirk's Ferry | *(Union Church)* | 1898 | claimed by UCC 1928 |
| Knowlton | **St Paul's** | 1842 | |
| Knowltonville | see Knowlton | | |
| L'Acadie | **Grace Church** | 1830 | |
| Lac Echo | see Echo Lake | | |
| Lachine | **St Paul's** | 1874 | |
| Lachine | **St Stephen's** | 1822 | |
| Lachute | **St Simeon's** | 1878 | |
| Lacolle | *St Saviour's* | 1838 | sold 1979 |
| La Corme | *(erected by Letters Patent)* | 1822 | congregation moved to New Glasgow |
| Lafleche | *St Andrew's* | 1961 | |
| Lakefield | **Holy Trinity** | 1820 | |
| Lakeside Heights | **St Augustine's** | 1954 | |
| La Prairie | *St Luke's* | c. 1830 | sold 1893 |
| Lasalle | **St Lawrence** | 1961 | |
| Lascelles | *Holy Trinity* | 1865 | to Dio of Ottawa 1965 |
| Laurel | **The Good Shepherd** | 1895 | |
| Laval West | *St George's* | 1930 | deconsecrated 1972 |
| Leslie | *St James'* | 1864 | to Dio of Ottawa 1965 |
| Lochaber | see Silver Creek | | |
| Longue Pointe | *St Chad's* | 1918 | deconsecrated 1972 |
| Longueuil | **St Mark's** | 1842 | |
| Louisa | **St Aiden's** | 1895 | |
| Lower Eardley | *St Augustine of Canterbury* | 1874 | to Dio of Ottawa 1965 |
| Maniwaki | *Christ Church* | 1884 | to Dio of Ottawa 1965 |
| Mansonville | **St Paul's** | 1856 | |
| Mascouche | *Grace Church* | 1840 | |
| Mascouche Heights | **St Margaret's** | 1945 | |
| Masham | see Lascelles | | |
| Mille Isles | **Christ Church** | 1861 | |
| Milton | *St Mark's* | 1851 | closed c.1918, and sold 1927 |

| | | | |
|---|---|---|---|
| Montebello | **Christ Church** | 1935 | |
| Montreal | see also Ahunsic, Bordeaux,Chomedy, Hampstead,Westmount, Verdun, &c. | | |
| Montreal | *All Saints* | 1889 | closed 1944 |
| Montreal | **Christ Church** | 1760 | Cathedral status 1850 |
| Montreal | *Church of the Ascension* | 1894 | sold 1991; becomes a municipal library |
| Montreal | *Church of the Redeemer* | 1870 | sold 1984; becomes 7th Day Adventist |
| Montreal | **Église de la Nativité** | 1973 | |
| Montreal | **Église du Rédempteur** | 1876 | new building of 1912 deconsecrated 1971 |
| Montreal | *Emmanuel Chapel* | 1902 | Hebrew Congregation of Christ; sold 1946 |
| Montreal | **Grace Church** | 1871 | |
| Montreal | **St Aiden's** | 1910 | in 1984 congregation merged with Re- deemer |
| Montreal | *St Alban's / Bishop Carmichael Memorial* | 1894 | burnt 1962 |
| Montreal | *St Ann's Chapel, see St Edward's, Mtl* | | |
| Montreal | *St Bartholomew's Reformed* | 1877 | closed c.1910 |
| Montreal | *St Basil's Mission / Marguerite Lindsay Memorial* | 1923 | closed 1937 |
| Montreal | **St Columba's** | 1907 | |
| Montreal | *St Cuthbert's* | 1910 | closed 1991 |
| Montreal | *St Cyprian's* | 1897 | closed 1986; becomes Église de Dieu |
| Montreal | *St Edward (first St Ann's, then St Stephen's)* | 1834 | closed 1950; demolished |
| Montreal | **St George's** | 1842 | |
| Montreal | **St Hilda's** | 1907 | in 1995 merges as St Cuthbert, St Hilda & St Luke's parish |
| Montreal | **St Ignatius'** | 1921 | |
| Montreal | **St James the Apostle** | 1864 | |
| Montreal | **St John the Evangelist** | 1861 | |
| Montreal | *St Jude's* | 1870 | closed 1969; becomes Pentecostal church |
| Montreal | *St Luke's* | 1854 | sold 1924; becomes Orthodox cathedral |

| Montreal | St Martin's | 1874 | closed 1954; demolished |
|---|---|---|---|
| Montreal | St Mary's Hochelaga | 1828 | expropriated and demolished 1890 sold 1947; parish disbanded 1970 |
| Montreal | **St Paul's,** Côte-des-Neiges | 1932 | |
| Montreal | **St Peter's,** Mount Royal | 1921 | |
| Montreal | **St Saviour's** | 1928 | |
| Montreal | St Stephen's, see St Edward's | | |
| Montreal | St Simon's | 1892 | closed 1950; demolished |
| Montreal | **St Thomas,** NDG. | 1841 | of 4 churches, 1st burnt 1852; 2nd sold 1906; 3rd becomes École de danse |
| Montreal | Trinity | 1840 | 3 separate buildings |
| Montreal | **Trinity Memorial** | 1919 | comprising old Trinity and Good Shepherd |
| Montreal North | see St Ignatius, Mtl | | |
| Montreal South | St Oswald's | 1908 | closed 1980 |
| Montreal West | **St Philip's** | 1891 | |
| Morehead | St John the Evangelist | 1864 | to Dio of Ottawa 1965 |
| Morin Heights | **Trinity** | 1861 | |
| Mystic | St George's | 1881 | deconsecrated 1946 |
| Napierville | see Lacolle | | |
| Nelsonville | see Cowansville | | |
| New Glasgow | **St John's** | 1837 | |
| Noranda | All Saints | 1925 | to Moosonee 1947 |
| North Clarendon | St Matthew's | 1902 | to Dio of Ottawa 1965 |
| North Ely | All Saints | 1863 | |
| North Gore | see Lakefield | | |
| North Onslow | St Matthew's | 1888 | to Dio of Ottawa 1965 |
| North Shefford | St Peter's | 1883 | closed c.1968 |
| Notre-Dame-de-Grâce | see St Thomas, Mtl | | |
| Noyan | **St Thomas'** | 1817 | |
| North Onslow | St Matthew's | 1888 | to Dio of Ottawa 1965 |
| Odanak | **St Francis Mission** | 1862 | |
| Ormstown | **St James'** | 1831 | |
| Otterburn Park | **St Martin's** | 1958 | |
| Otter Lake | St James' | 1864 | to Dio of Ottawa 1965 |
| Papineauville | St Stephen's | 1874 | deconsecrated 1973 |

| | | | |
|---|---|---|---|
| Park Extension | see St Cuthbert's, Mtl | | |
| Parkman | *St Alban's* | 1896 | to Dio of Ottawa 1965 |
| Philipsburg | **St Paul's** | 1811 | |
| Pierrefonds | **St Barnabas'** | 1958 | |
| Pierrefonds | **St Michael & All Angels** | 1961 | |
| Pierreville | see Odanak | | |
| Pigeon Hill | **St James the Less** | 1859 | |
| Plage Laval | see Laval West | | |
| Pointe Claire | **St John the Baptist** | 1923 | |
| Pointe St-Charles | see Grace Church, Mtl | | |
| Poltimore | *Christ Church* | 1869 | to Dio of Ottawa 1965 |
| Portage du Fort | *St George's* | 1856 | to Dio of Ottawa 1965 |
| Portland | see Poltimore | | |
| Potton | see Mansonville | | |
| Quyon | *St John the Evangelist* | 1856 | to Dio of Ottawa 1965 |
| Rawdon | **Christ Church** | 1820 | |
| Radford | *Holy Trinity* | 1900 | to Dio of Ottawa 1965 |
| River Desert | *Christ Church* | 1884 | to Dio of Ottawa 1965 |
| Rockway | **St George's** | 1912 | |
| Rosemere | **St James'** | 1953 | |
| Rosemount | *St Augustine's* | 1906 | became St Luke, 1927 |
| Rosemount | *St Luke's* | 1927 | closed 1995, merged with St Hilda's, Mtl |
| Rougemont | **St Thomas'** | 1840 | |
| Rouyn | *St Bede's* | c.1924 | to Moosonee 1947 |
| Roxboro | see Pierrefonds, St Barnabas | | |
| Roxham | *St John's* | 1855 | last service 1958 |
| Russeltown Flats | *Christ Church* | 1841 | |
| Sabrevois | **The Messiah** | 1848 | |
| Ste-Agathe-des-Monts | **Trinity** | 1899 | |
| St Amadée | *St John's* | 1874 | deconsecrated 1968 |
| St Andrew's | see St Andrew's East | | |
| St Andrew's East | *Christ Church* | 1812 | closed 1999 |
| Ste-Anne-de-Bellevue | **St George's** | 1893 | |
| St Armand East | see Frelighsburg | | |
| St Armand West | see Philipsburg | | |
| St Bruno | **Trinity** | 1958 | |
| St-Eustache | see Two Mountains | | |
| St Francis Indian Village | see Odanak | | |
| St-Hubert (Croyden) | **St Margaret of Antioch** | 1910 | |

| | | | |
|---|---|---|---|
| St Hubert (E. Greenfield) | *St Stephen's* | 1918 | deconsecrated 1988 |
| St-Hubert (Springfield Pk) | *St Saviour's* | 1915 | sold 1974 |
| St Hyacinthe | *Christ Church* | 1849 | sold c. 1972 |
| St-Jean-sur-Richelieu | **St James'** | 1816 | |
| St Johns | see St-Jean-sur-Richelieu | | |
| St-Lambert | **St Barnabas'** | 1877 | |
| St-Laurent | **St Mark's** | 1924 | |
| St-Luc | *St John's* | 1871 | sold and moved 1998 |
| Ste-Marguerite | *St Christopher's* | 1961 | sold 1985 |
| St Martin | *St Stephen's* | c.1841 | last service 1863 |
| St Remi | **St George's** | c.1843 | expropriated 1979 |
| St-Sauveur-des-Monts | **St Francis of the Birds** | 1951 | |
| Savanne | see St-Luc | | |
| Shawville | *St Paul's* | 1841 | to Dio of Ottawa 1965 |
| Shefford | *St John's* | 1821 | |
| Sherrington | *St James the Apostle* | 1843 | in ruins, sold 1905 |
| Shephard's Mill | see Abercorn | | |
| Shrewsbury | **St John's** | 1820 | |
| Silver Creek | *St Thomas'* | 1845 | to Dio of Ottawa 1965 |
| Sorel | **Christ Church** | 1784 | |
| South Bolton | **Holy Trinity** | 1860 | |
| South Roxton | *St Philip's* | c.1889 | closed 1967 |
| South Stukely | *St Matthew's* | 1850 | deconsecrated 1972 |
| Springfield Park | see St-Hubert. St Saviour | | |
| Stanbridge East | **St James the Apostle** | 1829 | |
| Stanbury | **St John the Evangelist** | 1898 | |
| Strathmore | *St Andrew's* | 1955 | closed 1972 |
| Sutton | **Grace Church** | 1846 | |
| Sutton Junction | **St Aiden's** | 1908 | |
| Sweetsburg | *Christ Church* | 1854 | rented out after 1964 |
| Temiskaming | *Holy Trinity* | 1920 | to Algoma in 1947 |
| Terrebonne | *St Michael's* | 1840 | deconsecrated 1980 |
| Terrebonne Heights | see Mascouche Heights | | |
| Tetreaultville | **St Margaret of Scotland** | 1907 | |
| Thorne Centre | *St George's* | 1864 | to Dio of Ottawa 1965 |
| Town of Mount Royal | see St Peter's, Mount Royal | | |
| Two Mountains | **All Saints** | 1945 | |

| | | | |
|---|---|---|---|
| Upper Eardley | *St Luke's* | | to Dio of Ottawa 1965 |
| Upton | *Christ Church* | 1864 | closed 1940s; graves moved to Acton Vale |
| | | | |
| Vale Perkins | *(chapel)* | | |
| Valleyfield | **St Mark's** | 1894 | |
| Valois | **The Resurrection** | 1924 | |
| Vaudreuil | **St James'** | 1841 | |
| Verdun | **All Saints** | 1949 | |
| Verdun | **St Clement's/Belcher Memorial** | 1897 | |
| Verdun | **St John the Divine** | 1929 | |
| Ville Emard | see Montreal, St Aiden | | |
| Villeray | *St Peter's* | 1911 | discontinued 1921 |
| Wakefield | *Good Shepherd* | 1865 | to Dio of Ottawa 1965 |
| Warden | *St John the Divine* | 1883 | deconsecrated 1993 |
| Waterloo | **St Luke's** | 1821 | |
| Weir | **The Redeemer** | 1908 | |
| West Brome | **Ascension** | 1864 | |
| Westmount | **The Advent** | 1890 | |
| Westmount | *Good Shepherd* | 1909 | absorbed into Trinity Memorial in 1920 |
| Westmount | **St Matthias** | 1873 | |
| Westmount | **St Stephen's** | 1900 | |
| West Shefford | see Bromont | | |
| Wexford | *St George's* | 1820 | expropriated 1980 |
| William Henry | see Sorel | | |
| Wright | *St James'* | 1882 | to Dio of Ottawa 1965 |
| Yamaska Mountain | see Abbotsford | | |

# SOURCES

## Preface and Introduction

J. Douglas Borthwick, *History of the Diocese of Montreal 1850–1910* (Montreal: John Lovell & Son Limited 1910), v; John Irwin Cooper, *The Blessed Communion: The Origins and History of the Diocese of Montreal 1760–1960* ([Montreal:] Archives Committee of the Diocese of Montreal 1960), iv 129–30; Thomas R. Millman, *A Short History of the Parish of Dunham* (Granby, QC: Granby Printing and Publishing Co. 1946); E.C. Royle, *An Historical Study of the Anglican Parish of Vaudreuil* (Hudson Heights, QC: n.pub. 1952); John Wilfred Netten, *The Anglican Church: Its Influence on the Development of Education in the Province of Quebec from 1760–1900*, Masters Thesis in Education, Bishop's University, 1965; Robert Merrill Black, *A Crippled Crusade: Anglican Missions to French-Canadian Roman Catholics in Lower Canada*, Doctoral Thesis in Theology, University of Toronto, 1989; Joan Marshall, *A Solitary Pillar: Montreal's Anglican Church and the Quiet Revolution* (Montreal & Kingston: McGill-Queen's University Press 1995); E[dward] H[allett] Carr, *What Is History?* (Harmondsworth, Middlesex: Penguin Books Ltd 1964), 12; H.R.S. Ryan, "The General Synod of the Anglican Church of Canada: Aspects of Constitutional History," *Journal of the Canadian Church Historical Society*, Vol. XXXIV no. 1 (Apr. 1992), 7, 25, 36–7; Oswald Howard, *The Montreal Diocesan Theological College: A History From 1873 to 1963* (Montreal: McGill University Press 1963), 7–8; M.E. Reisner, *Strangers and Pilgrims: A History of the Anglican Diocese of Quebec 1793–1993* (Toronto: Anglican Book Centre 1995), 77–9, 107, 150; John Irwin Cooper, *Montreal: A Brief History* (Montreal and London: McGill-Queen's University Press 1969), 94–5; Holly Ratcliffe, "Race Relations Committee," *Proceedings of the 135th Annual Synod of the Diocese of Montreal*, 1994, 87; "Hearing from the Dioceses: Report," ([Toronto: National Church Consultation 1998]), 2, 6, 9–10; Anthony Wilson-Smith, "Stopping the Bleeding," *McLeans*, 29 Nov. 1999, 68; *The Anglican Year Book* (1960), 99; Ibid, (1985), 51; *The Anglican Directory* (Toronto: Anglican Book Centre 2001), 84.

## Beginnings: 1760-1792

**1760: Chaplain to the Forces:** H.C. Stuart, *The Church of England in Canada, 1759-1793* (Montreal: John Lovell & Son 1893), 22, 23; *Classified Digest of the Records of the Society for the Propagation of the Gospel in Foreign Parts 1701–1892 (With Much Supplementary Information)*, C.F. Pascoe, ed., (London: Published at the Society Office 1893),136–7; A.R. Kelley, *The Church of England in Quebec 1759–1791: A Compendium of Church and State Papers* (Quebec: 1937), 7–8; Thomas R. Millman, "John Ogilvie," *Dictionary of Canadian Biography* (hereafter *DCB*), 13 vols (Toronto and Buffalo: University of Toronto Press 1966–), IV, 586.

1765: "What Footing Religion Is to Be Upon": Lambeth Palace Archives (hereafter LPA), SPG Papers II, ff 28-9, copy of a letter: Des Vœux to Pechell, 6 Apr., 1765; *A Sermon Preached Before the Incorporated Society for the Propagation of the Gospel in Foreign Parts, ... on Friday, February 20, 1767 By ... John Lord Bishop of Landaff* (London: 1767); James H. Lambert, "David Chabrand Delisle," *DCB*, IV, 138.

1768: "Peculiar Situations and Circumstances": LPA, Fulham Papers, I, ff 163–6.

1771: The First Appointment by the Crown: Kelley, *The Church of England in Quebec*, 18-19; Lambert, "David Chabrand Delisle," 138-9; Robin W. Winks, *The Blacks in Canada: A History*, 2nd ed. (Montreal & Kingston: McGill-Queens University Press 1997), 24; Daniel G. Hill, *The Freedom-Seekers: Blacks in Early Canada*, (Agincourt, ON: The Book Society of Canada Limited 1981), 9, 127; Pascoe, *Classified Digest*, 140; Brian Cuthbertson, *The First Bishop: A Biography of Charles Inglis* (Halifax, N.S.: Waegwoltic Press 1987), 11; letter of John Doty to Frederick Haldimand, 15 Sept. 1784, quoted in Walter S. White, *Governor's Cottage*, (Sorel, QC: Le Sorelois Ltée [1967]), 52; Frank Dawson Adams, *A History of Christ Church Cathedral, Montreal* (Montreal: Burton's Limited 1941), 18.

1788: Fruits of Patronage and Power: Adams, *A History of Christ Church Cathedral*, 33, 39-40; Thomas R. Millman, "David Chabrand Delisle, 1730–1794," parts I and II, *Montreal Churchman*, Vol. XXIX no. 2 (Feb. 1941), 14–15, and Ibid (Mar. 1941), 14–16; A.H. Young, "More Langhorn Letters," *Papers and Records*, Ontario Historical Society, Vol. XXIX, 1933, 4; LPA, Moore Papers, Foreign I, Jacob Mountain to Moore, 13 June 1803; Lambert, "David Chabrand Delisle," 138–40.

1789: The First Visitation: "Bishop of Nova Scotia's Minutes of Voyage to Quebec," in Kelley, *The Church of England in Quebec*, 47; General Synod Archives (hereafter GSA), Charles Inglis Papers, Mf 66–5, reel C-6, 1, "Bishop of Nova Scotia's Minutes of Voyage to Quebec"; Lucien Lemieux, "Etienne Montgolfier," *DCB*, IV, 542–5.

1792: Petitioners to Government: Montreal Diocesan Archives (hereafter MDA), Charles Inglis Papers, RG 1.2; Royal Letters Patent quoted in Adams, *A History of Christ Church Cathedral*, 176–86; Louis Rosenberg, *Chronology of Canadian Jewish History*, (n.pl.: National Bicentenary Committee of the Canadian Jewish Congress [1959]).

## An Episcopate for the Canadas: 1793-1835

1794: Jacob Mountain on the Road to Montreal: "From Quebec to Niagara in 1794: Diary of Bishop Jacob Mountain," *Rapport de L'Archiviste de la Province de Québec pour 1959–1960*, 129–35.

1796: Murder Will Out? MDA, Charles Abrahall, *A History of [the] Diocese of Montreal: 1850-1908*, (hand-written in two volumes, completed 1931) I, 96–7, 105–7; "Our Parishes and Churches, No. 11, Christ Church, Sorel (conclusion)" *The Canadian Church Magazine and Mission News*, Vol. I no. 15 (Sept. 1887), 358; White, *Governors Cottage*, 77–8. The belief that the wounds of a murdered person would bleed on being touched by the murderer persisted well into the 20th century, see *A Dictionary of Superstitions*, Iona Opie and Moira Tatum, eds (Oxford and New York: Oxford University Press 1989), 270.

**1809: Rural Psalmody**: Quebec Diocesan Archives (hereafter QDA), Unbound MSS, Index 123, Case T, folder 3: Jacob Mountain Letters 1802–25 (Private and Personal).

**1811: The Plight of a Bachelor Clergyman**: Missisquoi Historical Society Archives (hereafter MHSA), Stanbridge East, QC, V-449-3-13, typscript copies of letters from C.C. Cotton to his family in England: letter of 24 Sept. 1811 Cotton to his sister Fanny; Ibid, letter of 20 July 1814, Cotton to his sister Anna; Millman, *A Short History of Dunham*, 8–11, 18; Thomas R. Millman, "Charles Caleb Cotton," *DCB*, VII, 229–30.

**1814: Family Prayers**: Thomas R. Millman, "The Earliest Collection of Prayers Printed in the Canadas For the Use of Members of the Church of England," *Montreal Churchman*, Vol. XXXI, no. 10 (Oct. 1843), 10–11; QDA, Stewart Letters — Reid Collection. Vol. I, Stewart to James Reid, 29 July 1815; Charles James Stewart, *Two Sermons on Family Prayer, With Extracts From Various Authors [a]nd a Collection of Prayers ...* (Montreal: Nahum Mower 1814), 191–2, 337, 368–370; letters of 1 May 1813 and 1 Nov. 1813, in Thomas R. Millman, *The Life of the Right Reverend, the Honourable Charles James Stewart* (London, ON: Huron College 1953), 24–6.

**1817: Montreal Through American Eyes:** Joseph Sansom, *Travels in Lower Canada, with the Author's Recollection of the Soil, and Aspect; the Morals, Habits, and Religious Institutions of That Country* (London: 1820), iii, 21, 72–3.

**1819: Dreams of Establishment**: C.J. Stewart's Report appears in *A Sermon Preached Before the Incorporated Society for the Propagation of the Gospel in Foreign Parts ... Together with the Report of the Society for the Year 1819* (London: 1820), 132-3; MDA, Fulford Papers, Francis Fulford, *A Charge Delivered to the Clergy of the Diocese of Montreal, on the 20th January, 1852, at The Primary Visitation, Held in The Cathedral Church of Montreal* (Montreal: John Lovell 1852), 3.

**1820: Disciplinary Measures**: MDA, G.J. Mountain Papers, Resolution contained in letter from Micajah Townsend to Jacob Mountain, 7 Nov. 1815; letter from Micajah Townsend to Jacob Mountain, 22 Sept. 1820; letter from Micajah Townsend to G.J. Mountain, 29 Dec. 1820.

**1829: The Archdeacon Reports**: QDA, "E[astern] T[ownships] Visitation, G.J. Mountain," 124, Case II, folder 13 pp. 29–37; Millman, *The Life of ... Stewart*, 81; Armine W. Mountain, *A Memoir of George Jehoshaphat Mountain* (Montreal: John Lovell 1866), 132.

## A Bishop of Montreal: 1836-1850

**1836: Clergy Conditions:** *A Sermon Preached Before the Incorporated Society for the Propagation of the Gospel in Foreign Parts ... Together with the Report of the Society for 1836* (London: printed for the Society 1836), 125–6, 127, 128; Pascoe, *Two Hundred Years of the SPG*, 146–7.

**1836: Proto-Synod**: George Merchant, *History of St. Stephen's Anglican Church, Lachine, Quebec, Canada: 1822–1956*, rev. ed. ([n.pl.: n.pub, n.d.]), 128; [Thomas Brock Fuller,] *Thoughts on the Present State and Future Prospects of the Church of*

*England in Canada with Some Hints in Her Ecclesiastical Arrangements* (n.pl.: n.pub 1836), 4, 6, 10–11, 14–15, 16; *Summary Account of the Society for the Propagation of the Gospel in Foreign Parts Corrected to October 1847* (London: [1847]), 4–5; Millman, *The Life of ... Stewart*, 21, 122–3; 164. 165–6, 200; Owsley Robert Rowley, *The Anglican Episcopate of Canada and Newfoundland* (London: A.R. Mowbray & Co. 1928), 65.

**1837: Rebellion**: A.R.M. Lower, *Colony to Nation*, 4th ed. (Don Mills, ON: Longman Canada Limited 1964), 228–9; Donald C. Masters, *A Short History of Canada*, (Princeton, NJ: D. Van Nostrand Company, Inc. 1958), 24–5; J. Douglas Borthwick, *History of the Montreal Prison*, (Montreal: A. Periard, 1886), 23; Elinor Kyte Senior, *Redcoats and Patriotes: The Rebellions in Lower Canada 1837–38*, Canadian War Museum Historical Publication No. 20, (Stittsville, ON: Canada's Wings Inc 1985), 31, 36-7, 88, 108; Charles O. Jones, "The Moore's Corner Battle in 1837," *Fourth Annual Report of the Missisquoi County Historical Society for 1908–1909* (St. Johns, QC: News Typ. [1909]), 67–73; George H. Montgomery, *Missisquoi Bay (Philipsburg, Que.)* (Granby, QC: Granby Printing and Publishing Co. Ltd. 1950), 106–109; William Henry Atherton, *Montreal Under British Rule, 1730–1914*, II, (Montreal: The S.J. Clarke Publishing Company 1914), 150–3 and 157; *Report of the Incorporated Society for the Propagation of the Gospel in Foreign Parts for 1838* (London: W. Clowes & Sons, 1838), 117, 120, 130–1, 138; John Beswick Thompson, "Wolfred Nelson," *DCB*, IX, 593–7.

**1840: Coping with Scandal**: "Injunctions Given to the Clergy of the Province of Quebec at the Primary Visitation Holden in the City of Quebec, by the Right Reverend Charles, by Divine Permission Bishop of Nova Scotia," reproduced in Stuart, *The Church of England in Canada*, 73-4; Philip Carrington, *The Anglican Church in Canada: A History* (Toronto: Collins 1963), 50; Kelley, *The Church of England in Quebec*, 37; QDA Unbound Manuscripts, Reid-G.J. Mountain papers, originals, Case 2, folder 10, G.J Mountain to James Reid, 6 Nov. 1849; the same to the same, 1 Dec. 1840; Reid to Mountain, 31 Dec. 1840; Mountain to Reid, 3 Jan. 184[1]; the same to the same, 7 and 8 Jan. 1841; Reid to Mountain, 14 Jan. 1841; QDA, Diocesan Papers, Series B, Vol 2, Bedford, 98, endorsed "Rev. E. Burke's case, Rev. George Mackie, 31 Oct. 1840; *Report of the Incorporated Society for the Propagation of the Gospel in Foreign Parts for 1838* (London: W. Clowes & Sons 1838), 137; Archives nationales du Québec à Montréal (hereafter ANQ-M): Court Records: Court of King's Bench, April Term 1841, No. 155, William F. Stinehour Plff vs the Revd Robert P. Balfe; *St. James Church, Bedford, Quebec: One Hundred and Fortieth Anniversary (1832–1972)*, typescript, 1972, [2, 4]; Paige Knight, "Bedford Church Is One of the Oldest in the Area," *The Record* (Sherbrooke, QC), 18 Oct. 1990, 10.

**1842: Involving the Laity**: "Constitution of the Church Society of the Diocese of Quebec, adopted at a General Meeting of the Society, duly convened at Montreal, on 21st July, 1842" and "By-Laws of the Corporation of the Church Society of the Diocese of Quebec, adopted at a General Meeting of the Society, duly convened at Quebec, on the 22nd day of October, 1844," *Second Annual Report of the Church Society of the Diocese of Quebec*, (Montreal: Lovell and Gibson 1844) 17–19; Carman Miller, "Thomas Brown Anderson," *DCB*, X, 10–11; Reisner, *Strangers and Pilgrims*, 81.

**1846: Ministry to the Marginalized**: William Henry Atherton, *Montreal 1535–1914: Under British Rule 1760–1914*, III, (Montreal, Vancouver and Chicago: The S.J. Clarke Publishing Company 1914), 478–80; Pascoe, *Classified Digest*, 872; *The Montreal Witness*, Monday, 19 Apr. 1847 (Vol. II No. 16), 124; *Report of the Incorporated Society for The Propagation of the Gospel in Foreign Parts for the year 1845, with the Anniversary Sermon: and an abstract of receipts and payments for the year ending December 31, 1844* (London: printed for the Society 1845), cxxiv; "Auberge Madeleine," *Proceedings of the 136th Annual Synod of the Diocese of Montreal, Canada* (1995), 73–4.

**1847: Typhus**: Reisner, *Strangers and Pilgrims*, 200–205; Marianna O'Gallagher and Rose Masson Dompierre, *Eyewitness Grosse Isle 1847* (Sainte-Foy, QC: Carraig Books 1995), 53, 332, 336, 340; Armine W. Mountain, *A Memoir of George Jehoshaphat Mountain*, 257; *Montreal Transcript*, Vol XII no. 22 (19 June 1847), 2; Ibid, 1 July 1847, 4; Ibid, 8 July 1847, 4, copied from *The Pilot*; Ibid, 10 July 1847, 2; Carrington, *The Anglican Church in Canada*, 104; *Montreal Witness*, Vol. II no. 27 (5 July 1847), 212; Ibid, 12 July 1847, 218; Ibid, 19 July 1847, 228; Ibid, 26 July 1847, 236. Montreal *Gazette*, 10 July 1847.

**1848: Finding Books for Sale**: Adams, *A History of Christ Church Cathedral*, 156; *Report of the Society for Promoting Christian Knowledge for 1834* (London: J.G. & F. Rivington 1834), 45, 46–7; *The Sixth Annual Report of the Incorporated Church Society of the Diocese of Quebec* (Quebec: Thomas Cary 1848), 15–16; Robert W.S. Mackay, *The Montreal Directory: New Edition, Corrected in May, 1849* (Montreal: Lovell and Gibson 1849), 268; *Report of the Church Society of the Diocese of Montreal 1852* (Montreal: John Lovell, 1852), 21; MDA, Untitled, undated typescript history of the Diocesan Book Room, incorrecly attributed to A.R. Kelley.

**1849: The Future Diocese on View**: United Society for the Propagation of the Gospel Archives (hereafter USPGA) Ernest Hawkins' Manuscript *Journal of a Tour of Canada and America*,1849; "Advertisement for Donegana's Hotel," Montreal *Gazette*, 16 June 1847.

**1849: Who Will Be Bishop?** Trinity Church (Frelighsburg) Parish Records (hereafter TCPR), James Reid's Letterbook, 66–73; transcript of Reid's letter to G.J. Mountain, 29 Oct. 1849, Ibid, 74–7; MDA, James Reid Papers, diary, Vol. 25, 4586; Rowley, *The Anglican Episcopate of Canada and Newfoundland*, 35.

**1850: A Laywoman's Initiative**: MDA, James Reid Papers, diary, Vol. 23, 4075, 4079, 4083–4, 4087, 4141; Ibid, Vol. 36, 6240-41, 6243; All Saints' Church, Dunham, parish papers, Church Warden's Accounts Jan. 1843-Oct. 1852 and Church Account Book from 21 Apr. 1822; TCPR, copy of letter from James Reid to Ernest Hawkins, 9 Jan. 1864.

### Erection and Consolidation : 1850-1868
**1850: A Country Cleric Meets His Future Bishop:** Letter from George Slack to Isabella Ann Slack, 28 May 1850; the same to the same 16 July 1850; George Slack to Harriet Slack, 26 June 1874, private collection, quoted by kind permission of Richard Moysey; MDA, James Reid Papers, diary, Vol. 23, 4043 (11 Feb. 1850); [George Slack,] *Personal Memoirs of a Canadian Missionary S.P.G. in a Personal Letter Addressed to His Children*, (Montreal: John Lovell 1859), 11-23; "Rev. George Slack, Formerly Rector of Bedford," *MCHS 5th Report*, 98-101;

Borthwick, *History of the Diocese of Montreal*, 128–30; Fennings Taylor, *The Last Three Bishops Appointed by the Crown for the Anglican Church of Canada* (Montreal: John Lovell 1869), 42-5; Richard D. Moysey, "George Slack: A Pioneer Townships Clergyman, *Journal of Eastern Townships Studies*, No 13 (Fall-Winter, 1998-1999), 59-65.

**1850: Bishop Fulford Arrives**: MDA, Fulford Papers, Private Journal, Vol. I, R.G. 2.1 II; Rowley, *The Anglican Episcopate of Canada and Newfoundland*, 17; Service Booklet for the 150th Anniversary Celebrations at St-Jean-sur-Richelieu, 11 Sept. 2000; Taylor, *The Last Three Bishops Appointed by the Crown*, 42–5; Black, *A Crippled Crusade*, 255–6; John Irwin Cooper, "Francis Fulford," *DCB*, IX, 289-93; For the salaries of the Colonial Bishops, see "A Return of the Number of Colonial Bishops, stating the Salaries of each, and the Sources whence those Salaries are derived: Ordered, by The House of Commons, to be Printed, 31 July, 1855," *Documents Relative To The Erection and Endowment of Additional Bishoprics in the Colonies, 1841–1855*, Ernest Hawkins, ed., 5th ed. (London: S.P.C.K. 1855), 60.

**1851: Power Struggles at the Outset:** USPGA: Bound Correspondence: Letters Received, Montreal 1850–1859, from George Slack, 9 Dec. 1851; MDA, Francis Fulford, *A Pastoral Letter, Addressed to the Clergy of His Diocese* (Montreal: John Lovell 1851), 8–9, 15.

**1852: Anglican Standards:** MDA, James Reid Papers, diary, Vol. 25, 4515–6; QDA, Stewart Letters, Reid Collection, I, undated letter without sender or recipient's name, but in Stewart's hand, item 64, and C.J. Stewart to James Reid, 8 May 1832, II, item 113; Reisner, *Strangers and Pilgrims*, 101–2.

**1855: The Bishop in Request:** Stephen Inwood, *A History of London* (New York: Carroll & Graf Publishers, Inc. 1998), 612; Francis Fulford, "Some Remarks on Colonial Institutions," *Five Occasional Lectures* (Montreal: John Lovell 1859), 33, 34, 35–6, 37–8, 40–1, 40; MDA, James Reid Papers, diary, Vol. 25, 4682–3 (31 Jan. 1854).

**1858: A Ministry to Native People**: Robert L. Howard, "Why the Anglicans of Odenak Commemorate a Congregational Minister," undated typescript, 1-2, MDA, Parish papers, Odenak/Pierreville; Joseph de Mouilpied, "Report of a Visit to the Indian Village of St Francis," transcript of *Sixth Report of the Colonial Church and School Society for the Diocese of Montreal*, 1859, *loc. cit.*; [H.L. Masta] Address to the Right Reverend Lord Bishop of Montreal by the Abenaki Indians of St Francis, 29 Sept. 1883, 3-page MS, 2, *loc. cit.*; "Dedication of the Memorial for the Reverend Peter Paul Wzokhilain [Service Bulletin]," 5 Sept. 1982, *loc. cit.*; R[obert] C[enter] B[rewer], "St. Francis Indian Mission, Pierreville, Que.," *Montreal Churchman*, Vol. IV no. 2 (Dec. 1915), 12.

**1859: Montreal's First Synod:** Ryan, "The General Synod of the Anglican Church of Canada," 25; *Proceedings of the First Meeting of the Synod of the Diocese of Montreal, Canada, June 7 & 8, 1859* (Montreal: John Lovell 1859), *passim*; *Proceedings of the Conference of the Bishop, Clergy and Laity, of the Diocese of Montreal, Held on the 16th January 1856, at the National School House* (Montreal: John Lovell 1856), 3–4, 7–9, 24, 25, 26–7; Philip Carrington, *The Anglican Church in Canada*, 119.

**1863: Isolation:** Thomas W. Fyles, "Reminiscences of Forty Years Ago," *Programme of the Jubilee Celebration of the Parish of Nelsonville* (n.pl: n.pub. n.d. [probably 1904]), 43–4; Thomas W. Fyles, *An Account of the Early Days of the Mission of Iron Hill and West Brome in the Diocese of Montreal* (Levis, QC: [n.pub.] 1907), 5–6, 8, 9, 10–12; Canada Census Returns for 1871, District No. 126: Brome, p. 47, no. 176.

**1867: Church Music**: Philip Wood Loosemore, *Church Music: A Sermon Preached in Christ Church Cathedral, Montreal, On Sunday Evening, Jan. 27th, 1867* (Montreal: John Lovell 1867), 5–24; Adams, *A History of Christ Church Cathedral*, 92–3.

### An Elective Episcopate: 1868-1895

**1868: Church Debt**: MDA, parish papers: Abercorn, "Proceedings of the Abercorn Church of England Sewing Society," and "Proceedings of the Abercorn Church Building Society"; Audrey Martin McCaw, "Abercorn: Churches Change Hands But Keep Faith," *The Record* (Sherbrooke QC), 26 July 1990.

**1869: Oxenden up the Ottawa**: Ashton Oxenden, *My First Year in Canada*, (Montreal: Dawson Brothers 1871), 17, 28–32; G[eorge] Abbott-Smith, *I Call to Mind; Recollections and Impressions of the Last Three-Quarter Century* (Toronto: GBRE [1947]), 20-1; "Canon Abbott-Smith Retires After 52 Years as Clergyman," *Montreal Daily Star*, 30 Mar. 1939, 1; Borthwick, *History of the Diocese of Montreal*, 109–110; MDA, Clarendon Deanery Papers, Transfer Papers, Memorandum: Deanery of Clarendon, 1964.

**1870: Setting the Tone at Synod:** *Proceedings of the Eleventh Synod of the Diocese of Montreal* (1870), 10, 14, 19–20; Cooper, *The Blessed Communion*, 91; Carrington, *The Anglican Church in Canada*, 142–3; *Laus Deo 1878–1928: The Church of St John the Evangelist, Montreal* ([Montreal: 1928]), 25, 39, 42; *Centenary Book of the Parish of St. John the Evangelist, Montreal* ([Montreal: 1961]) 46; Parish papers of the Church of St John the Evangelist, Wood memorabilia; Rowley, *The Anglican Episcopate of Canada and Newfoundland*, 51.

**1875: Some Founding Mothers**: "In Memoriam: Laura Mudge," *Montreal Churchman*, Vol. XV no. 9 (July 1927), 3; Cooper, *The Blessed Communion*, 127, 212; Fennings Taylor, *Portraits of British Americans, By W. Notman, Photographer to Her Majesty, With Biographical Sketches*, 2 vols (Montreal: William Notman 1865), 1, 19; Bill McCarthy, *The Rev: Memoirs of Montreal's Old Brewery Mission*, Janet Hughson, ed. (Montreal: Robert Davies Publishing 1996), 7–8; MDA, Fulford Residence papers; "History etc.," typescript, [1977], 2. pp.; Ibid, "History of the Church Home of Montreal: 1855–1955," typescript [1955], 4 pp., Ibid, Hazel P. Harrington, typescript report [1988], 2pp.; Ibid, "Outline of Church Home: 1855-1870, typescript, 4 pp.; Ibid, "Church Home," printed flyer, 1888, 3 pp.; Ibid, "The Church Home," printed flyer, 1890, 4 pp.; Typescript history of Fulford Residence, supplied by Laurie Kirkpatrick, unsigned and undated, but after 1998, 2 pp.; Eve McBride, "I Want to Live in Guy St.'s Fulford House When I Grow Up," Montreal *Gazette*, 23 June 1994, A2; *Fulford Residence Newsletter*, no. 16 (Spring 2001), 6; personal communication with Laurie Kirkpatrick, 31 May and 8 June 2001.

**1877: Relations with Rome**: W.L. Morton, *The Kingdom of Canada*, 2nd ed. (Montreal and Toronto: McClelland and Stewart Limited 1970), 304, 357; Lower, *Colony to Nation*, 372–4; Charles Lindsay, *Rome in Canada: The Ultramontane Struggle for Supremacy Over the Civil Authority* (Toronto: Lovell Brothers 1877),

252, 254, 255–6, 260–1, 269; Philippe Sylvain, "Ignace Bourget," *The Canadian Encyclopedia: Year 2000 Edition* (Toronto: McClelland & Stewart Inc. 1999), 286.

**1882: La communauté du Rédempteur**: MDA, papers of the Comité de la pastorale francophone: RG 301; Gérard Lavallée, *Petite Histoire de l'anglicanisme dans la société francophone de Montréal et des environs* ([Montreal:]1997), *passim*; "Observations sur le ministère dans la ville et le diocèse de Montréal," personal communication from Gérard Lavallée, 23 Feb. 1999 and probably of the same date; "Anglicans react to PQ election," *Montreal Anglican*, Vol. 120 no. 8 (Oct. 1994), 1, 6; "Un vrais Québécois," Letters to the Editor, *Montreal Anglican*, Vol. 120 no. 9 (Nov. 1994), 15.

**1885: Smallpox:** Cooper, *Montreal: A Brief History*, 89, 90–1; William Boyman Howell, *F.J. Shepherd—Surgeon: His Life and Times* (Montreal and Vancouver: J.M. Dent and Sons Ltd. 1934), 62–3; *Historical Sketch of St. Luke's Church [Montreal]* [n.pl. n.pub n.d.], 12; *Laus Deo*, 42–3; Atherton, *Montreal Under British Rule*, II, 445; MDA, Bond Papers, RG 2.3, file 18 (Service Forms) "A Special Form of Prayer …" (Montreal: 1885).

**1886: The Woman's Auxiliary**: [Emily] Willoughby Cummings, *Our Story: Some Pages from the History of the Woman's Auxiliary to the Missionary Society of the Church of England in Canada, 1885–1928* (Toronto: Garden City Press [1928]), 7–8, 17–19, 24, 51; *Report of the Meetings Held in Montreal, Sept. 9th and 10th, 1886, Called by the Provisional Committee Which Was Authorised by the Board of Missions for the Purpose of Organizing a Woman's Auxiliary for the Board of Foreign and Domestic Missions of the Church of England in Canada* (Montreal: John Lovell & Son 1886), 11–12, 20–1; 27–8; Carrington, *The Anglican Church in Canada*, 181–2; Marshall, *A Solitary Pillar*, 87, 113, 141.

**1887: Domestic Missions:** "Parishes and Churches No. 9, part 2: Lachute and Arundel," *The Canadian Church Magazine and Mission News*, June 1887, 296; Cummings, *Our Story*, 63.

**1889: The Unique Style of Bishop Bond**: MDA, Bishop Bond Papers, R.G. 2.3, folder 5; MDA, W.H. Naylor papers, M.G. 2007, Box 4: Day Book for Jan. 1889 to Dec. 1894; *Proceedings of the Special Synod of the Diocese of Montreal, Canada … For the Election of a Bishop* (Montreal: Lovell Printing and Publishing Company 1878), 91; *Laus Deo*, 40; "Obituary Record: the Rev. Canon Empson," Montreal *Gazette*, 10 Nov. 1910.

**1890: Sisters of St Margaret:** Owen Chadwick, *The Victorian Church, Part I, 1829–1859*, (London, SCM Press Ltd, 1987), 212–213, 507, 509; Cooper, *The Blessed Communion*, 203–4; *Sisters of St. Margaret: Seventy-Five Years in Montreal*, ([Montreal:] n.pub 1958), 6, 8–9, 10; *Statutes of the Province of Quebec*, 54 Vict., [1890] cap LXIV, "An Act to incorporate the Sisters of St. Margaret"; Cathedral Service Bulletin, 24 May 1981, Evensong, with historical notes; MDA, Bond Papers, RG 2.3, file 15, MS memorandum appended to printed Private Bill, "An Act to incorporate the Sisters of St. Margaret," 1–3, unsigned; Ibid, printed address to Sister Sarah, 27 Oct. 1886; Ibid, unidentified newspaper clipping tentatively dated 1893 apparently a letter to the editor of the *Montreal Star*, signed "Another Episcopalian."

**1890: Christieville**: *Trinity Church, Iberville, Quebec: Centenary Souvenir* (n.pl.: n.pub. 1941), 6, 14; "Our Parishes and Churches No 69 — Christieville," *The*

*Canadian Church Magazine and Mission News* (Toronto) Vol VI, no 70 (Apr. 1892), 82–3; Black, *A Crippled Crusade*, 77–8; *Annual Report of the Church Society of the Diocese of Montreal for 1852*, (Montreal: John Lovell 1852), 39; Gretchen Cheung, "Epiphany House," *Proceedings of the 136th Annual Synod of the Diocese of Montreal*, 1995, 77; Jim Barnett, "Epiphany House Wind Down Committee," *Proceedings of the 135th Annual Synod of the Diocese of Montreal* (1994), 81–2.

**1895: "Women's Work":** *Woman's Work in St George's Church, Montreal: 1895-96*, (Montreal: Gazette Printing Company, 1896), in MDA, Parish Papers, St George's, Montreal, file 5; Royle, *An Historical Study of the Anglican Parish of Vaudreuil*, Ch. 6, 8; Grace Church, Sutton, Sewing Society Minutes, 1855–1881, MDA, Parish Papers, Sutton; Helen E. Williams, *Three Churches*, (Knowlton, QC: St Paul's Church 1941), 24–5; *St. James Church (Anglican): 125 Years, 1823–1948*, (Hull, QC: n.pub. 1948), 30; [John B. Hall,] *Dedication of St Mark's Anglican Church — Salaberry-de-Valleyfield, QC* (n.pl.: n.pub 1963); Marshall, *A Solitary Pillar*, 100–1, 113; [Gordon Hynes] *Down Through the Years: Grace Church, Montreal* (Montreal: Corporation of Grace Church 1982), 4; TCPR, Minutebook of the Ladies' Accumulating Fund 1860-71, [p.1]; *James Reid: The Diary of a Country Clergyman, 1848–1851*, M.E. Reisner, ed., (Montreal and Kingston: McGill-Queen's University Press 2000), 110–1: MDA, Parish Papers, Bedford/Mystic, Letter of 11 Dec. 1989, re Dunham, QC; "Editorial," *Montreal Churchman*, Vol. I, no. 1 (Nov. 1912), 6.

## Prosperity and Optimism: 1896-1914

**1897: Parochial Expectations:** QDA, Parish Histories: Diocese of Montreal: A.G. Walsh, undated typescript, "History of Trinity Church, Beauharnois," 21 pp; MDA, Parish papers: Beauharnois, Vestry Book, Trinity Church memorabilia.

**1898: The Evolution Controversy**: Alec R. Vidler, *The Church in an Age of Revolution: 1789 to the Present Day*, rev. ed., Pelican History of the Church, vol. 5 (Harmondsworth, Middlesex: Penguin Books, Ltd 1985), 114, 115–116, 117, 120, 121–2; James Carmichael, *Why Some Fairly Intelligent Persons Do Not Endorse the Hypothesis of Evolution: A Plea for Divine Intention in Creation* (Montreal: The Gazette Printing Company 1898), 12–13, 19–20, 22–3, 27, 28–30; "Bishop Carmichael," *The New Era: A Monthly Missionary Review*, Vol. VI no. 12 (Dec. 1908), 409; James Carmichael, *The Stone of Destiny, An Archæological Study: A Paper Read Before the Hamilton Association* (Montreal: n.pub. 1881), 2, 3, 4.

**1900: Diocesan Jubilee:** Borthwick, *History of the Diocese of Montreal*, vi, 37; "Closing Address," *Programme of the Jubilee Celebration of the Parish of Nelsonville (Trinity Church, Cowansville [and] Christ Church, Sweetsburg) August 21 to September 5: 1854–1904* (n.pl.: no pub. [1904]), 70.

**1902: Montreal's First General Synod**: *Journal of Proceedings of the Third Session [of General Synod], Held in the City of Montreal from September 3rd to September 12th, in the year of our Lord MDCCCCII* (London, ON: A. Talbot & Company 1902), 2-3, 5, 14–15, 29, 125.

**1905: Prisoners' Aid**: "Prisoners' Aid Association of Montreal, Thirteenth Annual Report, 1905," and "Report of the Woman's Auxiliary of the Prisoners' Aid Association," *Proceedings of the Forty-seventh Annual Synod of the Diocese of Mon-*

*treal* (1906), 132–6; Borthwick, *History of the Montreal Prison*, 225–6; Borthwick, *History of the Diocese of Montreal*, 177; MDA, Diocesan Council of Social Service papers, undated and unsigned report titled "Social Services Committee, Prisons, and Minutes of the Meeting of the Social Service Council, J.C. Flanigan, Chairman, held on 4 December 1944"; Douglas E. Norquay, "Établissement LaMacaza," *Proceedings of the 137th Annual Synod of the Diocese of Montreal* (1996), 115.

**1906: Carmichael's Itinerary**: MDA, Carmichael Papers, RG 2.4 Box 1, "Episcopal Acts," 1906, 20–31, 39–41. J[onathan P.] Noyes, *Sketches of Some Early Shefford Pioneers*, (Montreal: Gazette Printing Company 1905), 99.

**1908: Requiescat and After**: J. Philip DuMoulin, "Words of Loving Remembrance," *In Memory of the Right Rev. James Carmichael … and His Wife* (Montreal: Gazette Printing Company n.d.), 3-4; J.M.B., "His Last Service! His Last Sermon! His Last Blessing," reprinted from the *Standard* (Montreal), Ibid, 8, 12–13, 14, 15–17; James Carmichael, "The Bishop's Last Sermon," Ibid, 18; Oswald W. Howard, "An Appreciation," reprinted from the *Canadian Churchman*, 1 Oct. 1908, Ibid, 40, 41–2; S. Baring-Gould, "Through the Night of Doubt and Sorrow," The Book of Common Praise, hymn 566; Carrington, *The Anglican Church in Canada*, 118; Rowley, *The Anglican Episcopate of Canada and Newfoundland*, 77, 111, 123–4, 265.

**1908: "A Legend in the Musical World"**: *Laus Deo*, 65; Millman, *A Short History of Dunham*, 55; [Margaret D. Ellis], *Dunham History*, (Saint-Hyacinthe: Les Ateliers Jacques Gaudet Ltée 1968], 131; "In Memoriam Lynnwood Farnam," *Montreal Churchman*, Vol. XX no. 1 (Jan. 1932), 9; *Encyclopedia of Music in Canada*, Helmut Kallmann, Gilles Potvin, and Kenneth Winters, eds (Toronto, Buffalo and London: University of Toronto Press 1981) 316; *The International Cyclopedia of Music and Musicians*, Oscar Thompson, ed., 3rd ed., revised and enlarged (Philadelphia: Blakiston Co. 1944), 528; Christ Church Cathedral Archives (hereafter CCA), Music Committee Papers, "Organists of Christ Church Cathedral [1791-1922]," typescript; H.E. MacDermot, *Christ Church Cathedral: A Century in Retrospect* (Montreal: The Gazette Printing Company Limited 1959), 34; "Montreal to Host Organ Historical Society," *Montreal Anglican*, June 1999, 1, 3; personal communication from Charlotte W. Turner, 5 Dec. 1999.

**1910: A Spirit of Confidence:** Borthwick, *History of the Diocese of Montreal*, 8–9; Mireille Baillargeon, "Évolution des caractéristiques linguistiques des échanges migratoires interprovinciaux et internationaux du Québec depuis 1971," quoted in Marshall, *A Solitary Pillar*, Appendix A, tables 2 and 5.

**1911: Housing the Poor:** [John Paterson Smyth,] "Housing the Poor," *St George's Monthly: A Parish Chronicle and General Church Review*, Vol. 5 no 3 (Dec. 1911), 11–15; "St George's Church, Montreal," *Canadian Churchman*, 20 May 1943, 313; A.P. Gower-Rees, *Historical Sketch of St George's Church, Montreal and Its Constitution* (Granby, QC: Simms Printing Co. 1952), 63–4.

**1912: The Diocesan Paper:** T.R. Millman, "Canadian Anglican Journalism in the Nineteenth Century," *The Journal of the Canadian Church Historical Society* (Toronto), Vol. III no. 5 (Mar. 1958), 5–6, 16–17; [A.H. Moore,] "Editorial," *Montreal Churchman* (St Johns, QC) Vol. I no. 1 (Nov. 1912), 5, 6, 7; Ibid, "The Children of the Church," 10; "Congratulations," Ibid, Vol. I no. 4 (Feb. 1913),

6; "Charge Delivered to the Synod of the Diocese of Montreal," *idem*, 11; W.H. Naylor, "Work of the Sacred Ministry," *Montreal Churchman*, Vol. I no. 2 (Dec. 1912), 12.

**1914: Controversies and Confrontations**: Rosenberg, *Chronology of Canadian Jewish History*, 12; Cooper, *Montreal: A Brief History*, 94–5; "M.S.C.C.," *The Montreal Churchman* (St Johns, QC) Vol. I no. 8 (June 1913), 4, "The Montreal Jewish Mission," Ibid, Vol. II no 3 (Jan. 1914), 9, "Work Among Jews," Ibid, Vol. II no. 5 (Mar. 1914), 4; Frederick George Scott, *The Great War as I Saw It* (Toronto: F.D. Goodchild Company 1922), 15, 23–4; "Frederick George Scott," *Quebec Diocesan Gazette*, Vol. LI no. 1 (Feb. 1944), 11; John Cragg Farthing, *Recollections of the Right Rev. John Cragg Farthing* (n.pl.: n.pub n.d.), 163–4.

## In War and Depression: 1914-1933

**1916: In the Midst of War:** [John Cragg Farthing,] "A Message for the New Year," *Montreal Churchman* (St Johns, QC), Vol. III no. 3 (Jan. 1915), 1; "That They Should Be the Lord's People" [Bishop's Message for the New Year], Ibid, Vol. IV no. 3 (Jan. 1916), 1–2, and [Allan Pearson Shatford,] "With the Chaplains," 10; "Honour Rolls Unveiled," Ibid, Vol. IV no. 7 (May 1916), 4; "Annual Charge to the Synod," Ibid, Vol. V no. 5 (Mar. 1917), 9; "Canadian Chaplain Service," Ibid, Vol. V no. 6 (Apr. 1917), 1; "The Bishop's Message," Ibid, Vol. V no. 11 (Sept. 1917), 1 and [Allan Pearson Shatford] "A Message From the Front," 8.

**1918: Influenza:** Cooper, *Montreal: A Brief History*, 148, 149–50. "The Bishop's Message," *Montreal Churchman* (St Johns, QC), Vol. VII no. 1 (Nov. 1918), 3 and [A.H. Moore,] "Editorial," 5.

**1919: Episcopal Dress**: Cooper, *Montreal: A Brief History*, 91; Farthing, *Recollections*, 110–112, 140–1; *Laus Deo*, 40; "Recollections of W.S. Humphrey," Adams, *A History of Christ Church Cathedral*, 89, 91; Taylor, *The Last Three Bishops, Appointed by the Crown*, 82–3; W.P. Robertson, "The Venerable John Paterson Smyth: A Memoir," *Montreal Churchman*, Vol. XX no. 3 (Mar. 1932), 9.

**1921: Prayer Book Revision**: Carrington, *The Anglican Church in Canada*, 223, 235, 245, 252, 289–90; W.J. Armitage, *The Story of the Canadian Revision of the Prayer Book* (Toronto: 1922, 55, 86-7; Colin Cuttell, *Philip Carrington: Pastor, Prophet, Poet* (Toronto: Anglican Book Centre 1988), 140, 141–2; "Two Liturgies Ready for Church Testing: Our Bishop Urges Participation by Parishes," *Montreal Churchman*, Vol. 8 no 10 (Jan. 1967), 1; Marshall, *A Solitary Pillar*, 53, 54–5, 58, 59, and appendix A; Stephen Kohner, "Youth Synod 1986," *Montreal Churchman*, May 1986, 1; Stephen Kohner, "Youth Synod: A Clarification," Ibid, Oct. 1986, 2; Ann Cruickshank, "One Book, Two Books, Three or More?" *Montreal Anglican*, Oct. 2000, 3.

**1923: Who Was Welcome?** "An Extraordinary Life," *Montreal Anglican*, Apr. 1998, 1, 3; Anthony Jemmott, "Caribbean Anglicans," lecture delivered on 21 Nov. 2000 at Montreal Diocesan Theological College, [5]; personal communications from Richard Lord, 6, 28 and 30 Dec. 2000.

**1928: Finding Furnishings**: *Laus Deo*, 122; *The Parish Review, Church of St John the Evangelist*, Vol II no. 2 (Lent 1929), 13–14.

**1929: The Fellowship of the West:** Carrington, *The Anglican Church in Canada*, 267; [advertisement], "Great Missionary Meeting! The Forum," *Montreal Church-*

*man*, Vol. XVI no. 6 (May 1928), 16; H.M. Little, "The Challenge of the West," Ibid, Vol. XVI no. 7 (June 1928), 12–13; R.B. McElheran, "The Missionary Situation," *loc. cit.*, 14–15; "The Bishop's Charge," Ibid, Vol. XVII no. 7 (May 1929), 3; "The Fellowship of the West," Ibid, Vol. XVII no. 9 (July 1929), 8; Cooper, *The Blessed Communion*, 187; "The Fellowship of the West," *Montreal Churchman*, Vol. XVIII no. 7 (5 July 1930), 7, 10; MDA, R.K. Naylor Papers, diary; "Obituary: Mary Naylor," *Montreal Anglican*, Mar. 1997, 5.

**1931: Happy New Year?** [Reuben Kenneth Naylor,] "Editorial," *Montreal Churchman*, Vol. XIX no. 1 (Jan. 1931), 5.

**1932: Economies**: "Economy," *Montreal Churchman*, Vol. XX no. 6 (June 1932), 11; "Re-Organization," Ibid, Vol. XX no. 4 (Apr. 1932), 2; "The Bishop's Charge," Ibid (June 1932), 3, 13; Jane Reeve, "A Historic Memorandum of the Protestant Relief Society of the North End," June 1934, MDA, Church of England Central Council of Social Service and Emergency Relief, typescript, 4 pp; Helen C. Dunlop, "Report on Emergency Relief, 19 Feb. 1929, MS, 9 pp., *loc. cit.*; "The Bishop's Message," *Montreal Churchman*, Vol. XX no. 12 (Dec. 1932), 3; "The Bishop's Charge: A Marriage Annulment," Ibid, Vol. XX no. 7 (July 1932), 3.

## The Duplessis Years: 1933-1959

**1935: St Michael's Mission**: *Parish Review: The Church of St John the Evangelist* (Passiontide 1937), 7–8; Cooper, *The Blessed Communion*, 205–6; Gerry Lafferty, Jr, [Annual Report] St Michael's Mission, *Proceedings of the 137th Annual Synod of the Diocese of Montreal* (1996), 108.

**1937: The Padlock Law**: Lower, *Colony to Nation*, 532; "The Padlock Law," *Montreal Churchman*, Vol. XXV no. 4 (Apr. 1937), 5.

**1939: War Again**: MDA, David Victor Warner Papers, diary for 1939, 31 Aug.-17 Sept.; "Retired: The Rev. Canon D.V. Warner," *Montreal Churchman* (Granby QC), Vol. XXXIII no. 8 (Aug. 1945), 21; "Canon Warner Funeral to be Held Tomorrow," *Montreal Daily Star*, 15 Sept. 1949.

**1941: Financial Crunch**: "The Bishop's Message," *Montreal Churchman* (Granby, QC), Vol. XXIX no. 1 (Jan. 1941), 5. "The Bishop's Message," Ibid, Vol. XXIX no. 2 (Feb. 1941), 5; "The Bishop's Message," Ibid, Vol. XXIX no. 3 (Mar. 1941), 5; "The Bishop's Message," Ibid, Vol. XXIX no. 11 (Nov. 1941), 5; "The Bishop's Message," Ibid, Vol. XXX no. 1 (Jan. 1942), 5; "The Bishop's Message," Ibid, Vol. XXX no. 2 (Feb. 1942), 5.

**1942: Chaplains Overseas**: "Canadian Chaplain with Aid of 18 Canadian Sappers Rebuilds Bombed Church in England," *Montreal Churchman* (Granby, QC), Vol. XXXI no. 8 (Aug. 1943), 3–4. "He Paid the Supreme Sacrifice," Ibid, Vol. XXXI no. 9 (Sept. 1945), 8–10; "Our Chaplains Receive Decorations," Ibid, Vol. XXXIV no. 1 (Jan. 1946), 15; "St. George's Church, Granby, Honour Roll Dedicated by the Lord Bishop," Ibid, Vol. XXXIV no. 12 (Dec. 1946), 23–4; personal interview with Alexander D. Addie (brother of Major the Rev. Gordon Addie), 27 Sept. 2000.

**1944: A Voice Against Discrimination**: "Resolution Condemning Action of the Senate of McGill University—Barring Japanese of Canadian Birth—Passed at Alumni Meeting of Diocesan College," *Montreal Churchman* (Granby, QC), Vol. XXXII no. 11 (Nov. 1944), 7; "General Synod Board Meetings and Executive Council," Ibid, 21; *Crockford's Clerical Directory* (1957-58), 937.

**1944: Conference on Post-War Problems:** "The Bishop's Charge," *Proceedings of the 107th Annual Synod of the Diocese of Montreal* (1966), 24; [B.S. Robinson] "Editorial," *Montreal Churchman*, Vol. XXXII no. 12 (Dec. 1944), 7; "The Montreal Diocesan Conference on the First Post-War Problem," *idem*, 24–5.

**1945: A Portable Altar:** "The Ste. Agathe Portable Folding Altar," *Montreal Churchman* (Granby, QC), Vol. XXXII no. 5 (May 1944), 6; "New Altar Dedicated at St[e] Agathe Sanatorium," Ibid, Vol. XXXIII no. 2 (Feb. 1945), 25; [B.S. Robinson] "Editorial," Ibid, Vol. XXXIII no. 6 (June 1945), 6 and *idem*, Harcourt Fuller, "London Pride," 14; [B.S. Robinson] "Editorial," Ibid, Vol. XXXIII no. 9 (Sept. 1945), 6.

**1946: A Mission to Poland:** "The Rev. Adolph Louis Sergent," *Montreal Churchman* (Granby, QC), Vol. XXXIV no. 1 (Jan. 1946), 6; "The Rev. A.L. Sergent, L.Th.," Ibid, Vol. XXXIV no. 1 (Jan. 1945), 27; "Adolph Louis Sergent," Ibid, Vol. XXXIV no. 6 (June 1946), 6; "Rev. A.L. Sergent and Family Arrive Safely in Poland," Ibid, Vol. XXXIV no. 7 (July 1946), 20; "The Rev. A.L Sergent in Poland, Special Notice," Ibid, Vol. XXXIV no. 9 (Sept. 1946), 6; "The Rev. A.L. Sergent, in Poland," Ibid, Vol. XXXIV no. 11 (Nov. 1946), 72–3; "Prayers to be Used at All Meetings of the Society," *Report of the Church Society of Montreal, 1852* (Montreal: John Lovell, 1852), 3; "Work Among the Jews," *Montreal Churchman* (St Johns, QC), Vol. I no. 8 (June 1913), 4; "Bishop's Message," *Montreal Anglican*, May 2000, 2.

**1947: The Arundel Group:** "On Work, Not Theories, Says Bishop-Elect," MDA, Episcopal Papers: John Dixon, undated clipping marked "Standard, 1943"; Carrington, *The Anglican Church in Canada*, 268; "Report of the Arundel Conference," *Montreal Churchman* (Granby, QC), Vol XXXI No. 10 (Oct. 1943), 15–16; "The Second Arundel Conference," Ibid, Vol XXXII no. 10 (Oct. 1944), 17–19; [B.S. Robinson] "Editorial," Ibid, Vol. XXXII no. 12 (Dec. 1944), 7; S.L. Pollard, "Church Trends," Ibid, Vol. XXXIV no. 4 (Apr. 1946), 8–11; Andrew Wetmore, "The Briefcase Boys," *Journal of the Canadian Church Historical Society*, Vol. XXX no. 2 (Oct. 1983), 88–9; "The Bishop's Charge," *Proceedings of the 88th Annual Synod of the Diocese of Montreal* (1947), 32; "The Right Rev. Arthur Carlisle, DD, DCL, LLD, Late Bishop of Montreal," *Montreal Churchman* (Granby, QC), Vol XXXI no. 2 (Feb. 1943), 8–9; "Announcement Concerning the Consecration and Enthronement, May 3, 1943," Ibid, Vol. XXXI no. 5 (May 1943), 3.

**1951: Men For All Seasons:** *Chronicles of a Country Church: Holy Trinity, Lakefield, Québec, With Some Memoirs and Notes on the History of The Gore*, Louise Johnston, ed. (Lakefield, QC: Trenmore Printing Ltd n.d.), 16–17; Alison Ramsay, "Quebec Church Rises From Ashes," *Anglican Journal*, Vol. 123 no. 5 (May 1997), 17; Shirley E. Woods, Jr, *The Molson Saga: 1763–1983* (Toronto: Doubleday Canada Ltd 1983), 307; Bulletin of St. Francis of the Birds Anglican Church [n.d.]; "Lieut-Governor Visits Maison Emmanuel," *Montreal Anglican*, June 1999, 13; Horace G. Baugh, personal communication, 4 Mar. 1999.

**1952: "Her Gift of Music":** Jemmott, "Caribbean Anglicans," [3]; personal communication from Anthony Jemmott, 30 Nov. 2000; personal communications from Marita Archer, 4 and 13 Dec. 2000.

**1954: Deconsecrations:** MDA, Parish Papers: Berthier, hand written inventory, dated 7 Sept. 1954, initialed M.K.; Ibid, typewritten letter: J.F. Morris to Miss M. Kittson, dated 21 Sept. 1954; E.E. Dawson, "Berthier: St James' Church," 9 pp. typescript, with note by A.R. Kelley, dated 21 July 1955; "Montreal to Host Organ Historical Society," *Montreal Anglican*, June 1999, 1, 3.

**1954: New Congregations**: Personal communications from Mrs Elizabeth Howes, 21 Dec. 2000 and 4 Jan., 15 Feb., 12 Apr. and 13 Apr. 2001; "St. Barnabas, Roxboro," *Montreal Churchman*, May 1976, 3; personal communication from Mrs Connie Bridgeman, 14 Mar. 1999.

**1957: Exchange Scholarships to Diocesan College**: Oswald Howard, T*he Montreal Diocesan Theological College*, 124–5; Winks, *The Blacks in Canada*, 441; Joan Shanks, "'Dio' Bids farewell to a Dedicated Director," *Montreal Anglican*, June 2000, 4; personal communications from the Rev. Dr John McNab, 22 Nov. and 19 Dec. 2000.

**The Quiet Revolution and Vatican II: 1960-1976**
**1961: Choir Camp**: Marcia Hollis, "New Venture: Special Camp For Anglican Choirboys," Montreal *Gazette*, 2 Sept. 1961; P.D. Hannen, "[Report on] The Montreal Boys' Choir Camp," *Proceedings of the 114th Annual Synod of the Diocese of Montreal* (1973), 93; P.D. Hannen, "[Report on] The Montreal Boys' Choir Camp," Ibid, (1974), 94; Cynthia Hawkins,"[Report on] The Montreal Boys' Choir Course 1995," Ibid, (1996), 104-5.

**1963: The Old Brewery Mission**: Bill McCarthy, *The Rev: Memoirs of Montreal's Old Brewery Mission*, Janet Hughson, ed. (Montreal: Robert Davies Publishing 1996), 1, 6, 9, 102–3.

**1966: Reinstitution of the Cathedral Men and Boys Choir:** Roger S.W. Howard, *The Story of St. Martin's* (Montreal: published by the Corporation of St Martin's 1954), 8; Marshall, *A Solitary Pillar*, 90; CCA, Music Committee File, Gerald Wheeler, "A Report on the State of the Choirs of Christ Church Cathedral, Montreal," 27 Sept. 1985; Ibid, Proposed Music budgets for 1986 and 1987; Ibid, Correspondence; Gerald Wheeler, "Our Ambassadors in Washington," *Cathedral Script* [Newsletter of Christ Church Cathedral, Montreal], no. 208 (Nov. 1993), 2.

**1967: Expo '67:** "Synod Supports Expo '67 Participation," *Montreal Churchman*, Vol. 7 no. 8 (Oct. 1965), 1; "Diocese Centre Geared up to Care for Expo Visitors," Ibid, Vol. 8 no. 13 (Apr. 1967), 1-2; *idem*, "Canterbury Will Host Expo Guests," 4; "Bishop Welcomes Expo 67 Visitors to Montreal Diocese," Ibid, Vol. 8 no. 15 (June 1967), 1; *idem*, "Volunteers Face Heavy Summer," 1–2.

**1968: Closures and Amalgamations**: MDA Parish Papers: Bondville, letter dated 1 Apr. 1968, from George Beach to Kenneth Maguire, and the same to the same 8 Apr. 1968; Williams, *Three Churches*, 17–18; *Annual Report of Church Society of the Diocese of Montreal for … 1864*.

**1969: The Impact of Provincial Politics**: MDA, Parish Papers: Arundel, letter to Bishop Kenneth Maguire, 30 Dec. 1969.

**1970: The French Fact:** Marshall, *A Solitary Pillar*, 40, 156–7; "The Bishop's Charge," and "Policy and Programming Committee Report," *Proceedings of the 111th Annual Synod of the Diocese of Montreal* (1970), 21–22 and 84; "The Bishop Looks at the Future," *Proceedings of the113th Synod of the Diocese of Montreal* (1972),

35, 39; "Bishop's Address," *Proceedings of the 114th Synod of the Diocese of Montreal* (1973), 22; "Bishop's Charge," *Proceedings of the 115th Synod of the Diocese of Montreal* (1974), 27; "Bishop's Charge," *Proceedings of the 116th Annual Synod of the Diocese of Montreal* (1975), 43; Reginald M. Turpin, "The Church in Quebec: Report to General Synod 1977 on French-English Relations," typescript, 4, 8.

**1972: A Laywoman's Many-faceted Involvement:** John Gomes, "Eulogy for Pamela McBeth," delivered 30 Oct. 2000, St Mark's Church Dorval; "In Memoriam: Alice Pamela McBeth," *Montreal Anglican*, Dec. 2000, 3; John McNab, personal communications, 18 and 23 Nov. 2000; Mrs. Gloria Augustus, personal communications, 23 Nov. and 3 Dec. 2000.

**1975: La Nativité:** "New Congregation: Haitian Hopes," *Montreal Churchman*, Oct. 1975, 2; MDA, Papers of the Comité de la Pastorale française, conflation of "Partners in Mission Consultation" questionnaires by Gavin Elbourne, 25 Mar. 1980 and letter from C.P. Carr to Reginald Hollis, 19 June 1986; Marshall, *A Solitary Pillar*, 134, 135, 138–9, 161; "Bishop's Charge," *Proceedings of the 135th Synod of the Diocese of Montreal* (1994), 29, 30; "Project Haiti 1978," *Montreal Churchman*, Mar. 1978, 2; "Jésus, Quel Nom Merveilleux! SOMA's Mission to Haiti — Apr. 19–26, 1999," *Montreal Anglican*, June 1999, 14.

**Parti Québécois Victory at the Polls and After: 1976-2000**
**1977: The Turpin Report**: Turpin, "The Church in Quebec: Report to General Synod," 5, 10, 12-13; and personal communication, 6 Dec. 2000.

**1978: Multi-Ethnic Ministry**: Carrington, *The Anglican Church in Canada*, 127; Winks, *The Blacks in Canada*, 228, 333, 417, 439, 477; William N.T. Wylie, *Prospective Sites Relating to Black History in Canada* ([Ottawa:] Historic Sites and Monuments Board of Canada 1994), 58, 75; Hill, *The Freedom-Seekers*, 29; Margot Blackman, "St. Paul's Makes History," *Afro-Can* (Montreal) July 1981, 11; Jemmott, "Caribbean Anglicans," [3]; personal communication from Margot A. Blackman, 25 June 1999; John McNab, personal communications, 18 and 22 Nov. 2000.

**1978: The Ordination of Women to the Priesthood**: Reisner, *Strangers and Pilgrims*, 95, 116–7, 118; "Bishop's Charge," *Proceedings of the 107th Annual Synod of the Diocese of Montreal* (1966), 24; "Editorial: The Sessions of Synod," *Montreal Churchman*, Vol. X no. 7 (May 1922), 5; "Bishop's Charge," *Proceedings of the 115th Annual Synod of the Diocese of Montreal* (1974), 24; Lettie James, "The Ordination of Women to the Priesthood," delivered at Christ Church Cathedral, March 1975, typescript, 6–7, 8, personal papers of Dr. Lettie James; *Minutes of the Twenty-Seventh Session of the General Synod* (1975), M-50; *Minutes of the Twenty-Sixth Session of the General Synod* (1973), M-20; Bill Kokesch, "Protests threaten to mar ordination of woman priest,' Montreal *Gazette*, 29 Sept. 1978, 1; Bill Kokesch, "Protest Fails: Montreal Has Female Priest," Ibid, 2 Oct. 1978, 1, 3; "Bishop's Letter," *Montreal Churchman*, Nov. 1978, 2; "Ordination Reaction Muted," *idem*, 2; "Support Group for Women in Priesthood," *Montreal Churchman*, May 1976, 2; "Bishop's Charge," *Proceedings of the 135th Annual Synod of the Diocese of Montreal* (1994), 25; Lettie James, personal communication, 6 Dec. 2001.

**1979: Helping the Boat-People**: *St. Mary's News [Beaconsfield, QC]*, Vol. 18 no.

4 (Sept. 1979), 1, 3; Ibid, Vol. 21 no. 2 (Apr. 1981), 5; Ibid, Vol. 22 no. 7 (Feb. 1982), 7–8; Albert Noel and Aaron Derfel, "Community Grieves for Well-liked Pair," Montreal *Gazette*, 4 Apr. 1995, A-1, Katherine Wilton, "Boy Knew Murdered Couple—Police," Ibid, 6 Apr., A-1, A-2; Geoff Baker, "Judge Must Weigh Series of Factors Before Sending Case to Adult Court," *idem*, A-2; Levon Sevunts, "Toope Killer Gets Another 2½ Years," Montreal *Gazette*, 12 Apr. 2001; Glynis Williams, "Action Réfugiés Montréal," *Proceedings of the 136th Annual Synod of the Diocese of Montreal* (1995), 72.

**1981: Staying On**: Mireille Baillargeon, "Évolution et caractéristiques linguistiques des échanges migratoires interprovinciaux et internationaux du Québec depuis 1971," édition provisoire, Conseil de la langue Française, 1983, quoted in Marshall, *A Solitary Pillar*, 172; Catherine Hughes, Leslie Hughes, Florene Trentman and John Trentman, *A History of St Peter's Church* ([Montreal: n.pub 1981]), 11; personal communication from Catherine Hughes, 7 Apr. 1999.

**1983: Cathedral Place**: Personal interview with W.T. Duncan Shaddick, 20 Apr. 2000; Kathe Lieber, "Christ Church Cathedral: Old and New," *En Ville* (Montreal), Nov. 1988, 10–11; "Concrete Underpinning for Historic Stone Church," *RSIC/IAAC*, a publication of the Reinforcing Steel Institute of Canada (Willowdale, ON), Vol. 6 no. 1 (Winter 1992), 2; *Maison des Coopérants*, Promotional Brochure, n.d, copy in CCCA, 10–11; George A. Peer, "Church Uplifted by Caisson Legs," *Heavy Construction News*, 18 Jan. 1988, 18; Derek Drummond, "From Church's Fall into Temptation Comes Sin of Banality," Montreal *Gazette*, 24 Sept. 1988, K-14; G.M. Elbourne, "Anglican Cathedral Not Part of a Real Estate Sell-out," Ibid, 14 Oct. 1988, B-3; David Sherman, "God, Big Business and the Pursuit of Salvation in a Secular World," unidentified article in CCCA.

**1984: A Native Son for Bishop**: Rowena Blair, "Rev. James A. MacLean, Bishop Suffragan, Montreal, Retires," *The Watchman* (Lachute, QC), 29 Jan. 1990, 15; Byron Clarke, "Native Magdalen Island Bishops: The Right Reverend James Aubrey MacLean," *Gleanings on the Magdalen Islands* (Grosse Isle, QC: n.pub. 2000), 103–4; Monica Kirby, "James Aubrey MacLean, EGCLJ, LTh, DD, Bishop in the Church of God," *Montreal Churchman*, June 1992, 1; Harvey Shepherd, "Bishop's Retirement Will Be Anything But Complete, Montreal *Gazette*, 30 Dec. 1989, G-7; [David Yarrow], "A Bishop Comes Ashore," *Montreal Churchman*, Nov. 1989, 1; James Aubrey MacLean, *Living Hymns*, (n.p.: n.pub. 1992), 22, 42; personal communications from Mrs Jean MacLean, 17 Oct. and 14 Nov. 2000.

**1985: Parish Newsletters**: "[Parish] Newsletter [Arundel, QC]," 27 Aug. 1985, 1-2; Service Bulletin [Grace Church, Arundel], 14 June 1985; *Saint Mary's News* (Beaconsfield, QC), Vol 25 no. 2 (June-Aug 1985), 2.

**1986: "The Nature of Youth Work"**: *The Anglican Young People's Association Golden Jubilee* (Toronto: AYPA Office 1952), 26; Robin Guiness, *History of Crosstalk Ministries*, Brett Cane, ed. (Montreal: [typescript] 2000), 1, 3, 7; "Youth Synod," *Anglican Newsletter*, May 1975, 2; Minutes of the First Meeting concerning the Establishment of a Youth Drop-In Centre in Central Montreal [unsigned], 27 Apr. 1985: Quentin Robinson, personal papers, Ayer's Cliff, QC; Minutes of the Second Meeting [unsigned], 19 May 1985, *idem*; letter from Quentin Robinson and Valerie Paterson to parish Youth Leaders dated 30 May

1985, *idem*; Minutes of the Third Meeting [unsigned], 9 June 1985, *idem*; Minutes of the Fourth Meeting [unsigned], 20 June 1985, *idem*; Minutes of the Fifth Meeting [undated and unsigned], *idem*; Drop-In Centre Committee phone list, *idem*; letter from Quentin Robinson to the Corporation of St George's Church, Montreal, 14 Jan. 1986, *idem;* Minute Book of the Church of England Association for Young Men of Montreal, 1856–1860, MDA; *Fifth Annual Report of St George's Young Men's Christian Association* (1869), 3–4: MDA, Parish Papers, St George's, Montreal; Cummings, *Our Story*, 44, 107, 109; "Training Course for Anglican Girls' Leaders," *Montreal Churchman* (Granby QC), Vol XXXIV no 3 (Mar. 1946), 8; personal communications with Mercia Church, 9 Aug. and 9 Oct. 2000; personal communications with Quentin Robinson, 24 Mar. and 22 Apr. 2001.

**1987: Acknowledging Multicultural Needs**: "Varieties of Gifts But the Same Spirit; A Long Way to Go": The Message to the Anglican Church of Canada from the First National Symposium on Ministry in a Multicultural Society, 21st-24th October 1985 (1985), *passim*; "Called to Be Leaven," A Message to the Anglican Church of Canada from the Second National Symposium on Ministry in a Multi-Cultural Society, 19–22 Feb. 1987 (1987), passim; *Proceedings of the 138th Annual Synod of the Diocese of Montreal* (1997); John McNab, "Ministry in a Multi-Ethnic Context," a paper presented at Trinity College, Toronto, 28 Oct. 1998; communications from John McNab, 18 and 21 Nov. 2000.

**1991: Women's Plainsong**: Elizabeth Rowlinson, personal communication, 18 and 29 Nov., and 1 Dec. 2000; "Choral Evensong / Les Vêpres chantées," service bulletin, Christ Church Cathedral, 12 Mar. 2000.

**1992: "Under the Influence of the Liturgical Movement"**: [P. Harper,] *The Church of St John the Evangelist: Its Architectural History and Symbolism* (Montreal: The Liturgy and Music Committee of the Parish of St John the Evangelist 1992), [draft, section "A Ritualist Church," pages not numbered].

**1993: The Dilemma of Sexual Orientation**: "Speculation Surrounds Motive for Murder," *Anglican Journal*, Vol. 119 no 10 (Dec. 1993), 11; Carolyn Purden, "A Devoted Priest ... a Gay Man," Ibid, Vol. 120 no. 3 (Mar. 1994), 14–15; Douglas Chambers, "Priest's Death Was Violent, But Not Mindless," reprinted from *Globe and Mail* (Toronto) in *Integrator* (Toronto), Advent-Christmas, 1993, 6; "Making Church Communities Safe Places Around Sexual Orientation," *idem*, 2, the Rev John Doe [*pseud*], "My Gayness Is Not a Weakness, but a Strength, *idem*, 5; "Let's End the Bias, Bigotry and Ignorance: A Letter from the Family of Fr Warren Eling, Handed Out at the End of Synod," *idem*, 3; "The Bishop's Charge," *Proceedings of the 120th Annual Synod of the Diocese of Montreal* (1979), 24–5; Bruce Russell, "Report of the Diocesan Sexuality Commission," ([Montreal:] undated, probably 1999); personal communications from Chris Ambidge, 6 Jan. and 5 Feb. 2001; Aaron Derfel, "Anglican Minister Robbed, Murdered," Montreal *Gazette*, 11 Nov. 1993, A1; Harvey Shepherd, "Investigate if Pastor's Death Was Sex-related: Bishop," Ibid, 12 Nov., A3; Lisa Fitterman, "Priest's Killer Gets Life in Prison — Again," Ibid, 22 Feb., 1997, A3.

**1994: The Essentials Movement:** Sue Careless, "Gathering Will Look at Essentials," *Anglican Journal*, Vol. 120 no. 3 (Mar. 1994), 10; "Revenue Decline Continues," "Sexuality, the Future, Top Bishops' Agenda," and "Directors Leave

National Office," *idem*, 6; "An Inoffensive Church," Editorials and Comment, *idem*, 20; Carolyn Purden, "A Devoted Priest ... a Gay Man," *idem*, 14–15; "Priest Faces 17 Charges," *idem*, 3; [Lynn C. Ross,] "Essentials '94—Anglicans Search to Define Essentials of Faith," *Quebec Diocesan Gazette*, Sept. 1994, 1-2; M. Louise Cornell, Letter of Greetings, Essentials 94 Welcome Kit, [9]; Peter Hannen, "Our Faith Is Not Reflected Here," *Anglican Journal*, Vol. 120 no. 8 (Oct. 1994), 9; *The Challenge of Tradition: Discerning the Future of Anglicanism*, John Simons, ed. (Toronto: Anglican Book Centre 1997); W. Michael Birch, "Report on Essentials '94," *PBSC Newsletter: The Prayer Book Society of Canada*, No. 32 (Sept. 1994), 1-2; James I. Packer, Don Lewis and George Egerton, "From Essentials 94 to Essentials 2001: Challenges, Topics and Speakers," *Incourage* (Halifax, NS), Barnabas Anglican Ministries Vol. 14 no. 1, 2001, 4-6; "Lift High the Cross: Global Anglicanism and the Anglican Church of Canada," publicity flyer and registration form, Halifax, 2001.

**1995: The Ministry of Lay Readers**: "The Bishop's Charge," *Proceedings of the 136th Synod of the Diocese of Montreal* (1995), 23; Aloha Smith, "The Laos Institute for Lay Ministry [Annual Report]," Ibid, 83-4; Jan Dijkman, "Lay Readers' Association [Annual Report]," Ibid, 84; "Thirty Five Years as a Lay Reader," *Montreal Anglican*, Apr. 1999, 3; "In Memoriam: Frederick Cyril Grant Sheward," *The Church of St John the Baptist News* (Pointe Claire, QC), Mar. 1993, 1-2 and "Snippets," *idem*, 2; "The Bishop's Annual Charge," *Montreal Churchman* (St Johns, QC), Vol. XI no. 7 (May 1923), 4; "The Lay Readers' Day and Commissioning Service," *Montreal Anglican*, Dec. 2000, 7.

**1996: Mile-End Community Mission**: "A Brief Past and Present of Mile-End Community Mission [Montreal]," 13 Mar. 1997, [1]; John Beach, "Mile End Community Mission," *Proceedings of the 136th Annual Synod of the Diocese of Montreal* (1995), 85; Roslyn Macgregor, "Mile End Community Mission," *Proceedings of the 137th Annual Synod of the Diocese of Montreal* (1996), 103; "Mile-End Mission Communautaire / Community Mission [Annual Report for 1998]," (28 Feb. 1999), a-b, d; Joyce Sanchez, "A Letter of Thanks," *Mission Possible*, Vol. 1 no.1 (Autumn 1998), 3; Luboslaw H[rywnak], "A Vision of Hope and Involvement," *loc. cit.*; communication with Joyce Sanchez, 24 July, 10 Oct. 2001.

**1997: What Constitutes a Sphere of Mission?** "The Bishop's Charge," *Proceedings of the 135th Annual Synod of the Diocese of Montreal* (1994), 23; Website of the Diocese of Montreal: www.Montreal.anglican.org (Wednesday, 12 July 2000); Constitution of the Church Society of the Diocese of Montreal, *Report of the Church Society of the Diocese of Montreal, 1852* (Montreal: John Lovell 1852), 5.

**1998: The Ice Storm**: "Bishop's Message," *Montreal Anglican*, Feb. 1998, 2; "Stormy Weather," *idem*, 5–9; "Bishop's Message," Ibid, Apr. 1998, 2.

**1998: Common Praise:** Paul Gibson, personal communication, 12 Apr. 1999; Patrick Wedd, personal interview, 8 June 2000; *Common Praise* (Toronto: Anglican Book Centre 1998), 6–7, 906–7, 912, 922; Diane Paquette, "Singing the Praises of a New Hymn Book: Ten Years to Create, Worth Every Minute," *Anglican Journal*, Jan. 1999, 12; Patrick Wedd, "A New Hymnbook for Anglicans," *Montreal Anglican*, Apr. 1998, 1, 4; "Montreal Anglican and Lutheran Clergy Day: Top Ten Things I Like About Being Lutheran, and Top Ten Things I Like About Being Anglican," Ibid, June 2000, 7.

**1999: A Space Age Diocese**: "Cathedral Fanfare for Astronaut Julie Payette," *Montreal Anglican*, June 1999, 3.

**2000: The Context of the National Church**: Kathy Blair, "Committees to Discuss Plans for Church's Future," *Anglican Journal*, Vol 126 no. 2 (Feb. 2000), 1; Kathy Blair, "Ottawa, Not Natives, Behind Many Lawsuits," Ibid, Vol. 126 no. 4 (Apr. 2000), 1–2; David Harris, "A Funny Kind of Invitation From Ottawa," *idem*, 4; David Napier, "Sins of the Fathers," Ibid, Vol. 126 no. 5 (May 2000), *passim*; "Bishop's Message," *Montreal Anglican*, June 2000, 2.

**2000: Keeping the Feast**: Peter Hannen, "Therefore Let Us Keep the Feast," *Montreal Anglican*, June 2000, 1.

**2000: What Is a Church but the People?** "Rural Deanery Statistical Reports," *Proceedings of the 49th Annual Synod of the Diocese of Montreal* (1908), 188, 191, 192, 197, 199; *Memories and Stories from the Parish of St Cuthbert, St Hilda and St Luke* (Montreal: draft copy 2000), [1-2] and *passim*; Harvey Shepherd, "Congregation Leaves Church of the Ascension," Montreal *Gazette*, 13 July 1991, J-7; personal communication from Roslyn Macgregor, 4 Dec. 2000.

# NOTES ON
# ILLUSTRATIONS
# AND MAPS

*Plate 1.* I am indebted to the Ven. Peter Hannen, who supplied the heraldic information for this plate, for the following additional quotation: 'Several of the bishops of Montreal have been armigerous (i.e., have had a family coat-of-arms), and there are several examples of their personal arms impaled (i.e., side-by-side on a single shield) with those of the diocese. For example, the monument to our first bishop beside the Cathedral shows Fulford/Montreal, and the sedilia at the High Altar shows Carlisle/Montreal."

*Plate 2.* Charles Inglis's episcopate continued for twenty-three years beyond the period of his jurisdiction over the future Diocese of Montreal, until 1816; Jacob Mountain and Charles James Stewart had Montreal in their care throughout their episcopates. George Jehoshaphat Mountain, who was finally enthroned as Bishop of Quebec on 21 September 1850 after administering that Diocese as Bishop of Montreal for thirteen years, continued in his episcopate until his death in 1863.

*Plate 3.* The SPG publication in which this illustration appeared also furnished the following explanation: "For the drawing which is here engraved, the Society is indebted to one of its Missionaries, the Rev. G. Slack who visited England last summer, and who has delineated a scene with which his experience had made him familiar. Mr Slack is stationed in Granby, in Shefford, not far from the scene of the Yamaska, in the Diocese of Montreal. When the Bishop [G.J. Mountain] visited Granby in 1843, the district had neither a Church nor a Minister ... On Trinity Sunday in that year Mr Slack was ordained, and appointed to the district; and, at a subsequent visitation ... the Bishop had the gratification of consecrating a handsome church at Granby, and confirming 29 persons, in the presence of a congregation which numbered 250 souls ..." I am grateful to Richard Moysey, a Slack descendant, for supplying this illustration, and for his permission to reproduce it.

*Plate 4.* The old Christ Church on Notre Dame Street burned to the ground on 10 December 1856. The new cathedral, on its present site, was completed and opened for worship in 1859. This engraving reflects the "out-of-town" setting the new Cathedral enjoyed in its early years. It appeared in the February 1887 issue of *Our Mission News* (Vol. I, no. 8, page 183).

*Plate 5.* The MDA preserves seven such subscription booklets, which are hard-bound and contain pledges under original signatures totalling as much as $60 (from Chambly), or as modest an amount as $11 (from Portage du Fort). At Waterloo, the Rev. David Lindsay's confirmation class gave $11.55 for a total subscription of $37.05. Other booklets came from Berthier-en-Haut, St Andrew's East, and Sutton. The imposing gothic revival monument beside the Cathedral, restored in 2000 as part of the sesquicentennial celebrations of the Diocese, was erected in Fulford's memory with the help of these donations.

*Plate 6.* The Diocese has been associated with a number of schools for girls, including Dunham Ladies' College, instituted by act of the provincial parliament in 1875. Its ties with the Diocese were closer than those of the Boarding and Day School for young ladies at Berthier, but the latter institution, under the patronage of Bishop Oxenden and Dean Bond, is of particular interest because of its emphasis on French. The overleaf of the flyer states that "Special facilities will be offered to advanced pupils wishing to confine their studies to French alone; and during the year a course of Lectures on French Literature will be delivered by M. Calvin E. Amaron, of Montreal. ... Drawing and other accomplishments as desired. Physical Culture will not be neglected." The girls were to furnish their own "bedding, toilet linen and table napkins; also spoon, knife, fork, and napkin ring." There were four teachers on staff, including the Rev. W.C. Merrick, MA, lecturer in Holy Scripture and Church History, and the Rev. Edward McManus, instructor in Classics and Mathematics. Mlle Amaron taught French and Mme Amaron superintended "the household arrangements." Board and tuition were $160 per annum "payable quarterly in advance" with $20 extra, each, for music and washing.

*Plate 7.* Nineteenth-century church activities frequently involved cultural as well as social events: musical evenings, recitations, and lecture series. In their less ambitious forms, and often at a later date, they included skits, melodramas, and community singing (see plate 13). A literary and musical program similar to the one outlined here was offered at Synod Hall on Thursday evening, January 14th 1875. Both reflect the early association between the YMCA and specific Montreal Anglican Churches such as the Cathedral and St George's.

*Plate 8a.* According to the July 1935 issue of the *Montreal Churchman* (Vol. XXIII, no. 7, page 10), this picture was taken on 26 May 1885, the day on which the little wooden church was consecrated by Bishop Bond (seen at the top of the steps). The church and basement had been built within a year at a cost of $1,500, of which $800, no small sum in those days, was raised locally. On 26 May 1935, Bishop and Mrs Farthing attended the church's fiftieth anniversary celebrations and a similar photograph was taken. At that time many of those who had been present at the consecration were still alive and some took part in this special event. The two pictures are juxtaposed in the *Churchman*, together with an account of the celebrations.

*Plate 8b.* According to *Chronicles of a Country Church: Lakefield, Québec*, this beautiful, substantial stone church was completed in 1859. In 1860, when its debt was paid off, it was consecrated by Bishop Fulford. The photograph, according to the same source, dates from 1900. Tom Hodge, James Arnott, Allan Mount, Thomas Copeland "and others" are thought to be present in this wintry scene.

*Plate 9.* According to *Laus Deo* (the fiftieth anniversary history of the church of St John the Evangelist), when the present church was opened in 1878, the reredos behind the high altar "consisted of projected hangings of damask, red in colour." Before "the present magnificent reredos in carved oak" was erected, there was introduced, in the 1880s, a projecting canopy over a depiction of the crucifixion. The photograph, the same source suggests, was probably taken at an Easter festival in the 1890s. The eucharistic candles date from the early days, the altar cross was a memorial to the late Sister Maria Laetitia Holland, and the superfrontal was used in the first church.

*Plate 10.* This souvenir of the Diocese of Montreal's first Jubilee celebrations is preserved in the MDA. Beginning in upper left hand corner the portraits are of Bishops Oxenden, Bond and Fulford (in the centre). Below, left to right are Deans Bethune, Baldwin and Carmichael. Bishop Bond, who also served as Dean, 1872–1879, was elected Metropolitan in 1901.

*Plate 11a.* Sunday School Libraries formed an important part of the cultural and educational resources of Anglican parishes, especially rural ones, and a real effort was made by local incumbents to find the funds to stock their shelves. The Church of St Andrew's East, for example, had a particularly fine collection which was delivered to the MDA when the church closed in 1999. Its holdings included such titles as *The Christian Cottager's Triumph in Sickness and Death* (published in 1854 by the SPCK in London), *The Circle of Blessing and Other Parables from Nature* (published in 1861 by the General Protestant Episcopal Sunday School Union and Church Book Society in New York), *The Plan of Salvation, Made Familiar to Children* (a sermon preached to the scholars of Christ Church Sunday School at Reading, PA, by the Rector of the Church), and *The Lily of Treflis: A Sketch from Georgian Church History* (acquired by the library in 1863, apparently the 176th volume to be added to its collection). In most cases a Sunday School library was "under the immediate direction of the Minister of the Parish," who chose the books, and superintended their distribution and prompt return.

*Plate 11b.* Sunday School materials included schedules of lessons, together with verses and catechism to be committed to memory, for each Sunday. Some were especially sanctioned for the Diocese of Montreal, and adopted by the Committee of Synod on Sunday Schools (see the schedule for 1874–75 in the MDA). There were hand-out cards with the lesson on one side and a picture on the other, and leaflets for children of various ages. With poorer parishes having difficulty in paying for Sunday School materials (however modestly priced), wealthier parishes often collected their used ones and sent them on for use elsewhere in a subsequent year. Certificates of Faithfulness and rewards for attendance or proficiency, treasured as they no doubt were by the scholars, would have been beyond the means of many struggling Sunday Schools. This example, from, St George's Church, Montreal, is preserved in the MDA.

*Plate 12.* This page reproduces the original masthead of the *Montreal Churchman*. Since its first issue in November 1912, the *Churchman* had carried advertising, which moved to the front page as early as the December issue of that year. Henry Birks & Sons, Limited, who had a special ecclesiastical department, were among the paper's most faithful advertisers, as were Willis & Co, Limited ("Church and Chapel Reed Organs a specialty"). The back page, too, was almost entirely devoted to advertisements, often of an institutional nature, such as the Berthierville Grammar School ("for the Sons of Gentlemen"), and Dunham Ladies' College ("Residential Church School for Girls").

*Plate 13.* Parish fêtes included a wide range of activities such as oyster suppers, strawberry socials, lawn parties, and "gracious teas." Primarily fund raising events, they were particularly important in building community spirit, furnishing local entertainment and drawing new members to the church.

*Plate 14a.* This undated photograph, preserved in the MDA, is titled "For Our Christian Education." Individual pupils are not identified, but the two adults are Russell Aldcroft, the teacher, and his brother Geoffrey, a visitor.

*Plate 14b.* The presiding clergy, in this undated and otherwise unidentified photograph from the MDA of a confirmation service held at the Lasalle Mission, are Bishop Kenneth Maguire and the Rev. D. Lim Yuen. The social and cultural norms of the day, as represented in these two pictures, reflect the dramatic changes in the Diocese between the 1950s and the 1970s.

*Plate 15a.* The Sunday School and a few adults watch as the Rev. Murray Magor turns the first sod of Trinity Church's new hall in Ste-Agate-des-Monts in 1963.

*Plate 15b.* Bishop Reginald Hollis, Elizabeth McLaughlin and the Very Rev. Ronald Shepherd are seen taking part in French classes instituted for Diocesan clergy and staff in the 1970s in an effort to integrate the church more effectively into an increasingly francophone society.

*Plate 16.* This schematic map showing the location of the parish of North Clarendon's four churches appeared on the front page of the June 1965 issue of the *Montreal Churchman*. The Deanery of Clarendon, as of 1 July of that year, ceased to be part of the Diocese of Quebec, just in time for the centenary celebrations of the parish during the weekend of Saturday July 31st to Monday August 2nd.

*Plate 17.* The four young people who served as hosts at the Anglican House Hospitality Centre were Ann Taylor, Ian Bourne, Andrew Elliott and Joan Turner.

Volunteers from many parishes also staffed the Centre throughout this period. The Information Centre (the Diocese's Centennial Project) planned to be open every day for twenty-six weeks during the Expo period.

*Plate 18a.* This informal picture, taken in 1975 on the lawn in front of the former Synod office, shows a group of young people relaxing during a day of Prayer and Renewal. Although the ordination of women to the priesthood was far from a reality in Canada at this time, two of these young women — Mary Irwin, later Gibson (left of centre) and Heather Thomson (on her left) — were then enrolled as theology students at the MDTC, preparing themselves to be ready should General Synod sanction their vocation. Both would eventually receive ordination, the former in the Diocese of Montreal, the latter in the Diocese of Quebec.

*Plate 18b.* Montreal's French press as well as its English-language papers gave wide coverage to the ordination of Dr Lettie James to the priesthood. The present article appeared on 2 October 1978 in the *Journal de Montréal*, and took up most of the page.

*Plate 19a.* Dr Sheema Kahn, one of the speakers on Race Relations Day, 1997, gave a presentation on Islam. The general theme for the day's program that year was "Make All Things New." There were also presentations on Judaism, Sikhism and the Bahai faith.

*Plate 19b.* This candid photograph of two participants at Youth Synod, 1999, held at St George's, Montreal, reflects the increasingly relaxed atmosphere and informality of proceedings since the formation of this body in the 1980s.

*Plate 20.* This event involved a pageant, concert and songs from different nations. The adults shown with the children are Kathy Calder, Paula Merriman, Michele Wilson, and Wilma Cobb. It reflects Tyndale-St George's strong tradition of ministry to refugees and involvement in pre-school programs for the young.

*Plate 21a.* This 1999 photograph shows the street view of the Mile-End Mission's enlarged facilities at 87 Bernard ouest, Montreal.

*Plate 21b.* This special cake marked the celebration of the blessing of the enlarged, reorganized Mile-End Mission.

*Plate 22.* Liturgical dance has been an important part of worship in a number of Montreal churches since the mid-1980s, notably at St Matthew's, Hampstead. Their dancers have led workshops in a number of local parishes and prepared instruction videos for the Crosstalk Ministries Day Camp Program.

*Plate 23.* This particular Evensong was composed of portions taken from each of the authorized editions of the Book of Common Prayer and reproduced in the language of the day. It was intended as a precursor to the projected event of 13 June 1999, sanctioned by the Bishop, for the use of the 1549 Service of Holy Communion in churches throughout the Diocese. The Rev. David Curry, Vice-President of the PBSC, was the guest preacher.

*Plate 24a.* Perpetue Mukarugwiza's dancers, many of whom had fled to Canada from Rwanda, gave a stunning performance at the Annual PWRDF dinner.

*Plate 24b.* Shown left to right are Susana Alves Ribeiro, Robert Camara, Dr Marion Simpson, Bishop Jubal Neves (of Montreal's Companion Diocese of Southwestern Brazil) and his wife Eleca, Dr Ivan Harding, and Canon Jenö Kohner.

*Plate 25.* Special thanks are due to the McCord Museum for permission to re-produce the portrait of Ashton Oxenden which, although it is preserved in the MDA, forms part of the Notman Collection. It is interesting to note that the average length of completed episcopates in the Diocese has been fifteen and a half years.

*Plate 26.* These portraits are preserved in the MDA.

*Plate 27.* This map of Lower Canada was published by the SPG in 1822. With the erection of the Diocese of Montreal in 1850 the border between it and the Diocese of Quebec ran north from Vermont to include the townships of Potton, Bolton, Stukely, and Ely, then northward to William Henry (Sorel) and Berthier.

*Plate 28.* This plan appeared in the December issue of the *Montreal Churchman*, Vol. XII, no. 2, page 4.

*Plate 29.* This map, preserved in the MDA, was prepared for *The Blessed Communion* and appeared as endpapers in that volume.

*Plate 30.* Since 1990, further churches have become inactive: Iberville, and St Andrew's East among others. See Appendix B for further details.

# INDEX

Anglican Council of Emergency Relief and Social Service, 263
Anglican Fellowship for Social Action (AFSA), 294, 296
Anglican Foundation, 319
Anglican House, Montreal, 327
*Anglican Journal*, 168, 248, 388, 393, 394–5, 411, 413, 414
*Anglican Newsletter* (Montreal), 234
Anglican Renewal Movement (ARM), 393
Anglican Roman Catholic International Commission (ARCIC), 396
Anglican Young People's Association (AYPA), 373, 376
Anglo-Catholics, 26, 158, 187, 386–7
Archer, Adina, 302
Archer, Ethelbert, 302
Archer, Marita, 302–4
Arctic, Diocese of the, 345, 347
Aristophanes, 132
Armitage, W.J., 247
Armitage, William David, 216
Arnott, James, 486
Arthur William Patrick Albert, Duke of Connaught, 152
Arthur, Euline, 351
Arthurson, Charles, 382
Arundel Group, 285, 295–6
Arundel, QC, 180, 193, 211, 217, 234, 280, 294–5, 297, 371
Ascah, Augustus Clifford, 217
Ascah, Mrs Augustus Clifford, 217
Ascension, Church of the, Montreal, 378, 401-2, 419, 420-1
Ascension, Church of the, West Brome, 174
Asia, 350, 381
Associated Charities of Montreal, 187
Athabasca, AB, 256–7
Athabasca, Diocese of, 255
Atherton, William Henry, 86
Auberge Madeleine, 96–7
Augustus, Gloria, 340
Aurora, ON, 379
Avoca, QC, 254–5

Aylmer, QC, 152, 154
Aylwyn, QC, 280

**B**
Bach, Johann Sebastian, 224, 386
Bacon, Miss M.E., 193
Bahai, 488
Bairstow, Edward Cuthbert, 224
Baker, Henry, 83
Baker, Joel, 194
Balch, Lewis W.P., 146
Baldry family, 259
Baldry, Mrs, 258
Baldwin, Maurice Scollard, 204, 486
Balfe, Robert P., 87, 89–92
Balfour, Andrew, 85
Balkan states, 28
Ball, Thomas William, 217
Ball, Mrs Thomas William, 217
Bancroft, Charles, 102, 107, 113, 121, 122, 137, 139
Bancroft, Henry, 217
Band of Hope, 193
Bank of Montreal, 61, 93, 338
Bank of Quebec, 93
Baptists, 308, 329, 343, 420
Barbados, 301–2, 349, 351, 419
Bark Lake, QC, 371
Barnabas Anglican Ministries (BAM), 393
Barrett, S. Dawn, 407–8
Bartholomew, Harry, 259
Battle River, AB, 258
Baugh, Cyrus Wesley Palmer, 234, 297–8
Baugh, Ella (Mrs C.W.P. Baugh), 234
Baugh, Horace G., 297–9, 301
Baugh, William Jesse Palmer, 216
BBC (radio), 277–8
Beach, John, 401–2
Beattie, Jim, 259
Beaugrand, Honoré, 186
Beauharnois, QC, 73, 196–8
Beaurepaire, QC, 309
Beauvoir, Ogé, 342, 344
Beaver Lake, Montreal, 299
Bedford, QC, 82, 87–8, 90–2, 150, 213–14, 418

Chalk, Linda, 121
Chamberlain, Neville, 271
Chamberlin, Almira, 114–16
Chambers, Douglas, 388, 391
Chambly, QC, 33, 108, 113, 485
Champlain Presbytery of New York
and Vermont, 133
Champlain, Lake, 53, 59, 107, 120
Chapleau, Camp, QC, 321
Charbonnel, Armand-François-
Marie de, 123
Charles, a slave, 37
Charleston (Hatley), QC, 331
Chartrand, Doris, 403
Chastelain, John de, 326
Chatham, ON, 141
Chelsea, QC, 182
Chester, Bishop of, 88–9, 91
Chichester, Bishop of (A.T. Gilbert),
417
China, 261
Chippewa, ON, 220
Christ Church Cathedral, 26, 28,
135, 136, 138, 142, 145–6, 159,
162, 167, 168–9, 181-2, 188, 213,
217–20, 223–5, 246, 255, 256, 272,
274, 297, 318–19, 324–6, 327, 336,
344, 353, 357, 364–8, 368, 374,
378, 385–6, 403, 409, 413, 417,
484–5
Christ Church, Montreal, 40, 42, 44,
75, 102, 110, 123
Christ Church, Rawdon, 403
Christ Church, Sorel, 51, 86
Christ Church, St Andrew's East, 108
*Christian Sentinel and Anglo-Canadian
Churchman's Magazine, The*, 229
Christie's Manor (Clarenceville),
64–6
Christie, General Gabriel, 41
Christie, Major William
Plenderleath, 88, 189–91
Christieville, 189–90
Church Army, The, 394
*Church Chronicle of the Diocese of
Montreal*, 229
Church Extension Mission, 262
Church Home, *see* Fulford Residence

Church House (Toronto), 414, 417
Church of England Association for
Young Men of Montreal, 129, 376
Church Society of the Diocese of
Montreal, 23, 93, 106, 138, 189,
292, 330, 405–6
Church Society of the Diocese of
Quebec, 23, 79, 93, 99, 100, 105–6;
Book Depository of, 104–6; Lay
Committee of, 93
*Church Temporalities Act* (Quebec),
415
Church, Mercia (Tibbs), 377–8
Church, William Harold Morrison,
378
Churchill, Winston, 287
CKVL (radio), 309
Clarenceux king-of-arms, 11
Clarenceville, QC, 85, 305-6, *see also*
Christie's Manor
Clarendon (Shawville), 153, 154, 183
Clarendon, Deanery of, 22, 23, 154,
213, 216
Clark, Colonel, 59
Clarke, Alured, 44
Clear Prairie, AB, 258–9
Clench, Lieutenant, 37
Clergy Reserves, 23, 62, 72, 129
Clyd, AB, 257
Cobb, C. Cedric, 408
Cobb, Wilma, 384, 488
Coffin, Hubert, 214–215, 217, 262
Coffin, Mrs Hubert, 217
Coggan, Donald, Baron, 327
Colborne, Sir John, 82, 84
College of Arms (London, England),
11
Colonial Church and School Society,
124–5, 133
*Colonial Church Chronicle*, 179, 229
Colonial Church Society, 125
'Coloured Church,' The, *see* Union
United
Columbia University, New York, 270
Columbia, District of, 318
Comité de la pastorale francophone,
168
*Common Praise*, 409, 411, 413

Dunham, QC, 54, 56, 65, 108,113, 128, 194, 215, 222, 262
Dunn, Hon. Thomas, 38, 40
Dunn, Rev. Mr, 125
Dunsmore, James, 196
Duplessis, Emmanuel, 342
Duplessis, Maurice, 26, 267, 269
Duracin, Mgr Zaché, 344
Durham, John George Lambton, Earl of, 86
DuVernet, Edward, 233
Dylan, Bob, 362

**E**
East Farnham, QC, 262
East Grinstead (Sussex, England), 183
East Lansing, MI, 253
Eastern Newfoundland and Labrador, Diocese of, 251
Eastern Townships, 15, 22, 52, 59, 67, 71, 80–1, 108, 110, 116, 118, 215, 305, 378, 408
Eastman, QC, 214
Eaton, QC, 57
Eccleston, W.C., 257
Edmonton, AB, 256
Egerton, Arthur, 224 –5
Elbourne, G.M., 367
Elgin, James Bruce, 8th Earl of, 110
Eling, John Warren, 17, 387–9, 391–3
Elizabeth, Sister (of St Margaret), 173, 185
Elliott, Andrew, 328, 487
Emery, Miss (of New York), 178
Emmanuel Church, Boston, 223
Emporia, KS, 214
*Empress of Ireland*, SS, 220
Empson, John, 181–2
*En Ville* (Montreal), 364
England, 31, 35, 47, 53, 54, 56, 62, 72, 76, 79, 106, 108, 109, 113, 116, 138, 152–3, 158, 159, 199, 219, 221, 231, 236, 264, 291, 316, 359, 368, 377, 404, 419
Epiphany House, Iberville, 190–1, 385

Erechim (Brazil), 293
Essentials Movement, 393–7
Established Clergy Association of Lower Canada, 79
Evangelicals, 25, 26, 27, 57, 118, 121–2, 125, 137, 154, 157, 190, 393–7
Evans, Lewis, 167
Evans, Mrs H[enry] J[ames], 176, 179
Evans, Muriel, 254
Evans, Thomas Frye Lewis, 221, 244
Everett, Thomas, 215
Expo '67, 327–30, 487

**F**
Fairview, AB, 258, 259
Falloon, Daniel, 102, 233
Farnam, Lynnwood, 222–5
Farnham, QC, 108, 113, 216
Farnham (Surrey, England), 118–19
Farthing, Elizabeth Mary (Mrs J.C. Farthing), 485
Farthing, John Cragg (5th Bishop of Montreal), 25, 26, 158, 167, 195, 206, 213, 222, 224, 233, 235–8, 238–9, 241, 243, 244–6, 247, 256, 262–4, 271, 279, 399, 401, 422, 485
Fascism, 269
Fay, [Caroline] (Mrs [Robert] Fay), 147
Fay, R[obert] E., 148
Fellowship of the West, 255–60, 273, 279
Fénelon, François de Salignac de la Mothe, 114
Ferguson, William Aldworth, 313
Fergusson family, 259
Ferry, James, 388
Findlay, Eva, 159
Finlay, Terence, 389, 392
First Nations People, 24, 32, 37, 74, 132–5, 348, 381, 394, 414–15, 417
Flanagan, J. Cyril, 294
Flanagan, John, 139
Flanders, 270

Goodings, Allen, 311, 420–1
Gordon, Donald, 321
Gordon, Savanna, 403
Gore, Colonel Sir Charles, 81
Goulet, Mr., 305
Gower-Rees, Albert Philip, 253, 271
Grace Church, Arundel, 294, 371–2
Grace Church, Montreal, 192, 214,
  241
Grace Church, Sutton, 215, 373
Grace-Church-on-the-Hill, Toronto,
  297, 318
Granby, QC, 70, 109, 113, 116, 118,
  214, 407, 484
Grand Trunk Railway, 141
Grande Prairie, AB, 256
Grande-Ligne, QC, 85
Great Britain, 270–1, 273, 279, 337
Greek Orthodox Church, 329
Green, Michael, 393
Grenfell, Wilfred Thomason, 193
Grenville, QC, 217
Grey Sisters, 42
Grey, Henry R., 186
Griffintown, 129
Grosse Isle (Quarantine Station),
  97–9, 104
Grosse Isle, Magdalen Islands, 368
Groves, Byron, 259
Gudwin, Mark, 168
Guelph, School of Agriculture, 314
Guerout, Narcisse, 99
Guinness, Robin Gordon, 378, 393
Guiton, Geoffrey, 256–7, 263
Gutstadt, Jossi, 366

**H**
Haeckel, Ernst, 200
Haensl, Charles Lewis Frederick,
  122
Hague, George, 96
Haiti, 344, 361
Haiti, Diocese of, 344
Haitians, 170, 314, 340–4, 348
Haldimand, Sir Frederick, 37
Halifax, NS, 25, 41, 120, 393
Hall family, 258

Halle (Germany), 239
Hallerton, QC, 418
Hamilton Association of Montreal,
  202
Hamilton, Charles, 245
Hamilton, ON, 79
Hamilton, Senator John, 186
Handel, George Frederick, 417
Hannen, Peter Douglas, 10, 318,
  396, 484
Harding, Ivan, 416, 489
Harding, Malcolm Taylor McAdam,
  256
Harris, Barbara, 359
Harris, Mr (of Trinity Memorial),
  303
Harris, William, 216
Hartford, CT, 78
Harvard University, 282, 314
Hasell, Eva, 256
Hatley, QC, 57
Havergal, Frances Ridley, 370
Haviland, Richard, 257
Havill, Thomas, 305
Hawkins, Cynthia, 319
Hawkins, Ernest, 107–9, 115, 118
*Heavy Construction News*, 365
Heber, Reginald, 105
Heeney, William Bertal, 196
*Helen*, The, 104
Hemmingford, 418
Henderson, Mrs, 176
Henderson, William, 233
Henry Birks & Sons, Limited, 487
*Herald Tribune*, 223
*Hibernia*, SS, 120
High Church, 25, 118, 146
High School (of Montreal), 282
Hill, Daniel G., 349
Hill, William, 141
Hills, George, 245
Hinchinbrooke, QC, 418
Hitler, Adolf, 271, 292
Hobart, John Henry, 79
Hodge, Tom, 486
Hodgson, Frederick Hamilton, 398–9
Holden, Henry T., 257

James, Lettie, 253–9, 346, 488
James, Mrs Willis, 377
Japan, 177, 419
Jay Peak, VT, 317
Jemmott, Anthony Gordon Edwin, 252, 303–4, 351–2
Jessop, Henry, 93
Jesuits (Society of Jesus), 135
Jews and Judaism, 28, 45, 105, 235, 289–92, 367, 488
John Abbott College, 393, 395
*John Bakke*, SS, 290
Johnson, (probably John), 233
Johnson, F.G., 186
Johnson, Thomas, 69, 108, 109, 111, 113, 118
Jones, Charles O., 82, 85
Jones, Dora M., 107
Jones, James, 92, 108, 111, 113
Jones, William, 113
Joseph, Yves-Eugène, 342–4
Josephine Margaret, Sister (of St Margaret), 185
*Journal de Montréal*, 488
Judge, Percival E., 216

**K**

Kahn, Dr Sheema, 380, 488
Kahnawake, QC, 314
Kammerer, J.G., 197
Karg-Elert, Sigfrid, 224
Keble College, Oxford, 222
Keefler, Kathy, 321
Kelley, Arthur Reading, 306
Kemp, Oren Jocelin, 82–5
Kemp, Patience, 114–16
Ker, John, 214
Ketzbach's Station, 140
Kildare, QC, 306
Kilkenny (Ireland), 182
Kilkenny, QC, 74, 305–6
Kingdon, Hollingworth Tully, 247
Kingston College (Jamaica), 352
Kingston, ON, 248
Kinsale Village (Montserrat), 251
Kirby, Monica, 368–9
Kitson, Miss (of Berthierville), 304

Knapp, Grant, 257
Knowlton family, 214
Knowlton, QC, 140, 215
Knowlton, Paul Holland, 83–5
Kohner, Jenö George, 416, 489
Kootenay, Archbishop of (W.R. Adams), 280–1
Korean War, 319

**L**

L'Acadie, QC, 84
La Macaza, QC, 211, 372
La Prairie, QC, 107, 113, 123, 140
*La rencontre*, 168
La Rivière, Dollard, 167–70
Labrador, 24, 193
Lachine, QC, 37, 75, 151
Lachute, QC, 180, 217
Lacolle, QC, 104, 113
Laflèche, Mgr Louis, 164–5
Lakefield, QC, 174, 217, 297–8
Lalonde School, Roxboro, 309–10
Lambeth Conference, 27, 217, 220, 352, 356
Lambeth Palace, 34, 72, 118, 220
Langevin, Mgr Jean, 165
LAOS Institute, 398
Lapointe, Fr Lafond, 341
Laporte, Pierre, 333
Larivière, Louis-Vitalien, 134–5
Larivière, Mrs Louis-Vitalien, 135
Lasalle Mission, 300, 487
Latartigue, Mgr Jacques, 81
Latin America, 350
Laura, Sister (of St John the Divine), 265
Lausanne (Switzerland), 35
Lavallée, Gérard, 166–70
Lay Helpers' Association, 207
Lay Readers' Association, 398
*Le Devoir* (Montreal), 334
Le Foy family, 258
Leach, Louisa (Mrs William Turnbull Leach), 176
Leach, William Turnbull, 112–13, 151, 376
Leclerc, Roger, 388

Magil Construction Ltd, 366

Magor, Murray, 311, 320, 487

Maguire, Robert Kenneth (8th Bishop of Montreal), 25, 27, 180, 248–9, 312, 327, 329–30, 332, 333–6, 352–3, 378, 423, 487

Maine, 134

Maison des Coopérants, La, 28, 366, 369

Maison du Père (Montreal), 323

Maison Emmanuel, Val Morin, QC, 301

Malloch, Archibald, 385

Manchester (England), 88

Manitoba, 318

Manitoba, University of, 314

Manning, Ann (Mrs William Adolphus Fyles), 182

Manning, Henry Edward, 199

Mansfield, Lord, *see* William Murray

Maria II of Spain, 117

Marindin, Jean, 377

Marsden, Dr, 88

Marshall, Joan, 14, 178, 195, 249–50, 333, 343

Martin, J.E.F., 224

Marvin, Mrs, 57

Mary Queen of Peace, Roxboro, 312

Maskinongé, QC, 47–8

Maskinongé, Lake, 306

Massawippi, Lake, 378

Masta, Chief H.L., 134

Masters, Donald Campbell, 80

Matthews, Timothy John, 355

Matthews, Victoria, 359, 395

Maurice, Frederick Denison, 314

Maxwell, James Clerk, 200

May, Edward Geoffrey, 285, 289

Mechanics' Institute, Montreal 129–130

Medley, John, 24

Megantic, QC, 89

Memphremagog, Lake, 69

Merbecke, John, 316

Mercer, Miss, 215

Merrick, William Chad, 113, 485

Merriman, Paula, 384, 488

Messie, l'église du, Sabrevois, 167

Methodists and Methodism, 61, 64, 69, 83, 85, 127, 129, 159, 216, 226, 303

Mexico, 314

Michigan State University, 253–4

Michigan, 318

Mid-Japan, Assistant Bishop of (P.S.C. Powles), 280

Mile End (district), 319, 402–3

Mile-End Mission, 363, 400, 401–4, 488

Mille Isles, QC, 217

Miller family, 83

Millman, Thomas Reagh, 13, 40, 57, 60, 79, 229

Milton, QC, 116, 124

Mirabel airport, 299

Miramichi River, 104

*Mission Possible*, 404

Mission to Seamen, the, 394

Missionary Society of the Canadian Church (MSCC), 178, 235, 262, 275, 280

Missionary Society of the Church of England, London, 289

Missionary Society of the Protestant Episcopal Church, 173

Missisquoi (county), 79

Missisquoi Bay (as body of water), 83

Missisquoi Bay (mission), 54–5

Missisquoi Bay, *see* Philipsburg

Missisquoi Established Clergy Association, 79

Mohawks, 32, 37

Molson family, 186, 298

Molson, John, 298

Monk, Chief Justice James, 38

Mont Tremblant, QC, 371

Montgolfier, Étienne, 43

Montgomery, General Richard, 61

Montreal (city of), 11, 12, 22, 23, 24, 28, 31–3, 35, 36, 38, 40, 41, 43, 47, 54, 59, 60–2, 65, 81, 86, 92, 93, 99–104, 105, 107, 110–11, 123, 125, 129, 135, 140, 141, 156–7, 163, 170–3, 173, 175, 185, 209, 219, 225, 226, 228, 235, 242, 251, 261, 282, 296, 302, 319, 323, 325,

Powles, Percival Samuel Carson, 280–1, 295
Prayer Book Society of Canada (PBSC), 250, 393, 488
Presbyterians, 34, 40, 61, 106, 226, 240, 291, 308, 310–12, 329, 415
Price, Sir William, 237
Prideaux, Humphrey, 105
Primate's World Relief and Development Fund (PWRDF), 414, 489
Prisoners' Aid Association of Montreal, 207–9, 210
Pritchard, Glenn, 329
Programme Committee of the Diocese of Montreal, 168
Promenades de la Cathédral, Les, 28, 364–5, 367
Protestant Episcopal Church, the, 58, 77, 79
Protestant School Board of Greater Montreal (PSBGM), 325
Puerto Rico, 338
Pullin family, 258
Pullin, Bruce, 258
Pullin, Earl, 258
Pulman, James, 11
Purcell, Henry, 318
Pusey, Edward Bouverie, 183, 199
Puseyism, 118

**Q**

Qu'Appelle, Bishop of (Malcolm Taylor McAdam Harding), 256
Quakers, 37, 78
Quatrefages de Bréau, Jean Louis Armand de, 200
Quebec (city), 32, 35, 36, 40, 41, 43, 54, 60–2, 65, 67, 88, 93, 116, 141, 220, 236, 245, 253
Quebec (province), 24, 26, 38, 134, 154, 169, 241, 242-3, 250, 269, 318, 332-3, 335, 336, 337, 345, 347–8, 362, 406, 409
*Quebec Diocesan Gazette*, 394
*Quebec Gazette*, 32, 52
Quebec Liberal Party, 169

Quebec Lodge Camp, 378
Quebec, Bishop of (George Jehoshaphat Mountain), 22, 121; (Jacob Mountain), 38, 40; (Charles James Stewart), 67, 73
Quebec, Diocese of, 22, 23, 24, 28, 47, 93, 98, 107, 139, 176, 234, 250, 251, 295, 331, 347, 355, 378, 382
Queen's University, Kingston, 314
Quiet Revolution, The, 27, 333, 341, 418
Quinn Dressel Associates, 365

**R**

Race Relations Committee, 28
Radio Ville Marie (Montreal), 385
Rahard, Victor, 167
Rangoon University, 313
Raspberry, Chester, 259
Rauschenbusch, Walter, 314
Rawdon, QC, 181
*Rebellion Losses Bill*, 110
Rebellions of 1837-38, 80-6, 110, 163
Redeemer, Church of the, Côte St. Paul, 321
Redeemer, Church of the, Weir, 371
Rédempteur, la communauté du, 166, 169, 336
Reed, Ernest Samuel, 295
Reed, William, 222
Reford, K.T. (Mrs Robert Reford), 161
Regina, SK, 253, 355–6
Reid, Anthony Meredith, 311
Reid, Charles Peter, 99
Reid, Isabella (Mrs James Reid), 110
Reid, James, 85, 87–92, 110–13, 114–16, 127–8, 194
Reid, Nancy, 114–16
Renforth, NB, 251
Residential Schools, 24
Ribeiro, Susana Alves, 416, 489
Richards, Fr John, 104
Richelieu (district), 15, 22, 121
Richelieu River, 108, 120
Richelieu Valley, 80, 82, 85–6, 104

Sergent, Rachel (Mrs Adolph Louis Sergent), 290, 292
Sewell, Jonathan, 51
Shaddick, W.T. Duncan, 365
Shatford, Allan Pearson, 240, 242
Shawville, QC, 213, *see also* Clarendon
Shearith Israel Synagogue, 45
Shefford, QC, 69, 79, 109, 116, 484
Shefford, Deanery of, 213, 214
Sheltering Home for Protestants (Montreal), The, 95, 209
Shelton, Mary M. (Mrs Elijah Edmund Shelton), 96
Shepard, Mrs Richard, 147
Shepherd, Francis John, 170
Shepherd, Mary Cecilia (Mrs Robert Ward Shepherd), 96
Shepherd, Ronald Francis, 487
Shepherd, Thomas, 54
Sheppard, Frances, 358
Sheward, Frederick Cyril Grant, 398–9
Shrewsbury, QC, 297–8
Shufelt, John, 140
Sikhism, 488
Simons, John MacMillan, 396
Simpson, Marion, 416, 489
Simpson, Mrs (of Montreal), 147
Simpson, Mrs G.W., 161
Sir George Williams University, 314
Sixby family, 83
Skare, Elizabeth (Betty), 307–8
Skare, Olaf, 308
Slack, Emma Coulson (Mrs George Slack), 118
Slack, George, 109, 113, 116–19, 124, 124–6, 484
Slack, Isabella Ann (Mrs George Slack), 109, 116–19
Slack, Thomas, 117
Slater, Robert Henry Lawson, 313–15
Sligo (Ireland), 98
Smith family, 258
Smith, AB, 257
Smith, Alfred William, 262

Smith, John, 140, 147, 149
Smith, Mrs John, 148
Smith, Shubal, 127
Smith, Sir Donald, 186
Smyth, John Paterson, 227–9, 244, 246–7, 252–3
Social Service Committee of the Diocese of Montreal, 294–5, 296
Socialism, 228, 270
Society for the Promotion of Christian Knowledge (SPCK), 58, 104–5, 142, 406, 486
Society for the Propagation of the Gospel in Foreign Parts (SPG), 23, 31, 34, 36, 40, 41, 55, 57, 59, 63, 65, 68, 72, 73, 75–7, 85, 87, 91–2, 94, 96, 106, 107–8, 111, 124, 125-6, 196, 229, 484
Sœur de la Nativité (Mme Jetté), 95
Sœur St. Jeanne Chantal (Mme Galipeau), 95
Sœurs de la Miséricorde, 95
SOMA (Sharing of Ministries Abroad), 344
Somalia, 361
Sophocles, 132
Sorel River, 49
Sorel, QC, 33, 43, 49, 50, 54, 72, 81, 86, 122, 132, 141, 306
South America, 28, 339
South East Asia, 28, 359
South Merstham (Surrey, England), 277
South Roxton, QC, 262
South Stukely, QC, 214
Southwark, Bishop of, 278
Sparling, "old" Mr (of Bolton), 214
Sparling, Mrs, 214
Spencer, [Wealthy,] (Mrs Richard Spencer), 147–8
Spencer, Richard, 147–8
Sperry, John R., 393
Springate, George, 321
Springer, William, 256
Squires, William, 85
Stanbridge East, QC, 92, 216, 268
Stanbridge Lower Falls, 92

Stanbridge Upper-Mills, *see* Stanbridge East

Stanbridge, 87–9, 91–2, 110, 113

Stavert, A. Bruce, 121

Steinhower, William F., 91–2

Stephenson, John, 318

Stepney, Bishop of (Cosmo Lang), 221–2

Stevens, Brooke Bridges, 75, 229

Stewart, Bishop Charles James, 22, 39, 52, 53, 54, 56–60, 64–5, 67, 72, 75, 78–9, 80, 108, 109, 128, 331, 484

Stonhouse, Sir James, 58

Strachan, John, 23, 79, 124

Strite family, 54

Stuart, John, 37

Stuchberry, Ian, 311

Stukeley, QC, 69

Sullivan, Edward, 219

Sulpicians, 43

Sunday School, 15, 92, 103, 114–6, 180, 194, 254, 287, 303, 307, 312, 351, 377, 486, 487

Sutton, QC, 149, 191, 215, 216, 222, 485

Sutton, Edward George, 99

Suzanna, Jarquin-Olson, 403

Swanton, VT, 82, 83-4

Switzerland, 34

Symonds, Herbert, 218

Symonds, Kingsley, 107

*Synod Act* of 1856–57, 24

Synod of the Diocese of Montreal, 23, 27, 79, 93, 121, 135, 138–9, 151, 154–7, 187, 190, 205, 207, 231, 282, 295, 333, 352–3, 355–6, 373, 385, 390; Executive Committee of, 181–2, 214

Synod of the Diocese of Toronto, 391

Synods of the Ecclesiasical Provinces: of Canada, 154, 173, 176, 221, 262; Ontario, 262; Rupert's Land, 262

Synod Office, Montreal, 271, 321, 343, 378

*Syria*, The, 98

**T**

T. Eaton Company Ltd, 290, 292

Takata (Japan), 280

Taylor, Ann, 328, 487

Taylor, Fennings, 121–2

Taylor, Jeremy, 58

Taylor, Ralph, 82

Taylor, Rev., 57

Temiscaming, QC, 22, 347

Temple, Archbishop William, 294, 296, 314

Ten Eyck family, 54

Terreau, Marcel, 421

Terrick, Richard, 35

Thailand, 361

Thibault, Hon. Lise, 301

Thompson family, 258

Thompson, Alf, 257

Thomson, Heather Joan, 346, 488

Thorne, QC, 418

Thorold, ON, 79

Three Rivers, QC, 32, 35, 36, 47, 48, 54, 141, 163, 229

Tilton, Roberta Elizabeth, 173

Todd, Dan, 258

Tomkins family, 259

Toof family, 57

Toope, Frank Morris, 360–1

Toope, Jocelyn, 361

Toosey, Philip, 40

Toronto (city), 25, 79, 164, 173, 209, 235), 349, 253, 377, 382-3, 379, 393, 414

Toronto, Bishop of (John Strachan), 417; Suffragan Bishop of (Victoria Matthews), 359

Toronto, Diocese of, 23, 24, 79, 93, 109, 138, 176, 250, 316, 388

Toronto, University of, 314

Torrance, John S., 99

Town of Mount Royal (TMR), 362–4

Townsend, Micajah, 54, 64–7, 85, 111–13, 121, 137

Tractarians, 118, 157, 183, 387

Trinidad, 419

Trinity Chapel, Montreal, 96, 102–3, 113